MW00565382

CAIA Level II

CAIA Level II

Advanced Core Topics in Alternative Investments

Melissa Donohue
Urbi Garay
Ernest Jaffarian
Francois Lhabitant
Pierre-Yves Mathonet
Thomas Meyer
Richard Spurgin
Simon Stevenson

Edited by Kathryn Wilkens-Christopher

WILEY
John Wiley & Sons, Inc.

Published by John Wiley & Sons, Inc., Hoboken, New Jersey.
Published simultaneously in Canada.

For general information on our other products and services or for technical support, please contact our Customer Care Department within the United States at (800) 762-2974, outside the United States at (317) 572-3993 or fax (317) 572-4002.

Wiley also publishes its books in a variety of electronic formats. Some content that appears in print may not be available in electronic books. For more information about Wiley products, visit our web site at www.wiley.com.

ISBN 978-0-470-69426-8

A catalogue record for this book is available from the British Library.

Typeset in 10/12pt Times by Aptara Inc., New Delhi, India
Printed in the United States of America by Hamilton Printing

10 9 8 7 6 5 4 3

Contents

Preface

Since its inception in 2002, the Chartered Alternative Investment Analyst (CAIA) Association has strived to incorporate state-of-the-art reading material in its curriculum. This latest curriculum reading is part of the Chartered Alternative Investment Analyst Series and represents a milestone in our efforts to continuously improve and update our curriculum. To ensure that the material best reflects current practices in the area of alternative investments, the CAIA Association invited a group of leading industry professionals to contribute to the production of the series, covering core areas of alternative investments: hedge funds, managed futures, commodities, real estate and private equity. Similar to other books published by the CAIA Association, this book is grounded in the *CAIA Program Core Knowledge Outline*^{SM}. We are proud to make this book available to our candidates and alternative investment professionals. This first edition of the series is being launched in the year 2009 when more than 5,000 aspiring, as well as accomplished, alternative investment professionals will endeavor to master the material covered in this book as well as other readings as outlined in the CAIA study guides so that they can earn the prestigious CAIA designation.

In publishing the books in this series, we are guided by the Association's mission to provide its members with a comprehensive knowledge of alternative investments, advocate high standards of professional conduct, and establish the Chartered Alternative Investment Analyst designation as the educational "gold" standard for the alternative investment industry.

FOUNDATION

The quality, rigor, and relevance of this series derive from the ideals upon which the CAIA Association was based. The CAIA program offered its first Level I examination in February of 2003. We now have over 3,000 members, but in its first full year, only 43 candidates, who passed Level I and Level II exams and met the other requirements of membership, were invited to join the CAIA Association. Many of these founding members were instrumental in establishing the CAIA designation as the global mark of excellence in alternative investment education. Through their support and with the help of the founding co-sponsors, the Alternative Investment Management Association (AIMA) and the Center for the International Securities and Derivatives Markets (CISDM), the Association is now firmly established as the most comprehensive and credible designation in the rapidly growing sphere of alternative investments.

The AIMA is the hedge fund industry's global, not-for-profit trade association with over 1,100 corporate members worldwide. Members include leading hedge fund managers, fund of hedge funds managers, prime brokers, legal and accounting services and fund administrators. They all benefit from AIMA's active influence in policy development, its leadership in industry initiatives, including education and sound practice manuals and its excellent reputation with regulators.

The CISDM of the Isenberg School of Management of University of Massachusetts, seeks to enhance the understanding of the field of alternative investments through research, education, and networking opportunities for member donors, industry professionals, and academics.

I first attended one of the early annual CISDM Research meetings as a CISDM fellow and doctoral student over ten years ago, and recall being most impressed by the level and depth of discussion among the Center's sponsors regarding the need for education and research in the area of alternative investments. It has been truly rewarding to witness the development and growth of CAIA, starting from only an idea to meet a real need.

Led by Craig Asche, Executive Director of the Association; Dr. Thomas Schneeweis, Director of the CISDM; Florence Lombard, of AIMA; and a core group of faculty and industry experts who were associated with University of Massachusetts and AIMA, the CAIA program took shape and was introduced to the investment community through the publication of its first set of CAIA study guides in 2002. From the beginning, the Association recognized that a meaningful portion of its curriculum must be devoted to codes of conduct and ethical behavior in the investment profession. To this end, with permission and cooperation of the CFA Institute, we have incorporated its *Code of Ethics* and the *CFA Standards of Practice Handbook* in our curriculum. Further, we leverage the experience and contributions of our membership and other distinguished alternative investment professionals on our Board and Committees to create and update the *CAIA Program Core Knowledge Outline*^{SM}.

The CAIA Association has experienced rapid growth in its membership during the last seven years – a growth that has followed the expansion of the alternative investment industry into the mainstream of the investment industry. We strive to remain nimble in our process so that curriculum developments remain relevant and keep pace with the constant changes in this dynamic industry. Yet we never lose sight that we complement the still larger, traditional and established investment arena.

This series focuses on the core topics that comprise each of the basic areas of alternative investments, but our original philosophy to stay nimble will serve us especially well now. Given the recent turmoil in the markets, the ability to keep pace with the regulatory and economic changes is more important today than it has ever been in our history. This series, including the annually revised, most advanced material contained in our *Current and Integrated Topics*, reflects the current state of the industry.

BENEFITS

While the CAIA Association's origins are largely due to the efforts of professionals in the hedge fund and managed futures space, these founders correctly identified a void in the wider understanding the alternative investments space as a whole. From the beginning, the CAIA Curriculum has also covered private equity, commodities and real estate equally and always with an eye towards shifts in the industry. Today, several hundred CAIA members identify their main area of expertise as real estate or private equity; several hundred more members are from family offices, pension funds, endowments, and sovereign wealth funds that allocate across multiple classes within the alternative space. To accomplish this comprehensively, we have fully developed Curriculum Subcommittees that represent each area of coverage within the curriculum. Each of these alternative investment areas shares many distinct features such as the relative freedom on the part of investment managers to act in the best interest of their investors, alignment of interest between investors and management, relative illiquidity of positions for some investment products and deviations from some of the underpinning assumptions of modern portfolio theory. These characteristics necessitate conceptual and actual modifications to the standard investment performance analysis and decision making paradigms.

The reader will find the publications in our series to be beneficial whether from the standpoint of allocating to new asset classes and strategies in order to gain broader diversification or from the standpoint of a specialist needing to better understand the competing options available to sophisticated investors globally. In either case, the reader will be better equipped to serve his or her clients needs. The series has been designed to make studying more efficient relative to our past curriculum. Importantly, it is more relevant, having been written under the direction of the CAIA Association with the input and efforts of many practicing and eminent alternative investment professionals, as reflected in each publication's acknowledgements section.

THE CAIA PROGRAMS AND
CAIA ALTERNATIVE INVESTMENT SERIES

The CAIA Prerequisite Program is an assessment tool to determine a candidate's readiness to enter the CAIA program. These prerequisite materials cover the quantitative analytics commonly associated with traditional assets, as well as a blend of practical and theoretical knowledge relating to both traditional and alternative investments.

The first book in our series, *CAIA Level I: Introduction to Core Topics in Alternative Investments* is a revised edition of Mark Anson's *Handbook of Alternative Investments*. This new CAIA edition includes completely updated sections on hedge funds, managed futures and commodities, private equity, and credit derivatives, as well as new chapters on active management and real estate. Thus, the CAIA Level I required readings are contained in this one text, supplemented only by the CFA Institute's *Standards of Practice Handbook*. The reader should be aware, however, that the prerequisite program has been expanded, and that Level I candidates are assumed to have mastered all of its content in advance of sitting the Level 1 exam.

The second book in our series, *CAIA Level II: Advanced Core Topics in Alternative Investments*, also represents a significant improvement to the coverage of our curriculum. Specifically, each section was developed to incorporate the expert practitioner input which comprises the *CAIA Program Core Knowledge Outline*[SM]. We believe this new model of curriculum development accurately reflects the skill set required of industry practitioners.

The third book in the series, *CAIA Level II: Integrated Topics and Applications* is the result of the work of our Curriculum Task Force members. They reviewed the newly developed drafts of the first two new books in the series in light of the *CAIA Program Core Knowledge Outline*[SM], updated the Outline, prioritized and developed supplemental topics, and reviewed practice problems designed for the Level II examinations and included in this publication.

The fourth volume in this series is titled *CAIA Level II: Current and Integrated Topics*. It is updated annually and designed to address topics that cut across all areas of alternative investments, such as asset allocation and risk management techniques, as well as new developments in the alternative investment research space and in the industry itself.

Finally, we will continue to update the *CAIA Level I Study Guide* and the *CAIA Level II Study Guide* every six months (each exam cycle). These are freely available on our website. These guides outline all of the readings and corresponding learning objectives (LOs) that candidates are responsible for meeting. They also contain important information for candidates regarding the use of LOs, testing policies, topic weightings, where to find and report errata, and much more. The entire exam process is outlined in the *CAIA Candidate Handbook* and is available at http://www.caia.org/enroll/candidatehandbook/.

I believe you will find this series to be the most comprehensive, rigorous and globally relevant source of educational material available within the field of alternative investments.

June 2009   Kathryn Wilkens-Christopher, Ph.D., CAIA
                                                     Director of Curriculum
                                                     CAIA Association

Acknowledgments

We would like to thank the many individuals who played important roles in producing this book. Each section of this text was developed by a set of main authors, however several others were instrumental in bringing this project to its completion. Hossein Kazemi, Nelson Lacey, Donald Chambers, Craig Asche, Urbi Garay, David McCarthy and Kristaps Licis contributed greatly by providing and revising content in all sections, assisting with the development of the initial section outlines, which are based on the CAIA Core Knowledge Outline^{SM} (CKO), and reviewing several section drafts. Melissa Donahue, Michael Carolan, Meg Inners and Aileen Cummings were very helpful in the review stage. Jeanne Miller kept the project on schedule and we owe many thanks to Caitlin Cornish and Viv Wickham at John Wiley & Sons.

Main authors of the **commodities and managed futures section** are Rich Spurgin and Melissa Donahue (Commodities), and Ernest Jaffarian (Managed Futures). Hilary Till made significant contributions to the outline and section reviews. Ernest Jaffarian would like to thank several people as well. The entire team at Efficient Capital Management contributed to the final product, making this section truly a joint venture. Randy York put a dent in the nation's ink supply, compiling the content for this survey and putting it into writing. John Traylor, the lead designer, arranged, illustrated, polished, and segued the content. Joe Mitchell, the project manager, did the statistical analysis and worked as a communication liaison. Ryan Bunting provided research assistance and catalogued information sources. Ron Davis provided his expertise with regard to operations and industry history, while Donna Allen did the same with regard to regulation and compliance. Chad Martinson shared his knowledge of structured products, and Grant Jaffarian furnished information on how CTAs work and are evaluated. Marat Molyboga spent hours discussing trading strategy and providing a seasoned mathematician's perspective on risk analysis. Finally, Courtney Ellis brought her editor's eye to refine the work. To them, and to everyone at Efficient Capital, Ernest Jaffarian wants to give his heartfelt thanks for the dedication, professionalism, and enthusiasm they brought to this undertaking.

Francois Lhabitant is the main author of the **hedge fund section**, and he would like to thank Rebecca Chalmers and Caroline Farelly for their assistance. Jimmy Liew also contributed a chapter to this section, and Jim Gillies made valuable suggestions.

The main authors of the **private equity section** are Pierre-Yves Mathonet and Thomas Meyer. Didier Guennoc was instrumental in the review process and Linda Pells Calnan provided valuable input.

Simon Stevenson and Urbi Garay coauthored the **real estate section.** Bret Wilkerson and Peter Linneman were instrumental in the review process. Urbi Garay would like to extend a special gratitude to and Jaime Sabal for his invaluable help and support during the undertaking of this project. In particular, Urbi is grateful to Ben Branch, Kristap Licis, Raj Gupta and Edward Szado. He would also like to express his gratitude to those at John Wiley & Sons and to Jeanne Miller for their immense help.

About the Authors

Ernest L. Jaffarian is the Founder, President and Chief Executive Officer of Efficient Capital Management, LLC (*Efficient*). He is a veteran of over 20 years within the alternative investment industry in the areas of trading, portfolio construction, and risk management. In 1986 he joined Chicago Research & Trading Inc. (CRT) as a member of the proprietary trading group on the floor of the Chicago Board Options Exchange and rose to position of Senior Vice President for OTC Treasury Options. Immediately prior to founding *Efficient*, Mr. Jaffarian was responsible for the managed futures department of Hull Equity Management, LLC and for the allocation of Hull Trading Company, LLC's proprietary capital among trading advisors. Jaffarian is a CAIA® designee and a frequent speaker at alternative industry events.

Founded in 1999 by leaders from within the industry's preeminent trading organizations including CRT and Hull Trading, *Efficient* is dedicated to maximizing the unique benefits of cash-efficient "alpha" strategies for the institutional investor. *Efficient* presently allocates assets for a variety of global private bank, insurance company, funds of funds and private investor clients. It seeks and invests with more than 40 independent trading firms from 8 countries and 4 continents delivering broad diversification in more than 200 markets. Trading is limited to highly liquid and cash-efficient CFTC approved listed futures and futures/options contracts and generic interbank foreign exchange focused on non-directional sources of alpha returns. The market exposures capitalize on opportunities in currencies, interest rates, stock indices, energy, base and precious metals, and commodities. With a staff of over 40, *Efficient's* significant infrastructure is dedicated to exceeding the most rigorous demands of institutional investors. Available investment structures include private managed accounts and fund structures offering varying levels of capital funding efficiencies.

Francois-Serge Lhabitant, Ph.D., is the Chief Investment Officer of Kedge Capital. He was formerly a Member of Senior Management at Union Bancaire Privée, where he was in charge of quantitative risk management and subsequently, of the quantitative research for alternative portfolios. Prior to this, Francois-Serge was a Director at UBS/Global Asset Management, in charge of building quantitative models for portfolio management and hedge funds.

On the academic side, Francois-Serge is currently a Professor of Finance at the University of Lausanne (Switzerland) and at the EDHEC Business School (France), and a visiting professor at the Hong Kong University of Science and Technology. His research and publications primarily focus on asset management, alternative investments (hedge funds) and emerging markets. He is also a Member of the Scientific Committee of the *Autorité des Marchés Financiers*, the French financial markets regulatory body, a Member of the European Advisory Board of the International Association of

Financial Engineers (IAFE) and a Member of the Alternative Investment Management Association (AIMA) Investor Steering Committee

Kathryn Wilkens-Christopher received her Ph.D. in finance at the University of Massachusetts at Amherst in 1998 after receiving a Center for International Securities and Derivatives Markets (CISDM) fellowship in 1997. She was on the CAIA advisory board from the program's inception in 2002 through 2005. Prior to her current full time involvement with CAIA, she was an assistant professor at Worcester Polytechnic Institute and was awarded the 2002–2004 Teaching Technology Fellowship, which emphasized pedagogical issues in distance learning programs. She is now a CISDM Research Associate and has published chapters in *Intelligent Commodity Investing* (2007), *Hedge Funds and Managed Futures* (2006), *Funds of Hedge Funds* (2006), *Hedge Funds: Insights in Performance Measurement: Risk Analysis, and Portfolio Allocation* (2005), Commodity *Trading Advisors: Risk, Performance Analysis and Selection* (2004), and *Hedge Funds: Strategies, Risk Assessment, and Returns* (2003), as well as several journal articles. Dr. Wilkens-Christopher works with CAIA's membership, Advisory Board, Curriculum Committees, Subcommittees and Task Forces to develop the curriculum based on their expert collective knowledge of alternative investments. She is ultimately responsible for selecting and developing the required readings and outlining the learning objectives of the program.

Melissa Donohue is Senior Editor at Alternative Investment Analytics, a financial consulting firm in Amherst, Massachusetts. She was formerly a financial journalist with global news organizations Bloomberg News and BridgeNews. Melissa was also an associate in emerging markets debt trading at Wasserstein Perella, and a research analyst at Swiss Bank Corporation. She received a Masters of International Affairs with a specialization in banking and finance from Columbia University, and a Bachelor of Arts in government from Oberlin College. Melissa is currently pursuing a Doctoral Degree in Education with a dissertation focus on financial education at the University of Massachusetts.

Pierre-Yves Mathonet is heading the venture capital unit within the risk management division of the European Investment Fund, which is one of the largest investors in the European private equity market, having committed since 1996 to almost 300 funds.

He is also a member of the *Private Equity Subcommittee of the Chartered Alternative Investment Analyst*® Program.

Before that, he worked as an investment banker in the technology groups of Donaldson, Lufkin & Jenrette, and Credit Suisse First Boston, and, previously, for the audit and consulting departments of PricewaterhouseCoopers.

He co-authored two books often used as reference manuals by many private equity and venture capital professionals: *"Beyond the J Curve: Managing a Portfolio of Venture Capital and Private equity Funds"* and *"J Curve exposure: Managing a Portfolio of Venture Capital and Private equity Funds"*.

He holds a Master of Science cum laude in Finance from London Business School and a Master of Science magna cum laude in Management from Solvay Business School in Brussels. He is also a Certified European Financial Analyst cum laude.

Richard Spurgin is an Associate Professor of finance at Clark University in Worcester, Massachusetts. His research centers on investment strategies that use derivatives and on performance measurement for hedge fund strategies, commodities and managed futures. He has published more than thirty academic articles and has assisted in the design of a number of alternative investment benchmark products including the Dow Jones Hedge Fund indices and the Bache Commodity Index. He currently serves on the editorial board of the Journal of Alternative Investments and on the curriculum committee for the CAIA. He received an A.B. in mathematics from Dartmouth College and a Ph.D. in finance from the University of Massachusetts.

Simon Stevenson is Professor of Finance and head of the Real Estate Finance & Investment Group at Cass Business School, City University in London. He joined Cass in 2005 from the Smurfit School of Business, University College Dublin. Professor Stevenson's primary research interests are in the fields of real estate investment, housing economics and international portfolio management. He has published over 50 papers in journals such as the Journal of Housing Economics, Real Estate Economics, Journal of Real Estate Finance & Economics, European Journal of Finance, Emerging Markets Review and the Journal of Real Estate Research. Simon has received best paper awards three times at the annual meeting of the American Real Estate Society and once at the European Real Estate Society annual conference. He was awarded the 2006 International Real Estate Society Achievement Award "for outstanding achievement in real estate research, education and practice at the international level". He is on the editorial board of the Journal of Real Estate Portfolio Management and was President of the International Real Estate Society in 2008. In a recent ranking of real estate researchers Professor Stevenson was ranked 2nd in Europe, 20th globally and 5th of non-US affiliated researchers.

Dr. Thomas Meyer (tmeyer.mba33@london.edu) Thomas is a director of the European Private Equity & Venture Capital Association and a member of the Chartered Alternative Investment Analyst Association's (CAIA©) private equity sub-committee. He studied computer science at the Bundeswehr Universität in Munich followed by doctoral studies at the University of Trier. He holds an MBA from the London Business School as well as an MA in Japanese Language and Society from the University of Sheffield and is a Shimomura Fellow of the Development Bank of Japan's Research Institute of Capital Formation. After 12 years in the German Air Force he worked for the German insurance group Allianz AG in corporate finance and as the regional Chief Financial Officer of Allianz Asia Pacific in Singapore. He was responsible for the creation of the European Investment Fund's risk management function with focus on the development of valuation and risk management models and investment strategies for venture capital fund-of-funds.

Together with Pierre-Yves Mathonet he authored *"Beyond the J Curve: Managing a Portfolio of Venture Capital and Private Equity Funds"* and *"J-Curve Exposure: Managing a Portfolio of Venture Capital and Private Equity Funds"*, both by John Wiley & Sons, Chichester.

Urbi Garay is currently a Full Professor of Finance at IESA Business School in Caracas (Venezuela) and was a visiting researcher at the Center for International Securities and Derivatives Markets (CISDM) and a visiting professor at the Isenberg School of Management at the University of Massachusetts, Amherst (2007–08). He has been a consultant to the Chartered Alternative Investment Analyst Association (CAIAA) since 2008. He received a Ph.D. in Finance from the University of Massachusetts, Amherst, a M.A. in International and Development Economics from Yale University, and a B.A. in Economics from *Universidad Católica Andrés Bello* (Caracas).

Urbi's research and publication focus on alternative investments (primarily real estate, closed-end funds and hedge funds), emerging markets, international finance and corporate governance. He has written two finance textbooks and has published several articles in leading journals, including *The Journal of Alternative Investments*, and an article in *Investor Protection and Corporate Governance* (a recent book edited by F. López-de-Silanes and A. Chong, and published by Stanford University Press).

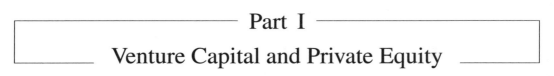

Part I
Venture Capital and Private Equity

Pierre-Yves Mathonet and Thomas Meyer

Introduction

In the broad sense, private equity is a term that includes any type of equity investment in a firm which is not listed on an exchange. Private equity investment strategies increasingly represent a significant component of institutional portfolios (Center for International Securities and Derivatives Markets, 2006). The growing interest in this alternative investment asset class has risen in part as a result of its superior historical long-term returns when compared to those of public equities and by its diversification benefits. The sources of the higher return opportunities provided by private equity have risen because of their ability to invest in privately-held companies not available in the traditional investor arena as well as their capability to create value by proactively influencing the management and operations of the invested firms.

The private equity section in Level II consists of eleven chapters. Chapter 1 presents a description of the private equity market landscape, including a review of important concepts such as the relationship lifecycle between limited and general partners, buyout and venture capital funds and the (in)famous J-curve. Chapter 2 offers a discussion of the different routes into private equity investments using either private equity funds or private equity funds-of-funds as intermediaries. Chapter 3 describes the structure of private equity funds, from the limited partnership agreement and its key features to a discussion of potential conflicts of interest. Chapter 4 discusses the idiosyncrasies of the private equity investment process and introduces concepts pertaining to the risk management of a portfolio of private equity funds. Chapter 5 compares and contrasts the bottom-up and top-down approaches to private equity portfolio design and highlights issues surrounding private equity diversification.

Chapter 6 explores the fund manager selection process, its impact on performance and the essential steps to conducting proper due diligence. Chapter 7 presents the main performance measures and benchmarks used to evaluate individual private equity funds (including the important concept of the interim internal rate of return) and portfolios of funds. Chapter 8 discusses the benefits and drawbacks of monitoring, as well as important related issues such as style drift and transparency. Chapter 9 compares and contrasts the net asset value and economic value approaches used to value private equity funds. Chapter 10 deals with the empirical issues that arise when attempting to estimate the discount rate applicable to private equity investments, including the different methods used to calculate private equity fund betas. Finally, Chapter 11 delineates the principles of liquidity management in private equity funds (including the concept of over-commitment), describes the main sources of liquidity and outlines the various methods of making cash flow projections for private equity funds.

This section of the CAIA curriculum covers advanced topics in private equity investing. The reader is assumed to be familiar with the private equity chapters in the Level I readings. Whereas the emphasis there was on introductory concepts and historical performance, the emphasis in Level II is on the management of portfolios of private equity funds.

CAIA Association 2009

1
Private Equity Market Landscape

The growing interest in private equity investing has arisen in part as a result of its superior historical long-term returns when compared to those of public equities, and by the diversification benefits it provides. Investments in private equity funds offer access to privately-held companies not available in the traditional investor landscape and expertise in creating value by proactively influencing the management and operations of the invested firms.

Institutional investors typically focus on the organized private equity market, where professional management is provided by intermediaries. There is also an informal private equity market, which is composed of angel capital and, not without justification, which is often called family, friends and fools. Companies can also get funding from the founder's savings and efforts, commonly referred to as blood or sweat equity. The number of investments made in the informal private equity market is probably several times larger than the organized private equity market, but it is difficult for institutional investors to gain the information necessary to invest in these markets effectively.

MAIN STRATEGIES

Private equity funds refer to a multitude of investment strategies with varying risk profiles, liquidity requirements and returns. The primary, and most important, three types of funds are: venture capital (VC), buyouts and mezzanine funds. These funds form the bulk of a typical institutional investor's private equity portfolio.

Venture capital funds invest alongside management in young and/or potentially fast-growing companies and are often active in technology sectors such as telecommunications, life sciences and clean-tech. Venture capital has two sub-categories depending on the stage of development of the funded company:

- **Early stage.** Early stage companies are riskier because of their small size and unproven ability to generate profits. This stage is further split into seed[1] and start-up stages.
- **Expansion stage.** Companies in this stage have already established the technology and market for their product, but require further financing to allow greater, or more rapid, growth.

VC investments are not comparable with traditional financial investments and have characteristics that make it difficult to apply traditional portfolio management techniques. These investments are still generally in their cash-burning stage and may be several years away from an exit.

Buyout funds[2] invest in established businesses (generally privately held or spin-offs from public companies) that need financial capital in connection with a change of ownership. Buyout is a generic term that comprises notably: management buyouts (MBO), where the current management acquires the company; management buy-ins (MBI), where new managers come from outside the company; and public-to-private transactions where companies are de-listed when a private equity company acquires their shares. In all of these cases, a buyout fund may intervene as an intermediary owner,

---

[1] The seed stage takes place before there is a real product or the company is organized.

[2] Some investors in the investment industry use the term "private equity" to refer only to buyout fund investing, while others, as we do in this book, refer to both venture and buyout investing as "private equity" investing.

usually alongside the management. In buyout funds, portfolio companies are established, have tangible assets and are normally beyond the cash-burning stage, which allows the use of debt to finance part of the transaction. In these cases, buyouts are referred to as leveraged buyouts (LBO).

Mezzanine funds invest in established companies (usually privately held and/or below investment grade) seeking expansion or transition capital through the issuance of subordinated debt with warrants or conversion rights to purchase the common stock. Mezzanine financing is halfway between equity and secured debt. While mezzanine financing gives a more predictable cash flow profile, it is unlikely to provide capital returns comparable to other private equity financing forms.

MAIN DIFFERENCES BETWEEN VC AND BUYOUT FUNDS

VC and buyout funds differ in several significant aspects, notably in terms of their business model, deal structuring, roles of the general partner and valuation. These and other differences are summarized in Table 1.1 and discussed below.

The classic argument presented for diversifying among private equity classes, and especially between buyout and VC funds, is that they often exhibit negative correlations and differ in terms of growth and value investing. To begin with, buyout transactions are largely debt-financed and tend to perform well during depressed public equity market periods, when debt is cheap. However, if depressed equity prices are accompanied with a widening of credit spreads (e.g. the financial crisis of 2008–2009), then leveraged buyout transactions may not be feasible. Second, VC relies on the stock market as the main exit route and therefore close to exit, often shows strong correlation with small-cap indices. Consequently, VC would be expected to do better during equity bull markets. Historically, buyouts have provided more stable returns with an orientation towards minimizing risk, while VC occasionally produces higher rates of return in certain markets but also the possibility

Table 1.1 Buyout–Venture Capital comparison

	Buyout	Venture capital
Sector	Established industry	Cutting-edge technology or rapidly growing sectors
Stage	Stable growth and mature	Seed, start-up and expansion
Approach	Financial engineering, corporate restructuring	Industry know-how, product development and commercialization
Uncertainties	Risk is measurable	Risk is difficult to measure
Source of returns	Leverage, company building, multiple arbitrage	Company building, finding follow-on investors
Selection	Intensive financial due diligence	Limited financial due diligence but extensive sector/product due diligence
Valuation constraints	Cash flow projections overlooked by credit lenders	None; often no non-VC third party oversight
Business model	High percentage of success with limited number of write-offs	A few winners with many write-offs
Financing/deal structure	Club deals and large investments	Limited syndication with several investment rounds
Monitoring	Cash-flow management	Growth management
Success factor	Backing experienced managers	Backing entrepreneurs

of higher losses. Thus, investors seeking long-term stable returns would be inclined to overweight buyout funds, while those seeking higher returns would do so through increased exposure to VC.[3]

Business model

Attractive VC investment opportunities can be difficult to assess and are usually concentrated in a few high technology sectors, which often results in a relatively high number of small investments being done initially. Returns stem from taking large risks to develop new businesses and concentrating efforts and capital through several incremental funding rounds. The goal is to build companies that can be sold or taken public with a high multiple of invested capital.[4] These few big wins need to compensate for many failures. VC-funded companies can be seen as works in progress, with intermediate stages of completion. These stages of completion are often distinguished by milestones such as rounds of financing (e.g. rounds A, B, C, ...) or, in the case of a biotech company, perhaps phases of clinical trials (Phases I, II, III and IV). In this respect, they are development projects that cannot be prematurely exited without risking the loss of most, if not all, of one's invested capital. Thus, VC funds should be viewed as long-term investments, which explains why fund managers often impose rigid restrictions on the transferability of interests in their funds.

Large capital requirements and lower risk levels result in most buyout firms making a smaller number of investments compared to VC. There is also a multitude of different approaches that can be combined in a transaction, such as divestment of unrelated businesses, financial engineering, company turnaround, and vertical or horizontal integration through acquisition. Buyout managers need to give extensive strategic and business planning advice. They tend to focus on consistent rather than outsized returns. Because they target established enterprises, buyout firms experience fewer outright failures but have more limited upside potential.

Deal structuring

VC funds typically utilize no debt and gain control of a company over time through a series of equity investments. Returns stem from building companies and from managing growth. Valuation is complicated by the lack of appropriate comparisons, and explains why venture capitalists carry out only limited financial due diligence. They typically provide not only financing for building businesses, but also industry know-how and management expertise. The investments can be relatively small[5] and are overwhelmingly equity or quasi-equity financed with little or no leverage.[6] Successful exit strategies require VC managers to secure follow-on investors or syndications.

Buyout funds, on the other hand, typically use debt financing to purchase all or most of a company's equity. Assets of the acquired company are used as collateral for the debt and the cash flow of the

---

[3] There exist more "rules of thumb" for determining the private equity allocation that best positions investors with regard to risk and return. According to Venture Economics, between 1990 and 2000, the commitment ratio of buyouts compared to venture capital was somewhere between 3:1 and 2:1. Because of the costs involved, institutional investors who are looking to put large amounts of money to work into the private equity sector should consider committing 75% of their private equity allocation to buyout funds and 25% to VC funds (Giacometti, 2001).

[4] The term "multiple" is defined as the return earned by investing in early stage companies expressed as a *multiple* of the original investment. For example, a multiple of 2x means that investors receive a return of two times their original investment.

[5] Initial stakes in the area of €100,000 are not uncommon.

[6] One could argue that there is implicitly "leverage" through the intensive use of option-like mechanisms and through the fact that there is constrained financing: Start-ups are never fully financed and seldom do funds have the financial resources to fund all their investments.

company is used to pay off the debt. Buyout managers conduct intensive financial due diligence and rely occasionally on sophisticated financial engineering. The ability to analyze a company's balance sheet and extract operational efficiencies, as opposed to the implementation of financial legerdemain, are the primary drivers of a successful transaction. Generally, there are few limitations to investment size, given the high number of stable growth and mature companies that can be targeted.

Role of general and limited partners

General partners are the managers of private equity funds but depending on the type of fund, their role can differ dramatically. Venture capitalists look to launch new or emerging companies while buyout funds focus on leveraging an established company's assets. Venture capitalists back entrepreneurs whereas buyout funds deal with experienced managers. General partners of VC funds often play an active role in the companies in which the funds invest, either by sitting on the board of directors or becoming involved in the day-to-day management of the company. Investors in funds assess how much value general managers can add to the portfolio of companies. Thus, in VC, the choice of general manager is a key driver of returns.

In buyout funds, a greater proportion of time and manpower is spent analyzing specific investments and adjusting the business model. Buyout partners look to leverage their expertise in turning around underperforming businesses, to improve profitable businesses, or to optimize the balance sheet and the financing of the companies. General partners typically engage in hiring new management teams or retooling strategies. In an operating company it is easier to give guidance to a seasoned management team, while in early-stage investments one often needs to build and coach the management team from the ground up.

Limited partners are simply investors with little or no influence on the day-to-day management of the fund. The interests of the limited partners are aligned with those of the general partners through a shared financial commitment to the fund, including the **carried interest**[7] (or profit share) of the manager.

Valuation

The valuation of VC investments can pose significant problems given their often limited operating history, and is compounded in cases where the company has yet to generate a profit. Traditional valuation methods can only be applied to VC by making numerous assumptions often using unreliable information. The valuation of a VC investment is mainly based on the analysis of intangibles, such as patents or the founders' entrepreneurial skills, competence and experience; as well as the assessment of the expected market size for the portfolio company's products or the presumed exit value relative to existing comparable public companies. Thus, investment valuation is usually based not on cash flow or earnings but rather on multiples where comparable companies exist. Where they do not, valuation becomes even more difficult to quantify.

There are relatively few investors (i.e. sources of capital) and little or no consensus on valuation. A lack of third-party oversight can make venture capital prone to losses from overvaluation. In addition, because the value placed on a young company cannot be verified except through future rounds of investment,[8] it may take years to uncover overinflated and unsustainable valuations.

---

[7] Carried interest is a share in the fund's profits received by the fund manager.

[8] While for later stage private equity the investors' relationship to the portfolio company may have little influence on its valuation, this is clearly not the case for venture capital investments: Their realizable "value" is heavily influenced by the

Buyout funds typically use debt financing with significant leverage to purchase all, or most, of a company's equity. Assets of the acquired company are posted as collateral for the debt while the company's cash flow is used to service the debt. In buyout funds, valuation risk is more limited. First of all, the valuation of portfolio companies is more straightforward enabling one to draw upon a rich toolbox of accepted instruments for quantitative analysis, such as discounted cash flow projections. The leverage required for the transactions leads to scrutiny from a syndicate of commercial lenders and often due diligence by underwriters of a high-yield bond offering. The influence of these credit providers eliminates some of the potential risks inherent in the leverage. There will be restrictions on the amount of leverage they provide which implicitly sets an upper boundary on the total valuation for the targeted business.

THE RELATIONSHIP LIFECYCLE BETWEEN LIMITED AND GENERAL PARTNERS

There is a symbiotic relationship between limited and general partners. A limited partner's investment strategy is built around a small number of general partners who focus on specific segments, such as stages or sectors, of the market. This specialized focus can often limit the scalability of a particular fund, particularly in the case of VC, where limited partners may find it difficult to identify and access additional fund managers of comparable quality.

General partners, on the other hand, want financially strong, dependable, knowledgeable and long-term limited partners. Limited partners should have industry expertise and familiarity with the nuts and bolts, particularly valuations and benchmarking, of the private equity business. Adverse selection exists in the private equity market. Poor quality funds, be they inexperienced ones or old dog firms in decline, will court inexperienced investors. Because of the bad results, both will sooner or later exit the market.

To maintain continuous investment in portfolio companies, general partners need to raise new funds as soon as the capital from the existing partnership is fully invested (or reserved for follow-on investments), which means about every three to five years. Therefore, relationships between limited and general partners follow a lifecycle and are forged through various rounds of investment, eventually resulting in a virtuous circle of growing experience and fund size.

Investors as well as fund managers depend on forging long-term relationships. Anecdotal evidence suggests that experienced market players profit over protracted time periods from these relationships. Initial criteria are very stringent and fund managers usually cannot get rich through their first funds. A favorable track record and experience is an asset in itself. Fundraising is less costly for more reputable funds. To minimize their expenses, fund managers generally turn first to those who invested in their previous partnership, provided that the fund's performance was satisfactory.

While it is obvious that fund managers greatly benefit from a loyal and reliable investor community, long-term relationships can also be advantageous for limited partners as well:

- In the opaque private equity market, the search for and due diligence of funds is a costly exercise and often limited partners prefer familiar fund managers to unproven investment proposals.
- For an investor it is especially desirable to hold on to good fund managers, as the best teams will have an established investor base which may eliminate the need to seek out new funding sources.

---

bargaining power of their venture capital investor. Only a financially strong investor can sustain longer negotiation periods. A weak VC fund is in no position to "shop around" for several months while its portfolio burns the remaining liquidity.

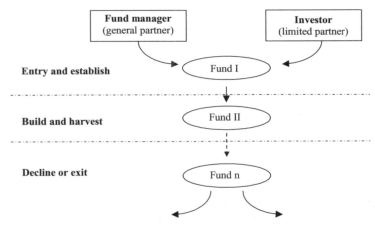

Figure 1.1   Fund manager–investor relationship lifecycle

- There is likely to be better planning, as limited partners make clear their intentions to participate in follow-on funds. As limited partners form a network, even if they do not have the means to continue, they often refer other investors to a good team. Predictable closings put money to work more efficiently.

The lifecycle of the fund manager–investor relationship (see Figure 1.1) can be divided into three phases: 1) entry and establish; 2) build and harvest (or growth and compete); and 3) decline (lost competition), exit (gave up or made it), or transition to new managers (spinouts). The main differences between these phases are summarized in Table 1.2.

During the "entry and establish" phase, significant entry barriers into the private equity market exist for both general and limited partners. Lacking a verifiable track record, new teams find it difficult to raise their first fund. Furthermore, analysis of historical benchmark data supports the hypothesis that new teams suffer from higher "mortality" than established or institutional-quality

Table 1.2   Fund manager–investor relationship lifecycle model

Fund's characteristics	Entry and establish	Build and harvest	Decline or exit
Investment strategy	Differentiation	"Star" brand	Unexciting
Fundraising	Difficult fundraising	Loyal limited partner base	Limited partners leave and are replaced by other types of investors (secondary plays, new entrants in market)
Performance	Unknown: either "top" or "out"	Likely "top" performer	Not "top" but consistent performer
Size	Fund is too small	Fund size is right	Fund size too large/too many funds
Economies of scale	Fund is too small to get rich	Best alignment of interests	Senior managers made it
Management team	Management team forming	Management team performing	Succession issues, spinouts

fund management. First-time funds note the importance of differentiation as it applies to fundraising and thus often pursue specialized investment strategies.[9]

New limited partners also face entry barriers. They normally suffer from the initial informational disadvantages that afflict all limited partners and make it extremely difficult for them to identify or gain access to the best managers, particularly where managers are oversubscribed. For limited partners, it takes the disciplined execution of a long-term investment strategy to build up a portfolio of funds that gives attractive and sustainable returns.

Since investors are mainly interested in the cash returned, the fund manager–investor relationship tends to be relatively stable throughout the "build and harvest" phase. Lerner and Schoar (2004) presented evidence on the high degree of continuity in the investors of successive funds and the ability of sophisticated investors to anticipate funds that will have poor subsequent performance.

It is an oversimplification to assume that investors only invest in top performers and that below-average funds are unable to continue.[10] As in most relationships, there is a certain degree of tolerance for mistakes and failures, at least over some time. It is clear that there are limits to disappointing results but, all things being equal, investors will tend to go with fund managers they already know or who have been referred to them through their network even if their performance at times is sub-par.

Eventually the relationship ends in the decline or exit phase. Not surprisingly, the terms marriage and divorce are often used in the context of relationships between fund managers and their investors. A gradual decline may occur as a result of past successes which potentially decrease the financial motivation of senior fund managers, or perhaps due to an improperly planned succession which leads to the departure of middle management. Also, the limited partners eventually may end the relationship if they lose confidence or trust in the team, for example if the team becomes arrogant or fails to deliver. Some limited partners do not invest in follow-on funds and may be replaced by less deep-pocketed investors, or by secondary investors who choose to invest as a one-off financial play.

THE J-CURVE

One of the first private equity fund concepts that investors will encounter is the (in-)famous "**J-curve**" – also referred to as the "hockey stick" (see Figure 1.2). The European Venture Capital and Private Equity Association (EVCA) defines the J-curve as the "curve generated by plotting the returns generated by a private equity fund over time (from inception to termination)". The common practice of paying the management fee and start-up costs out of the first drawdowns causes book value to be lower than the sum of the contributions. As a result, a private equity fund will initially show a negative return. When the first realizations are made, the fund returns start to rise quite steeply. After about three to five years the Interim IRR (IIRR) will give a reasonable indication of the definitive IRR.[11] This period is generally shorter for buyout funds than for early stage and expansion funds.

---

[9] See Thompson (1999).

[10] See Hellman and Katz, 2002: "Just as one fight shouldn't wreck a marriage, one bad fund should not ruin a long-standing relationship between a fund manager and an investor. But, in order to strengthen the relationship, both sides need to be able to recognize and discuss what went wrong and how things will change going forward to maximize the chance of success for all."

[11] The (traditional) IRR is the implied discount rate that makes the net present value of all cash flows zero. The interim IRR (IIRR) is the IRR of unliquidated funds, as it considers fund distributions during each period t, the net asset value of the fund at the end of period T, and capital contributions or drawdowns during each period t. Therefore, IIRRs are only estimates rather than realized rates of returns. The IIRR is the rate of return of a fund before the final termination date. It can also be thought of as the IRR that is calculated assuming that the residual value of the private equity fund is the final cash outflow. Chapter 7 presents the formal definition and an example of the calculation of this important concept.

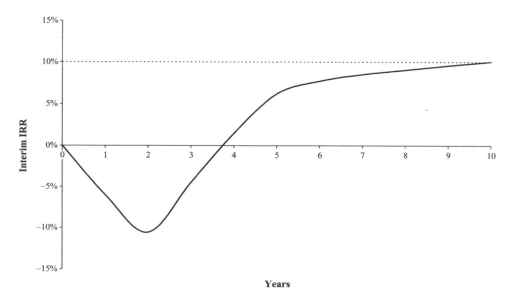

Figure 1.2   Fund standard J-curve

The classical fund performance J-curve is mainly caused by the fact that valuation policies followed by the industry and the uncertainty inherent in private equity investments prevent revaluing promising investments upwards until quite late in a fund's lifetime, while fees, costs and expenses are quickly deducted. As a result, private equity funds tend to demonstrate an apparent decline in value during the early years of existence, the so-called "valley of tears", before beginning to show the hoped-for positive returns in the later years of the fund's life.

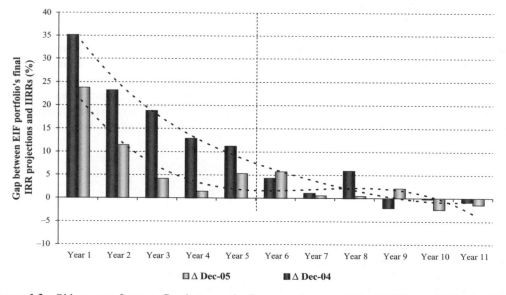

Figure 1.3   Old vs. new J-curve. Gap between the European Investment Fund (EIF) portfolio's final IRR projections and IIRRs as of December 2005 vs. December 2004 (Source: Mathonet and Monjanel, 2006 and EIF)

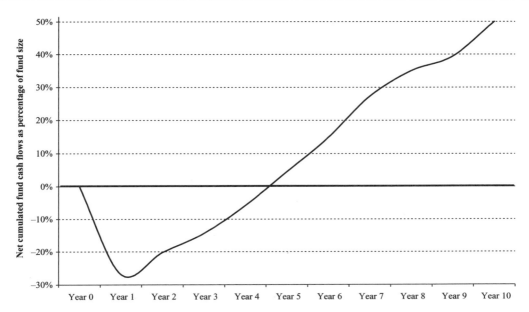

Figure 1.4   Fund cash flows J-curve

Some time ago,[12] it was postulated that the introduction of the new International Private Equity and Venture Capital Valuation Guidelines (IPEV guidelines)[13] in 2005 would drive the J-curve to extinction as a truly fair value for funds would eliminate the conservative bias caused by early expensing of costs and deferred recognition of increases in the values of promising investments. Instead, Mathonet and Monjanel (2006) found that the gap between the final IRR (or the expected in Figure 1.3) and the IIRR narrowed in years one thru five, after which the IIRR became on average a reasonably reliable estimator of the final performance (see Figure 1.3).

But other J-curves can also be observed in private equity funds: the **cash flow J-curve** and the **net asset value (NAV) J-curve**.[14] The **cash flow J-curve** is a representation of the evolution of the net accumulated cash flows from the limited partners to the fund, which are first increasingly negative during the early years of existence before making a U-turn and becoming positive in the later years of the fund's life. This is explained by the fact that, in standard private equity fund structures, commitments are drawn down as needed, or just-in-time. When realizations are made, after having successfully developed these newly-found companies, they are distributed as soon as practical (see Figure 1.4).

---

[12] See Meyer and Mathonet (2005).

[13] Available on www.privateequityvaluation.com [accessed October 2007].

[14] The net asset value (NAV) of a fund is calculated by adding the value of all of the investments held in the fund and dividing by the number of outstanding shares of the fund. The NAV J-curve is a representation of the evolution of the NAV versus the net paid-in (NPI), which first decreases during the early years of existence before improving in later years of the fund's life.

2

Routes into Private Equity

There are different routes for investing in private equity (see Figure 2.1). Few institutions have the experience and the incentive structures that would allow them to invest directly in non-public companies and most of them seek intermediation through the limited partnership structure. For institutions, the most relevant approaches to investing in private equity are through fund-of-funds specialists as intermediaries, or through similarly structured, dedicated in-house private equity investment programs who invest directly in funds. Other routes are via publicly-quoted private equity vehicles, or through opening a dedicated account managed by a private equity specialist.

PRIVATE EQUITY FUNDS AS INTERMEDIARIES

The organized private equity market is dominated by funds, generally structured as limited partnerships, which serve as principal financial intermediaries. Fund management companies, also referred to as private equity firms, set up these funds. Private equity funds are unregistered investment vehicles in which investors, or limited partners, pool money to invest in privately-held companies. Investment professionals, such as venture capitalists or buyout investors (known as general partners or fund managers), manage these funds. Tax, legal and regulatory requirements drive the structuring of these investment vehicles with the goal of increasing transparency (investors are treated as investing directly in the underlying portfolio companies), reducing taxation and **limiting liability** (investors' liabilities are limited to the capital committed to the fund). From a strictly legal standpoint, limited partnership shares are illiquid, while in practice **secondary transactions** occasionally take place where investors sell their shares before the termination of the fund. Private equity funds principally serve the following functions:[1]

- pooling of investors' capital for investing in private companies;
- screening, evaluating and selecting potential companies with expected high-growth opportunities;
- financing companies to develop new products and technologies, to foster their growth and development, to make acquisitions, or to allow for a buy-out or a buy-in by experienced managers;
- controlling, coaching and monitoring portfolio companies;
- sourcing exit opportunities for portfolio companies.

While the specific terms and conditions and investor rights and obligations are defined in non-standard partnership agreements, the limited partnership structure — or comparable structures used in the various jurisdictions — has evolved over the last decades to include the following standards (see Chapter 3 for more details on fund structures).

- The fund usually has a **contractually limited life** of 7–10 years, often with a provision for an extension of two to three years. The fund manager's objective is to realize all investments before or at the liquidation of the fund.

---

[1] See also Thalmann and Weinwurm (2002).

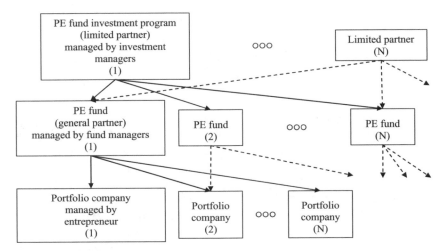

Figure 2.1 Private equity funds investment program

- Investors — mainly institutions such as pension funds, endowments, private equity, funds-of-funds, banks or insurance companies, or high net worth individuals or family offices — are the **limited partners** and commit a certain amount of money to the fund.
- The main part of the capital is drawn down during the **investment period**, typically the first three to five years, where new opportunities are identified. After that, during the divestment period, only the existing portfolio companies with the highest potential are further supported, with some follow-on funding provided to extract the maximum value through exits. The manager's efforts during this time are concentrated on realizing or selling the investments.
- **Commitments** (i.e. capital pledges by investors in private equity) are drawn down as needed, i.e., just-in-time, to make investments or to pay costs, expenses or management fees. Because private equity funds typically do not retain large pools of uninvested capital, their general partners make capital calls once they have identified a company to invest in.[2] Therefore, the main part of the **drawdowns** (i.e. the use or call of capital committed or pledged) gets invested immediately.
- When realizations are made, or when interest payments, dividends or recapitalizations are received, they are distributed to investors as soon as feasible. Thus, the fund is self-liquidating as the underlying investments are realized. However, these returns come mostly in the second half of the fund's lifetime. **Distributions** to investors can also be in-kind as securities of a portfolio company, provided that these securities are publicly tradable.
- The **management fees** depend on the size of the fund. They generally range from 2.5% of committed capital for funds of less than €250 ($300) million, to 1.5% for the larger funds. The fees are often scaled down once the investment period has been completed and adjusted according to the proportion of the portfolio that has been divested. There are considerable differences from one fund to the next regarding directorship fees or transaction costs. These can have an impact on the returns and often account for material differences between gross and net returns.
- The main incentive for the general partners comes in the form of carried interest, typically 20% of the profits realized by the fund. Carried interest is usually subject to a **hurdle rate** or **preferred**

---

[2] Private equity firms collect or "call" the needed capital for investment from the limited partner in a series of tranches called "capital calls".

return, so that it only begins to accrue once investors have received their capital back and a minimum pre-agreed rate of return.[3]

- There is a private equity **fundraising cycle** which begins anew each time the general partners need to raise capital for another fund. Typically, limited partnership agreements do not allow follow-on funds by the same manager before the end of the initial fund's investment period or until a large part of the initial fund has been invested.

PRIVATE EQUITY FUNDS-OF-FUNDS AS INTERMEDIARIES

Many institutions outsource their private equity fund investment program either through a dedicated account or by pooling assets with other investors. The private equity funds-of-funds are probably the most common type of institutional investment program. The authorizing entity for a private-equity fund investment program is the principal who provides the resources, while the manager of the program is his agent and conducts the investments in private equity funds as a limited partner.

Funds-of-funds, which are generally organized by banks, asset managers, insurance groups, or specialists, are vehicles that pool funds from a group of investors to invest in a diversified portfolio of funds. Some funds-of-funds specialize in certain private equity sectors or geographies, while others follow a more generalist approach. Funds-of-funds manage the following, often complementary, activities:

- Primary investments in newly-formed limited partnerships. Because of the "blind pool" nature of such investments, the assessment of the fund management team's skills is key (see Chapter 6).
- Selectively makes direct co-investments alongside the primary investments. This activity requires direct investment experience and skills.
- Secondary investments in existing funds or portfolios of direct investments. While this is generally a niche activity for most funds-of-funds, in recent years secondary specialists have emerged, such as Coller Capital, Green Park Capital, and Lexington Partners. For co-investments, direct investment experience, skills for the assessment of the companies already in the portfolio and the ability to quickly execute the transaction are very important.

While investment in a particular private equity fund can have a "blind pool" nature, a fund-of-funds can have established relationships with fund managers via existing investments. Therefore, its future portfolio is somewhat predictable and is not necessarily a blind pool investment. A newly-created portfolio is likely to be largely comprised of follow-on funds raised by these known managers. In fact, funds-of-funds are marketed on either a partially blind or a fully informed basis. For a partially blind pool some of the intended partnership groups are identified, while for a fully informed pool, virtually all of the intended partnerships have been identified to the investors.

Private equity funds-of-funds costs

Funds-of-funds are often seen as less efficient because of the additional layer of management fees. This double layer is perceived to be one of the main disadvantages of this structure. Funds-of-funds would have to outperform by 0.7–3.4% to compensate for this additional layer of fees.[4] However,

---

[3] Hurdle rates, also called preferred return, are defined as the minimum rate of return which must be attained before the manager of the private equity fund can collect any carried interest payments.

[4] Jo (2002) analyzed 48 U.S.-based funds-of-funds launched between 1992 and 1999 (13 asset managers, 15 banks and 20 independent funds). For asset managers the author found an average carried interest of 3.8% (only 5 of the 13 asset managers charged a carried interest) and an average management fee of 0.85%. For investment and commercial banks,

given the resources required to manage a portfolio of private equity funds internally, investing through a fund-of-funds structure might well prove more cost-efficient in the end. Not necessarily so argues Smith (2000) who found that expenses for in-house teams are comparable to the management fees charged by funds-of-funds.

An additional cost of outsourcing to a fund-of-funds is the carried interest. Whether an in-house program can work without investment performance-related incentives is debatable. According to Otterlei and Barrington (2003), the annual costs of an in-house team can be significant compared to a typical fund-of-funds. Even with a 5% carried interest charged by the fund-of-funds manager, these authors find that the fees have an insignificant impact on the net returns of the investor. Information is an asset in the often opaque environment of private equity. Taking the fund-of-funds route versus that of direct investor can lead to a loss of information and control, essentially a cost in itself. Because private equity programs follow a learning curve, inexperienced institutions initially may have little option other than to go through a fund-of-funds vehicle. Ultimately they can become limited partners in funds and with increasing sophistication build their own portfolio of companies, either through co-investing or by independently sourcing deals. In conclusion, funds-of-funds are often used as a first step into private equity and may well be worth the additional layer of fees in exchange for avoiding expensive learning curve mistakes and/or for providing access to a broader selection of funds.

PRIVATE EQUITY FUNDS-OF-FUNDS VALUE-ADDED

Diversification and intermediation

Funds-of-funds can add value in several respects and are seen as safe havens for private equity investors. Especially in the case of new technologies, new teams, or emerging markets, a fund-of-funds allows for a reasonable downside protection through diversification. Not surprisingly, various studies have shown that, because of their diversification, funds-of-funds perform similarly to individual funds but with less pronounced extremes (see Weidig and Mathonet, 2004, or Mathonet and Meyer, 2007). In the absence of funds-of-funds, smaller institutions may have difficulty achieving meaningful levels of diversification. Even for larger institutions, investments in private equity funds and especially VC funds may be too cost-intensive when the size of such investments is small compared to the administrative expenses. A fund-of-funds can mediate these potential size issues either by scaling up through pooling smaller investors, or by scaling down through investing a large commitment to the fund-of-funds.

Resources and information

Funds-of-funds can provide the necessary resources and address the information gap for inexperienced private equity investors through their expertise in due diligence, monitoring and restructuring. Investing in private equity funds requires a wide-reaching network of contacts in order to gain access to high-quality funds, trained investment judgment and the ability to assemble balanced portfolios. The liquidity management can also be quite challenging. This demands a full-time team with insight and an industry network, adequate resources, access to research databases and models, and skills and experience in due diligence, negotiation, and contract structuring. Depending on the overall market

---

management fees were in the range 0.88–1.25%; 12 of the 15 banks charged a carried interest, average carry was 6.6%; typical was just 5% carry. At the end of the 1990s annual management fees were in the region of 0.8% and 10% carried interest; five years later the difficult market environment brought that down to 0.7% and a carried interest of 5%.

situation, access to quality funds can be highly competitive and pose a significant entry barrier for a newcomer to the market. Funds-of-funds are continuously involved in the private equity space, speak the language and understand the trade-offs in the industry.

Selection skills and expertise

Investors expect funds-of-funds managers to be able to invest in top-performing funds, either by having access to successful "invitation only" funds, or by identifying the future stars among the young and less-known ones. They may also play the role of educator in explaining to comparatively unsophisticated investors that the fund, despite apparently suffering "horrible losses" in the early years, is still viable and merely reflecting the early stages of its J-curve. While funds-of-funds are more willing to give the fund managers sufficient latitude to focus on their portfolio companies, they are often better skilled and experienced in restructuring failing funds, if that is ultimately required. In turn, fund managers often welcome funds-of-funds investors as a more stable source of cheap, pooled capital.

Incentives, oversight and agreements

For institutional investors, direct investment is problematic because such institutions cannot offer their employees adequate performance-related pay. For typical conservative and seniority-based institutions like banks, pension funds, or insurance companies, a theoretically unlimited carried interest does not fit into the compensation scheme. While institutional investors do not lack staff with the intellectual caliber to evaluate investment proposals and to structure transactions, generating profitable exits in private equity programs requires very hard work over protracted time periods. Moreover, the lack of incentives to take risk and to find value will affect investment decisions. Furthermore, there is a significant learning curve and, without performance-related pay, employees may jump ship as soon as they are competent in the area and understand their opportunities better.

Finally, for larger institutions, intermediation through funds-of-funds allows them to focus on their core businesses. This advantage tends to outweigh most cost considerations.

3
Private Equity Funds Structure[1]

Regulatory changes in the U.S. in the late 1970s permitted greater private equity investment by pension funds, but it was mainly the intermediation through limited partnerships that fostered a widespread adoption of private equity in institutional portfolios. According to Prowse (1998), the growth of private equity shows how organizational innovation, assisted by regulatory and tax changes, can create new possibilities and ignite activity in a particular market. The limited partnership as the dominant structure in private equity investment results from the extreme information asymmetries and incentive problems that arise in the private equity market. While the limited partnership structure does not exist in all jurisdictions, most local legislation allows for this well-established form to be utilized.

For the private equity fund, the **limited partnership agreement** (LPA) defines its legal framework and its terms and conditions. The LPA primarily addresses the allocation of capital gains or losses among partners, allocation of interim distributions, management fees for the general partner, possible investment restrictions and major governance issues. LPAs are continuously evolving given the increasing sophistication of fund managers and investors, new regulations and changing economic environments. In essence, the LPA lays out conditions aimed at aligning the interests of fund managers with their investors, and discouraging "cheating" (moral hazard), "lying" (adverse selection), or "opportunism" (hold-up problem) in whatever form. Incentives are designed so that the fund manager's focus is to maximize terminal wealth and performance and that contractual loopholes are not exploited by producing overly-optimistic interim results.

One private equity management company can act as a group, managing several such partnerships in parallel. Typically, LPAs do not allow follow-on funds by the same manager before the end of the investment period or before a high percentage (usually more than 70%) of the active fund has been invested.

For the general partner, an operating agreement sets the division and vesting of carried interest among individual fund managers. The management company enters into agreements with all employees and with the general partners. For the management company, an additional operating agreement may be required to define the division of management fees and the licensing of name and trademark.[2]

The main documents of the fund offering are the privae placement memorandum which describes the general investment proposal, the subscription agreement which contains the contractual capital commitment and securities law exemptions, and the LPA.

Figure 3.1 presents a summary of the typical private equity limited partnership structure, where the relationship between the management company, the general partner, the limited partners and the fund are outlined. These relationships are further explored in the next chapter. Needless to say, intensive communication between general and limited partners at all stages of the investment process is the most effective non-structural method for creating alignment and avoiding surprises.[3]

---

[1] This section was not written by lawyers. It contains information of a general nature and is meant only to illustrate principles.

[2] See Muller (2004).

[3] See Hellman and Katz (2002): the "increased communication enables GPs and LPs to better understand each other's actions and motives, creating an atmosphere of long-term partnership that both sides profess to desire". Investors also demand transparency related to co-investors and co-investment terms and conditions.

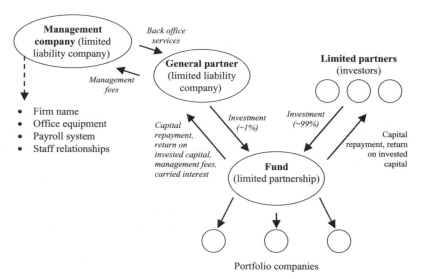

Figure 3.1   Limited partnership structure

KEY FEATURES

The limited partnership in its current form is viewed as a good fit for the existing market environment; however the environment is never static but continuously evolving. Yet given the success of the current limited partnership structure, it is more likely we will see adjustments to the LPA terms and conditions rather than broad structural changes. For example, in the highly fragmented private equity market, competition and variations in local regulations can precipitate different fund terms and conditions in the LPA. As the industry develops, fund sizes may diverge and specialist players emerge, rendering standard terms inappropriate for ensuring the alignment of interests in all situations. Deviations from the mainstream or even newly evolving best practices arise out of the need for new fund managers to differentiate themselves. In addition, new terms and conditions can result from changes to the regulatory and economic environment. Ultimately though, it is the general partners who, having control over who can invest in their funds, are best positioned to dictate these terms.

It is through the proper alignment of investor and investment manager economic interests not just through the LPA covenants, the advisory boards, or the committees composed of limited partners – that one can eliminate many of the problems associated with the principal–agent relationship in various scenarios, especially in those scenarios that cannot be foreseen. To be successful, the structure must address management fees, performance-related incentives, hurdle rates and, most importantly, commitments by the general partners of significant portions of their wealth alongside the limited partners. Additional clauses may be required to cover such issues as reinvestments, clawbacks and noneconomic terms such as key person provision, joint-and-several liability and disclosure obligations.[4] Together, these provide limited partners with moderate control over the management of the fund.

---

[4] **Clawbacks** are liabilities triggered when, at the end of a fund's life and assuming a 20% carried interest structure, the limited partners have received less than the sum of contributed capital and 80% of the fund's profits.

Corporate governance in private equity

The law and the LPA define and restrict the limited partners' degree of control over the general partners' activities. Such controls relate mainly to waiving or accepting investment restrictions, extending the investment period, valuations, conflicts of interest, or key person-related issues. The limited partners can only make decisions either with a simple majority (e.g., the decision to extend the investment period or the fund's duration) or with a qualified majority[5] (e.g., the decision to remove the general partner without cause). In limited partnership structures, an overactive limited partner could become reclassified as a general partner, thereby losing his/her limited liability.

Further, corporate governance bodies that may be specified include the investors committee, the advisory board and the board of directors. An audit and valuation committee may also be meaningful in the corporate governance process. Occasionally, limited partners may be offered positions on an investment committee. However, it is not clear that limited partners should take on this role. Generally, international industry professionals recognize that fund managers should make investment and divestment decisions without the direct involvement of investors, so as not to dilute their responsibility or create potential conflicts of interest with non-participating investors. Also, investors do not normally have the legal rights nor the required skills and experience to make such decisions.

Another important element of corporate governance is the reporting to limited partners. Various private equity and VC associations, such as the European Private Equity and Venture Capital Association (EVCA), the British Venture Capital Association (BVCA) and the Association Française des Investisseurs en Capital (AFIC)[6] or the Private Equity Industry Guidelines Group (PEIGG)[7], have released guidelines for valuation and reporting. The obligation to disclose in line with these guidelines is increasingly being made part of the contractual agreements. Still, reporting fund managers may follow different approaches. While some general partners reduce the level of detail provided to the bare minimum and share it with all limited partners, others share different levels of detail depending on the specific type of investor.[8]

Investment objectives, fund term and fund size

In LPAs, the description of investment objectives should be specific, but not too narrow. Lerner (2000) argues that private equity funds are blind pools for a reason. Investors should not attempt to put overly-restrictive limits on a fund manager's flexibility that may block the fund manager's ability to profit from unanticipated opportunities. Further, with uncertain investments, severe information asymmetry and difficulties in monitoring and enforcing restrictions, fund managers may simply find ways around narrow restrictions.

Fund terms of typically 7–10 years, with possible extensions of up to three years, represent the trade-off between a better IRR, sufficient time to invest and divest, and degree of illiquidity still acceptable for the investors. Normally the extension of the fund's life is approved annually, one year at a time versus two or more at once, during which time management fees are either reduced or eliminated altogether to stimulate quick exits.

---

[5] A qualified majority is generally more than 75% of the limited partners as opposed to the 50% required for a simple majority.

[6] See www.privateequityvaluation.com/ [accessed October, 2007].

[7] See www.peigg.org/valuations.html [accessed July, 2007].

[8] Associated with the Freedom of Information Act debate in the U.S. on transparency for public institution limited partners, this approach was seen as a way out of the dilemma. It went even so far as to oblige such limited partners to destroy the material provided by the fund manager as soon as it is practical for them to do so.

The fund size, in terms of capital committed by the limited partners, needs to be in line with these investment objectives. On the other hand, various factors such as management resources or number of potential opportunities implicitly set a maximum size of the fund.

Normally, proceeds are distributed to investors as soon as feasible after the realization of or distribution of a fund's assets but, in some cases, limited partners grant the fund managers the discretion to reinvest proceeds that are realized during the investment period.

Management fees and expenses

In private equity, compensation is overwhelmingly performance driven and there is a consensus that general partners should not be able to make significant profits on fees. Management fees provide a base compensation so the fund manager can support the ongoing activities of funds. They need to be reduced to a level that ensures the fund manager is primarily motivated by the carried interest, but sufficient to avoid their departure to greener fields.[9] Fees are on a commitment basis rather than only being levied against capital that has been invested. If fees were based only on invested capital the management might have an incentive during the investment period to pursue volume instead of quality. Also, the fees on committed but uninvested funds can be viewed as paying for the staffing required for due diligence during the investment period. Fees ramp down at the end of the investment period or with the raising of subsequent funds.

When management fees are low, the fund manager may be looking for other compensation, such as fees for sitting on the boards of directors of portfolio companies, for providing consulting or management services, or for advising or structuring transactions. To counter these incentives for distraction from investment management, LPAs mandate that these fees be fully or partly set off against the management fees.

Carried interest

As mentioned previously, carried interest is the share in the fund's profits received by the fund manager. It remains largely uncontested over time that the fund manager's main incentive is performance-based through the realization of carried interest. Carried interest is calculated either on a "fund-as-a-whole" or a "deal-by-deal" basis. In both cases, the carried interest is normally payable if the IRR of a fund exceeds the hurdle rate or preferred return. In the majority of cases, previous losses and overall portfolio performance are also taken into account. It is generally accepted that a 20% share carried interest aligns the manager and investor interests appropriately.[10] Typically, limited partners favor the fund-as-a-whole over the deal-by-deal basis for carried interest calculations, as it further aligns manager and investor interests.

Preferred return or hurdle rate

The preferred return – often called the hurdle rate – has become a standard limited partnership term. The rationale for its introduction was to ensure that general partners are only compensated for over performance (see Maxwell, 2003). Therefore, the limited partners have the first priority to receive all distributions up to their commitment (or capital invested), plus the preferred return, before the

---

[9] On fees, Bushrod (2003) commented that, at least according to U.S. data, there is no direct correlation between salary and bonus paid and the performance of the fund.

[10] It is not unheard of that a few "star" funds manage to garner carried interest percentages larger than 20% (25% or even 30%). However, these are exceptions.

general partner gets access to carried interest.[11] In theory then, the preferred return is an annual compound interest rate on the invested capital that is set well above the currently prevailing risk-free rate of return, but at or below the historical performance of public equity.

If hurdle are set too low, they become meaningless as incentives and just create administrative problems. There are also some conceptual issues with preferred returns. General partners are faced with the dilemma of whether to realize an investment over a short period of time to optimize the IRR, or hold on for longer and try to optimize the multiple. For example, is it better to generate a 50% IRR for a period of 3 months which yields a 1.11× multiple on capital invested, or only a 10% IRR for a period of 3 years, leading to a 1.33× multiple. The standard preferred return, being based on the IRR, gives incentive to the former.[12]

While high hurdle rates aim to give an incentive for fund managers to outperform, they can also have the opposite effect. Managers of struggling funds can be demotivated if it becomes unlikely that they will receive carried interest. High hurdle rates may also lead to excessive risk taking. Incentive fees are used to reward managers when the fund does well, but alone they do not provide punishment when the manager behaves badly. With this structure, the more risk a manager takes, the greater the upside potential, with little immediate downside impact from losses.

General partners' contribution

Excessive risk-taking can be reduced or eliminated if the manager has a significant portion of his personal wealth in the fund. The manager, being directly exposed to fund losses, no longer has the incentive to take extraordinary risks or to abandon ship once the prospects for generating carry and launching a follow-on fund become highly unlikely.

Typically, investors in private equity funds see 1% as a standard and acceptable general partners' contribution, also known as "hurt money".[13] However, in the case of wealthy managers, 1% may sometimes be too low.[14] To better understand this relationship, it makes sense to look at the general and limited partners' relative exposure. Typically, the general partners' contribution to the fund is a significant share of their personal wealth; whereas, although in absolute terms far higher, the limited partners' investment typically represents an immaterial share of the institution's overall assets. It is a challenge to determine the appropriate contribution level for the general partner that provides a reasonable incentive but is not onerous. An analysis of previous fees that have been received, profits that have been earned from past investments, salaries and so forth may provide useful information for determining a contribution level that is appropriate for a particular general partner.

---

[11] The risk-free rate was deemed to be the yield on a Treasury with similar maturity to the weighted average life (6–7 years) of a private equity partnership.

[12] While the preferred return works reasonably well for later stages with only one round of finance, this approach can be less effective for early stages with multiple rounds of funding, many of which are subject to meeting milestones. According to Maxwell (2003), the preferred return is more confusing than useful. He proposes an alternative model that builds on a flexible carried interest schedule and believes that this aligns the interests better than the classical preferred return.

[13] See Bushrod (2003): "This is usually referred to as 'hurt money', which means it is enough to materially impact the lifestyle of the venture capitalist if it is lost, which in private equity terms means that the fund does not make enough profit for there to be any carry element for the venture capitalist."

[14] See Meek (2004): "Those that offer to put up the standard one per cent of the fund just because that is the standard, for example, are unlikely to convince investors that they truly believe in the investments they make [...] Adveq's Andre Jaeggi agreed. 'The appropriate level of contribution depends on the fund manager's circumstances. If Kleiner Perkins partners agreed to put in ten per cent of the fund, that's a very significant amount, but it might not hurt the partners as much as a one per cent contribution made by newer players [...] The general partner has to be at risk'. Or, in the words of another investor: "I'm not interested in what the percentage is. I'm interested in how much it hurts the manager to lose the contribution'."

Key person provision

If one of the named key persons departs the team, stops committing sufficient time to the management of the fund, or sells his interests in the management company, the **key person provision** allows limited partners to suspend contributions and investment/divestment activities until a replacement is found. The limited partners can even terminate the fund if they so choose. Depending on the size, experience and depth of the team, the inability of one or more of the key persons to carry out their duties could have a significant adverse effect on the partnership. Key person clauses are also put in place in anticipation of the retirement of senior fund managers.

While traditional management firms depend on key personnel as well, investors in private equity funds may find it costly or impossible to exit these investments without the key persons, due to the illiquidity of private equity investments. The key person clause is important to ensure that the individuals entrusted with investing the fund's capital actually stay around to do so. The clause is more common and pertinent to private equity, where the judgment and trust of key persons is critical in safeguarding the investments.

Termination and divorce

LPAs may foresee a "for-cause" removal of the general partner and include a "**bad-leaver clause**". If exercised, investments are suspended until a new fund manager is elected or, in the extreme, the fund is liquidated. In practical terms, conditions leading to a for-cause removal are difficult to define and determine. In private equity very little can be legally enforced: issues are highly subjective and taking matters to court carries high legal risk for an investor as it is very difficult and lengthy to prove wrongdoing.

The "without-cause" or "**good-leaver**" termination clause enables the investors to cease funding the partnership with a vote requiring a **qualified majority** – generally more than 75% of the limited partners. The clause provides a clear framework for shutting down a partnership that is not working, or when confidence is lost. The good-leaver clause sometimes provides for compensation amounting to six months to one year of management fees, while in the case of bad leaver, no such compensation provision exists. Normally both clauses include a vesting schedule for the carried interest so that part of the carry remains available to incentivize the new team being hired.

In deciding whether to exercise one of these clauses, reputation considerations play a key role, because the market consists of a small number of players that repeatedly interact with each other. General partners that are removed with or without cause may subsequently be unable to raise funds or participate in investment syndicates with other partnerships. To avoid such disastrous outcomes, general partners are often inclined to agree on a fund restructuring to prevent being removed.

Distribution waterfall[15]

Exits realized by the fund are distributed according to a **distribution waterfall**. Normally, the limited partners are first returned all the capital invested plus fees and expenses (i.e. all drawn capital), or sometimes the total commitment (drawn and undrawn capital). Then they receive the preferred return on the investment, or hurdle rate, normally compounded per annum. This is followed by the catch-up period, during which time the general partner receives all or the major share of the distributions. The catch-up period ends when the agreed **carried-interest split** or stated share of the fund's profits to be received by the general partner and the limited partners is reached. Thereafter, distributions are

---

[15] A more detailed description of distribution waterfalls can be found in Mathonet and Meyer (2007).

shared between fund managers and investors in the proportion agreed to in the legal documentation, normally 20% for the general partners and 80% for the limited partners. This mechanism is also not standardized (e.g. whether an interest rate such as a hurdle rate is compounded on a quarterly or on an annual basis). Sometimes there is a 100% catch-up, while other agreements may foresee only a partial catch-up or no catch-up at all. With a 100% catch-up the limited partners are effectively excluded from all new distributions until the general partner has fully recovered its agreed share of the profit.

The simplest and, from the viewpoint of the limited partner, the most desirable solution is that general partners do not take carried interest until all invested, or sometimes even committed, capital has been repaid to investors. But it could take several years before the fund's team sees any gains and it could lead to demotivation. An accepted compromise is that general partners take lower percentages of early distributions until contributed capital is returned, either distributing the excess to limited partners directly or putting it into an escrow account. Investors often require that fund managers escrow typically 20–30% of their carried interest proceeds as a buffer against potential claw-back liability.[16]

As mentioned before, clawback is a liability triggered when, at the end of a fund's life, the limited partners have received less than the sum of contributed capital and a certain amount of the fund's profits. Clawback is relevant in situations where early investments do well but later investments fail. It assures that the managers will not receive a greater share of the fund's distributions than they are entitled to. Responsibility for payment of the clawback rests with the persons or entity who received the carried interest distributions. In such a case, the general partner is required to return some proceeds to make the investor whole.

But clawback can also exist for limited partners. It is triggered when, at the end of a fund's life, the general partners have received less than their share of the fund's profits. Such clawback is relevant in situations where a portion of the committed capital has not been drawn and limited partners have received full repayment of their commitment plus hurdle before the general partner has access to its carry.

CONFLICTS OF INTEREST

Consulting activities, previous funds, new fundraising activities, chairmanships, or personal participation in individual portfolio companies provide a fertile breeding ground for conflicts of interest. Walter (2003) differentiates between two types of conflicts of interest. In private equity funds "Type 1" conflicts – "between a firm's own economic interests and the interests of its own clients, usually reflected in the extraction of rents or mispriced transfer of risk" – are usually addressed or mitigated through an alignment of interests. "Type 2" conflicts of interest – "between a firm's clients, or between types of clients, which place the firm in a position of favoring one at the expense of another" – are more problematic, as fund managers may have multiple relationships with various clients.

Conflicts of interest need to be minimized to focus the fund manager's attention on the fund. Even if such outside activities are not directed against the limited partners, investors want to ensure that the management team is completely dedicated and that the day-to-day management of a fund is not left to the less-experienced team members. There are also inherent conflict-of-interest issues in

---

[16] Associated with this is the joint-and-several liability: If a manager leaves the fund and the fund ends up with a liability, such as clawback to its limited partners, this clause makes the remaining team members responsible for the departed person's share of the liability.

Table 3.1 Net return to limited partners as a function of management fees and carried interest (Source: Flag Venture Management (2003b))

		Net IRR (assuming 20% gross multiple)		
		Carried interest		
		20.0%	25.0%	30.0%
Management fee	2.0%	11.98%	11.49%	10.99%
	2.5%	10.57%	10.12%	9.66%

Note: These calculations are based on the break even analysis described in Mathonet and Meyer (2007) which is based on the Yale model (see Takahashi and Alexander (2001). Standard fund cash flow patterns as well as terms have been used. The gross IRR is a measure of the total performance of a fund's investments (both realized and unrealized), and the net IRR is the same measure but considering the cost of the fund structure, mainly the effect of carried interest and management fees.

so-called captive, or sponsored, funds linked, for example, to a bank or a financial group. Here the independence of the management team is a prerequisite for securing investment commitments.

In conducting due diligence, the objectivity as well as the expertise of a partnership's management needs to be scrutinized. Conflicts of interest are often not obvious and require looking beyond the fund proposal. Even if the current fund is structured to align interests and to avoid conflicts with previous or parallel funds, if market conditions are changing or more interesting opportunities emerge, the manager may get distracted.

While investors attempt to reduce such potential for conflicts by crafting appropriate LPAs, the interests of fund managers may diverge from those of limited partners, even with the most carefully considered deal structures. Consequently, continuous monitoring[17] is needed to identify the emergence of diverging interests in time to prevent problems.

FINDING THE BALANCE

The LPA sets the economic incentives and penalties that make the fund managers perform in line with their principals' interests. Fund managers as individuals should do well if the funds they manage perform well and not otherwise. They must establish a favorable track record to raise new partnerships. With poor performance, they will be put out of business. There is a series of trade-offs and it becomes clear that for a limited partner a perfect fund structure does not exist. According to Meek (2004), sophisticated investors recognize the importance of ensuring that fund managers receive the correct incentives to outperform. They are not looking for cheap private equity. Instead, they are looking for an appropriate and fair balance – a legitimate alignment of interests achieved through terms that are suitable to fund type, size and investment style.

The alignment of interests also requires compromises between the parties, as general and limited partners are in a kind of prisoners' dilemma. Even if limited partners in a difficult fundraising environment could theoretically negotiate highly favorable terms, those terms do not guarantee fund manager attention to the fund. For example, if economic conditions change, fund managers have a strong incentive to quickly raise another fund with more favorable conditions, potentially from another group of investors, and not focus their attention on their old fund any longer. On the other hand, if the general partners can base management fees on contractual conditions, they are often quite

---

[17] See Chapter 8 for a more detailed discussion on monitoring.

accommodating in order to maintain the relationship with their investors for follow-on funds. The magnitude of any fee changes also has to be taken into account. Flag Venture Management (2003b) refers to an analysis showing that a 50 bps reduction in management fees can boost net returns to limited partners by 100 bps or more (see Table 3.1). Surprisingly, this exceeds the impact investors would realize from a reduction in the carried interest from 25% to 20%. We can conclude that achieving the appropriate fee structure is challenging, and requires a continuous balancing process which takes into account the level of capital commitments to a fund, the value of fund's assets, the carried interest and other fund terms and conditions.

4

The Investment Process

In general, an investment process consists of a number of steps that result in an initial investment strategy and portfolio allocation. There are challenges at all steps of the private equity investment process and no process is ideal or optimal in all cases. The most appropriate process for a given manager depends on the manager's objectives and tolerance for risk. This means that trade-offs are inevitable. The idiosyncrasy of private equity – the long-term nature, the illiquidity and the peculiarity of its risks – means that a balance must be found between the various components of the process such as over-diversification and superior fund selection. Figure 4.1 illustrates the process.

PROCESS DESCRIPTION

The main decisions to address in the investment process include strategic asset allocation, fund selection, level of diversification and liquidity management. The challenge of managing the investment program requires an appropriate balance between the return driver selection and efficient allocation of capital. Being highly selective and only investing a restricted share of the total amount earmarked for private equity in a few funds of top quality would maximize the expected returns, but ignore the impact of undrawn commitments. Being highly diversified smoothes the cash flows and allows for a nearly full investment of the allocated capital for private equity, thereby lowering risk and enhancing total return but at the expense of potentially eliminating extreme positive returns.

For private equity, the three key performance drivers are portfolio design (see Chapter 5 regarding the management of diversification), management of liquidity (see Chapter 11) and fund manager selection (see Chapter 6).

Because of the length of time required to realize returns in private equity, it can be difficult to quantify the risks involved. Due to the opaque nature of the industry, not all outcomes are known, information is difficult to assemble and the quality of data is generally very poor. This is most notable in the case of technology-focused VC funds which face rapid industry advances, newly evolving business models, short boom-to-bust-periods and long investment periods, making it very difficult, if not impossible, to systematically collect data with any statistical merit.

That said, there is a significant number of assessable or even measurable factors in private equity, more than is typically perceived, that can be used in place of quantitative risk measures (e.g. VC vs. buyout, vintage year). A clearer differentiation between risk and uncertainty can be a useful tool for the management of a private equity investment program. Experts can put lessons learned into a new or changed context and extrapolate from their experience. While a precise quantification is nearly impossible, except in very specific situations, experts can associate experiences and opinions on various dimensions with categories for return expectations. For these categories an approximate quantification can be estimated and used to manage the uncertainty-return trade-off. For example, experts might grade funds subjectively with regard to risk and return, then use the grades to select an appropriate aggregate risk.

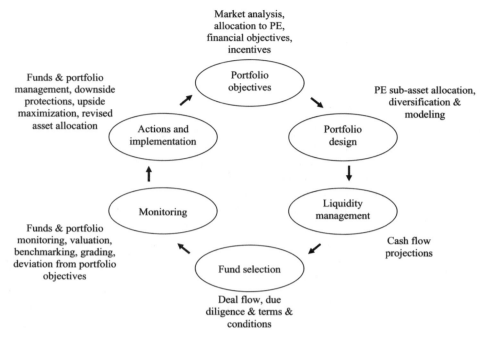

Figure 4.1 Investment process

Portfolio objectives

The starting point of any investment process is the definition of the portfolio objectives. These objectives should be set, or at least agreed upon, by the authorizing entity. Identifying trends in the market and the amount of capital that can be profitably invested is crucial for establishing the investment strategy and setting targets. Construction of the portfolio requires the identification of attractive sectors and the best strategies. As with the structuring of funds, it is important that the investment program manager receives the proper incentives to align his interests with those of the authorizing entity. The result of this analysis is a formalization of portfolio objectives that should ideally include the level of allocation to private equity, the targeted private equity markets, the financial objectives (e.g. desired risk/return profile) and the high-level strategy to achieve them (e.g. core/satellite, diversification, co-investments).

Modern Portfolio Theory provides the theoretical basis for investors' acceptance of alternative assets. According to this theory, adding noncorrelated assets, such as private equity, to a portfolio of publicly quoted securities can improve the portfolio's risk and return characteristics. According to Steers (2002), it is almost impossible to use standard risk–return optimization models to determine the appropriate allocation to private equity because it is difficult to estimate the correct risk premium and correlation with other asset classes.

Therefore, institutions typically apply a **naïve allocation** by committing equal amounts to the different funds and cap their private equity exposure at around 5–10%, although some foundations have as much as 30% allocated to private equity.[1] This naïve allocation can be estimated based on the analysis of the following basic dimensions.

---

[1] Naïve diversification is the optimal strategy when there is no information that allows differentiation among assets.

- If the allocation is not large enough, it will not allow for the establishment of a dedicated team, which is a required condition if one expects to achieve above-average performance. Conversely, if the allocation is too large, it may not be possible to find sufficient investment opportunities or it may drive the performance down in the case where lower quality funds are selected.
- If the allocation is not large enough versus the overall portfolio, it will have an insignificant impact on the overall portfolio performance. If the allocation is too large compared to the overall portfolio, the investor risks being under-diversified and overexposed to private equity-specific risk such as illiquidity.
- The benefit of adding private equity has to be analyzed in the context of the existing portfolio. The goal is to determine the various risk dimensions that the investors would like to diversify (e.g., industry sector, country, company size) and to assess the impact of the private equity allocation on these dimensions within the overall existing portfolio. For example, a high-tech early stage allocation will have a more important diversification impact on a portfolio invested mostly in the "old" economy.
- The institution's liquidity needs[2] should be part of the analysis. The constraint essentially depends on the institution's regular liquidity needs to support their on-going business. An investor with high regular liquidity needs and no excess capital is not well-placed to launch a private equity program. The lower the on-going liquidity needs and the more excess capital, the more funds an investor can allocate to private equity. In general, the more mature a private equity program, the more liquidity it is likely to be generating, again increasing the funds available for allocation to private equity.
- Finally, if in doubt, it is always worth tracking other institutions' allocations as a gauge for how attractive they perceive private equity as compared to other asset classes.

Portfolio design

The objective of the above analysis is to determine the appropriate allocations to the various private equity markets[3] and estimate the optimal level of diversification. Modern Portfolio Theory (MPT) suggests that under-diversified portfolios have a higher risk without an adequate compensation in expected returns. However, there are challenges to utilizing MPT in the world of private equity.

MPT employs rigorous mathematical techniques for designing portfolios. For the model to work, one must be able to quantify each asset's expected return and risk as well as the correlations of each asset's return relative to all other assets' returns in the portfolio. While public market managers have reliable statistical data to support their analysis, private equity and in particular VC managers lack such data. Indeed, the analysis of private equity returns, volatility and correlations is limited by the relatively short time series of publicly-available data. Those data are not fully representative of the market and are often biased by the survivorship issue.[4]

Most of all, data do not fully capture the uncertainty inherent in innovation-driven asset classes such as VC, since relevant past data would rarely be available on investments that emphasize new concepts. Additionally, the standard IRR performance measure used for private equity funds is

---

[2] For a more detailed description, see Mathonet and Meyer (2007), Chapter 16.

[3] The classification of the various private equity markets should be driven by the different risk profiles (see Chapter 6). The classical ones are identified by their stage focus (venture capital vs. buyout) and geography (U.S., EU, and Asia) but some more refined classifications are also used, including the less developed – but often important for the portfolio design – emerging niche markets.

[4] The **survivorship bias** is the tendency for failed companies to be eliminated from performance studies because they no longer operate.

capital-weighted, whereas for public market assets it is traditionally time-weighted (for more on IRR in private equity investments see Chapter 7). This means that an analysis of the correlations between private equity and other asset classes is not possible without making significant adjustments such as computing private equity returns under an assumption that intervening cash flows are invested in public market indices.

Moreover, MPT assumes a normal return distribution which clearly does not hold for private equity. In fact, the distribution of private equity returns departs significantly from the normal distribution. Empirical results on private equity indicate large standard deviations of period returns, as well as significant skewness and excess kurtosis.[5] As a result, it is questionable whether private equity can be integrated into the MPT framework or what modifications would be permissible to do so.

Some practitioners believe that asset and sub-asset allocations are key investment policy decisions and that private equity portfolios should be managed more like public equity portfolios, drawing on many of the same tools and accepted principles while adjusting for market specificities. Using this approach, practitioners rely upon adjusted historical risk, return and correlation figures as reasonable approximations of the future when incorporating private equity investments in their portfolio models.[6] The common argument is that by adding private equity to a portfolio of publicly-quoted stocks and bonds, one can move the portfolio closer to the efficient frontier i.e. improve the risk–return trade-off.[7]

Public and private equity returns may be more closely correlated than is commonly believed. The biases and the infrequent revaluations common to private equity result in an artificial dampening of both volatility and correlation analysis relative to public equities. Indeed, the uncertainty and imprecision of valuation (see Chapter 9) of private equity might not only mask the natural correlation between public and private equity, but also blur the inherent risks. According to *The Economist* (2004), "to say that private equity is less volatile and thus less risky is a bit like saying that the weather does not change much when you stay inside and rarely look out of the window." Barber and Zage (2002) argue that there are more similarities between public and private equities than differences and certainly more similarities than many private equity practitioners acknowledge. "[Regardless of] whether buyouts or VC, poor private equity practice is likely to produce higher correlations with the public markets, since it involves 'surfing the wave' rather than creating value." The idea is that high-quality private equity investing practices may achieve "alpha" (that is not correlated with market performance), while poor practices may have high systematic risk because returns are dominated by public equity market trends.

At the end of the day, private companies operate in the same economic environments as public companies. They face the same trading conditions, interest rates and regulatory regimes. Furthermore, exiting through trade sales (sales of shares to another company) or IPOs is generally dependent on public markets to provide valuation reference points and needed liquidity. Therefore, although low, at least some degree of correlation between public and private equity returns is to be expected.

Liquidity management

Liquidity management is one of the key performance drivers in private equity. (See Chapter 11 for a description of the various approaches used by practitioners.) It can be a difficult task to steer between putting money efficiently to work while simultaneously maintaining a balance in the portfolio composition and quality of the individual fund investments.

---

[5] See Mathonet and Meyer (2007).

[6] See Simons (2000), Arthus and Teïletche (2004), and Kaserer and Diller (2004).

[7] See, for example, Fort Washington Capital Partners (2004).

Just looking at the capital invested in portfolio companies does not tell the full picture of a fund's performance. Investors are rightly concerned with the total return on all resources dedicated to private equity which includes undrawn capital. If a large part of the capital remains uninvested or parked in Treasury bills for instance, the resulting drag on total return can be significant. To keep a program permanently and fully invested in portfolio companies, the so-called **overcommitment strategy** needs to be employed, whereby more commitments are signed than can be met with existing capital resources as discussed in Chapter 11.

Funds-of-funds certainly may lose investors if they fail to deliver sufficiently attractive returns, but they can go bust – and some have already experienced significant problems in this area – because they have not mastered the management of liquidity required to run such overcommitment strategies. There is anecdotal evidence that repeatedly funds-of-funds have been struggling with this issue and that overcommitment strategies have not worked out.[8] The high degree of uncertainty regarding the timing of cash flows render funds investing and liquidity management exceptionally challenging.

Fund selection

Gaining access to so-called top-quartile performers is critical to the fund selection process. According to Raschle and Ender (2004), in recent decades the top quartile of U.S. VC funds has achieved returns that were twice as high as the average VC fund. This fund-selection skill is often considered the core competence of private equity specialists and is seen as a key performance driver for generating attractive returns for a portfolio of funds, which helps to explain why private equity investing is predominantly characterized as an "alpha-seeking" exercise. A more detailed description of the fund selection process is provided in Chapter 6.

Monitoring

Limited partners should monitor the composition of their portfolio, identify trends within the private equity markets and track their peer group's allocations to private equity on an ongoing basis. For a limited partner, monitoring should include the specific fund investments, as well as the overall composition of the relationships managed. Only through ongoing monitoring and reviewing of investment vehicles and the overall portfolio can a limited partner make informed, proactive portfolio decisions.

Analyzing concentration across all partnerships in the portfolio, for example by industry, stage, geography, **vintage years** and cross-holdings between funds, can provide valuable insights. Stress tests can provide early warning signals and increase the transparency of the portfolio.[9] Tracking overall commitment level, contributions and distributions, return on investment to date, or expected final return on investment is also important for portfolio management. Identifying overexposures may lead to a review or adjustment of investment objectives and, where severe imbalances exist, may require active management to mitigate.

At the individual fund level, compliance with contractual terms and investment style need to be tracked. Fund monitoring is based on regular meetings with all parties involved and should include the following: tracking planned versus implemented strategy; reviewing the fund's financial investment, valuation and divestment information; analyzing the impact of relevant market trends;

---

[8] See Mathonet and Meyer (2007), Chapter 4, for a detailed description and analysis of a real-life example.

[9] Vintage year is the year in which the first flow of investment capital is drawdown from investors and delivered to a company.

assessing the risk of both individual investments and the overall portfolio; measuring/benchmarking performance (see Chapter 7); and verifying legal and tax compliance.

Monitoring may also be relevant for liquidity planning (see Chapter 11). A more detailed description of the monitoring process is provided in Chapter 8.

Actions and implementation

The last step in the investment process is the implementation of the portfolio management decisions. These decisions can be taken at three different levels: individual fund, portfolio composition and portfolio objective, which in turn can impact the rest of the investment process.

Active management is constrained because private equity assets are long term, illiquid and only offer limited (in quality and over time) opportunities to invest or sell. Co-investing, secondary transactions, securitization and restructuring of funds are the common means of actively managing the portfolio. The main purpose of fund restructuring is to stop value destruction rather than to create new opportunity. In practice, these tools can only be applied sparingly, as rebalancing the portfolio through buy-and-sell transactions can be very expensive and opportunities relatively scarce.

RISK MANAGEMENT

The approach to risk management for a portfolio of private equity funds rests on the pillars of measurement, control and mitigation.

Risk-measurement framework

When discussing risk and return expectations of any investment, the starting point is a proper valuation of the asset. There is a difference between an accounting rules-based valuation approach and a market-based concept of the economic or financial value of a fund. Modeling the economic reality as closely as possible is key to efficient management. Typically, fund values are estimated by valuing every single portfolio company individually, aggregating these valuations to a portfolio value and finally by calculating the investor's respective share in the fund. In Chapter 9, we demonstrate why this approach often does not reflect the economic reality.

In line with financial theories and secondary market practices, private equity funds should be valued through a discounted cash flow approach. Such an approach provides risk managers with several cash flow scenarios (see Chapter 11) and discount rate estimates (see Chapter 10.)

Risk control

There is no definitive risk-adjusted pricing available for primary private equity fund investing. The lack of data, the blind pool nature of the investments, and the fact that virtually all private equity is highly risky make differentiation and quantification of risks in private equity difficult at best. For buy-and-hold investments, the quality of the asset determines the returns to the investor. Within the private equity universe, we can only use the non-quantitative approach to risk control by constraining managers to invest only in assets of equivalent risk. Since risk differentials cannot be measured, it is neither possible nor meaningful to try to select funds based on risk control issues so long as the investments are restricted to institutional-quality private equity funds. Therefore, being highly selective is the typical approach to fund selection. How the cut-off is set depends on the accessible universe of funds and portfolio objectives.

The private equity fund market is unable to differentiate precisely between the amount of risk found in different industries or geographical sectors, and can only offer broad comparisons of the risk inherent to buyout versus VC funds. Within the institutional private equity asset class, traditional quantitative measures like beta cannot distinguish reliably between differences in risk and therefore investors must defer to their own judgment.

For primary investments into funds, an efficient risk-adjusted price setting (comparable to high-yield bonds, where – at least in theory – the greater the risk, the higher the interest rate) does not exist.[10] All primary positions are bought at par (i.e., without premium or discount) and there is no predefined coupon payment but only a predefined cost structure and uncertain performance. While fund structure and management fees are occasionally revisited, the variations are insufficient to cover the risks. For such a blind pool investment, the uncertainty does not allow a full risk adjustment in pricing. Rather, this is accomplished more through an industry-wide adjustment of terms driven by currently prevailing market conditions rather than a differentiated pricing mechanism.

Risk mitigation

In principle, one mitigates risks by choosing to avoid, to support, to control, or to transfer them. Risk avoidance, or significant changes in investment proposals with special contract provisions, is the most commonly-used approach to mitigating risk in private equity. In other words, by rigorously weeding out inferior proposals, investors hope to minimize risks.

Clearly, risk taking cannot be avoided entirely. One reason is that the supply of institutional quality teams is insufficient to meet industry demand and the number of top funds with a verifiable track record is lower than the numbers that eventually perform in the top quartile. Also, an index-tracking passive investment approach is not available and may not be possible in such an illiquid market.

Many risks in private equity need to be evaluated, accepted, monitored and perhaps controlled. A possible adverse impact can be mitigated through diversification or controlled through monitoring. On a portfolio of funds level, risk transfer mechanisms, such as overdraft facilities, can be used to manage liquidity risk. Securitization is another risk transfer mechanism. However, this financial engineering technique is generally only applicable on a portfolio of funds level. For the private equity investments themselves, a risk transfer is difficult to implement. On the individual portfolio company level there are occasionally guarantees, such as those provided by the Société Française de Garantie des Financements des PME in France, or the scheme run by the German TBG (since abandoned). Generally, risks cannot be quantified to a degree that allows for the application of sophisticated risk-transfer tools used elsewhere in the financial industry. Some degree of risk sharing can be achieved through relationships with co-investing limited partners. With their financial strength, they can step in when other investors are defaulting. Co-investing limited partners can help to address operational issues and may even lead to reduced expenses through sharing of monitoring efforts. They impose market discipline and can assist in facilitating continuity as follow-on funds with the same managers can be closed more quickly.

---

[10] For secondary transactions, however, premiums – or more often discounts – are applied. Here, even for low quality investments, profits can be made.

5
Private Equity Portfolio Design

PRIVATE EQUITY PORTFOLIO CONSTRUCTION TECHNIQUES

The construction of a private equity portfolio can begin once an investor (typically an institutional investor) has decided what portion of his total portfolio of assets will be allocated to this alternative asset class and what objectives are set for this allocation. Private equity portfolio construction approaches are usually described as either bottom-up or top-down. The **bottom-up approach** is fund manager research-based, where the emphasis is on screening all investment opportunities (including intensive analysis and due diligence) and picking the perceived best fund managers. A **top-down approach** analyzes the macroeconomic conditions surrounding the portfolio and then determines the strategic asset allocation (i.e. the combination of industry sectors, countries and fund style that are best for the likely scenarios).

While appearing to be in opposition, the bottom-up and top-down approaches are complementary and are therefore typically used in tandem. This method is called a **mixed approach** and starts with a bottom-up strategy, to which one adds increasing top-down optimization (which will be explained later). Finally, investors that claim to have a top-down, a bottom-up or a mixed approach all stress the importance of a proactive approach in fund selection (see Chapter 6). Investors cannot just wait for investment opportunities to arrive but must proactively search for the funds that fit their investment guidelines and start making contact with these funds before they go to the market to raise capital. This requires a constant monitoring of the environment.

Bottom-up approach

As private equity is characterized by a high differential between top-quartile and lower-quartile fund performance, investing in the asset class requires good selection skills.[1] Therefore, investors do generally follow a bottom-up approach, as it is widely believed that the quality of the fund management team is the most essential criterion, much more significant than other factors like sector or geographical diversification. The starting point of a bottom-up approach, also called the "screening technique" (see Figure 5.1), is the identification of suitable investments.[2] This is followed by an intensive analysis and due diligence in order to rank the funds by their attractiveness[3] and identify which managers are the likely top performers. The investor selects those funds perceived to be the best. The investor then analyzes the structuring of the limited partnership agreements, the inclusion of covenants and the post-commitment monitoring and conducts the necessary due diligence leading to the final fund investment decision.

The bottom-up approach has several compelling features. As it depends solely on ranking, this approach is simple, easy to understand and robust. It enhances the expected performance by concentrating the portfolio in the highest "alpha" funds (i.e. funds with the highest expected performance uncorrelated with the market), while it controls for risk by diversifying across multiple funds.

---

[1] See Chapter 6 on fund selection process.

[2] By suitable investments, we mean all potential investment opportunities available during the investment period and compliant with the portfolio strategy and restrictions.

[3] We describe the due diligence process for private equity in Chapter 6.

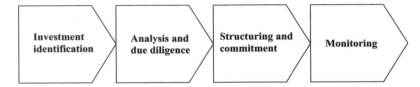

Figure 5.1 Bottom-up approach

However, the bottom-up approach is not without problems. As it is very opportunistic, it can lead to an unbalanced portfolio (e.g. a portfolio excessively concentrated in a specific sector), carrying considerably more risk than intended.

Top-down approach

The top-down approach (see Figure 5.2) takes the "big picture" as the starting point as opposed to individual fund selection. Investors who follow a top-down approach place more emphasis on the management of the strategy, the asset allocation and the diversification of the portfolio.

As we mentioned at the beginning of the chapter, the top-down approach is a process that analyzes the macroeconomic conditions surrounding the portfolio and attempts to determine the strategic asset allocation (i.e. the combination of industry sectors, countries and fund styles that will benefit most under the likely scenarios). The main criteria used in the evaluation process are political, economic and currency risks. Other criteria examined include the extent to which each particular market has accepted private equity as a form of financing and investment, and the degree to which the environment is conducive to entrepreneurial activity. In this context, factors influencing the ability to invest, such as due diligence standards, accounting and tax issues, and the enforceability of legal rights (this last issue is particularly relevant in the case of many emerging markets), are taken into account. Finally, the availability of attractive investment opportunities and the availability of exit opportunities for investments are considered. In the broadest sense, the decision to allocate commitments to vintage years could also be considered as part of a top-down approach.

After establishing the strategic asset allocation, the investor next determines what resources will need to be committed to the fund. This commitment planning depends on the investor's desired exposure level, risk tolerance and the available resources for investing. Then the final commitment strategy is determined based on cash flow projections and stress testing. Finally, one looks for funds that best fit the desired allocation.

There are also investors who aim to imitate the top-down approach adopted with public equity, whereby past performance of the assets in terms of risk and return measures is used as a proxy for future investment performance. They ultimately hope to exploit perceived low levels of correlation in different private equity segments across geographical regions. While such an approach certainly has its merits, there are practical problems associated mainly with the limited availability and quality of financial data for private equity. As data only become reliable for fully liquidated funds close

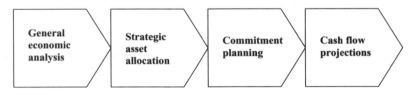

Figure 5.2 Top-down approach

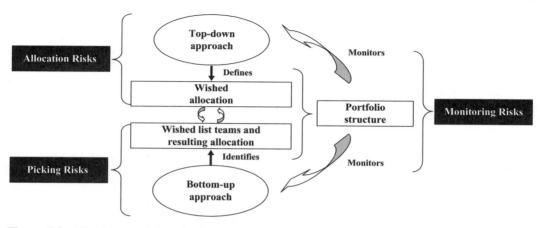

Figure 5.3   Mixed approach (see also Jaeggi, 2005)

to realization, any quantitative approach based on historical data reflects an outdated economic environment and will be even less indicative of the future. Even without being overly rigid or quantitative, a top-down approach can be used to generate alpha (by trying to spot the next "big thing" in private equity) or as a sanity check that helps to avoid fads. Based on pre-screening criteria derived from this high-level allocation, investors can limit the time they spend on analyzing individual investment proposals.

Apart from the questions associated with determining the weight of sub-portfolios, the major shortcoming of a top-down approach is that, in reality, strict allocations are not possible. This is because in practice it may be difficult to find and have access to a sufficient number of superior managers to fill in each predetermined sub-class allocation.[4] Indeed, often only one or two superior managers operate in a particular sector and they raise capital only every three to four years. Therefore, in order to adopt a top-down approach, investors cannot just wait for investment opportunities to arise but must proactively search for them to have a sufficiently large number of funds available to fill in their desired allocations.

Mixed approach

As both pure bottom-up and pure top-down approaches are not without problems, most investors follow a combined or mixed approach (see Figure 5.3). Even a strong believer in the top-down approach would rarely invest in funds that are not of high quality just to fulfill a target allocation. Likewise, no fund picker would commit all his money to a single sector based solely on the opportunity to invest in outstanding teams. Investors are conscious of the importance of diversification, but instead of diversifying on the basis of the correlation among the different asset classes, they define their target allocation on the basis of the investment strategies of the funds in which they invest. Basically, the mixed approach is a top-down approach where the capital is allocated equally to the different asset classes without making adjustments for any view on the future performance of the asset classes.[5]

---

[4] These sub-class allocations may be defined by industry sectors, countries, and fund styles.

[5] Rod Selkirk, Head of Private Equity, Hermes Pension Management, from an interview in *AltAssets*, 11 March 2003: "I want to stress that our investment strategy is more a framework than a rigid allocation. We would never invest in substandard funds simply because our asset allocation model dictated that we had to have a certain amount committed to a particular type of fund." (AltAssets, 2003)

Shearburn and Griffiths (2002) follow an investment strategy that can be considered representative of many private equity funds-of-funds. They invest exclusively in established private equity markets such as the U.S., UK and selected European economies; target the premier league of private equity funds in Europe and the U.S.; and diversify by stage, focus, geography and time. The goal is to create a portfolio that is diversified according to specified investment strategies or dimensions. In this portfolio, all the strategies or dimensions have equal weight. More specifically, these authors describe an approach that "consists in creating a portfolio of unique private equity strategies that are diversified from one another over multiple dimensions. These dimensions might include industry focus, investment size, geographic focus and private equity sub-asset class (such as leveraged buyouts, venture capital, growth capital and distressed investments)." Then, they assemble a portfolio of superior managers capable of generating extraordinary returns, with each manager's strategy being as distinct as possible from all the other strategies in the portfolio. Investors using this approach weight each strategy equally in the portfolio in order to minimize the concentration of funds. This means, for example, investing the same amount in a London-based, large buyout private equity manager as in a Silicon Valley-based early stage venture capitalist. This manager-driven, equally weighted approach to portfolio construction also drives the weighting of private equity sub-sectors, even where an investor may have a strong point of view.

Finally, there is an evolution in the adoption of the different approaches. For the early stages of an investment program, one of the main objectives is to put capital quickly to work in the best available teams in order to minimize idle liquidity. As young programs cannot count on an established relationship, the available universe of investment opportunities is restricted to a limited number of accessible wish-list funds. This makes a top-down approach difficult to implement, as allocation targets would make little sense. Once a sizeable portfolio has been built, however, a top-down approach becomes a more appropriate means of identifying concentration (e.g. in sectors or in teams).

RISK-RETURN MANAGEMENT APPROACHES

The goal of portfolio design is to combine assets that behave in fundamentally different fashions to optimize the risk–return relationship. But because many of the traditional analytical approaches are not fully relevant to private equity, additional techniques are required. For example, by dividing the portfolio into two or more sub-portfolios, the management of the risk–return relationship can be improved. Similarly, as discussed below, understanding the benefits and limitations of diversification for portfolios invested in private equity funds can lead to improved risk–return management.

Core–satellite approach

The **core–satellite approach** is a way of allocating assets to protect and grow wealth. The portfolio is structured in various sub-portfolios, which can then be designed using one of the construction techniques (e.g. bottom-up or top-down). Such an approach is based on Behavioral Portfolio Theory, where portfolios can be constructed as layered pyramids. A well-diversified core or bottom layer provides downside protection for the portfolio (risk aversion), while a less-diversified satellite or top layer looks to generate upside gains (risk seeking).[6] This approach aims to increase risk control, lower costs and add value.

---

[6] See Statman (2002): "The desire to avoid poverty gives way to the desire for riches. Some investors fill the uppermost layers with the few stocks of an undiversified portfolio like private individuals buy lottery tickets. Neither lottery buying nor undiversified portfolios are consistent with mean-variance portfolio theory but both are consistent with behavioural portfolio theory."

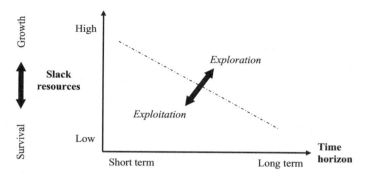

Figure 5.4   Trading off exploitation against exploration

This may be an effective strategy for institutions that want to diversify their portfolios without giving up the potential for higher returns generated by selected active management strategies. Another advantage is the flexibility to customize a portfolio to meet specific investment objectives and preferences. The core–satellite approach also provides the framework for targeting and controlling those areas where an investor believes he is better able to control risks or is willing to take more risk. What constitutes core versus satellite depends on the investor's focus and expertise. Some see VC as "satellite", while others view a balanced buyout and VC funds portfolio as "core". Finally, another benefit to this approach is that it facilitates spending more time on the satellite portfolio, which is expected to generate excess performance, and less time on the "less risky" core portfolio.

One option is to structure the portfolio in two sub-portfolios (see Figure 5.4):[7]

- The core portfolio typically aims to "exploit" relationships with institutional-quality firms raising funds that are expected to generate a predictable base return. If there is no change in the current environment, such mainstream funds are perceived to be the safe bet. A solid core of high-quality relationships allows limited partners to stay in the game long enough to seize the golden opportunities, but the exclusive reliance on the core leaves them susceptible to a long-term decline.
- The satellite portfolio can be interpreted as a bet on radical changes and aims to "explore" new opportunities. Funds in the satellite portfolio typically are comparatively small and will, for the most part, have only a limited impact on the portfolio. Rather, they should be seen as real options; having no value if not exercised from time to time.[8]

The balance between exploitation and exploration can be based on the following:

- The *time horizon* for the private equity funds investment program. The more long-term oriented, the higher the value of the option and therefore the higher the degree of exploration that should be undertaken.
- The *resources available*. With a larger reserve buffer a higher degree of exploration is possible. The initial stages of a private equity funds investment program are dominated by a primarily exploitation-oriented bottom-up approach to build up slack resources that enable exploration going forward.

---

[7] For more details see Mathonet and Meyer (2007).

[8] Real options can be defined as an alternative (hence the term "option") that becomes available with an investment opportunity, and are referred to as "real" because they are typically associated with tangible assets rather than with financial securities.

- The *anticipated volatility* of the private equity market environment. The more disruptive an expected market environment is, the more one needs to spread out one's options; whereas in a stable environment, exploration can be reduced to a minimum.

Diversification

Diversification is another area where limited partners attempt to manage the risk–return relationship in private equity funds. Diversification should be increased as long as the marginal benefit of adding a new asset to a portfolio (i.e. the marginal contribution of the asset towards portfolio risk reduction) exceeds the marginal cost (i.e. basically the transaction costs and the time and money spent on researching the asset). Therefore, another key question related to the portfolio design is the optimal number of positions. For private equity funds it is difficult to determine this optimum diversification level. To answer this, a series of other questions need to be addressed first:

- What is the investor's ability to identify and – even more importantly – access top teams?
- What trade-off is the investor searching for between risk-taking and profit-seeking. What is the investor's risk appetite? Arguably, fund-of-funds managers who co-invest their own personal wealth and have the fund-of-funds' full resources allocated to the asset class are in a different risk position than an institution that allocates an immaterial share of its assets to private equity. Additionally, the risk appetite of both investor groups may differ significantly.
- Does the investor have other non-commercial or strategic objectives, such as promoting technologies or creating employment?

Empirical evidence shows that the distribution of private equity fund returns is quite dissimilar to the normal distribution.[9] It exhibits a relatively high probability of a large gain (i.e. positive skewness) and a relatively high probability of extreme outcomes, (i.e. excess kurtosis, see Figure 5.5). Diversification has two impacts: it lowers risk as long as asset returns are not perfectly correlated and, due to the law of large numbers, may bring the distribution closer to normal. For private equity funds, the distributions of returns share characteristics with lotteries: a few extraordinary winners will compensate for many small losses. As in a lottery, where buying all lots (tickets) guarantees picking the winner but also that associated costs exceed the total gain, being invested in too many funds assures that the few top performers cannot adequately compensate the many funds with mediocre or substandard returns.[10] Therefore, in VC as in a lottery, a common strategy is to make few bets under the assumption that luck or selection skills will deliver the winners without having to support too many losers.

There is no formulaic answer to the diversification question, but research suggests that, for most assets, sufficient diversification is achieved with 20 positions in whatever one is seeking to diversify.[11] Figures 5.6 and 5.7 illustrate the situation for U.S. and European VC fund portfolios, but the conclusions are similar for buyout funds:

- 80% of the standard deviation is diversified away with a portfolio of 20 to 30 funds.
- Skewness decreases more or less at the same rate as standard deviation.
- 80% of the kurtosis is diversified away with a portfolio of five funds.

---

[9] We are more likely to encounter symmetrical return distributions where there is equilibrium between supply and demand and many market participants push prices in one or the other direction. Therefore it is not surprising that for private equity, return distributions are asymmetric.

[10] See Waters (2005): "Yet the big gains are concentrated in a handful of funds, leaving most investors with mediocre returns."

[11] See Flag Venture Management (2001), Weidig and Mathonet (2004), and Meyer and Mathonet (2005).

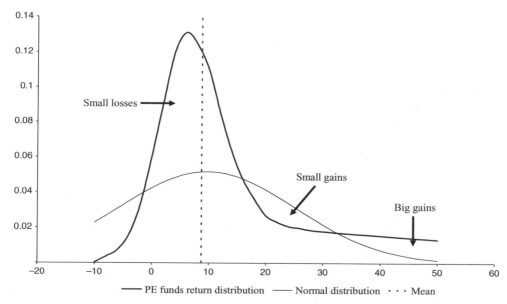

Figure 5.5 Private equity funds return distribution vs. normal distribution

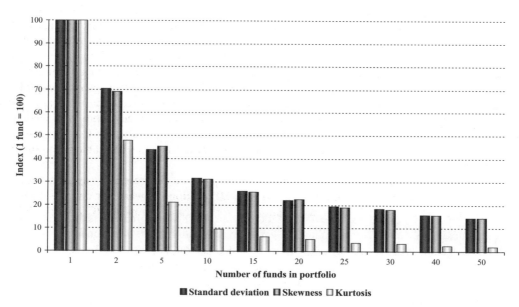

Figure 5.6 U.S. standard deviation, skewness and kurtosis of portfolio of funds returns with increasing diversification

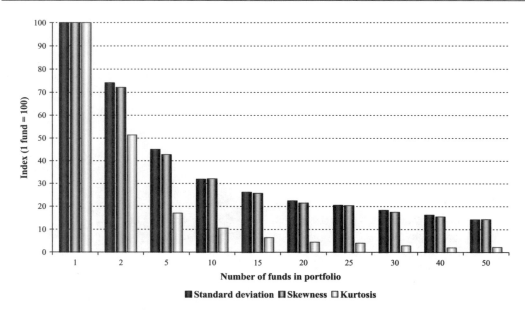

Figure 5.7   European standard deviation, skewness and kurtosis of portfolio of funds' returns with increasing diversification

The simulations done in Figure 5.6 suggest that there is no need to have more than 20 to 30 funds in a portfolio. In fact, when investors are seeking diversification that will not eliminate the desired skewness and kurtosis, it does not make sense to have more than five funds in a portfolio.

Probably the strongest argument against a high level of diversification is the quick fading of the fund quality. There are simply too few excellent fund management teams within a vintage year peer group. Over-diversification therefore not only leads to a reduction in positive skewness and kurtosis, but also depresses the portfolio's expected return. The fading of quality and the loss of positive skewness and kurtosis is more of an issue for VC than for leveraged buyouts. For buyouts, the distribution function looks more symmetrical and there are usually more high-quality teams. Finally, these "notions" only hold for the plain vanilla limited partnership stakes in funds. Real options, like co-investment rights, can justify a higher level of diversification.

Naïve diversification

Due to the poor quality of the available data, Markowitz's "big D" diversification is difficult to apply to the private equity arena. An alternative is naïve diversification.[12] As mentioned before, naïve diversification is the optimal strategy when there is no information that allows differentiation among assets.[13] Lhabitant and Learned (2002) further argue that Modern Portfolio Theory is seldom applied

---

[12] See King and Young (1994) on an application of naïve diversification to real estate fund portfolios. For a review of Markowitz's Mean-Variance Theory see Bodie, Kane and Marcus (2008).

[13] However, naïve diversification approaches can be refined. Brands and Gallagher (2003) found for equity funds-of-funds that investment strategies that ensure equal representation across investment styles perform better than a naïve sampling approach. See also Shearburn and Griffiths (2002): "Finally, these investors choose a sufficient number of strategies to provide diversification and spread risks. Based on quantitative analysis, Goldman Sachs pursues this approach to portfolio construction, targeting 18–25 different strategies in the broad-based private equity portfolio we manage."

to the full degree[14] and that naïve diversification (also called "1/N heuristics") in practice usually produces reasonably diversified portfolios that are somewhat surprisingly close to the efficient frontier.

Albeit less rigorous than traditional portfolio models, naïve diversification is nevertheless valuable to the prudent investor, as it can avoid extreme concentrations by ensuring an even distribution among the following dimensions:[15]

- number of fund managers and stage focus;
- vintage years and calendar years;
- industry sectors.

In general, a diversification strategy that doesn't take into account the specificities of this asset class can be quite inefficient. Over-diversification may lead to capping the upside. Furthermore, just investing in many teams without managing the diversification of other dimensions, like industry sectors and geography, can seriously damage the portfolio. Diversification sets in more slowly when funds are highly correlated. An unbalanced portfolio (e.g. one with a high exposure to early-stage investments or specific vintage years) works against diversification benefits. There are also diseconomies of scale. The number of investments, rather than the invested amounts, sets the cost base – such as legal expenses, due diligence and monitoring effort – of a portfolio of funds. It also becomes increasingly difficult to identify and gain access to suitable funds, as the number of quality opportunities is limited. Consequently, for private equity fund portfolios, diversification may be of reduced use for the management of risk versus return.

Market timing and cost-averaging approaches

The best investment practice is simply to define an investment strategy and to stick to it, regardless of whether the current environment is seen as good or bad. In order to get a good level of diversification, many investors have adopted what is called a **cost-averaging approach**. This proven method of **vintage year diversification** consistently invests a fixed amount of money throughout all years and steadily commits to the best funds around. This disciplined approach helps minimize overexposure to vintage years with high valuations. The cost-averaging principle sets an annual investment target for each private equity fund type, or a more or less constant target throughout funding cycles, thus avoiding any inclination to try to time the cycles.

The **market timing approach** involves varying investment levels across vintage years in an effort to invest more in years with better prospects and less in years with inferior prospects. It is too dangerous to assume that what has worked well in the past will continue to do so: emotional expectations are shaped by one's most recent experience. Also, the private equity market overreacts and experiences disruptions in trends. During market upswings, it is important to go for quality and

---

[14] See Lhabitant and Learned (2002): ". . . very few investors effectively take correlations (that is, the non-linearity of risk) into account when making complex portfolio decisions. Rather, they prefer to allocate assets using simpler rules, such as dividing allocations evenly among the assets available . . . Many respondents even admitted to having no asset-allocation strategy at all!"

[15] Standard and Poor's conducts ratings for structured notes backed by a portfolio of private equity funds. The basis of the rating is the analysis of a portfolio of private equity funds' diversification level in a multidimensional fashion. The following dimensions signal how diversified a portfolio is: number of fund managers or general partners and number of funds or limited partnerships, vintage years and calendar years, type of private equity funds or strategies, industry or sector, geography, and single investment exposure. In Standard and Poor's opinion, mainly the portfolio diversification provides downside protection to the holders of the rated notes (Erturk, Cheung and Fong, 2001).

be more restrictive than other investors; while during depressed market conditions, it could make sense to be more flexible, as very often the overall vintage year quality can turn out to be attractive.

Investing in secondaries could help in situations where the portfolio is unbalanced in terms of adequate exposure to all the vintage years. It is important to stick to the budgeted allocation as new opportunities to invest in VC or buyout funds tend to coincide with the rise and fall of returns of each strategy. Careful investors avoid the temptation to overweight commitments to the hot strategy of the moment and stick to a long-term plan.

6

Fund Manager Selection Process

While a wide divergence between top- and bottom-quartile performers may provide an opportunity to perform extremely well by selecting the top-performing managers, it also exposes the portfolio to a high degree of underperformance risk. If an institution is unlucky or unskilled enough to pick a bottom-quartile manager, the returns will likely prove to be very disappointing.

Manager selection and access is seen to be one of the keys to sustainable outperformance in private equity. It forms a distinct part of the investment process that can be efficiently structured. Manager selection is not mechanical, but requires industry experience and resources to conduct both research and due diligence. Unfortunately, this is easier said than done and the advice to focus on top funds is probably as helpful as the observation that "to become rich one needs to earn a lot of money". Further, it is more difficult to identify superior managers than it is to weed out obviously inferior managers. The key is to be highly selective and to strike a proper balance between seeking exposure to top funds and diversification. A thorough, consistent, detailed analysis and discipline in the due diligence process are critical.

To make matters worse, few investors, advisors and consultants have experience and familiarity with the unique aspects of private equity. Because the industry and its practices are continuously evolving, categorizations are fuzzy and there are no clear do's and don'ts. That makes the identification and evaluation of fund managers more important and also more challenging in the private equity universe. Consequently, one needs a different selection process for fund managers in private equity (Figure 6.1) than for fund managers of publicly-quoted assets.

DETERMINATION OF THE "WISH LIST" OF FUND CHARACTERISTICS

The development of an investment strategy is important to efficiently manage the process and it forms the starting point for the fund manager selection. Based on the investment strategy of the investor and the resulting portfolio design, a wish list of fund characteristics needs to be established. The wish list defines the types of proposals that are consistent with the investment strategy of the investor.

Next, an active deal-sourcer will identify wish-list funds to be specifically targeted for investment. Investors make a market mapping, where all management teams are ranked by their perceived attractiveness (see Figure 6.2).

Attractive teams are normally those that have been able to generate top performance during several market cycles and are the most likely to continue to do so in the future. One way to classify the manager teams is to rank them based on this dual-dimension approach: the quality of the track record from bottom to top performer, and the duration of their joint experience from none to several market cycles' joint experience. From this the following classification emerges:

- A blue chip team is a team that has been able to generate a top quartile performance for all its funds through at least two business cycles (i.e. a sequence of more than three funds).
- An established team is a team that has been able to generate a top quartile performance for most of its funds (more than three funds) through at least two business cycles.

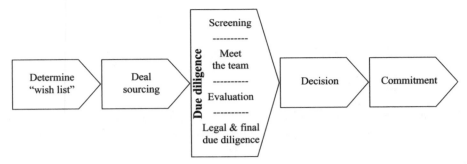

Figure 6.1 Private equity fund manager selection process

- An emerging team is a team with limited joint history but with all the characteristics to become at least an established team.
- A re-emerging team is a previously blue chip or established team that has been through a restructuring following recent poor performance or some significant operational issues and has regained the potential to re-emerge as established or blue chip.
- Not interesting are all the teams not included in the other categories.

DEAL SOURCING

Investors in private equity funds need to use their network of industry contacts to identify and establish contact with high-quality fund managers. It is critical to get as many opinions and leads as possible. This can be achieved through discussions with other investors or entrepreneurs, by employing advisors and consultants, and by researching the press.

Reactive deal sourcing, where investors often get showered with investment proposals, is not an efficient way of approaching selection. With this approach, literally hundreds of private placement memoranda need to be checked as to whether they comply with the set wish list characteristics or

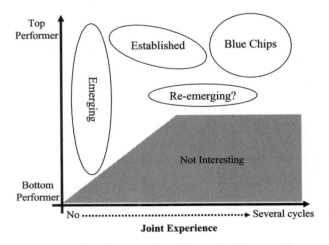

Figure 6.2 Market mapping of fund performance through several business cycles

investment criteria. First-time teams often have to approach as many investors as possible anyway, but top teams typically get referred to limited partners by word of mouth and therefore need to be actively sourced. Developing long-term relationships as well as exploring opportunities that fit the set criteria are critical. For this purpose teams have to be identified and approached even before they start their fund raising. This process requires establishing a calendar of when these teams are expected to go to the market.

A historical review of private equity performance reveals two important trends: 1) median private equity returns tend to underperform public equity indices; and 2) as was mentioned before, there is a wider gap between top-quartile and bottom-quartile returns than for funds of quoted assets. Under the assumption that past and future performance of a team are correlated,[1] funds raised by teams that have performed well in the past tend to be oversubscribed. If returns have been high, limited partners from prior funds are highly motivated to commit to follow-on funds and general partners will reward their loyalty with virtually guaranteed access to future funds.

In fact, private equity is a closed community where past relationships provide access to funds in high demand, while newcomers are often turned away. Frequently, when a team with a strong track record raises a new fund, investors in previous funds quickly commit often leading to oversubscription. General partners are interested in maintaining the relationship with the existing limited partnership base. Searching for new limited partners is an expensive exercise and it creates uncertainty regarding the timing of closing and future relationships.[2] Consequently, fund managers tend to avoid this exercise whenever possible. In the extreme, it will not even be known to outside parties that the team may be raising a new fund. Having access to a network of contacts is required to identify top teams and to know about the timing of their fundraising activities. While top teams give priority allocations to their previous investors, they may also allocate a share of the new fund to investors who could add value, such as deal flow, exit opportunities, industry expertise, etc. Nonetheless, access is far less of a problem for limited partners who are financially strong and have demonstrated that they are long-term players in the market. For newcomers however, this is a significant barrier to entry.

DUE DILIGENCE: IMPORTANCE AND LIMITATIONS

As fund selection is one of the key performance drivers in private equity, due diligence is a requirement for prudent investors as well as the basis for better investment decisions. The due diligence process covers all the activities associated with evaluating an investment proposal and is commonly defined as "the process of investigation and evaluation, performed by investors, into the details of a potential investment, such as an examination of operations and management and the verification of material facts".[3]

---

[1] It is generally believed that there is a high degree of repeatability or "persistence" of top-quartile performance in private equity. See, for example, Rouvinez (2006).

[2] See also Lerner and Schoar (2004). The authors presented the theory that, by choosing the degree of illiquidity of the security, private equity fund managers can influence the type of investors the firm will end up attracting. This allows managers to screen for "deep-pocket" investors (i.e. those that have a low likelihood of facing a liquidity shock), as they can reduce the general partner's cost of capital in future fundraising efforts. Their analysis is based on the assumption of an information asymmetry about the quality of the manager between the existing investors and the market. The general partner faces a lemons problem when he or she has to raise funds for a subsequent fund from outside investors, because the outsiders cannot determine whether the manager is of poor quality or whether the existing investors were hit by a liquidity shock. Transferability constraints are less prevalent when private equity funds have limited partners that are known to be subject to few liquidity shocks (e.g. endowments, foundations, and other investors with long-term commitments to private equity).

[3] Source: www.investorwords.com/1596/due_diligence.html [accessed October 2007].

Due diligence as a requirement for originators

According to Camp (2002), the concept of "due diligence" essentially denotes a legal obligation imposed on parties involved with the creation of prospectuses (directors, officers, underwriters, lawyers, accountants and others) to use due diligence to ensure that they contain no material misstatements or omissions. In the context of private equity funds, the phrase "due diligence" is used slightly differently. Funds are issuing securities privately and are therefore not required to provide their investors the same level of information as they would if they were selling the same securities in the public markets. However, in practice, the level of disclosure often ends up to be much more important.

Due diligence as a basis for better investment decisions

By consistently and methodically performing their due diligence, investors hope to make better investment decisions. Every fund promises a top-quartile performance. According to Kelly (2002), the marketing line most often heard is that one's fund is in *"the first quartile of returns"*.[4] While this may often be genuinely believed, new funds, in particular, are difficult to benchmark. Likewise, every fund-of-funds manager claims to follow a methodical and thorough due diligence procedure. In essence there are few differences in the processes followed but investors agree on the desired characteristics: a skilled and experienced management team, a good track record, a sensible and consistent strategy and an alignment of interests between investors and fund managers.

As information on private equity funds is not publicly available, it is necessary to collect data on the funds considered for investment. The management of this activity is seen as the main source of competitive advantage – even to the extent that other tasks critical to the success of the investment program, such as liquidity management, are overshadowed by this activity.

Limitations

Due diligence is generally based on cross-referencing and cross-checking, but often the lack of suitable comparables and information makes the analysis highly subjective. The high reliance on qualitative aspects and judgment can become a liability. Without proper incentives, investors have the tendency simply to raise the thresholds higher and higher to avoid personal exposure to criticism. As a result, potentially good investment proposals might be rejected. For example, in many cases newer partnerships are avoided, not necessarily because the fundamentals are not right or because the investment proposal is not convincing, but simply because not all points of the due diligence can be supported with tangible evidence.[5] An open mind towards new ideas is required and clear reasons why certain fund characteristics are to be avoided need to be stated.

Once a reputable institution has committed itself to invest in a fund, other investors tend to believe that it has carried out a proper due diligence. However, one should not rely on other investors' findings and judgments. Information provided by other limited partners also needs to be taken with a grain of salt. It could well be that an individual investment manager who has committed to an investment subconsciously tries to protect himself by bringing other institutions to commit: if others make the same mistake, he may be less subject to blame.

---

[4] See Meek (2004): "As one investor says: 'we always take the "top quartile" claim with a huge pinch of salt' ".

[5] Most limited partners make a distinction between first-time management teams and first-time funds. They usually have no interest in first-time teams (see AltAssets, 2002a, 2002b, 2003), but invest on a selective basis in first-time funds. However, in new technologies or new markets, first-time teams often cannot be avoided.

Private equity fund due diligence: step by step process

To reduce uncertainty to the minimum, a study of the entire market would be necessary. To assess the quality and relative performance expectations of funds, a professional manager can analyze hundreds of factors, the majority of them being qualitative rather than quantitative. As this is associated with significant costs, every investor will approach the due diligence process from a cost–benefit perspective. The due diligence process can be structured in the following stages: screening, meeting the team, evaluation, and final and legal due diligence.

Screening

Due diligence requires significant time and effort, and there are many more managers than can be analyzed in detail. Therefore, the first step of the due diligence process consists in a preliminary screening. The objective is to quickly eliminate proposals that do not fit or that are to be avoided based on the criteria and objectives laid out under the portfolio design. This could be because these proposals are in the wrong industry sector, stage or geographical focus, or do not meet minimum quality requirements. Deals screened out are *de facto* not worth spending further time and effort on.

Assuming that no knock-out criteria are detected, there is a preliminary evaluation of the fund manager's proposed investment strategy, the management team's overall quality, its track record, the fund's structure and its main terms. Appropriate analysis for this phase involves determining whether the fund's strategy is convincing; whether it differentiates itself from other proposals and, most importantly, whether there is potential for future success.

Proposals should be taken forward only if there is a good fit with the investor's portfolio strategy and if the wish list criteria are met. This screening process narrows down investment opportunities to a manageable few that merit a more in-depth due diligence.

Meeting the team

Paraphrasing real estate, where the three key components of investment success are "location, location, location", in private equity they are "team, team, team". Consequently, the next step in the due diligence process is a meeting with the fund management team to better understand the personalities, experience, dynamics and qualifications of the members. Attributes to examine in this phase include the overall management team quality and competencies, member synergies, team cohesion, the fairness of the incentives and the motivation of the team and the individual team members. The organizational structure and the decision-making process need also to be understood. This evaluation is highly subjective and can only be performed by an experienced investment manager.

There should also be a detailed analysis of the team's track record – both of the group and of the individuals. The expected drivers of performance need to be identified. Potential "deal breakers" need to be identified and clarified. These involve items related to proposed terms and conditions, alignment of interest factors, potential conflict of interests that the team is unwilling to negotiate, or where a gut instinct tells the investor not to go forward.

The comfort level with the fund manager is also important to ascertain. This is because the limited partner will be monitoring the fund manager for years. Hence, incompatible views can create instability in this relationship. At the other extreme, there is a danger that personal aspects can blur the picture. One should not forget that a limited partner often commits more than €10 million to a fund and of this – through management fees and carried interest – a few million might end up in the team's pockets. Who would not try to show his best side to potential investors under these circumstances?

Evaluation

In the next step, the proposal is evaluated against other opportunities on the limited partner's long list. As no funds are equivalent, this is the critical step. In this phase, it is important to examine the relative performance among fund managers on the long list, as well as the funds' positions in the competitive landscape.

In private equity, there exists an high degree of uncertainty as investment decisions must often be based on incomplete information and data. This implies that the entire due diligence process is of an imprecise nature. Therefore, the assessment of investment proposals not only requires expertise, but also involves pattern recognition. Camp (2002) argued in the context of direct investments, but the same applies to funds, that perhaps "the most important thing that separates [a] good venture capitalist from the rest of the pack is a dependable gut". Unfortunately, this is the point where, faced with high uncertainty levels, most investment managers would tend to throw all analytical rigor overboard and start to rely entirely on their judgment and their gut instinct.

Limited partners usually do not attempt to value a private equity investment proposal as they would do in the case of traditional asset classes. As primary positions in private equity funds are bought at par, the investment decision is either "yes" or "no" and, apart from negotiations around terms and conditions, there is no meaningful pricing mechanism to adjust for perceived risks. As a result, institutions have the tendency to impose an ever-growing list of criteria in the hope that this will help them to avoid mistakes. We believe that this is fundamentally wrong and only leads to homogeneity and quasi-standardization in an asset class that requires innovation and evolution. Instead, we propose a structured assessment of the following two main dimensions of a fund's value:

- The fund's expected economic value is mainly dependent on the quality of the proposal. We propose basing the assessment on a grading methodology that comes from qualitative scoring. The purpose of the qualitative scoring is to benchmark the fund against best practices for the private equity market. Dimensions assessed are management team skills, management team stability, management team motivation, conflicts of interest, structuring and costs, and validation through other investors.
- Second, there can be a real option value associated with the investment in the fund. For example, investing in a first-time fund is generally perceived to be more risky than investing in an established firm, but normally allows access later on if the fund becomes a top performer and is oversubscribed in subsequent fundraisings.

Grading private equity funds requires classifying all funds into specific unambiguous classes where all members share similar characteristics. As the private equity industry thinks in terms of top-quartile funds, the quartile statistics form the basis for an intuitively simple grading scale. Due to the scarcity of reliable data on the private equity market, grades finer than these values do not appear to be meaningful. Under the assumption that the fund's ranking does not change within its peer group and that it maintains its current quartile position within its peer group, its return is expected to fall into the respective quartile of the benchmark. That leads to the definition of the expected performance grades that is presented in Table 6.1.

Grades can be assigned based on the evaluation of both quantitative and qualitative criteria. It is a relative ranking within the fund's specific peer group that combines a quantitative scoring, a qualitative scoring, a method to combine the two evaluations, the internal age, and a final review leading to an adjustment of the grade if necessary (Meyer and Mathonet, 2005). In essence, this system is based on general considerations and experience and not on sophisticated mathematical modeling. It cannot be regarded as precise and it also clearly relies on the judgment of the evaluators.

Table 6.1   Grades description

Grade	Description
P–A	At the time of the grading the fund's rank falls into the first quartile of the peer group.
P–B	At the time of the grading the fund's rank falls into the second quartile of the peer group.
P–C	At the time of the grading the fund's rank falls into the third quartile of the peer group.
P–D	At the time of the grading the fund's rank falls into the fourth quartile of the peer group.

The grading is based on the assumption that all investors are treated *pari-passu* (i.e. with the same rights) and relates to the assessment of the fund, not to the structuring of the investment. For example, secondary transactions are often at a steep discount to the NAV. This, however, does not affect the fund's grade, as it may be the reflection of other variables. Furthermore, a fund with poor performance becomes a sunk cost once the purchase price has been paid and it is only the intrinsic quality of the fund that will support the future cash flows.

Finally, it has to be kept in mind that a fund with the highest ex-ante grade of P–A may also fail and that funds with the lowest grading of P–D can well turn out to be spectacular winners. Moreover, simply funding all P–A graded funds should not be equated with selectivity: an ex-ante P–A grading states that the proposal is closely complying with best market practices for funds, but does not address the question of whether there are better funds around.

Assessing the value of intangibles is difficult, particularly in the case of the real option value. Therefore, this valuation cannot be precise. But given the context of intangibles, a structured process is helpful and techniques such as qualitative scoring can improve the quality of the decision.[6]

At this stage an investor may have formed a hypothesis that the proposal fits the private equity funds investment program's strategy and that it is of acceptable quality. The in-depth due diligence aims to confirm this hypothesis.

Final and legal due diligence

This last step of the selection process before decision and commitment is an exhaustive and costly exercise. It comprises the legal due diligence and final in-depth due diligence. Often limited partnership agreements incorporate unique terms or, in the case of funds operating offshore, are structured to comply in the jurisdiction's unique rules. Therefore, such agreements need to be drafted by experts, something that is very expensive to do too early in the process when the final investment decision is still very uncertain. On the other hand, any negotiation and changing of terms and conditions is only meaningful before investing and therefore all sides often have to work under serious time pressure.

The next phase of this final analysis focuses on a more detailed analysis of the key issues identified previously. This due diligence, any negotiations, and a detailed track record analysis also offer an opportunity for getting to know the team better and set the theme for future monitoring activities.

Finally, investors in private equity funds need to use their network of industry contacts to do independent reference checks. It is advisable to get second opinions from co-investors in the portfolio, entrepreneurs, competitors, or industry advisors. Also, existing investors' commitments should be verified. In addition, contact with the other prospective limited partners may help expedite changes to the fund's terms and conditions.

---

[6] See, for example,. Edvinsson and Malone (1997) or Chapter 15 in Meyer and Mathonet (2005).

DECISION AND COMMITMENT

Due diligence can be seen primarily as information gathering and evaluation and not as a decision-making tool. In practice, the distinction is seldom made: due diligence is used to weed out inferior funds and accept the remaining proposals. The results of the due diligence should only be used as input for a decision-making process that takes into consideration not only the quality of the investment proposal but also the program's portfolio composition.

Finally, this is not a one-sided decision. Teams may have their own due diligence criteria for selecting potential investors. They should examine whether the investor's commitment is long term; if the investor understands the business, if the investor has a reputation of being difficult, or if the investor is a "defaulting investor" (one who has previously reneged or is anticipated to renege on capital commitments). In a case where public institutions seek to become limited partners, their investment restrictions (particularly those related to industry sectors and geography) and their transparency requirements need to be acceptable to the fund managers.

7
Benchmarking in the Private Equity World

Benchmarking aims to evaluate the performance of a specific entity by comparison to a standard or a point of reference. In the case of private equity funds, the analysis is normally done on the past financial performance of a particular fund manager and, as such, it forms part of the due diligence process. However, benchmarking can also cover the current financial performance and is thus also used in the monitoring process. Benchmarking is not the only tool that is used in the track record analysis. Many other tools exist, such as the portfolio performance dispersion or the winners' dependence analyses used to assess the level of risk.[1] The most intuitive approach is to compare a private equity fund against a group of funds that have a similar risk profile (i.e. that have the same style or specialization, also called a peer group). Ideally these funds should represent the closest competitors of the fund to be benchmarked.

SPECIFIC ISSUES

In the case of private equity there exists an ongoing discussion on the validity of benchmarks. According to Geltner and Ling (2000), appraisal-based peer universe benchmarks are, in principle, valid and useful tools for investment performance evaluation purposes. However, Kelly (2002) sees private equity as an *"asset class nearly impossible to benchmark"*. The author raises the issue that there are sometimes too few observations within one vintage year to benchmark. Furthermore, he also mentions that very often the general partners are vague regarding the methodology used for calculating the reported returns, rendering the comparison somewhat questionable.[2] Bailey, Richards and Tierney (1990) define the so-called **Bailey criteria** as a grouping of characteristics to gauge the appropriateness of investment benchmarks. We now proceed to present these criteria and how they apply to private equity:

- *Unambiguous/knowable. Are the names and weights of assets that comprise the benchmark clearly identifiable?* Private equity benchmarks only provide aggregate data and thus do not give a complete representation of the available asset set.
- *Investable. Is the option being analyzed available by forgoing active management and simply holding the benchmark assets?* It can be in public, but not private, equity markets.
- *Measurable. Is it possible to frequently calculate the benchmark performance?* The data provided by private equity funds do not allow one to accurately measure their risk and return characteristics. Valuation guidelines such as those put in place by various VC associations define an appraisal policy to improve the coherence and consistency, making the comparison between funds more meaningful. However, the industry uses several different performance measures, such as IIRR or multiples, that can sometimes offer varied pictures.
- *Specified in advance. Is the benchmark constructed and mutually agreed upon prior to the manager evaluation?* Private equity is considered to be an absolute-return asset class. Consequently, benchmarks are of less relevance for the evaluation of managers, whose incentives are not normally based on an index.

---

[1] For a more detailed description of track record analysis see Chapter 10 in Mathonet and Meyer (2007).

[2] This important issue would probably arise as a result of the due diligence process presented in the previous chapter.

- *Appropriate. Is the benchmark consistent with the manager's investment style?* As the private equity market is continuously evolving, there is a risk of using an inappropriate evaluation benchmark. If a benchmark does not represent well the style or specialization of the fund (e.g. in the case of emerging markets funds, or new technologies not yet represented in the benchmark), comparisons can be problematic.

Private equity benchmarks suffer deficiencies in nearly all of these dimensions. However, most of the time practitioners can live with these shortcomings, or see them as inconsequential. Thomson Financial, Venture One, Cambridge Associates and Private Equity Intelligence are database providers for private equity investors. These databases contain peer groups that can serve as benchmarks. However, it must be noted that private equity funds provide performance information predominantly on a voluntary basis.[3] For this reason, these databases do not necessarily capture the same data which can result in reported returns differing by as much as several percentage points for some peer groups. Another common criticism is **survivorship bias**,[4] which refers to the fact that managers or funds that perform poorly tend to go out of business and therefore drop out of the peer universe. As a result, statistical data will only cover the currently existing funds and present an average historical performance that is likely upwardly biased. On the other hand, according to Geltner and Ling (2000), it is not necessary to have a fixed and constant set of funds in the benchmark, and Swensen (2000) argues that survivorship bias may be less of a problem for long-term-oriented illiquid investments, e.g. private equity, as this population does not change rapidly. Indeed, managers of private equity funds enter and exit the benchmark statistics with considerably less frequency than their counterparts focusing on traditional marketable securities, since the limited partnership structure precludes an easy departure from the industry.

We now proceed to describe the main performance measures for individual funds and, later, for portfolios of funds.

INDIVIDUAL FUNDS

Performance measures

As mentioned before, the internal rate of return is the implied discount rate that makes the net present value of all cash flows equal to zero. According to Born (2004), the IRR is the most accurate method for calculating the returns of VC, as this performance measure incorporates the time value of money. (It also assumes that cash is reinvested at the IIRR, which may be unrealistic. The Modified IRR assumes a given reinvestment rate and is therefore preferred by some investors.) The IIRR, which is the IRR of unliquidated funds, is a cash flow-based return measure which considers the residual value or NAV of the partnership's holdings as a final cash inflow. **Interim IRRs (IIRRs)** are only estimates rather than actual realized rates of returns. Mathematically, the IIRR is found by solving this equation for IIRR:

$$\sum_{t=0}^{T} \frac{D_t}{(1 + IIRR_T)^t} + \frac{NAV_T}{(1 + IIRR_T)^T} - \sum_{t=0}^{T} \frac{C_t}{(1 + IIRR_T)^t} = 0$$

---

[3] See Shearburn and Griffiths (2002) "Precisely because private equity is private, published data in the field is not particularly reliable."

[4] It is to be noted that though the survivorship bias is often raised in the context of private equity, this issue is also relevant for public equity. Databases on private equity must also face the problem that they do not contain the performance data of all active fund managers. This is because some private equity managers may decide not to provide information to databases as they would prefer to maintain exclusivity. Another problem is that private equity returns are usually not adjusted for the statistical problems caused by the inherent market's illiquidity of private equity investments and the consequent infrequent pricing.

where: D_t is the fund distribution during the period t; NAV_T is the net asset value of the fund at the end of its lifetime (T); C_t is the capital contribution or drawdown during the period t; and $IIRR_T$ is the investors' net interim internal rate of return at time T.

VC associations and the CFA Institute deem the Interim IRR,[5] which is a cash-weighted IRR, to be the most appropriate return measure for VC and private equity funds.[6] Implicit in this decision is the recognition that, when a management contract calls for a series of investments to be spread out over time at the discretion of the manager, a rate of return-based performance measurement and evaluation that is time-weighted is not appropriate.

Use of the IRR to compare investment alternatives implicitly assumes that reinvestment can be made at the IRR. Further discussion of this appears in Chapter 9, where we assess the components of IIRR.

The IIRR is not the only performance measure used by the industry. The following represent some of the other commonly-used performance measures:

- The **total value to paid-in ratio** (**TVPI** or total return), which is a measure of the cumulative distribution to investors plus the total value of the unrealized investments relative to the total capital drawn from investors:

$$TVPI_T = \frac{\sum_{t=0}^{T} D_t + NAV_T}{\sum_{t=0}^{T} C_t} = DPI_T + RVPI_T$$

- The **distribution to paid-in ratio** (**DPI**, or realized return), which is a measure of the cumulative distribution to investors relative to the total capital drawn from investors:

$$DPI_T = \frac{\sum_{t=0}^{T} D_t}{\sum_{t=0}^{T} C_t}$$

- The **residual value to paid-in** (**RVPI**, or unrealized return), which is a measure of the total value of the unrealized investments relative to the total capital drawn from investors:

$$RVPI_T = \frac{NAV_T}{\sum_{t=0}^{T} C_t}$$

Note that these ratios are measures of net returns to invested capital and therefore do not take the time value of money into account, as distinct from the IIRR. It should also be stressed that the

---

[5] Note that as database providers are focusing on net return to the limited partners, it is the fund's net IIRR and not the gross that has to be benchmarked. Also note that the NAV is sometimes a "gross" figure (i.e. before deduction of a possible carried interest for the general partner), while the cash flows are "net" to the limited partners.

[6] See Geltner and Ling (2000): "In 1993, AIMR proposed performance measurement guidelines that recommended a time-weighted approach. After investors and fund managers expressed concerns, a special sub-committee of private equity industry investors and experts appointed by AIMR studied the applicability of time-weighted returns to the private equity industry. They recommended that fund managers and intermediaries present their private equity performance results on the cash-weighted IRR basis."

private equity industry does, in effect, attempt to appraise the NAV at the end of each quarter (see discussion in Chapter 9). IIRRs, TVPI and RVPI are computed based on these residual values. Their estimations are the most problematic components of return evaluation and are among the main reasons a quantitative benchmarking should be complemented by a qualitative analysis.

Classical relative benchmarks

Many investors attempt to apply traditional public equity methodologies to private equity. In efficient markets, managers can decide to be passive or active, depending on whether or not they structure a portfolio to closely mimic the market. In less efficient markets, such as those in which private equity operates, managers have to be active as they cannot track a benchmark given the aforementioned deficiencies.

Following an active investment strategy implies, by definition, that the risk level taken by the manager will be changing. This changing risk can be controlled in one of the following two ways: non-quantitatively, by constraining the manager to invest only in assets having the same risk profile as the benchmark; and quantitatively, by adjusting the manager's ex-post returns to reflect the market's price of risk. In theory, risk can be controlled by using risk-adjusted return measures in both the benchmark and the fund.[7] But in private equity only the non-quantitative approach to controlling for risk can be used.[8]

It is common practice in private equity to use a vintage, geographic and stage focus-specific benchmark, often referred to as "peer-group cohort" (e.g. 1995 European buyout funds), and to express the result in terms of the quartile it lies in within the benchmark group. The quartile is a relative measure and does not reflect any qualitative assessment. A top performer in a dismal vintage year may barely return the invested funds, while in some spectacular vintage years even fourth-quartile funds have returned double-digit returns. Figure 7.1 shows one example of an individual fund benchmarking. The benchmarked fund starts as a fourth-quartile fund and moves after several quarters into the first-quartile area to peak with a 25% IIRR. Then, it goes down into the second quartile and ends its life at the boundary between the first and second quartiles.

A top quartile fund by definition belongs to the 25% best funds in its peer group, which erroneously leads to the conclusion that only 25% of funds may legitimately be qualified as top quartile. The fact is that many more funds in the market are being labeled top quartile.[9] One reason is that, except for the 25% ratio itself, nothing else in this definition is cast in stone. Whether best performance refers to total value or IIRR, net (i.e. IIRR of a portfolio or fund considering the effect of management fees and carried interest), gross (i.e. IIRR of a portfolio or fund without taking into account the effect of management fees and carried interest), realized (i.e. based on historical data) or not realized (i.e. based on historical and/or estimated data), is open to interpretation. The composition of the peer group may vary between analyses resulting in different funds being identified as being in the top quartile. Also, because several return measures exist, each with their advantages and disadvantages, a fund can wind up in different quartile positions depending on which measure is employed. It is thus a good practice to benchmark the fund using a variety of measures, but also to use judgment.

---

[7] Returns must be adjusted for risk in the way that the capital market prices risk. This is done on the basis of, for example, the Treynor ratio: portfolio's excess return over risk-free investments divided by its systematic risk as presented by its beta.

[8] As will be described in Chapter 10, it is very difficult to reliably measure the risk level in private equity investments.

[9] The "best of category" issue is also observed in other asset classes, where the choice of benchmarks, performance measure, etc. can used to try to convince investors that the considered asset belongs to the "best of category".

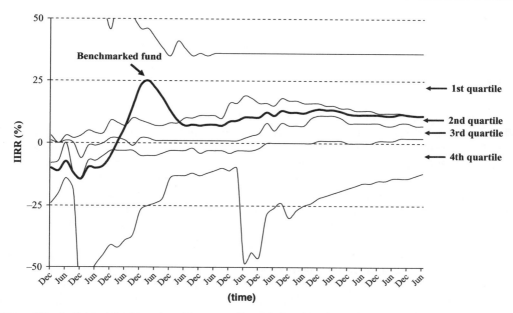

Figure 7.1   Individual fund benchmarking: quartile evolution since inception

Other relative benchmarks

In some cases, there are simply not enough funds to obtain a meaningful peer-group cohort. As the industry is private, the data providers mostly rely on voluntary participation, which can mean that certain markets are not effectively covered. In these cases, more general or alternative benchmarks must be used.

Extended peer group. When a representative peer-group cohort is too limited, it is simplest to extend the peer universe to the most similar funds. For example, if the number of 2005 European early stage funds is not sufficient, the universe of all 2005 European VC funds or the universe of the 2004–2006 European early stage funds could potentially be used as alternatives.[10]

Public market equivalent. The goal of the public market equivalent methodology is to calculate a private equity equivalent public index return, which provides a basis for comparison. The methodology[11] involves the estimation of a public market equivalent terminal value, which is substituted for the NAV in the IIRR calculation. Each actual cash flow is hypothesized to have been invested in a public index (for cash contributions) or divested from the same public index (for cash withdrawals). The size of the terminal position is the accumulation of this hypothetical program of buying and selling units of the public index using the fund's actual cash flow schedule.[12] Once the final number of units is estimated, it is valued using the index's concurrent value. Then the NAV is replaced by this terminal value (i.e. the number of units times the index value) and the private equity equivalent public index return is calculated. The resulting return is a cash-weighted return indicating

---

[10] The vintage year may be a less important differentiator than type of VC funds since two consecutive vintage years have on average eight common years in their existence.

[11] See, for example, Cheung et al. (2003).

[12] The fact that the fund's cash flow schedule is used explains why only the terminal value has to be changed for the calculation of the public market equivalent IRR.

hypothetical performance if the investor had invested the actual cash flows in a public index rather than in the private equity.

Absolute benchmarks

Private equity is often perceived as an absolute return asset class. Therefore, it is meaningful to use absolute return targets to evaluate performance. The most straightforward one is the comparison of the fund performance against the private equity investment program target or required rate of return. Until recently, it was not uncommon to have target rates of return of 30% or even more. Such high rates of return targets may no longer be meaningful because the levels were both temporary and unsustainable. Another often-used absolute benchmark is a target expressed as a premium over public equity (e.g. 300–500 bps over public equity). This benchmark is a hybrid, being both a relative (public index)[13] and absolute (premium) benchmark. Its use is justified by the fact that often the private equity allocation is obtained at the expense of public equity, and can thus be considered a sort of perceived opportunity cost to private equity.

Finally, the performance can be measured against the absolute returns of the historical peer group cohort for all the vintage years or the mature ones.

Let us take a look at an example to illustrate the use of the formulas just presented. Suppose that we have the following values for distributions, contributions and NAVs for two French private equity funds (named "1" and "2") that belong to the vintage year 2000-stage focus buyout (amounts in Euro millions):

	2000	2001	2002	2003	2004	2005	2006
PE Fund 1	(200)	(800)	200	(2.000)	(600)	2.000	3.500
PE Fund 2	(1.500)	(1.500)	(800)	(200)	500	1.500	5.000

Positive numbers correspond to years in which investors received net distributions, negative numbers correspond to years in which investors made net contributions and the figures for 2006 correspond to the NAVs of each of the two funds at the end of that year. We have to:

1. Calculate the IIRR, the TVPI, the DPI and the RVPI for the two funds.
2. Perform a classical benchmark analysis based on the following information collected for 31 European private equity funds categorized as vintage year 2000-stage focus buyout, from inception to December 31, 2006:
   a. the maximum return (measured using the IIRR) registered by a private equity fund was 34.80%;
   b. the highest quartile of PE funds had a return of 13.20% or more;
   c. the median return was 6.50%;
   d. the lowest quartile funds had returns of 0% or less; and
   e. the minimum return was −9.50%.
3. Compare the returns offered by the two private equity funds to those of public securities (as measured by the French stock exchange using the CAC 40 Index as benchmark), calculating the

[13] As we explain in Chapter 10, private equity funds are most likely to be correlated, at least to some degree, with public equity. For example, in a recent article by the Center for International Securities and Derivatives Markets (2005) the correlation between private equity and the S&P 500 was 0.55 (1991–2007).

gap between the IIRR of each private equity (PE) fund and the *public market equivalent*. Note: The value of the CAC 40 Index during the 2000–2006 period was:

	2000	2001	2002	2003	2004	2005	2006
	1	2	3	4	5	6	7
CAC 40	5926	4625	3064	3558	3821	4715	5542

Solution to 1: Calculate the IIRR, the TVPI, the DPI and the RVPI for the two funds

Recall that the Interim IRR (IIRR) is defined as the discount rate that makes the present value of the distributions, the contributions and the NAV equal to zero. Therefore, in the case of PE Fund 1, the IIRR is found as the solution to:

$$\sum_{t=0}^{T} \frac{D_{(t)}}{(1 + IIRR_T)^t} + \frac{NAV_T}{(1 + IIRR_T)^T} - \sum_{t=0}^{T} \frac{C_t}{(1 + IIRR_T)^t} = 0$$

$$\times \frac{(200)}{(1 + IIRR)} + \frac{(800)}{(1 + IIRR)^2} + \frac{200}{(1 + IIRR)^3} + \frac{(2,000)}{(1 + IIRR)^4} + \frac{(600)}{(1 + IIRR)^5} + \frac{2,000}{(1 + IIRR)^6}$$

$$+ \frac{3,500}{(1 + IIRR)^7} = 0$$

Solving this equation using a financial calculator or Excel (function IRR) we obtain an IIRR = 16.53%. Following the same procedure for PE Fund 2, we find that its IIRR is a lower 12.53%. As can be seen, PE Fund 1 is more profitable than PE Fund 2 by exactly 4%. Notice that we would need to compare these IIRRs to the discount rates or required rates of return applicable to each private equity fund to determine whether these returns were greater than the required minimum returns (further discussion on the discount rates applicable in private equity appears in Chapter 11).

TVPI: In the case of PE Fund 1, the TVPI is:

$$TVPI_T = \frac{\sum_{t=0}^{T} D_t + NAV_T}{\sum_{t=0}^{T} C_t} = \frac{(200 + 2,000) + 3,500}{200 + 800 + 2,000 + 600} = 1.58$$

In the case of PE Fund 2 the TVPI is 1.75. Thus, PE Fund 2 has a higher ratio of total distributions and NAV to total contributions between 2000 and 2006 than PE Fund 1. As we mentioned before, this measure does not take into account the time value of money. Also, note that even though the drawdowns or paid-in had a negative sign in the table (given that they represent a use of cash to private equity funds), we used their values expressed in positive numbers in the denominator of the equation. We followed this convention because it generates a more meaningful sign (i.e. a positive value) for the TVPI index that is more easily interpreted as benefit-to-costs ratios are usually expressed and interpreted. We followed the same procedure when calculating the total value of drawdowns in the case of the next two indices (DPI and RVPI).

DPI: In the case of PE Fund 1, the DPI is:

$$DPI_T = \frac{\sum\limits_{t=0}^{T} D_t}{\sum\limits_{t=0}^{T} C_t} = \frac{200 + 2{,}000}{200 + 800 + 2{,}000 + 600} = 0.61$$

In the case of PE Fund 2 the DPI is 0.50 Therefore, PE Fund 1 has a higher ratio of total distributions to total commitments than PE Fund 2 between 2000 and 2006. As we mentioned before, this measure does not take into account the time value of money.

RVPI: For PE Fund 1, the RVPI is:

$$RVPI_T = \frac{NAV_T}{\sum\limits_{t=0}^{T} C_t} = \frac{3{,}500}{(200 + 800 + 2{,}000 + 600)} = 0.97$$

Whereas in the case of PE Fund 2 the formula gives us a RVPI of 1.25. It can be seen that PE Fund 2 has a higher ratio of NAV to total contributions than PE Fund 1. Again note that this measure does not consider the time value of money.

Solution to 2: Perform a classical benchmark analysis based on the following information collected for vintage year 2000-stage focus buyout European private equity funds

Based on the information provided, we can construct the following table to help visualize the performance of Private Equity Funds 1 and 2 using a classical benchmark analysis:

Individual funds: Classical relative benchmarks
Vintage year 2000 - Stage focus Buyout

VentureXpert Stage Buyout - EU - VY 2000 - Date 31/12/2006

Benchmarh (IRR)

From	To	Sample Size	Max	Upper	Med	Lower	Min
Inception	12/31/06	31	34.80	13.20	6.50	-	-	9.50

PE Fund 1   16.5%-> Q1

PE Fund 2   12.5%->Q2

It can be seen that PE Fund 1 had an excellent return when compared to its peers, as its IIRR was located between the upper and the maximum return corresponding to the 31 European private equity funds used in the sample. In the case of PE Fund 2, the observed return was less impressive, although its IIRR was still above the median private equity fund return of the sample.

Solution to 3: Compare the returns offered by the two private equity funds to those of public securities (as measured by the French stock exchange using the CAC 40 Index), calculating the gap between the IIRR of each PE fund and the public market equivalent.

The IRR of PE Fund 1 is 16.5%. The growth in the CAC 40 from 2000 to 2006 is −6.5%. CAC 40 units are defined as the PE funds cash flows relative to the CAC 40 values. The absolute value of

		Individual funds: Other relative benchmarks							Return
		2000 1	2001 2	2002 3	2003 4	2004 5	2005 6	2006 7	
PE Fund 1	(1)	(200)	(800)	200	(2.000)	(600)	2000	3500	16.5%
CAC 40	(2)	5926	4625	3064	3558	3821	4715	5542	−6.5%
CAC 40 units	(3) = (1)/(2)	(0.03)	(0.17)	0.07	(0.56)	(0.16)	0.42	0.44	
PME	(4) = (3)*(2)	(200)	(800)	200	(2000)	(600)	2000	2419	9.1%
GAP									7.4%
PE Fund 2		(1500)	(1.500)	(800)	(200)	500	1500	5000	12.53%
CAC 40		5926	4625	3064	3558	3821	4715	5542	−6.5%
CAC 40 units		(0.25)	(0.32)	(0.26)	(0.06)	0.13	0.32	0.45	
PME		(1500)	(1500)	(800)	(200)	500	1500	2471	2.5%
GAP									10.0%

the sum of each year's CAC 40 units for PE Fund 1 is 0.44. Multiplying this sum by the value of the CAC 40 at the end of the period yields \$2,419, which represents the amount an investor in the CAC 40 would hold on a public market equivalent (PME) basis. This contrasts with the PE Fund 1 investor who holds \$3,500 at the end of the period. The IRR for the public market equivalent is 9.1%. We find that the gap, or excess IRR, for the PE Fund 1 relative to the PME is 7.4%. For PE Fund 2, the gap (10%) is calculated by subtracting the IRR of the PME (2.5%) from the IRR of the fund (12.5%) is 10%.

PORTFOLIO OF FUNDS

Performance measures

Because a private equity portfolio is an aggregation of funds, its performance measures are simply the aggregation of the ones used for the individual funds (IIRR, TVPI, DPI or RVPI), and can be calculated based on one of the following methods.

Simple average. The arithmetic mean of the private equity funds' performance measures.

$$IIRR_{P,T} = \frac{1}{N} \sum_{i=1}^{N} IIRR_{i,T}$$

Here, $IIRR_{p,T}$ is the IIRR of the portfolio at the end of periot T, $IIRR_{i,T}$ is the IIRR of fund i at the end of time period T, and N is the number of funds in portfolio.

Median. The value appearing halfway in a table ranking the performance of each fund held in the portfolio.

Commitment weighted. The **commitment weighted** average of the funds' performance measures.

$$IIRR_{P,T} = \frac{1}{\sum_{i=1}^{N} CC_i} \sum_{i=1}^{N} CC_i * IIRR_{i,T}$$

Here, CC_i is the commitment made to fund i.

Pooled. Portfolio performance obtained by combining all individual funds cash flows and residual values together as if they were from one single fund, and solving the equation for $IIRR_{p,T}$:

$$\sum_{t=0}^{T}\sum_{i=1}^{N}\frac{CF_{i,t}}{\left(1+IIRR_{P,T}\right)^{t}}+\sum_{i=1}^{N}\frac{NAV_{i,T}}{\left(1+IIRR_{P,T}\right)^{T}}=0$$

Here, $CF_{i,t}$ is the net cash flow at the end of time period t between the fund i and the investor, T is the number of periods, $NAV_{i,T}$ is the latest NAV of the fund I, $IIRR_{P,T}$ is the IIRR of the portfolio P at the end of time period T and N is the number of funds in the portfolio.

Arguably, the pooled measure gives the "true" financial return of the portfolio. However, it may also make sense to use the others, depending on what one wishes to measure. For example, the simple average can be a good indicator of the selection skills, while the commitment-weighted average can be useful in assessing the added value resulting from the decision of what size commitment to make to each specific fund.

Benchmark of private equity fund portfolios

To benchmark a portfolio of private equity funds, the portfolio needs to be compared against another portfolio of private equity funds. But there are two problems with this comparison: first, publicly-available database providers report too few funds-of-funds to make a comparison meaningful. Second, these funds-of-funds implement various investment strategies, have a different portfolio composition and, most of all, usually have a different vintage year structure. To circumvent these problems, synthetic portfolios can be generated with the same allocation to the various sub-asset classes (e.g. vintage year, stage and geographies) as the one to be benchmarked. Such benchmarking allows one to evaluate the portfolio managers selection skills, (i.e. how good was he or she at selecting the best fund managers within the defined allocations). If the portfolio is composed of 40% buyouts and 60% VC, the synthetic portfolio would need to have this same 40-60 split.

As the performance of a portfolio is the aggregation of the individual funds' performances, the benchmarking of a portfolio is simply the extension of the benchmarking of an individual fund. In doing so, it is important to use the same aggregation method for both the portfolio and the benchmark.

Commitment weighted benchmark

The portfolio benchmark is constructed using the commitment weighted average of the benchmark for each individual fund comprising the "peer group cohorts" (e.g. the same vintage, geographic and stage focus):

$$BM_{P,T}=\left(\frac{1}{\sum\limits_{i=1}^{N}CC_{i}}\right)\sum_{i=1}^{N}CC_{i}*BM_{i,T},$$

where $BM_{P,T}$ is the portfolio benchmark at the end of time period T, CC_{i} is the commitment to the fund i, N is the number of funds in the portfolio and $BM_{i,T}$ is the benchmark of fund i at the end of time period T. To compare apples to apples, one must compare the commitment weighted portfolio performance to that of the commitment weighted benchmark.

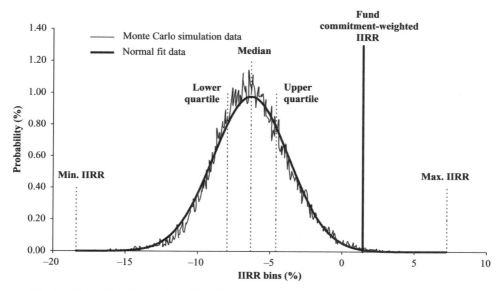

Figure 7.2   Portfolio of funds benchmarking: Monte Carlo simulation

Monte Carlo simulation

The Monte Carlo simulation[14] is one technique that can be used to generate portfolios similar to the one to be benchmarked. This is done by drawing, at each simulation run, the same number of funds as in the portfolio out of all the relevant peer group cohorts and weighting the performances by the commitment sizes of the funds in the portfolio. For example, for a portfolio composed of eight early stage funds and five later stage funds, the simulation will draw for each run eight funds out of the early stage cohort and five out of the later stage cohort. After weighting the performance of each fund drawn according to a corresponding commitment size, a portfolio performance is obtained. This is repeated many times so that a distribution can be created, which is then used to benchmark the portfolio. The commitment weighted IIRR of the portfolio is then compared against this synthetic benchmark (see Figure 7.2).

The results obtained from this approach should be analyzed with care. This is because, by construction (meaning the random picks), it is implicitly assumed that the fund manager knows and has access to the entire population of the peer group cohorts. Furthermore, it is also implicitly assumed that the manager makes no decision on the allocation among the various peer group cohorts or the level of diversification, which in reality is often not the case. These limitations can be resolved by running a simulation better reflecting the flexibility granted to or the constraints imposed on the manager. For example, while a portfolio can be composed of 60% buyout funds and 40% VC funds, the composition of benchmark portfolios might range between 50% and 75% of buyout funds and 25% and 50% of VC funds, if this is what is prescribed in the investment policy imposed on the assessed manager.

---

[14] A description of a Monte Carlo simulation can be found in Weidig and Mathonet (2004).

8

Monitoring Private Equity Investments

While investors in private equity funds may assume that little can be done to prevent problems once the due diligence process has been completed, ongoing monitoring throughout the life of a private equity investment is a necessary control mechanism. In such a long-term business, initial due diligence findings quickly become obsolete, while changes to the economic environment can fundamentally alter the balance between investor and fund manager interests. The information asymmetry and moral hazard-related problems associated with such changes can be lessened through monitoring.

APPROACH TO MONITORING

Monitoring involves the routine and systematic collection of information. According to Robbie, Wright and Chiplin (1997), private equity limited partners typically engage in few monitoring actions. The authors expected this to continue as a more proactive approach often raises questions about cost-effectiveness.

Monitoring as part of a control system

Monitoring involves more than simply the issuance of warnings. Instead, it should be seen as part of a larger control system (see Figure 8.1) within the investment process. Its role is to observe, verify and control in an attempt to make the portfolio perform in a desired way.

The monitoring process involves identifying problems and developing a plan to address them. Because of the illiquidity of a private equity fund, the investor's ability to react to identified problems is somewhat limited. In many situations a solution will require finding a consensus with the fund manager and the other co-investors, or building alliances with co-investors to exercise pressure and act jointly.

The trade-offs of monitoring

The appropriate approach and level of intensity of monitoring is not inconsequential. Investing in and monitoring of private equity investments involves more effort and higher costs relative to an otherwise equivalent quoted investment. Such costs need to be weighed against the potential benefits. Turning the monitoring findings into management actions and choosing the appropriate time and degree of intervention poses a dilemma. This is because intensive monitoring and the associated interventions can effectively dilute the fund manager's responsibility, lead to limited partners being reclassified as general partners and, in an extreme case, negate their limited liability status. Private equity in particular requires the long-term view and limited partners should avoid overreacting to bad news, especially during the early years of a fund's lifetime. On the other hand, the private equity investor's reaction, when necessary, is typically too little, too late to prevent further deterioration of the investment.

The limited partnership agreement's terms and conditions in many ways reflect a trade-off in various dimensions. It is neither possible nor meaningful to anticipate the expected behavior of the

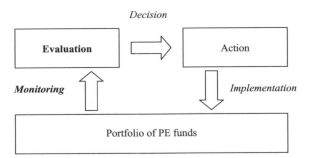

Figure 8.1   Control system

general partner over a time frame of ten or more years. Market conditions fluctuate, fund management teams evolve, co-investors change, investments do not materialize as planned and new opportunities arise. In hindsight, limited partners may conclude that certain provisions of the agreement were overly restrictive and worked against their interests, while other issues may have not been addressed in sufficient detail. The monitoring exercised by the investors is intended to bridge this gap.

THE MONITORING OBJECTIVES

While monitoring is an important instrument to assure compliance with the limited partnership's terms and conditions and to gather information, it is not necessarily linked to the performance of the fund. Monitoring should not be confused with the management of portfolio companies, an activity in which, in accordance with industry practices, limited partners have no involvement. Rather the limited partner is responsible for managing the portfolio of funds and monitoring the fund managers.

Monitoring to protect downside

Limited partners monitor the fund managers in order to minimize risks. In conventional asset classes, reducing risk means moving money into safer investments. But unlike most investors, limited partners cannot easily withdraw their commitments. Through monitoring activities, however, a limited partner may be able to identify severe shortcomings in time to reduce downside risks, either through a restructuring or by selling the position on the secondary market.

Investments are done in the context of a general portfolio strategy. As a result, monitoring must encompass not only individual funds but also the limited partner's overall portfolio composition. Indeed, while a detailed asset allocation process can promote effective diversification and eliminate the problems associated with haphazard fund selection, in the case of private equity it is often problematic to obtain equal weightings across funds and, at the same time, be represented in all key market segments. In addition, significant changes in investment valuations due to market fluctuations and distribution activity may cause the allocation to private equity to rise above or fall below the desired limits. To ensure that the allocation remains within the established ranges, limited partners must consistently monitor and adjust the portfolio structure.

Monitoring the risk of style drift

Monitoring is also important for assuring style discipline. As limited partners are investing in a blind pool, the investment is mainly based on the fund managers' declared investment strategy. Funds will not necessarily adhere to it nor should they in certain instances. For example, in a difficult market environment, it makes sense to deviate from the declared investment strategy and to look for investments in more promising areas. While style-tracking in private equity is not as applicable as in the context of the hedge fund industry, limited partners nevertheless need to ensure that fund managers stay within the confines of their core expertise and style. Limited partners should be concerned with any change to a private equity fund strategy. Indeed, a style shift (drift) may have serious consequences for the risk–return profile of the fund and can create unexpected exposures for limited partners. This reinforces the need to constantly monitor and adjust the portfolio structure.

Style drift describes the tendency for investment managers to deviate over time from their initially stated and agreed-upon investment style. In private equity, fund managers explain their investment practices and their strategies during the initial due diligence. Limited partners expect fund managers to be reasonably consistent in following them. However, adherence to a stated investment style may not always hold true in the world of private equity funds, where secrecy and flexibility are critical to success. Cumming, Fleming and Schwienbacher (2004) researched this issue and found that in private equity, style drift is more common than was previously perceived.

In order to alleviate the risk of style drift, the upfront design of the limited partnership agreement is important, as the covenants guide the behavior of the fund manager. Because of the blind pool nature of private equity fund investing, it is crucial for limited partners to set the risk profile of their investment at the time of commitment. Moreover, given private equity's lack of liquidity, the limited partner cannot easily adjust portfolio holdings or rebalance them if general partners undertake actions that are inconsistent with governing documentation. That said, there are risks associated with adhering too closely to a declared investment strategy, especially when market conditions change significantly, creating new opportunities.

Changes in style are often observed in geographical focus, or between buyout and VC focus. The skill sets required for fund managers and investment objectives of buyouts and VC funds differ in important ways. While related, the two fields are sufficiently distinct to make the transfer of skills difficult. Nevertheless, there is anecdotal evidence that VC funds that raised excessive amounts of money were not able to resist the temptation to put the money to work in buyouts, rather than return the unutilized commitments to investors.[1] When deal flow dries up, fund managers often consider other markets. VC funds may look for investments in Europe, while European VC funds try to gain access to Silicon Valley. Limited partners view this geographic drift with skepticism because, particularly in the case of VC, hands-on involvement of the fund manager is essential. Moreover, with the change in geography, investors may become exposed to foreign exchange rate risks they had not accounted for previously.

Other reasons for changes in investment style exist. A motivation of fund managers could be to engage in potential "window dressing" (e.g. moving private equity investments to later stages to create earlier exits).[2] Finally, style drift may be used to camouflage substandard investment management by further diversifying within the fund to reduce the chances of substantially underperforming peers.

Creating value through monitoring

For fund investments, the management of the upside is primarily delegated to the fund managers, assuming that appropriate incentives have been provided. This underscores the importance of

---

[1] Likewise in buyouts; see Henderson Global Investors (2002): "The opportunistic buoyancy of sentiment upon which many of today's large private equity funds were raised has contributed to the 'style drift' (e.g CLECs, PIPEs, IT incubators) and subsequent portfolio problems evident amongst some of the highest profile managers in the asset class."

[2] See Cumming, Fleming and Schwienbacher (2004), who specifically examined shifts in allocation to investment stages.

selecting the right teams. While the general partner is able to create value at the individual private equity fund level, the limited partner can create significant value through monitoring activities at the portfolio of funds level, as illustrated in the following six situations.

- Intensive contact with the fund managers is important when deciding whether to invest in a follow-on fund. It improves the due diligence and can lead to a quicker finalization of contracts, after incorporating improvements based on the previous experience with the fund manager. Moreover, a strong relationship can extend to junior team members ready to spin out and set up their own fund.
- The study undertaken by Lerner, Schoar and Wong (2004) suggests that investors in private equity owe their success to superior reinvestment skills. The authors specifically refer to the example of endowment funds. These funds were found to be less likely to reinvest in a partnership, but if they did invest in the follow-on fund, its subsequent performance was significantly better than those of funds that they let pass. This finding underlines the importance of monitoring for improving decision-making.
- Networking and liaising with other limited partners is an important instrument for gathering intelligence on the overall market and gaining knowledge of other funds,[3] and may help an investor gain access to deals that otherwise might not appear on the institution's radar screen. It can also improve access to secondary opportunities in advance of the less favorable auction process.
- In the context of a co-investment strategy, monitoring is important for screening interesting investment opportunities that may arise through the activity.
- Lessons learned from monitoring can also be applied in the future to improve the due diligence and the selection of future investments.
- Access to information may enable a limited partner to optimize the management of commitments and treasury assets through more precise cash-flow forecasting.

INFORMATION GATHERING IN THE MONITORING PROCESS

The private equity sector is called "private" for good reason and transparency has its limitations. The typical monitoring process follows a dual approach (see Figure 8.2), separating formal from informal reporting. There is a tendency for larger investors to differentiate between obtaining specific qualitative data by direct interaction with the investment managers and obtaining quantitative or standardized data provided by the back office.[4] As the reporting quality and detail vary considerably among different funds, the monitoring needs to focus on filling the gaps present in the reporting. To avoid the risk of reporting overloads, an appropriate balance must be struck between the provision of specific information and the provision of standardized information to the limited partners.

Transparency

While reporting to investors can often be more transparent for private equity investments than for public ones, this transparency is normally kept to a minimum for non-investors. Indeed, private

---

[3] Being perceived as a professional and serious investor also increases negotiation power vis-à-vis the fund managers. In a comparatively small industry, a strong network is a credible "threat" against a team that otherwise would be unwilling to compromise.

[4] According to Diem (2002), the vast majority of limited partners "agreed that the most valuable information is acquired by nurturing personal contacts between limited partners and general partners, which was also considered to be the only feasible way of overcoming [the problem of limited] data availability."

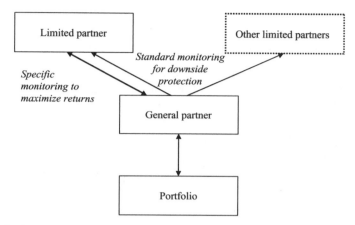

Figure 8.2   Monitoring process

investments were generally exempt from registration with authorities such as the Securities and Exchange Commission (SEC) in the U.S., the Financial Services Authority (FSA) in the UK, or the Autorité des Marchés Financiers (AMF) in France.[5] Thus, the development of valuation and reporting standards in private equity was driven more by industry players than regulatory bodies, although this could change with a tightening of regulatory regimes for alternative investments worldwide.

Historically, the appearance of private equity as unregulated was the by-product of a careful balancing of specific exemptions from certain aspects of regulation and from the sustained efforts of VC associations to maintain high standards of investment conduct by private equity fund managers. In the U.S., private equity fund managers, like hedge fund managers, have historically relied upon the same exemption from registration under the Advisers Act. Given the lack of a clear delineation that many times arises between hedge funds and private equity funds, both are now subject to regulatory changes taking place in 2009.

The information required for the management of the portfolio is, in principle, the same as that needed for the investment decision (i.e. the information gathered through the due diligence). This information is supplied by the fund managers but also collected from outside sources.[6] While a significant amount of the information should be provided in a low-cost standardized manner, proprietary information can lead to a competitive advantage. For example, some limited partners conduct quarterly conference calls to compile estimates from the fund managers, which are then used to improve cash-flow forecasting for liquidity and commitment planning.

Standard monitoring information

Monitoring is built around the information supplied in the fund management reports. Therefore, reliable, appropriate and timely management information is crucial. VC associations' reporting guidelines, such as those issued by EVCA, BVCA and AFIC, define the standard level of information to be provided. Generally, investors in private equity funds complain about inadequate disclosure, inconsistent reporting and the often significant time lag in receiving this information. Major problems

---

[5] This refers only to the private equity investments, and in some jurisdictions, to private equity companies. In the case of fund managers in some jurisdictions (e.g. UK, France, Italy) registration is an obligation.

[6] Also, the administration of capital calls and distributions by general partners offers opportunities to conduct monitoring by limited partners, as in this context, for example, contractual terms can and should be checked.

with a portfolio company eventually appear in the reporting. But often by then the damage has been done and little corrective action remains possible. This raises the question of whether large institutional investors will become more active or proactive in addressing the following issues:

- Incomplete information creates uncertainty and consequently increases risks. Should institutions, possibly together with VC associations, persuade industry players to provide more detail and transparency in the reporting?
- Transparency in reporting is tied to the question of valuation and risk. Can investors get a truer and fairer picture of their investments through more detail and better quality investment reporting?

There is overall agreement among industry players that formal accounting-related information should be standardized. EVCA reporting guidelines are seen as sufficient in general, but the information reported depends very much on the general partner's willingness to disclose this information in its reporting framework.

Increased disclosure appears to be an admirable objective, especially to those accustomed to public markets. However it needs to be kept in mind that there are practical obstacles to disclosure. The answers to these questions need to be pondered against the background of the private equity market's dynamics and from a cost–benefit viewpoint:

- In private equity, information collection and analysis can be prohibitively expensive and there are market forces that work against transparency.[7] Any attempt to go against these dynamics would be expensive, time-consuming and may ultimately be unsuccessful.
- The huge information asymmetry in private equity explains and justifies the need for intermediation. An increased level of detail will not allow a non-expert to verify the fund manager's appraisal. Moreover, due to its imprecise character, any qualitative information is, by definition, of low quality. If one does not want to rely on the intermediary's judgment, the only alternative is direct investing, which requires an entirely different approach and skill set.
- As private equity fund investments are buy-and-hold and illiquid, a fund's limited partners are unable to react quickly to new information. Moreover, for such a long-term-oriented investment, short-term developments do not, most of the time, materially affect the fund's valuation.

Based on these points, one could conclude that while a higher degree of transparency would be desirable, the public market cannot be seen as the benchmark. It is mainly the limited partners' monitoring that can overcome the non-transparency and the reporting time lags of this asset class.

Specific information

General partners are extremely reluctant to disclose all information to the investors. Their dilemma is obvious: on the one hand, there is an obligation to disclose information so that the investors are able to understand the portfolio's progress; but on the other hand, further information, especially at a level of detail that allows an independent risk assessment, potentially reduces the chance that the limited partners commit to follow-on funds. There is also the investment rationale for maintaining a high degree of confidentiality. Indeed, a fund with a niche strategy that consistently yields above-average returns will attract competition. General partners fear that too much information given to the outside helps competitors imitate their strategy, access their deal flow, or jeopardize their negotiating

---

[7] We expect that information targeting downside protection will be more likely to be standardized and be shared among all limited partners. Ultimately, to remove the fund manager, a majority of the limited partners is required. Therefore, it is in all investors' interests that everybody knows how the portfolio is performing.

position. Cullen (2004) cites an example where a limited partner was given financial information regarding a deal that was later shared with a competitor and ultimately caused the fund to lose the deal.

Moreover, if disclosed to a wider audience, information can be highly damaging. It may even have an adverse impact on the trading ability of a portfolio company as it could result, for example, in reduced credit lines, or lead the company's potential clients to choose to partner with the competition. Conversely, news of success may breed competitors. In the extreme, the fund manager might even be sued for disclosing harmful information.

Interestingly, however, it is not only the fund managers but also the limited partners who may prefer to limit the degree of transparency. Making "star funds" public knowledge may attract competitors. Limited partners need to protect their privileged access to follow-on funds or to new teams that set up their own vehicles outside the old fund. As private equity funds are not scalable, limited partners may be concerned about being locked out of follow-on funds because, as suggested by Lerner and Schoar (2004), general partners have a preference for "deep pocket investors". Better to keep the information quiet than attract a feeding frenzy of competing investors.

ACTIONS RESULTING FROM MONITORING

Results of the monitoring and its evaluation can lead to decisions on a series of possible actions. These can range simply from changing the monitoring intensity to intervention at the individual fund or perhaps even portfolio level. The monitoring intensity should be a function of the total exposure of a private equity fund, its final expected performance and its operational status (see Figure 8.3).

It does not make sense to spend too much time on monitoring funds that are already quite advanced in their life cycle or beyond recovery. It is also not money well spent to focus scarce monitoring resources on teams that are highly professional or on funds where other experienced limited partners

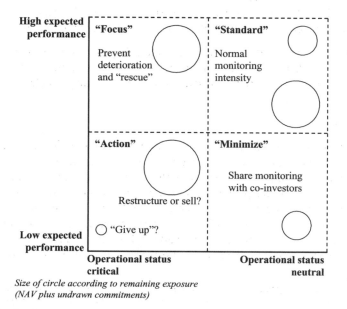

Figure 8.3   Monitoring intensity management

already exercise significant oversight. In these cases, if one is dissatisfied, one would simply not invest in the follow-on fund. Finally, the cost of control must be relative to the size of the asset.

Limited partners want to influence the actions being taken as a result of changed circumstances. This often means taking part in the decision-making process, vetoing decisions[8] or simply exercising pressure on the fund manager. One of the more obvious and common monitoring actions is the increased use of renegotiations of management fees and fund size towards the end of a fund's life.

Due to the illiquidity of private equity funds, the toolset for the management of the portfolio is comparatively restricted. Active trading of positions through the secondary market to significantly rebalance the portfolio in line with allocation targets is often not feasible. At the fund level, the first approach to adjusting the portfolio structure is the continuous review of the ongoing investment pipeline in primary fund investments. However, this strategy may be restricted by the availability of suitable investment opportunities, or by delays in closing the deals. Moreover, when the private equity portfolio is large, the adjustment via primary transactions may be insufficient.

Another approach for investors is to attempt to exit their investments in private equity funds before maturity. There are two main exit routes:

- *Secondary transactions.* A secondary market for limited partnership shares exists, although it is expected to remain rather inefficient and illiquid.[9] Often the stake in a private equity fund cannot be sold off without the consent of the general partners and possibly that of other limited partners.
- *Securitization.* Transfer of the limited partnership share to a **special purpose vehicle** (**SPV**) for a collateralized fund obligation.[10] The SPV is a distinct legal entity that issues senior and junior notes and uses the proceeds from the issuance for investment in a private equity fund-of-funds (for such securitizations, see Chapter 19 in Mathonet and Meyer, 2007).

However, the above transactions require expertise and opportunities are often scarce. Alternatively, co-investing alongside the fund managers is a tool for increasing exposure to certain sectors, but also requires specific skills. Finally, a further option is to adjust allocations using public small-cap equities as a proxy for private equity investments. This could be a meaningful investment where a significant pool of undrawn commitments needs to be managed.

Active involvement mainly relates to individual funds and can take, for example, the following forms:

- In situations where a fund management team has clearly demonstrated that they are not up to the job or that they are not cooperating with their limited partners, the simplest and most obvious action of a limited partner is not to commit to the follow-on fund. This is also most feared by the fund managers, as often the loss of a reputable investor sends a clear negative signal to the market. Not only would the team need to go back to the capital market for fundraising, but they would do so with a tarnished reputation.
- Limited partners can, to some degree, use their negotiating power to reduce the new fund's size, or use the new agreement to address issues that created risks in the previous fund. Stronger funds may resist such changes, however.

---

[8] An illustrative list of considerations would be the appointment and the remuneration of the managers, the approval of annual reports, the approval of the budget, decisions on unforeseen investments (loans or "side funds"), issues of new shares, extension of the investment period, etc.

[9] See McCune (2001): "[...] to speak of a market is a misnomer—there is not a market in a conventional sense. No established market rules, forms, procedures or customs exist."

[10] A special purpose vehicle is a special company, typically located in tax- and/or legal-efficient offshore location, that is established by a company to answer a certain financial or legal problem (e.g. to pay lower taxes).

- During the lifetime of a fund, agreements are not carved in stone. If it becomes clear that the original investment strategy cannot be successfully implemented and no credible alternative is brought forward, investors can influence the fund manager to reduce management fees or even release limited partners from portions of their commitments. More often than not, general partners give in to reducing fund size. This investor-friendly behavior can build up goodwill and ease the next fundraising exercise. Moreover, from a purely financial viewpoint, it increases the likelihood that fund managers will receive carried interest.
- Of course, firms have the right to refuse such voluntary actions. However, this often results in pressure, activism and even lawsuits from limited partners who want some or all of their money back. In the extreme, and if there is an agreement between the limited partners, the fund management team can be terminated "for good cause". Even without recourse to such extreme measures, the threat of action or the noise of complaints from investors can be highly damaging to the reputation of a fund manager. This in turn can have serious implications for future fundraising ambitions.
- Investor default is questionable, as it constitutes a contractual breach, but it may be the instrument of last resort if the fund manager is clearly incompetent.[11]

---

[11] See Meek (2003): "In one instance the limited partners of a U.S. fund have simply refused to honor any future drawdowns, taking the view that to do so would simply be throwing good money after bad."

9
Private Equity Fund Valuation

In a discussion on the International Financial Reporting Standards (IFRS) fair-value treatment for private equity funds, an anonymous auditor suggested, slightly provocatively, that there be a debate on the sense of the whole exercise. As previously mentioned in the context of monitoring, it is also fair to say that there is a trade-off in terms of costs and benefits to private equity fund valuation. This trade-off also exists between the valuation's level of precision (i.e. trying to minimize errors) and timeliness.

When discerning the value of private equity funds, it is necessary to differentiate between the following concepts:

- A valuation for accounting purposes that primarily aims to assure the timeliness of the reported value and its compliance with accounting standards and/or valuation guidelines such as the International Private Equity and Venture Capital Valuation Guidelines (IPEV guidelines)[1] produced by the AFIC, the BVCA and the EVCA.
- The economic value of limited partnership shares that can be used for portfolio management purposes.

In this chapter we describe the two main approaches employed to value private equity funds, namely, the net asset value (NAV) approach and the economic value approach.

NET ASSET VALUE (NAV)

Limited partnership shares have been traditionally valued by multiplying the NAV of the private equity fund by the percentage of shares owned in the fund. In private equity, the NAV is often referred to as a fund's residual value, as it represents the value of all investments remaining in the portfolio, minus any liabilities and net of fees and carried interest as of a specific date. This is a bottom-up technique where individual companies are valued (normally according to industry valuation guidelines) and then aggregated to compute the private equity fund value.[2] Generally, many investors appear to look at NAVs because they prefer current and reliable information over information that is based on expectations about the future

In private equity, and especially in VC, the "break-up" assumption underlying a bottom-up valuation approach has to be challenged. This is because the goal of private equity investing is to earn attractive long-term returns, rather than to try to profit from short-term movements. Private equity is instead a buy-and-hold investment where companies are developed over a substantial time period and where the general partners have a fair chance of timing the exit.[3] From the limited partner's viewpoint, valuations will be very different, depending on whether the investment is held until maturity, or if an exit is intended before the end of a fund's lifetime.

---

[1] Available on www.privateequityvaluation.com [accessed October 2007].

[2] For the sake of completeness some other asset or liability items such as net cash have also to be taken into account to get to the fund's value.

[3] See Lerner (1994).

When the fund's NAV has been estimated in compliance with accounting standards or guidelines such as the IPEV guidelines, it can normally be used for accounting purposes. However, the NAV can produce a result that is often quite distinct from the economic reality of the fund. In order to be really fair, such value should equal the present value of the fund's expected cash flows. Even assuming the fair value of the individual companies can be established, their aggregation often does not provide the limited partners with the economic value of a private equity fund for the following reasons:

- *Undrawn commitments.* The expected future cash flows of a private equity fund are generated not only out of the NAV but also out of investments still to be made.[4] During the first years of a fund's life, the main value to be created will depend on the fund manager's future activities. For successful teams, the fair value of the existing portfolio may fall short in expressing the total value to be created. And for "lemons," writing down the portfolio to its fair value may be insufficient to cover the existing losses, as well as the losses to be expected from the future investments.
- *Private equity fund added (or deducted!) value.* If one accepts that the management team of a private equity fund adds significant value to the private equity companies, this value-added should be reflected.
- *Future fund expenses.* As these portfolio companies will not be realized now but over the remaining lifetime of the fund, additional management fees, expenses and eventually catch-up and carried interest will be charged against their fair value and reduce the cash flows to the investors and, therefore, the fund value.[5]
- *Capital constraints.* Even if a portfolio company theoretically has a value during the early investment stages, success will depend on the fund's intentions going forward. Most of the time portfolio companies are technically insolvent, as financing is typically done through various rounds with ratchet mechanisms and milestones. At any time, the fund might exercise the implicit option to abandon should better projects emerge. Ultimately, valuation is a matter of negotiation, where much depends on a fund's position in the market. In the extreme, where a fund has no liquidity left it is either forced to abandon a promising investment or has to accept a highly unfavorable valuation.

It is important to differentiate between the value of the portfolio companies, as seen from the viewpoint of the general partner, and the value of the fund, comprising not only the portfolio companies but also the undrawn commitments and the quality of the general partner. Under a break-up assumption, the NAV is too high, as the portfolio companies cannot be liquidated at the ascribed valuation, while as an estimate of the fund's terminal wealth, it will often be too low.

INTERNAL RATE OF RETURN (IRR)

The "traditional" IRR for a project completed at time T can be found by solving the following equation for IRR:

$$\sum_{t=1}^{T} \frac{CF_t}{(1 + IRR)^t} = 0$$

---

[4] This view is also supported and therefore more consistent with the treatment of undrawn commitments under the New Basel Accord. According to the Basel Committee on Banking Supervision, the undrawn commitments to private equity funds also need to be risk-weighted (http://www.bis.org/bcbs/qis/qis3qa_o.htm) [accessed October, 2007].

[5] Some reporting guidelines, such as the ones published by the EVCA, recommend reporting valuation net of management fees and carried interest. But this netting only refers to past management fees and carried interest plus, eventually, the carried interest implied by the current portfolio.

Table 9.1 IIRR components assessment

IIRR component	Assessment
Past cash flows	Quantitative only
Current portfolio (NAV)	Quantitative, but qualitative review recommended
Future cash flows	Qualitative, based on historical data and scenarios

Here, CF_t is the net cash flow at time t, and T in this case is the lifetime. In Chapter 7, it was shown that the interim IRR (IIRR) is a rough but widely-used estimation of IRR performance and forms the basis of most published performance statistics in private equity prior to the termination of the investment. For active funds, the IIRR is computed by taking the NAV as the last cash flow at time T:

$$\sum_{t=1}^{T} \frac{CF_t}{(1 + IIRR_T)^t} + \frac{NAV_T}{(1 + IIRR_T)^T} = 0$$

As we explained before, the IIRR usually follows a J-curve as it is low or negative and later converges to the final, and likely much higher, IRR.

Notice that, in theory, the IIRR equation can be divided into three parts: the past cash flows from the portfolio (up to and including time T), the future distributions of the current portfolio and the future drawdowns and distributions for new investments that generally cannot be stopped without the investor defaulting or selling the position.

$$\sum_{t=1}^{T} \frac{CF_t^{PAST}}{(1 + IIRR_T)^t} + \sum_{t=T+1}^{\infty} \frac{CF_t^{PORT}}{(1 + IIRR_T)^t} + \sum_{t=T+1}^{\infty} \frac{CF_t^{NEW}}{(1 + IIRR_T)^t} = 0$$

Also, notice that whereas the NAVs approximate[6] the middle expression of the above equation, the use of NAVs in IIRR computations neglects the right-hand term (i.e. the future investments' cash flows), even though the weight of these factors changes over time. Therefore, taken at face value, the NAV may lead to short-term thinking in the portfolio management. This is because the expected future cash flows of a fund are generated not only out of the existing portfolio companies, but also out of the investments to be made, like the undrawn commitments. During the first years of a fund's life, the majority of the value to be created will depend on the investments still to be made. Therefore, to estimate the expected investment performance for a fund's entire lifetime, all three components of the IIRR need to be assessed (see Table 9.1).

For the current portfolio, limited partners should have a valuation review policy in place, such as the one described in Mathonet and Monjanel (2006). Such a policy should take the quality of the appraising fund managers into consideration. Finally, for the assessment of the fund's future

---

[6] See Cheung et al. (2003): "Private equity values represent the opinions of general partners rather than market-traded values and do not address the cash flow amount and timing, which are relevant in the securitization and must be addressed in the rating in a probabilistic framework"; or Blaydon and Horvath (2003): "They are an interim report on the performance of the fund and rely on the GP's assessment of unrealised current portfolio company values [...] The IRRs, publicly reported or not, are only as good as these underlying assessments [...] But what is missing is sufficient discussion of how the underlying assessments of company value are arrived at, other than to note that some funds may have widely differing assessments of the value of the same company, much to the frustration of LPs to whom these assessments are reported."

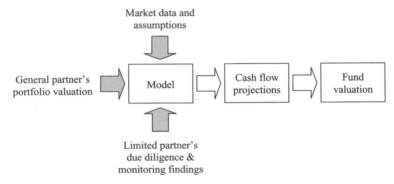

Figure 9.1   Funds cash flows and valuation modelling process

cash flows (as represented by the third part of the equation), a qualitative assessment of the general partner's quality is also required.

ECONOMIC VALUE APPROACH

To work around the NAV's shortcomings, some limited partners use models to determine the economic value of a private equity fund. Examples of the **economic value approach** used in practice are based on a so-called modified bottom-up and a modified comparable approach. Both approaches try to forecast cash flows using either a bottom-up or a top-down rationale (see Figure 9.1).

These two economic value approaches seem to come much closer to the economic reality of funds. However, they cannot be used for accounting purposes as they fail to meet accounting standards requirements.

Bottom-up cash flow projection

To obtain a more useful valuation, a fund can be modeled bottom-up by analyzing its main value drivers in detail and aggregating these individual components into a big picture. Here an investor must first obtain information on the quality of the fund managers, the legal structure of the partnership and the current portfolio holdings. Next, exit projections for the underlying portfolio companies are determined, including exit multiples and timing, along with future capital calls resulting in company-level cash-flow streams. These cash-flow streams are then combined and filtered through the partnership structure to arrive at a series of net cash flows, which represent the cash flows the limited partner can expect to receive. These cash flows must then be discounted, typically by the target return rate or the cost of capital (see Chapter 10), to arrive at a present value for the fund.

However, limited partners may have difficulty determining exit scenarios for individual companies, especially in cases where even the general partner is unable to provide meaningful exit guidance. Furthermore, even if a limited partner was able to project accurate portfolio company exit values on a consistent basis, institutions with large portfolios would have to conduct extensive due diligence on potentially thousands of companies every quarter, which may not be feasible from a resource perspective. This high workload calls for practical solutions, such as the modified bottom-up approach described in detail in Mathonet and Meyer (2007).[7] In this approach, when it is difficult or

---

[7] The "modified bottom-up approach" was developed by Cogent Partners, an international investment bank specializing in transactions of private equity secondary assets, private equity research and the investment of alternative assets.

too costly to determine specific exit scenarios for individual companies, various alternative inputs are used at the fund manager or market level, including fund manager track record data or broad VC secondary market insight. Based on these inputs, global exit scenarios are determined and used for individual companies without specific scenarios, as well as for undrawn capital. Then, as before, these cash flow streams are combined, possibly adjusted depending on the partnership structure and discounted to yield a present value for the fund.

Top-down cash flow projection

Meyer and Mathonet (2007) have described in detail another option for valuing a fund, the Grading-based Economic Model (GEM) which could be seen as a modified comparable approach.[8] The GEM does not rely on the projection of individual portfolio company exit values but rather on a high-level evaluation of the overall private equity fund and on information on the past performance or cash flows of comparable funds. This technique is based on the assumption that the comparable funds' historical performance or cash flows are representative and that the grading (see Chapter 6) allows for an identification of these comparables. To apply this relative valuation technique, it is necessary to identify the best comparable peer group and obtain its historical cash flows or performance data. The grading is used to control for any qualitative differences between the funds that might affect the value. After the relative position of a fund within a peer group has been estimated and a grade determined, the expected IIRR of the fund and cash flows are forecasted based on the peer group historical cash flows and performance data.

Forecasting cash flows for any alternative asset class is a challenge and requires significant effort and experience. Typically practitioners need to utilize a number of complementary approaches such as estimates, projections and scenarios, which are further described in Chapter 10.

---

[8] See Chapter 16 in Meyer and Mathonet (2007).

10

Private Equity Fund Discount Rate

Discount rates are particularly difficult to estimate in the case of private equity, but they are important. As with any financial asset, it is only worth investing in a private equity fund if its expected rate of return is at least equal to the investors' required rate of return. Moreover, when cash flows can be projected, the discount rate allows estimating the economic value of a fund, as we saw in the previous chapter. Therefore, the question of how to set this rate is of high interest for private equity investors. Finance theory postulates that the risk in an investment should be the risk borne by a well-diversified investor and that the return to be expected should be commensurate with this risk.

THE CAPITAL ASSET PRICING MODEL (CAPM)

The CAPM model defines the relationship between risk and return using the following equation:

$$E(R_A) = R_f + \beta_A[E(R_M) - R_f]$$

Here, $E(R_A)$ is the expected return of asset A, R_f is the risk-free rate of return, β_A is the beta or systematic risk of asset A, and the term $[E(R_M) - R_f]$ is the market risk premium. If we know an asset's systematic risk, the risk-free rate and the market risk premium, we can use the CAPM to observe its expected return.

Even though in theory the CAPM holds whether we are dealing with financial assets or real (physical) assets, it is not clear that it can be applied to private equity funds. The CAPM assumes that investors hold well-diversified portfolios. Knowing that the vast majority of the private equity fund investors are large and sophisticated institutions, such an assumption appears sensible. The model also assumes that there are no transaction costs, that buyers and sellers are fully informed, that assets are tradable and that the market is always in equilibrium. Obviously, these assumptions are not necessarily accurate in the context of private equity. However, if the objective is to estimate a fair value as defined in the International Accounting Standards, it is implied that parties are knowledgeable and willing, and that the transaction is at arm's length. Given this, such assumptions may appear to be more plausible.

Assuming for the moment that the CAPM can be used for private equity funds, it is necessary to get access to the required data. Indeed, accuracy depends not only on the model used but also on the availability and the quality of the financial data used in the model. And as we just saw, the CAPM requires three inputs: the risk-free rate, the expected equity risk premium and the beta.

The risk-free rate and the equity risk premium

The risk-free rate in the CAPM equation is an estimation of the "pure time value of money." In the case of the U.S., the returns on Treasury securities issued by the federal government with maturities similar to those of the projects being analyzed are the preferred estimation for the risk-free rate.

The CAPM does not reflect the total risk that an investment carries but only quantifies the marginal risk that it adds onto a diversified portfolio. This is explained by the nature of the total risk, which can be broken down into two components: the investment-specific (or idiosyncratic) and the market (or systematic) risks. As the former can be diversified away while the latter cannot, diversified investors require an excess return for being exposed to the latter. Such a distinction is important and explains why investors in private equity funds often have a misperception of the risk taken. Indeed, many investors expect a premium as compensation for the fund's total risk, while only its systematic portion should be rewarded. However, although this approach is perfectly acceptable when investors are diversified, it is much less so in the context of an investor holding only one (e.g. the entrepreneur) or a few positions.

Moskowitz and Vissing-Jørgensen (2002) have analyzed the returns to private equity. The analysis that they conducted was based on data derived from the U.S. Survey of Consumer Finances and various national income accounts and predominantly relates to non-intermediated investments in non-public companies, as opposed to intermediated investments undertaken by private equity funds. They estimated that the additional premium required to compensate an investor for the risk of holding a single position was at least 10% per year. Using recent high-tech IPOs, Kerins, Smith and Smith (2001) estimated that the required additional premium for an entrepreneur with 25% of her wealth in a single VC project is in the range of 25%. This is a good illustration of the importance of the additional premium required by an investor exposed to total risk, or at least to a significant portion of it, compared to a fully diversified investor exposed only to systematic risk.

In the CAPM, this extra return over the risk-free rate is estimated based on a measure of the relative risk added by an asset to a diversified portfolio (i.e. the beta) and on the risk premium over the risk-free rate expected by a diversified investor holding the market portfolio. This premium is normally estimated either by using historical data or by extracting the data implied by the current market prices. In the U.S., the premium estimated with historical data from 1926–2007 is 8.5%. Although this approach is commonly used, there are some limitations to it. First, there can be surprisingly large differences in the estimated premium,[1] notably due to differences in the time period used,[2] in the choice of the risk-free security[3] and in the use of arithmetic versus geometric averages. Second, the survivorship bias that was described in previous chapters has an impact on market data and results in higher estimates than the real historical risk premiums. Third, while it is already difficult to estimate a reliable premium based on historical information for mature markets such as the U.S., it becomes even more challenging for markets with short and more volatile histories. One solution is to consider the U.S. premium as a basis and to adjust it in order to account for the additional country systematic risk.

The alternative to the historical risk premium is to estimate the equity risk premium implied by the current market prices. Obviously, the implied equity premium changes over time much more than the long-term historical. Applied to the U.S. market, the average implied premium is in the range of 4%.[4]

---

[1] According to Damodaran (2001) investment banks, consultants and corporations estimate the risk premium in the U.S. markets to range from 4% at the lower end to 12% at the upper end.

[2] Shorter periods are used to provide an estimate that will better reflect the current risk aversion of the average investor. In doing so, it is assumed that the risk premium is changing over time and, therefore, using a shorter time period will provide a more accurate estimate.

[3] The risk-free rate to be used in order to estimate the discount rate should be the government zero-coupon bond rate with a maturity equal (or at least, similar) to the private equity fund's duration. Therefore, to be consistent, the same risk-free rate should be used when estimating the equity risk premium.

[4] The difference with the historical premium could be due to the survivor bias.

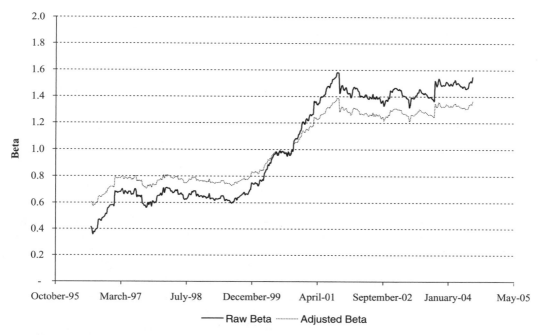

Figure 10.1   3i PLC: Historical beta (*Source:* Bloomberg)

Undoubtedly, the equity risk premium discussion will continue. Some argue that the premium is probably below the 6% annual premium figure estimated in much of the financial literature.[5] Using an expected equity risk premium in the range of 4–5% can be considered reasonable.

PRIVATE EQUITY FUND BETAS

Not being specific to private equity, the risk-free rate and the equity risk premium are not problematic and they can be determined with relative ease using publicly-available market information. This leaves us with only the private equity fund beta to estimate.

Estimation based on quoted comparable

When an asset is not publicly traded, it is common practice to use the beta of a similar quoted asset as proxy. As the most liquid stock in the European private equity industry is probably 3i, its beta can give an indication (see Figure 10.1). 3i is a world leader in private equity and VC and is listed on the London Stock Exchange. It focuses on buyouts, growth capital and VC, and invests across Europe, the U.S. and in Asia Pacific. As of March 2004, its portfolio was roughly composed of 51% buyouts, 31% growth capital, 12% VC, and 6% quoted equity, and amounted to £4326 million. In terms of geography, the split was 58% UK, 35% continental Europe, 5% U.S., and 2% Asia. Although not free from bias, 3i is potentially a good comparable for a portfolio of European private equity funds, but less fitting for VC funds. Nevertheless, it is still worth looking at it in more detail.

---

[5] See Siegel (1999).

Table 10.1 PTPE betas against major indices

Index	Volatility (ann.)	Implied PTPE beta
MSCI	12.35%	1.08
S&P 500	14.47%	0.92
NASDAQ	21.33%	0.63
STOXX	15.37%	0.87
Russell 2000	15.88%	0.84
PTPE (Overall without Incubators)	13.37%	1.00

Datasource: Datastream/Bloomberg (1988–05/2000)
Source: Bauer, Bilo and Zimmermann (2001) and author calculations

The evolution of 3i's beta over time, which is presented in Figure 10.1, remained relatively stable over two clearly differentiated periods, before and after the internet bubble of the late 1990s. Before the bubble, the beta was in the 0.6–0.8 region, supporting the hypothesis that an investment in private equity was an effective way to diversify a portfolio. Post-bubble the picture changed, with betas ranging from 1.20 to1.60, supporting the alternative hypothesis that an investment in private equity is correlated with public equity and somewhat risky.

3i is not the only quoted private equity asset. For instance, Bauer, Bilo and Zimmermann (2001) researched other publicly-traded private equity (PTPE). They classify PTPE into three groups: listed companies whose core business is private equity (e.g. 3i, mentioned above), quoted investment funds (e.g. Schroeder Ventures Trust) and specially structured investment vehicles (e.g. Castle Private Equity). They identified more than 200 PTPEs and, after liquidity constraints, more than 100 that were considered to be acceptable for their investigations. Over the period January 1988–May 2000, the authors calculated the volatilities of the various public equity indices and PTPEs. The PTPE volatilities were similar to those observed in the public markets. In their study, they did not calculate correlations or betas. However, assuming that all the PTPE risk is systematic, betas can be easily calculated by comparing the volatility levels. Following this procedure, and making the strong assumption that the correlation of a stock (X) with the market (M) is equal to 1, the estimation of the beta can be simplified as follows:

$$\beta = \frac{\text{cov}_{XM}}{\text{var}_M} = \frac{\text{corr}_{XM} * \text{vol}_X * \text{vol}_M}{\text{vol}_M^2} = \frac{1 * \text{vol}_X * \text{vol}_M}{\text{vol}_M^2} = \frac{\text{vol}_X}{\text{vol}_M}$$

The betas obtained with this approach are in the range 0.63–1.08 (see Table 10.1). For example, the beta of PTPE with respect to the S&P 500 index was 0.92 (i.e. 13.37%/14.47%) between 1988 and 2000. This result suggests that the stocks of publicly-traded private equity companies were slightly less risky than the market, as measured by the S&P 500 Index.

They further refined their analysis by splitting the PTPE into the following sub-classes: incubators (27), ventures[6] (39), private equity funds (28), buyout houses (12) and balanced funds (12). Making the same assumption as above (i.e. that all the risk is systematic), betas can be calculated for these sub-classes (see Table 10.2). For VC, the betas were in the range of 1.40–2.42, with a mean of 1.94.[7]

---

[6] Bauer, Bilo and Zimmermann (2001) defined Venture as follows: "They invest directly in early or expansion stage companies which are active in technology- and innovation-driven sectors and have great growth potential."

[7] These results call for a judgment on which of these indices gives the best beta estimate. In short, indices that are market-weighted and that include more securities should be favored.

Table 10.2 Breakdown of PTPE betas by stage

	Ventures	Incubators	Buyouts	PE-Funds	Balanced	Overall	Overall (without Inc.)
Sample size	39	27	12	28	12	124	97
Volatility (ann.)	29.9%	41.8%	9.4%	13.8%	17.1%	16.9%	14.6%
Betas							
MSCI	2.42	3.39	0.76	1.12	1.39	1.37	1.18
S&P500	2.07	2.89	0.65	0.96	1.18	1.17	1.01
NASDAQ	1.40	1.96	0.44	0.65	0.80	0.79	0.69
STOXX	1.95	2.72	0.61	0.90	1.11	1.10	0.95
Russell 2000	1.88	2.63	0.59	0.87	1.08	1.07	0.92
Max	2.42	3.39	0.76	1.12	1.39	1.37	1.18
Min	1.40	1.96	0.44	0.65	0.80	0.79	0.69
Mean	1.94	2.72	0.61	0.90	1.11	1.10	0.95

Datasource: Datastream/Bloomberg (PTPE: 05/1996 - 02/2001 & Public indices: 1986–2000)
Source: Bauer, Bilo and Zimmermann (2001) and author calculations

These results support the hypothesis that VC is more risky and buyouts less risky than publicly-quoted equity. Assuming a market risk premium of 5%, VC requires a risk premium in excess of 400 bps over public equity. Final conclusions cannot be drawn based on this analysis, as the sample used is limited and most likely not fully representative of the VC market. Finally, there are several important dimensions that have not been taken into account in the study that may be key factors for estimating betas, such as geographical location or industry sector.

Recently, Zimmermann et al. (2004) further researched the risk and return of PTPE. This work, which is the continuation of the work of Bauer, Bilo and Zimmermann (2001), defines and discusses different indices for PTPE. Based on this work, a new benchmark for private equity, called LPX 50, has been created. The benchmark is either value-weighted (VW) or equally-weighted (EW). The 50 PTPEs that compose the index have been selected based on several liquidity criteria.[8] The index is then constructed out of the 50 most capitalized companies. Although they have not calculated correlation coefficients, betas can still be calculated by making the same assumption as before (i.e. that all the risk is systematic). The betas are in the range of 0.55–1.25, depending on the index chosen (see Table 10.3).

Alternatives to the "standard" regression betas

As indicated above, the performance of private equity funds cannot be easily compared to public equity, mainly due to differences in return measurement practices. As funds have little historical data and almost no comparables that have been listed for any significant period of time, the conventional approaches to estimating risk parameters cannot be easily utilized. However, there are some alternatives to simple regression betas. The first requires development of an alternative measure of relative risk to beta. The second is to estimate bottom-up betas, which reflect the businesses a firm is operating in and its current financial leverage. The third approach is to modify and correct the return data to make the estimation of the beta possible.

---

[8] A minimum of 30 weekly observations, a market value of minimum $20 million, a relative trading volume of 0.1% per week, a bid–ask spread smaller than 8% and a continuity of trade of 15%.

Table 10.3   LPX 50 (Source: Bloomberg)

	LPX50 VW	LPX50 EW	MSCI world	Nasdaq
Volatility	18.50%	15.04%	14.76%	27.44%
Implied beta versus MSCI world	1.25	1.02	1	N/A
Implied beta versus Nasdaq	0.67	0.55	N/A	1

Base date: Dec. 31 1993–July 2, 2004

Relative risk measures

Relative risk measures require assumptions about the nature of risk. For example, the relative volatility measures the volatility of an asset relative to the average volatility across all assets in that market. Relative volatilities are standardized around 1. A relative volatility greater than 1 indicates above-average risk, while a relative volatility less than 1 indicates below-average risk. The relative volatility can be used in much the same way as the traditional beta estimate to compute expected returns. The relative volatility measure does not require a correlation measure and hence is less noisy. However, this comes at a cost. The relative volatility measure is based upon the assumption that total risk and market risk exposures are perfectly correlated. This is the same approach we used above to estimate betas.

Bottom-up beta

Another alternative, the **bottom-up beta** approach, consists of estimating risk parameters using the financial characteristics of the portfolio companies. Such an approach is based on a feature that betas possess: The beta of two assets put together is a weighted average of the individual asset betas, with the weights based upon market value. Consequently, the beta for a fund is a weighted average of the betas of all of the different businesses the fund has invested in and can be estimated as follows:

1. Identify the type of businesses (industries) that make up the private equity fund's portfolio.
2. Estimate the unleveraged beta(s) for each type of business.
3. Calculate the leverage for each portfolio company, using market values if available. If not, use the target leverage (which is preferred) specified by the management of the company, or industry-typical debt ratios.
4. Estimate the leveraged beta for each portfolio company using the unleveraged beta from step 2 and the leverage from step 3. Note that in the VC industry there is no debt but the deal structuring often implies leverage.
5. Calculate the unleveraged beta for the fund (i.e. the beta for the fund ignoring the fund's own leverage) by calculating the weighted average of the portfolio companies' leveraged betas, using the market values. If the market values are not available, use a reasonable proxy, such as the last reported valuation or the cost.
6. Calculate the fund's leverage, using market values, if available. If not, use the target leverage specified by the management (which is better) or industry-typical debt ratios, which for VC funds is normally zero.
7. Estimate the fund's leveraged beta using the unleveraged beta from step 5 and the fund's leverage from step 6.

This approach provides better beta estimates for funds for three reasons. The first is that while regression betas are noisy and have large standard errors, averaging across regression betas reduces the noise in the estimate. The second advantage is that the beta estimates reflect the fund as it exists today, since it is computed based upon current weightings of its different businesses. The final advantage is that the leveraged beta is computed using the current financial leverage (or even better the expected or target one) of the firm, rather than the average leverage over the period of the regression. This approach is generic and can be applied to funds in any market. The dark side of this approach is that it remains difficult to identify quoted companies that are comparable to VC companies and that, as for many private equity funds, future cash flows are generated not only from existing investments but also from investments yet to be made. Such an approach requires an assumption on the nature of these future investments.

Ljungqvist and Richardson (2003) used a bottom-up approach to estimate betas based on a private database of actual cash flows of VC and buyout funds over the last two decades. This dataset was composed of 73 funds raised over the period 1981–1993, composed of 88.2% buyout and 11.8% VC funds. In terms of geography, the breakdown was 91.1% U.S., 7.4% EU and 1.5% Latin American funds. They looked at each fund's investments in detail, assigning industry betas to the portfolio companies in order to estimate the fund's risk. In doing so, they made the simplifying assumption that the leverage of the private company coincides with that of the industry, which allowed them to use the industry-leveraged beta based on one of 48 broad industry groups chosen by Fama and French (1997). They then used the capital disbursements as weights to calculate the funds' weighted average betas. The results are presented in Table 10.4, where weighted portfolio betas and weighted Fama and French industry risk premia are presented for all private equity funds, venture funds and non-venture-funds.[9] These estimates suggest that buyout funds (non-venture funds) are riskier than the market (beta of 1.08) but less than VC funds (beta of 1.12). However, no final conclusion can be drawn, as buyout funds typically use more leverage than the industries they invest in, and VC funds use less to no leverage.

Beta based on modified and corrected data

The absence of a market with continuous trading leads to the use of appraisals as prices. The resulting difficulties of stale pricing or smoothing make the measurement of true volatilities and correlations with other asset classes difficult. In order to measure betas, data need to be corrected and adjusted. Arthus and Teïletche (2004) estimated the optimal share of private equity in the portfolio of diversified European portfolios. In doing so, they had to estimate all the required inputs to estimate betas. To obtain a time-weighted return as required for the CAPM, the authors did not use final IIRRs, but rather "periodical aggregated returns built on the sum of all the funds for a specific period of time (i.e. the sum of the cash flows and NAVs between the starting and the ending dates of the chosen period)." Then they corrected these aggregated quarterly return data generated by the smoothing process, using an autocorrelation analysis. The authors acknowledge that the results obtained did not lead to a fully satisfactory solution (see Table 10.5).

Kaserer and Diller (2004) complemented the study of Arthus and Teïletche (2004) by focusing on individual cash flows, which are not impacted by the smoothing process and therefore do not require any correction. To obtain a time-weighted return, they constructed a benchmark for returns,

---

[9] Following Fama and French, industry risk premia were calculated by multiplying industry betas by the equity risk premium.

Table 10.4 Portfolio risk

	All funds (1981–1993)					Venture funds (N = 19)					Non-venture funds (N = 54)				
	Mean	St. dev.	First quartile	Median	Third quartile	Mean	St. dev.	First quartile	Median	Third quartile	Mean	St. dev.	First quartile	Median	Third quartile
Weighted portfolio betas	1.09	0.10	1.05	1.10	1.14	1.12	0.06	1.09	1.12	1.16	1.08	0.11	1.04	1.09	1.13
Weighted FF industry risk premia (%)	5.55	0.52	5.38	5.63	5.82	5.70	0.31	5.56	5.73	5.93	5.50	0.57	5.32	5.58	5.78

Source: Ljungqvist and Richardson (2003)

Table 10.5   Risk, performance, correlation and betas of European private equity

Returns (%)	Venture capital	Buyouts	Equities
Average	11.3	9.9	7.7
Std deviation	34.0	10.0	20.6
Correlation matrix			
VC	1.00	0.33	0.50
BO	0.33	1.00	0.11
Equities	0.50	0.11	1.00
Beta			
vs. Equities	0.83	0.06	1.00

Sources: Arthus and Teïletche (2004) and author calculations

based on the assumption that the distributions are reinvested in either quoted securities or bonds (Table 10.6).

The results obtained from these two studies, although quite interesting, most probably contained other imperfections through their corrections and adjustments. We do not believe that these results can be used in order to estimate VC fund discount rates. However, it is worth stressing that when the data are corrected, the betas of VC tend to come closer to 1, further supporting the notion that VC is not much different from public equity.

THE ALTERNATIVES TO THE CAPM

Other asset pricing models exist in addition to the CAPM, such as multi-factor models. But as they are more complex and often require more input or analysis, they likely will bring no more insight into the VC funds discount rate discussion. Regardless, there does not appear to have been empirical analyses performed using these other models. In addition to the CAPM approach, there are two other approaches to consider: the opportunity cost of capital and the historical performance approaches.

The opportunity cost of capital

The discount rate is also often called the opportunity cost of capital because it is the return forgone by investing in one asset versus another. Therefore, an alternative way to estimate a discount rate is by using the rate of return expected by investors in any securities of similar risks. As most of the

Table 10.6   Risk, performance, correlation and betas of European private equity

Returns (%)	PE (equity reinvestment)	PE (bond reinvestment)	MSCI Europe
Average	9.8	8.1	11.5
Std deviation	19.0	9.0	18.1
Correlation matrix			
PE (equity reinvestment)	1.00	n.a.	0.90
PE (bond reinvestment)	n.a.	1.00	0.04
MSCI Europe	0.90	0.04	1.00
Beta			
vs. MSCI Europe	0.94	0.02	

Sources: Kaserer and Diller (2004) and author calculations

Table 10.7 Public equity: historical performance

Countries	Index	Beginning Date	Beginning Price	Ending Date	Ending Price	Annual Return
France	CAC 40	Dec 87	1000.0	Dec 03	3557.9	8.26%
Germany	DAX	Dec 87	1000.0	Dec 03	3965.2	8.99%
Japan						
UK	FTSE 100	Dec 87	1712.7	Dec 03	4476.9	6.19%
U.S.	S&P 500	Dec 87	247.1	Dec 03	1111.9	9.86%

Source: Bloomberg. (Dec. 1987–Dec. 2003)
Note: The prices of the CAC 40 and DAX indices were set equal to 1000.0 at the beginning date of December 1987.

investors give an allocation to private equity funds to the detriment of public equity and often small caps, the return to this asset class can be used for estimating a minimum required discount rate.

One common mistake is to add distorted factors to the discount rate obtained via public equity, to offset things that could go wrong with the proposed investment but cannot be measured. The correct approach is to think about the determinants of betas. Often, as in the case of VC funds, the characteristics of high- and low-beta assets can be observed when the beta itself cannot, e.g. by analyzing the industry sectors that compose the portfolio (Ljungqvist and Richardson, 2003). Another approach is to try to identify specific public equity indices that are closer to the risk profile of the VC funds in the portfolio, such as small cap or industry sector indices. Table 10.7 shows some of these indices and their annual returns. Not surprisingly, these indices have historically yielded different returns. Therefore, depending on their portfolio composition, investors may want to use different minimum required discount rates.

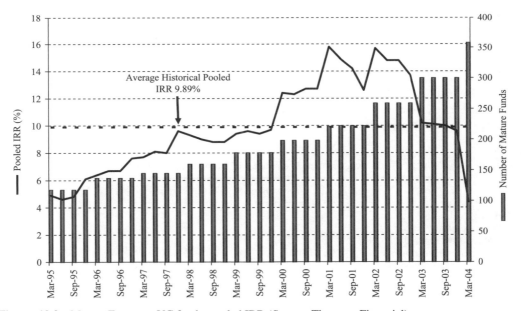

Figure 10.2 Mature European VC funds: pooled IRR (*Source:* Thomson Financial)

The historical performance

For the opportunity cost of capital, the historical performances of the assets that are perceived as alternatives to private equity funds were used to estimate the discount rate. Similarly, it is worth looking directly at the funds' historical performance, which could then be used as the discount rate. For funds, there are several problems with using such an approach. First, there are not sufficient data in terms of quantity and quality. Indeed, there are no time series available and the relatively short period covered appears insufficient to provide acceptable statistics. However, the funds' historical performance can still provide some useful indications of the adequate discount rate. Figure 10.2 shows the evolution of the historical "pooled" IRR for mature funds. Mature funds are often defined as funds whose vintage year is five years before the measurement year (e.g. in 2004, up to vintage year 1999).[10] As of March 2004, the IRR was 9.89%. With a risk premium of 5% and an EUR risk-free -rate around 4%, such an IRR implies a premium over public equity of 89 bps. However, this analysis is overly simplified in comparing cash flow-weighted returns with time-weighted returns.

---

[10] This is based on several studies that showed that after five or six years, on average, the IIRR becomes a reliable estimator of the final performance. See Burgel (2000) and Mathonet and Monjanel (2006).

11

The Management of Liquidity[1]

Investments in private equity funds have proved to be risky for a number of reasons, but principally because of the long time frame of the investment and the lack of liquidity. Managing the liquidity of a private equity fund investment program needs to take into account the existing interdependencies among the overall investment strategy, the management of the undrawn capital, the available resources and aspects of timing. It is a difficult task to put money efficiently to work while maintaining a balance in the portfolio composition and the quality of the individual fund investments. Therefore, modeling the cash flows of such investments is an important part of the management process, and potentially allows one to:

- improve investment returns for the undrawn capital;
- increase the profit generated by the private equity allocation through overcommitment;
- calculate an economic value, when a discount rate is available; and
- monitor the cash flows and risk-return profiles of a portfolio of private equity funds.

Achieving a high total return for the overall investment program is a complex task that requires not only quantitative modeling and financial engineering skills, but also a high degree of judgment and management discipline. There is no quick fix for this and only a disciplined approach can deliver small improvements that eventually add up to a significant impact. As a result, it is likely to take many years before an investment program is able to reach sustainable high total return levels.

OVERCOMMITMENT

Around 20% of a limited partner's commitments are invested per year on average. Therefore, investors have to find ways to minimize the opportunity cost of the non-productive investment. Timing and size of cash flows to and from a single private equity fund are not known until they are announced. But for a diversified private equity fund investment program they follow a predictable pattern. Therefore, limited partners can implement an overcommitment strategy in which more than the available resources are committed in order to achieve the target investment level.

$$\textbf{Overcommitment ratio} = \frac{\text{Signed commitments}}{\text{Resources available for commitments}}$$

An overcommitment ratio of less than 100% suggests an inefficient use of resources. Overcommitment ratios of 125–140% have been documented.[2] The investment phase of a program usually involves an aggressive overcommitment strategy, because capital needs to be quickly put to work. After the build-up of the portfolio, programs that have a long-term orientation and foresee

---

[1] The authors are grateful to Juan Delgado-Moreira PhD, CFA, Hamilton Lane, and Dr. Michael Jean Gschrei of Dr. Gschrei & Associates GmbH for their valuable comments and suggestions. The views expressed in this section are the authors' and are not necessarily shared by the aforementioned contributors.

[2] Examples: Schroders Private Equity Fund-of-Funds (listed on Dublin stock exchange), 130% overcommitment ratio; VCH Best-of-VC, 140% overcommitment ratio. Hewitt Investment Group recommended overcommitment ratios of 125–135% (see Schwartzman, 2002).

reinvestments or new commitments are constrained by the portfolio's average return, which sets a cap on the overcommitment ratio.

An overcommitment strategy is not simply setting a maximum allocation of commitments per year, but needs to be underpinned by a detailed understanding of the cash flow profiles of private equity funds. The overcommitment ratio can be determined on the basis of empirical data. Assuming that, on average, not more than 70% of the commitments are actually called, an overcommitment level of around 140% would be feasible.[3] But the reality can be significantly different and large fluctuations around averages can be observed, notably during some overheated market conditions. The time lag between commitment and actual investment can be reflected in the maturity profile of the treasury investments to give some extra basis points of return. Other sources of liquidity also have to be taken into account. To achieve a higher overcommitment level, the limited partner's portfolio needs to be diversified over several vintage years. As distributions begin to come in, they theoretically supplement resources available to be spent on new capital calls. If there is no vintage year diversification in the extreme, all private equity funds achieve their maximum investment level simultaneously.

In a diversified private equity portfolio, cash flow patterns of various fund types can be exploited within a portfolio approach. Buyout and mezzanine funds typically draw down commitments more quickly than VC funds that tend to stretch drawdowns in parallel with their stage financing approach.[4] Buyout and mezzanine funds also tend to start distributing more quickly, as they usually have annual income components, such as interest on subordinated debt or dividends on preferred stock. They also invest in established companies requiring fewer years to exit.

The implementation of a successful overcommitment strategy and investment strategy for the undrawn capital largely depends on the quality and precision of the cash flow projections. Also, the limited partners' overall portfolio composition has an impact on such projections: A highly diversified portfolio of private equity funds, particularly if representing several vintage years, can significantly contribute to the smoothing of net cash flows. As Figure 11.1 shows, diversification over time is essential for an overcommitment strategy. For investment programs that only have a short lifetime, this can become problematic.[5] Consequently, achieving a high level of resources actually invested in private equity is a very challenging task, as it needs to take all these interdependencies into consideration. A real-life case study in Mathonet and Meyer (2007) further highlights the perils of overcommitting and should serve as a warning that just looking at simple ratios is not sufficient for controlling risk.

SOURCES OF LIQUIDITY

Commitments are generally met through cash inflows, supplemented by assets readily convertible to cash, or are met through a company's capacity to borrow. To achieve a competitive total return on committed capital, the investor needs to manage the investment of uncalled capital during the drawdown period and the reinvestment of distributed capital. The maturity structure of Treasury

---

[3] See Schaechterle (2000): "Analysis of statistical data from Venture Economics funds that invest in private equity have a peak level of 65% leaving the remainder of the investors' committed capital invested in short-term investments. The resulting opportunity costs dilute the overall performance of an investor's private equity allocation by approximately one-third. Swiss Re and Partners Group have developed a proprietary over-commitment model as part of (their) investment strategy."

[4] See Maginn and Dyra (2000) about the U.S. market.

[5] See Steers (2002): "Institutional investors have discovered that they need to commit as much as 30–40% more than their policy allocation to private equity in order to get capital working. According to the author, in 2001 continental investors had over-committed around 40% of their strategic allocation in an attempt to get more capital actually invested; UK investors had an over-commitment level of 16%."

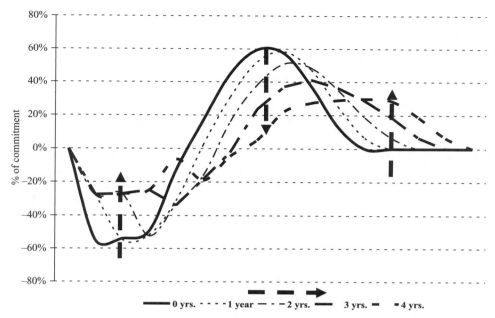

Figure 11.1 Time diversification. Cumulative cash flows (as percent of commitment) over time for a portfolio of two private equity funds with commitments made with a 4, 3, 2, 1, or 0 years gap between the two funds

assets and private equity funds should be matched and there should be well-diversified and stable sources of funding, such as:

- *Follow-on funding.* In the case where the mandator is managing the liquidity, he may be able to step in as a provider of follow-on funding, which is especially meaningful, as repayment of liquidity may take time.
- *Liquidity lines.* A short- and medium-term borrowing facility could be managed either by the mandator or by the program manager. Cash needs to be available to meet capital calls, but a liquidity line is used should these resources run out. Structuring a sensible liquidity line needs to reflect factors such as the expected amount and timing of cash needs, or the rating of the liquidity provider.
- *Maturing investments.* While it is tempting to maintain undrawn capital in short-term instruments, such a policy is likely to adversely impact the total return. To achieve higher returns, the profiles of the private equity fund cash flows need to be predicted and matched with those of an investment portfolio composed of assets with the same maturities, but also expected to produce a return above short-term instruments. Because of the uncertain schedule, a maturity structure can only have a limited match.
- *Realizations of investments.* With such a mismatch, the risk of illiquidity increases. Therefore, cash cannot simply be provided for by maturing assets only, but occasionally requires a liquidation or realization of exisiting positions. To limit the potential for losses resulting from market fluctuations, strict criteria for the eligibility of investments needs to be applied.
- *Sell-off of limited partnership shares.* Private equity funds are illiquid investments and an early redemption is usually not allowed. Limited partners are generally prohibited from transferring, assigning, pledging, or otherwise disposing of their limited partnership interests or withdrawing from the partnership without the prior consent of the general partners, who can grant or withhold consent at their sole discretion. However, there is a growing secondary market where seasoned

fund investments may be liquidated. But a realization of limited partnership shares in an attempt to increase liquidity is problematic as it takes considerable time to identify buyers and negotiate the transaction.

- *Distributions from private equity funds.* A reinvestment plan should be established that takes into account the uncertainty inherent in the timing and magnitude of distributions from private equity funds. As investments in private equity funds are speculative and require a long-term commitment, there is no certainty regarding timing and amounts of distributions. It is also possible that part or all of the return is received as **distribution-in-kind** in the form of marketable restricted securities. Consequently, reinvestment planning exposes one to considerable liquidity risks.
- *Limited partner default.* If several capital calls cannot be met simultaneously, the last resort is for the investor to default.[6] However, ignoring the reputation damage for the defaulting limited partner, there are stiff penalties associated with not meeting a drawdown request. These penalties include the termination of the limited partner's right to participate in the fund's future investments, the loss of entitlement to distributions or income but not its liability for losses or partnership expenses, the mandatory transfer or sale of its partnership interests, the continuing liability for interest in respect of the defaulted amount, the partial or total forfeiture of the partnership interest, or the liability for any other rights and legal remedies the fund managers may have against the defaulting investor.

CASH FLOW PROJECTIONS

Investments in illiquid assets present particular challenges for portfolio management, as there is a high degree of uncertainty inherent in the timing and amount of cash flows. The main objective of a strategic commitment steering is to build up and maintain a balanced and stable portfolio in line with the investment strategy. The portfolio balance depends not only on the level of commitments to fund investments, but also on the rate and timing of drawdowns and distributions. Effective management of a private equity program requires a reasonably accurate assessment of the individual fund's future cash flow pattern to enable the steering of commitments and portfolio balance.

Maximizing the return on undrawn commitments will often require taking positions in assets with limited liquidity. A profitable realization of such positions may take two to three months or more. This process needs to be started as early as possible. Thus, the establishment of efficient liquidity management relies heavily on projection and planning methodologies. Projection models have to be simple and sensible on a theoretical basis. They should be able to incorporate and respond to actual cash flow experience and valuations. Such models should also be able to analyze the portfolio impact of varying return scenarios and changing rates of investments and repayments. Projections need to consider existing deals with known characteristics and future deals with unknown characteristics or characteristics yet to be chosen (such as commitment levels).

Sophisticated alternative investment and fund-of-funds managers have developed proprietary approaches[7] that take a series of inputs into consideration:

- *Market and empirical data.* These data come mainly from data services such as Thomson Financial, but internal data can also form the statistical input for forecasting expected drawdowns and distributions. They are complemented by an assessment of the vintage year quality and the investment and exit environment (empirical data on expected drawdowns and repayments).

---

[6] This has also a "spill-over" effect on the other investors in the private equity fund, as they have to step in for the defaulting partner. Therefore, an important part of due diligence is the assessment of the other limited partners' financial strength and commitment to this asset class.

[7] The Partners Group's model (see Wietlisbach, 2002) differentiates between strategic and tactical commitment steering. Its private equity management approach rests on the four pillars, "empirical data," "actual data," "investment advisory," and "quantitative management."

Table 11.1   Approaches to projecting cash flows

	Estimates	Forecasts	Scenarios
	Tactical		Strategic
Term	Short-term (~3 to 6 months)	Medium-term (~1−2 years)	Long-term (over 2 years)
Based on	Current market situation	Specific market environment	Uncertain market environment
Approach	Data gathering and analysis	Quantitative modeling	Planning

- *Expert judgment*. As purely quantitative approaches have their limits, significant judgment is required for estimations and valuations. The main problem is the quality of data in an opaque market. It is only with a high level of expertise that the accurate interpretation of empirical and observed data is possible.
- *Fund data*. These data on actual drawdowns and distributions form the basis for the valuation of individual private equity fund investments (monitoring input on actual drawdowns and distributions). Also, monitoring of the portfolio quality is of relevance; for example, although write-offs are not immediately relevant for cash flows, they can reduce further financing needs.
- *Models*. Projections are generated with the help of various models. Generally, the accuracy of predictions is higher for mature funds than during the first years of a new fund. Also, estimating exits in the early stage segment is extremely difficult.

Very simplistically, one can differentiate three approaches to carrying out projections:

- Estimates utilize an assessment of current conditions to identify possible future events. The priority is accuracy, which requires a relatively short time horizon.
- Forecasts go beyond the short-term horizon, primarily relying on trend-based analysis. Often expert opinion is required for making an assessment concerning the continuity or modification of current trends.
- Scenarios can be thought of as a range of forecasts, but both their construction and intent are more complex. They aim to describe different environments based on plausible changes in current trends.

There is a significant difference between scenarios and forecasting. Presumably, forecasts are attempts to predict the future, while scenarios aim to enable better decisions about the future. Of course, the distinction is not as clear-cut as depicted in Table 11.1, and typically projection tools combine elements of all of these approaches.

Estimates

To estimate is to form an opinion based on imperfect data, comparisons or experience. Because statistics are of lesser value over the short term (or for a single position), in this situation estimation techniques can be more meaningful than forecasts. Estimates can be applied to new commitments in private equity funds to be signed within the next few months and to liquidity events in the near future within private equity funds already committed, as follows:

- New commitments in private equity funds and their first drawdowns can be derived from deal pipeline analysis with reasonable accuracy for a period of three to six months ahead. Investment managers typically are already in discussions with potential investors. They have a good understanding of the current fundraising environment, the resulting likelihood of commitments to materialize and the size of these commitments.

• There is a series of liquidity events that is either known or is reasonably likely to happen. Occasionally exits (e.g. in the form of IPOs) are even publicly announced, and possible price ranges are discussed.

A regularly updated calendar of such events forms the starting point for estimating short- and medium-term liquidity needs. Such an approach is also appropriate for pricing secondary transactions but using estimates until full liquidation of the positions. The use of this technique for long-term purposes tends to be quite time- and information-consuming, leading to significant costs that cannot necessarily be justified for classical portfolio projections, but may be appropriate in the case of secondary transactions where higher benefits can be expected.

Example for estimation techniques

Distributions from the private equity funds to their investors are obviously more sensitive to short-term information and changes. Estimates can be significantly improved through closer interaction with general partners and through incorporating judgment.

Baring Private Equity Partners (BPEP) has pioneered a cash flow model with the objective of generating the most accurate possible projections of net capital flows from BPEP directly managed funds to investors. In order to measure the uncertainty of exit values and dates, the model has incorporated a probabilistic methodology. BPEP investment managers are routinely asked to provide an early, expected and late exit date, and a low, median and high exit value, as well as the attached probabilities for each event and the basis for these estimates. Such an estimate will take the following form (see Figure 11.2), with:

$$p_{a;\min} + p_{a;med} + p_{a;\max} = 1 \text{ and } p_{t;\min} + p_{t;med} + p_{t;\max} \leq 1$$

where: $p_{a;\min}$, $p_{a;med}$ and $p_{a;\max}$ are the probabilities of the minimum, median and maximum cash flow amount occurring and $p_{t;\min}$, $p_{t;med}$ and $p_{t;\max}$ are the probabilities of the earlier, median and latest cash flow date occurring.

That these probabilities for cash flow dates do not necessarily add up to 1 allows the situation where the cash flow is not certain to take place at all. BPEP applies this estimation exercise consistently and rigorously using valuations arrived at in compliance with EVCA guidelines. This approach calls for the following comments:

• The accuracy of the model's projections depends on the estimates for price and date of portfolio exits and therefore is subject to the uncertainties of market conditions and buyer sentiment.

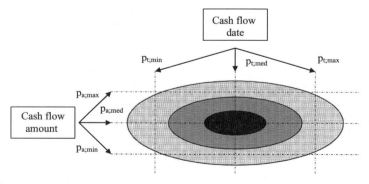

Figure 11.2   Estimation "grid" according to BPEP

- Exit values and dates are uncertain and continuous variables. Since they are based on established valuation methods, estimates of exit values forecasts are more likely to be accurate than those of exit dates.[8]
- Exit dates can be estimated only over a short time frame. Typically, after more than one year, estimates cease to be of relevance and forecasting techniques become more important.

This approach is successfully applied by BPEP for its portfolios of directly managed investments. In this situation BPEP as general partner has privileged access to information. A limited partner, however, needs to overcome significant barriers to access timely information of sufficient quality that allows a bottom-up analysis and precise projections. For a limited partner, a bottom-up analysis – due to the lack of detailed information – is usually only possible with limitations, and estimates will often lack precision.

Generally, the fund managers will feel reluctant to disclose information on likely financing or exit events before the deals actually close, in order to protect their negotiation position. Consequently, this is not made part of the regular standard reporting, and only in rare cases, such as with an IPO, are investors informed in advance. However, there are various analytical techniques that can be used to form educated guesses (as was the case in evaluating secondary transactions). For the limited partner, it is either a good questioning technique or an educated guess that leads to the estimates. The basis for such an estimate could be discussions with the fund's management on possible new investments or planned realizations, or an assessment of the maturity of the fund and the current exit conditions.

The combination of three exit values and three dates gives nine possible outcomes per portfolio company. Just combining 10 companies would give $9^{10} = 3.5$ billion different outcomes. A relatively simple Monte Carlo simulation helps to determine the range for possible outcomes. With a sensitivity analysis (taking into account longer or shorter time periods or lower or higher realization levels) the robustness of results can be checked using the following three methods:

- The estimates can be interpreted as inputs for a discrete distribution. Volatility, as expressed by the standard deviation of the returns and therefore a judgment on risk, is implied by the inputs.
- Another approach would be to take the investment managers' inputs as a continuous distribution. Their average estimate is taken and a normal distribution is assumed as to both value and timing, with a set standard deviation for the exit value and for the exit timing.
- A third alternative used by BPEP is a non-normal probability distribution created ad hoc, following the shape of the curves defined by the three exit values/times and the associated probabilities. Here each deal can have a different curve.

If applied consistently, this too, despite its simplicity, can be highly useful in assessing likely cash flow patterns over a short time frame. A structured analytical process and interview technique, possibly with a scoring to link categories to probabilities, can further improve the quality and consistency of estimates and allow for calibration of the model.

When aggregating the estimates into projections, the private equity fund's structure is also relevant. For example, the preferred return or hurdle rate can heavily distort the cash flow to the limited partner. With 100% catch-up, once the limited partners have the preferred return they cease to share further new realizations until the general partner has made a full recovery.

---

[8] Increasing standardization of valuation approaches in private equity (see the IPEV guidelines) will further improve the comparability between various private equity funds.

Implementation issues

For short-term estimates in a bottom-up approach, the private equity funds and their portfolio companies are analyzed in detail. It is obvious that a thorough bottom-up analysis is a resource-intensive exercise and therefore, especially for large portfolios, all companies cannot be continuously reviewed. Also, different general partners will provide information with varying levels of detail and reliability or will not even respond to requests at all. However, in most cases it is possible to split the portfolio into parts with higher and lower probabilities of cash flows and focus attention on the parts of the portfolio with higher activity levels (e.g. mature companies in booming market segments are more likely to exit than recently funded and young companies). Even in more active market situations, many funds can be eliminated from such an exercise right away, such as:

- some funds are so early in their life that no positive cash flows can be expected;
- some funds in later stages have portfolio companies that are too young to be likely candidates for exits; and
- some market segments may be comparatively flat.

In a real-life situation such a bottom-up analysis would need to be combined with a macro view that takes into account, for example, the different private equity funds' geographical orientation, age, industry and stage focus as a starting point. This narrows the population down to a meaningful list of funds to be analyzed. For the relatively idle part of the portfolio, simplistic techniques like "next quarter's forecast is equal to last quarter's realized cash flow", in combination with medium-term forecasts, can be applied. Even if estimation techniques occasionally lack precision, they are always an indispensable tool for anticipating liquidity shortfalls and serve as an early warning system to supervise limits. For an illiquid asset class such as private equity, it is critical to continuously monitor developments and initiate changes as early as possible.

Forecasting

All forecasts are based on the assumption that the past can be extended into the future and build on statistical extrapolation of variables. Such approaches are mainly quantitative and aim to predict over the medium term. For private equity funds, a forecasting approach needs to factor in, among other items, criteria such as the fund's life-cycle characteristics, its age, empirical data for comparable funds, or market data such as stock market indices.

A private equity fund's life cycle characteristics are typically modeled through cash flow libraries based on historical fund data. This could be data from one's own investments or provided by data services such as Thomson Financial. The underlying assumption is that the pattern (timing, amount of cash flows) is the same for each fund or quality of fund, and that a scaling such as described in Weidig (2002) can be applied.

This approach is meaningful, especially for drawdowns, as capital calls depend on investments in young companies not ready for exits and therefore the link to markets is less important. Drawdowns tend to follow a reasonably predictable schedule but show marked differences between investment environments (see Figures 11.3 and 11.4).

Although the private equity market is very cyclical, any environment does not necessarily resemble another historical period. For example, in the late 1990s, venture capitalists drew down capital at unprecedented rates with atypical returns. Historical data for any previous period provided a poor template for modeling these vintages. Moreover, there is little historical data available for European funds. For distributions, the pattern appears to be less predictable than for contributions. Differences are even more pronounced for the U.S. market (see Figures 11.5 and 11.6). These limitations, the incompleteness of the cash flow library and the non-availability of data in general, pose restrictions

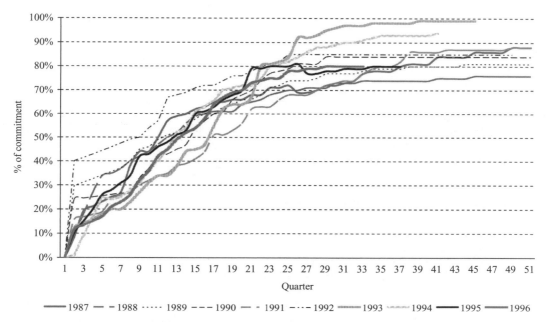

Figure 11.3 EU VC funds (vintages 1987 until 1996): cumulative paid in (Source: Thomson Financial)

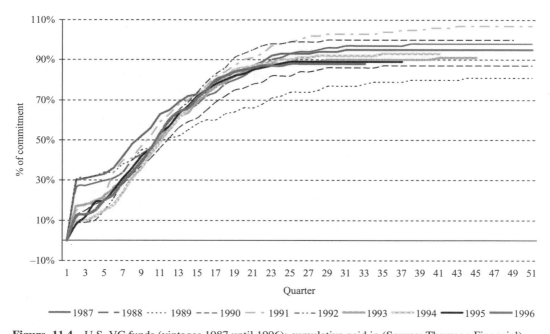

Figure 11.4 U.S. VC funds (vintages 1987 until 1996): cumulative paid in (Source: Thomson Financial)

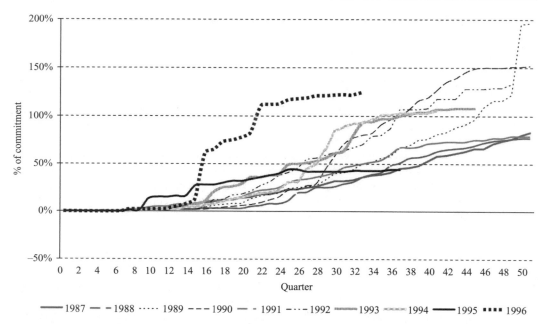

Figure 11.5   EU VC funds (vintages 1987 until 1996): cumulative distribution (Source: Thomson Financial)

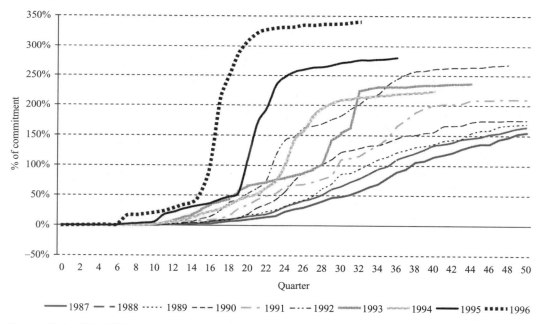

Figure 11.6   U.S. VC funds (vintages 1987 until 1996): cumulative distribution (Source: Thomson Financial)

to such approaches and, therefore applications should monitor feedback and utilize expert opinion as well.

One alternative is to use public market indices as part of an econometric model. Small company equity markets generally serve as the primary exit vehicle for private equity investments either through IPO or via company valuation in the case of mergers and acquisitions. Despite its plausibility, the above analysis of cash flow data over the time period 2001–2004 has not revealed a strikingly clear and simple relationship between VC fund exit patterns and small cap indices. To be of any predictive value, econometric forecasts need to consider several explanatory variables and therefore carry significant model risk, made worse by the low availability and quality of private equity data.

A continuous review and validation of input parameters and results is critical. Consequently, it is important that all trend-based forecasting approaches be used only with a stern warning, and only in conjunction with alternative approaches as reality checks. For example, results should be consistent with the assumed scenario. Blindly following econometric models representing a specific market environment is an accident waiting to happen.

Scenarios

While forecasting gives the most likely picture of the future against which plans can be judged, long-term projections in particular are fraught with considerable uncertainty, regardless of the kind of forecasting problem. If the environment changes radically, statistical extrapolation techniques fail. As forecasts do not communicate uncertainty – especially in the VC industry which thrives on innovation – reliable forecasting has its natural limits. The nearer term one looks, the more predictable the future is. In the very short-term most people are inclined to estimate or forecast, whereas long-term planning relies on scenarios. Scenarios are a set of reasonably plausible but structurally different futures and are a useful tool for setting out a course in the face of significant uncertainty.[9]

Scenarios can be an individual's isolated opinion or can be discussed in groups.[10] This approach is built on the assumption that some people can be more expert than others in predicting what will happen, or in excluding what will not happen. This expertise is based on experience, closeness to markets and access to privileged information. Another feature of scenarios is that they are abstract, simplified and do not consider the same level of detail as forecasts. Consequently, their results lack precision and often cannot differentiate between the natures of cash flows. The assumptions underlying the scenarios need to be documented. Also "intervention points" need to be defined; for example, under which circumstances should the scenario be seen as invalid and a new round of scenario development required? Scenario development helps users to think through the process, to understand the environment better and to enhance the capability to recognize unexpected events.

Partners Group analyzed empirical cash flow patterns of U.S. VC funds during different time periods and found marked differences between averages of the periods 1981–1985, 1986–1990 and 1991–1995.[11] For illustration, three different time periods with the scenarios "normal" (pre-1990), "emerging" recession (1990–1993) and post-1993 "boom" are presented. Figure 11.7 suggests that scenarios can be quite different. While differences for the European VC market are not as pronounced as those of the U.S. (see Figure 11.8), they nevertheless can be significant and form the basis for a scenario discussion.

---

[9] See van der Heijden (1996).

[10] Surowiecki (2004) argues that the collective also beats the individual expertise in smaller groups, and identified as necessary conditions the diversity and independence of experts and well-defined mechanisms for aggregating and producing collective judgment.

[11] See Wietlisbach (2002).

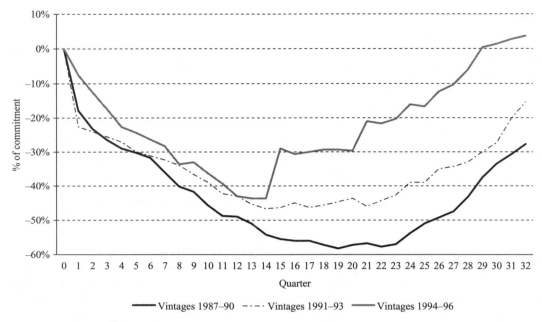

Figure 11.7 EU VC funds: Cumulative cash flow scenarios (Source: Thomson Financial)

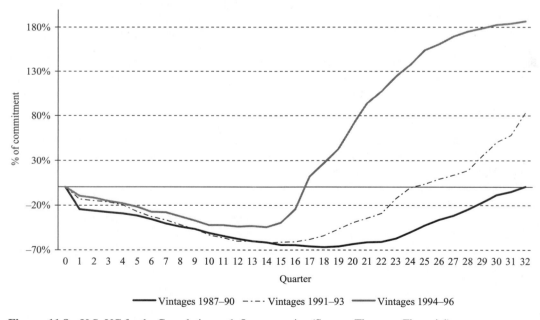

Figure 11.8 U.S. VC funds: Cumulative cash flow scenarios (Source: Thomson Financial)

For a private equity funds investment program, a scenario-based tool like the Yale Model (Takahashi and Alexander, 2001) could aid the strategic commitment steering. This model considers NAVs, commitments, drawdowns, repayments, funds' lifetimes, exit patterns and growth rates. It does not give variances but only averages. The variety of possible outcomes is not described by volatilities, but approximated through the choice of scenarios.

CONCLUSIONS

To conclude, we would like to make a final observation that, as is often stated in this industry, investing in private equity has a lot in common with wine making. In talking about wine, some authors argue that only those civilizations that drank wine survived when the overall water quality turned poor, as it did regularly. Similarly, we believe that when traditional asset classes enter turbulent market conditions, investors that have invested in private equity, and venture capital in particular, and used the approaches and tools discussed in this material, will be better equipped to navigate through these turbulences.

In private equity, some claim to have found ways to rapidly generate above market returns – but we remain skeptical. As with making wine, there is a series of obstacles to overcome and if you give up, then this effort will go entirely unrewarded. Inevitably, some vintage years will be disastrous. But your wine cellar will help you to survive these downturns and eventually the spectacular vintages will make the effort worthwhile. For these reasons, you can not switch into and out of winemaking – it is a decision for your life (and most probably that of your children). The same applies to private equity: to some extent it could be seen as a decision for your professional life – and most probably that of your successor.

References

AltAssets. *Institutional Investor Profiles: Volume I*. London, AltAssets. www.altassets.com. 2002a.

AltAssets. *Institutional Investor Profiles: Volume II*. London, AltAssets. www.altassets.com. 2002b.

AltAssets. *Institutional Investor Profiles: Volume III*. London, AltAssets. www.altassets.com. 2003.

Arthus, P. and J. Teïletche. "Asset Allocation and European Private Equity: A First Approach Using Aggregated Data." Brussels, EVCA. 2004.

Bailey, J. V., T. M. Richards, and D. E. Tierney. "Benchmark Portfolios and the Manager/Plan Sponsor Relationship." *Current Topics in Investment Management*. F. J. Fabozzi and T. Dessa Fabozzi eds. New York, Harper and Row. pp. 71–85. 1990.

Barber, J. and L. Zage. *Moving in Tandem?* London, Helix Associates. 2002.

Basel Committee on Banking Supervision. "Risk-Sensitive Approaches for Equity Exposures in the Banking Book for IRB banks." Working Paper. Basel. August 2001.

Bauer, M., S. Bilo, and H. Zimmermann. "Publicly Traded Private Equity: An Empirical Investigation." 2nd Draft, Working Paper No. 5/01. Universität St. Gallen, Swiss Institute of Banking and Finance. May 2001.

Blaydon, C. and M. Horvath. "LPs Need to Trust General Partners in Setting Valuations." *Venture Capital Journal*. March 2003.

Brands, S. and D. R. Gallagher. "Portfolio Selection, Diversification and Funds-of-Funds." School of Banking and Finance, The University of New South Wales, Sydney. 2003.

Burgel, O. "UK Venture Capital and Venture Capital as an Asset Class for Institutional Investors." London, BVCA. 2000.

Bushrod, L. "Fees: Unable to Move Out of the Spotlight." *European Venture Capital Journal*. July/August 2003.

Camp, J. J. *Venture Capital Due Diligence*. New York, John Wiley & Sons, Inc. 2002.

Center for International Securities and Derivatives Markets (CISDM), The Benefits of Private Equity (Accessed at http://cisdm.som.umass.edu/research/pdffiles/benefitsofprivateinvestment.pdf). 2006.

Cheung, L., C. Howley, V. Kapoor, and A. Smith. "Rating Private Equity CFOs: Cash Flow Benchmarks." Standard and Poor's CDO Research. Special Report. January 2003.

Cullen, A. "Locating Venture Capital Returns." Boston, HBS Working Knowledge. 2004.

Cumming, D. J., G. A. Fleming, and A. Schwienbacher. "Style Drift in Private Equity." Working Paper. Center for International Securities and Derivatives Markets. May 2004.

Damodaran, A. *The Dark Side of Valuation. Valuing Old Tech, New Tech, and New Economy Companies*. Upper Saddle River, NJ, Financial Times Prentice-Hall. 2001.

Diem, G. "The Information Deficiency Problem of Private Equity Funds-of-funds: A Risk and Monitoring Management Perspective." MBA Thesis. University of Birmingham. MBA 2002.

Edvinsson, L. and M. S. Malone. *Intellectual Capital*. New York, HarperBusiness. 1997.

Erturk, E., L. Cheung and W. Fong. *Private Equity Fund-of-Funds: Overview and Rating Criteria*. New York, Standard and Poors Publication. 2001.

Fama, G. and G. French. "Industry Costs of Equity." *Journal of Financial Economics*. 43, pp. 153–193. 1997.

Flag Venture Management. "The Right Level of Diversification." Venture Insights. Stamford, CT. Flag Venture Management Special Report. 1st Quarter, 2001.

Flag Venture Management. "Evaluating Funds-of-Funds." Stamford, CT. Flag Venture Management. Special Report. 3rd Quarter, 2003a.

Flag Venture Management. "Let's Talk Terms." Stamford, CT, Flag Venture Management Special Report. 4th Quarter, 2003b.

Fort Washington Capital Partners. "Investing in Private Equity through a Fund of Funds." White Paper. Cincinnati, OH. Ford Washington Capital Partners. 2004.

Geltner, D. and D. Ling. "Benchmark and Index Needs in the U.S. Private Real Estate Investment Industry: Trying to Close the Gap." RERI study for the Pension Real Estate Association. 2000.

Giacometti, M. *Asset Allocation in Private Equity*. Institute for Fiduciary Education. 2001.

Hellman, R. B. and E. Katz. *The Evolution of Partnership Terms − Aligning GP and LP Interests*. Institute of Fiduciary Education. 2002.

Henderson Global Investors. "The Case for Smallest Sized Private Equity Funds." Chicago, IL, Henderson Global Investors. Heppner 2003. http://www.altassets.com. 2002.

InvestorWords.com. http://www.investorwords.com/1596/due_diligence.html. Accessed October 2007.

Jaeggi, A. P. "Successful Risk Management for LP's Private Equity Portfolios." Presentation, Super Investor. 17 November 2005.

Jo, H. "Perspectives and Problems of Private Equity Funds-of-Funds." Leavey School of Business and Administration. 2002.

Kaserer, C. and C. Diller. "European Private Equity − A Cash Flow-based Performance Analysis." EVCA. May 2004.

Kelly, T. G. "Private Equity: A Look at a Maturing Asset Class." Presentation to Chicago GSB Finance Round Table. 2002.

Kerins, F., J. K. Smith, and R. Smith. "New Venture Opportunity Cost of Capital and Financial Contracting." Working Paper in Economics, Claremont Graduate University. 2001.

King, D. A. and M. S. Young. "Why Diversification Doesn't Work." *Real Estate Review*. Vol. 25, No. 2, pp. 6–12. Summer 1994.

Lerner, J. "The Future of Private Equity: Research and Hypotheses." Boston, MA, Harvard Business School and National Bureau of Economic Research. 2000.

Lerner, J. "The Syndication of Venture Capital Investments." *Financial Management*. 23, pp. 16–27. 1994.

Lerner, J. and A. Schoar. "The Illiquidity Puzzle: Theory and Evidence From Private Equity." *Journal of Financial Economics*. Vol. 72, No. 1, pp. 3–40. 2004.

Lerner, J., A. Schoar, and W. Wong. "Smart Institutions, Foolish Choices? The Limited Partner Performance Puzzle." Working Paper. Harvard Business School. 2004.

Lhabitant, F. S. and M. Learned. "Hedge Fund Diversification: How Much is Enough?" Research Paper No. 52. Geneva, International Center for Financial Asset Management and Engineering. July 2002.

Ljungqvist, A. and M. Richardson. "The Cash Flow, Return and Risk Characteristics of Private Equity." Finance Working Paper No. 03-001. New York University. http://ssrn.com/abstract=369600. January 2003.

Maginn, J. and G. Dyra. "Building Private Equity Portfolios." Summit Strategies Group. www.summitstrategies.com. 2000.

Mathonet, P.-Y. and G. Monjanel. "Valuation Guidelines for Private Equity and Venture Capital Funds: A Survey." *Journal of Alternative Investments*. Vol. 9, No. 2, pp. 59–70. Fall 2006.

Mathonet P.-Y. and T. Meyer. *J-Curve Exposure: Managing a Portfolio of Venture Capital and Private Equity Funds*. Chichester, UK, John Wiley & Sons Ltd. November 2007.

Maxwell, R. *To Disclose or Not to Disclose? That is the Question*. London, AltAssets. March 2003.

McCune, A. "Looking at the Nuts and Bolts of the Secondary Market for LP Interests." Venture Economics. 2001.

Meek, V. "Bottom of the Pile." London, AltAssets. April 2004.

Meek, V. "Time to Deviate From the Standard?" London, AltAssets. May 2003.

Meyer, T. and P-Y Mathonet. *Beyond the J-Curve: Managing a Portfolio of Venture Capital and Private Equity Funds*. Chichester, UK, John Wiley & Sons Ltd. July 2005.

Moskowitz, T. and A. Vissing-Jørgensen. "The Returns to Entrepreneurial Investment: A Private Equity Premium Puzzle?" *The American Economic Review*. Vol. 92, No. 4, pp. 745–778. September 2002.

Muller, K. W. "Formation and Operation of Venture Capital/Private Equity Funds." Presentation. Cooley Godward LLP. 2004.

Otterlei, J. and S. Barrington. "Alternative Assets − Private Equity Fund-of-funds." Special Report. Piper Jaffray Private Capital. 2003.

Piper Jaffray Private Capital. "Alternative Assets − Private Equity Fund-of-funds." Special Report. Piper Jaffray Private Capital. 2003.

PrivateEquityValuation.com. http://www.privateequityvaluation.com. Accessed October 2007.

Prowse, S. D. "The Economics of the Private Equity Market." *Economic Review.* Federal Reserve Bank of Dallas. Third Quarter, pp. 21–34. 1998.

Raschle, B. E. and R. Ender. "Absolute Returns or Private Equity Asset Allocation?" Zurich, Adveq Management. 2004.

Robbie, K., M. Wright, and B. Chiplin. "The Monitoring of Venture Capital Firms." *Entrepreneurship Theory and Practice.* 214, pp. 9–28. 22 June 1997.

Rouvinez, C. "Top Quartile Persistence in Private Equity." *Private Equity International.* pp. 76–79. June 2006.

Schaechterle, S. "Taking Away the Disadvantages." Baar-Zug, Switzerland, Partners Group. 2000.

Schwartzman, T. J. "Alternative and Liquid Alternative Assets — Structuring and Oversight." Presentation to Investment Management Institute's Endowment and Foundation Forum. Atlanta, GA, Hewitt Investment Group. http://www.hewittinvest.com/pdf/IMIAlternative%20Assets012002.pdf January 2002.

Shearburn, J. and B. Griffiths. "Private Equity Building Blocks." *Pension Week* in association with Goldman Sachs. April 2002.

Siegel, J. "The Shrinking Equity Premium." *Journal of Portfolio Management.* Fall 1999.

Simons, K. "The Use of Value at Risk by Institutional Investors." *New England Economic Review.* November/December 2000.

Smith, M. D. "Private Equity Funds-of-Funds: Getting What You Pay For." Presentation at Asset Alternatives' Fund-of-Funds Summit. Atlanta, GA, Hewitt Investment Group. http://www.hewittinvest.com/pdf/AssetAlternativesFoFSummit10122000.pdf. October 2000.

Statman, M. "How Much Diversification is Enough?" Leavey School of Business, Santa Clara University. September 2002.

Steers, H. "Special Rules of the Game." Frank Russell Company. AltAssets. 2002.

Surowiecki, J. *The Wisdom of Crowds.* New York, Doubleday. 2004.

Swensen, D. F. *Pioneering Portfolio Management — An Unconventional Approach to Institutional Investment.* New York, Simon and Schuster. 2000.

Takahashi, D. and S. Alexander. "Illiquid Alternative Asset Fund Modelling." Yale University Investments Office. January 2001.

Thalmann, O. and U. Weinwurm. "Public Equity or Private Equity?" Paper prepared for doctorate seminar in corporate finance, University of St. Gallen. 2002.

The Economist. "Once Burnt, Still Hopeful." November 2004.

Thompson, D. B. "Are There Too Many Private Equity Funds? Survival of the Fittest?" Sacramento, CA, Institute of Fiduciary Education. 1999.

Van Der Heijden, K. *Scenarios — The Art of Strategic Conversation.* Chichester, John Wiley & Sons Ltd. 1996.

Walter, I. "Strategies in Banking and Financial Service Firms: A Survey." New York University, New York. December 2003.

Waters, R. "The Biggest Gains are Concentrated in a Handful of Funds." *Financial Times.* 15 February 2005.

Weidig, T. "Risk Model for Venture Capital Funds." European Investment Fund. November 2002.

Weidig, T. and P.-Y. Mathonet. "The Risk Profiles of Private Equity." Brussels, EVCA. January 2004.

Wietlisbach, U. "Private Equity Fund-of-Funds Management: A Strategic Approach." London, AltAssets. June 2002.

Zimmermann, H., M. Degosciu, H. Christophers, and S. Bilo. "The Risk and Return of Publicly Traded Private Equity." Working Paper No. 6/04. WWZ/Department of Finance, University of Basel. April 2004.

Introduction

This section consists of six chapters and covers advanced topics in commodity investment analysis. The reader is assumed to be familiar with commodity futures pricing as covered in the CAIA prerequisite materials and commodity investments chapters in the CAIA Level I curriculum. This section's emphasis is on concepts rather than performance information. This is not because performance of commodity investments is unimportant, but because this topic is covered well in other parts of the program.

Key concepts are presented in Chapter 12. These include the differences among real and financial assets, the nature of commodities futures contracts, the convenience yield and the cost of carry. The discussion of commodity forward curves assumes familiarity with the various theories that explain the term structure of interest rates. Chapter 13 discusses the role of commodity futures in asset allocation and reviews the results of major studies in the area.

Chapter 14 discusses various methods of delivering long commodity exposure. Most direct commodity investments are made through derivatives contracts such as futures contracts, forward contracts, swaps, and options. Other methods of delivering long commodity exposure include indirect investments through companies involved in the production of commodities, commodity mutual funds and ETFs, long-biased hedge funds and private commodity partnerships. Chapter 15 describes methods of delivering commodity alpha which often involve trading commodities. The chapter provides an overview of these strategies and details the use of commodity futures and options spreads. Many of the strategies for generating returns in the commodities markets are standard hedge fund or managed futures strategies, and are covered extensively in other sections and parts of this book.

Chapter 16 reviews several commodity indexes, providing an overview for each as well as more details such as their launch date, roll periodicity, average maturity, allocation to energy, and performance. Chapter 17 discusses various commodity-linked investment vehicles and concludes with some final words on allocations to commodities.

CAIA Association 2009

12

Key Concepts in Commodity Market Analysis

The Bear a good contango loves,
The Bull a backwardation
Society (UK) September 3, 1880[1]

The study of commodity investments is complicated by the fact that commodities are fundamentally different from traditional securities. Most alternative investment strategies are natural extensions of traditional investments because they involve buying and selling financial securities. For example, hedge funds typically utilize publicly-traded stocks and bonds. Private equity strategies are closely related to public equity strategies. However, commodities are not securities, but simply materials used in the production of goods and services. This fundamental difference means that investment strategies that are effective when applied to traditional assets may not be effective when applied to commodities. The opposite is also true. Some strategies that seem to work well in commodity markets do not work efficiently in traditional markets. While some of this is due to differences in the way commodity and securities markets are organized, it is mostly due to the fundamental difference between securities and commodities.[2]

REAL ASSETS AND FINANCIAL ASSETS

Commodities are real assets. **Real assets** are sometimes called economic assets as they can be used or consumed. They are tangible assets with intrinsic value that offer a reasonable expectation of inflation protection. Real estate, factories, patents, certain types of real options, and human capital are examples of real assets. Economists distinguish between two types of real assets — durable and non-durable. **Durable assets** are employed in the production of wealth but are not consumed in the process. *Materials* are used during production and can be either durable or non-durable. For example, production of airplane travel uses durable assets (airplanes, airports) as well as non-durable assets that are used up in the production process (jet fuel, roasted peanuts, etc.). Many other inputs are also required for airplane travel, of course, including human capital (pilots, ground crews) and management of these assets by corporate executives.

Financial assets are claims on the income that is derived from the use of real assets. A financial asset may also have an ownership claim on the real assets themselves. For example, the stockholders of an airline company are entitled to share in the income generated by using real assets such as airplanes, jet fuel, and peanuts. If the airline company owns the airplanes, the stockholders will also share in the profits or losses when airplanes are sold.

---

[1] As quoted in the Oxford English Dictionary.

[2] The returns in commodity futures investing are due to highly nuanced factors. For background, see Till (2006) and Kazemi *et al.* (2007).

THE NATURE OF COMMODITY FUTURES CONTRACTS

While commodities themselves are real, tangible assets like crude oil, wheat, and gold trade in the derivatives markets in the form of futures contracts. A commodity futures contract, which is a contract for delivery of a commodity at some date in the future, is generally considered to be a real asset, particularly when collateralized. Continuing with the air travel example, an airline can sell tickets on a route, schedule the airplane, and purchase the fuel many months in advance of the flight. In this example, the fuel for the flight could be purchased today and stored until needed, or purchased in the futures market for delivery when needed. If purchased in the futures market the fuel is still a real asset because the airline is purchasing a tangible asset. The difference is that the airline will take physical possession of the fuel at some date in the future, rather than at the time of purchase.

Some argue that a commodity futures contract is more appropriately defined as a financial asset. This argument is based on the definition of a financial asset which holds that a financial asset is a contractual claim of ownership that derives its value from real assets. A commodity futures contract clearly satisfies this definition. While technically correct, this argument is not very useful because it requires defining ownership more strictly than in common business usage.[3] Further complicating this discussion is the fact that some commodity futures contracts are cash-settled. For example, the Chicago Mercantile Exchange (CME) Lean Hogs futures contract, which is cash-settled to a published index of hog prices, is an example of a futures contract that is based entirely on a financial instrument. While it is important to recognize that commodity futures contracts exhibit some properties of financial assets, they are predominantly real assets.

THE ROLE OF INVESTORS IN COMMODITY MARKETS

Investors in commodity markets have historically been called *speculators*. The term *speculation* is applied differently in commodity markets vis a vis the traditional financial markets, where it has negative connotations because it can be viewed as mercenary trading activity that causes market distortions that harm investors. Speculators in commodity markets play an important economic function because their investment adds liquidity to the market, which makes it easier for other participants to manage risk. This function of speculators is often compared to insurance, in that speculators are willing to accept risks that commercial firms would prefer not to bear. The following definitions of a *speculator* and of the quantity of a commodity held by a speculator (*speculative stocks*) come from one of the seminal articles on commodity markets entitled "Speculation and Economic Stability," which was published by economist Nicholas Kaldor in 1939.

> "*Speculation* . . . may be defined as the purchase (or sale) of goods with a view to re-sale (re-purchase) at a later date, where the motive behind such action is the expectation of a change in the relevant prices . . . and not a gain accruing through their use, or any kind of transformation effected in them or their transfer between different markets."

> "*Speculative stocks* of anything may be defined as the difference between the amount actually held and the amount that would be held, if other things being the same, the price of that thing were expected to remain unchanged." [Emphasis added]

---

[3] It is normal for accounting purposes to recognize purchases and sales of assets at the time the sale takes place rather than when delivery takes place. Similarly, ownership of a commodity is considered to be transferred when a commodity futures contract is purchased – even if the purchaser has no intent of taking delivery.

In Kaldor's view, there were only two types of positions: speculative trades and non-speculative trades. Speculators always speculate. Non-speculators buy or sell commodities for reasons that may include an expectation of profit from a change in price, but must include some other reason such as traditional, business-related activities like production, transportation, and warehousing. It may also apply to certain non-commercial investors in commodity markets. An investor who holds commodities for reasons other than price appreciation is not speculating. These reasons could include inflation hedging, currency hedging, and hedging against a change in other asset prices. The key, according to Kaldor, is to determine the quantity and variety of commodities an investor would hold "if the price of that thing were expected to be unchanged." That portion of an investor's commodity holdings would be deemed non-speculative. The remainder (positive or negative) would be considered speculative stocks.

Other seminal studies in this area include articles by Holbrook Working (1949) and Paul Cootner (1960). They take an approach slightly different from Kaldor's, defining hedging as any futures activity conducted by those who handle the physical commodity, and speculative trading as any activity that is not hedging. The difference between these approaches is subtle, but important. While both definitions would reach the same conclusion about the vast majority of hedging and speculative positions, there are some noteworthy exceptions. For example, an investment bank that enters into over-the-counter commodity index swaps and then uses the futures market to hedge these positions is considered a hedger under the Cootner definition, since the bank has access to the physical markets. However, the risk is ultimately held by the swap counterparty, who may be a speculator. These positions would be considered speculative under the Kaldor definition, since the motivation for the positions is a change in the price of the commodity. Another example is a pension fund that uses commodity investments to hedge inflation or to hedge against a decline in equity markets. Cootner would consider these positions to be speculative, because the investor does not handle the physical commodities. Kaldor would define this as a hedge, since the reasons for the positions will be evaluated using factors other than the price of the commodities.

CONVENIENCE YIELD

All real assets have a **convenience yield**, which is the benefit that comes from physical possession of an asset. It is literally a measure of the convenience of having the asset available to use. Alternatively, it is a measure of how much a buyer would pay to avoid the inconvenience of constantly ordering new quantities of the asset and worrying that the supply of the asset will not arrive when needed. It is an economic benefit, not a monetary benefit. Continuing the airline example, the convenience yield of having sufficient fuel for an airplane is quite high if the airline has routes that need to be flown. If the airline has more airplanes than it needs given travel demand (as in October 2001, for example), the convenience yield of available fuel for an additional airplane is quite low, or possibly almost zero.[4] However, if the number of airplanes held by an airline is equal to traveler demand, the convenience yield for materials such as jet fuel is quite high since the production of air travel is impossible without it.

Measuring the convenience yield of a real asset is difficult because it differs for every user and may be different for the same user from one day to the next. Alternatively, what can be measured using market prices is the *marginal* convenience yield, which is the lowest convenience yield that will match buyers with sellers. Buyers who have a higher convenience yield will earn a

---

[4] Common practice is to require that the convenience yield be non-negative except for assets such as nuclear waste that have negative market price and are not easily disposed. The cost associated with maintaining and storing a surplus airplane is accounted for under carrying costs, not as part of the convenience yield.

consumer surplus. A consumer surplus is the difference between the highest price a buyer would be willing to pay (his reservation price) and the actual market price. If the price is lower than the reservation price, the buyer earns a surplus. Because we cannot observe the reservation price of each buyer, we cannot measure the total amount of convenience yield that is earned.

The convenience yield of a commodity is often compared to the dividend stream paid by a stock, because in both cases there is a return that is paid to the owner of the asset which is not paid to owners of derivatives based on the asset. Owners of equity futures contracts or stock options do not receive cash dividends. Similarly, owners of commodity futures contracts do not receive the convenience yield. Owners of stock options and equity futures contracts can earn implicit dividends, since the size and frequency of stock dividends is captured by derivatives pricing models. Similarly, owners of commodity futures contracts implicitly earn a portion of the commodity's marginal convenience yield, because the marginal convenience yield is incorporated into commodity futures pricing equations. However, comparing a convenience yield to a dividend yield overlooks some important differences between commodities and equities. Most significant is that convenience yield is unique to the user of the asset, while dividend yield is the same for all holders of a share of stock.

COST OF CARRY

The **cost of carry** is equivalent to the cost of storing a commodity. The major components of the cost of carry include:

- *Financing costs*. The standard assumption is that storage is fully financed, and that the financing cost is the cost of capital the firm applies to working capital.
- *Storage costs*. Rental of storage facilities, insurance, inspections, transportation costs, maintenance costs (e.g. cattle feed).
- *Spoilage*. The loss of value that may naturally occur through storage.

In Table 12.1, if the commodity is needed three months in the future, in theory the buyer would be indifferent between paying $4.25 today and also paying $0.31525 in storage costs or paying a futures price of $4.5625 for delivery in three months' time. For these calculations, we ignore commissions and transaction costs.

Table 12.1   Cost of carry

Cost of carry = Financing cost + Storage cost + Spoilage cost

Cost of carry example		Monthly carry cost
Spot price/bushel	4.25	
Storage costs/month	0.0300	0.03000
Insurance/month	0.0150	0.01500
Spoilage rate/month	0.50%	0.02125
Financing rate/month	0.60%	0.02550
Total monthly cost/bushel		0.09175
Transport to/from storage	0.020	
Total storage costs for 3 months		0.27525
Transportation cost (round trip)		0.04000
Total cost of carry		0.31525
Break-even futures price (spot + carry)		4.56525

If the futures price were higher than $4.5625 then the buyer could profit by purchasing more of the commodity than needed and simultaneously selling the additional quantity in the futures market. This trade is known as **cash-and-carry arbitrage**.

If the futures price is below $4.5625, then the buyer may choose to use the futures market for delivery or may choose to purchase the commodity today. The choice will depend on the buyer's convenience yield. If the buyer's convenience yield is 0.10/month, then the breakeven futures price would be $4.2625 (the spot price plus storage costs minus convenience yield).

As with the convenience yield, the cost of carry for a commodity varies from user to user. The cost of carry also depends on seasonal factors and on the amount of the commodity in storage at a particular time. For example, when crude oil stocks are low, the cost of storage is relatively low, since there is ample capacity in storage facilities. Conversely, when stocks are high, the cost of storing increases as storage capacity is in scarce supply.

THEORIES OF COMMODITY FORWARD CURVES

The price of a commodity for delivery in the future can be higher or lower than the price of that commodity for immediate delivery. When the price for delivery in the future (the *future price*) is higher than the price for immediate delivery (the *spot price*), we say that the **forward curve** is *upward sloping*. This is also termed **contango**.[5] When the future price is below the spot price, we say the forward curve is *downward sloping*, or in **backwardation**.

The theories for why commodity forward curves slope up or down are similar to theories that try to explain why yield curves slope up or down. In the context of commodity markets, non-speculative or commercial accounts are typically segregated into *producers* and *users* of the commodity. In fixed-income markets, we can think of borrowers as *producers* of bonds, and lenders as *users* of bonds. To expand on this analogy, borrowers typically have a preferred maturity date in mind when issuing bonds, but are willing to shorten or extend that maturity date if market conditions dictate. Also, a borrower may increase the quantity of bonds issued if the price is attractive. Similarly, buyers of bonds (lenders) typically consider the prices of bonds with differing maturities when making decisions.

Borrowers and lenders also make hedging decisions. A borrower can decide to lock in the interest rate today for a project that will be funded in the future. Alternatively, the borrower can wait until the project begins to issue bonds. These decisions are similar to a commodity producer's decision to sell future production in the forward market or to wait and sell the commodity at the future spot price. The literature on commodity forward curves and yield curves has tended to use different terminology, but both are ultimately trying to explain the interaction between producers, users, and speculators in establishing forward prices.

Rational expectations

The **Rational Expectations Hypothesis** holds that the price of an asset for delivery in the future must be the same as the market's current forecast of the spot price of the asset on the future delivery date.[6]

---

[5] This awkward term is 19th-century British equity trading jargon for a fee that was paid by the buyer of shares to the seller on the settlement date in order to defer payment for the shares until some future date – a trade similar to today's repurchase agreement. It is assumed to be derived from the word "continuation." On some occasions, either because of a large short interest that was being rolled or due to dividend payments, the contango fees would be negative, or backwards, which gives us the equally awkward term "backwardation."

[6] Rational expectations models have been explored by a number of researchers across many fields, including fixed income and commodity pricing. Hicks (1939) is commonly credited with applying these concepts to forward commodity prices,

For example, assume that a survey of participants in the copper market (appropriately weighted for the relative impact of each on the overall market) found that the price in one year was expected to fall by 5%. The rational expectations model would predict that the price for delivery of copper in one year would be 5% below the current spot price. Any other price would violate the hypothesis.

Rational expectations models hold up well in laboratory settings – perfect markets with no transactions costs, taxes, or borrowing constraints and markets in which some portion of the traders are risk-neutral. Rational expectations models have not proven to be a useful method for explaining commodity forward curves. This does not mean that commodity markets are irrational, but merely that the assumptions about perfect markets and risk neutrality are too strong for these markets.

The mechanism that drives rational expectations models is *relative value arbitrage*. Speculators who identify prices on the forward curve that deviate from their expected value can either purchase or sell those commodities outright or enter into spread trades by purchasing the commodity at one point on the curve and selling at another.

Normal backwardation/preferred habitat

The economist John Maynard Keynes argued in 1930 that commodity futures prices should typically be lower than the rational expectations prices defined in the previous section. Keynes defined **normal backwardation**[7] as the tendency of commodity futures contracts to trade at prices below the rational expectations price.

This argument was based on the assumption that producers of a commodity have a strong incentive to lock in a price today for future production by selling futures contracts, but that users of the commodity have a strong incentive to purchase at spot prices. If there is a natural oversupply of futures contracts, then speculators will enter the market to purchase the excess supply – but only at a discount. Alternatively, discounts for future delivery may entice more users to lock in the price.

The economic rationale for this theory is that producers of a commodity have predictable production costs, so locking in a future price for their goods is equivalent to locking in a profit margin. Users, on the other hand, prefer the flexibility offered by the spot market.[8] In the fixed-income world, this argument is similar to the **Preferred Habitat Hypothesis**. This hypothesis holds that producers of bonds (borrowers) prefer long maturities while consumers of bonds (lenders) prefer short maturities. Producers offer attractive yields, which would mean low bond prices, to entice borrowers to extend their maturity, or to induce speculators to borrow at short maturities and lend at long maturities.[9]

Storage models

The relationship between spot and forward prices for a commodity depends to a large degree on the relationship between current storage levels and expected storage levels in the future. Storage

---

although according to Evans and Honkapohja (2001) the phrase "rational expectations" was first used in a 1946 article by Hurwicz.

[7] *Normal backwardation* and *backwardation* are similar but not identical terms. A market is in *backwardation* if the futures price is lower than the spot price. A market is in *normal backwardation* if the futures price is lower than the expected spot price. Since the expected spot price cannot be observed, we can never know if a market is in normal backwardation.

[8] This theory is more applicable in markets where costs are easily passed along to final consumers. For example, the owner of a gasoline station has no incentive to lock in the wholesale price of gasoline six months forward, since any price increase is easily passed along to customers. An airline, on the other hand, has a stronger incentive to lock in the cost of jet fuel since fuel costs are difficult to pass along to buyers of airplane travel.

[9] An upward sloping yield curve is the same as a downward sloping forward curve for bond prices.

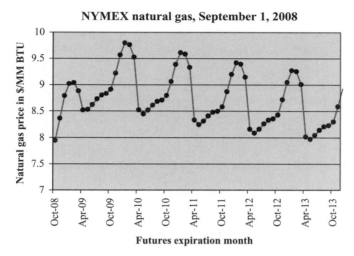

Figure 12.1 Forward curve for natural gas illustrates the storage effect

models also consider the cost and feasibility of storing a commodity for an extended period of time and of transporting it to other locations for delivery. Commodities which can be either expensive or difficult to store, such as natural gas and live cattle, can have forward curves with steep positive or negative slopes. This is because relative value arbitrage trades can be very difficult to hedge with physical positions. In the case of natural gas (see Figure 12.1), storage is feasible but becomes quite expensive as physical storage capacity limits are approached. Inadequate storage capacity for peak winter demand results in exceptionally steep positively sloped forward curves during the fall–winter period in the natural gas futures curve (Till, 2008a). In comparison, live cattle are arguably non-storable. The animal degrades after getting to market weight, resulting in a historical tendency for backwardation (Helmuth, 1981).

Storage models of a commodity forward curve predict that the curve will be upward-sloping when the current inventory levels are beyond the threshold levels of demand and that it will be downward-sloping when inventories are tight. Storage models are unique to real assets and do not have a corresponding model in fixed income because storage and transportation of bonds is effectively free.[10]

Another factor incorporated into storage models is the risk of **stock-out**. Stock-out occurs when storage drops effectively to zero, and consumption is dependent entirely on production and transportation networks. The risk of a stock-out typically occurs in markets with peak seasonal demand such as natural gas or heating oil, or annual crop cycles such as grains. To avoid stock-out, users of a commodity have an incentive to hedge more actively at points on the forward calendar that are most susceptible to stock-out. These would be the months just before harvest for annual crops, and the later part of the heating season for natural gas and heating oil.

Other models and special cases

In certain markets, the users of a commodity rarely use the forward market to hedge future supplies. These particular markets typically are for products that are directly consumed by the public, such as

---

[10] The cost of financing a position is a component of both storage models and fixed income models, but that is not generally considered a storage cost. Storage costs for bonds would consist of custody services.

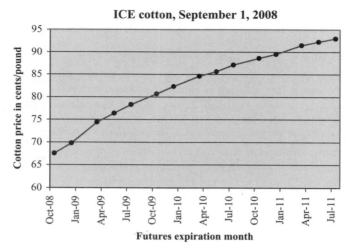

Figure 12.2   Upward sloping commodity curve (normal contango)

gasoline. This phenomenon is explained by the **Liquidity Preference Hypothesis**. It is an extreme case of the Preferred Habitat Hypothesis, in which there is an insufficient commercial long position in the futures markets and any long positions are owned by speculators.

Another special case is a **segmented market**. Segmented markets are markets for the same product that, due to geography or other market frictions, operate relatively independently of each other, and consequently the price of the product in one market does not influence the price in the other.[11] A market can be segregated across *time* as well. For example, the spot market for a product may be dominated by one set of buyers and sellers and the market for delivery in the future dominated by a different set of buyers and sellers. When this happens, the forward curve for the commodity provides little useful information, as spot market players ignore what is happening in the futures market, and vice versa.[12]

In certain markets the users of the commodity have a stronger need to hedge than the producers. This is the opposite of normal backwardation, where it was assumed that the producer had the strongest incentive to hedge. When this occurs, the forward curve would be upward-sloping, as users of the commodity would need to entice sellers to sell the commodity in the forward market rather than the spot market. Keynes (1930) called this **normal contango.** The natural gas market in the U.S. may exhibit this property. Utilities are believed to purchase more natural gas in the forward market than they are likely to need, in order to plan for spikes in demand. When this demand does not materialize, the utilities sell the surplus gas in the spot market. This results in an upward sloping curve. The cotton market was in contango in September 2008 (Figure 12.2).

The crude oil futures curve can often be humped, which means the market is in normal contango in the short term but gives way to inverted markets for longer maturity contracts (see Figure 12.3).

Option-based models of the term structure focus on two types of real options embedded in commodity markets. The first is the option to extract a natural resource. A copper mine can be shut

---

[11] Good examples of this are the natural gas markets in North America and in Europe. Because the cost of shipping liquefied natural gas (LNG) from Europe to America is high, the markets are effectively segregated. Markets for water are typically segregated across much smaller geographical regions.

[12] There is reasonable empirical evidence that the long-term market for crude oil (beyond 18 months) is segmented from shorter-term delivery. See Lautier (2005) for a discussion of this research.

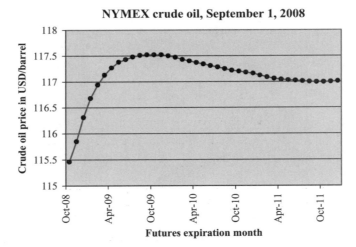

Figure 12.3   A humped forward curve

down if the price of copper falls below the marginal cost of production. While there may be times when the spot price of copper falls below its marginal cost of production due to a temporary glut, producers will not sell forward production below cost – they will shut down the mine. The option to extract the resource dampens the volatility of commodity prices for future delivery.

The second real option embedded in the commodity forward curve is related to inventories. Commodity markets generally have higher volatility when prices are rising than when they are falling. This is because shortages tend to cause more problems than surpluses. The volatility asymmetry favors owning physical inventory (or short-dated futures contracts) over longer-dated futures contracts. All things equal, this factor will tend to make commodity forward curves slope down.

13

Role of Commodities in Asset Allocation

REVIEW OF MAJOR ARTICLES AND STUDIES

It was not until the 1970s that academic studies appeared highlighting the positive role commodities could play in institutional investor allocation (Schneeweis, 2006). A steady evolution of research and commodity index development, accompanied by results that went beyond pro forma, indicated that commodity investment was not only a good buffer for inflation, but could also provide a profitable source of returns on its own. In addition and of equal importance, it was later demonstrated that adding commodities to a portfolio helped mitigate risk (Till, 2007a).

In a seminal article published in the *Journal of Portfolio Management* in 1978, Robert Greer tackled the issue of perceived risk in commodity futures. He showed that risk in a commodity position could be lowered significantly by its full collateralization. Using a dataset from 1960 to 1974, Greer calculated the returns of an unleveraged, collateralized commodity futures program, including the collateral returns. He showed that such an index had higher returns and a lower maximum drawdown than an index of equities. Greer also pioneered efforts to demonstrate the benefit of diversifying an equities-only portfolio with the addition of commodity futures, by showing that a rebalanced portfolio of stocks and commodities would have provided a steadier and higher rate of return than a stock-only portfolio (Greer, 1978).

Moving forward in time, Zvi Bodie and Victor Rosansky in 1980 echoed Greer's 1978 findings by showing that an equally weighted basket of commodity futures (constructed using 1950–1976 data) produced equity-like returns, as long as collateral returns were included. Of equal importance, the mean of the annual loss on their portfolio was also significantly lower than if it held only equities.

The Goldman Sachs Commodity Index (GSCI) was launched 10 years later, on the heels of research published by David Walton in 1991. The GSCI is a production-weighted index largely comprised of commodity futures that historically had downward-sloping forward curves. Walton showed that commodity futures with downward-sloping forward curves are generally markets whose products have smaller stocks and are thus more prone to supply disruptions, leading to a frequent premium in the spot market for physical possession (Walton, 1991).

Sudhakar Satyanarayan and Panos Varangis (1994) of the World Bank brought to the fore the issue of portfolio diversification with commodities and its impact on the portfolio's risk-return ratio, or efficient frontier. Specifically, they researched how the efficient frontier changed if commodities were added to international portfolios. Using the GSCI as a proxy for commodity investments, they found that adding commodities to a portfolio of global stock and bond indices provided the same level of return with less risk. In 1995, Kenneth Froot showed that a commodity index needs to be oil-dominated in order to reduce the risk of bond and equity investments (Froot, 1995). A decade later, Thomas Idzorek published a study for Ibbotson that showed that the efficient frontier for a diversified portfolio would have been improved with commodity futures contracts (Idzorek, 2006).

The benefits to commodity investment were broken down further by Mark J.P. Anson, who published an article in 1998 that examined the component parts of commodity futures investment return: the spot return, roll yield (as defined later), and collateral return. Examining data that spanned 1985–1997, Anson showed that the spot return provided a diversification benefit, while the roll yield and collateral return were responsible for the bulk of a commodity investment's total return (Anson, 1998).

The potential role of commodity investment in institutional portfolios was further clarified by Jelle Beenen, who in 2005 published a study that showed that commodities could assist in an institution's pursuit of matching future asset returns with its expected liabilities. His study resulted in meaningful allocations to commodities, given their diversification and risk reduction potential when combined with other holdings in a pension plan (Beene, 2005). The diversification potential of commodity investment was further explored by Gary Gorton and Geert Rouwenhorst in an article in 2006 that showed that an equally weighted index of commodity futures was negatively correlated with equity and bond returns, but positively correlated with inflation. All of these correlations were found to be most pronounced at five-year holding periods. Gorton and Rouwenhorst also found that the commodities index had about the same return and Sharpe ratio as U.S. equities (Gorton and Rouwenhorst, 2006).

Erb and Harvey (2006) took a look at rebalancing (an action that brings portfolio's allocations back into line with target allocations), by examining the returns of 16 commodity futures contracts from 1982 to 2004. They found that when correlations are low and asset variances are high, the diversification return from rebalancing can be high. The return from rebalancing (sometimes called **diversification return**) is not unique to commodities. The term was first coined by Booth and Fama (1992), and has been studied for equities, bonds, emerging markets, and multi-asset class portfolios. Commodities seem particularly well suited for this type of return for two reasons. Diversification returns are highest when the individual assets in a portfolio are highly volatile and the correlation among those assets is low. Frequently rebalancing a portfolio of these assets will result in higher geometric growth rates (as compared to infrequently rebalancing). Historically, commodities have satisfied these criteria. To understand the effects of diversification on geometric (i.e. compounded) returns on a portfolio of commodities, consider the approximate relationship between arithmetic return and geometric return. The two figures are calculated as

$$R_A = \frac{1}{T}(r_1 + r_2 + \ldots + r_T)$$

$$R_G = \sqrt[T]{(1+r_1)(1+r_2)\ldots(1+r_T)} - 1$$

Here, R_A is the arithmetic mean return of the portfolio, R_G is the geometric mean return of the portfolio, and r_i is the annual rate of return on the portfolio for year i. In this case there are T observations (years). There is an approximate relationship between these two estimates, expressed as

$$R_G = R_A - \frac{1}{2}Var$$

The annual volatility of the return on the portfolio is denoted by Var. Notice that the arithmetic average return of a portfolio will be equal to the average of the arithmetic averages of returns on N individual commodities futures. That is,

$$R_A = \sum_{j=1}^{N} weight_i \times R_{A,j}$$

Here, $R_{A,j}$ is the arithmetic mean return on commodity j. Therefore, given the arithmetic mean returns on individual commodities, the geometric mean return of the portfolio will be higher the lower the volatility of the portfolio. It is well known that the volatility of the portfolio will be low if the commodities included in the portfolio are not highly correlated with each other. Further, if the individual commodities are not highly correlated, the geometric mean return of the portfolio will be significantly higher than the average of the geometric means of the individual commodities. The reason is that the volatility of the portfolio will be smaller than the average of the volatility of individual commodities. In fact, a study by Erb and Harvey (2006) shows that although the geometric means of individual commodities are historically close to zero, the historical geometric mean of a rebalanced portfolio of commodities is significantly greater than zero.

Frequent rebalancing (reducing the weight of commodities that have increased in value, and increasing the allocation to commodities that declined in value) will also provide better returns if asset values exhibit mean reversion. Several studies of rebalancing in commodity markets have concluded that the optimal rebalancing window is once every twelve to eighteen months, which is consistent with the hypothesis that commodities exhibit long-run mean reversion.[1]

Gorton, Hayashi, and Rouwenhorst (2007) found that commodity futures risk premiums vary across commodities and over time. They found that a major determinant of the risk premium is the amount of a given commodity held in storage. Using a comprehensive dataset on 31 commodity futures and physical inventories between 1969 and 2006, they showed that price measures, such as the futures basis, prior futures returns, and spot returns, reflect the state of inventories and provide useful information about commodity futures risk premiums.

SOURCES OF RETURN TO COMMODITY INVESTMENT

Spot, collateral income, and roll

Returns on commodity futures contracts stem from three sources: a **spot return**, a risk-free **income return**, and a **roll return**. Spot prices increase over time, although historically they have remained below inflation (Burkart, 2006). Spot returns result from changes in the value of the underlying cash commodity and are generally driven by classic market factors like fluctuations in supply and demand for that asset. These factors can be the result of weather patterns or crop sizes for agricultural commodities; seasonal issues like weather or driving patterns for energy; and growth in real demand for base metals. Anson (1998) points out that periods of financial and economic distress can lead to market conditions that are often favorable for spot commodity prices. Because spot commodity prices tend to mean-revert over longer time horizons, spot prices cannot usually be positive sources of return over longer periods (Till, 2006).

The income return of a commodity investment results from the return of the cash collateral, which is usually a Treasury Bill rate in the U.S., although the cash collateral can also be in other forms like TIPS, money market securities, and other liquid assets. As indicated above, most commodity trading programs include a collateral feature.

Because commodity investors generally are not in the market to take ownership of the actual physical commodity they are trading, a futures position needs to be closed out or rolled prior to expiration. Rolling involves selling a futures contract that is close to expiration and opening a new position in a contract that expires at a later date. The difference between the prices of these two futures contracts is called the **roll return**. If the forward curve for the commodity slopes down, the investor will sell a contract with a higher price than the one being purchased in the "roll," so the roll return will be positive. If the forward curve slopes up, then the roll return will be negative (Burkart, 2006).

---

[1] Rebalancing returns has been analyzed and discussed by Greer (2000), Gorton and Rouwenhorst (2006), and Till (2006).

Scarcity

Scarcity in commodity markets can provide a source of return to commodity investors, but the difficulty can be in determining when this market pattern is occurring. Using the forward curve, relative price differences of futures contracts across delivery months can be measured. If the forward curve is downward-sloping, meaning spot prices are higher than those in the future, this price pattern can indicate scarcity, as a premium is being offered for the immediately deliverable commodity. This price pattern may also indicate that there is not an excess of commodity inventories (Till and Eagleeye, 2005).

THE STATISTICAL PROPERTIES OF COMMODITY PRICES

The historical performance of commodity investments can provide useful information for forecasting future returns, volatility, and correlations with other asset classes. However, the recent transformation of many commodity markets from purely commercial markets into markets with a significant investor presence leads to concerns that the historical track record may be of questionable value in projecting future returns.

The first question researchers ask is whether the long-run return to commodity investments has been positive or negative. Evidence is inconclusive. While commodity prices have trended higher over the past century in nominal terms, the inflation-adjusted prices of many commodities have actually declined. There is conflicting empirical evidence on the existence of a long-term positive return in commodity prices. Cuddington (1992) found little evidence to support the view that prices of primary commodities were on a declining path over the long term. Evidence also fails to support a long-term positive drift in commodity prices. Cashin and McDermott suggest that such evidence of a low long-term expected return may be of little significance since it is dominated by the variability of prices (Cashin and McDermott, 2002; Cashin, McDermott and Scott, 1999). Another complication arises from currency effects. While most research focuses on performance measured in U.S. dollars, investors who measure performance in different currencies may observe either a long-run positive drift or a negative drift, based on the historical performance of the home currency exchange rate (Black, 2008; Till, 2008b).

Difficulty in measuring a long-run return is not unique to commodity markets. Commodity investment, like most alternative investment strategies including hedge funds, managed futures, and private equity, has a relatively short history of clearly defined performance. For example, crude oil futures were first listed on a futures exchange in 1983. Data for energy markets prior to 1983 have been assembled by researchers from over-the-counter sources and from spot market transactions.

Over the past century there have been long periods of rising commodity prices in real terms and also extended periods of declines. Commodity prices have risen, in real terms, over the past two decades, but questions about the very long-term performance remain inconclusive.[2]

Another important question is what factors influence performance. Williams and Wright (1991) studied the implications of storage on the time series of commodity prices. They find that the time series of spot prices for major commodities have two features in common: (1) considerable positive autocorrelation, and (2) spikes in prices. Williams and Wright point out that both the autoregressive structure of commodity time series and the excess skewness and kurtosis are the natural result of storage.

Another area of research on momentum in commodity markets relates to the persistence of volatility shocks. Research finds strong evidence of the volatility of commodity futures over time

---

[2] For additional arguments see Heap (2005) and Till and Gunzberg (2005).

(Elder and Jin, 2007; Baillie *et al.*, 2007). There is both theoretical and empirical evidence of a positive relationship between volatility and convenience yield. An important part of the convenience yield is the risk premium. All things equal, an increase in commodity price volatility will cause the risk premium to increase. The risk premium can be positive or negative. During periods of positive risk premium, a volatility shock will cause the risk premium and convenience yield to rise. In periods of negative risk premium, the risk premium and convenience yield would be expected to decline. So, to the degree that spikes in volatility exist and persist over time, and that such spikes in volatility are consistent with the existence of convenience yield, strategies such as momentum models that are positively related to volatility may capture excess returns.

Finally, many active managers in commodity markets employ momentum strategies. The profitability of momentum-based trading rules has been examined for a number of commodity futures markets (Schneeweis *et al.*, 2008). Empirical research on momentum models to test for weak-form efficiency in commodity markets dates back several years. A series of articles published more than 30 years ago found evidence of pricing patterns that differed from simple random walks.[3] However, they did not address the theoretical or behavioral causes for the existence of such pricing patterns. In commodity markets, the structural friction that may lead to momentum profits is frequently linked to problems associated with storing and transporting commodities.

Given the importance of storage in many commodities, it is not surprising that recent empirical research (Gorton *et al.*, 2007) has concluded that profitability of momentum and backwardation strategies is related to storage in particular commodities. Storage is not the only basis for momentum in commodity futures. Similar to the source of pricing patterns in other futures markets, government intervention, macroeconomic shocks, and differing risk appetites among investors may all lead to commodity prices following various pricing patterns.

In summary, the historical track record for commodity markets is inconclusive on the question of whether the long-run risk premium has been positive, although it has been positive in recent decades. There is evidence that commodity prices exhibit short-term autocorrelation. There is also evidence of price shocks, which lead to excess kurtosis in commodity returns. There is considerable evidence that volatility in commodity markets varies over time. Researchers have also rejected the hypothesis that commodity markets are weak-form efficient, as simple trading rules based on storage or momentum have been shown to deliver excess returns after adjusting for transactions costs.

---

[3] For example, see Cargill and Rausser (1975), Leuthold (1972), and Peterson and Leuthold (1982).

14

Methods of Delivering Long Commodity Exposure

DIRECT PHYSICAL OWNERSHIP OF COMMODITIES

Most investors avoid holding physical commodities because storage can be cumbersome and expensive. For example, barrels of oil would require a storage tank, as well as transportation from the purchase site. In short, real assets such as commodities require a degree of active management in order to maintain their value. As a result, most direct commodity investments are made through derivatives contracts such as futures contracts, forward contracts, swaps, and options. This allows the owner to benefit from price changes in the commodity without the need to store it. Precious metals, particularly gold, are exceptions to this. Gold investors have historically held physical gold rather than gold derivatives.

INDIRECT OWNERSHIP

Another method of obtaining commodity exposure is through **indirect commodity investments**. Most investors actually have this type of exposure embedded in their traditional investment portfolios. These are investments in companies that are involved in the production, transportation, and marketing of commodities. Some of these investments have returns that are highly correlated with specific commodities, while others do not. For example, the returns of integrated oil companies (like Exxon) and mining companies are highly correlated with the price of crude oil, but the returns of food companies such as Kraft Foods typically have only a modest correlation with the prices of grains and livestock.

Indirect commodity investments derive at least some of their returns from the active management of commodities. Investing in stocks or bonds issued by commodity producers is the most common indirect strategy, though there are many others. Many of these other strategies involve purchasing commodities or commodity futures contracts using active management to deliver both exposures to the underlying commodities as well as trading profits.

Commodity mutual funds and exchange traded funds

Another way to gain exposure to commodities is through a commodity mutual fund. Mutual funds and exchange traded funds (ETFs) mirror the performance of direct investment in various commodity indices. Commodity mutual funds can include commodity indices, equities of commodities-based companies, or actual commodity futures (Schneeweis, 2006). While these funds provide exposure to the commodities markets, they have fees and cost structures in line with mutual funds in general (Burkart, 2006). Commodity-based exchange-traded funds are another method of indirect ownership of commodities. ETFs are listed on an exchange, but are index-linked rather than actively managed.

Long-biased hedge funds

Hedge funds are active players in the commodity markets. Before 2000, commodity hedge funds and managed futures funds were primarily focused on absolute return and relative value strategies. However, in response to the rise in institutional investment in commodities, a number of firms have launched long-biased commodity hedge funds or managed futures programs.

There are two categories of long-biased funds. The first group is similar to long-only equity funds. Funds in this group look to identify undervalued commodities to purchase and hold in unhedged portfolios. These funds have been successful in attracting assets that would otherwise be placed in commodity index funds. Active managers may be able to avoid unfavorable rolls and to overweight or underweight commodities based on fundamental or systematic strategies. The fund managers are typically benchmarked to a particular index with compensation schemes tied to their performance relative to its benchmark. For the most part, these managers hold futures contracts rather than physical commodities. Lockups are short, and liquidity and transparency high.

The second group of long-biased funds is involved in the physical markets. These funds are engaged in the purchase, storage, and transportation of commodities. Because they limit their use of hedging, their returns are influenced by the direction of commodity prices. These managers tend to specialize in particular commodities or commodity sectors. Investors in these funds are seeking returns generated through a combination of active management (alpha) and commodity beta. Investments with these managers are fairly illiquid, often requiring long notice periods prior to redemptions. Competitors include trading companies, shipping firms, and the commodity trading desks of major financial firms.

Private commodity partnerships

Private commodity partnerships offer long-term ownership of real assets used in mining and energy markets. Commodity partnerships are similar to real estate investment trusts (or REITs). Whereas REITs typically own buildings, commodity partnerships might own the extraction rights to a natural gas field, a pipeline, rail cars, storage facilities, or refining operations related to natural resource extraction.

Partnerships are organized as pass-through entities. The income from ownership of the assets is distributed to the partners, typically without taxation at the corporate level. Income can be in the form of rental income, for example if the partnership owns a pipeline, or from the sale of commodities such as crude oil or natural gas. In either case, the income paid by the partnership is usually correlated with the price of some commodity, so investors see partnerships as a substitute for direct commodity investments.

The partnership market has expanded rapidly since 2000. For example, as reported by Alerian Capital Management, the market capitalization of the Alerian Master Limited Partnership index increased from $15.7 billion at the end of 2000 to $80.6 billion at the end of 2008. Demand for all commodity-linked investments has increased, which explains much of the growth. However, other factors are also at play. Infrastructure and other real asset investments have become an important strategic part of institutional portfolios. The long duration of partnership investments is attractive to pension funds. Another factor in the growth of commodity partnerships is the public listing of partnership units. Like REITs, commodity partnerships can be listed on public exchanges if they adhere to regulations governing payout ratios and make appropriate filings with the SEC. This has greatly increased the liquidity and transparency of partnerships and expanded the potential investor base. As with REITs, the principal advantage of the Master Limited Partnership (MLP) structure is in avoiding corporate taxation. Income from qualifying MLPs is distributed directly to investors.

Commodity trade financing and production financing

Financing the production, storage, and transportation of commodities has historically been provided by merchant banks and by vertically integrated commodity firms. A number of private investment pools have been organized to compete in the high-margin segments of this business.

The strategy can be executed in a number of ways. Most commonly, investment funds will provide financing for the extraction or shipping of bulk commodities, with the commodities pledged as collateral for the loans. Other strategies involve purchasing commodities for future delivery directly from the producers. In effect, the producers are borrowing money that will be repaid with commodities. This provides working capital to the producers and an effective hedge against a decline in the price of the commodity. For the investment funds, these transactions typically have higher margins than are available simply by purchasing commodity futures, as they are custom transactions and frequently involve both default and political risk. Many commodity producers are located in parts of the globe with elevated political risk. While a commodity futures contract is settled daily and guaranteed by the futures exchange, purchasing commodities for future delivery from many producers carries considerable risk. These risks, and the resulting profits, have traditionally gone to multinational banks and other financial intermediaries. As the financial system has become more risk-averse, the opportunities for disintermediation by investment funds have grown.

Public commodity-based equities

Owning the securities of a firm that derives a significant part of its revenue from the sale of physical commodities is another way of gaining exposure to commodities. The disadvantage of this is that it provides the investor with significant stock market exposure. In addition to the underlying commodity risk associated with direct investment in a given commodity, an investor who takes a position in the equity securities of companies engaged in the sale of physical commodities is also subjected to the company's underlying business risk (Schneeweis, 2006).

According to the widely-read 2006 article "Facts and Fantasies About Commodity Futures" by Gary Gorton and Geert Rouwenhorst, an index of equities of companies involved in producing commodities had about the same long-run return as an index of commodity futures contracts. The study also showed that the volatility of the commodity futures index was lower than that of the commodity equity portfolio, and that the commodity index correlation with the S&P 500 was lower than that of the commodity equity portfolio. Their conclusion is that commodity company stocks behave more like equities than like commodity futures and thus, in terms of performance, are not a good proxy for an investment in commodity futures (Gorton and Rouwenhorst, 2006).

Bonds issued by commodity firms

Similarly, investors can gain exposure to commodities through owning bonds issued by firms that derive a significant part of their revenue from the sale of commodities. However, if these are high-grade bonds, the yield on these bonds generally has only a small exposure to the commodity market in which the company is involved. Specifically, the risk of holding the bond will not fluctuate with the value of the commodities that provide the basis of the firm's revenue. In contrast, for high-yield bonds, where the default or political risk is high, the price of the bonds will tend to be more highly correlated with the commodity being produced by the firm.

15

Methods of Delivering Commodity Alpha

Commodity markets offer numerous potential opportunities to generate profits. Most of these involve trading commodities or trading the stock of companies that are involved with commodities. This chapter provides an overview of these strategies. Many are standard hedge fund or managed futures strategies and are covered extensively in other sections of this book.

Commodity trading strategies can be separated into two broad groups: directional and relative value. Directional strategies take outright positions based on a forecast of market direction. Relative value strategies attempt to identify mispriced assets or securities and to hedge away some or all of the market exposure.

DIRECTIONAL STRATEGIES

Directional strategies are strategies that express a view on market direction, resulting in either long or short positions. They can utilize listed commodity futures and options as well as over-the-counter (OTC) derivatives such as forward contracts or swaps. Some strategies also involve holding physical commodities, though this is much less common.

Fundamental directional strategies are based on an analysis of supply and demand factors for commodities or commodity sectors. They can be based on macroeconomic factors such as economic growth, interest rate forecasts, and currencies, or on industry-specific factors such as the number of cattle in feed lots.

Quantitative directional strategies use technical or quantitative models to identify overpriced and underpriced commodities. These strategies are similar to managed futures strategies discussed in other sections of this book.

RELATIVE VALUE STRATEGIES

Relative value strategies in commodity markets are best understood as businesses rather than as trading strategies. Relative value managers combine investment capital with expertise in a particular sector to provide economic value-added. They generally compete for profits with vertically integrated commodity firms, merchant banks, shipping companies, and trading firms.

Relative value strategies in commodities can be executed across three risk dimensions: *location, correlation,* and *time*. The same commodity can have different prices at different locations in the world. The prices of two similar commodities can diverge from historical norms. The price of the same commodity can be different based on when the commodity is scheduled to be delivered. For example, consider a spread trade that is long crude oil for delivery in October in the UK and short heating oil for delivery in December in the U.S. This trade has three risk dimensions: location, correlation, and time.

In contrast, relative value strategies in equity and fixed income markets are generally limited to a single dimension: correlation. A share of stock, when expressed in the same currency, sells at essentially the same price everywhere in the world, so there is no location dimension. Similarly, the price for delivery of a share of stock in the future is determined by its price today and the cost of financing, so there is no time dimension. Commodity traders have more degrees of freedom when designing strategies, which leads to a richer set of relative value opportunities than is available in debt or equity markets.

Commodity futures and options spreads

Commodity spreads are strategies that take advantage of trading opportunities that can be executed entirely in derivatives markets. They can involve futures contracts, forward contracts, OTC swaps, and options.

Time spreads

Perhaps the simplest strategy is a **calendar spread**, which involves taking opposing positions in the futures market for delivery at different times in the future. These trades can be designed to provide liquidity or insurance against an unforeseen event.

For example, a typical calendar spread trade involves selling natural gas futures for delivery in March and taking a long position for delivery of natural gas in April. This spread could be profitable in a very mild winter and lose money in a very cold winter. Utilities purchase more natural gas for delivery in March than they expect to need to ensure adequate supplies. If the winter is mild, they will sell the excess gas towards the end of the season, which will push down the price for delivery in March. Traders who hold this spread are writing a synthetic weather derivative. They will earn a premium if the weather is mild and take a loss if weather is severe. Traders may also take the other side of this trade by buying natural gas for March delivery and selling it for delivery in April. If a natural gas shortage develops due to an exceptionally cold winter or supply disruptions, this trade will be profitable.

Other common calendar spreads are designed to provide liquidity. For example, in 2005–2006 it was common for traders to buy crude oil futures for delivery two months forward and hedge this position by selling crude oil for delivery three months forward. This trade was designed to take advantage of the growth in commodity index investments. Since most commodity index investments are designed to hold futures for near-term delivery, there was a surplus of these contracts on dates when the indices were selling their short-maturity futures positions and a corresponding shortage of next-month futures when the indices were buying the second-deferred futures positions. Speculators responded by designing a calendar spread that offered liquidity to the indices at prices that could provide a reasonable expected profit to the speculators.

In general, investors can enter two types of calendar spreads – bull spreads and bear spreads – depending on their market views. In a **bull spread**, the investor is long the nearby (near-term) contract and is short the distant (long-term) contract. In backwardated markets the investor is hoping for the spread to narrow, whereas in inverted (contango) markets the bull-spread investor is hoping for the price difference to widen. The losses of a bull-spread investor are limited because, in an efficient market, price differences cannot exceed carrying costs. If, at some point, the differences do exceed carrying costs, arbitrageurs would drive prices down to a level reflecting fair carrying costs.

In a **bear spread**, the investor is long the distant (long-term) contract and is short the nearby (near-term) contract. In backwardated markets the investor wants the spread to widen, whereas in inverted (contango) markets the bear-spread investor wants the price difference to widen. If prices move against the investor's position, the bear spread faces unlimited risk since the nearby contract theoretically can rise without an upper limit; consequently the bear spreader would have to deliver or offset at any price.

Example of spread P&L calculation

The profit and loss (P&L) from a spread position can only be calculated after the spread is closed. Assume the following scenario. In March, a spreader observes an unusually steep backwardation in the crude oil forward curve. Anticipating a flattening of the curve and narrowing of the spread, the trader goes long three July Light Sweet Crude Oil futures (traded on NYMEX) at $44.37 simultaneously shorting three December Light Sweet Crude Oil futures at $50.78. In April and May, oversupply of crude in the world markets causes prices to slump across the board. At the beginning of June, the spreader closes out the July contract at 35.18 and December contract at 38.16.

P&L calculation per barrel is shown below.

	July (1st leg)	December (2nd leg)	Total
March, Open	LONG: −$44.37	SHORT: + $50.78	
June, Close	SHORT: +$35.18	LONG: −$38.16	
Net per barrel	−$9.19	$12.62	$3.43

P&L calculation for the whole position can now be determined. Since the size of the NYMEX light sweet crude oil contract is 1000 barrels whereas the size of the trader's spread position is three contracts, the total gain of his position is $10,290.

$$\text{position P \& L} = \text{P \& L}_{barrel} \times \text{contract size} \times \text{position size}$$
$$= \$3.43 \times 1000 \times 3 = \$10,290$$

Correlation spreads

Processing spreads seek to take advantage of the relative price difference between a commodity and the products produced using the same commodity. For example, processing spread strategies can involve crude oil and its products. A common processing spread involves buying crude oil futures and selling a combination of heating oil and gasoline futures. Another example of a processing spread involves buying soybeans and selling a combination of soybean meal and soybean oil.

Processing spreads are used by producers to lock in favorable margins. For example, a soybean processor may wish to "buy" the spread (buy soybean futures, sell soybean meal and soybean oil futures). However, there are no natural "sellers" of this spread. Instead, there are three separate natural participants on the other side of the spread; farmers who sell the soybean futures, livestock feed producers who buy the soybean meal, and vegetable oil consumers who buy the soybean oil. Speculators may provide liquidity by selling the spread to permit the processor to lock in a favorable margin, and then attempt to find buyers or sellers to unwind the individual components of the spread trade. They can also hold the spread intact and hope to unwind the entire transaction at a more favorable price.

In summary, there are two conditions which hold for all producers: 1) producers take long futures positions to hedge against rising input prices; 2) producers take short future positions to hedge against falling output prices.

It should be noted that futures exchanges set lower margins for *bona fide* hedging spreads, in which a producer goes long futures on the input and goes short futures on the output. On the flip side, a spread investor who goes long the output and shorts the input is subject to higher margin requirements. A few examples of typical processing spreads follow.

Crack spread: A crack spread is a hedge typically used by oil refineries. The typical producer hedge position would involve going long crude oil futures (to hedge future input purchases) and short gasoline and heating oil to hedge against potential decreases in the price of the outputs (distillates).

It is a common practice to express the crack spread in terms of a ratio as "X:Y:Z" where X represents the number of barrels of crude oil, Y represents the number of barrels of gasoline, and Z represents the number of barrels of heating oil, subject to the constraint that $X = Y + Z$. Typical crack spreads are 3:2:1, 5:3:2, and 2:1:1 (examples of benchmarks: "Gulf Coast 3:2:1," "Chicago 3:2:1").

Financial intermediaries have custom products that facilitate entering scaled crack positions. For example, NYMEX offers virtual crack spread futures contracts by aggregating a basket of underlying NYMEX futures contracts corresponding to a crack spread ratio. It is possible to obtain even more customized products in the over-the-counter market.

Crush spread: A crush spread is a hedge typically used by soybean processors. A typical crush spread would involve going long soybean futures (to insure the processor against potential input price increases) and short soybean oil futures and soy meal futures (to insure against potential output price decreases). The reason behind the name of this spread is that historically soybeans were crushed to produce oil and meal.

Crack spread, Example 3:2:1

The following example has been partially adapted from New York Mercantile Exchange's publication *Crack Spread Handbook* (2001). An independent refiner is concerned about the possibility of increasing oil costs (input) and falling refined product prices (output). In other words, the refiner is subject to the risk that his refining margin will be less than anticipated. However, using a crack spread hedge, the producer can effectively lock in the current refining margin as demonstrated in the following example.

On June 15, the refiner enters an obligation in the cash market to buy 60,000 barrels of crude oil on July 15 at prevailing market prices. He has also entered an obligation to sell 840,000 gallons (20,000 barrels) of heating oil and 1,680,000 gallons (40,000 barrels) of gasoline on August 27 at prevailing market prices.

That same day, June 15, the refiner initiates a long hedge in crude oil and short hedges in heating oil and gasoline to fix a substantial portion of his refining margin through a 3:2:1 crack spread. He does this by going long 60 August crude oil futures contracts at \$44.34/bbl. while selling 20 September heating oil contracts at \$55.77/bbl. and 40 September gasoline futures contracts at \$55.04/bbl. Each one of these contracts is for the equivalent to 1000 barrels. The table below reflects the refiner's 3:2:1 crack spread of three crude, two gasoline, and one heating oil parts.

Date	Cash market	Action	Futures Market
June 15	Light, sweet crude oil: \$44.79/bbl	Agrees to buy at prevailing prices: 60,000 bbl. light, sweet crude on July 15	Goes long 60 Aug light, sweet crude contracts at \$44.34/bbl.
	Gasoline: NY Harbor: \$1.3274/gal. (\$55.75/bbl.)	Agrees to sell at prevailing cash market prices: 1,680,000 gal. (40,000 bbl.) NY Harbor gasoline on August 27	Shorts 40 Sep NY Harbor gasoline contracts at \$1.3105/gal. (\$55.04/bbl)
	Heating oil: NY Harbor: \$1.3148/gal. (\$55.22/bbl.)	Agrees to sell at prevailing cash market prices: 840,000 gal. (20,000 bbl.) NY Harbor heating oil on August 27	Shorts 20 Sep NY Harbor heating oil contracts at \$1.3279/gal. (\$55.77 bbl.)

In this case, the futures crack spread is calculated as:

[(Number of gasoline futures contracts sold short × Gasoline futures price) + (Number of heating oil contracts sold short × Heating oil futures price) – (Number of long crude oil contract × Crude oil futures price)] / Total number of contracts long or short

Thus, the futures crack spread on June 15 is:

$$[(40 \times \$55.04) + (20 \times \$55.77) - (60 \times \$44.34)]/60 = \$10.94/bbl.$$

In this example, the cash market margin is calculated as:

[(Number of gasoline futures contracts sold short × Gasoline cash market price) + (Number of heating oil contracts sold short × Heating oil cash market price) – (Number of long crude oil contracts × Crude oil cash market price)] / Total number of contracts

Thus, the NY Harbor cash market margin is:

$$[(40 \times \$55.75) + (20 \times \$55.22) - (60 \times \$44.79)]/60 = \$10.78/bbl.$$

The $10.94/bbl. crack spread has ensured that refining crude oil will be at least as profitable in August as it was in June, regardless of whether the actual cash margin narrows or widens. A decline in the cash margin is offset by a gain in the futures market. Consider the following two scenarios.

Scenario A: Rising crude, falling distillates, stable basis, refiner puts on the spread

Date	Cash market	Action	Futures market
July 15	Light, sweet crude oil: $45.03/bbl	Buys 60,000 bbl. light, sweet crude at $45.03/bbl.	Shorts 60 Aug light, sweet crude contracts at $45.03/bbl.
August 27	Gasoline: NY Harbor: $1.1746/gal. ($49.33/bbl.)	Sells 1,680,000 gal. (40,000 bbl.) NY Harbor gasoline for $1.1746/gal. ($49.33/bbl.)	Goes long 40 Sep NY Harbor gasoline contracts at $1.1805/gal. ($49.58/bbl)
	Heating oil: NY Harbor: $1.2409/gal. ($52.12/bbl)	Sells 840,000 gal. (20,000 bbl.) NY Harbor heating oil for $1.2409 gal. ($52.12 bbl.)	Goes long 20 Sep NY Harbor heating oil contracts at $1.2445/gal. ($52.27 bbl.)

Futures crack spread: $[(40 \times \$49.58) + (20 \times \$52.27) - (60 \times \$45.03)]/60 = \$5.45/bbl.$
Futures profit = Initial crack spread − Closing crack spread = $10.94 − $5.45 = $5.49/bbl.
NY Harbor cash market margin: $[(40 \times \$49.33) + (20 \times \$52.12) - (60 \times \$45.03)]/60 = \$5.23/bbl.$
Realized margin: cash margin + futures profit = $5.23 + $5.49 = $10.72/bbl.

Scenario B: Falling crude, rising distillates, stable basis, refiner puts on the spread

Date	Cash market	Action	Futures market
July 15	Light, sweet crude oil: $41.47/bbl	Buys 60,000 bbl. light, sweet crude at $41.47/bbl.	Shorts 60 Aug light, sweet crude contracts at $41.47/bbl.
August 27	Gasoline: NY Harbor: $1.4459/gal. ($60.73/bbl.)	Sells 1,680,000 gal. (40,000 bbl.) NY Harbor gasoline for $1.4459/gal. ($60.73/bbl.)	Goes long 40 Sep NY Harbor gasoline contracts at $1.4600/gal. ($61.32/bbl)
	Heating oil: NY Harbor: $1.2739/gal. ($53.50/bbl.)	Sells 840,000 gal. (20,000 bbl.) NY Harbor heating oil for $1.2739 gal. ($53.50 bbl.)	Goes long 20 Sep NY Harbor heating oil contracts at $1.2800/gal. ($53.76 bbl.)

Futures crack spread: $[(40 \times \$61.32) + (20 \times \$53.76) - (60 \times \$41.47)]/60 = \$17.33/bbl.$
Futures loss = Initial crack spread − Closing crack spread = $\$10.94 - \$17.33 = -\$6.39/bbl.$
NY Harbor cash market margin: $[(40 \times \$60.73) + (20 \times \$53.50) - (60 \times \$41.47)]/60 = \$16.85/bbl.$
Realized margin: cash margin − futures loss = $\$16.85 - \$6.39 = \$10.46/bbl.$

In summary, the cash market refining margin on June 15 was $10.78. Unhedged, under scenario A, the refiner would have experienced a 50% drop in his refining margin. If the hedge were applied, his loss would have been reduced to less than 1%. On the other hand, the hedge would have eliminated the refiner's potential gain under scenario B. Note that the hedge was not perfect in this case; the imperfection was caused by the fact that the refiner had to buy in July and deliver in August, whereas the futures maturities happened in different months.

Substitution spreads are trades between commodities that can be substituted for one another. There are two types of substitution. A producer may use the same capital equipment to produce different products. Also, a consumer may be able to substitute one commodity for another based on their relative prices. Examples of producer substitution include corn and soybeans − land suitable for growing soybeans is usually also suitable for growing corn. Oil refineries can also vary the mix of refined products. A refinery can be adjusted, within limits, to favor production of heating oil, jet fuel, or gasoline depending on seasonal demand. Consumers of commodities can often substitute a less expensive commodity. Utilities can utilize different fuels for electricity generation. For example, natural gas can be substituted for oil-based fuels. Cattle and hogs are also substitutes. Substitution spread trades are generally riskier than processing spreads or calendar spreads, since they depend on historical correlations that may not persist in the future.

The general premise of substitute spreads is that the relationship between easily substitutable commodities should be stable. If the price of one becomes too expensive, the consumers will switch to the substitute. This results in a price drop for the original and a rise for the substitute, forcing the ratio back to normal. To "normalize" ratios of contracts with different pricing specifications and contract sizes, one can study natural logs of the ratios of prices. For example, one might look at the natural log of a series of Heating Oil/Natural Gas price ratios, such as:

$$\text{substitute test statistic}_t = \ln\left(\frac{\text{close price (Heating Oil)}_t}{\text{close price (Natural Gas)}_t}\right)$$

For the purposes of illustration, let's assume that the nearest maturity NYMEX Heating Oil (HO) yesterday has closed at $1.2810 per gallon, while the same maturity NYMEX Henry Hub Natural Gas (NG) has closed at 4.056 per 10,000 million British thermal units (mmBtu). The HO/NG test statistic for yesterday would be estimated as follows:

$$\text{substitute test statistic}_{\text{yesterday}} = \ln\left(\frac{HO_{yesterday}}{NG_{yesterday}}\right) = \ln\left(\frac{1.281}{4.056}\right) = -1.15$$

To determine whether the spread has experienced a change significant enough to warrant a spread trade, a measure of stability is required. One such measure at traders' disposal is "difference from 100-day moving average", calculated as follows:

$$100\text{-day statistic} = \frac{\text{close} - 100\text{-day moving average of closes}}{100 \text{ day standard deviation of closes}}$$

The critical values of the statistic that would trigger entering/exiting a spread position are determined statistically (optimizing over historical series of logs of price ratios of the related securities). For the purposes of example, assume that the critical value for entry is 2.75 while the critical value for exit is 0. A long entry into the spread would be triggered if the 100-day statistic fell below -2.75, whereas a short position in the spread would be established if the 100-day statistic rose above 2.75. Long spreads are exited when the 100-day stat rises above zero, and short spreads are exited when the 100-day stat falls below zero. Note that "entering spread long" means going long the product in the numerator of the price ratio and shorting the product in the denominator. The assumption of the long spread position is that the product in the denominator has become too expensive relative to the numerator. "Shorting the spread" means the opposite: shorting the product in the numerator and going long the product in the denominator. The assumption of the short spread position is that the product in the numerator has become too expensive relative to the product in the denominator.

Quality spreads are similar to substitution spreads, except that the spread is across different grades of the same commodity. A common quality spread executable in futures markets involves spring wheat and hard red winter wheat. Most other quality spreads involve OTC transactions. For example, there is a liquid OTC market in jet fuel, which is very similar to diesel fuel/heating oil. Similarly, there are many grades of coffee that are traded OTC but only a few grades that are listed on futures exchanges.

Quality spread traders provide liquidity to producers in the OTC market and then hedge by using other OTC markets or listed futures contracts. Most quality spreads have historically had relatively low price risk. There has been little chance that the spread between jet fuel and heating oil would undergo a major structural change, because refineries have easily switched production between heating oil and jet fuel if a demand imbalance takes place. Rather than list separate futures contracts for diesel fuel, jet fuel, and heating oil, liquidity in the futures markets is combined into a single market (heating oil), and users of the other two commodities utilize quality spreads to provide an effective hedge.

Location spreads

Location spreads are trades that involve the same commodity but different delivery locations. A common location spread involves Brent crude oil, delivered in the UK, and WTI crude oil, delivered in the U.S. Location spreads are primarily traded using OTC derivatives, though some location spreads, such as the Brent/WTI spread, can be executed using listed futures contracts (Pringle and Fernandes, 2007, p. 316).

Some location spreads have an arbitrage component. For example, if the Brent crude/WTI crude trade is executed with a one-month lag, then it is possible to take delivery in one location and make delivery in another location. However, if the location spread is made without a lag, then the trade is a correlation trade.

Intra-market relative value strategies

Many of the strategies utilized by active commodity managers and hedge funds combine trading **commodity derivatives** with trading the underlying commodities in the physical or spot markets. These strategies utilize commodity futures markets the same way that commercial users do: as hedging vehicles to minimize the exposure of a particular transaction to unexpected market risk.

Storage strategies utilize leased storage facilities to hold physical commodities for delivery at a later date. These strategies are more complex than futures-based strategies, and are both labor- and capital-intensive. Storage strategies are typically hedged transactions, involving a simultaneous purchase of the physical asset and sale of the commodity in the futures or OTC forward market. The strategy can also be an unhedged or directional trade in anticipation of an increase in the commodity price, though this is less common. A **storage strategy** is equivalent to a calendar spread in that the transaction involves holding the same commodity over time.

Transportation strategies utilize spot commodity markets to execute location trades. The strategy involves leased transportation services such as tankers, bulk shipping, or pipelines to physically move a commodity from a location where the commodity is in surplus to a location where it is in shortage.

Transportation and storage strategies carry risks that futures-based strategies do not. For example, the investors must be willing to assume the attendant credit risk of the OTC counterparties used in these transactions (Till and Eagleeye, 2005). The investors must also be prepared to bear the risks associated with storing and transporting potentially hazardous commodities, including the potential headline risk. Market participants must also make sure that these strategies do not give the appearance of physical-market manipulation. Till (2008c) describes a CFTC and U.S. Department of Justice action against a major international oil company where the company was fined $303-million for attempting to manipulate one U.S. delivery location's physical propane market. The firm's positions were initially entered into through the forward OTC markets. This case was particularly striking since the firm had *actually failed* in this attempted manipulation and had lost at least $10-million in attempting to carry out this "market corner."

Commodity-based equity and debt strategies

Equity-based commodity strategies involve hedging the commodity price risk associated with the share price of a particular company. They can also involve buying the commodity to hedge a production input. An example of this would be buying jet fuel as a hedge for an airline stock.

Commodity-based corporations are typically valued as the sum of the firm's **commodity rights** and its **enterprise value**. Commodity rights reflect the current value of untapped commodity assets such as oil reserves. The enterprise value is the residual value of corporate assets. If an analyst determines that the enterprise value of a particular firm is overpriced, a common strategy is to sell the firm's equity short and buy commodity futures to hedge out exposure to the commodity rights. Conversely, if the enterprise value is underpriced, the strategy involves buying the equity and selling futures to hedge the commodity rights.

Debt strategies use commodity futures and options to hedge the default risk of commodity producers and consumers. Because default risk is highly nonlinear, commodity options are commonly utilized for this type of hedge. For example, a lender to a copper producer might purchase put options on copper to hedge this exposure. The owner of airline bonds would buy call options on jet fuel to hedge the negative effect on margins of higher fuel costs.

Commodity Indices

COMMODITY INDICES COMPARED TO SECURITIES INDICES

Commodity indices are an effective and efficient means for gaining access to the benefits of commodities. A **commodity index** is a group of commodity futures contracts that are rolled. Commodity indices provide returns comparable to passive long positions in listed futures contracts. They attempt to replicate the returns one would generate through holding long positions in agricultural, metal, energy, or livestock futures contracts, without requiring the investor to actively manage the positions.

The number of commodity indices available to investors has multiplied since the year 2000. There are now more than 10 publicly-available commodity indices. All indices offer a diversified exposure to commodity markets through the use of commodity futures contracts. The indices differ in composition, commodity selection criteria, rolling mechanism, rebalancing strategy, and weighting scheme.

Commodity index performance can be a function of the methodology of the index, combined with the impact of market factors on the index components. As a result, commodity index performance can vary across indices, and market environments. The methodology of the index can have an impact on volatility levels (Kazemi *et al.*, 2008). Also, research from Kazemi *et al.* (2008) showed that even though indices can be highly correlated, they can also have very different returns.

VALUE-BASED VS. QUANTITY-BASED

Commodity indices can be value-based or quantity-based. A value-based index has fixed component weights. The number of futures contracts in the index changes dynamically to maintain constant weights. A quantity-based index holds a fixed quantity of each commodity, so that the index weights change each day. For example, the S&P 500 stock index is quantity-based since the number of shares of each company in the index only changes when the index constituents are changed. Conversely, a benchmark that consists of 60% stocks and 40% bonds is value-based.

TOTAL RETURN VS. EXCESS RETURN

There are two types of return indices available to investors. A **total return index** is a fully collateralized investment strategy, with the collateralization generally taking the form of Treasury Bills. In a total return index, the overall calculation of the index return includes the cash return from the collateral. Generally, total return indices have returns comparable to stock or bond markets. An **Excess return index** provides returns over cash and are linked to the price movements of a basket of commodity futures contracts (Blanch and Scheis, 2006).

SOURCES OF RETURN

Commodity indices can benefit from multiple sources of returns, many of which tend to be uncorrelated. These can include spot, roll, beta, momentum, rebalancing, and T-Bill returns. Additional factors like diversification, commodity component weighting, and roll schedule can also impact the index return. We now proceed to explain these return sources.

Commodity beta: For a given market commodity beta can be defined as the return to holding the active futures contract until the contract roll date and then rolling to the next active futures contract. With respect to liquidity and transparency, this is the simplest way to hold commodities, and thus is the benchmark against which other methods of holding commodity futures are measured.

Roll return: The profits or losses generated from the rolling of futures contracts. These have a direct impact on index performance. Roll returns will be positive when the commodity forward curve persistently slopes down and will be negative when the forward curve persistently slopes up. Some commodities, such as gold, very nearly always have a negative roll yield. The cost of carry for gold has been larger than the convenience yield, so the forward curve has been upward-sloping.

Spot return: The difference between the excess return of an index and the roll return is referred to as the spot return.

Dynamic asset allocation: Some commodity indices incorporate dynamic asset allocation models. These models determine which commodities to overweight and which to underweight. Momentum is a commonly used asset allocation rule. Momentum models overweight commodities that are increasing in price and underweight commodities that are declining in price. Another common strategy for dynamic asset allocation includes mean reversion. This strategy reduces the allocation to commodities that have increased in value and increases the allocation to commodities that have declined in price. Typically, momentum-based asset allocation rules are based on short-term models and mean reversion strategies are based on price changes over a time horizon greater than one year.

Diversification: The greater the number of commodities, the more diverse the index, which makes it less sensitive to price increases or decreases in a particular commodity or a commodity subsector.

Commodity weights: Higher index returns may result from overweighting commodity futures that are increasing in value and underweighting those that are falling in value. However, risk and volatility can increase in an index that allocates a large weight to a small subset of commodities. A commodity weighting scheme should also have an economic rationale to avoid designing an index that optimizes based solely on past performance.

Maturity: Using longer maturity contracts tends to increase roll returns and consequently total returns, but may not significantly affect spot returns. Investing in longer maturity contracts can also effectively enhance risk-adjusted returns as measured by the Sharpe ratio. Long-maturity futures contracts tend to be less volatile. Events that may cause a dramatic change in the spot price of a commodity will probably have a more subdued influence on the price for delivery six or 12 months in the future. As a result, an index based on these futures contracts will be less volatile. The drawback to this approach is that liquidity is much more variable in long-maturity futures contracts, so it may be more difficult to exit a large index position in a short period of time.

Treasury (collateral): In total return indices, the amount invested in futures is set aside as collateral and earns interest.

A PRIMER ON COMMODITY INDEX CALCULATION: SPOT, ROLL, EXCESS, AND TOTAL RETURNS

The four measures of return that are commonly published by commodity index providers are *spot return*, *roll return*, *excess return* and *total return*. Each of these measures of commodity performance has an important use in evaluating the performance of different commodity investment strategies. This section introduces these concepts by calculating a hypothetical commodity index over the course of two trading days. The sections that follow will focus on analysis of these return measures.

Three index values are calculated: excess return index, total return index, and spot index. The industry convention is to compute index returns the following way:

- **Spot return:** percentage change in market value of futures contracts held in the index at the end of the day, *after accounting for any index changes.*
- **Excess return:** percentage change in the market value of the futures contracts held in the index at the end of the trading session *but before accounting for any index changes.*
- **Total return:** excess return plus the risk free return (usually Treasury Bills).
- **Roll return:** excess return minus spot return.

There will be a difference between spot and excess return when the index composition changes, either because a contract is rolled forward or because the weights are changed. For most indices, rolls only take place on a few days per month and weights change once per year, so for most days the roll return is zero. On any date when the index changes, the excess return will measure the return on the positions before the changes take place, and the spot index will measure the value of positions after the changes take place.

The following example shows the return calculations for a simple commodity index comprised of two commodities. The first panel below shows return calculations on a date when the index does not change any positions (i.e. does not roll or rebalance). The two tables at the top show the values that will be used to calculate index values, returns, and weights for August 29 2008. The key figures are the Index Multipliers. These values are fixed each year in most indices, and represent the number of "contracts" held for each commodity in the index.

Settlement Prices for Simple Index Calculation			Index Values on 08/28/08	
CRUDE OIL (NYMEX)	08/28/08	08/29/08	Index	28-Aug
Oct '08	114.12	115.46	SPOT INDEX	94.43
Nov '08			EXCESS RETURN INDEX	118.21
			TOTAL RETURN INDEX	231.41
COPPER (COMEX)	08/28/08	08/29/08		
Dec '08	340.25	338.70	Index Multipliers (Contracts per Index Point)	
Mar '09				
			Commodity	Multiplier
3 Month TBill Return	08/28/08	08/29/08	CRUDE OIL	0.0063372
Basis Points/Day	0.80	2.41	COPPER	0.0008135
			Index Weights on 08/28/08	
			Commodity	% of Index
			CRUDE OIL	72.32%
			COPPER	27.68%

1. Compute New Index Values

Excess Return Index: $118.21 \times (115.46 \times 0.0063372 + 338.70 \times 0.0008135) = 119.06$
Total Return Index: $(231.41 \times (115.46 \times 0.0063372 + 338.70 \times 0.0008135)) \times (1 + 0.000080) = 233.10$
Spot Index: $94.43 \times (338.70 \times 0.0008135 + 115.46 \times 0.0063372) = 95.11$

2. Calculate New Weights

Copper Weight: $(338.70 \times 0.0008135) \times 94.43/95.11 = 27.36\%$
Crude Oil Weight: $(115.46 \times 0.0063372) \times 94.43/95.11 = 72.64\%$

3. Calculate Index Returns

Excess Return: $119.06/118.21 - 1 = 0.723\%$
Total Return: $233.10/231.41 - 1 = 0.731\%$
Spot Return: $95.11/94.43 - 1 = 0.723\%$
Roll Return: $.0723\% - .0723\% = 0$

Since there is no roll return in this example, the Spot Index uses futures with the same expiration months used in calculating the Excess Return and Total Return indices.

In the example above, the price of copper declined and the price of crude oil rose on the evaluation date (8/29/08). There were no index changes so spot return and excess return are the same. Roll return is zero. Crude oil has a higher weight in the index, so all three indices gained in value. Note that the weight of crude oil rose in the index. This is because the index holds a fixed position in each commodity, so with crude oil rising more than copper, the portion of the index represented by crude oil increased as well.

The example below shows the same set of calculations on a date when the index "rolls." On a roll date, futures contracts nearing expiration are replaced in the index by new contracts. The changes take place after the futures markets close. In the example below, crude oil for October delivery is replaced with a contract for November delivery. Also, copper for December delivery is replaced with a contract for delivery the following March. The changes are assumed to take place after the close of trading on September 1.

Settlement Prices for Simple Index Calculation			Index Values on 08/29/08	
CRUDE OIL (NYMEX)	08/29/08	09/01/08	Index	29-Aug
Oct '08	115.46	111.00	SPOT INDEX	95.11
Nov '08		111.38	EXCESS RETURN INDEX	119.06
			TOTAL RETURN INDEX	233.10
COPPER (COMEX)	08/29/08	09/01/08		
Dec '08	338.70	330.60	Index Multipliers (Contracts per Index Point)	
Mar '09		328.00		
			Commodity	Multiplier
3 Month TBill Return	08/29/08	09/01/08	CRUDE OIL	0.0063372
Basis Points/Day	2.41	0.78	COPPER	0.0008135
			Index Weights on 08/29/08	
			Commodity	% of Index
			CRUDE OIL	72.64%
			COPPER	27.36%

1. Compute New Index Values

Excess Return Index: $119.06 \times (111.00 \times 0.0063372 + 330.60 \times 0.0008135) = 115.78$
Total Return Index: $(233.10 \times (111.00 \times 0.0063372 + 330.60 \times 0.0008135)) \times (1 + 0.000241) = 226.68$
Spot Index: $95.11 \times (328 \times 0.0008135 + 111.38 \times 0.0063372) = 92.51$

2. Calculate New Weights

Copper Weight: $(328.00 \times 0.0008135) \times 95.11/92.51 = 27.43\%$
Crude Oil Weight: $(111.38 \times 0.0063372) \times 95.11/92.51 = 72.57\%$

3. Calculate Index Returns

Excess Return: $115.78/119.06 - 1 = -2.762\%$
Total Return: $226.68/233.10 - 1 = -2.754\%$
Spot Return: $92.51/95.11 - 1 = -2.733\%$
Roll Return: $-2.762\% - (-2.733\%) = -0.029\%$

In this example, the excess return index is calculated based on the original contracts (October crude and December copper). The spot return index uses the new contracts (November crude and March copper). Using these values, the spot return is slightly higher than the excess return (−2.733% vs. −2.762%). The difference of .029% (or −2.9 basis points) represents the roll return. Note that on the next day – September 2, both the spot and excess indices would be calculated using the new contracts.

DESCRIPTION AND UNIQUE FEATURES OF THE MAJOR COMMODITY INDICES

The current grouping of major commodity indices is listed below, along with an overview of the index, the specific methodology used and the factors impacting performance. This section describes several indices that have been published since the beginning of 2007. Indices revise their methodology and weighting schemes from time to time. These descriptions are current as of February 2009 (Schneeweis *et al.*, 2009).

S&P Goldman Sachs Commodity Index (SPGSCI)

Overview: The SPGSCI – a quantity-based, world production-weighted index – currently holds six energy products, five industrial metals, eight agricultural products, three livestock products and two precious metals. The index has the flexibility to hold any number of contracts so long as the particular contract meets the liquidity criteria. Contracts are weighted by the average worldwide production in the last five years of available data. The SPGSCI is dominated by energy, with roughly a 68% allocation to the energy sector as of the beginning of 2009. There is also a series of indices that use the same convention and hold the same components as the SPGSCI, including the SPGSCI Reduced Energy, Light Energy, and UltraLight Energy sub-indices. The SPGSCI Reduced Energy Index uses one-half of the SPGSCI contract production weights for the energy components, while the SPGSCI Light and SPGSCI UltraLight Energy indices use one quarter and one eighth of the contract production weights for the energy components respectively.

The SPGSCI Enhanced Commodity Index is another variant of the SPGSCI. It holds the same basket of commodities as the SPGSCI but tries to address the issue of negative roll yield due to dominance of contango markets in recent years.

- *Launch date:* November 1991.
- *Roll:* The SPGSCI rolls from the front to the next contract between the fifth and ninth business day of the month prior to delivery. Rebalancing of the index takes place once a year after the weights are reviewed by the index committee. However, these weights typically do not vary much from year to year due to the five-year evaluation period.
- *Average maturity:* The weighted average maturity of futures contracts in the SPGSCI is less than two months, the shortest average maturity of all commodity indices.
- *Energy allocation:* Because the SPGSCI does not have sector-weight constraints, the index methodology generates the largest energy allocation of any commodity index.
- *Outperformance:* This index is expected to do well in times of rising energy prices. It will also perform quite well when commodity markets are in backwardation because it holds the shortest average maturity contracts of any major commodity index.

Dow Jones-AIG Commodity Index (DJAIG)

Overview: The DJAIG, a quantity-based commodity index, predefines a set of criteria to prevent any sector from becoming dominant in the index. It limits the maximum weight of any commodity to 15% of the index, any sector to 33% of the index, and any commodity along with its downstream products to 25% of the index. This index currently holds 19 commodity futures of which seven are agricultural products, four are energy products, four are industrial metals, two are precious metals and two are livestock products. A combination of liquidity and production measures is used to assign weights to individual commodities. Liquidity has twice as much influence as production in deciding the overall weights. Use of the production data has the drawback of underweighting commodities like gold that are storable over a longer time horizon.

In January 2009, UBS Investment Bank announced that it entered an agreement to purchase the commodity index business of AIG Financial Products Corp., including AIG's rights to the DJAIG. If the transaction closes as expected by May 2009, the DJAIG will be known as the Dow Jones-UBS Commodity Index.

- *Launch date:* July 1998.
- *Roll:* The DJAIG follows a similar roll strategy similar to that of the SPGSCI, and rolls from the 4th to the 8th business day of the month, from the front to the next contract.
- *Average maturity:* The DJAIG has the same average maturity for agricultural markets as the SPGSCI but longer average energy and metal maturities because it skips every other expiration in commodity markets that trade on a monthly expiration schedule.
- *Energy allocation:* The DJAIG methodology has a cap of 33% on the energy sector, lower than almost all of the other commodity indices.
- *Outperformance:* The DJAIG will tend to outperform other indices when agriculture and metal prices rise more than energy. This index will also do better when agriculture and metals are experiencing greater backwardation than energy.

Bache Commodity Index (BCI)

Overview: The BCI is composed of 19 commodities that are traded on seven major futures exchanges located in the United States and the United Kingdom. The primary objective of the BCI is to provide broad-based exposure to global commodity markets, low turnover[1] and strong risk-adjusted returns. Commodities for the index are chosen based on their importance to the global economy and on liquidity measures. The BCI also focuses on commodity markets that have potential to function as a hedge against inflation and exhibit low correlations to traditional assets. The BCI is designed so that the index does not become dominated by a single commodity sector or by several commodities by employing upper and lower bounds on the commodity weights and through frequent rebalancing.

- *Launch date:* January 2007; pro forma returns available from January 1991.
- *Roll:* The index utilizes a continuous roll methodology.
- *Average maturity:* Three weeks more than the average maturity of the same commodity in the SPGSCI.
- *Energy allocation:* The index can have as much as 50% allocated to energy, depending on the performance of the energy markets.
- *Outperformance:* When markets are in contango, the BCI will outperform most traditional indices, and when markets are declining, it will experience smaller drawdowns than the other indices. It will have smaller drawdowns compared to any other indices in declining markets.

Rogers International Commodity Index (RICI)

Overview: The RICI – a quantity-based, world production-weighted commodity index designed by investor Jim Rogers – was launched in July 1998. The index is one of the most diverse commodity indices consisting of 36 commodities from 10 exchanges in five countries. The RICI currently holds six energy products, seven industrial metals, three precious metals, 18 agricultural products and two livestock products. The components are subject to change by the RICI Committee. Inclusion

---

[1] On a daily basis, this index rolls only a small portion of its positions as needed and therefore the overall turnover is low.

of a commodity in the index is determined by its significance in worldwide consumption. Each commodity is rebalanced at the start of each month toward initial weights, determined annually by the RICI Committee. The index is rolled at the end of each month to contracts that are expected to be the most active during the next month. The index calculation methodology is reviewed annually by the index committee during its meeting in December and possibly amended thereafter. The initial value of the RICI was set to 1000 on July 31, 1998.

- *Launch date:* July 1998.
- *Roll:* The RICI usually rolls over three days, from the day prior to the last RICI business day of the month to the first RICI business day of the following month. During the roll period, the index is shifted from the first to the second nearby baskets at a rate of 33.33% per day. On the last roll day, the roll is completed unless the roll period is extended for a component as a result of a market disruption event such as futures prices hitting the limits set by the exchange (i.e., a limit day).
- *Average maturity:* RICI has the same average maturity as the SPGSCI prior to the roll periods for the contracts common in both indices, except for industrial metals. Between the RICI roll period and the SPGSCI roll period, the average maturity of energy products in the RICI is about one month more than the average maturity of energy products in SPGSCI. Industrial metals have an average maturity of three months and forward contracts are used in calculating the contribution of industrial metals to the RICI.
- *Energy allocation:* The target allocation for energy in the RICI is 44%.
- *Outperformance:* This index will perform better than the other indices when the agriculture sector performs better than the energy and metals sectors. With a very low allocation to natural gas, the RICI will also perform better than other major indices when the price of natural gas futures declines. The RICI is one of the few commodity indices with direct exposure to exchange rate fluctuations. A decline in the value of the U.S. dollar relative to Japanese Yen, Canadian Dollar, and Australian Dollar will boost the performance of the index.

Merrill Lynch Commodity Index eXtra (MLCX)

Overview: The MLCX is a quantity-based index introduced during the commodity bull run of the middle part of 2006. The distinguishing characteristic of this index is the longer average maturity compared to the SPGSCI and DJAIG. Commodity contracts are selected based on liquidity and then weighted based on the importance of each commodity in the global economy with an emphasis on downstream commodities. Diversification of the index is ensured by setting maximum and minimum weights for sectors in the index. Currently, the cap for any sector is set at 60% and the floor is set at 3%. Due to its allocation to the energy sector of 60%, this index will do well when energy prices are rising. In 2009, the MLCX added Gasoil, Soybean Oil, and Cotton and removed Heating Oil and Soybean Meal.

- *Launch date:* June 2006.
- *Roll:* It rolls over a period of fifteen days from the first to the fifteenth business day of the rolling month, and rolls from next to second next contract instead of more conventional front to next contract.
- *Average maturity:* Rolling one month ahead of the SPGSCI and DJAIG gives the MLCX an average maturity of about one month longer than the DJAIG and six weeks longer than the SPGSCI.
- *Energy allocation:* The index can have as much as 60% allocated to energy at the start of each year, which is larger than any other index besides the SPGSCI.
- *Outperformance:* This index will do better when markets are in contango due to its longer average maturity.

Reuters/Jefferies-CRB Index (CRB)

Overview: The CRB index, established in 1957, is a value-based index with the longest history of all the commodity indices. However, the usefulness of the long track record has been reduced by the high number of revisions in methodology. The CRB index was modified in 2005 to form the Reuters/Jefferies CRB index. Over the years, the number of commodities in the index was lowered to its current level of nineteen.

- *Launch date:* Revised in 2005.
- *Roll:* During the last revision, the index committee decided to move to monthly rebalancing and a traditional rolling mechanism. At present, the roll takes place over a four-day window between the 1st and 4th business days of the rolling month.
- *Average maturity:* The CRB average maturity is about the same as SPGSCI.
- *Energy allocation:* The index's energy allocation is low, 39% at the start of 2007.
- *Outperformance:* This index has the largest allocation to agriculture of any index, thus it will outperform the other indices when agriculture does best. Also, by trading a few days ahead of the SPGSCI and DJAIG, the CRB can benefit from markets that are in contango.

Deutsche Bank Liquid Commodity Index (DBLCI)

Overview: The key feature of the DBLCI is its low number of markets compared to the other indices. It is a value-based index. This index consists of only six highly liquid commodities with each commodity having large weights compared to other indices. Commodities included in this index are WTI crude oil, heating oil, aluminum, gold, wheat, and corn. Aluminium creates exposure to industrial metals while gold create exposure to precious metals.

- *Launch date:* February 2003.
- *Roll:* This index has a dual rolling strategy: energy products are rolled each month while the others are rolled once a year during the annual rebalancing period, between the second and sixth business day of November. During this rebalancing period, energy products are rolled into contracts expiring in two months while the other contracts are rolled into contracts expiring in December of the next year.
- *Average maturity:* The longest of any of the conventional commodity indices, the DBLCI has a considerable variation in maturity during the year. It is shorter in the fall just before the annual rolls and long in winter just after the rolls.
- *Energy allocation:* The index target is 55% in energy and 22.5% each in agriculture and metals.
- *Outperformance:* Low diversification means that the DBLCI could perform very well if its subset of commodities does well. It has a heavy allocation to grains, no soft commodities (e.g. cocoa, sugar, coffee, etc.) or livestock and no natural gas. The DBLCI will benefit from upward-sloping forward curves, as it holds long maturities and rolls ahead of the SPGSCI and DJAIG.

Diapason Commodities Index (DCI)

Overview: The DCI, a value-based index, is one of the broadest commodity indices available, with 48 components representing four major raw material sectors. The significance of the commodity in world trade constitutes one-third of weighting, while the remaining two-thirds is determined by its liquidity. Weights in the index are rebalanced monthly to the predetermined level set at the beginning of the year. Unlike most of the other indices, the DCI has some very thinly traded commodities like coal, electricity, lumber, and ethanol, which might prove to be an impediment at large investment flows. At present, the index holds 13 energy products, seven industrial metals, four precious metals, four livestock products, and 20 agricultural products. While an interesting approach to indexing the commodity markets, the DCI is not really an investable index given that even a small investment (e.g. $100 million) would create liquidity problems for an index-tracking product.

- *Launch date:* June 2006.
- *Rolls:* The DCI rolls contracts from the front to the next during the last three business days of the month two months prior to expiration (about two weeks before the SPGSCI and the DJAIG). The index is rebalanced at the same time that rolls are executed.
- *Average maturity:* Due to an accelerated roll, the average maturity of the DCI is longer than the SPGSCI and DJAIG. The index also holds some contracts with a small number of contract rolls per year.
- *Energy allocation:* For the first part of 2009, the target allocation to the energy sector was set at 54.58%, roughly equal to the average allocation among commodity indices.
- *Outperformance:* Significant weight is allocated to small, illiquid markets that appear in none of the other indices.

JP Morgan Commodity Curve Index (JPMCCI)

Overview: JPMCCI introduced a new concept in commodity index investing by holding the entire commodity curve as opposed to holding only the front contracts held by the more popular indices. This index holds exposure along the entire commodity curve in proportion to the open interest of each tenor. The index included 33 commodities when it went live in 2007. Two more commodities were added to the index at the beginning of 2008. The energy sector had the highest weight among the component sectors with an allocation of approximately 46% at the beginning of 2009. The index contains some less liquid contracts like NYBOT Orange Juice, LIFFE White Sugar, and MGE Spring Wheat. This index has a Light Energy version, which holds the same commodities as the main index but caps allocation to the energy sector at 33%.

- *Launch date:* November 2007.
- *Rolls:* The index rolls on the first to tenth business day. The major roll occurs from the expiring contract to the next contract, and other contracts rebalance during the roll period.
- *Average maturity:* Average maturity varies among different groups of futures. The average maturity is close to six months for energy contracts, two to three months for precious metals, and around four months for industrial metals.
- *Energy allocation:* Around 46% at the beginning of 2009.
- *Outperformance:* The JPMCCI will outperform when deferred contracts perform better than front contracts, and could also perform better than other indices in high negative roll periods.

UBS Bloomberg Constant Maturity Commodity Index (CMCI)

Overview: UBS and Bloomberg L.P. have created a series of value-based commodity indices that seek to keep the weighted average maturity of any particular commodity in the index at a constant value ranging from three months to five years. CMCI indices from four to five years are available only for a specific number of commodities. Constant maturity is attained by holding two contracts expiring around the target maturity in a proportion that makes the weighted average of the contract maturities match the target maturity. This method involves a continuous rolling mechanism that is expected to reduce the negative roll yield in adverse markets. The weight for each commodity is determined by a combination of economic factors like CPI, PPI, GDP, and liquidity factors.

The three-month maturity holds 26 components of which seven are in the energy sector, 10 are agricultural commodities, five are industrial metals, two are precious metals, and two are livestock products. The index holds two contracts of both crude oil and sugar. The number of commodities in different CMCI indices declines as the maturity of the index increases. The index with a maturity of four years holds only five commodities whereas the one-year maturity index holds 20 commodities.

- *Launch date:* February 2007.
- *Roll:* The index utilizes a constant-maturity roll method similar to the BCI. It slowly rolls forward in each of the target maturities to maintain a constant weighted average maturity. The shortest maturity, three months, rolls about a month ahead of the SPGSCI and DJAIG.
- *Average maturity:* The main selling point in this index is its emphasis on average maturity. The design is much closer to a constant-duration bond index than an equity index. It remains to be seen if there is sufficient liquidity in the deferred contracts to support a significant level of tracking products.
- *Energy allocation:* The CMCI energy allocation is low. For the first part of 2009, target allocation to the energy sector is 34.81%, which is close to the target allocation of energy sector of the DJAIG Commodity Index.
- *Outperformance:* The outperformance is difficult to measure since there are many versions of the CMCI. The three-month CMCI version has been used for recently announced index-tracking products, so it seems likely that this version will come to dominate. The three-month CMCI will outperform during periods when agriculture and metals do better than energy products due to the low CMCI energy allocation. All versions, including the three-month CMCI, have a longer average maturity than the SPGSCI and DJAIG. So, the index will outperform the SPGSCI and DJAIG during contango.

17

Investment Vehicles and Asset Allocation

Most commodity investments are delivered through index-linked structures. These include not only vanilla, delta-one structures such as swaps and structured notes, but also an array of complex structures such as principal-protected notes, levered notes, and options.[1]

DELTA-ONE INDEX-LINKED STRUCTURES

Commodity index swaps

A **commodity index swap** is an exchange of cash flows in which one of the cash flows is based on the price of a specific commodity index, and the other cash flow is based on an interest rate. Commodity index swaps are the preferred vehicle for most institutional commodity investments. Swaps are competitively priced, with multiple dealers making markets in swaps on several major commodity indices. Competition among vendors ensures liquidity and provides multiple counterparties to spread the default risk that stems from OTC swap transactions.

Investors sometimes prefer this structure because it allows them to maintain control of their cash. While most indices include a collateral return equal to that of Treasury Bills, most investors can achieve higher collateral returns by managing the cash themselves. The cash can also be utilized in portable alpha strategies or, if desired, held in Treasury Bills. The principal drawback of OTC swaps is that only a small number of investors have access to this market, which is limited to large, highly creditworthy investors. Most commodity investors are excluded from directly participating in these structures. Also, the secondary market for commodity swaps is not liquid, so early termination or modification of swap agreements typically requires negotiating with the counterparty.

Index-linked notes and exchange-traded notes

The **commodity index-linked note** market is somewhat more expensive than swaps but offers a number of advantages. These include a secondary market and much smaller minimum investments. Index-linked notes appeal primarily to investors who prefer to hold bonds, often for regulatory purposes. Many investors are obligated to own securities and have difficulty owning futures contracts. Furthermore, futures contracts and swaps require frequent margin and/or collateral postings. Index-linked note structures do not require collateral since the structure is already fully collateralized. Finally, there is a secondary market for index-linked notes. A swap contract cannot generally be transferred, but ownership of notes is easily transferred.

Exchange-traded funds (ETFs) linked to commodity indices have been successfully launched on a number of exchanges. ETFs offer a liquidity advantage over other index-linked structures

---

[1] One can find a myriad of payoff structures in various commodity-linked notes that commercial and investment banks have been issuing via the EDGAR/SEC database.

because they are easily arbitraged. If the price of the commodity ETF falls below fair value, it can be profitable for commodity trading desks to purchase shares in the fund and sell the index short to lock in the profit.

Exchange-traded notes (ETNs) are index-linked notes that are listed on major stock exchanges. ETNs are frequently referred to as *prepaid forward contracts*, because the notes are economically equivalent to fully collateralized forward contracts for delivery of the index value. The advantage of the ETN structure is primarily related to taxation. Commodity indices have a high turnover rate, so profits and losses are usually treated as short-term income. However, since an ETN is based upon the index value (rather than futures contracts), an ETN may qualify for capital gains tax treatment if held for a long enough period of time. One disadvantage of ETNs is credit risk exposure. This risk is generally higher than the counterparty risk inherent in a commodity index swap. In a swap contract, the counterparty posts collateral at regular intervals so counterparty risk is usually no more than a few percent of the total notional size of the swap.

Fully margined, long-maturity futures contracts on several commodity indices are also available. These are economically equivalent to ETNs, except that they are listed on futures exchanges rather than stock exchanges. The key difference between these contracts and typical commodity futures contracts is that long-maturity index-linked futures contracts are fully margined. The investor must post 100% collateral at the time of investment (market-makers and other commercial users of these contracts are required to post much smaller margin amounts). Index-linked futures contracts offer one of the least expensive solutions for retail investors. Furthermore, there is less credit risk associated with futures exchanges than with ETNs.

LEVERAGED AND OPTION-BASED STRUCTURES

Leveraged notes

Many index-linked notes offer leveraged exposure to commodity indices. These are referred to as leveraged notes. A common structure offers three times leveraged exposure to a commodity index. Because these notes can default (a decline of more than 33% in the index would result in default), there is also an embedded put option that protects the issuer against default (the cost of this put option is embedded in the upfront fees).

The main benefit of leveraged notes is the high commodity exposure. In a three-time leveraged note, each $1000 note controls $3000 of commodity exposure, so an investor can add exposure without committing large amounts of capital. These notes provide a middle ground between an index-linked swap (no up-front capital commitment) and ETN structures (100% collateralized at purchase).

Principal-guaranteed structures

Many investors prefer **principal-guaranteed notes**. These notes offer investors the opportunity to profit if commodity prices rise, combined with a guarantee that the principal amount will be returned at the maturity of the structure. These structures are popular with retail investors but have generated little interest from institutional investors. This is because a steep decline in commodity prices will cause the issuer to shift 100% out of commodities and into bonds. This feature of principal-protected notes ensures that the investor will not lose principal, but if the notes are shifted into bonds, it prevents the investor from benefiting from the diversification properties of commodities.

For example, investors holding notes that were shifted into bonds during 2006 would have missed out on the commodity bull market in 2007 and 2008.

HEDGE FUNDS AND FUNDS-OF-FUNDS

Hedge funds that focus exclusively on commodity investment have attracted significant levels of investment. Hedge funds are familiar with commodity investments and provide pure alpha, pure beta, and alpha-plus-beta options in various hedge fund products. Hedge fund alpha is available through a number of methods, including cash management, long-short positions, and instrument choice (Burkart, 2006). A detailed discussion of the types of strategies used by commodity hedge fund managers is in the Commodity Alpha section of this chapter.

In an actively managed hedge fund, there is no guarantee that a manager will maintain a long position in commodities, as most hedge funds utilize a core risk management principle of managing total risk by neutralizing systematic risk through hedging (Till and Eagleeye, 2005). Commodity hedge funds also utilize market timing strategies. Historically, the correlation between commodity hedge fund returns and the returns of the underlying commodities has been low.

ASSET ALLOCATION

Commodities have been proven to enhance the risk-adjusted returns of diversified portfolios. Commodity returns have low correlations to stocks and bonds, and a higher correlation with inflation, particularly unexpected inflation and the rate of change in inflation. Research has shown that an allocation to commodities can improve the efficient frontier, or risk-adjusted return of the portfolio (see Chapter 13, Review of Major Articles). Additionally, research has shown that commodities have a low and sometimes even negative correlation with each other, and so can offer uncorrelated investment opportunities across various commodity markets. In particular, the energy sector is frequently negatively correlated to the non-energy sectors, because higher energy prices can weigh on economic growth and depress demand for other commodities. This correlation pattern can potentially help lower the risk of a diversified commodity portfolio (Till and Eagleeye, 2005).

Gorton and Rouwenhorst (2006) found that for time horizons longer than one month, an equally weighted commodity futures portfolio was negatively correlated with the return on the S&P 500 and with the return on long-term bonds. Although the hypothesis that the correlation of commodity futures with stocks is zero at short horizons cannot be rejected, their findings suggest that commodity futures are effective in reducing the risk of equity and bond portfolios. The negative correlation of commodity futures with stocks and bonds tends to become more negative as the holding period increases. This pattern suggests that the diversification benefits of commodity futures may only be realized at longer horizons (Gorton and Rouwenhorst, 2006).

Commodity futures returns are positively correlated with inflation, and correlation has been shown to increase over longer time horizons. Because commodity futures returns are volatile relative to inflation rate, the long-term correlations better capture the inflation hedging properties of commodity investments. While stocks and bonds are negatively correlated with inflation, the correlation of commodity futures with inflation is positive at all horizons and statistically significant at the longer horizons. Commodity futures' opposite exposure to (unexpected) inflation may help to explain why commodity futures do well when stocks and bonds perform poorly (Gorton and Rouwenhorst, 2006).

The optimal portfolio allocation to commodities will be largely determined by the expected risk premium. The statistical properties of commodities are attractive for most investors, providing diversification benefits and a positive correlation with inflation. For this reason, most investors can justify a commodity allocation even if the risk premium is low.

In addition to providing hedging against unexpected changes in inflation, commodity indices may provide exposure to long-term growth in world demand that may also result in increasing demand and prices for certain commodity products (Greer, 2000).

References

Anson, M. "Spot Returns, Roll Yield, and Diversification with Commodity Futures." *Journal of Alternative Investments*. pp. 1–17. Winter 1998.

Baillie, R. T., Y.-W. Han, R. J. Myers, and J. Song. "Long Memory Models for Daily and High Frequency Commodity Futures Returns." *Journal of Futures Markets*. Vol. 27, Issue 7, pp. 643–668. 2007.

Beenen, J. "Commodity Investing: A Pension Fund Perspective." *Futures Industry Magazine*. September/October, pp. 18–22. 2005.

Black, K. "The Role of Institutional Investors in Rising Commodity Prices." Ennis Knupp + Associates. 2008.

Blanch, F. and S. Scheis. "Merrill Lynch Global Commodity Paper #4: Selecting a Commodity Index." Research Report. Merrill Lynch. 2006.

Bodie, Z. and V. Rosansky. "Risk and Return in Commodity Futures." *Financial Analysts Journal*. Vol 36, pp 27–39. May/June 1980.

Booth, D. G. and E. F. Fama. "Diversification Returns and Asset Contributions." *Financial Analysts Journal*. Vol. 48, No. 3, pp. 26–32. May/June 1992.

Burkart, D. W. "Commodities and Real-Return Strategies in the Investment Mix." CFA Institute. December 2006.

Cargill, T. F. and G. C. Rausser. "Temporal Price Behavior in Commodity Futures Markets." *Journal of Finance*. Vol. 30, pp. 1043–1053. September 1975.

Cashin, P. and C. J. McDermott. "The Long-Run Behavior of Commodity Prices: Small Trends and Big Variability." IMF Staff Papers. Vol. 49, pp. 175–199. 2002.

Cashin, P., C. J. McDermott, and A. Scott. "Booms and Slumps in World Commodity Prices." IMF Working Paper, (99/155). 1999.

Cootner, P. H. "Returns to Speculators: Telser Versus Keynes." *Journal of Political Economy*. Vol. 68, Issue 4, p. 396. 1960.

Cuddington, J. T. "Long-Run Trends in Primary Commodity Prices: A Disaggregated Look at the Prebisch-Singer Hypothesis." *Journal of Development Economics*. Vol. 39, pp. 207–227. 1992.

Elder, J. and H. Jin. "Long Memory in Commodity Futures Volatility: A Wavelet Perspective." *Journal of Futures Markets*. Vol. 27, Issue 5, pp. 411–437. 2007.

Erb, C. and C. Harvey. "The Strategic and Tactical Value of Commodity Futures." *Financial Analysts Journal*. Vol. 62, No. 2, pp. 69–97. 2006.

Evans, G. and S. Honkapohja. *Learning and Expectations in Macroeconomics* (Frontiers of Economic Research). Princeton, NJ, Princeton University Press. 2001.

Froot, K. "Hedging Portfolios with Real Assets." *Journal of Portfolio Management*. Summer, pp. 60–77. 1995.

Gorton, G. K. and G. Rouwenhorst. "Facts and Fantasies About Commodity Futures." *Financial Analysts Journal*. Vol. 62, No. 2, pp. 47–68. 2006.

Gorton, G. B., F. Hayashi, and K. G. Rouwenhorst. "The Fundamentals of Commodity Futures Returns." Yale ICF Working Paper No. 07-08. 2007.

Greer, R. J. "Conservative Commodities: A Key Inflation Hedge." *Journal of Portfolio Management*. Summer, pp. 26–29. 1978.

Greer, R. J. "The Nature of Commodity Index Returns." *Journal of Alternative Investments*. Summer, pp. 45–52. 2000.

Heap, A. "China: The Engine of a Commodities Super Cycle." Research Report. Citigroup Global Markets. 2005.

Helmuth, J. W. "A Report on the Systematic Bias in Live Cattle Futures Prices." *Journal of Futures Markets*. Vol. 1, No. 3, pp. 347–358. 1981.

Hicks, J. R. *Value and Capital*. London, Oxford University Press. 1939.

Hurwicz, L. "Theory of the Firm and Investment." *Econometrica*. Vol. 14, No. 2, pp. 109–136. 1946.

Idzorek, T. "Strategic Asset Allocation and Commodities." Ibbotson Associates White Paper. March 2006.

Kaldor, N. "Speculation and Economic Stability." *Review of Economic Studies*. Vol. 7, Issue 1, pp. 1–27. 1939.

Kazemi, H., T. Schneeweis, R. Spurgin, and G. Martin. "Real Assets in Institutional Portfolios: The Role of Commodities." Alternative Investment Analytics LLC Research Report. 2007.

Kazemi, H., T. Schneeweis, and R. Spurgin. "The Benefits of Commodity Investment." Alternative Investment Analytics LLC Research Report. 2008.

Keynes, J. *A Treatise on Money*. London, MacMillan. 1930.

Lautier, D. "Term Structure Models of Commodity Prices: A Review." *Journal of Alternative Investments*. Summer, pp. 42–64. 2005.

Leuthold, R. M. "Random Walk and Price Trends: The Live Cattle Futures Market." *Journal of Finance*. Vol. 27, Issue 4, pp. 879–889. September 1972.

Peterson, P. E. and R. M. Leuthold. "Using Mechanical Trading Systems to Evaluate the Weak Form Efficiency of Futures Markets." *Southern Journal of Agricultural Economics*. Vol. 14, Issue 1, pp. 147–151. July 1982.

Pringle, A. and T. Fernandes. "Relative-Value Trading Opportunities in Energy and Agriculture." *Intelligent Commodity Investing: New Strategies and Practical Insights for Informed Decision Makings*. H. Till and J. Eagleeye (eds). London, Risk Books. pp. 313–340. 2007.

Satyanarayan, S. and P. Varangis. "An Efficient Frontier for International Portfolios and Commodity Assets. Policy Research Working Paper 1266. World Bank. March 1994.

Schneeweis, T. "The Benefits of Commodities – 2006 Update." Working Paper. Center for International Securities and Derivatives Markets. 2006.

Schneeweis, T., H. Kazemi, and R. Spurgin. "Momentum in Asset Returns: Are Commodity Returns a Special Case?" *Journal of Alternative Investments*. Spring 2008.

Schneeweis, T., R. Spurgin, S. Das, and M. Donohue. "Comparison of Commodity Indices: Multiple Approaches to Return." Alternative Investment Analytics Working Paper. 2009.

Till, H. "Structural Sources of Return and Risk in Commodity Futures Investments." Working Paper. EDHEC Risk and Asset Management Research Centre. 2006.

Till, H. "Part I of a Long-Term Perspective on Commodity Futures Returns: Review of the Historical Literature." *Intelligent Commodity Investing: New Strategies and Practical Insights for Informed Decision Makings*. H. Till and J. Eagleeye (eds). London, Risk Books. pp. 39–82. 2007a.

Till, H. "Part II of a Long-Term Perspective on Commodity Futures Returns: Term Structure as the Primary Driver of Returns." *Intelligent Commodity Investing: New Strategies and Practical Insights for Informed Decision Makings*. H. Till and J. Eagleeye (eds). London, Risk Books. pp. 83–94. 2007b.

Till, H. "Amaranth Lessons Thus Far." *Journal of Alternative Investments*. Spring, pp. 82–98. 2008a.

Till, H. "Long-Term Sources of Return in the Commodity Futures Markets: Evidence From the Grain Markets." *Hedge Fund Review*. pp. 45–46. October 2008b.

Till, H. and J. Eagleeye. "Commodities: Active Strategies for Enhanced Returns." *Journal of Wealth Management*. pp. 42–61. Fall 2005. Also in R. Greer (ed.), *The Handbook of Inflation Hedging Investments*. New York, McGraw-Hill. pp. 127–157. 2005.

Till, H. and J. Gunzberg. "Absolute Returns in Commodity (Natural Resources) Futures Investments." Working Paper. EDHEC Risk and Asset Management Research Centre. 2005.

Till, H. "Case Studies and Risk Management Lessons in Commodity Derivatives Trading," a chapter in *Risk Management in Commodity Markets: From Shipping to Agriculturals and Energy* (Edited by H. Geman), Chichester: John Wiley & Sons Ltd., pp. 255–291. 2008c.

Walton, D. "Backwardation in Commodity Markets." Working Paper. Goldman Sachs. 1991.

Williams, J. and B. Wright. *Storage and Commodity Markets*. Cambridge, Cambridge University Press. 1991.

Working, H. "The Theory of the Price of Storage." *American Economic Review*. Vol. 39, pp. 1254–1262. 1949.

Crack Spread Handbook. New York Mercantile Exchange. http://www.nymex.com/broch_main.aspx. June 4, 2001.

Section B
Managed Futures
Ernest Jaffarian[1]

[1] Please see the acknowledgements in the Preface for a list of employees at Efficient Capital Management as well as others who made significant contributions to this section.

Introduction

With $200 billion in assets under management, 902 entities registered as commodity trading advisors (CTAs) and another 397 registered as Commodity Pool Operators (CPOs), the managed futures industry plays a vibrant role in the alternative investment industry, and more broadly in global investing. While still relatively small compared to other investment categories, its size and strong performance during the recent financial crisis (both absolutely and relative to equities and other hedge fund styles) indicate that managed futures will continue to attract the attention of many investors. This section, which consists of five chapters, covers core concepts and issues related to CTAs and CPOs.

The first chapter in this section, Chapter 18, describes the development and regulation of the futures markets and the managed futures industry. It delineates the roles and responsibilities of the major participants in the futures markets including introducing brokers (IBs), futures commission merchants (FCMs), commodity trading advisers (CTAs), and commodity pool operators (CPOs). Generally, the term "managed futures" refers to various systematic trading strategies applied to futures markets and, in the case of foreign exchange, to cash/forward markets. Chapter (19) describes major trading strategies and focuses on three main systematic strategies: trend following, non-trend following and relative value.

Much of the same work that provides a framework for measuring investment risk in other strategies (e.g. Value at Risk (VaR) and stress tests), has been applied to managed futures as well. However, the industry has developed some idiosyncratic ways of measuring and describing risk (e.g. margin to equity ratio, capital at risk and maximum drawdown) and these are discussed in Chapter 20. It also covers two basic approaches to research on the performance of managed futures: the profitability of trading strategies used by CTAs and the profitability of CTAs and CPOs themselves.

Chapter 21 begins by considering five attributes that, as a group, tend to distinguish managed futures from other hedge fund styles, particularly those involving less liquid securities: liquidity, no directional bias, optionality, implicit leverage, and transparency. It continues by reviewing CTA indices. Some of the difficulties in assessing the performance of the CTA universe as a whole are summarized in Chapters 20 and 21. The most important drawback of using published indices as a benchmark is that there is no single database that encompasses the entire industry. When looking at indices of CTA performance, therefore, researchers must take into account that, while perhaps representative, not all managers will be included in a particular index. Instead, the index will represent the performance of only those CTAs who reported to the database at that time. This may give rise to certain biases such as selection bias or survivorship bias, which are discussed as well. Chapter 21 presents various types of indices, including investable indices.

The final chapter in this section, Chapter 22, illustrates an investment process commonly used by firms when allocating to managed futures. In general, this process does not differ materially from the one employed by other hedge fund investors (covered in more detail in Part IV). It begins by describing the qualitative and quantitative analysis of the investment strategy of a manager, which leads to an investment recommendation, and then discusses a formal due diligence process that focuses not on the investment strategy, but on the required documentation and operations of the investment fund. The chapter concludes with a discussion of performance monitoring.

There is considerable overlap and contradictory views on the classification of managed futures. In particular, "managed futures" is sometimes referred to as a type of hedge fund strategy and sometimes as a strategy distinct from hedge funds entirely; sometimes it is treated as synonymous with global macro hedge fund strategies, and sometimes described as a hybrid of the two strategies. In the CAIA curriculum, we treat managed futures in a comprehensive manner: we refer to it as a type of hedge fund strategy but devote a distinct section to it outside of the discussion of other hedge fund strategies. From our perspective, managed futures strategies are distinct from global macro hedge funds strategies because global macro hedge funds trade in a wider range of instruments than futures contracts. In addition, global macro hedge funds tend to be more discretionary whereas CTAs tend to be more systematic. The strategies are similar in that they both trade in many of the same underlying markets, but returns to these strategies are not highly correlated.

CAIA Association 2009

18

Managed Futures Industry Development and Regulation

The Chicago Board of Trade (CBOT), founded in 1848, is the oldest existing futures exchange in the world. Initially established for hedgers (those who use the market to reduce risk of an existing position), the exchange experienced a much-needed boost in liquidity when speculators (those who work to predict market direction) became active participants. Market makers (those who make a living by meeting bid-ask spreads) then provided bids and offers to hedgers and speculators, vastly improving the efficiency of the markets.

Other futures exchanges in North America and Europe date to the latter half of the 1800s. The London Metals Exchange was established in 1876, the New York-based Coffee, Cocoa, and Sugar Exchange opened in 1882, and the Winnipeg Grain Exchange began in 1887. Markets became truly global in the 20th century with the opening of more exchanges in North America, Asia, and Europe. Examples include: the Chicago Mercantile Exchange (1919), the Commodity Exchange (COMEX) in New York (1933), the Tokyo Grain Exchange (1952), Sydney Futures Exchange (1960), London International Financial Futures and Options Exchange (LIFFE) (1982) and Marché à Terme International de France (MATIF) in Paris (1986).

U.S. governmental regulation of the U.S. futures markets began in 1920 with the creation of the Grain Futures Administration. The U.S. government from nearly the outset delegated certain regulatory powers to the industry itself. For instance, it considered setting limits on daily price movements itself, but by 1925 had given that power to the CBOT board of directors. This aspect of partial self-regulation continues to be a part of the U.S. futures industry.

The managed futures industry developed as individual firms began trading on behalf of clients. The earliest recorded futures fund dates back to 1948. In the 1970s, such firms numbered in the hundreds and as of December 31, 2008, there were 902 entities registered with the U.S. Government as **Commodity Trading Advisors (CTAs)**.

The term "managed futures" has often been used interchangeably with CTAs. However, this is not entirely accurate. CTA refers to the U.S. regulatory category of Commodity Trading Advisor – an entity that is required to register with the U.S. **Commodity Futures Trading Commission** (CFTC). As defined, a "CTA is an individual or organization which, for compensation or profit, advises others as to the value of or the advisability of buying or selling futures contracts or commodity options." (**National Futures Association** (NFA) website 2008, definition of Commodity Trading Advisor). All entities managing money using futures contracts for U.S.-based investors must register with the CFTC. This includes both trading firms themselves and other entities such as funds-of-funds who allocate assets to futures traders, but who do not directly trade themselves.

It may be useful to introduce the managed futures industry in terms of the trading styles most often employed. Generally, managed futures refer to various systematic trading strategies applied to futures markets and, in the case of foreign exchange, to cash/forward markets. Also, there are a relatively small number of CTAs who classify themselves as having a discretionary trading style. These managers will be close to global macro managers in terms of their trading style. However, as stated above, global macro hedge funds trade in both cash and futures markets and therefore have more discretion in implementing their trading programs.

The dominant managed futures trading style is referred to as trend following (e.g. see Fung and Hsieh, 1997). Trend followers use various systematic approaches to establish long and short directional positions in individual futures markets. As the name implies, these strategies attempt to profit from extended price trends. It is important to note that empirically, trend following strategies and market timing strategies display the same properties and cannot be distinguished from each other (see Fung and Hsieh, 1997). However, in theory and implementation these are distinct strategies. Hedge funds that classify themselves as market timers use various statistical techniques to predict trends in security prices before those trends are established. Trend following CTAs, on the other hand, establish positions once a trend has already been observed. A "perfect" market timer will capture all potential profits of a trend, while a "perfect" trend-following CTA will be somewhat "late" and therefore would miss the potential profit associated with the initial stage of the trend.

Managed futures also include other systematic futures trading strategies. For instance, some strategies concentrate on very short-term futures price patterns, relying on high frequency price data as short as individual "tick" data and where the short-term movement being analyzed may be measured in seconds to frequencies of just few days. These strategies are referred to as "short term" or "systematic non-trend" trading. Historically, these short-term strategies have shown very low correlation to longer-term trend following strategies because they take advantage of short-term trends that may have no relationship with current long-term trends. For example, while the current long-term trend may indicate that oil futures will rise over the next 30 days, short-term traders may profit from certain intra-day declines in prices.

DEVELOPMENT OF FUTURES MARKETS

Until the 1960s, futures markets were comprised primarily of contracts related to agricultural products. This began to change with the introduction of precious metals futures. Silver had been deregulated in the United States in 1893, but the U.S. Mint continued to coin it until 1964. The elimination of silver coinage and silver certificates meant that the marketplace was now free to determine the value of silver, and in 1969 silver futures were introduced by COMEX. The U.S. government then abolished the gold standard in 1971, allowing its price to fluctuate with the market rather than being set by the government, and in 1974 futures contracts based on the price of gold were also introduced by COMEX. The removal of the gold standard also led to broader fluctuations in the value of foreign currencies relative to the U.S. dollar. In 1972, the Chicago Mercantile Exchange (CME) created the International Monetary Market (IMM) to trade futures on a range of international currencies.

With the broadening of futures markets beyond contracts on physical commodities, futures exchanges began to introduce interest rate products into the mix. The CBOT introduced the U.S. Government National Mortgage Association (GNMA) contract in 1975, followed by the CME's introduction of a Treasury-bill contract. In 1977, the CBOT began trading the U.S. 30-year Treasury bond contract, which became the highest volume futures contract in the world. The energy complex rounded out this mix with the introduction of crude oil futures on the New York Mercantile Exchange (NYMEX) in New York City in 1983, following President Reagan's decision to lift U.S. oil price and allocation controls. Europe, too, began offering interest rate products with the opening of both the LIFFE and MATIF exchanges in the 1980s.

Table 18.1 shows the three largest futures and options contracts, as measured by annual volume of contracts traded, in each of five market sectors: interest rates, equity indices, energy products, agricultural products and metals.

It's useful to note that the trading volume of a contract on an exchange will be influenced by the notional size (i.e. total monetary value represented by one contract) of the underlying instrument

Table 18.1 Top futures and options contracts – 2007 total annual volume (millions of contracts)

Interest Rate Futures and Options	
Eurodollar Futures	621
10 Year Treasury Note Futures	349
Euro-Bund Futures	338
Equity Index Futures and Options	
Kospi 200 Options	2643
E-Mini S&P 500 Futures	415
DJ Euro Stoxx 50 Futures	327
Energy Futures and Options	
Light Sweet Crude Oil Futures	121
Brent Crude Oil Futures	59
WTI Crude Oil Futures	52
Agricultural Futures and Options	
Soy Meal Futures	65
Corn Futures (DCE)	59
Corn Futures (CBOT/CME)	55
Metals Futures and Options	
High Grade Primary Aluminum Futures	40
Gold Futures	25
Copper Futures	21

Source: Futures Magazine, March/April 2008

that the contract represents. This is particularly important when looking at equity index and options trading volume. Looking at Table 18.1, it is interesting to see how financial futures (e.g. interest rate and equity contracts) have come to dominate more traditional commodity futures. This dominance can also be found in the trading allocations of many managed futures traders, where risk allocations to commodities in a diversified trend-following program might represent only 15% to 25% of total risk. The balance would be allocated to fixed income, equity indices, and foreign exchange (often traded in the interbank markets).

The creation of an array of futures contracts led to the development of a variety of strategies to invest and trade in these markets. Hedging strategies continue to be a mainstay of trading volume but the opportunity for speculative profits in futures markets attracted a number of new participants in the 1980s and 1990s. This was supported by advances in information technology, allowing wider access to real time futures price data at reasonable costs. This increase in computing power and wider access to data permitted researchers to analyze price patterns in increasingly sophisticated ways and ultimately led to the development of trading systems based on their findings.

DEVELOPMENT OF THE MANAGED FUTURES INDUSTRY

Speculative trading in futures markets has long been associated with individual traders on the "floor" of commodity exchanges. As speculative interest increased, some market participants recognized that their talent could be applied across multiple futures contracts and market sectors, thereby increasing the opportunity set for their trading (i.e. markets traded) while simultaneously diversifying their risk. Given the structure of futures markets (i.e. multiple exchanges, cities, and time zones), implementing a multi-market strategy from the "floor" of any single exchange was difficult and inefficient, leading some participants to "move upstairs".

The first commodity futures fund, Futures Inc., was established in 1948 by Richard Donchian, who developed the concept of "trend following" in futures and is considered to be the father of systematic commodities trading and the managed futures industry. His idea of diversifying some risks of traditional portfolios through allocations to commodities has generated much debate over the years within academic and industry circles. In fact, there are a number of academic journals largely dedicated to studying the futures industry (e.g. *The Journal of Futures Markets*). Much published work has been done on both the micro structure of these markets as well as the profitability of various investment strategies utilizing futures contracts. At an academic level, this debate continues. However, the growth of the managed futures industry itself indicates that futures trading has gained broad investor acceptance.

The managed futures industry grew slowly from its origin in Richard Donchian's fund. In the late 1960s, a number of entities were formed that would ultimately shape the industry into what it is today. It has been reported that the introduction of the first futures price database occurred in 1967, allowing researchers to perform systematic trading strategy analysis (Chandler 1994, p.17). Shortly there after the, Commodities Corporation (eventually bought by Goldman Sachs) was founded. Described as a "commodity think tank", Commodities Corporation funded and supported the investment research of futures traders and provided a number of trading support services as they developed their managed futures trading strategies. A number of leading global macro and systematic hedge fund managers, such as Bruce Kovner and Wim Kooyker, began their careers with Commodities Corporation.

These developments in the U.S. had their counterpart in Europe. In 1972, Conti-Commodities "began trading customer money in a trend following system. . .and became what is widely believed to be the first non-U.S. based CTA" (Chandler 1994, p18). By 1975, there were approximately 225 commodity trading advisers from around the world registered with the CFTC.

The 1980s saw significant acceleration in the growth of the managed futures industry, spurred by the creation of retail-based managed futures funds. Both the number of futures funds and the number of individually managed accounts increased dramatically, fueling a five-fold increase in assets under management in just five years (from $2 billion in 1983 to more than $10 billion in 1988). This growth in assets under management has continued over the past 20 years and by some estimates reached $200 billion by the end of 2008.

This growth in assets has intensified the academic debate over whether investing in futures constitutes an attractive investment option. There have been two threads to this debate. The first has centered on whether long-only portfolios of commodity futures belong in a diversified efficient investment portfolio. While investor allocations to these strategies remain small, at least as a percentage of an overall portfolio, there is substantial academic literature supporting the diversification benefits of long only commodity investing (e.g. Gorton and Rouwenhorst, 2006). This literature has provided an underpinning to the significant increase in investable long only passive commodity indices (e.g. S&P/Goldman Sachs Commodity Index).

The second thread to this debate has centered on whether an **actively managed** portfolio of futures can enhance return and contribute to portfolio diversification. A later chapter reviews some of the academic work looking at this issue. In summary, arguments in favor of active futures investing rely on reported good performance results, the low average correlation of managed futures to traditional investments such as stocks, and the strong asset growth of the industry as anecdotal evidence of investor support of managed futures. Others, though, argue that managed futures is not an asset class in any traditional sense since managed futures traders are as likely to hold long futures positions as short positions at any time. Therefore, any return to managed futures investing must stem from manager skill rather than a return to the asset (i.e. futures contract) itself. Further, reported performance figures may be affected by certain biases (e.g. survivorship bias), which inflate observed figures. This leads the critics of managed futures to point out that the empirical evidence of this skill is inconclusive.

Despite this debate, with $200 billion in assets under management, 902 entities registered as CTAs and another 397 registered as Commodity Pool Operators (CPOs), the managed futures industry plays a vibrant role in the global investment industry. While still relatively small compared to other investment categories, its size and its strong performance during the recent financial crisis (both absolutely and relative to equities and other hedge fund styles) assures that managed futures will continue to attract the attention of many investors.

INDUSTRY REGULATION

Asset growth in the managed futures industry moved in tandem with the growth of regulatory oversight (Note: this section offers an example of a regulatory structure based largely on the current U.S. system; rules in other countries will differ). While the U.S. government has regulated some futures trading since the 1920s, the U.S. Congress acted in 1974 to create the CFTC as a federal regulatory agency for all futures and derivatives trading. The CFTC's efforts were later joined by the NFA, an independent, industry supported self-regulatory body created in 1982, and the U.S. futures exchanges.

The NFA, in regulatory partnership with the CFTC, provides the primary oversight in the auditing of member firms. The NFA, as a self-regulatory organization, acts as the principal overseer of **futures commission merchants** (FCMs), **introducing brokers** (IBs), **commodity pool operators** (CPOs), and CTAs. It carries the primary responsibility to conduct audits, though the CFTC conducts audits as well. The NFA also provides an arbitration program for resolving disputes in the futures industry.

Foreign exchange (FX or Forex) is one area of the managed futures industry that remains largely unregulated. Futures trading in international currencies came under the purview of the CFTC in 1972 when the International Monetary Market (IMM) was founded in Chicago, but the great majority of currency trading is conducted in the over-the-counter, inter-bank spot and forward markets. Presently, it is subject only to limited regulation. Security futures, which can be either Single Stock Futures (SSF) or Narrow-Based Security Index Futures, began trading in 2002 on exchanges such as One Chicago in the U.S. and DTB (Eurex) in Europe. In the U.S., these products are regulated jointly by the Securities and Exchange Commission (SEC) and the CFTC.

As noted, there are a number of regulated entities that participate in the managed futures industry. Some of these are shown in Table 18.2 below.

If a CTA or a CPO has U.S. investors, it is subject to CFTC regulations and must register with the NFA. If a futures trading firm does not have any U.S. investors, it is not regulated by the CFTC nor is it required to register with the NFA, even if the investments are being traded on U.S. exchanges. Other exemptions to CTA and CPO registration exist. For a current listing, see the CFTC's website (www.cftc.gov).

Trading on behalf of U.S. investors in futures contracts listed on an exchange outside the United States must be approved by the CFTC; but approval is not required for trading outside the United States on behalf of non-U.S. investors. However, those trading on exchanges outside the United States may be subject to local/national regulatory agencies that oversee those exchanges. For example, the Financial Services Authority (FSA) in London regulates all investment products traded in the UK, including derivatives such as futures and options.

It is useful to distinguish the roles and responsibilities of CTAs vs. CPOs. Table 18.3 delineates some of these responsibilities.

A firm's registration (CTA or CPO) is dependent on the activities in which a company is engaged. A firm that trades directly for U.S. investors registers as a CTA. On the other hand, CPOs pool investors' funds into a collective vehicle, such as a fund or limited partnership, and then allocate the

Table 18.2   CTA, CPO, FCM, and IB definitions

CTA	Commodity Trading Advisor	A person who, for pay, regularly engages in the business of advising others as to the value of commodity futures or options or the advisability of trading in commodity futures or options, or issues analyses or reports concerning commodity futures or options.
CPO	Commodity Pool Operator	A person engaged in a business similar to an investment trust or a syndicate and who solicits or accepts funds, securities, or property for the purpose of trading commodity futures contracts or commodity options. The CPO either itself makes trading decisions on behalf of the pool or engages a commodity trading advisor to do so.
FCM	Futures Commision Merchant	Individuals, associations, partnerships, corporations, and trusts that solicit or accept orders for the purchase or sale of any commodity for future delivery on or subject to the rules of any exchange and that accept payment from or extend credit to those whose orders are accepted.
IB	Introducing Broker	A person (*other than a person registered as an Associated Person of a FCM*) who is engaged in soliciting or in accepting orders for the purchase or sale of any commodity for future delivery on an exchange who does not accept any money, securities, or property to margin, guarantee, or secure any trades or contracts that result therefrom.

capital to one or more CTAs. Funds-of-funds would be CPOs in this regard, although a CTA is also considered a CPO when it creates a fund on its own behalf.

The two most common investment vehicles in the managed futures industry are **managed accounts** and **funds**. Compared to funds, managed accounts are simpler and less expensive to establish and operate. To open a managed account, an investor goes to an FCM, completes all related paperwork and disclosure statements and negotiates the commission rate, after which the account is ready to use. In order to place and execute trades on behalf of a customer in a managed account, a CTA must possess a limited power of attorney granting such authority. The minimum investment required for an individual to open a managed futures account is generally quite high, usually $10m to $20m or more. This effectively prevents smaller investors from accessing CTAs through a direct managed account

Managed accounts have the advantage of being completely transparent, liquid, and under the investor's control but the disadvantage of having potentially unlimited financial liability should a trader lose more than 100% of the value of the account. A **futures fund**, on the other hand, requires

Table 18.3   Comparison of CTA and CPO responsibilities

CTA Responsibilities	CPO Responsibilities
Developing trading strategies.	Selecting CTAs and determining allocations to them.
Monitoring performance and reporting to investors.	Monitoring the performance of individual CTAs.
	Monitoring pool performance and reporting to investors.
Ensuring the completion of audited financial statements for submission to the NFA.	Ensuring the completion of audits for submission to the NFA.
Ensuring that funds and managed accounts meet the requirements of the CFTC and NFA.	Ensuring that the pool meets the requirements of the CFTC and NFA.
Ensuring that the investors meet all necessary requirements.	Ensuring that the investors meet all necessary requirements.
Complying with all rules and regulations of the CFTC and NFA.	Complying with all rules and regulations of the CFTC and NFA.

legal representation, a private placement memorandum, an annually audited financial statement and often an outside administrator to provide independent reporting to investors. These services come with a cost to the fund which, depending on the fund size, typically runs anywhere from 10 to 50 basis points annually. On the plus side, futures funds have two advantages over managed accounts. First, they limit the investor's financial liability to the amount invested in the fund. Second, through the pooling of assets, they may allow for greater access to managers requiring high minimum investments and allow the manager to create and manage a more diversified portfolio. On the down side, they offer reduced transparency, liquidity, and investor control.

The 1980s saw a sharp rise in the number of futures funds. While initially these funds allocated assets to a single CTA (and were often organized by the CTA itself), there grew over time funds (i.e. funds-of-funds (FOFs)) that allocated assets to multiple CTAs. This permitted the assets of the fund to be diversified across a broader spectrum of trading styles. As these diversification benefits were more widely identified (see Irwin and Brorsen, 1985), the role of CPOs grew in importance. Funds organized by CPOs offer investors the advantage of a customized mix of trading programs to meet their investment objectives. A CPO also offers the investor its services in trader selection, asset allocation, and portfolio rebalancing.

CTAs typically prefer that investors choose to invest in a fund versus a managed account as trading a number of individual managed accounts can be a burden to a CTA. Moreover, a pooled fund is simpler from the standpoint of trade allocation, auditing, tracking brokerage expenses, etc. In addition, the transparency of managed accounts has the potential of giving investors access to proprietary information, making reverse-engineering of trading strategies theoretically possible, thereby raising trust and security issues. As a result, some CTAs do not offer managed accounts but require that investments be placed in their own fund.

Once the decision has been made to invest either in a fund or in a managed account, the money to be invested does not go to the CTA directly. In the case of a managed account, the funds are deposited into a bank account in the investor's name through an FCM. In the case of a fund, the money is sent to the bank account at the fund's administrator. FCMs are futures brokerage houses regulated by the CFTC and NFA and are subject to auditing by the exchanges. Investor money must be segregated by the FCM.[1]

Fees and commissions charged by FCMs have been under constant pressure over the years. In the 1980s, brokerage charges were as high as $50 per round turn. (A round turn is the cost of entering and then exiting a single futures contract.) Today, the round turn commission is usually under $10. With this reduction in commissions, FCMs needed increased volume to make up the difference in their revenue. Hence, FCMs have become more involved in raising investment money by introducing potential investors to CTAs and CPOs in much the same way capital introduction groups connect investors to hedge fund managers. These introductions help traders grow the amount of money under management, thereby increasing trading volume and commissions

The integrity of the marketplace itself is guaranteed by the exchanges where futures contracts are traded and their clearing members. In the U.S., futures contracts are guaranteed by the exchanges, which in turn are guaranteed by FCMs, who in turn guarantee each other. In the United Kingdom, a default fund is in place, which is funded by general clearing members. If the fund is depleted because of the failure of a clearing member, then additional equity is raised from among the members to satisfy the remaining debt. Such structures vary around the world, but increasing standardization is occurring with the mergers of more and more exchanges, banks, and other trading industry entities.

---

[1] Investor money must be held in an account separate from the general funds of the FCM.

U.S.-based CTAs and CPOs also offer investment vehicles to non-U.S. clients, as do non-U.S.-based managed futures firms. These investment vehicles are typically investment companies and are organized in a range of countries. Popular countries to register fund vehicles include the British Virgin Islands, Cayman Islands, Luxembourg, and the Channel Islands. These investment companies may or may not be listed on a stock exchange. The Irish Stock Exchange, for example, is used to list a number of these non-U.S. investment companies.

19

Managed Futures Strategies

Development of trading strategies begins with information. In the case of managed futures, the information set is twofold: fundamental and technical. One way to view these two types of information is to recognize that the fundamental trader is concerned with identifying price value, while the technical trader is concerned with price movement itself.

Fundamental analysis attempts to determine the value of an underlying security, such as a futures contract, through the use of economic and price indicators. These inputs can be economic statistics, such as quarterly economic growth, inflation, unemployment, and individual commodity supply and demand data. Estimated price values can also be impacted by: (a) changes to the monetary or fiscal policies of individual countries; (b) natural events such as a storm or disease that affects farm commodity futures; (c) "unnatural" events such as the Chernobyl nuclear accident or the terrorist attacks of September 11, 2001; (d) market factors such as depth and liquidity; and (e) market rumors.

Technical analysis focuses on price movements. It quantitatively analyzes the price history of futures contracts with the hope of identifying exploitable price patterns. Technical analysis works from the assumption that prices already incorporate known economic information but exhibit patterns that may be identified and profitably traded. For instance, if there is asynchronous global economic growth, one might find exploitable price movements (e.g. in exchange rates) as national and global economies adjust to a new equilibrium. It may even be possible to exploit price movements (e.g. price trends) resulting from government actions (e.g. intervention in FX markets or gradual changes in monetary policy). To the extent these patterns exist, and are repeated, the systematic trader need not be concerned with analyzing all of the factors at work on the market or the causes of these patterns, but concentrate instead on identifying the price pattern itself. This more focused approach allows technicians the flexibility to analyze trading opportunities simultaneously across a wide set of markets.

From these analytic approaches, managed futures strategies are developed. These can be broadly classified as either **discretionary strategies**, which employ fundamental and/or technical analysis to arrive at individual trading decisions, or **systematic strategies** (often referred to as "black box" trading models), which use quantitative methods to analyze price and/or broader economic factors. The primary difference between the two approaches is that discretionary traders use their own day-to-day judgment in determining which trading positions to establish. In doing so, they use any or all of the information that fundamental and technical analysis might use. Systematic strategies, on the other hand, are rules-based strategies leaving the trader with little or no room for discretionary input into individual trades. Instead, the discretionary aspect of the trading only arises in the original model development, in deciding when and how to revise the model over time, and how much risk or leverage to assume.

While managed futures include both discretionary and systematic trading styles, the latter is most commonly associated with the managed futures industry (whereas discretionary traders often fall into the category of global macro). Much of the discussion below will concentrate on systematic strategies given their dominance in the managed futures industry.

SYSTEMATIC TRADING

Systematic trading is usually quantitative in nature and is often referred to as computer-based or model-based trading. Systematic trading models apply a fixed set of trading rules in determining when to buy and sell futures contracts. Deviation from the rules is generally not permitted. Specific trading rules are generally derived from recurring price patterns that are identified and verified through a quantitative analysis of historical futures prices. These analyses are generally referred to as "back-tests" of individual trading strategies. The process of back-testing managed futures trading strategies is integral to the industry. While systematic traders generally apply individual trading strategies consistently, it should be noted that they rarely employ only a single trading system. Over time, managers may add new systems to their mix, drop others, or apply current systems to new futures markets. For example, a trading strategy could be a combination of a medium-term and a long-term trading system. The signals generated by these two systems would form the basis of the trading strategy. This is important to keep in mind when attempting to interpret the historical performance of systematic strategies and managers.

There are three useful questions to ask when evaluating an individual trading strategy:

- What is it and how was it developed? Here, one is looking to understand the broad underlying trading approach (e.g. trend following vs. countertrend) and specific characteristics of the strategy itself. It is also important to understand the research methods followed in developing the strategy since quantitative analysis can lead to overfitting of historical data (i.e. a historical price series may appear to have a recurring pattern when it may really be random). Only well-developed research efforts are likely to successfully distinguish between the two.
- Why does it work and why it may not work? It is important to understand the underlying hypothesis of a specific trading strategy. Such understanding is important in and of itself but is also critical in identifying market conditions (e.g. trend accompanied by low volatility) supportive of the strategy. While it may be difficult to forecast market conditions, understanding what impact various market conditions are likely to have on the strategy's performance is important in interpreting the potential success or failure of a strategy over time.
- How is it implemented? Many operational factors contribute to a successful systematic trading strategy including the selection of data sources, determination of periodicity of data, establishment of protocols to "clean" data, processing of the data into a trading signal, trade placement, trade record keeping and broker reconciliation.

Developing a systematic trading strategy is often dependent on a limited set of data. Strategy researchers hope that the data sample they use is broadly representative of past price behavior. They consider various market conditions and attempt to estimate possible performance outcomes for each strategy. However, these strategies are based on the expectation that historical price patterns will recur in the future. This does not generally prove to be the case. This means that many trading systems that appear to perform well using backtested data end up performing poorly when they are implemented in real time.

SYSTEM VALIDATION AND POTENTIAL FOR DEGRADATION

Systematic managed futures strategies rely on quantitative research methods that backtest using historical price data. Choosing the periods for backtesting is an art in itself. A strategy researcher will use many different time periods and methods of testing to identify robust trading parameter sets (i.e. specific trading rules). This backtesting never stops because continuous improvements to systems require ongoing validation. Further, once a profitable price pattern is identified and exploited by a large number of CTAs, it may disappear, or then reappear in a different form. A trading model or trading strategy that has been successful over the past ten years may not be profitable over the next ten. Managed futures traders continually assess the durability of any individual trading strategy. This assessment requires consideration of the following four factors:

- *How quickly will competitors discover this exploitable edge and replicate it?* This can directly affect the speed of **degradation** of the trading strategy over time.
- *How are the trades executed?* Poor execution can cause slippage resulting in immediate degradation.
- *How does the trading manager handle asset growth?* This is a multifaceted question covering style, strategies, and research. At its core is a recognition that some futures markets (particularly some of the futures for physical commodities) have limited market liquidity. This has proven to have significant implications for strategy performance as asset size increases. Indeed, some well-known hedge fund failures (e.g. Amaranth) have been caused by position sizes that were too large relative to their underlying markets (see Gupta and Kazemi, 2007).
- *Is there evidence of **overfitting**?* That is, is the data sample used to develop the strategy proving to be unrepresentative of current market conditions? Overfitting can also take place if the parameters of a trading model are estimated using a relatively short performance history. In such a case the parameters would give the researcher "too many" degrees of freedom and thus the model appears to fit the data rather well. However, the model will lose all of its explanatory or forecasting power when applied to a new set of observations.

SYSTEMATIC TRADING STYLES

Systematic trading strategies are generally categorized into three groups: trend following, non-trend following and relative value.

Trend-following strategies

Trend-following strategies are designed to identify and take advantage of momentum in price direction (i.e. trends in prices). All trend-following strategies use recent price moves over some specific time period (e.g. ranging from a few days to several hundred days) to identify the existence of a price trend. **Moving average** strategies identify these trends by comparing the current price of a futures market to a "smoothed" series of lagging prices. Once the current price or some moving average of historical prices moves above (below) a certain level, which could be a function of other moving averages, it may signal the beginning of a trend and a long (short) position would be initiated. **Break-out strategies**, on the other hand, focus on identifying the commencement of a new trend by observing the range of recent market prices (e.g. looking back over a specific time period). If the current price is above (below) all prices in the range, the strategy would identify this as the beginning of a trend and a long (short) position would be initiated

Many observers have described trend-following strategies as "long volatility" strategies. This is not a completely appropriate description. Trend following works best when there is an extended move in the price of a futures contract from one level to another and when that move is accompanied by low daily price volatility. This low volatility makes it less likely that the trend-following manager will be whip-sawed; i.e. forced to liquidate a position solely due to a short-term correction, only to reestablish the same position at less attractive levels once the underlying trend has reasserted itself. The higher the daily volatility of the futures price, the more likely is the occurrence of a "whip-saw." Another practical indicator that trend-following strategies are not "long volatility" is the fact that

Table 19.1 Futures markets examined by Miffre and Rallis (2007)

Agricultural Futures:	
Cocoa	Coffee C
Corn	Cotton #2
Milk	Oats
Orange Juice	Soybean Meal
Soybean Oil	Soybeans
Sugar #11	Wheat
White Wheat	
Livestock	
Feeder Cattle	Frozen Pork Bellies
Lean Hogs	Live Cattle
Metals	
Aluminum	Copper
Gold 100 oz.	Palladium
Platinum	Silver 1000 oz.
Oil and Gas	
Heating Oil	Light Crude Oil
Natural Gas	Regular Gas
Unleaded Gas	
Miscellaneous	
Diammonium Phosphate	Lumber
Western Plywood	

many trend followers use volatility to filter trade entry signals. That is, in periods of high volatility, their systems will act to filter out signals to enter some new trades.

There has been considerable academic debate over the viability of trend-following strategies. Some of this is reviewed later. One paper, which looked specifically at momentum strategies in commodity markets, serves as a useful example of the research being conducted in this area.

Miffre and Rallis (2007) examined 31 U.S.-based commodity futures contracts for evidence of short- and longer-term price momentum or reversal characteristics. The specific contracts they examined are shown Table 19.1.

Miffre and Rallis (2007) analyzed the price behavior of these futures contracts for the period January 31, 1979 through September 30, 2004. As noted by the authors, certain contracts were dropped whenever average daily trading volume fell below 1000 contracts. As a result, sample size in any single year varied between 22 and 27 contracts (Miffre and Rallis, 2007).

They began by computing the investment return from holding a position in each futures contract over a range of months (running from 1 to 60 months and referred to it as the Ranking Period). Based on the return for each ranking period, they then ranked the contracts. Next, the futures contracts were separated into quintiles. Contracts in the top and bottom quintile for each ranking period were then equally weighted and examined over a subsequent time period, referred to as the Holding Period. These periods also ranged from 1 to 60 months. Adjustments were made to avoid the problem of overlapping periods.

Results from their analysis show that 13 of the momentum strategies they examined were profitable for the period of their analysis. In fact, portfolios that held long positions in the top quintile of contracts and short positions in the bottom quintile of contracts were profitable in all but one combination of ranking and holding periods of as long as one year. Returns ranged from −3% (12-month ranking period, 12-month holding period) to 14.6% (12-month ranking period, 1-month

Table 19.2   Simple moving average definition

	Simple Moving Average (SMA)
Description	In the simple moving average, the daily prices are equally weighted. As each new price observation is added to the series, the oldest observation falls away, creating a fresh average price that is then plotted on the chart.
Signals	Enter long if price > average. Enter short if price < average.
Equation	$SMA_t(n) = \dfrac{1}{n} P_t + \dfrac{1}{n} P_{t-1} + \cdots + \dfrac{1}{n} P_{t-(n-1)}$

holding period). Reward-to-risk ratios[1] ranged from -0.1670 (for the single losing period) to a high of 0.6681 (1-month ranking period, 6-month holding period). The average return across all of the 1–12 month ranking/holding periods was 7.6%, with an average reward-to-risk ratio of 0.41.

The results of Miffre and Rallis (2007) are presented to provide some research context for the following discussion of trend-following strategies. There are many variants of trend-following strategies and two of these, moving average and breakout, are discussed below.

Moving averages represent the average price of a futures contract over a given time period. Like the underlying market itself, the average changes every day and moves along the price chart as a lagging indicator. The shorter the time period used to calculate the moving average, the more closely it will match the movement of the market price itself. Conversely, the longer the time period, the more gradually the moving average will adjust to changes in the contract price. Simple moving averages, defined in Table 19.2 , as well as weighted and exponential moving averages are employed by trend followers.

Though simple moving averages are the most commonly-used measures, exponential moving averages have the advantage of assigning larger weights to the most recent prices. A common representation of the exponential moving average is given below:

$$EMA_t(\lambda) = \lambda \times P_t + (1 - \lambda) \times EMA_{t-1}(\lambda)$$
$$EMA_t(\lambda) = (1 - \lambda)\left(P_t + \lambda \times P_{t-1} + \lambda^2 \times P_{t-2} + \ldots\right)$$
$$0 < \lambda < 1$$

Here, λ is the parameter that determines how much weight is assigned to current price relative to past prices. Since λ is less than 1, the weights assigned to previous prices decline as we move back in time. We can see from the first line that today's exponential moving average is a weighted average of the current price and yesterday's exponential moving average.

Common applications of these moving averages in trend following include:

- Identifying a buy signal when the price is above a given moving average or a set of moving averages, or a sell signal when the price dips below those levels.
- Identifying a buy signal when a shorter-term moving average crosses up and over a longer-term moving average or a sell signal when a shorter-term moving average crosses down under a longer-term moving average.
- Identifying a buy signal when a set of moving averages align upward (i.e. are all in the same direction), or a sell signal when they align downward.

---

[1] Reward–to-risk ratio is represented by the ratio of average return to standard deviation of returns.

Moving Average Example
10-day and 45-day SMA with price data

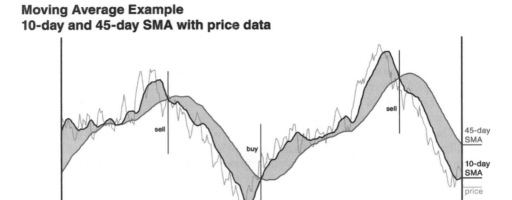

Figure 19.1   Simple moving average example

Figure 19.1 illustrates a strategy employing two moving averages to generate trading signals. In the example, the strategy uses a 10-day and 45-day moving average as the shorter-term and the longer-term indicators.

The first discrete signal in the example is a sell signal (i.e. signal to short the futures contract) because the 10-day moving average line crossed below the 45-day moving average line. Some days later, a buy signal emerged when the 10-day moving average line crossed above the 45-day moving average line. And a final sell signal occurred when the 10-day moving average line crossed below the 45-day moving average line.

Note that one characteristic common to moving average systems (indeed, nearly all trend following systems) is that they are not designed to forecast a market's future price levels or predict the beginning or end of a trend. They are actually agnostic on the expected movement in price, at least in any forecasting sense. Rather they hold positions until the most recent trend no longer exists as evidenced by a sustained reversal in the price direction. As a result, trend managers following a reversal system (i.e. one that always holds either a long or short position), will always "give back" part of the unrealized trading profit as they unwind old positions and enter new positions based on a new emerging trend. Underlying these "give backs" is the intuition that only a significant change in the direction of price can conclusively indicate the end of a trend.

Breakout strategies observe ranges of prices over specific time periods and lead to long (short) trade entry points when prices break above (below) these ranges. The concept can apply to both price and volatility breakouts and, indeed, these are often used in tandem. Table 19.3 describes a simple **channel breakout** strategy.

The simplest way to think of this is in terms of a "**look back**." For example, a 20-day look back means that the trading system observes today's price in relation to all prices over the past 20 days. If today's price is higher than the upper bound (i.e. higher than all prices over that period), the system initiates a long position in that futures contract. If the price is below the lower bound of the same period, a short position is initiated. If it is within the range, then the system might continue to hold the previous position, in the case of a reversal system, or no position at all. Figure 19.2 uses a price channel to illustrate a simple breakout strategy.

Table 19.3   Channel breakout definition

	Channel Breakout
Description	Channels are created by plotting the range of new price highs and lows. When one side grow disproportionally to the other, a trend is revealed.
Signals	Buy when channel breaks upward. Sell when channel breaks downward.
Equation	UpperBound = HighestHigh(n) LowerBound = LowestLow(n) most commonly, $n = 20$ days

In this example, one observes a trend until the price consolidates in a range as indicated in the highlighted box. After some time, the futures price breaks through the upper bound of the shaded range triggering a buy signal. After a period of upward trending prices, the price once again settles into a trading range with no clear directional trend. This is highlighted in the second gray box. This price consolidation may lead some traders to exit the long position and wait for a new breakout in either direction. This eventually occurs at the end of the second shaded area. Here, the futures price declined below the lower boundary, thereby generating a sell signal.

Trend following is the dominant strategy in managed futures, both by number of managers and industry assets. This can be casually observed through an analysis of any of the leading managed futures indices (e.g. Barclay's). Correlations between this index and most of the leading known trend followers are reasonably high (e.g. 0.50 or more). Further academic work such as that conducted by Fung and Hsieh (1997) confirm trend following as the dominant style employed by CTAs.

Even when properly and regularly calibrated, trend following systems based on moving average rules usually suffer from two drawbacks (see Lhabitant, 2008). First, they are slow. Because of the inherent lag in moving average compared to market prices, they tend to enter late in a trend and exit late, that is, after the trend has reversed and losses have occurred. The second drawback is that

Channel Breakout

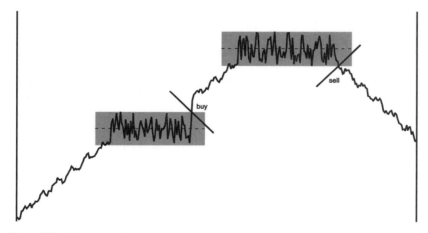

Figure 19.2   Channel breakout example

moving average rules are designed to exploit momentum in commodity prices. In order for them to be effective, returns should exhibit significant autocorrelations. This is obviously the case in trending markets, but moving average rules perform poorly in markets that evolve in a narrow range without any real trend. In this case, moving average rules tend to generate useless and costly signals; that is, the trader may end up buying high and selling low.

As mentioned above, there are trading rules that may use more than one moving average and may use moving averages that assign different weights to different observations. Below we highlight some of these more sophisticated moving average rules (see Lhabitant, 2008).

Variable length moving average rules are usually based on the comparison of two or more moving averages. One average would be the short term and the other would be long term. Long term moving average moves slower and has lower volatility when compared to short term moving average. However, in a trending market they tend to point to the same direction but at different rates. This causes the values of the two moving averages to become equal to each other or cross one another. These are called cross-over points. A buy (sell) signal is generated, then the short term average crosses the long term average from below (above).

Fixed length moving average rules are similar to variable length moving averages except that the position established following a signal is only maintained for a fixed holding period. This method is used to reduce potential losses resulting from a trend reversal.

High-low moving averages run two moving averages; one for the high prices (e.g. daily high prices) and one for low prices (e.g. daily low prices). This creates a channel of prices. These two moving averages will not cross over. They are rather used to identify support (moving average of low prices) and resistance (moving average of high prices) areas.

Triple moving average rules use three moving averages at the same time. When the shorter moving average of a commodity price crosses above a medium moving average, and the medium moving average crosses above a longer moving average, a bullish signal is generated.

Non-trend following strategies

Non-trend following strategies are designed to exploit inconsistencies in market movements such as inconsistent relative moves in prices of related commodities (e.g. oil and gasoline). They generally fall into major categories of countertrend or pattern recognition. **Countertrend** strategies use various statistical measures, such as price oscillation or a **Relative Strength Index** (RSI), to identify range trading, rather than price trending, opportunities. Pattern recognition systems look to capture systematic abnormal market behavior, identified as shapes in price or market volatility.

To illustrate a common non-trend following approach, an example of a countertrend strategy employing an RSI indicator is shown in Table 19.4.

It is useful to observe that the RSI can be used with any periodicity (i.e. unit of time). In the exhibit above, the periodicity, n, is defined as 14 days. But, it could equally have been expressed in hours, minutes, or in terms of individual price "ticks." Figure 19.3 below illustrates the use of an RSI graphically.

In its application, when an RSI is less than 30 the market is usually considered to be oversold and a long position would be taken. When its value is more than 70, the market is considered overbought and a short position taken. As can be seen in the above example, the price of the futures contract declined sharply early in the series, eventually reaching a level for which the corresponding RSI was less than 30, indicated by the dark shaded area below the 30% RSI horizontal line. At this level, this countertrend strategy would buy (i.e. go long) the futures contract and hold the position (subject to other risk management rules in the strategy) until the RSI moved back into its mid-range where it would be liquidated. As prices continued to move higher, so did the RSI, eventually reaching

Table 19.4   Relative strength indicator definition

	Relative Strength Index (RSI)
Description	Relative Strength Index (*RSI*) is an oscillator based on an index of 0 (*absolute market bottom*) to 100 (absolute market top), with 50 being neutral. The RSI attempts to determine the relative market strength of the current price of the underlying. To do this, the RSI compares the average price change of all up moves to the average price change of all down moves.
Signals	Buy when RSI < 30 (*oversold market*). Sell when RSI > 70 (*overbought market*).
Equation	$RSI = 100 - \dfrac{100}{1 + \frac{U}{D}}$ U = average of all up days for the last n days D = average of all down days for the last n days most commonly, $n = 14$

levels associated with an overbought market. The strategy would now require the trader to establish a short futures position, once again hoping to liquidate the position when the RSI returned to its mid-range.

Two aspects of countertrend trading are useful to highlight. First, non-trend following strategies trade frequently, usually much more often than most trend following systems (clearly, short-term trend-following strategy is likely to have high turnover as well). In their 2007 analysis, Miffre and Rallis found that while a number of momentum strategies were profitable, this was not the case for longer-term countertrend strategies. Recall that this study only looked at periods of one month or longer. In the managed futures industry, most countertrend strategies operate within a much shorter time frame, using periods ranging from minutes to only a few days. This higher frequency price sampling, at least relative to trend followers, more often than not results in significantly higher

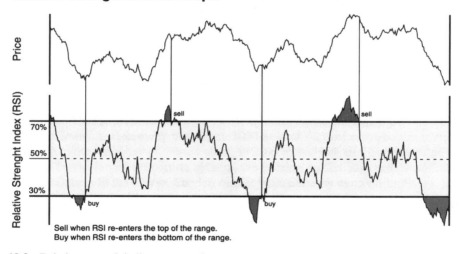

Figure 19.3   Relative strength indicator example

daily trading volumes. For instance, many trend followers trade between 1,000 and 2,000 contracts annually per $1m of assets under management whereas non-trend managers frequently trade 5,000 or more contracts per $1m.

Second, non-trend following strategies thrive in markets with reasonably high, but stable, volatility. High volatility is necessary for the strategy to have an attractive positive expected profit for each individual trade. Slow moving markets may trend for several days without signaling overbought or oversold conditions. On the other hand, the same move over a short period of time would create a signal and to the extent that those sharp moves are reversed, the non-trend following strategy would be profitable. Further, higher volatility means that the entry/exit price difference will be larger, leading to potentially higher profits. Stable volatility is beneficial because it allows the price range that the system is examining to be well formed, offering attractive trading opportunities at both extremes of the range. However, spikes in volatility after a range has formed may lead to a position being prematurely established at one end of the recent price range, only to be closed out later when the market moves outside this previously defined range.

Relative value strategies

Relative value strategies look to capture inefficient short-term price divergences between two correlated futures contracts. As in countertrend trading, RSIs can be applied to the price spread between related contracts. Table 19.5 outlines a definition of this approach.

Relative value strategies are built on the assumption that price responses in individual futures contracts to new information or changes in market liquidity can be inefficient. In managed futures, relative value strategies can focus on short time frames (e.g. measured in seconds to days) or long time frames (e.g., measured in months). Relative value strategies analyze correlation structure between two or more futures contracts and attempt to exploit deviations in prices as individual futures contracts respond differently to new information or to liquidity imbalances.

Figure 19.4 illustrates a relative value futures trade. It depicts the price evolution of two contracts, "A" and "B," which are assumed to be highly correlated (e.g. oil and gasoline). Early in the series the prices of both contracts behaved very similarly. However, after reaching an initial low, the price of contract "A" rose much faster than the price of contract "B." Relative value strategies would look to exploit the price gap that developed between these two contracts by selling (i.e. going short) contract "A" and buying (i.e. going long) contract "B." The trade would be unwound as the two price series converged.

Table 19.5 Relative value strategy definition

	Arbitrage
Description	Arbitrage strategies exploit the price differences of two correlated contracts. The contracts can involve different markets or different expirations of the same underlying at market neutral ratios.
Signals	Buy spreads when market will have to correct up. Sell spreads when market will have to correct down.
Equation	$\text{difference}_t = \text{Close}_t (A) - \text{Close}_t (B)$ $= \text{Price of } A_t - \text{Price of } B_t$ $RSI \text{ (difference)} < 30, \text{ Buy } A, \text{ Sell } B$ $RSI \text{ (difference)} > 70, \text{ Sell } A, \text{ Buy } B$

Relative Value

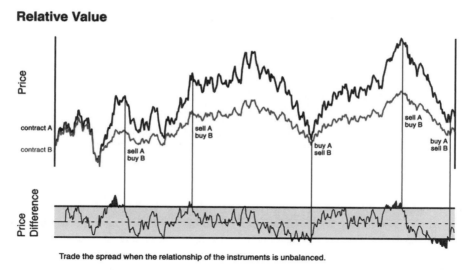

Trade the spread when the relationship of the instruments is unbalanced.

Figure 19.4   Relative value strategy example

The strategies outlined above are just a few of those used in managed futures trading. In practice, these trading strategies are often quite complex with a variety of rules and filters, entries, exits, position sizing and risk management.

DIVERSIFICATION ACROSS TRADING STYLES

Managed futures offer substantial opportunities for investment diversification. This is particularly true relative to traditional equity investing. The high correlation among individual equity securities and among equity mutual funds is widely acknowledged. With the predominance of computer-based trading, a managed futures strategy can be applied to a large number of futures contracts and markets simultaneously. It is not uncommon to find these strategies applied to more than 100 separate futures markets. Table 19.6 displays just a sample of futures markets that may be traded in a managed futures strategy.

Table 19.6   Futures sectors

	Sectors	
Commodities	Grains	Corn, Wheat, Soybeans, etc.
	Meats	Live Hogs, Feeder Cattle, Pork Bellies, etc.
	Metals	Gold, Silver, Copper, etc.
	Softs	Coffee, Cocoa, Cotton, etc.
	Energies	Crude oil, Natural Gas, Heating Oil, etc.
	Miscellaneous	Lumber, Dairy, Rubber, etc.
Financials	Interest Rates	Bonds, Bunds, Eurodollars, etc.
	Currencies	Euros, British Pounds, Japanese Yeh, etc.
	Equity Indexes	S&P, KOSPI, DAX, etc.
	Insurance	Carvill Hurricane Index, Nationwide Catastrophe, etc.

Table 19.7   Correlation of Returns of Selected Futures Contracts (1/2/07 to 1/29/09)

	Corn	Gold	Crude Oil	Soybeans	S&P 500
Corn	1				
Gold	0.3	1			
Crude Oil	0.4	0.4	1		
Soybeans	0.6	0.29	0.4	1	
S&P 500	0.17	−0.03	0.25	0.12	1

Futures contracts exhibit far less correlation among themselves than individual equities. This can be seen in Table 19.7 which presents the correlations of a sample of futures contracts. One sees in this table a wide range of individual correlations, ranging from −0.03 to 0.60. These relatively low correlations allow for portfolios of futures to have higher diversification potential than many other financial markets. The potential for diversification is further enhanced by the fact that managed futures strategies are equally likely to be long or short in any of these markets at a given time.

Managed futures strategies also achieve diversification by incorporating multiple time frames in their trading models. Industry participants acknowledge, for instance, that you cannot know beforehand whether a 45-day breakout system will outperform a 25-day breakout system. Managers address this by incorporating a number of time frames into their models, thereby diversifying their trading across time. Finally, managed futures strategies diversify across styles of trading models. For instance, some strategies may incorporate both trend-following and countertrend systems, perhaps using different time periods for each. In this case it is hoped that the diversification across styles will lead to steadier long-term performance than relying only on a single trading style.

This diversification may also be captured by funds-of-funds investing with multiple managed futures traders. For example, Table 19.8 compares a snapshot of actual currency positions held by a trend-following CTA and a relative value CTA.

Note that of the five currency positions held by these two managers, only two were in the same direction (i.e. long positions in Swiss Franc and Australian Dollar). Combining independent strategies such as these into a single approach offers diversification benefits.

This diversification and the fact that managed futures take long and short positions have contributed to one of the important characteristics of managed futures (i.e. their time varying correlation to equity markets such as the S&P 500).

Figure 19.5 shows the 24-month rolling correlation of the CASAM CISDM CTA Asset Weighted Index to the S&P 500 from 1990 through 2005, and a graph of the performance of $1 invested in the S&P 500 at the beginning of 1990. The time varying relationship of CTAs to equities is clearly displayed here. CTAs had positive correlation during equity bull markets and sharp negative

Table 19.8   Sample of Currency Positions Held Relative to the U.S. Dollar By Two Managed Futures Traders (May 31, 2006)

	Trend Following Manager	Relative Value Manager
Euro	Long	Short
Swiss Franc	Long	Long
Japanese Yen	Short	Long
British Pound	Long	Short
Australian Dollar	Long	Long

Correlation to Managed Futures During Bull & Bear Markets

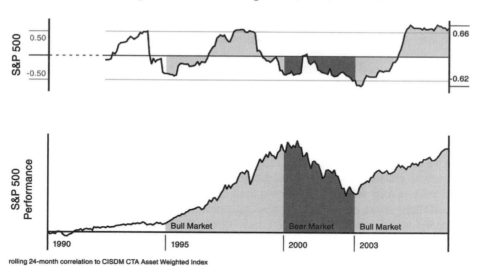

rolling 24-month correlation to CISDM CTA Asset Weighted Index

Figure 19.5 Correlation during bull and bear markets.

correlation during the bear market of the early 2000s. This pattern repeated itself during the bull market that developed in the mid 2000s and, not shown on the graph, is the fact that CTA correlation to the S&P turned negative in 2007 and 2008, as equity markets again declined.

The marketing literature provided by managed futures firms often refers to their low average correlation to equities. In fact, average correlations are indeed quite low. But this masks the fact that correlations have ranged in almost a symmetrical fashion between −0.60 and +0.60 as Figure 19.5 shows. This means that over short periods of time the correlation could be fairly high and thus the short-term diversification benefits of CTAs may be overestimated.

20

Risk and Performance Measurement in Managed Futures Strategies

Managed futures strategies have the same elements of risk found in all investment strategies. Much work has been done to provide a framework for measuring investment risk (e.g. Value at Risk (VaR)) and this work has been applied to managed futures. However, the industry has developed some idiosyncratic ways of measuring and describing risk and it is worthwhile to discuss some of these as well.

RISK EVALUATION

Margin to equity

The **margin to equity ratio** is computed as the amount of **initial margin** (which can be held in the form of cash or Treasury Bills) that must be in an account at a broker (FCM) in order to trade a specific set of futures contracts, expressed as a percentage of the net asset value of the investment account. Minimum initial margins are set by the exchanges for each futures contract. This initial margin, which is generally only a small percentage of the notional value of the futures contracts, is related to the volatility of the underlying futures contract and can change over time. More volatile contracts require larger margins. Table 20.1 displays the initial margin requirements for selected futures contracts as of January 28, 2009.

If the investment account holding the positions in Table 20.1 was valued at $1,000,000, then the margin to equity ratio would be 6.2% (i.e. $61,582/$1,000,000). It is often difficult to interpret margin-to-equity ratios. High levels could indicate highly levered trading, or could equally result from a portfolio diversified across many futures markets where margin offsets are not available (e.g. partially offsetting positions at different exchanges).

In certain circumstances, the initial margin required to be held with the broker may be less than the sum of the initial margins of the individual futures contracts. Futures exchanges take into account the fact that the manager is holding both long and short positions in related contracts. Since such spread positions may have less risk than outright directional positions, the exchanges apply a lower spread margin. For instance, a relative value trader might be long a nearby futures contract (say Long March Corn) and short a distant contract (say, Short September Corn). In such cases, spread margins would apply; in this case a margin of only $270.

Capital at Risk (CaR)

Managed futures traders almost always employ stop loss rules in their trading programs. These stop losses are specific prices at which the strategy will exit a futures position should the price move adversely. In the case of "reversal" systems, stops are effectively the price at which the system liquidates an existing directional position and establishes a new position in the opposite direction. Capital at Risk (CaR) represents the total loss that would be incurred should each position hit its stop loss price level on that day. Table 20.2 displays the CaR of a sample portfolio of long futures

Table 20.1   Margin to equity ratio selected futures contracts (as of January 28, 2009)

Futures Contract	Initial Margin Requirement For Trading One Contract
S&P 500 Stock Index	$30,938
Corn	$2,025
Soybeans	$4,725
Eurodollars	$1,485
U.S. Long Bond	$4,320
Crude Oil	$8,100
Gold	$5,399
Japanese Yen	$4,860
Total Initial Margin of a Portfolio Holding	
1 Contract in Each of the Futures Markets Above	$61,852
Assumed Size of Investment Account	$1,000,000
Margin To Equity Ratio	6.19%

positions. It assumes that each stop loss is set at 1% of the notional value of each contract (i.e. the position would be liquidated upon a 1% adverse price move based on February 4, 2009 prices).

The usefulness of CaR is dependent on the stop loss level established for individual futures positions. If this level is quite close to the current market price, the CaR might underestimate the real risk of loss since unanticipated price volatility could lead the futures price to "gap" through the stop loss level, resulting in a greater loss than that being reported by the CaR. This is a particularly important risk in less liquid markets such as futures on agricultural commodities. In another sense, though, CaR often overstates a portfolio's risk since it does not account for the possibility that a portfolio may hold both long and short futures positions, which might offer some offset should significant price moves occur. That is, it is unlikely for all positions to hit their stop loss levels simultaneously.

Table 20.2   Leverage and Capital at Risk (CaR) of a sample portfolio (February 4, 2009)

Contract	Notional Contract Value	Loss at 1% Price Change
S&P 500 Stock Index	$207,250	($2,073)
Corn	$17,913	($179)
Soybeans	$47,475	($475)
Eurodollars	$987,650	($9,877)
U.S. Long Bond	$126,640	($1,266)
Crude Oil	$40,320	($403)
Gold	$90,166	($902)
Japanese Yen	$139,636	($1,396)
Size of Notional Positions	$1,657,050	
Total CaR Value		($16,571)
Assumed Account Value:	$1,000,000	
Notional Leverage	166%	
Capital at Risk	−1.66%	

Value at Risk

Value at Risk (VaR) is a method of measuring potential loss in an investment portfolio, given a particular holding period, with no changes to the portfolio during the holding period, and at a particular confidence level. The most common confidence levels used are 95% and 99%. A portfolio's one-day VaR of $3 million at a 95% confidence level means that there is a 95% probability that losses sustained by the portfolio over the next day will not exceed $3 million, and a 5% chance that losses will be greater than that.

Using the portfolio shown in Tables 20.1 and 20.2 above (i.e. one long contract in each of the individual markets), a one-day VaR can be computed over a continuous 60-day period ending December 14, 2007. At a 99% confidence level, the one-day VaR would be $9,453, or approximately 1% of the assumed portfolio of $1,000,000. That is, one would expect that 99% of the time, the daily loss on this portfolio would be less than $9,453.

As a method of calculating risk, VaR is useful but should be used in conjunction with additional risk measurement techniques. Its reliance on specific estimates of correlations and volatilities makes it prone to underestimating potential tail risk.

Maximum drawdown

Maximum drawdown is calculated as the relative value of the last peak price to the all-time low price since the peak was reached. Suppose we wish to calculate the maximum drawdown for a CTA using performance figures covering January 2005–December 2008. Then we estimate the maximum drawdown using the following expression:

$$\text{Max Drawdown} = \left[\text{Min} \left(\frac{NAV_{t+i}}{NAV_t} \right) - 1 \right] \times 100$$

where t is any date between January 2005 and December 2008 and $t+i$ is any date between t and December 2008. For example, suppose the NAV of a CTA at the end of June 2007 was 120 and the NAV of the same fund was 90 at the end of August 2008. The ratio would be $(90/120) = 0.75$, which turns out to be the lowest value that can be obtained using the fund's NAVs between January 2005 and December 2008. In this case, the maximum drawdown of the fund is calculated to be -25%. Maximum drawdown is a useful measure of risk because it shows how sustained are the losses experienced by a manager, and may be used to determine if the manager has the skill to reevaluate his/her model and make appropriate adjustments when losses are increasing. Maximum drawdown may be used by risk managers as well. For example, a risk manager may follow the maximum drawdown of a fund and decide that whenever the fund's maximum drawdown reaches some predetermined level, the fund should significantly reduce its leverage or reevaluate the fund's trading system.

Stress tests

A **stress test** is a market simulation applied to a portfolio to determine how it will perform under different market scenarios. Commonly, these try to focus on extreme market events, both those historically encountered (e.g. the financial crisis in the summer of 1998) and simulated financial stress. Often this technique is used in conjunction with VaR since it examines scenarios where volatility and correlations are assumed to change.

Table 20.3 illustrates a stress test under simplified assumptions. It analyzes the demand on cash in an investment account should a set of futures positions simultaneously have an 8 standard deviation

Table 20.3 Portfolio stress test: 8 standard deviation price move; doubling of initial margin (February 4, 2009)

Contract	Notional Contract Value	One Standard Deviation Move In Price	Potential Loss From 8 Standard Deviation Price Move	Initial Margin Requirement
S&P 500 Stock Index	$207,250	1.24%	−$20,559	$30,938
Corn	$17,913	1.68%	−$2,408	$2,025
Soybeans	$47,475	1.45%	−$5,507	$4,725
Eurodollars	$987,650	0.08%	−$6,005	$1,485
U.S. Long Bond	$126,640	0.63%	−$6,383	$4,320
Crude Oil	$40,320	2.17%	−$7,000	$8,100
Gold	$90,166	1.26%	−$9,089	$5,399
Japanese Yen	$139,636	0.66%	−$7,373	$4,860
Total Loss From 8 Standard Deviation Price Move			−$64,322	
Total Required Initial Margin				$61,852
Potential Total Cash Demand:				
8 Standard Deviation Price Move	$64,322			
Initial Margin at 2X Levels	$123,704			
Total	$188,026			
Assumed Account Value:	$1,000,000			
Potential Total Cash Demand as Percent	18.7%			

adverse price move and, at the same time, futures exchanges double the required initial margins on these same positions. Recall from the preceding exhibits that these futures positions have a Margin to Equity Ratio of 6.19%, a CaR of 1.66%, and a VaR of 1%. However, under the conditions assumed in the stress test, the portfolio could lose over 6.4% on that day. This is significantly higher than indicated by the CaR or the VaR. In addition, the doubling of the initial margin creates a further demand on cash of 12.3% of the account value. The combined impact would be an 18.7% usage of cash in the portfolio over one day. While this may be an unlikely scenario, the purpose of stress tests is to examine the potential impact of low probability events. It has been seen in the past (e.g. Long Term Capital Corp. or Lehman Brothers) that these low probability events do occur.

Understanding investment risk in any portfolio requires constant interpretation of multiple risk factors. This is no less true in managed futures. But doing so in managed futures is made somewhat easier because these strategies typically only trade futures contracts listed on major exchanges or liquid over the counter foreign exchange. In both cases, pricing of these instruments is transparent and continuous, thereby permitting the risk of these portfolios to be monitored and measured on a real time basis.

RESEARCH ON PERFORMANCE OF MANAGED FUTURES

Academic research has focused on the managed futures industry from two perspectives. The first analyzes individual investment strategies in futures markets in order to identify potentially abnormal returns from these strategies. Usually, this involves identifying and analyzing various momentum and/or contrarian investment strategies. The second approach analyzes the actual performance results of managed futures traders.

Research on performance of individual trading strategies

Schneeweis, Kazemi and Spurgin (SKS) (2008) review of a number of published studies that examine trading strategies in futures markets. They note that this research follows from similar work done on traditional asset markets such as individual equities. Some studies (e.g. Grundy and Martin (2001), Jegadeesh and Titman (2002), Griffin, Ji and Martin (2003)) identify the presence of momentum in individual equities. Other studies (e.g. Cooper, Gutierrez and Hameed (2004), Lesmond, Schill and Zhou (2004), Hwang and Rubesam (2007)) indicate that profits from momentum strategies, if they do exist, may not cover transaction costs, may not be present under certain market conditions and may not be present in all segments of the market (e.g. large versus small cap stocks).

The research on **momentum** in futures markets follows from this research in individual equities. Here, a number of studies conclude that momentum exists in several futures markets during various time periods and under many market conditions. Okunev and White (2003) looked at momentum-based strategies in currency markets. As noted in SKS (2008), Okunev and White ". . . used data from eight countries over the 1975–2000 period. They showed that it is possible to generate momentum trading profits in foreign exchange markets without frequent trading." Similarly, Bhojraj and Swaminathan (2006) examined currency and equity markets for the presence of momentum and reversals. Their results find "currency momentum profits up to three years after portfolio formation when the data sample contains emerging markets and profits up to six months after portfolio formation when only the data of developed countries is applied." (SKS, 2008).

Pirrong (2005) and Miffre and Rallis (2007) also find evidence of momentum in futures markets. Pirrong examined global financial and commodity futures markets and identified profitable momentum and reversal trading strategies. Miffre and Rallis (2007), analyzing commodity futures prices, examined 56 momentum and contrarian strategies. They did not find the contrarian strategies to be profitable but noted that ". . .13 momentum strategies are found to be profitable . . ." (Miffre and Rallis, 2007).

Other studies (e.g. Corredor, Muga and Santamaria, 2006) have resulted in different conclusions. They find that after transaction costs or risk adjustments, profitability on an individual strategy disappears, at least in certain markets, such as stock futures contracts in small equity markets. However, one major reason cited by other researchers as to why momentum strategies may be more successful in futures markets is the low transaction cost of trading futures relative to the contract size. This is a result of low direct costs of trading futures contracts (e.g. brokerage commissions of $5–7 for a round turn trade).

Research on performance and benefits of managed futures

A more direct way to examine the attractiveness of a managed futures investment is to directly analyze the performance of managed futures traders. In 1983, John Lintner presented one of the first academic papers on this topic. His analysis was designed to examine the risk/return characteristic of managed futures accounts or funds. In this study, Lintner concluded that "the combined portfolios of stocks (or stocks and bonds) after including judicious investments. . .in managed futures accounts (or funds) show substantially less risk at every possible level of expected return than portfolios of stocks (or stocks and bonds) alone."

Lintner's work provided an initial academic basis for investing in managed futures. Other early studies that followed his both challenged and supported his results. A series of studies by Elton, Gruber, and Rentzler (EGR, 1987, 1989, and 1990) examined public commodity pools and found little evidence of the benefit of managed futures. These EGR studies are more fully discussed in the Level I review material. Other analyses of managed futures supported the inclusion of managed

Table 20.4   Comparative performance of CTAs and traditional assets (1991 to 2008)

Index	CISDM CTA Equal Weighted Index	S&P 500 Index	Lehman Government/Corporate Bond Index
Annualized Return	8.7%	7.9%	7.0%
Annualized Standard Deviation	9.2%	14.4%	4.9%
Information Ratio	0.94	0.55	1.81
Maximum Drawdown	−9.4%	−44.7%	−5.1%
Correlation with CISDM CTA Equal Weighted Index	1.00	−0.11	0.23

futures in investment portfolios (see McCarthy, Schneeweis and Spurgin, 1996, Edwards and Park, 1996, Schneeweis, Spurgin, and Potter, 1997). Some of these later analyses attempted to address data issues in the EGR studies. EGR looked at public commodity pools, known to have been a very expensive way to invest in managed futures. Later analyses examined the returns of managed futures traders directly and found evidence that on average managed futures provide attractive risk-adjusted returns, especially if the performance is measured in the context of a diversified portfolio of stocks and bonds.

Academic research in this area continues today. In "The Benefits of Managed Futures: 2009 Update," a research paper produced by the Center for International Securities and Derivatives Markets, the performance of a number of managed futures indices is examined for the period from 1991 through 2008. The main results from their analysis are shown in Table 20.4.

Here, the performance of an equally weighted CTA portfolio (the CISDM CTA Equal Weighted Index) is compared to indices of traditional asset classes (i.e. S&P 500 and the Lehman Government/ Corporate Bond Index). For the period examined, 1991 to 2008, CTAs outperformed equities (annualized return of 8.7% vs. 7.9%) and bonds (annualized return of 8.7% vs. 7.0%). Considering risk as measured by standard deviation of monthly returns, CTAs fall between stocks and bonds (standard deviations are 9.2%, 14.4%, and 3.9%, for CTAs, stocks, and bonds respectively). On a risk-adjusted return basis, CTAs show a higher Information Ratio than the S&P 500 and a lower Information Ratio than bonds. CTAs are also found to be essentially uncorrelated to both equities and bonds. The individual correlations to the S&P 500 and the Lehman Government/Corporate Bond Index were −.11 and .23 respectively.

The CISDM paper offers significant insight into the performance of managed futures. Its findings of the relative return and risk of CTAs vs. traditional asset classes, and the correlation among these asset classes, provide a strong argument supporting the growth of the managed futures industry. However, researchers who have looked at managed futures, and hedge funds generally, confront a number of difficulties.

Principal among these difficulties is the lack of a central database of individual hedge fund performance. This problem is discussed in Bhardwaj, Gorton and Rouwenhorst (BGR, 2008). They note that there is no single repository of performance data for managed futures traders. Instead, there are multiple data vendors with each reporting performance figures of individual managers. The set of managers covered by these databases may have significant overlap but they would also include managers that are unique to each database. Performance reporting to these data vendors by CTAs is entirely voluntary. Some managers may report only to one database and not to others; some report only to their investors and not to any database. As a result, analyses of managed futures may differ depending on which data source is used for the analysis.

Beyond the data source issue, several other problems encountered in analyzing the performance of managed futures are discussed in BGR (2008). Again, these problems stem from the lack of uniform standards in collecting and reporting performance data. They note that there are a number of potential sources of bias in hedge fund/CTA databases. The first is **selection bias**. This stems from the voluntary nature of the data reporting process. Funds that achieve strong performance may choose to provide data to one or more databases while those with weak performance may choose not to report at all. Or, successful managers may discontinue reporting their performance as their need to attract new investment capital decreases. As a result, it can be difficult to assess the representativeness of the database.

A second issue is the **look-back bias**. This also results from the voluntary nature of performance reporting. For example, a fund may stop reporting after a period of poor performance. If performance improves, the fund may begin reporting to the vendor again. If poor performance persists, the fund may not report any further results. This pattern of selective reporting, after knowing performance results, may create an upward performance bias in average performance of the managers that report to a database. Note that the look-back bias is not likely to impact published indices that are based on these databases because most index providers do not revise the history of their index as managers decide to report their past performance.

A third issue relates to **survivorship bias**. This occurs when a fund's performance data are removed altogether from the database as a result of the fund shutting down (or, perhaps, resulting from the fund requesting that its data be removed from the database). The effect of such a removal is that the database only reflects the performance results of the "surviving funds." That is, it includes the performance only of those funds that continue to stay in business, presumably at least in part due to better-than-average investment performance. Again, this may lead to an upward bias in the estimate of the average performance of the managers reporting to a database. Similar to look-back bias, this bias is not likely to impact performance of published indices.

Most significantly, perhaps, is the issue of **backfill bias**. BGR (2008) refer to this bias as the "instant history" bias (p. 6). Backfill bias occurs when a fund decides to provide its investment performance to a vendor and, in addition to providing performance data from that date forward, it provides figures on its past performance to the database as well. The reasonable concern here is that backfilled data will be stronger for funds that eventually report to a database than funds that might have existed over the same time period but never reported their performance data (again, presumably due to poor performance). Again, this bias is not likely to impact the published values of most indices. Note that an index may have an instant history bias as well if the index is created in, say, January 2000, but the index provider decides to create a history going back to 1990. However, going forward, the index will not suffer from this bias unless the index provider decides to revise the history of the index (a rather uncommon practice).

These biases combine to make it difficult to comprehensively analyze performance results of all hedge funds, including managed futures. It is an issue that needs to be understood in interpreting the results of any performance analysis.

21

Benchmarking and Investment Products

As noted in Chapter 20, a consistent finding of various studies of managed futures industry has been their very low correlation to traditional assets and other hedge fund investment styles. This chapter focuses on the performance of managed futures by examining the performance of one of the industry's leading CTA indices for the period 1991 to 2008. The chapter begins with a discussion of some general investment characteristics of managed futures and then moves to a performance analysis and potential portfolio benefits.

ATTRIBUTES OF MANAGED FUTURES

While not completely unique, investments in managed futures have certain attributes that tend to distinguish them from other hedge fund styles, particularly those involving less liquid securities. Five such characteristics will be discussed: liquidity, no directional bias, optionality, implicit leverage, and transparency.

Liquidity

The growth in the number of futures contracts available to trade worldwide and in the total volume of futures contracts traded has provided managed futures access to an efficient and reliable marketplace. While market liquidity differs across individual contracts (e.g. agricultural futures are far less liquid than financial futures), CTAs have been able to achieve considerable diversity within their trading portfolio. Many CTAs trade 40–60 futures markets and a few trade more than 100 markets. For the trader, greater liquidity in an individual market means lower **slippage costs** (i.e. the risk that the actual transaction price of a trade will differ from the expected price when the order was placed). For the investor, the liquidity of futures markets means that investment lock-up periods are usually not required, liquidity is frequent (usually monthly, sometimes daily) and the imposition of any type of redemption restriction or gate is rare.

No directional bias

As noted earlier, managed futures strategies take both long and short positions in futures contracts. Most strategies have no directional bias built into the system and are equally likely to take a long or short position for an equivalent move up or down in a market. This is not true of other hedge fund styles as is illustrated in Figure 21.1, which shows the 12-month rolling correlation of returns from selected hedge fund styles vs. the S&P 500. As can be seen, only the CTA index demonstrates a correlation pattern that is symmetrical and centered around zero. The other hedge fund indices demonstrate a distinct long equity bias. While convertible arbitrage has shown some negative correlation at times, only CTAs have done this during times of equity market declines (excluding short sellers, who obviously have negative correlation with equity markets).

This time-varying correlation pattern provides CTAs with the opportunity (but not certainty) of profiting from rising and falling futures prices. Such a return and correlation pattern illustrates the benefit of having an investment style with no directional bias in a portfolio. There have been times,

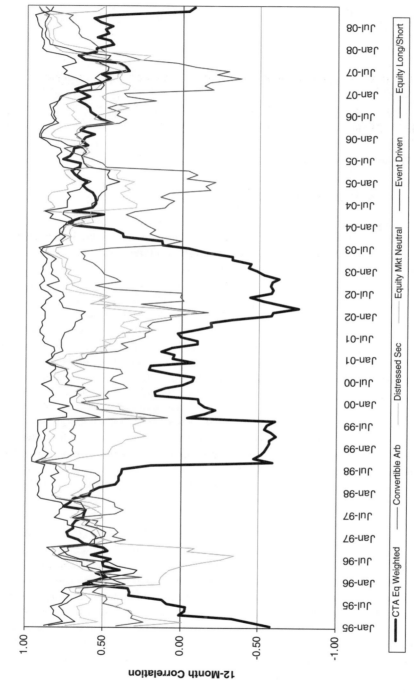

Figure 21.1 Twelve-month rolling correlation of hedge fund returns against S&P 500 returns (Source: CASAM/CISDM)

in broad equity market rallies for instance, when CTAs have been positively correlated and other times, such as broad market declines (1998, 2002, 2008), when they have been negatively correlated.

Optionality

Futures markets have long been perceived by traditional investors as being too volatile. A significant danger in a volatile market is a short-gamma position, i.e. the increase and/or decrease of market exposure as prices change. A short-gamma position loses money at an increasing rate when the market moves against the trade. Many CTAs, particularly trend followers, have a long-gamma aspect to their trading. Trend-following exposure tends to grow as the market trend develops. A move in the opposite direction of the trade will result in stop-loss orders or trade reversals that minimize the potential loss from any single trade. In a sense, traders may be able to replicate the payoff from an option through dynamic trading.

Implicit leverage

Futures markets offer levered trading with no borrowed money. This can be demonstrated by examining the cash required to trade a single Corn futures contract (in this case, on February 4, 2009). On February 4, 2009, the futures price of the March Corn Contract was $3.58. One futures contract of corn represents 5,000 bushels. So, the notional dollar value of one such contract on that day was $17,900 (i.e. the notional value of a contract equals the price per unit of the contract times the number of units the contract represents, or $3.58/bushel × 5,000 bushels). Also on that day, the initial margin required by the broker to trade one corn contract was $2,025. The implicit leverage in this position was 8.8 times (i.e. the notional value of the contract divided by the initial margin, or 17,900/2,025). Other comparative leverage numbers on that date were: S&P 500 – 6.7 times; Crude Oil – 5.0 times; and Gold – 16.7 times. It is important to note that these leverage ratios vastly overestimate the actual leverage employed in CTA trading. The ratios above are calculated using only the initial margin required to trade a contract. CTAs would also hold additional cash balances to meet margin calls on these positions should unrealized losses on the positions occur due to adverse price moves. In fact, since initial margin typically represents 10–20% of a CTA's investment account (e.g. the balance being held in cash or Treasury Securities), the actual leverage (i.e. notional value of the futures positions divided by the size of the investment account) is much less, usually running 2 times to 3 times. Unlike most other hedge fund styles, though, actual borrowing is not required to achieve this leverage. CTAs, then, are not beholden to banks for lines of credit.

Transparency

Exchange-traded futures and options prices are continuously updated and made available to the public on a tick by tick real-time basis. Market depth and volume are tracked and published by the futures exchanges and carried by data services such as Bloomberg, Reuters, and CQG. In this way, market moves are immediately known everywhere and to all. Add to this the transparency of the managed account, in which all futures positions are known, and it means that the value of a portfolio can be calculated and verified at any time. For the trader, transparency means that historical data are available for research, real-time market prices are available to use for generating trading signals, and market "color" (depth, volume, open interest, market sentiment, etc.) is available for the decision-making process. For the investor, the level of transparency is dependent upon the way the investment is structured. Funds often have limited levels of transparency, while managed accounts offer complete transparency, offering the investor full knowledge of all positions in the account and their value at any time.

PERFORMANCE OF MANAGED FUTURES INDICES

There are a variety of ways one can analyze the performance of the managed futures industry. For example, one can attempt to assess the performance of the universe of CTAs as a whole. Some of the difficulties of doing this were summarized in Chapter 20. The most important difficulty in doing this is that there is no single database that encompasses the entire industry.

A second approach is to examine indices of CTA performance. These indices are usually created from the performance of funds reporting to a single database and will be subject to selection bias, and − depending on how these indices are calculated and reported − they could be subject to other biases as well. However, as noted in Chapter 20, since the index value in any month is representative of those managers who reported to the database in that month, performance values of indices are not subject to most of the biases (e.g. backfill, look-back and survivorship biases).

The following analysis will use the CASAM CISDM database. The funds in this database accounted for approximately \$29 billion in assets in 1994. This grew to approximately \$150 billion at the end of 2008. CASAM CISDM offers a number of indices and sub indices. The data in this section examine the performance of the CASAM CISDM CTA Equal Weighted Index (CTA EQ) as reported in "The Benefits of Managed Futures," CISDM Benefits Research Series (2009).

Table 21.1 presents the performance of selected indices, including the CISDM CTA Equal Weighted Index (CTA EQ), for the period of January 1, 1991 to December 31, 2008.

Over the 1991 to 2008 period the performance of CTAs has been very competitive with traditional asset classes. The CTA EQ earned 8.7% per annum (p.a.), beating both the S&P's return of 7.9% and the Lehman Aggregate's return of 7.0%. In terms of risk, the CTA index had an annualized standard deviation and a maximum drawdown between those of the S&P 500 and the Lehman indices. This resulted in a strong risk-adjusted outperformance of the CTA index relative to equities over this period, while bonds performed better than equities and CTAs in risk-adjusted terms.

Table 21.1 also notes the low average correlation of CTAs to the S&P 500 over this time period, though as Figure 21.1 illustrated, this pattern is time varying. The correlation of CTAs to the Lehman bond index has been positive, though not overly high. This generally results from the fact that bonds had an extended bull market rally over the period analyzed and CTAs benefited from this extended trend.

One of the arguments supporting investments in managed futures has been the attractive portfolio effect they offer. Table 21.2 illustrates this argument.

Table 21.1   Comparative performance of CTAs and traditional assets (1991 to 2008)

	CASAM/CISDM CTA Equal Weighted Index	S&P 500 Index	Lehman Aggregate Bond Index
Annualized Return	8.70%	7.90%	7.00%
Annualized Standard Deviation	9.20%	14.40%	3.90%
Sharpe Ratio	0.46	0.24	0.66
Maximum Drawdown	−9.40%	−44.70%	−5.10%
Corelation with CASAM CISDM CTA Equal Weighted Index	1.00	− 0.11	0.23

Table 21.2   Comparative portfolio performance: traditional assets and CTAs (1991 to 2008)

	Portfolio I	Portfolio II	Percentage Change
Annualized Return	7.70%	7.90%	2.60%
Annualized Standard Deviation	7.60%	6.90%	−9.21%
Sharpe Ratio	0.43	0.50	16.28%
Maximum Drawdown	−21.00%	−17.30%	−17.62%
Portfolio I: Equal weight S&P 500 and Lehman Aggregate			
Portfolio II: 90% Portfolio I and 10% CASAM/CISDM Equal Weighted Index			

Table 21.2 shows two portfolios. Portfolio I represents an equal allocation to equities and bonds. Portfolio II is comprised of Portfolio I plus a 10% allocation to the CTA EQ. Adding CTA EQ to Portfolio I improves each measure of risk and return. The improvement in performance is only marginal, but portfolio risk is significantly reduced, with the standard deviation and the maximum drawdown both being lower, and risk-adjusted return increasing by approximately 16%.

More recently, the outperformance of CTAs relative to traditional assets has been more striking. Tables 21.3 and 21.4 examine performance for the period from 2001 to 2008. Note that equities lost money for this 8 year period (i.e. −2.9%) while bonds earned a return of 5.7%. CTA EQ returned 9.2% over the same period. In terms of risk measures, CTAs performed better than equities, with bonds exhibiting less risk than equities or CTAs. Not surprisingly, the benefits of adding CTAs to a traditional portfolio of stocks and bonds are quite pronounced over the period from 2001 to 2008, with all return and risk measures achieving double digit percentage improvements.

In light of the stand alone performance of CTAs and the potential benefit they offer to portfolios of traditional assets, it is sometimes surprising that this asset class has not won broader investor acceptance. To some extent this may result from some of the issues in assessing managed futures performance (e.g. no single performance database). It may also stem from reluctance in the investment community to embrace quantitative strategies. But the strong absolute and relative performance of managed futures overall, in equity market downturns in particular, offer an argument for broader use in investment portfolios.

BENCHMARKING

Over time, there have been three approaches to benchmarking managed futures performance. The first has been to use an index of long only futures contracts. Since managed futures traders are as likely

Table 21.3   Comparative performance of CTAs and traditional assets (2001 to 2008)

	CASAM/CISDM CTA Equal Weighted Index	S&P 500 Index	Lehman Aggregate Bond Index
Annualized Return	9.20%	−2.90%	5.70%
Annualized Standard Deviation	8.20%	15.00%	4.00%
Sharpe Ratio	0.68	−0.40	0.64
Maximum Drawdown	−8.70%	−40.70%	−3.80%
Corelation with CISDM CTA Equal Weighted Index	1.00	−0.26	0.17

Table 21.4 Comparative portfolio performance: traditional assets and CTAs (2001 to 2008)

	Portfolio I	Portfolio II	Percentage Change
Annualized Return	1.70%	2.50%	47.06%
Annualized Standard Deviation	7.50%	6.60%	−12.00%
Sharpe Ratio	−0.20	−0.11	45.00%
Maximum Drawdown	−21.00%	−17.30%	−17.62%
Portfolio I: Equal weight S&P 500 and Lehman Aggregate			
Portfolio II: 90% Portfolio I and 10% CASAM/CISDM Equal Weighted Index			

to be long as to be short, this approach has not been found to be particularly useful. Schneeweis and Spurgin (1997) note, "There appears to be little connection between the returns of major commodity indices and the returns of CTA indices. . . results presented suggest that CTA-based indices provide a better benchmark for an actively managed futures portfolio than either passive or active long only commodity based performance indices."

Instead, managed futures are most commonly benchmarked to indices representing active or passive futures trading. **Active benchmarks** of futures trading reflect the actual performance of a universe of CTAs. The leading indices of CTA performance are briefly described in Table 21.5.

As noted previously, there are a number of issues one needs to be aware of when using hedge fund databases, including those reporting CTA performance. Recall that many funds only report to one of these providers and not others. Indeed, some of the best CTAs have no incentive to report to any database. It is interesting to note that one of the indices shown, the Edhec-Risk CTA Global

Table 21.5 Leading CTA performance indices

Index	Provider	Start Date	Number of Managers (12/31/08)	Weighting Scheme
AlternativeEdge Short Term Trader Index	Newedge	2008	25	Volatility Equal Weighted
Barclay CTA Index	BarclayHedge	1980	491	Equal
CASAM CISDM CTA Equal Weight Index	CASAM CISDM	1980	307	Equal
Credit Suisse/Tremont Managed Futures Index	Credit Suisse/Tremont	1994	31	Assets
Greenwich Global Futures Index	Greenwich Alternatives Investments	2005	266	Equal
HFN CTA/Managed Futures Index	HedgeFund.net	1976	625	Equal
Newedge CTA Index	Newedge	2000	20	Volatility Equal Weighted
Edhec Alternative Indices: CTA Global*	Edhec-Risk	1997	4	Principal Components

*The Edhec-Risk CTA Index is combination of four of the CTA indices shown above: Barclay's, CS/Tremont HFN, and CISDM

index, is actually an index of four of the other indices in Table 21.5. The Edhec-Risk CTA index is designed to capture CTA performance across various indices.

Some index providers offer sub indices within the managed futures space. Both CASAM CISDM and BarclayHedge offer sub indices of CTAs, broken down in some cases by markets (e.g. currency-only CTA series vs. agriculture-only CTA series) and in other cases by the style of trading (e.g. systematic vs. discretionary). In addition, some firms also offer investable CTA indices. These would generally include a subset of the managers open to new investment who are already part of the full index as listed in Table 21.5 (e.g. in the case of BarclayHedge, Credit Suisse/Tremont, and Greenwich Alternatives). Alternatively, the investable index may be comprised only of managers who invest through managed accounts at a specific firm. This would be true of Lyxor, which offers the Lyxor CTAs Long Term Index and the Lyxor CTAs Short Term Index, and AlphaMetrix which offers the AlternativeEdge Short Term Traders Index Tracker Fund. Investable indices may suffer from **access bias,** which could have an adverse impact on the performance of these indices. The access bias arises because some managers may not wish to be part of an investable index because of the restrictions that such indices may impose on them. For example, the manager may be prevented from increasing or decreasing leverage outside a predetermined level, or managers may have to agree to reduce their fees. Therefore, only those managers that have difficulty raising funds outside the investable index platform may agree to be part of the platform.

CTAs are also commonly compared to **passive benchmarks** of futures trading. These passive indices represent the performance of an individual trading system, as opposed to the performance results of CTAs themselves. The case for doing this, and a methodology, is described in "Benchmarking Commodity Trading Advisor with a Passive Futures-based Index," Spurgin, Schneeweis and Georgiev (2001).

In managed futures, passive indices have been created primarily for trend-following strategies. The oldest and most prominent of these is the MLM Index. Mt Lucas Management has published the MLM Index since 1988. The index represents the daily performance of a 252-day moving average trend-following system applied to 22 futures markets. Such an index can be quite useful because it provides the return that can be achieved from a simple trend-following trading model. This return can then be compared to the performance of active trend-following managers in order to examine the value added of more active (and expensive) strategies.

While benchmarking trend-following CTAs can be a reasonably straightforward exercise due to the high correlation among trend-following strategies, the same is not true of other managed futures trading styles such as non-trend following and relative value. There is considerable heterogeneity among managers in both of these styles. For example, one fund-of-funds noted that among the 30 trend-following CTAs it examined, the average paired correlation of the 30 managers was 0.56, but of the 25 non-trend followers examined, the average paired correlation was zero, indicating no common trading style among these managers. Finding or creating useful indices to benchmark non-trend follower CTA styles remains a significant challenge. A recent paper by Kazemi and Li (2009) examines the performance of both trend-following and non-trend following managers using portfolios of futures contracts. The portfolios are created using the Shape Style analysis approach whereby returns of individual CTAs are regressed against total returns of a set of futures contracts. Kazemi and Li report that the resulting portfolios have significant explanatory power when performance of trend-following managers are analyzed (the R-squares are as high as 45%). On the other hand, performance of non-trend following managers can be hardly explained with the average R-square being about 6%. However, non-trend following managers displayed higher alphas in comparison to trend following managers.

22

Investment Analysis in Managed Futures

This chapter outlines a process often used by investors to identify and analyze managed futures traders. It is offered from the perspective of an investor examining individual managed futures traders. The outline below is not meant to be comprehensive, but rather to highlight certain steps and issues that would be common across most approaches to these investments.

SOURCING MANAGERS

There are a variety of approaches to **sourcing** potential investment candidates in the managed futures industry. One of the best ways is through referrals from knowledgeable industry participants. These could be individual managers themselves who are willing to suggest others in the industry. Alternatively, they could come from fund-of-funds managers or consultants whose business is to follow the managed futures industry. Obviously, the referral approach requires that a potential investor already has a network to draw on when considering an investment in this asset class.

Building from this, one can look at public information sources. These can include publications and/or futures brokers. For instance, *Absolute Return Magazine*, a publication of Hedge Fund Intelligence, reports the monthly returns of approximately 169 CTA investment programs and another 76 Global Macro programs. Newedge Financial Inc. makes available to its clients the monthly performance of approximately 581 CTAs.

A more common way to source managers would be through subscription to one or more database services. These are some of the same names that offer performance indices of CTAs (see Table 21.5) and include: Hedgefund.net, BarclayHedge and CASAM CISDM.

QUALITATIVE ANALYSIS OF MANAGERS

As in all investing, the quality of the firm's management and organization will contribute to its success. Some of the key factors in assessing a firm and its staff include:

- Firm
  - Principals
    - Biographies
    - References
  - Organization
    - History
    - Regulatory registrations
    - Track record
- Organizational strength and depth
  - Trading
    - Principal traders
    - Backup personnel
    - Systems
  - Back office
    - Personnel

- Systems
- Service providers
- References
  - Current and past investors
  - Banks
  - Auditors
  - Legal
  - Regulatory
  - Credit
- Goals and objectives of the firm
  - Relative to trading
    - Investment styles
    - Markets traded
    - Personnel
  - Assets under management
  - Development of new products and business lines

Consideration of the above factors is important in assessing the strengths and stability of any investment firm. Doing this assessment successfully requires significant effort and resources as well as a fully developed investment process.

QUANTITATIVE ANALYSIS OF MANAGERS

There are a number of different approaches to quantitatively analyzing individual manager performance. They all share the common element of examining the time series of a manager's performance. These time series come in many forms and can include any of the following.

- *Composite track record of many programs rather than an individual investable program.* Since firms often offer multiple investment products, it is not uncommon for them to publicize a composite performance series. However, one should analyze the performance of the product or the fund which is actually under investment consideration.
- *Actual track record of an individual product or fund.* This would be the performance series of the investment product under consideration. While this is always appropriate to analyze, these may be somewhat short, particularly in the case of new managers.
- *Pro forma or simulated track records.* New investment managers often put together pro forma performance records. In systematic trading, these are created by applying a current trading system to a series of historical prices and computing the results as if the system had been trading at that time. While the performance data generated by such an analysis are useful, and may be the only data a manager is able to show, they should be used with a great deal of caution. Most importantly, pro forma results are always subject to the issue of data fitting. That is, the performance results reflect a system whose trading parameters work over the time period tested, but are not profitable over other time periods. Even in the case of discretionary managers, pro forma records are often presented. Sometimes these represent a "carve out" of a manager's results when working for another firm (e.g. an investment bank). These results are very difficult to assess because it is never entirely clear what the manager's actual capital base was at the previous firm, whether the manager had total discretion over the trades being shown, or whether there were trades excluded from the track record.

The analysis of any performance track record can be straightforward or relatively complex. At one end of the scale is an analysis that looks at common performance measures such as return, standard deviation, drawdown and risk-adjusted returns. At the more complex end, the quantitative

Table 22.1   Comparative Performance: Selected CTA's and the S&P 500 (January 2001 to December 2008)

Performance Measure	CTA A	CTA B	CTA C	S&P 500
Annualized Return	9.60%	13.20%	14.00%	−2.90%
Annualized Standard Deviation of Monthly Returns	14.00%	15.90%	15.90%	15.10%
Sharpe Ratio	0.38	0.56	0.60	−0.44
Drawdown	−26.80%	−23.10%	−17.20%	−46.70%
Best Single Month	14.00%	14.50%	12.90%	8.80%
Worst Single Month	−7.70%	−14.00%	−12.60%	−16.80%
Average Positive Month	3.51%	3.26%	3.90%	2.60%
Average Negative Month	−2.70%	−3.40%	−3.10%	−4.10%

analysis might examine the full distribution of returns, the importance of single months or periods in overall return, and look at performance as a function of specific market conditions. Increasingly, various forms of factor analysis have been applied to managed futures performance. This has gained momentum as researchers apply investment replication techniques in their analyses.

Table 22.1 provides a simple performance analysis of three managed futures traders for the period from January 2001 through December 2008. Included in this table is the performance of the S&P 500 for the same period. Manager A is a relative value trader, Manager B is a non-trend following trader and Manager C is a long-term trend follower. Annualized returns for these managers have ranged from 9.6% to 14.0%; risk, as measured by standard deviation, ranged from 14.0% to 15.9%. Risk-adjusted returns, as measured by the Sharpe Ratio, ranged between 0.38 and 0.60. The performance of these three managers compares quite favorably against the S&P 500 over the same period, which had a return of -2.9%, a standard deviation of 15.1%, and a Sharpe Ratio of −.44. Not surprisingly, these managers exhibited little correlation to equities over this period. Correlations of managers A, B and C to the S&P 500 were −0.05, −0.37 and −0.35, respectively.

The outperformance of these three managed futures traders relative to equities over this period is quite striking, as illustrated in Table 22.1. One might have thought that since they had all outperformed equities so strongly they might have done so following similar strategies. However, the correlation matrix in Table 22.2 demonstrates that this is not the case. Here, one can see that the correlations of these managers' returns to each other are quite low.

There are other aspects of the return and risk profile of these three managers, and all managers in general, that are important to analyze. In particular, one would wish to understand to the fullest extent possible what market conditions contributed to the managers' returns. Through a thorough analysis of performance relative to specific market conditions, one might begin to develop insight into the probabilities of future outcomes that would support individual and portfolio investment decisions. In that regard, and concluding this section on quantitative analysis, it is interesting to see what the portfolio return of an equally weighted allocation to these three managers would have been from January 1, 2001 through December 31, 2008.

Table 22.2   Comparative Correlations: Selected CTA's and the S&P 500 (January 2001 to December 2008)

	Manager A	Manager B	Manager C	S&P 500
Manager A	1.00			
Manager B	0.24	1.00		
Manager C	0.30	0.26	1.00	
S&P 500	−0.05	−0.37	−0.35	1.00

Table 22.3   Portfolio Return: Selected CTA's and the S&P 500 (January 2001 to December 2008)

Performance Measure	CTA A	CTA B	CTA C	Equal Weight CTA Portfolio	S&P 500
Annualized Return	9.60%	13.20%	14.00%	12.40%	−2.90%
Annualized Standard Deviation of Monthly Returns	14.00%	15.90%	15.90%	11.00%	15.10%
Sharpe Ratio	0.38	0.56	0.60	0.68	−0.44
Drawdown	−26.80%	−23.10%	−17.20%	−15.60%	−46.70%
Best Single Month	14.00%	14.50%	12.90%	8.40%	8.80%
Worst Single Month	−7.70%	−14.00%	−12.60%	−8.70%	−16.80%
Average Positive Month	3.51%	3.26%	3.90%	2.80%	2.60%
Average Negative Month	−2.70%	−3.40%	−3.10%	−2.30%	−4.10%

Table 22.3 demonstrates the diversification that may be achieved by allocating to multiple CTAs following different trading styles. An equally weighted portfolio of the three CTAs has a standard deviation and drawdown well below any of the CTAs individually and, in fact, considerably below the average across the same group of CTAs (a 27% reduction and a 30% reduction, respectively). Again, for comparative purposes, performance statistics for the S&P 500 are also presented in Table 22.3.

INVESTMENT RECOMMENDATION

After analyzing individual managers both qualitatively and quantitatively, the investment process in most firms eventually moves on to a formal **investment recommendation**. Investment firms, such as funds-of-funds, have their own formal process for recording these recommendations, but most of these would include:

- General Manager information
  - Name of firm and contact information
  - Name of specific investment fund/product being recommended
  - Assets under management of the firm and the fund/product
- Description of the management company and regulatory registrations
- Biographical information of key staff
- Investment references
- Description of the investment strategy, including markets traded, liquidity, time frames, and full discussion of investment style
- Quantitative review of investment strategy
- Discussion of investment risk
- Discussion of current portfolio activities
- Subscription/redemption terms of the fund along with its fee structure, and information about whether investments can be "side pocketed," or redemption restrictions ("gates") be imposed
- Specific amounts to be invested
- Evidence of investment recommendation approval (i.e. authorized signature)

Again, the specific information and level of detail included in a formal investment recommendation differ from firm to firm. However, the existence of a formal process, backed by independent due diligence, is widely felt to be a required "best practice" in the industry.

DUE DILIGENCE

Firms, such as funds-of-funds, have increasingly separated the functions of investment analysis from the **due diligence** appraisal. A due diligence review focuses on the legal documents of an investment vehicle and back office operations of an investment firm. The skills required for a due diligence review, such as legal, accounting and operational risk assessment, are often not the same in assessing the investment strategy of a manager. Assessing the strategy will require knowledge of markets and the macro economic environment, and involve a fair degree of sophisticated quantitative analysis. These are different skills than those required to review managers' documents or accounting systems.

The formal due diligence process begins with a review of all of the documents and counterparties involved in an individual investment. It also includes a review of the internal procedures of the investment manager. As an example, the due diligence process is likely to review the entire applicable fund documents discussed below.

Offering documents

Offshore and onshore hedge funds are marketed to investors through an **offering document**, referred to as an Offering Memorandum or Private Placement Memorandum. The offering document is similar to a mutual fund prospectus. It summarizes the terms of the investment product including a description of the fund's structure (e.g. where it is domiciled, what laws govern it, whether it is listed on an exchange), investment goals and objectives, management team, fees and expenses, and subscription and redemption terms. The offering document serves a marketing purpose and is not the legally operative document of a fund. The operative documents are the articles of association or bylaws, in the case of an offshore fund, and the limited liability company (LLC) agreement or the limited partnership agreement (LPA), in the case of a U.S. fund. A full due diligence review will examine all of these documents for consistency and completeness.

Subscription agreement

Investors in a hedge fund need to complete a **subscription agreement**. This includes detailed information about the investor. As anti-money laundering (AML) rules have been adopted in many legal jurisdictions, subscription agreements have increasingly asked for proof of the identity of the investor. For individual investors, this has been in the form of certified copies of passports and proof of address. Requirements for investment by a legal entity (e.g. a trust) will often include the entity's incorporation or registration document, proof of identity of directors/general partner/trustees, authorized signatory lists, etc. In the case of U.S. investment products, subscription agreements include a number of questions designed to ascertain whether the investor is "qualified," that is, whether the investor has sufficient income and/or assets to legally qualify as eligible to participate in certain investments.

Redemption form

A **redemption form** is provided to investors at the time of their initial investment. This usually provides information about redemption terms and restrictions. This would include the frequency at which redemptions are allowed (e.g. monthly, quarterly or annually), the notice period required for a redemption (e.g. 90 days before the redemption date), special terms such as whether a penalty can be imposed on redemptions of investments not held for minimum periods of time (e.g. a 5% redemption penalty on investments held less than one year), lockup periods (e.g. periods of time after the initial investment during which no redemption is permitted), and whether redemptions may be suspended and under what conditions.

Investment advisory agreement

For offshore funds, the investment manager will sign an **investment advisory agreement** with the fund itself. The agreement will describe the obligations of the investment manager with regard to that investment vehicle. In the case of a U.S. limited partnership, the investment manager generally acts as the general partner and the obligations are set forth in the limited partnership agreement.

Administration agreement

Most offshore funds, and increasing numbers of U.S. limited partnerships, use outside **administrators** for certain tasks. These include the responsibility for receiving subscriptions into the funds and paying out redemptions. In addition, and importantly, it also includes valuing the fund on a periodic basis, most commonly on a monthly basis. For managed futures, this valuation process is normally straightforward since most of the instruments traded are readily priced on a transparent futures exchange. The administration agreement is important in that it outlines the obligations of the administrator relative to this pricing process.

Audited financial statements

Both offshore funds and onshore partnerships undertake an **annual audit**. These audits are provided to current and prospective investors. It is common for prospective investors to request at least three years of audits prior to formally deciding to invest. These audits are reviewed to verify information provided by the manager, to assure that there is an unqualified audit letter and to discern whether there has been a change in auditor over this period. While there are often simple explanations as to why an auditor has been replaced, prospective investors usually wish to discuss the reasons with a manager and often with the audit firm directly.

NFA or other regulatory websites to confirm registrations

In the U.S., CTAs are required to register with the CFTC through the self-regulatory body, the NFA. On its website, the NFA provides information on each of its registered firms including the current registration status of the firm and its history, a list of the principals of the firm, and whether the firm has been subject to any regulatory or arbitration actions.

Upon successful review of these documents and the onsite review of a manager's operations, a formal due diligence will be issued and signed by the head of the due diligence process. For most investment firms, an approved recommendation and an approved due diligence report are necessary for an investment to be made.

PERFORMANCE MONITORING

After an allocation to a managed futures trader is made, most firms institute a formal monitoring and review process. However, most have the following central elements.

On a regular basis, each investment will be quantitatively compared on the basis of its realized return and its risk, as well as on the basis of its correlation structure to its history, to some designated peers and to manager benchmarks. Here, deviations from expectations and/or historical performance are identified. While such a review is usually done on a continuous basis, the degree of idiosyncratic performance of managed futures traders usually leads to a more formal review on a periodic (usually semi-annual or annual) schedule. At that time, other aspects of the investment are also reviewed. These would typically include reviewing changes in any of the following areas: strategy/markets traded, key personnel, risk, operations, liquidity and counterparties.

Also, on a periodic basis (usually annually), a due diligence review is performed. On a formal basis, the investment would then be formally re-approved for the next investment horizon.

The above examples of an investment process are presented as an illustration of practices found in firms allocating to managed futures traders. They do not differ materially from the practices one would find in other hedge fund investment styles.

References

Bhardwaj, G., G. Gorton, and K. G. Rouwenhorst. "Fooling Some of the People All of the Time: The Inefficient Performance and Persistence of Commodity Trading Advisors." Yale ICF Working Paper No. 08-21. 2008.

Bhojraj, S. and B. Swaminathan. "Macromomentum: Returns Predictability in International Equity Indices." *Journal of Business*. Vol. 79, Issue 1, p. 429–451. January 2006.

Center for International Securities and Derivative Markets. "The Benefits of Managed Futures: 2009 Update." CISDM "Benefits of" Series. 2009.

Chandler, Beverly. "Managed Futures, An Investor's Guide," John Wiley & Sons, 1994.

Cooper, M. J., R. C. Gutierrez, and A. Hameed. "Market States and Momentum." *Journal of Finance*. Vol. 59, No. 3, p. 1345–1365. June 2004.

Corredor, P., L. Muga, and R. Santamaria. "The Profitability of Momentum Strategies Using Stock Futures Contracts in Small Markets." *Applied Financial Economics Letters*. Vol. 2, Issue 3, 173–177. 2006.

Edwards, F. and J. Park. "Do Managed Futures Make Good Investments." *Journal of Futures Markets*. p. 475–517. 1996.

Elton, E., M. Gruber, and J. Rentzler. "Professionally Managed, Publicly Traded, Commodity Funds." *Journal of Business*. Vol. 60. No. 2, p. 175–199. 1987.

Elton, E., M. Gruber, and J. Rentzler. "New Public Offerings, Information and Investor Rationality: The Case of Publicly Offered Commodity Funds." *Journal of Business*. Vol. 62, No. 1, p. 1–15. 1989.

Elton, E., M. Gruber, and J. Rentzler. "The Performance of Publicly Offered Commodity Funds." *Financial Analysts Journal*. July/August, p. 23–30. 1990.

Fung, W. and D. Hsieh. "Empirical Characteristics of Dynamic Trading Strategies: The Case of Hedge Funds." *Review of Financial Studies*. Vol. 10, No. 2, p. 275–302. 1997.

Gorton, G. K. and G. Rouwenhorst. "Facts and Fantasies About Commodity Futures." *Financial Analysts Journal*. Vol. 62, No. 2, p. 47–68. 2006.

Griffin, J. M., X. Ji, and J. S. Martin. "Momentum Investing and Business Cycle Risk: Evidence From Pole to Pole." *Journal of Finance*. Vol. 58, No. 6, p. 2515–2547. December 2003.

Grundy, B.D., and J.S. Martin. "Understanding the Nature of the Risks and the Source of the Rewards to Momentum Investing." *Review of Financial Studies*. 14, p. 29–78. 2001.

Gupta R. and H. Kazemi (2007), "Factor Exposures and Hedge Fund Operational Risk: The Case of Amaranth." CISDM Working Paper.

Hwang, S. and A. Rubesam. "The Disappearance of Momentum." Working Paper. 2007.

Irwin, S. H., and B. W. Brorsen. "Public Futures Funds" *Journal of Futures Markets*. Vol. 5, No. 3, p. 463–485. 1985.

Jegadeesh, N. and S. Titman. "Cross-Sectional and Time-Series Determinants of Momentum Returns." *Review of Financial Studies*. Vol. 15, No. 1, p. 143–157. 2002.

Kazemi, H. and Ying Li, "Market Timing of CTAs: An Examination of Systematic CTAs vs. Discretionary CTAs," CISDM Working Paper 2009, forthcoming *Journal of Futures Markets*.

Lehman Brothers. "Alternative Portfolio Solutions." New York, Lehman Brothers Inc. 2006.

Lesmond, D. A., M. J. Schill, and C. Zhou. "The Illusory Nature of Momentum Profits." *Journal of Financial Economics*. Vol. 71, No. 2, p. 349–380. 2004.

Lhabitant, F., " Commodity Trading Strategies: Examples of Trading Rules and Signals from CTA Sector," In *The Handbook of Commodity Investing* Edited by F. Fabozzi, R. Füss and D. Kaiser, Wiley and Sons. 2008.

Lintner, J. "The Potential Role of Managed Commodity – Financial Futures Accounts (and/or Funds) in Portfolios of Stocks and Bonds." Presented at the Annual Conference of the Financial Analysts Federation. Toronto Canada. May 1983.

McCarthy, D., T. Schneeweis, and R. Spurgin. "Investments in CTAs: An Alternative Managed Futures Investment." *Journal of Derivatives*. 1996.

Miffre, J. and G. Rallis. "Momentum Strategies in Commodity Futures Markets." *Journal of Banking and Finance*. Vol. 31, No. 6, p. 1863–1886. 2007.

Okunev, J. and D. White. "Do Momentum-Based Strategies Still Work in Foreign Currency Markets?" *Journal of Financial and Quantitative Analysis*. 38, p. 425–447. 2003.

Pirrong, S. C. "Momentum in Futures Markets." Working Paper. Bauer College of Business, University of Houston. 2005.

Richard Davoud Donchian Foundation. "Founder Biography." The Richard Davoud Donchian Foundation. http://www.rddonchian.org/.

Schneeweis, T., H. Kazemi, and R. Spurgin. "Momentum in Asset Returns: Are Commodity Returns a Special Case?" *Journal of Alternative Investments*. Vol. 10, No. 4, pp. 23–36. Spring 2008.

Schneeweis, T. and R. Spurgin. "Comparisons of Commodity and Managed Futures Benchmark Indices." *Journal of Derivatives*. Vol. 4, No. 4, pp. 33–50. Summer 1997.

Schneeweis, T., Spurgin, R., and M. Potter. " Managed Futures and Hedge Fund Investment for Downside Equity Risk Management." in *The Handbook of Managed Futures*, Ed. By Carl Peters and Ben Warwick, Irwin Publishing. p. 79–97. 1997.

Spurgin, R., T. Schneeweis, and G. Georgiev. "Benchmarking Commodity Trading Advisor Performance with a Passive Futures-Based Index." Working Paper. Center for International Securities and Derivatives Markets. 1999.

Part III

Real Estate

Urbi Garay and Simon Stevenson

Introduction

Real estate investment strategies represent a significant and dynamic component of institutional portfolios. The definition of real estate has not changed: it is land and everything "permanently" affixed to it. However, the methods of investing in real estate have undergone dramatic transformations. The physical real estate market and direct investing in real estate have been characterized by a relative lack of liquidity, high management costs, high information costs, high transactions costs and product heterogeneity. However, some of these costs of investing in real estate are being reduced through innovations such as those in the property derivatives markets to enhance liquidity. Other innovations include real estate investment trusts (REITs), mortgage-backed securities and increased use of mutual funds, hedge funds, closed-end funds, and exchange-traded funds to facilitate ownership of real estate.

The real estate section of the Level II curriculum covers advanced topics in real estate investment analysis. The reader is assumed to be familiar with the material specified by CAIA's Prerequisite Materials and covered in *Investments* by Zvi Bodie, Alex Kane and Alan J. Marcus (2008), as well as CAIA's Level I curriculum – especially the material regarding real estate. The emphasis of the Level II curriculum on real estate is on understanding concepts – especially as they relate to institutional investment in real estate.

The real estate material in Level II consists of nine chapters. Chapter 23 introduces the material by describing the characteristics of real estate as an asset class, as well as the main characteristics of various types of real estate investments.

Four chapters focus on specific types of real estate investments: Chapter 25 details real estate equity and its three main valuation approaches; Chapter 27 describes mortgage markets; Chapter 28 covers mortgage-backed securities; and Chapter 30 discusses alternative real estate investment vehicles.

Four chapters focus on activities or processes involved in real estate investments: Chapter 24 discusses indices; Chapter 26 details the main risks intrinsic to real estate investing and offers an introduction to due diligence; Chapter 29, focuses on the role of real estate in an investor's asset allocation and, finally, Chapter 31 addresses the topic of real estate development.

CAIA Association 2009

23
Real Estate Investments

In this first real estate chapter we describe the main characteristics of various real estate investments along two dimensions: private vs. public, and equity vs. debt (i.e. mortgage). We begin with private commercial real estate equity and then public commercial real estate equity. We conclude with private commercial real estate debt and public commercial real estate debt. We expand our discussion of real estate debt investments in other chapters including alternative real estate investment vehicles.

As an asset class, real estate has the following characteristics:

- Real estate is a highly *heterogeneous asset*. Not only are the physical features of the individual property unique in terms of location, use and design, but also varying lease structures can lead to large differences in income streams. This high level of heterogeneity is a major contributor to the lack of correlation between a number of real estate investments, as we will detail later. This heterogeneity is particularly troublesome in some international markets, such as the UK, where long-term leases and relatively infrequent rent reviews lead to situations where rental income can differ substantially from shorter-term market levels among otherwise similar properties.
- The second key characteristic of real estate is that of *indivisibility* of direct ownership. While the growth in REITs (Real Estate Investment Trusts, introduced in Level I) and in a number of alternative real estate investment vehicles has led to divisible investment opportunities at an indirect ownership level, investors at a single property level are still faced with the choice of buying the entire asset or not. The indivisible nature of real estate assets leads to problems with respect to high unit costs (i.e. large investment sizes) and relatively high transaction costs.
- The final major implication relates to the *liquidity* of real estate. As a private non-exchange-traded asset with a high unit cost, real estate is highly illiquid, especially when compared to stocks and bonds. We will have more to say about an important implication of illiquidity when we discuss the so called "illiquidity induced bias" (Chapter 24) that is present in many real estate databases.

All three of the above characteristics complicate performance measurement and evaluation.

REAL ESTATE INVESTMENT CATEGORIES

Private real estate is also known as physical, direct or non-exchange-traded real estate. Private real estate may take the form of equity through direct ownership of the property or debt through mortgage claims on the property. A mortgage is a debt instrument collateralized by real estate.

Public real estate is also known as securitized, financial, indirect or exchange-traded real estate. Public real estate is a financial claim in the form of equity and/or debt positions, and may be claims on underlying private real estate positions and/or on underlying public real estate positions. Thus public real estate *intermediates* the ownership of private real estate through one or more levels of contracts designed to facilitate real estate ownership and reduce costs and/or increase liquidity relative to direct ownership. For example, securitization has significantly increased the liquidity and accessibility of real estate investments.

For institutional investors, the two distinctions (equity vs. debt and private vs. public) of this asset class create the following four categories: private commercial real estate equity, public commercial real estate equity, private commercial real estate debt, and public commercial real estate debt (see Hudson-Wilson, Fabozzi and Gordon, 2003; and Idzorek, Barad and Meier, 2007).

The traditional distinction between equity claims and debt claims rests in the legal distinction between a residual claim and a fixed claim. However, the economic distinctions are not so clear in real estate since the performance of each one of the four real estate investment categories will reflect a mix of equity and debt behaviors. This is illustrated by the following two examples, adapted from Hudson-Wilson, Fabozzi and Gordon (2003). First, consider the case of a private real estate equity asset, such as an office, that has been leased to a single high quality tenant for a long period of time. The lease payments in this case will reflect the fixed payments usually associated with a bond, and the value of this property to the investor will also fluctuate in response to the same factors that affect the value of a bond (e.g. inflation, interest rate changes, and creditworthiness of the tenant). Now, consider the case of an equity position in an empty, speculative building. The value of this real estate asset will be determined in the market by the supply and demand for space, that is, by the forces that affect the price of an equity position. As the building becomes more fully leased, this real estate investment changes from pure equity to a debt-equity hybrid. As the property becomes fully leased to long-term tenants the investment becomes very debt-like.

Exposure to the equity side of the real estate market can be achieved via the two principal modes of investment mentioned above, namely private and public. Private real estate equity investment involves the acquisition and management of actual physical properties. Public real estate investment entails the buying of shares of real estate investment companies (REITs) and investments in other indirect forms of real estate (including futures and options on real estate indices, exchange-traded funds based on real estate, and non-exchange-traded investments such as partnerships, joint ventures, and syndications).

Private real estate equity[1]

We first detail the private side of the real estate equity market and then proceed to the public side. The private real estate market comprises several segments. These include housing or residential real estate properties, commercial real estate properties, farmland and timberland. The following are, in general, the relative advantages of investing in the private side of real estate equity (Idzorek, Barad and Meier, 2007): investors have the ability to choose specific properties; they have direct control of their investments; and, finally, they enjoy the potential for tax-timing benefits. We will discuss each of these segments in the following sub-sections and then discuss respective indices available on them in Chapter 24.

Housing or residential real estate properties

Residential real estate includes many property types, such as single family homes, townhouses, condominiums, mobile, and manufactured homes. According to Bianco Research LLC (2008), the value of residential real estate properties in the U.S. totaled U.S.$21.78 trillion at the end of second quarter of 2008, representing 114% of U.S. GDP. This is comparable to the U.S.$19.36 trillion held in domestic equities (which included some U.S.$200 billion invested in REITs) at that time.

Commercial real estate properties

Commercial real estate properties include, among others, the following categories: shopping centers, office buildings, restaurants, manufacturing, businesses, hotels, warehousing, investment properties such as multi-family apartment buildings, and land (both developed and undeveloped

---

[1] Part of this section is based on Garay (2008) and Garay and ter Horst (2009).

parcels). According to Bianco Research (2008), the market value of all domestic commercial real estate at the end of the second quarter of 2008 was estimated to be around U.S.$ 16.23 trillion.

Farmland

The Farmland Protection Policy Act (FPPA) states that **farmland** comprises prime farmland, unique farmland, and land of statewide or local importance and does not have to be currently used for cropland to be classified as farmland. Farmland can be forest land, cropland, pastureland, and certain other land types but cannot be covered by water or located in urban built-up areas.

Timberland

Timberland includes forests of tree species typically used in the forest products industry, such as ponderosa pine. Timber is a unique investment, characterized by the illiquidity and long-term nature of the investments involved and by its particular risk and return determinants. According to Akers (2002), the main risk factors in timber investments are changes in timber prices and harvest quantities. Neither of these factors is perfectly correlated to changes in the fundamental determinants of stocks and bonds. In addition to the general economy, timber prices are affected by regional supply and demand forces, seasonality, trade patterns, and weather. The supply of timber is affected by natural disasters (fire, hurricane, insect infestation, etc.) and by the growth of the forest.

According to Timberland Investment Resources, institutional investors own approximately 8% (around $18 billion) of the investable timberland in the U.S. The main owners of U.S. timberland are private, non-industrial landowners ($150 billion) and the forest products industry ($50 billion). This large investible timberland base represents a continued investment opportunity for institutional investors, particularly as private landowners and forest products companies continue to liquidate their timber holdings.

Real Estate Investment Trusts (REITs)[2]

Real estate investment trusts (REITs) are a form of public real estate. The relative advantages of investing in public commercial real estate (as opposed to private) include liquidity, greater investor access, relatively low transaction costs, the potential for better corporate governance structures, and the transparency brought by pricing in public capital markets (Idzorek, Barad and Meier, 2007). In this section, we discuss issues related to the recent growth in REITs, and in Chapter 25 we discuss the three main valuation methods.

REITs are subject to the following two main restrictions: 75% of the income they receive must be derived from real estate activities, and the REIT is legally obliged to pay out 90% of its taxable income in the form of dividends. Other restrictions relate to the ownership structure of the REIT. At present no more than 50% of the REIT shares can be held directly or indirectly by any group of five or fewer investors (based on a "look through" principle wherein a corporation with many owners is not generally counted as a single owner). As long as a REIT is in compliance with the relevant restrictions, it may deduct dividends from its income in determining its corporate tax liability (i.e. it pays corporate income taxes only on the retained income).

REITs can invest in the private real estate market (equity REITs) and also in real estate based debt (mortgage REITs). Generally, if a REIT has 75% of its assets in the private real estate market it is viewed as an equity REIT; if over 75% of assets are invested in real estate debt it would be viewed as a mortgage REIT. REITs that invest in both markets and do not comply with either 75% cut-off are termed hybrid REITs. This distinction is important in return analyses. For example,

---

[2] Part of this section is based on Garay (2008) and Garay and ter Horst (2009).

unlike equity REITS, mortgage REITs tend to move in line with bank stocks due to their underlying asset base. Equity REITs dominate the REITs sector, both in terms of number available and market capitalization.

The REIT market grew rapidly in the early 1990s. This growth was due in part to the poor underlying market conditions present at that time which, together with the drying up of traditional sources of debt capital, meant that many participants in the U.S. real estate market were forced to look at REITs as a financing alternative.

Another major factor behind the growth of U.S. REITs in the early 1990s was the development of the UPREIT (Umbrella Partnership REIT) structure. The UPREIT structure is composed of two vehicles: a REIT and an operating partnership. The rationale behind this structure is that it allows those who hold properties in a partnership structure to obtain units in the operating partnership on a tax deferred basis. Units in the partnership are subject to tax only if they are swapped for REIT shares. Therefore, existing investors can effectively defer capital gains tax liabilities. The actual underlying properties are owned by the operating partnership, in which the REIT owns units. As a result, the REIT only indirectly owns those properties in its portfolio.

Two further key changes occurred in the late 1990s: the REIT Simplification Act of 1997 and the 1999 REIT Modernization Act. The first piece of legislation contained a number of changes to the rules regulating REITs, including the elimination of the rule that prevented REITs from earning more than 30% of their gross income on the sale of assets not held as long-term investments. The major change that occurred with the 1999 REIT Modernization Act was that the minimum dividend payout was reduced from 95% to 90% of taxable income.

Figure 23.1 details the number of REIT Initial Public Offerings (IPOs) in the U.S. In 1993 and 1994 alone, 95 REIT's IPOs took place, the majority of which were equity IPOs.

Figure 23.2 illustrates the increasing dominance in the number of equity REITs relative to the number of mortgage or hybrid REITs. The reduction in the number of listed REITs in recent years is primarily due to consolidation within the industry, with a large amount of mergers and acquisitions activity taking place. Recently, privatization has been the overwhelming trend as private equity investors with substantial amounts of capital saw REITs as large and accessible pools of real estate assets.

Figure 23.3 indicates total market capitalization of REITs through time. Figure 23.3 illustrates the relatively small size of the sector prior to the early 1990s and the tremendous growth in overall

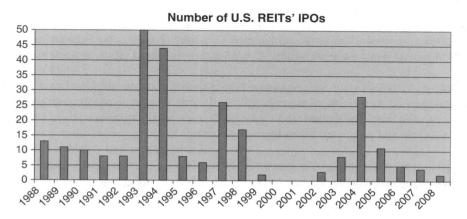

Figure 23.1   Number of U.S. REIT IPOs (Source: NAREIT)

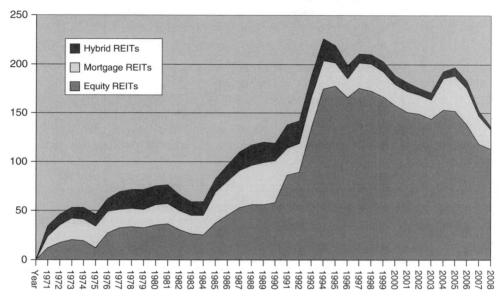

Figure 23.2 Number of traded U.S. REITs (Source: NAREIT)

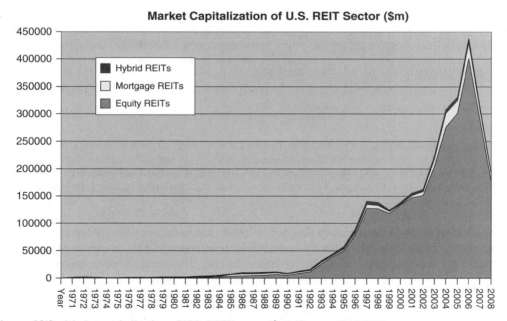

Figure 23.3 Market capitalization of U.S. REIT sector ($m) (Source: NAREIT)

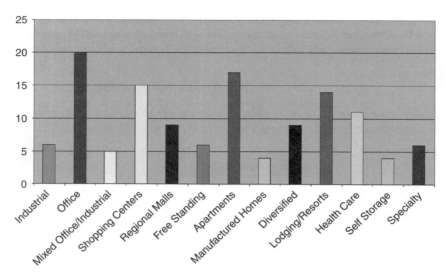

Figure 23.4   Specialization of U.S. equity REITs (December 2006) (Source: NAREIT)

market capitalization (until recently) despite the declines in the number of REITs illustrated in Figure 23.2. The financial and real estate crisis that started in 2007 had the effect of decimating the market values of REITs, including mortgage REITs which were caught with illiquid assets and short-term liabilities. Finally, Figure 23.4 shows the specialization by sector of the U.S. equity REITs market, where offices represent the main category, followed very closely by apartments and shopping centers.

In Chapter 30 we describe public real estate investments other than REITs (including options and futures on real estate indices, exchange-traded funds based on real estate indices, and closed-end real estate mutual funds). We also describe pools of private real estate investments (open-end real estate mutual funds, private equity real estate funds, commingled real estate funds, syndications, joint ventures, and limited partnerships).

Private and public commercial real estate debt

Private commercial real estate debt can be held as either directly issued whole loans, commingled vehicles or commercial mortgages held in funds. Public commercial real estate debt is primarily comprised of **commercial mortgage-backed securities** (CMBSs).

A CMBS consists of many single mortgage loans that are pooled or grouped together and transferred to a trust. The trust then issues bonds, or tranches, that may vary in yield, duration and payment priority. Interest collected from all of the pooled loans is paid to investors, starting with the highest rated tranches, until all of the interest that has accrued on those highest rated tranches has been paid. Interest is then paid to those investors holding the next highest rated tranches and so on. The same procedure is followed with principal payments as received. Credit rating agencies assign ratings to the various bond classes or tranches. Investors choose which CMBS bonds to purchase based on the combination of credit risk, duration and yield that best accommodates their needs.

Although CMBSs represent a form of real estate debt, some of the lower rated bonds or tranches may exhibit an equity-like behavior. This is because in the CMBS market the tranches vary from high-grade cash flow characteristics in the senior tranches to more equity-like cash flow character-istics in the most subordinate pieces for which receipt of interest and principal payments contains substantial uncertainty. Chapter 28 is dedicated to the analysis of mortgage-backed securities.

There also exist derivatives on real estate debt positions. For example, there are swaps based on indices of the CMBS market and private real estate debt derivatives, such as credit default swaps (CDSs).

24

Real Estate Indices

This chapter describes the main indices used to measure the returns of real estate investment categories presented in Chapter 23. It also discusses real estate database biases as well as their potential to adversely affect the reliability of inferences from index usage.

DESCRIPTION OF THE MAIN REAL ESTATE INDICES

Here we offer a brief description of the main real estate indices available, divided into three categories: private real estate equity, public real estate equity, and real estate debt (both public and private).

Private real estate equity

Housing or residential real estate properties

The values of U.S. homes or residential real estate properties are tracked by the Standard and Poor's (S&P) and Case-Shiller Home Price Indices that consist of 20 metropolitan regional indices, two composite indices and a national index. The indices are constructed using a methodology known as **repeated-sales pricing**, a process that involves recording sale prices of specific single-family homes in any region. When a home is sold twice within the database, the new sales price is combined with the previous sales price to form a "sale pair." The price differences in the sale pairs within a particular region are measured and used to infer changes in the levels of the index for that region. We expand on the methodologies used to construct real estate indices later in this chapter.

The CME Group, the combined entity created by the 2007 merger of the Chicago Mercantile Exchange (CME) and the Chicago Board of Trade (CBOT), offers futures contracts based on the S&P/Case-Shiller Home Price Indices for the following 10 U.S. cities: Boston, Chicago, Denver, Las Vegas, Los Angeles, Miami, New York, San Diego, San Francisco, and Washington, D.C., as well as on the Composite Index of all 10 cities.

Commercial real estate properties

The National Council of Real Estate Investment Fiduciaries (NCREIF) Property Index (NPI) is one of the most widely used commercial real estate property indices in the U.S. The NPI is an **appraisal-based index** (i.e. property valuations are based on appraisals rather than transactions). The NPI is a quarterly total return index of the investment performance of a large pool of individual commercial real estate properties acquired in the private market for investment purposes only. The NPI return provides an estimate of the quarterly internal rate of return (IRR) earned by an investor assuming that a property was purchased at the beginning of the quarter and sold at the end of the quarter (at appraised values) and with the investor receiving all the corresponding net cash flows (net operating profits – capital expenditures) during the quarter.

Returns based on appraisal-based indices deviate from returns based on market prices. The use of appraisals tends to smooth estimated price changes to the extent that the appraisals lag actual market changes in valuation. The smoothed prices tend to cause downwardly biased estimates of return volatility. Further, index returns based on smoothed prices tend to lag market returns and to demonstrate meaningless correlations with returns of other asset classes that are based on market prices.

Another index that measures the performance of institutional commercial properties is the MIT Transactions-Based Index (TBI). The purpose of this index is to measure market movements and returns on investments based on transaction prices of properties sold from the NCREIF Index database. Unlike the NPI, the TBI is a transactions-based index. Currently, no derivative products based on this index are being offered.

In November 2006, Standard and Poor's announced that it was teaming up with Global Real Analytics to develop and publish the S&P/GRA Commercial Real Estate Indices (SPCREX indices). There is a total of 10 indices with five representing regions in the United States (Pacific West, Desert Mountain, Midwest, Northeast and Mid-Atlantic South), four representing national property sectors (Office, Retail, Warehouse and Apartments) and one representing the entire U.S.

Farmland

The NCREIF Farmland Index is a quarterly appraisal-based index that measures the investment performance of a large pool of individual agricultural properties acquired in the private market solely for investment purposes. Only income-generating agricultural properties are included in the index. According to NCREIF, all properties in the Farmland Index have been acquired, at least in part, on behalf of tax-exempt institutional investors, the great majority being pension funds. As such, returns reflect properties held in a fiduciary environment.

Timberland

The NCREIF Timberland Index is a quarterly index that measures the investment performance of institutional timberland investments. To qualify for the index, a property must be held in a fiduciary environment and marked-to-market at least once per year. The lack of quarterly appraisals for many properties in this timberland index makes the annual return series more reflective of changes in the market than the quarterly series.

Public real estate equity

The FTSE NAREIT (National Association of Real Estate Investment Trusts) U.S. Real Estate Index Series consists of a family of REIT performance indices that covers the different sectors of the U.S. commercial real estate space. Constituents of the FTSE NAREIT Composite Index are classified into the following three investment sectors: Equity REITs, Mortgage REITs, and Hybrid REITs.

Other widely-used public real estate equity indices are the S&P U.S. REIT Composite Index, the Dow Jones Wilshire Real Estate Investment Trust DJW REIT, the Real Estate Securities Index (RESI), the Real Estate Investment Trusts Index (REIT), and the MSCI U.S. REIT. The main characteristics of the major private and public real estate equity indices are presented in Table 24.1.

Private and public real estate debt

The performance of commercial mortgages can be measured using the Giliberto-Levy Commercial Mortgage Performance Index. This index allows investors to evaluate total returns on a

Table 24.1 Main characteristics of U.S. real estate equity indices

Name	Type	Available data	Frequency	Methodology
1 Equity private				
S&P/Case-Shiller Home Price Indices	Residential properties	1990	Monthly	Repeat-sales
NCREIF Property Index	Commercial properties	1978	Quarterly	Appraisal-based
MIT/CRE Transactions-Based Index	Commercial properties	1994	Quarterly	Hedonic
NCREIF Farmland Index	Farmland	1992	Quarterly	Appraisal-based
NCREIF Timberland Index	Timberland	1987	Quarterly	Appraisal-based
2 Equity public				
FTSE NAREIT U.S. Real Estate Index	REITs	1979	Daily	Rule-based
S&P U.S. REIT Composite	REITs	1997	Daily	Rule-based
Dow Jones Wilshire REITs	REITs and REOCs	1996	Daily	Market cap weighted
Real Estate Securities Index (RESI)	REITs and REOCs	1977	Daily	Market cap weighted
Real Estate Investment Trusts (REIT)	REITs	1977	Daily	Market cap weighted
MSCI U.S. REIT	REITs	1996	Daily	Market cap weighted

marked-to-market basis. This index is calculated quarterly using aggregate returns on a pool of traditional fixed-rate loans that are collateralized by commercial real estate. The pool of mortgages underlying the Giliberto-Levy Commercial Mortgage Performance Index totals around $200 billion. Returns arising from public commercial real estate debt structured as commercial mortgage-backed securities (CMBS) are usually measured using the Lehman Brothers CMBS Index.

POTENTIAL BIASES IN REAL ESTATE INDICES

Real estate databases suffer from a number of potential biases. Here we describe the sample selection bias and the illiquidity induced bias, and comment on the effects of both data smoothing and real estate index construction methods on reported real estate returns and volatilities.

Sample selection bias

Transactions-based real estate indices suffer from **sample selection bias** to the extent that the properties that are transacted during a particular period and used to calculate these indices may not be representative of the entire universe of properties. While the effects of sample selection bias also affect residential property indices, it is likely to be especially severe for commercial properties because only a small portion of the universe of commercial properties is transacted in any particular time period. This is because the effects of randomness on the attributes of a sample tend to be larger when the sample is small.

There is another reason to be concerned about sample selection bias other than the idea that the sample of properties with transactions will deviate from the universe of all properties due to randomness. Haurin (2005, pp. 232–234) points out that "in a normal market, the real values (i.e. deflated values) of some properties will rise while others may decline. If the owners of properties with falling values tend to choose not to sell their properties, while owners of properties with rising values tend to choose to sell (or vice versa), then the sample of transacted properties is clearly not random and is biased towards a particular price outcome. It is also plausible that the choices of whether to sell properties with rising and falling values change over the real estate cycle and thus the nature of the sample selection bias will change over time. This changing bias results in an estimated transaction-based price index that differs from a theoretical price index that would track market values of the stock of all properties."

Illiquidity induced bias

Real estate is an inherently illiquid investment, especially when compared to publicly traded stocks and bonds. This is because real estate is transacted infrequently (the typical property trades once every seven years) and because it is not traded in an organized market. Furthermore, transaction costs for real estate (e.g. fees payable by one or both parties to brokers, accountants and lawyers, as well as potential taxes payable on a property transaction) are high and investment time horizons tend to be long. As a result, it is argued that total returns generated from real estate investments should reflect a liquidity premium (i.e. should be higher to compensate for the illiquidity).

The length of the real estate sales process is due to the complexities involved. For instance, while sellers will typically have to prepare the relevant documentation and hire a brokerage firm to market the property, potential buyers will often have to spend a considerable amount of time searching, dealing with the due diligence and with the financing aspects on the property. Furthermore, negotiations between the two parties can take a considerable amount of time.

Data smoothing

Data smoothing has occurred in a return series when the volatility of a proxy used as an input to the computation of returns has been dampened relative to the volatility of the true input variable. In the case of real estate indices, if appraisals are used in place of true values, and if the appraisals provide dampened price changes due to lags or a reluctance to recognize value changes, then the resulting return series will consistently underestimate the volatility of the true return series. Marcato and Key (2007) view **data smoothing** as a phenomenon that not only causes compressed volatility in valuation-based real estate indices when compared to the underlying property market prices, but also generates a lag effect wherein value changes are recognized by indices on a delayed basis. Smoothing can arise as a result of many factors, most notably in the appraisal process from "anchoring" new appraisal values to past values when the appraiser is concerned that definitive support for the current market prices is missing. Inaccurate appraisals are exacerbated by lack of reliable current market information about property values.

An important consequence of smoothing is its impact on asset allocation decisions because smoothing affects the estimation of risk-return profiles of various assets employed to design efficient portfolios. For instance, portfolio models based on Modern Portfolio Theory and using smoothed volatility data would recommend allocating a sub-optimally high weight to real estate equity investments when appraisal-based real estate indices are used and result in artificially low levels of measured risk. However, institutional investors have historically utilized a real estate weight of only between 5% and 10% of their portfolios rather than the high weights suggested by models using the smoothed return volatilities. An explanation of the difference is frequently attributed to institutional investors being aware of the underestimation of risk in available real estate indices.

Infrequent trading is another characteristic of real estate that can cause a downward bias in the measurement of real estate return volatility (i.e. real estate investments appear to possess relatively low return volatility). More on the issue of allocation to real estate assets is included in Chapter 29.

CONSTRUCTING REAL ESTATE PRICE INDICES: APPRAISAL METHODS AND TRANSACTION-BASED METHODS

As detailed above, returns computed from appraisal-based indices suffer from deficiencies, such as smoothed or lagged estimated price changes. As a result, appraisal-based indices tend to underestimate actual property volatility.

There are various methods of using property transactions to construct a price index. The most frequently used are the "repeat-sales" method, which is explained earlier in this chapter, and the "hedonic-price" method (see Haurin, 2005). Each of these two methods uses econometric regressions to explain real estate prices and then uses the results to generate a price change index for a "typical" property.

In the case of the repeat-sales method, the index's computation only requires that a portion of the properties in the database has at least two transaction prices through time. The two prices for each property included in the analysis are used to infer a return, and the resulting returns of various properties are analyzed to infer returns for the index. The repeat-sales technique has been criticized because, for example, it assumes that relative property values (or property attributes) do not change during the period of time between the two observed transactions, and because relatively few data points are available to create a database when following this methodology. In the case of the **hedonic-price method**, valuations are not dependent on two transactions occurring for the same property. Index returns are estimated based on observing and estimating the fundamental relationship between every transaction price and the characteristics of the underlying property, such as its structure and location. A model is used to adjust observed prices for property characteristics so that overall underlying price changes through time can be estimated.

When observing the volatility of a real estate series, it is important to remember that real estate is typically financed with substantial levels of debt (required initial investment as a percent of the property value will vary across deals and through time, but a 10% down payment is not unusual). This high degree of leverage causes the actual volatility of an investor's returns on equity to be substantially larger than the volatility of the returns of the underlying real estate assets.

25

Real Estate Equity Valuation

This chapter details the private and public sides of commercial real estate equity valuation. First, we present the three main approaches used for valuing private commercial real estate equity: the income approach, valuations based upon comparable sale prices, and the profit approach. Second, we discuss the three main approaches used for valuing public commercial real estate equity, concentrating our analysis on the valuation of real estate investment trusts: the net asset value assessment, the discounted cash flow valuation, and the dividend discount method.

VALUATION OF PRIVATE COMMERCIAL REAL ESTATE EQUITY

In the case of private commercial real estate equity, asset valuations have idiosyncrasies. These arise because the respective assets are not exchanged traded (as opposed to stocks or bonds of public companies), and also because each real estate asset is unique and has unique risk and income characteristics. Real estate assets are also notorious for their illiquidity, as an individual property may not be traded for a considerable number of years. A valuation is an estimate of the market value of a property and should be reflective of the price at which an average investor would either buy or sell that property. Bearing these aspects in mind, we now proceed to discuss the three main approaches that are usually employed for valuing private commercial real estate equity: the income approach; valuations based on comparable sale prices; and the profit approach.

The income approach

The value of a certain property depends on the benefits it can offer to its owner. The net revenues that the property is expected to generate are the future incomes that are expected over the life of the property being held as a standing investment. The income approach to real estate valuation consists of forecasting a property's future expected yearly revenues and expenses and then discounting the income at an appropriate rate (r) to find an estimate of the property's value. The income real estate valuation approach is based on the time value of money principle, which postulates that a certain amount of money is worth more today than if it is received in the future. This approach is also known as the Discounted Cash Flow (DCF) Method.

In the case of a property, the *investment value* (*IV*) or intrinsic value will be based not just on one single cash flow but on the expected cash flows, $E[CF_t]$, for each time period, t, as is illustrated in this equation:

$$IV = \frac{E[CF_1]}{(1+r)} + \frac{E[CF_2]}{(1+r)^2} + \cdots + \frac{E[CF_{T-1}]}{(1+r)^{T-1}} + \frac{E[CF_T]}{(1+r)^T} + \frac{NSP}{(1+r)^T} = \sum_{t=1}^{T} \frac{E[CF_t]}{(1+r)^t} + \frac{NSP}{(1+r)^T}.$$

The final term in the above equation is the present value of the **net sale proceeds** (NSP), or expected selling price minus selling expenses, arising from the sale of the property at time T. In the case of real estate, cash flows are usually estimated using the concept of net operating income (NOI), which is calculated as the property's rental income minus all expenses associated with maintaining and operating the property. Equating the expected cash flow at time t, $E[CF_t]$, with the net operating income, $E[NOI_t]$, generates the following equation:

$$IV = \frac{E[NOI_1]}{(1+r)} + \frac{E[NOI_2]}{(1+r)^2} + \ldots + \frac{E[NOI_{T-1}]}{(1+r)^{T-1}} + \frac{E[NOI_T]}{(1+r)^T} + \frac{NSP}{(1+r)^T}$$

$$= \sum_{t=1}^{T} \frac{E[NOI_t]}{(1+r)^t} + \frac{NSP}{(1+r)^T}.$$

We illustrate the income approach using the following example. Suppose that an investor is considering the purchase of an office building. The **potential gross income** (or gross income that could be potentially received if all offices in the building were occupied) in the first year of operations has been estimated at $300,000. However, it is unlikely that the building will be fully occupied all year round. In the case of multi-office or multi-apartment properties there typically needs to be some consideration for possible vacancies and therefore the loss of rental income. Assuming a 10% **vacancy loss rate** and no other income, the **effective gross income** from the building in the first year will be: $300,000 − ($300,000 × 0.1) = $270,000.

To be able to estimate the net operating income we would now need to estimate the *operating expenses* arising from the property. Operating expenses can be classified as fixed and variable. *Fixed expenses*, examples of which are property taxes and property insurance, do not change directly with the level of occupancy of the property. Variable expenses, on the other hand, change as the level of occupancy of the property varies. The following are examples of variable expenses: maintenance, repairs, utilities, garbage removal, management, and supplies. In the previous example, let us assume that fixed and variable expenses were estimated at $42,000 and $75,000, respectively, for a total operating expense of $117,000 or 43 1/3% of effective gross income. Therefore, the net operating income arising from this property in the first year is estimated to be:

$$NOI = (\text{Potential gross income} - \text{Vacancy loss}) - \text{Fixed expenses} - \text{Variable expenses}$$

or

$$NOI = \text{Effective gross income} - \text{Operating expenses}$$
$$NOI = \$270,000 - \$117,000 = \$153,000.$$

Now, assuming that the investor expects to maintain the property for seven years and that he has estimated that rents will increase by 4% per year, that the vacancy loss rate will remain constant at 10%, and that annual operating expenses will continue to represent the same fraction of effective gross income (117/270), the projected annual net operating income for the seven year period will be:

	Year 1	Year 2	Year 3	Year 4	Year 5	Year 6	Year 7
Potential gross income	$300,000	$312,000	$324,480	$337,459	$350,958	$364,996	$379,596
Vacancy loss	−$30,000	−$31,200	−$32,448	−$33,746	−$35,096	−$36,500	−$37,960
Effective gross income	$270,000	$280,800	$292,032	$303,713	$315,862	$328,496	$341,636
Operating expenses	−$117,000	−$121,680	−$126,547	−$131,609	−$136,873	−$142,348	−$148,042
Net operating income	**$153,000**	**$159,120**	**$165,485**	**$172,104**	**$178,988**	**$186,148**	**$193,594**

We now assume that the net sales proceeds in year 7 have been estimated to be $1,840,000. Finally, to be able to calculate the investment value of the office building we would need to estimate a discount rate to compute the present value of the expected cash flows. The expected cash flows include each year's net operating income as well as the net selling proceeds at year 7. In the case of real estate investments, the discount rate can be estimated using the following formula:

$$r = [1 + R_f] \, [1 + E(R_{LP})][1 + E(R_{RP})] - 1 \approx R_f + E(R_{LP}) + E(R_{RP})$$

where r is the required return on the respective real estate investment, R_f is the risk-free rate of return (the return or yield on a Treasury security of similar maturity to the real estate investment), $E(R_{LP})$ is a liquidity premium that is inherent to direct real estate investments, and $E(R_{RP})$ is the required risk premium or extra return demanded for bearing the remaining risks of investing in the specific real estate project.

Let us assume that U.S. Treasury notes with a seven-year duration are currently yielding 6.8%, that the liquidity premium is 1% per year, and that the required risk premium for a real estate project is 1.2% per year. With these numbers, the required rate of return for this real estate project is approximately 9%. This approximation to the above formula is formed by summing the three rates rather than inserting them into the exact formula and multiplying them (i.e. 6.8% + 1.0% + 1.2% = 9%).

Therefore, using a discount rate of 9%, the investment value of the office building is:

$$IV = \frac{\$153,000}{(1.09)} + \frac{\$159,120}{(1.09)^2} + \frac{\$165,485}{(1.09)^3} + \frac{\$172,104}{(1.09)^4} + \frac{\$178,988}{(1.09)^5} + \frac{\$186,148}{(1.09)^6} + \frac{\$193,594}{(1.09)^7}$$
$$+ \frac{\$1,840,000}{(1.09)^7}$$
$$IV = \$1,863,772.$$

In practice the DCF estimates would involve a far more detailed projection of cash flows than were illustrated in the example given above. Full pro-forma appraisals usually incorporate the following key elements:

- Income:
  - Rental income on a lease by lease basis
  - Other sources of income
- Expenses:
  - A deduction for factors such as allowances for unanticipated vacancies, as well as "downtime" between leases in a given space
  - Building operating expenses
  - Capital items
  - Tenant improvements
  - Leasing commissions

For large properties the rental income calculations can become complicated if the property has multiple leases. In such a case, the total rental income is estimated by calculating and summing the annual rental income received for each lease in the property. The ability to forecast future demand and supply dynamics in the real estate market in question and their impact on the cash flows of the property is a vital concern. As the largest factor in the cash flows will be the net rental income, it is important that their estimates be as realistic as possible. A simplistic approach is to assume that rents will increase through all of the years at an estimated and fixed rate of inflation.

The expenses incurred by the property operations include a wide variety of different items. Some of them, such as general property management expenses, will be recurring and contracted and therefore can be regarded as fixed expenses. Other expenses are considered to be variable because they depend on the level of property vacancy. It is important to take into consideration the terms of the leases, as some leases may be gross and some may be net. In a net lease the tenant is responsible for some of the operating expenses.

The other major expense items on the pro-forma cash flow are primarily related to capital improvements and leasing costs. These are irregular payments which are dependent on factors such as the lease terms and the condition of the property. In addition, it is common to include a capital reserve for the anticipated level of unexpected costs.

The issue of tenant improvements will depend on the exact nature of the property. However, generally office and retail space will be offered in such a condition as to allow tenants to tailor it to their own needs. It is common for a landlord to at least partially contribute to these fitting out costs. The extent to which this is a major cost will largely be dependent not only on the magnitude of the costs, but also on the frequency of tenant turnover in the property. The final major item, leasing commissions, is constituted by the costs payable to the brokerage firm for marketing the space.

In summary, the income approach involves projecting all cash flows, including a terminal value (net sales proceeds) and discounting the cash flows using the investment's required rate of return. The accuracy of the approach depends on the accuracy of the cash flow projections and the accuracy of the estimation of the required rate of return.

Valuations based on comparable sale prices

For non-income producing properties, such as an owner-occupied single family residence, a DCF approach is not viable. In these cases, where sufficient transaction data are available, valuations are typically based on the comparable sale prices approach. Comparable sales data are generally readily available for a finished property that is for sale to end users, such as, for example, mid-size single family houses in a particular area.

This method, however, is not viable when the number of relevant real estate transactions is limited. This can occur for highly specialized properties, such as in the case of some industrial properties that are highly specific in their use, or in the case of properties of large scale that cannot be compared in terms of zoning, topography, and other factors that influence value. An alternative approach in these cases is based on the following two components: first, the replacement construction costs of the structure and, second, indications of the market value of the site, assuming it is being employed for its most profitable use.

The profit approach

The profit approach is typically used for properties with a value driven by the actual business use of the premises. This is effectively a valuation of the business rather than a valuation of the property itself. The valuation approach is related to the comparable sale prices method but focuses on value from the business use.

VALUATION OF PUBLIC COMMERCIAL REAL ESTATE EQUITY: REITS

In this section, we present the three methods that are most often used to value REITs: the net asset value (NAV) assessment, the discounted cash flow valuation, and the dividend discount method. We concentrate on the second, as many analysts agree that this is the most often recommended method to value a REIT. To illustrate the methods, we present the example of a hypothetical real estate investment trust named *High Rise*. Table 25.1 presents summarized financial information of this REIT, as well as the stock market.

Table 25.1 *High Rise*: Some key financial numbers (December 31, 2009)

Number of shares outstanding: 82,578,000
Stock market price: $8.52
Net Asset Value: $9.51
Dividends per share: $1.00
Earning per share: $1.04189
Return on equity: 10.96%

Beta: 0.70
Risk-free rate: 6.5%
Stock market risk premium: 6%

We will also present a summarized income statement and other financial data corresponding to *High Rise* later.

The Net Asset Value (NAV) Assessment

NAV, which is an accounting measure of the value per share of a REIT's net assets, is a very important valuation indicator for REITs. This is because NAV endeavors to quantify the market value of the property assets, which fluctuate with anticipated property cash flows and applicable discount rates. The NAV assessment approach involves starting with the NAV and estimating the adjustments, if any, that should be made to the NAV in valuing each REIT share.

Nussbaum (2006) cautions that NAV tends to be computed more as if the REIT is going to be liquidated rather than as an ongoing concern with the potential for added value from superior management. This problem is particularly important when we consider a REIT whose management team has demonstrated their capability to generate value and to earn returns higher than the returns of a passively managed portfolio of properties.

According to Nussbaum (2006) other concerns regarding the use of NAV when valuing a REIT are:

- REITs frequently realize gains on the sale of assets after the funds either redevelop a property or profitably lease the assets before they sell them. Often these gains, which are the result of value created by management, are not anticipated and incorporated in the computation of the NAV.
- General and administrative expenses represent an important cash flow deduction (from 5−20% of a REIT's annual revenue). The future effects of these expenses are not explicitly included in NAV.
- There are important accounting inconsistencies across REITs about how capitalization rates (or "cap rates") are calculated.[1]

In spite of these concerns regarding NAV, past research suggests that the relation between the market price of a REIT and its NAV may be useful in predicting future returns from investing in REITs. For example, Gentry, Jones and Mayer (2004) observed that, using REITs' data since 1990, REITs' stock prices deviated considerably from their NAV. They found that there appears to be high volatility and predictable behavior in the relationship between the market price and the NAV of a REIT. Specifically, the relationship appears to contain short-term mean reversion (the tendency of extreme values to return towards past averages). They found that a strategy of buying

---

[1] For REITs, capitalization rates are calculated as the ratio between the cash flow produced by a property and the original price paid to purchase the property. Cap rates are a very important determinant to valuation estimates.

REITs that trade at a discount to NAV and shorting REITs trading at a premium to NAV generated superior returns even after accounting for transaction costs and after including short-sale constraints. Estimated alphas from this trading strategy are between 0.9% and 1.8% per month, with little risk.

In the case of *High Rise*, Table 25.1 lists that the NAV is $9.51. The NAV is 11.62% above the latest stock market price ($8.52). These values indicate that the market price of *High Rise* is trading at a discount of 10.41% to its NAV. One view of this discount, based for example on the research by Gentry, Jones and Mayer (2004) discussed above, is that it can be used to identify inefficiencies in the market prices of REITs. In this view and in the absence of further information, the larger the discount, the more underpriced and attractive the REIT is believed to be as an investment opportunity. Another view is that most or all of the differences between REIT market prices and NAVs can be explained by characteristics such as management fees and errors in computing NAV. An important source of error in NAV computations is the use of "cap rates" to value properties. Since many properties have few comparable properties with reliable market values, the estimation of these cap rates and, indeed, the entire NAV estimation may be little better than educated guesses. We believe that the discounted cash flow method, which we present next, is the most appropriate approach to value REITs because REITs are typically actively managed going concerns with value that is often not captured through NAV computation techniques.

The discounted cash flow valuation

Most analysts agree that discounted cash flow (DCF) valuation is a better method for estimating the value of a REIT than the NAV assessment approach. The core fundamental issues in the investment analysis of a REIT are the nature of the underlying cash flows and the expected growth rate in the cash flows. Understanding these issues begins with an examination of the current performance of the REIT's portfolio of properties. The future growth potential of the REIT's portfolio depends on factors such as the performance of the markets to which the REIT is exposed. An analyst should estimate the potential growth rate based on underlying factors such as occupancy demand as well as competitive supply issues in order to obtain the expectations of rent and occupancy levels. In addition to these factors, the lease structures in place in the portfolio will also need to be considered in order to assess the extent to which the firm will be affected by macroeconomic and real estate market factors. Finally, the investment strategy of the firm is an important element. Here, an analyst would consider factors such as the REIT's level of trading activity and plans to change its geographic market focus.

In addition to the common accounting numbers used *for stock* analysis (such as earnings per share and dividends per share), a commonly-used measure of operational performance in the case of REITs is the firm's **funds from operations** (FFO). The FFO is a widely-used earnings benchmark and can be estimated as:

Net Income + Property Depreciation − Gain on Sales from Depreciable Property
+ Losses from Property Sales

The rationale behind using FFO in the case of REITs is that **depreciation** distorts the earnings figures of REITs substantially downward when it is subtracted in the determination of income. Depreciation is deducted from revenues because Generally Accepted Accounting Principles (GAAP) require REITs to depreciate over time the properties in which they have invested even if the properties are actually appreciating in value through time. Notice that real estate is different from most equipment or fixed-plant investments in that property rarely loses value and often appreciates. For this reason, the required depreciation expense tends to make net income appear to be artificially low in the case of underlying real estate assets that are growing in value through time. Also, traditional income measures can be volatile due to the temporary impact that a few large transactions may have

Table 25.2   *High Rise* REIT: Summarized income statement

High Rise REIT (All numbers in thousands)	2007	2008	2009
Revenues			
Income (rents)	$750,621	$811,471	$839,610
Fees and asset management	$2,343	$2,003	$2,543
Total revenues	**$752,964**	**$813,474**	**$842,153**
Minus Operating Expenses			
Property and maintenance	−$256,432	−$265,400	−$266,756
Property, fee and asset management	−$2,132	−$2,564	−$3,212
Insurance	−$8,765	−$8,879	−$9,234
Depreciation	−$201,094	−$215,432	−$223,432
General and administrative expenses	−$32,345	−$34,543	−$35,459
Total operating expenses	**−$500,768**	**−$526,818**	**−$538,093**
Operating Income	**$252,196**	**$286,656**	**$304,060**
Other income/expenses net	$20,343	$14,564	$18,976
Gain on Depreciable Property Sales	$134,560	$150,443	$156,765
Earnings before interest and taxes	**$407,099**	**$451,663**	**$479,801**
Minus Interest expense	−$337,961	−$371,007	−$391,330
Income before tax	**$69,138**	**$80,656**	**$88,471**
Minus Income tax expense	−	−$2,343	−$2,434
Net Income	**$69,138**	**$78,313**	**$86,037**

on income in the case of REITs. Accordingly, the effects of gains and losses from property sales are deducted from net income to determine FFO as it is assumed that these gains and losses will not be recurring and therefore do not add to the long-term potential dividend-paying capability of the REIT (remember that REITs are required to pay out 90% of their taxable income in the form of dividends).

Continuing with the discounted cash flow valuation, let us look at the following example, which illustrates how to calculate the FFO for *High Rise*. Table 25.2 shows a summarized income statement for the past three years (end-of year numbers) for this REITs.

It can be seen that, from 2007 to 2008, *High Rise*'s net income grew by 13.3% (it grew from $69,138,000 by $9,175,000), and then from 2008 to 2009 net income grew by a slower 9.86% (it grew $7,724,000). However, and as we mentioned above, depreciation can distort the earnings figures of REITs when the portfolio of properties is actually appreciating in value. Therefore, it is recommended that an analyst calculate the funds from operations for the REIT which, relative to earnings, deducts depreciation and also deducts (adds) any gains (losses) arising from property sales. Table 25.3 provides the summarized calculation of the FFO for *High Rise* (some other minor items are not presented in the figure to help illustrate the main concepts).

Table 25.3   *High Rise* REIT: Funds from operations

High Rise REIT (All numbers in thousands)	2007	2008	2009
Net income	$69,138.00	$78,313.00	$86,037.00
Plus depreciation	$201,094.00	$215,432.00	$223,432.00
Minus gain on depreciable property sales	−$134,560.00	−$150,443.00	−$156,765.00
Funds from Operations (FFO)	**$135,672.00**	**$143,302.00**	**$152,704.00**

Table 25.4 *High Rise* REIT: Adjusted funds from operations

High Rise REIT (All numbers in thousands)	2007	2008	2009
Funds from Operations (FFO)	$135,672.00	$143,302.00	$152,704.00
Minus capital expenditures	−$56,435.00	−$62,046.00	−$67,321.00
Adjusted Funds from Operations (AFFO)	**$79,237.00**	**$81,256.00**	**$85,383.00**

It can be seen that as depreciation, which is usually a large component in a REIT's income statement, is added back and gains in property sales are deducted from net income, *High Rise*'s FFO (in thousands) equals $135,672 (2007), $143,302 (2008), and $152,704 (2009), for a 5.62% growth in 2007–2008 and a 6.56% growth in 2008–2009.

Analysts argue that an even more accurate measure of financial performance for REITs is the **adjusted funds from operations** (AFFO). The AFFO of a REIT is calculated as the REIT's funds from operations (FFO) plus any adjustments made for recurring capital expenditures used by the REIT to sustain the quality of its properties.[2] Therefore, the AFFO represents a more accurate metric of residual cash flow available to the REIT's shareholders and should be a better forecaster of the REIT's future power to pay dividends. Again, some argue that the approach ignores retention of some of the cash. Table 25.4 shows a summarized calculation of the AFFO for *High Rise* (once again, some other minor items are not shown in the table for the ease of exposition and to help illustrate the main concepts).

It can be seen that, as capital expenditures are subtracted from net income, *High Rise*'s AFFO equals $79,237 (2007), $81,256 (2008), and $85,383 (2009).

An analyst attempting to value this REIT using this approach would try to project future values for AFFO using an estimate of normalized capital expenditures since previous capital expenditures may be abnormally high or low. To estimate future values for AFFO the analyst would need to estimate the expected growth in AFFO. More specifically, the analyst needs to estimate future rent increases, any possible plans to upgrade the properties, vacancy rates, and potential acquisitions/dispositions of properties.

We will now show how the AFFO can be used to determine whether the stocks of *High Rise* are under- or overvalued in the market, remembering first that returns from stock investing (an example of which are REITs' stocks) come from two sources: dividends and stock price appreciation. In turn, the stock price appreciation component of a REIT can be divided into the following two parts: expected growth in AFFO, and expansion (compression) in the price-to-AFFO multiple. In the case of *High Rise*, the price-to-AFFO multiple at the end of 2009 was equal to 8.24 (i.e. 82,578,000 × $8.52 / 85,383,000). This ratio would need to be compared to *High Rise's* industry peers in the real estate investment trust's arena. Similar to the case of stocks, an investor would be hesitant to invest in a REIT whose multiple is too high, unless there are special circumstances explaining such a high multiple (for example, an expected rate of growth in AFFO for a particular REIT that is higher than its peers).

As we mentioned before, the potential stock price appreciation of a REIT can come from two sources: the growth in AFFO and/or an expansion in the multiple (price-to-AFFO ratio). For example, if AFFO grows at 20% and the current multiple of 10× is maintained, then the stock price of the REIT will grow 20%. But if the multiple expands 10% to 11×, then the REIT's stock price appreciation will be approximately equal to 30% (20% AFFO growth + 10% multiple expansion).

---

[2] Capital expenditures can be obtained from the cash flow statement. However, they are usually based on normalized capital expenditures, as those corresponding to any year may be abnormally high or low.

Harper (2006) recommends using the reciprocal of the price-to-AFFO multiple (i.e. 1 / [Price/AFFO] = AFFO/Price) to determine the convenience of an investment in a particular REIT. In the case of *High Rise*, this equals 12.14% (1/8.24). This ratio is known as the "AFFO yield." To evaluate whether the price of a REIT is under- or overvalued, an analyst would then compare the AFFO yield to (1) the market's capitalization rate, or "cap rate," and (2) her estimate for the REIT's growth in AFFO. A market cap rate of, for example, 7%, implies that investors are generally paying 14.28 times (1 / 7%) the net operating income (NOI) of the average real estate property.

Assuming that the market cap rate is 7%, and that the growth expectation for *High Rise's* AFFO will be equal to the average growth recorded during the past two years (i.e. about 4%), then, given the calculated AFFO yield of 12.14%, it seems that the stocks of *High Rise* are undervalued in the stock market. This is because the AFFO yield is higher than the market cap rate and, even more promising, the growth that the analyst is expecting should translate into both higher dividends and stock prices in the future.[3]

The dividend discount method

This is a third method that can be used to value a REIT. The dividend discount method is useful if an analyst is able to forecast dividends accurately and if the relevant discount rate can also be estimated with a degree of confidence. In this case, the Gordon Growth Model (also known as the Constant-Growth Dividend Discount Model), can be used to value real estate investment trusts using their dividends.

Before we continue, we must warn that while some authors argue that this method should not be used in the case of REITs because of the difficulty in forecasting future dividends, others (e.g. Damodaran, 2002) contend that, since REITs must pay out 90% of their earnings as dividends, the earnings per share growth will be small, thus allowing for the use of the Constant-Growth Dividend Discount Model (CGDDM).

As we can see in Table 25.1 *High Rise* had earnings per share of $1.04189 in 2009, out of which it paid $1.00 per share in dividends. The estimated *payout ratio* or percentage of the earnings per share that were paid in the form of dividends is therefore:

$$\frac{\$1.00}{\$1.04189} \approx 95.98\%$$

The *retention ratio* (RR), which is the percentage of the earnings per share that remain in the company after the dividends are paid to stockholders, is calculated as: 1 − *payout ratio*. For *High Rise*, the retention ratio is equal to: 1 − 0.9598 = 0.0402 = 4.02%

Information available on Table 25.1 also indicates that *High Rise* had a return on equity (ROE) of 10.96% in 2009. Therefore, we can now estimate *High Rise's* *sustainable rate of growth in dividends* (*g*) which, according to some applications of the Constant-Growth Dividend Discount Model, is equal to the retention ratio (RR) multiplied by the return on equity (ROE):[4]

$$g = RR \times ROE$$
$$g = 0.0402 \times 0.1096 = 0.44\%$$

---

[3] Following Harper (2006), we have ignored the potential effects of debt in our example. This is a reasonable approach to follow when a REIT's debt burden is relatively small and/or similar to its industry peers. If a REIT's leverage were above average, an analyst would need to make some adjustments to consider the added risk implicit in the additional debt.

[4] The method that we present here offers only a rough estimation of the sustainable rate of growth in dividends of a REIT. A more accurate estimation would consider the effects of expected inflation, leases, and debt maturities, among other variables.

It can be seen that the sustainable rate of growth in dividends for *High Rise* is estimated to be very small, just 0.44% per year given the purest assumption of the Constant-Growth Dividend Discount Model. In a more theoretically correct interpretation of that model, the earnings of the firm would be adjusted to reflect any appreciation in the assets of the firm due to inflation or increases in the real values of real estate. Thus, the above formula would vastly understate growth rates in actual REITs since most asset gains and other sources of growth have been assumed away. The tiny estimated growth rate of 0.44% is not surprising since *High Rise* pays about 96% of its earnings in dividends, thus reinvesting only 4% to finance just the type of growth that is permitted in this simplistic illustration of the computation of the sustainable rate of growth in dividends.

With these values, and given that we have previously estimated that *High Rise*'s discount rate is 10.7% (see Table 25.1, where the discount rate was calculated as 6.5% + 0.7 × 6%), we can now proceed to value the stock using the CGDDM:

$$V_0 = \frac{1.00(1.0044)}{0.107 - 0.0044} = \$9.78$$

According to the dividend discount method the value of *High Rise*'s stock is $9.78. This value is about 15% higher than the latest stock market price of this stock ($8.52). Therefore, according to the dividend discount method, *High Rise*'s stock is undervalued.

We conclude this section summarizing the main findings of this exercise. The three methods (NAV assessment, the discounted cash flow valuation, and the dividend discount method) suggest that the shares of *High Rise* are currently undervalued in the stock market given that the market price of $8.52 is lower than the values assessed using these three methods. The consistency in this finding across the three methods yields more confidence in the valuation analysis just presented.

Does being listed cause REITs to behave more like the stock market?

An important valuation concern specific to REITs is the extent to which these exchange-traded investment vehicles echo the behavior of the overall stock market rather than only reflecting the dynamics of the underlying private real estate market. At least in the short run, REIT indices appear to respond more substantially to fluctuations in the overall stock market than do private real estate equity indices. But it is difficult to ascertain whether the difference is attributable to true pricing behavior differences in the underlying assets or to biases introduced by the use of non-transaction-based indices for private real estate equity. Notwithstanding the recent introduction of transaction-based indices, traditional performance measurement in private real estate has been driven by indices constructed with appraisal data. In contrast, indices of listed securities, such as REITS, are priced on an ongoing transaction-based basis. Giliberto and Mengden (1996) show that the underlying income streams are nearly the same for REITs and NCREIF. Therefore, any differences in behavior must be caused by factors other than changes in income streams.

There are key differences between the methods that are used to value the private and listed real estate sectors. The private markets are valued according to the approaches discussed at the beginning of this chapter. The methods of pricing REITs are fundamentally different and could lead to substantial divergences in the estimated values, measured return performance and measured risks of private vs. listed assets, even in cases where the same underlying assets are involved.

Another feature of REITs is their substantially greater liquidity. Since investors in REITs have the ability to buy or sell reasonably sized blocks rather quickly on exchanges with much lower transaction costs than in the private market, the added liquidity could create valuation and performance differentials.

REITs and private real estate equity may be subject to different broad investment dynamics. If the majority of REIT investors are effectively dedicated real estate investors (i.e. either sector-specific mutual funds, or targeted allocations from pension funds), it may be that the share prices of the REITs would reflect and track very closely the underlying private market fundamentals. If, however, the majority of the trading is undertaken by broader equity fund managers and traders, their valuation decisions may be more linked to the valuation decisions being made in the broader equity markets.

A commonly-used argument in relation to the behavior of the listed sector relative to the private real estate market is that, over the long run, REITs do provide returns comparable to the underlying assets (i.e. private real estate). A number of studies examining the U.S. real estate markets have found, for example, evidence that the private and listed markets are cointegrated, thereby implying a long-term common trend (e.g. Campeau (1994) and Glascock, So and Lu (2002)). However, it is important to note that if over an extended time horizon REITs provide returns similar to the private market, then a private real estate investor is giving up the liquidity benefit from owning a listed security.

26

Real Estate Investment Risks and Due Diligence

This chapter deals with the main risks inherent with real estate investing, which we categorize as business risk, financial risk, liquidity risk, inflation risk, management risk, and legal risk. We then present an introduction to the due diligence process in the context of real estate investments, a concept that is especially related to legal risk. Finally, we discuss the use of real estate derivatives for risk management purposes.

REAL ESTATE INVESTMENT RISKS

Business risk

This is the risk that investors may incur a loss as a result of fluctuations in economic conditions. Real estate markets follow cycles that tend to be distinct from overall economic and business cycles. Cycles and other fluctuations generate variability in the income produced by real estate investments. It is important to note that various types of properties react differently to changes in economic conditions and the business cycle in particular. For example, a property that has a well-diversified tenant population is likely to be less subject to business risk (Brueggeman and Fisher, 2006). Another example is a property with leases that provide the owner with safety against changes in the rate of inflation. Investments in these types of properties would have less business risk. Ling and Naranjo (1997) found that the following economic risk factors drive real estate markets: the growth rate in consumption, real interest rates, the term structure of interest rates and the unexpected inflation rate.

Financial risk

Financial risk can be defined as any risk associated with financing. In the case of real estate, financial risk will be higher as the quantity of debt on a real estate investment (i.e. the leverage) increases. Financial risk will also be determined by the cost and structure of the debt. For example, a property financed using a variable-rate loan will typically have a higher degree of financial risk than a property acquired using a fixed-rate loan. The real estate crisis of 2007–2008 highlighted this risk when the majority of defaulting loans of properties were of the variable-rate type. A refusal of lenders to refinance can also be regarded as an important type of financial risk. An investor that entirely finances their real estate acquisitions with equity would pose almost no financial risk but would still be vulnerable to business risk.

Liquidity risk

This risk arises from the difficulty in selling a property on a timely basis and at a competitive price. Real estate assets, as opposed to stocks of publicly traded companies, are typically highly illiquid and therefore expose investors to high liquidity risk. Illiquidity is higher during periods of weak real estate demand, when the selling of a property can take up to a year or more. In this type of market, the owner of a property may need to offer a substantial discount to increase the chances of selling the property promptly. Case and Shiller (2003) report that, in the case of residential owner-occupied properties, fewer real estate transactions occur in a bear real estate market. They also argue that prices do not tend to fall at the beginning of a bear market, because owners usually set minimum reservation prices below which they are unwilling to sell. Similarly, Genovese and Mayer (2001), analyzing data from downtown Boston in the 1990s, contend that loss-aversion (or aversion to realize losses on an investment) is an important determinant of the behavior of sellers in the housing market. They similarly find that the real estate market exhibits a positive price-volume relation.

Inflation risk

This risk can be described as the likelihood that the real value of real estate holdings or rental income will decrease because of the effects of unanticipated inflation. The inflation-hedging capabilities of real estate investments have been examined in the literature with mixed findings. In theory, real estate should provide a hedge against the risk of inflation in periods when demand for real estate space is high and vacancy rates are low, because landlords would have a greater capability to raise the nominal value of leases as inflation accelerates. Moreover, the replacement cost of property holdings typically increases with inflation. In a recent article covering the 1978–2004 period, Goetzmann and Valaitis (2006) find that U.S. residential real estate can serve as an inflation hedge, especially over the long-term.

Management risk

Most real estate investments require the management of properties in order to maintain occupancy rates, to preserve the value of the property and to control expenses. Brueggeman and Fisher (2006) argue that management risk is driven by variability in management's competence, its talent to innovate, its reactions to competitive situations, and its ability to operate efficiently. Some properties demand a higher level of management skill than others and are therefore more subject to management risk.

Legal risks

Investors in real estate need to verify that when they pay for a property they are obtaining a good title, free of encumbrances and liens. In theory, title insurance in the U.S. can often provide protection against the legal risks of property acquisition. However, legal risks vary from country to country. For example, Girgis (2007) documents that real estate fraud has become a very real menace in recent years in places such as Ontario. Specifically, as a result of identity theft, homeowners' titles have been illegally transferred and mortgages have been registered against those titles, all without the homeowners' knowledge or consent. Management of real estate legal risks is closely related to many of the aspects of the real estate due diligence process, which we discuss next.

REAL ESTATE DUE DILIGENCE

Roulac (1995) defines due diligence in an institutional real estate setting as an evaluation of the procedures, policies, and results of an organization's structure, portfolio construction, and selection and monitoring of specific real estate investments. The due diligence process attempts to replicate the process that a prudent investor would apply prior to making a major financial commitment. The real estate investment due diligence should consider the following elements as part of the process: legal/documentation factors, investment factors, borrower/developer attributes, property characteristics, economic factors, market factors, and financial factors. Successful real estate due diligence practices can improve investment performance and reduce the risk of loss for investors.

Roulac (2000) argues that due diligence in real estate investments has become more important through time because (1) institutional investing has grown to be a more central part of the real estate market, and (2) investors are now further removed from the decisions regarding specific real estate properties. The reasons that investors are further removed from decisions include increased securitization through commercial mortgage-backed securities and REITs, and growth in non-exchange-traded real estate investments such as commingled real estate funds and real estate limited partnerships (which are discussed in Chapter 30). Poor performance of real estate investments implies the possibility of a poorly or deficiently conducted due diligence process. Thus, due diligence can be regarded as an absolutely essential input to the real estate investment process.

Roulac (2000) conducted a study based on interviews of institutional investors and found that due diligence was much more rigorous and time-consuming in the hard conditions of the real estate market of 1993 than in the more optimistic and lenient market conditions of 1987, thus suggesting that the state of the real estate market does affect the care and discrimination of the due diligence process and the importance that institutional investors assign to it. When the real estate market enters into a recession, capital becomes more difficult to find, and those investors that are willing to commit capital become more discriminating concerning their due diligence approach.

Wieder (2008) argues that many buyers fail to do a comprehensive check when it comes to due diligence in real estate transactions. The following elements should be considered by any investors interested in private real estate equity investments: financial due diligence, document production and review, and property condition and environmental assessments.

The financial due diligence process should check existing documents, such as rent records, mortgages, and tax records. Other financial aspects include, in the case of an existing commercial property: the percentage of the property that is rented, the level of current rents with respect to current market values, and whether and when existing leases are due to being renewed. Due diligence requires that a check of all relevant public records be conducted. This review may expose unsettled problems that must be addressed. The property condition due diligence consists of assessing the state of the property being considered to determine whether capital expenditures are necessary and to estimate the possible costs. Finally, the purpose of the environmental due diligence is to understand the extent, if any, to which the property may be affected by environmental concerns such as hazardous substances and materials (e.g. asbestos).

BASICS OF REAL ESTATE DERIVATIVES AND RISK MANAGEMENT

As is described in Chapter 30, the last few years has seen considerable growth in the quantity and diversity of alternative investments that are available in the real estate sector. There are now numerous mutual funds (both open-end and closed-end funds), exchange-traded funds and hedge funds that offer exposure to the real estate investment space. As these relatively new investable real estate products gain acceptance among market participants it is expected that there will be a considerable increase in transparency and liquidity in the real estate market in forthcoming years. It is expected that the recent introduction of property derivatives will also facilitate an increase in transparency, liquidity and risk management capabilities in the real estate market in the forthcoming years, as these new investable real estate products become available and achieve acceptance among market participants.[1] For Shiller (2008), the near nonexistence of markets for real estate derivatives, until very recently, has been a cause for great concern. Derivatives facilitate risk transfers including synthetic short selling and the ability to lay off risks without divesting assets (through hedging) that can ameliorate asset bubbles. The efficient and precise hedging of risks arising from real estate investments is important since enhanced abilities to transfer and control all economic risks (not only stock and bond risks) generate the well known benefits of economic exchange. Furthermore, we believe that the recent sub-prime crisis might be attributable to failures of market participants to manage risk appropriately. Case, Shiller and Weiss (1995) had already demonstrated through a model that investors in residential mortgage portfolios could have, at least in theory, hedged part of the risk of default by investing in derivatives markets for residential real estate during the period of 1975–93.

---

[1] In May 2006 the Chicago Mercantile Exchange launched futures and options markets on the Standard and Poor's/Case-Shiller Home Price Indices. The futures contracts possess a February quarterly cycle of expiration dates, are settled at $250 times the index, and were launched for 10 U.S. cities and for an aggregate index. This market has been much more successful than other previous efforts, such as the introduction of a property futures market in the London Futures and Options Exchange in 1991. More on real estate derivatives will be given in Chapter 30.

27

Residential and Commercial Mortgages

This chapter of the real estate section describes the basic structure of the residential and commercial mortgage markets. Much of the material presented in this chapter is introductory and CAIA Level II candidates should already be familiar with it. The next chapter, which deals with the securitized residential and commercial mortgage-backed securities markets, builds on the topics covered in this chapter.

RESIDENTIAL MORTGAGES

The residential and commercial mortgage real estate markets differ in a number of ways, both in terms of the structure of the actual loans and also with regard to the characteristics of the securitized market. A key difference in terms of the actual loans is the nature of the borrower. Residential mortgage loans are typically taken out by individual households. Furthermore, the property, if owner-occupied, generates no explicit rental income. Therefore, mortgage payments, as well as the initial amount borrowed, depend on the borrower's income and financial position. In contrast, commercial mortgage loans are largely taken out by corporations or other legal entities. Thus commercial mortgages are backed by different financial characteristics of the borrower relative to residential mortgages and, if the property is held for investment purposes, this means that there will be rental income that can be used to make the mortgage payments. Another feature of residential mortgage loans is their tendency to be far more homogenous in terms of their price behavior than commercial loans. This partly reflects the unique characteristics of individual commercial properties and also reveals the fact that residential property markets, particularly when looking within the metropolitan level, tend to be more homogenous than commercial property markets.

A mortgage loan can be simply defined as a loan secured by property. The property effectively acts as collateral against the amount borrowed. If the borrower defaults on the loan then the lender can take possession of the property. It is the mortgage deed that formally ties the property to the loan. In the U.S., states operate broadly under two main systems with respect to the mortgage deed. In the first case, the mortgages operate under what is referred to as **lien theory**. Under lien theory, the lender, or mortgagee, has the right to force a **foreclosure** if default occurs. The foreclosure and sale of the property would therefore allow the lender to recover the outstanding debt (or part of the debt if the property price has fallen extensively.) Under **title theory,** the title, and therefore ownership of the property, is actually transferred to the lender. The borrower, or mortgagor, only has the right to use the property while the loan is being repaid. The advantage to this system is that the lender can take possession of the property faster.

Another important characteristic of mortgages is that the principal of a mortgage can usually be partially or fully prepaid before the contractual due date. These partial **prepayments** are made by borrowers to save on future interest payments. The most typical reasons for full prepayments are sale of the property or refinancing with the objective to lock-in a lower interest rate. However, lenders may add prepayment penalties to mortgages to discourage borrowers from refinancing when interest rates decline.

Fixed rate mortgages

The majority of residential loans in the U.S. are **fixed-rate constant payment, fully amortized loans** (with equal monthly payments throughout the life of the loan). These loans also give the residential mortgage market some of its unique characteristics, as will be discussed later in the chapter. The fixed-rate and constant payment nature of these loans also has the implication that, during periods of high inflation, while the monthly payments remain constant in nominal terms they are actually declining in real terms. The monthly payments (*MP*) of a fixed rate loan can be calculated using the formula for the present value of a constant annuity (with the payment amount factored onto the left hand side):

$$MP = MB \left[\frac{i (1 + i)^n}{(1 + i)^n - 1} \right]$$

where *MP* is the constant monthly payment, *MB* is the total amount borrowed, *i* is the monthly interest rate and *n* is the number of months in the term of the loan.

The **effective cost of a mortgage** is the actual cost (usually expressed as an annual percentage) that a borrower bears for taking out a mortgage, including the financing costs. The effective cost of the loan is determined by including any loan fees that the lender may charge as cash flows in an IRR computation. If loan fees do not exist, the effective cost of the loan is the same as the stipulated interest rate in the contract.

Example of a fixed-rate, constant payment, fully amortized mortgage

Assume that a borrower takes out a \$100,000, 25-year mortgage (i.e. 300 months), at a 6% annual nominal interest rate (i.e. a monthly interest rate of 6%/12 or 0.5%). The monthly payments can be calculated using the formula directly as follows:

$$MP = \$100,000 \left[\frac{0.005 \, (1.005)^{300}}{(1.005)^{300} - 1} \right] = \$644.30.$$

Or, using a financial calculator, the monthly mortgage payment is calculated imputing the following values: *n* (number of periods) $= 12 \times 25 = 300$ months, *i* (interest rate per period) $= 6\%/12 = 0.5\%$, *PV* (present value) $= -\$100,000$, *FV* (future value) $= \$0$, and solving for (compute) *PMT* (payment). Some calculators do not use an opposite sign between the PV and FV entries. Spreadsheets contain functions analogous to the calculator functions that are demonstrated throughout this chapter. Note that payment amounts are rounded to the nearest penny.

An important feature of the fixed-rate mortgage is that the proportion of the monthly payments that will repay the principal and the proportion that consists of interest charges will change over the lifetime of the loan. In particular, in the early years of the mortgage, the largest portions of the monthly payments represent interest payments rather than principal repayments. The interest component at each month is equal to the monthly interest rate multiplied by the outstanding loan amount from the previous month. The principal repayment component is the residual between the total payment and the interest portion. Table 27.1 illustrates the amortization schedule for the example just presented: a \$100,000 mortgage with a fixed-rate (6% a year or 0.5% a month), constant payment (\$644.30 per month), that is fully amortized (the balance is \$0 at the end of the life of the mortgage).

As can be seen in Table 27.1, the first interest payment is equal to: $\$100,000 \times 0.5\% = \$500.00$. Given that the fixed monthly mortgage payment is \$644.30, the principal repayment in the first month will be: $\$644.30 - \$500.00 = \$144.30$ and, therefore, the end of month mortgage balance

Table 27.1   Amortization schedule for a fixed-rate (6% per year), constant payment ($644.30 per month), fully amortized 25-year mortgage ($100,000 mortgage).

Month	Beginning of month mortgage balance	Mortgage payment	Interest payment	Principal payment	End of month mortgage balance
1	$100,000.00	$644.30	$500.00	$144.30	$99,855.70
2	$99,855.70	$644.30	$499.28	$145.02	$99,710.68
3	$99,710.68	$644.30	$498.55	$145.75	$99,564.93
4	$99,564.93	$644.30	$497.82	$146.48	$99,418.45
.	.	.	.	.	.
.	.	.	.	.	.
.	.	.	.	.	.
59	$90,318.50	$644.30	$451.59	$192.71	$90,125.79
60	$90,125.79	$644.30	$450.63	$193.67	$89,932.11
61	$89,932.11	$644.30	$449.66	$194.64	$89,737.47
.	.	.	.	.	.
.	.	.	.	.	.
148	$68,782.90	$644.30	$343.91	$300.39	$68,482.51
149	$68,482.51	$644.30	$342.41	$301.89	$68,180.62
150	$68,180.62	$644.30	$340.90	$303.40	$67,877.23
151	$67,877.23	$644.30	$339.39	$304.91	$67,572.31
152	$67,572.31	$644.30	$337.86	$306.44	$67,265.87
.	.	.	.	.	.
.	.	.	.	.	.
299	$1,279.28	$644.30	$6.40	$637.90	$644.30
300	$641.37	$644.30	$3.21	$641.09	$0.00

(outstanding principal) will decline from $100,000 by $144.30 to $99,855.70. As the months pass, the monthly interest payment declines because the outstanding mortgage balance on which interest payments are calculated decreases. The last months of the mortgage life illustrate that the last mortgage payments go almost entirely to amortize the remaining mortgage balance as this outstanding balance is very small and, therefore, generates very small interest charges. Figure 27.1 further illustrates this phenomenon. Starting with a $500 interest payment in the first month, interest payments then decline at an increasing rate until the last interest payment (of just $3.21) is made in the last month at the end of the mortgage life (on month 300). On the other hand, principal repayments start at a low $144.30 for the first month and then grow at an increasing rate throughout the life of the mortgage.

Fixed-rate mortgages are exposed to interest rate risk because their market values will change inversely when market interest rates change. More specifically, as market interest rates rise, the value of a fixed-rate loan decreases. In our previous example of a 25-year, 6%, $100,000 fixed-rate mortgage, the monthly payment was $644.30. Suppose now that, 5 years (60 months) later, the market rate is 7.5% for 20-year, fixed-rate mortgages. According to Table 27.1, the outstanding value of this mortgage (in month 61) in terms of remaining principal is $89,932.11, five years after the loan has been taken out. If the appropriate market interest rate remained at 6% per year, the market value of the mortgage would be equal to this outstanding principal balance. However, at the new and higher market interest rate of 7.5% the market value of the mortgage is equal to $79,978.33 (using a financial calculator: $n = 12 \times 20 = 240$, $i = 7.5\%/12 = 0.625\%$, $PMT = 644.30, $FV = 0, solve for PV). Therefore, we can see that, in this example, the market value of the mortgage is substantially lower than the outstanding principal balance or book value five years after the mortgage was taken. This decrease in value takes place whether the lending bank keeps the

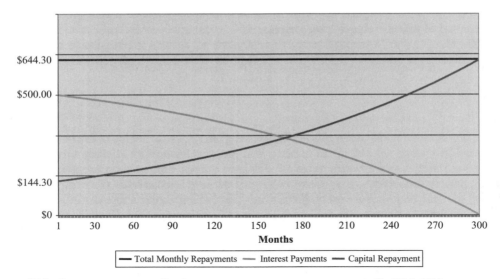

$644.30

$500.00

$144.30

$0

Months

— Total Monthly Repayments —— Interest Payments —— Capital Repayment

Figure 27.1   Repayment structure for the constant payment mortgage presented in Table 27.1

loan in its portfolio or sells it in the secondary markets, a possibility that will be discussed in the next chapter.

Some fixed-rate mortgages are **interest-only mortgages** (i.e. the monthly payments consist of only interest payments) for some initial period. The two most widely-used interest-only loans are, first, the 30-year mortgage that starts with a 10-year interest-only period and is followed by a 20-year fully amortizing period. This type of loan is known as "10/20." The second is the 30-year loan that starts with a 15-year interest-only period and is followed by a 15-year fully amortizing period. This type of loan is known as "15/15." Assuming that the previous example was structured as a 10/15 interest-only mortgage, and assuming the same yearly rate of 6%, for the first 10 years the monthly payments, which are interest-only, would have been equal to $500 (i.e. $100,000 × 0.5%). Between years 11 and 25, the monthly fixed payment necessary to fully amortize the mortgage for the remaining 15 years would have been equal to $843.86 (using a financial calculator: $n = 12 \times 15 = 180$, $i = 6\%/12 = 0.5\%$, $PV = -\$100,000$, $FV = \$0$, solve for PMT). Notice that interest-only mortgages have the advantage that the monthly payments during the interest-only period are lower than those in the case of a fully amortized loan (e.g. $500 versus $644.30). However, monthly payments are then higher (i.e. $843.86 versus $644.30) during the amortization period as the borrower has fewer years to amortize the loan (15 years versus 25 years).

Variable rate mortgages

Recent years, particularly during the period 2004–2006, saw a partial shift in the U.S. market towards **variable** or **adjustable rate mortgages** (ARM) away from fixed-rate mortgages. While the initial payments in the case of ARMs are calculated in the same manner as with the conventional fixed-rate loans, the payments are not necessarily constant during the lifetime of the loan as the interest rate will be periodically adjusted by the lender, generally to reflect changes in underlying short-term market interest rates. The obvious advantage of a variable rate type of mortgage to a lender is that it protects him from the situation where short-term rates rise and the borrower's interest payments do not rise accordingly. A variable rate loan provides advantages to the borrower as well. When interest

Table 27.2   Amortization schedule for a variable-rate, variable payment, fully amortized 25-year mortgage ($100,000 mortgage).

Year	Index rate +	Margin rate	= Interest rate	Beginning of year mortgage balance	Monthly mortgage payment	End of year mortgage balance
1			7%	$100,000.00	$706.78	$98,470.30
2	8.5	1.5	10	$98,470.30	$903.36	$97,430.75
3	10	1.5	11.5	$97,430.75	$1,006.05	$96,515.25
4	8	1.5	9.5	$96,515.25		
.	.	.	.	.	.	.
.	.	.	.	.	.	.
.	.	.	.	.	.	.

rates fall borrowers benefit from reduced payments, although it is also fair to say that fixed-rate loans also allow borrowers to refinance to gain the advantage of lower monthly payments. However, due to the higher interest rate exposure that a lender faces in lending at fixed rate terms these rates are generally higher than variable rates. This particularly occurs during periods when the yield curve in the money markets is upward sloping.

Example of an adjustable rate mortgage

Let us take a look at a simple example of an adjustable rate mortgage. Suppose that once again a $100,000, 25-year mortgage is taken out. The initial interest rate, which will apply for the first year, is 7% per year compounded monthly. This implies that the monthly mortgage payment during the first year is $706.78 ($n = 12 \times 25 = 300$, $i = 7\%/12$, $PV = -\$100,000$, $FV = \$0$, solve for PMT), and that at the end of the first year the mortgage balance will be equal to $98,470.30 ($n = 12 \times 24 = 288$, $i = 7\%/12$, $PMT = \$706.78$, $FV = \$0$, solve for PV). This information is presented in Table 27.2.

The monthly payments in this mortgage are based on an adjustable rate that applies starting in month 13. This variable rate, which applies for the whole year, is based on an **index rate**, which fluctuates freely in the money markets and can be based, for example, on the yield of one-year Treasury securities, plus a **margin rate** of 1.5%. This margin rate is determined as part of the original terms of the mortgage and is added to compensate for the expected or assessed degree of riskiness of the borrower. As it can be seen in Table 27.2, the monthly mortgage payment that the borrower would have to make during the second year, and for which a higher index rate of 8.5% applies, is equal to $903.36 ($n = 12 \times 24 = 288$, $i = 10\%/12$, $PV = -\$98,470.30$, $FV = \$0$, solve for PMT). Notice that the rise in interest rates between the first and the second year has caused a substantial increase (27.81%) in the monthly payment that the borrower is obliged to make. The mortgage balance at the end of the second year is equal to $97,430.75 ($n = 12 \times 23 = 276$, $i = 10\%/12$, $PMT = \$903.36$, $FV = \$0$, solve for PV). This process of computing the remaining mortgage balance and using that balance to compute the new monthly payments (considering the new interest rate that applies each year) continues over the life of the mortgage.

It is also common for interest rates in ARMs to be capped (also known as **capped interest rates**). In our example, suppose that the increase in interest rates was capped to 2% during any one year (the adjustment interval that we have been using) and to a total increase of 3% during the life of the mortgage. The effect of these interest rate caps on the mortgage balance and on the monthly payments is shown in Table 27.3. The initial rate (used in the first year) is now assumed to be higher

Table 27.3 Amortization schedule for a variable-rate, capped rate, variable payment, fully amortized 25-year mortgage ($100,000 mortgage).

Year	Index rate	Margin rate	Interest rate	Beginning of year mortgage balance	Monthly mortgage payment	End of year mortgage balance
1			8%	$100,000.00	$771.82	$98,691.38
2	8.5	1.5	10	$98,691.38	$905.38	$97,648.61
3	10	1.5	11	$97,648.61	$973.56	$96,657.80
4	8	1.5	9.5	$96,657.80		
.	.	.	.	.	.	.
.	.	.	.	.	.	.
.	.	.	.	.	.	.

(i.e. 8% versus the previous 7%) to compensate the lender for the potential negative effects that the cap rates may have on its future income from the mortgage should future uncapped interest rates rise above the mortgage's cap. It can also be seen that the monthly payment on the third year ($973.56) is now lower than it was in the previous example ($1,006.05), reflecting the fact that the rate for the third year has been capped at 11% in this new example (versus the 11.5% rate applicable in the previous example).

Other types of mortgages

Fixed and variable rate mortgage loans also have other variations. For example, it is common, particularly with variable rate loans, for the initial interest rate to be low (when compared to available short-term market rates) and fixed for a set period, say two years. After this initial time period, the mortgage rate is calculated based on the lender's standard variable interest rate. As we will discuss in the next chapter, the extensive use of this type of mortgage in the past few years, particularly during the 2004–2006 period, has been blamed for detonating the recent mortgage and ensuing financial crisis in the U.S. and elsewhere (2007–2008). It has also been increasingly common to observe **graduated payment loans**. These are loans made at an initially fixed interest rate where the initial interest rate is relatively low but is scheduled to increase slowly over the first few years. Both of these variations are designed to aid in the qualifying ability and initial payment ability of borrowers. This is because historically defaults in mortgage loans tend to be concentrated in the first few years of a loan. Therefore, by offering a reduced rate for the first period, the lender is not only using the lower rate as a marketing tool in attracting business, but it is also attempting to mitigate the default risk to which it is exposed.

Another variation has been that of **option adjustable rate mortgage loans** or **option ARMs**. An option ARM is an adjustable rate mortgage that provides the borrower with the flexibility to make one of several possible payments on her mortgage every month. Option ARMs typically offer low introductory rates and allow borrowers to defer some interest payments until later years.

A further mortgage variation that has attracted increased interest in recent years is a loan that includes some form of **balloon payment**. The balloon payment is a large promised future payment. Rather than amortizing the mortgage to $0 over its lifetime (e.g. 25 years), the mortgage is amortized to the balloon payment. This means that at the end of the loan there is an outstanding principal amount due equal to the balloon payment. The balloon payment allows for a lower monthly payment given the same mortgage rate. Balloon payments due in a relatively short time period (compared to traditional mortgage maturities of 15 to 30 years) may lower the risk to the lender and permit a lower mortgage rate.

To illustrate balloon payments, assume that the borrower and the lender in our original example decide that the $100,000 loan made at the fixed-rate of 6% per year compounded monthly for 25 years will have a $70,000 balance on the 25 year maturity date (rather than being fully amortized to $0). This amount of $70,000 is known as a balloon payment and will be due at the end of 25 years. In this case, the monthly payment would be equal to $543.29 (using a financial calculator: $n = 12 \times 25 = 300$, $i = 6\%/12 = 0.5\%$, $PV = -\$100,000$, $FV = \$70,000$, solve for PMT). Notice that the $543.29 monthly payment is less than the $644.30 payment that was computed for the case of the fully amortizing loan even though the interest rates in both mortgages are equal to 6%.

An extreme example of a balloon payment mortgage is where the loan payments only comprise interest and no principal repayments are required. Therefore, at the end of the loan the entire capital is due. The interest-only form is often used by buy-to-let investors in residential property. The interest-only nature of the payments reduces their monthly payments, which hopefully can be covered by rental income. In an ideal scenario the capital appreciation of the actual property's value will be substantial and will represent profit to the borrower when realized, frequently from the sale of the property. Examples of other types of mortgages can be found in Brueggeman and Fisher (2006).

COMMERCIAL MORTGAGES

In contrast to the relative standardization of residential mortgage loans, there is far greater variety when it comes to mortgages in the commercial sector, a fact that has hindered the development of the commercial mortgage-backed securities market. Mortgage loans on commercial real estate differ in a number of other respects from those in the residential market. Almost all commercial loans involve some form of balloon payment on maturity since the loan term is almost always shorter than the time required to fully amortize the loan at the required payment. For the most part, residential properties do not generate income, in contrast to the commercial sector; therefore residential lenders are primarily worried about the income of the borrower in any analysis concerned with the servicing of the loan. In contrast, commercial properties will be expected to have rental income that can be used to service the loan. Furthermore, due to the large size of commercial real estate, few individuals participate in this market. Most of the borrowers are commercial or financial firms that possess greater financial sophistication than the average homeowner.

An important distinction when examining commercial mortgages is the nature of the loan and, in particular, whether it is for *investment* or for *development purposes*. Most commercial loan securitization tends to be focused on loans taken out for ongoing investments. The reason is that development loans tend to be short-term in nature because of the short duration inherent in the development process. As a result, few development-based loans are securitized. In addition, most development loans are *phased*, where the developer only draws down funds when required during the construction phase. This is in contrast with loans for investment purposes, which tend to have a longer horizon, usually in the region of five to ten years, and where the full amount of the loan is drawn immediately.

In general, the **covenants** contained in a commercial mortgage are more detailed than those in a corresponding residential loan document. Covenants are promises made by the borrower to the lender that act to protect the lender (presumably in exchange for better terms). Although many of the covenants will be similar between residential and commercial mortgages (for example, the commitment to pay and the right of the lender to take possession in the event of a default), commercial loans will, however, contain far more detail concerning issues such as the seniority of the loan. As with all debts, particularly at the corporate level, all lenders will need to know their position with respect to seniority in the event of default or financial difficulty. For instance, it may be the case that if the loan is senior or is the original debt on the property, the lender has to provide permission before subsequent debts can be incurred. This can happen even if the loan is subordinate/junior. Likewise, a key element in any corporate debt is the level of *recourse* that the lender has to the actual borrowing company. A related issue is whether the loan is explicitly secured against the asset. If so, then generally the recourse is to the pledged asset. If this is not the case, then the lender will probably not be entitled to possession in the event of a default and the ability to pursue recourse to the corporate body would become more important. It is also more likely with commercial loans for explicit guarantees to be put in place, again further securing the lender's position. One further method for lenders to increase their security is to insist on restrictions on the distribution of the rental income from the property, with perhaps a certain proportion being redirected to a reserve account rather than straight to the investor. Lenders may also insist on a minimum deposit to be maintained in an account with them.

In addition to explicit covenants with regard to the debt, the loan may come attached with a *proviso* (i.e. condition or limitation) relating to the management and operation of the property. Lenders may insist that minimum levels of cash flow, net operating income and earnings before interest and taxes need to be achieved or that rental levels may not fall below a previously specified level. Such provisions are designed to ensure that the property will be able to generate sufficient income on an ongoing basis so that the borrower can service the loan. Lenders may even insist on having some form of either control or consultation with regards to leasing policies. This could involve examination of new lease terms, allowing credit checks to be conducted on potential tenants.

Finally, a **cross-collateral provision** is commonly used by banks to mitigate the risk to which they are exposed. The term cross-collateralization is used when the collateral for one loan is also utilized as collateral for some other loan. For example, if someone has borrowed using a home loan from a bank, secured by the property, and has borrowed an auto loan, secured by the car, from the same bank, and if there were a cross-collateral provision, then both assets would be used as collateral for both of the loans. If this person fully pays off the car loan and wishes to sell the car, the bank may veto the transaction because the car is still used as collateral to the home loan.

Financial ratios for commercial mortgages and default risk

As with residential loans the **Loan-to-Value** (LTV) ratio, both at the origination of the loan and on an ongoing basis, will be a key measure used by lenders. The LTV is the ratio of the amount of the loan to the value (either market or appraised) of the property. Financial institutions tend to lend only at lower LTVs on commercial property in comparison to the residential sector. It would be rare for senior debt in commercial properties to be lent at an LTV in excess of 75%. The LTV at which a lender will issue a loan will vary depending on the property sector and geographic market in which the property is located, as well as the stage of the real estate cycle and other circumstances such as the borrower's creditworthiness.

Given that commercial real estate generates rental income, lenders will also examine a variety of income-based measures, in addition to the LTV, when assessing the credit risk of the loan. For instance, lenders will typically examine the **Interest Coverage Ratio**, which can be defined as the property's net operating income divided by the loan's interest payments. This allows the lender to inspect the level of protection that they have, in terms of the borrower's ability to service the debt, purely from the property's operating income. In the case of senior secured debt lenders, it will usually be required that they meet a minimum coverage ratio of 1.2. This means that the net income is 20% greater than the interest payments due. A related measure is the **Debt Service Coverage Ratio** (DSCR). While the Interest Coverage Ratio is just concerned with the coverage of the interest payments, the DSCR is concerned with the coverage of all loan payments including the amortization of the loan. A final typically-used key ratio is the **Fixed Charges Ratio**. This ratio further extends the outgoings included in the ratio to include all fixed charges that the investor pays annually.

In summary, the measures used in assessing credit risk are:

$$\text{Loan to Value (LTV)} = \text{Amount of the mortgage loan/Value of the property}$$

$$\text{Interest Coverage Ratio} = \text{Property's net operating income/Loan's}$$
$$\text{interest payments}$$

$$\text{Debt Service Coverage Ratio (DSCR)} = \text{Property's net operating income/Loan's interest and}$$
$$\text{principal payments}$$

$$\text{Fixed Charges Ratio} = \text{Property's net operating income/All fixed charges that}$$
$$\text{the investor pays annually}$$

The risk of default needs to be constantly monitored by lenders. Research by Esaki (2002) notes that default rates of commercial mortgages are highly cyclical and tend to be explained by both market conditions and lender policies. Loans taken out, for example, during the real estate boom of the late 1980s, a period that witnessed not only a booming real estate market but also liberal lending policies (including LTVs greater than 100%), eventually recorded high default rates. For instance, loans issued in 1986 saw a lifetime default rate of 28%. In contrast, loans issued between the early 1990s and the beginning of this century recorded much lower default rates. This was in part due to more conservative lending policies during that later period. The nature of the underlying market cycle also comes into play. When the market is in the early stages of an upward cycle both the lender and the borrower are less exposed to possible future falls in property values. A major difference between residential and commercial lending is that it is far more likely that defaulting commercial loans will be restructured rather than moved directly to foreclosure. This is in part due to the size of the individual loans. For instance, Esaki (2002) found that 40% of defaulting commercial loans were restructured.

28

Mortgage-Backed Securities

This chapter discusses the mortgage-backed securities markets. **Mortgage-backed securities or MBSs** are a type of asset-backed security that is secured by a mortgage or pool of mortgages. In recent years there was substantially increased use of MBSs which can be explained by the spectacular rise in real estate prices that started in the late 1990s and peaked in the second half of 2006. While most attention has been focused on the residential MBS market, there was substantial growth in the **Commercial MBS (CMBS)** market in the years up to the real estate and financial crisis of 2007–2008.

There are a number of basic types of mortgage-backed securities, although all of them share the common structure of receiving cash flows based on mortgage loan payments. The cash flows received into MBSs share a number of common elements. One of the most important is that the size of the cash flows received each time period is dependent on the amount of unscheduled repayments of the principal (i.e. prepayments), which is not entirely predictable.

A **pass-through MBS** is perhaps the simplest MBS and consists of the issuance of a homogeneous class of securities with pro-rata rights to the cash flows of an underlying pool of mortgage loans. **Collateralized Mortgage Obligations (CMOs)** extend this MBS mechanism to create different bond classes called *tranches* that have different priorities to receiving cash flows and therefore have different risks.[1] We discuss the main characteristics of CMOs later in this chapter.

RESIDENTIAL MORTGAGE-BACKED SECURITIES MARKET

The U.S. **residential mortgage-backed securities** (RMBS) market is dominated by the following three main mortgage agencies: the Government National Mortgage Association (Ginnie Mae), the Federal National Mortgage Association (Fannie Mae), and the Federal Home Loan Mortgage Corporation (Freddie Mac).

Ginnie Mae, Fannie Mae and Freddie Mac were, until recently, U.S. publicly traded, stockholder-owned, government sponsored corporations, authorized to provide both loans and loan guarantees, and thus providing liquidity to mortgage originators. The main activity of these corporations consisted in buying mortgages on the secondary market, creating pools of them, and selling these pools as mortgage-backed securities to interested investors. As of 2008, Fannie Mae and Freddie Mac guaranteed or owned close to half of the U.S.'s $12 trillion mortgage market. The financial health of the two corporations was severely damaged by the housing market downturn of 2007–2008, about which we will comment at the conclusion of the chapter. In September 2008 the Federal Government adopted the unprecedented move of taking over the two companies and placed them into the "conservatorship" of the Federal Housing Finance Agency (FHFA). There are also private corporations that provide guarantees for loan issues.

Investors, and also credit rating agencies, examine a number of issues when analyzing an MBS. Probably the biggest concern with respect to investment dynamics is the prepayment behavior of the underlying pool. With MBS issues, when households prepay some or all of their mortgage loans, the principal repayments are distributed to the MBS investors. These unscheduled prepayments create

---

[1] The word 'tranche' is French for slice, portion, or section.

uncertainty on the part of investors regarding the timing of the principal repayments that they will receive and the longevity of the interest payments that they will receive.

Prepayments, single mortality rates and conditional prepayment rates[2]

Full mortgage prepayments are made for a variety of reasons. For example, mortgage loans must be repaid when homeowners sell their home to move to another home (or sell for any other reason except in the very rare case of assumable loans). While the home sellers may take out a new mortgage with respect to their new home this does not replace the old loan in the mortgage pool. The other main reason behind full prepayments is refinancing, particularly in the case of changing interest rates and fixed-rate mortgages. For example, assume that a borrower takes out a mortgage when the prevailing interest rate is 10%. If rates fall to, say, 7%, since the original loan is fixed-rate and interest on that loan continues to be assessed at 10%, it typically would make sense for the borrower to "exercise the option" to refinance the mortgage. The borrower would prepay the old loan in full using the proceeds of the new loan and would benefit from the lower rate on the new mortgage. From the perspective of the investor in the MBS, the loan having been prepaid provides the investor with early return of principal but takes away their ability to earn the original interest rate (10%) on the old mortgage. Similarly, if a borrower does not fully prepay a loan but merely makes additional (unscheduled) partial principal repayments, the investor experiences similar effects to the full prepayment scenario but at a smaller magnitude.

Other reasons leading to prepayments include default (with mortgage insurance proceeds providing the principal repayment) and the destruction of a home (with homeowner's insurance providing the principal repayment). As noted above, prepayments do not just affect the cash flows relating to the principal but also to the interest payments. Therefore, prepayments are perhaps the most important element leading to uncertainty in the cash flows received by investors in MBS since ultimate receipt of principal is typically not in jeopardy due to mortgage insurance.

It is therefore important that investors take into account the speed of prepayments, which can be measured by the **Conditional Prepayment Rate (CPR)**, and calculated using the following formula that is based on annualizing a monthly prepayment rate:

$$CPR = 1 - (1 - SMM)^{12},$$

where SMM is the **single monthly mortality rate**, which is calculated as:

$$SMM_t = \frac{\text{prepayment in month } t}{\text{beginning mortgage balance for month } t - \text{scheduled principal payment in month } t}.$$

For example, suppose that, for a hypothetical mortgage-backed security, in month 29 the beginning mortgage balance was \$447,634,562; the scheduled principal payment was \$372,234, and the prepayment made by borrowers was \$2,297,31. Then, the SMM for month 29 is equal to:

$$SMM_{29} = \frac{\$2,297,231}{\$447,634,562 - \$372,234} = 0.005136 = 0.5136\%.$$

This implies that, in month 29, 0.5136% of the anticipated outstanding mortgage balance (i.e. the total dollar amount that is anticipated to be available to be prepaid at the end of the month) was actually prepaid.[3] The formula of the CPR, found above, allows market participants to annualize the

---

[2] This section is adapted from Fabozzi (2006).

[3] Notice that we are using four decimals to calculate the SMM. We are doing this because it is recommended to use a very precise number in coming calculations.

SMM. This is important as investors usually prefer to refer to prepayment rates on an annual instead of on a monthly basis. Using the *CPR* formula for our initial example we find that

$$CPR = 1 - (1 - SMM)^{12} = 1 - (1 - 0.005136)^{12} \approx 0.0599 = 5.99\%.$$

In other words, excluding scheduled principal payments, approximately 5.99% of the outstanding mortgage balance at the beginning of the year is projected to be prepaid by the end of the year.

In addition to computing the *CPR* from the *SMM*, the *SMM* can be computed from the *CPR*:

$$SMM = 1 - (1 - CPR)^{1/12}.$$

Further, the *SMM* formula can be used to estimate the prepayment amount for a particular month based on the projected *SMM* and factoring the *SMM* formula as follows:

$$\text{Projected prepayment for a particular month} = SMM \times (\text{Outstanding mortgage balance}$$
$$- \text{Scheduled principal payment}).$$

For example, suppose that an investor possesses an MBS in which the outstanding mortgage balance at the beginning of month 31 is $195 million and the scheduled principal payment for that month is $2.1 million. Assume that the investor projects that the *SMM* for month 32 will be 0.5136%. Therefore, the projected prepayment for month 32 will be:

$$0.005136 \times (\$195,000,000 - \$2,100,000) = \$990,734.$$

The **Public Securities Association (PSA)**, which was established in 1976 and later became the Bond Market Association, carried out a study to determine the pattern of prepayments that a typical mortgage pool had over its life. As a result of this study, the PSA established the *PSA Prepayment Benchmark*, which has become the conventional approach used by market participants to measure and predict prepayments. The benchmark assumes that, for a 30-year mortgage, a *CPR* of 0.2% will apply for the first month of the security. This *CPR* then increases by 0.2% per month for the next 30 months until it reaches a figure of 6%, where it is kept constant at this rate for the rest of the life of the mortgage. The reason behind the gradual increasing *CPR* rate is that only a few borrowers will be expected to prepay in the early years of their loans (e.g. due to moving from their houses or refinancing) since their circumstances (and market interest rates) have had little time to change since making the decision to take the loan out. This standard PSA benchmark is referred to as "100% PSA." For example, according to the PSA Benchmark, the *SMM* for the 7th and 40th months are:

For the 7th month:

$$CPR = 0.2\% \times 7 \text{ (i.e. 0.2\% per month multiplied by the 7 months)} = 1.4\%$$
$$SMM = 1 - (1 - CPR)^{1/12} = 1 - (1 - 0.014)^{1/12} \approx 0.001174 = 0.1174\%$$

For the 40th month:

$$CPR = 6\%$$
$$SMM = 1 - (1 - CPR)^{1/12} = 1 - (1 - 0.06)^{1/12} \approx 0.005143 = 0.5143\%$$

If however prepayments are currently running at levels in excess of the PSA benchmark, the prepayments are expressed as a rate relative to which the analyst expects faster prepayments, and vice versa if prepayments are currently running below the PSA benchmark. For example, "200 PSA" means that prepayments are occurring at a rate 2 times faster than the *CPR* of the PSA prepayment benchmark, and "75 PSA" means prepayments are at three-quarters of the *CPR* of the

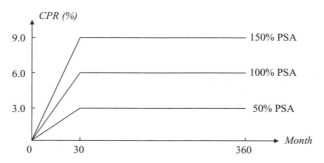

Figure 28.1 PSA benchmark models

PSA prepayment benchmark. Figure 28.1 illustrates the effect on the *CPR*, for future months up to 30 years of modeling different prepayment speeds relative to the PSA benchmark.

For example, assuming a "200 PSA," the *SMM*s for the 7th and 40th months would have been: For the 7th month:

$$CPR = 0.2\% \times 7 = 1.4\%$$
$$200 \text{ PSA} = 2 \times (0.014) = 0.028 = 2.8\%$$
$$SMM = 1 - (1 - CPR)^{1/12} = 1 - (1 - 0.028)^{1/12} \approx 0.002364 = 0.2364\%$$

For the 40th month:

$$CPR = 6\%$$
$$200 \text{ PSA} = 2 \times (0.06) = 0.12$$
$$SMM = 1 - (1 - CPR)^{1/12} = 1 - (1 - 0.12)^{1/12} \approx 0.01060 = 1.060\%.$$

Factors affecting prepayment rates

The rate of prepayments will be affected by a number of factors. The first and most important factor is the current level of mortgage rates relative to the rates being charged on loans in the pool. Borrowers will have a greater incentive to refinance when current mortgage rates are low relative to the rates on the existing mortgages. Second, not only does the current level of mortgage rates affect the rate of prepayment speed, but also the path that mortgage rates have followed to arrive at the current level. For instance, when mortgage rates drop further after already having declined substantially in the recent past, refinancing may not occur at a rapid rate since those who ascertained a benefit from refinancing at lower interest rates will probably have done so already (when the mortgage rate first dropped). This phenomenon is known as **refinancing burnout**.

Other issues related to the characteristics of the underlying pool affect prepayment rates. The type of loans in the pool is extremely important. In addition, there are also a number of other factors such as the maturities of the mortgages, the rates of the fixed rate mortgages and the terms of the variable rate mortgages. Another factor is the geographic location of the pool. In the context of the U.S. this is important due to the divergences present in regional prepayment tendencies, regional economic performance and their impact on prepayment speeds. Geography also comes into play in relation to factors such as the risk of destruction of properties. For example, if a large number of properties in the pool are located on the Southeastern seaboard, there is a greater risk of destruction due to hurricanes (which can speed prepayments of insured mortgages). Analysts build fundamental models of prepayment speeds and analyze past prepayment rates in their attempts to predict future prepayment rates. The effects of the recent crisis in the sub-prime sector of the mortgage market have once again highlighted the importance of analyzing the characteristics of the underlying pool when attempting to predict prepayment rates.

Collateralized Mortgage Obligations

As mentioned at the beginning of this chapter, Collateralized Mortgage Obligations divide the cash flows of mortgage pools (or other mortgage-related products) and distribute them into different classes of securities called tranches. CMOs can be issued by agencies (e.g. Fannie Mae) or they can be non-agency issues. A CMO issuer will structure these different tranches so that they will have different cash-flow seniorities, expected lifetimes, coupon rates and risks, and in so doing will attempt to create tranches that will be attractive to specific clienteles of investors. The CMO issuer receives the monthly mortgage payments (principal and interest payments) from homeowners and, after collecting its fees, the issuer "passes" the payments on to investors (hence the name passthrough securities) following the schedules previously defined in the CMO prospectus (for additional discussion of CMOs see Fabozzi (2006)).

Sequential-pay CMOs

The **sequential-pay collateralized mortgage obligation** is the simplest form of CMO. In a sequential-pay CMO each tranche receives a prespecified share of the interest payments (based on the tranche's coupon) and potentially receives principal based on seniority. The "first-pay" tranche (i.e. tranche "A") will receive all principal repayments until the tranche's face value has been repaid. A tranche will mature once it has received, either through a scheduled repayment of principal or through prepayments, its share of the principal. The next senior tranche then receives the entire principal payments until it, in turn, matures (i.e. it is paid off), and so on. There is a final tranche (typically tranche Z) that receives any residual cash flows. The interest payments received on each tranche decline to maturity as the tranche is repaid through principal repayments.

CMOs allow the design of bonds possessing dissimilar exposures to the risk of prepayment. This offers investors a new and diverse array of risk/return patterns. For example, an investor seeking short-term, low risk securities may purchase a highly senior tranche while a longer-term investor might seek a tranche with a longer maturity, higher yield and greater uncertainty of cash flow timing. Since principal is often guaranteed, risk is driven by interest rates and prepayment uncertainty. If interest rates increase, then prepayments by homeowners will be fewer. As a result, the life of most tranches will be extended, thus expanding the lifetime of the tranche further than originally expected. This phenomenon is known as **extension risk**. On the other hand, as interest rates decrease, the likelihood of prepayment increases and the life of the tranche will be shortened. This is because, in this case, borrowers will try to refinance their mortgages to be able to contract at the new lower interest rate. This phenomenon is known as **contraction risk**.

Example of a two-sequential pay tranche CMO

Consider the two-sequential pay tranche CMO structure that is presented in the following table, where principal payments are made first to Tranche A and then to Tranche B.

Tranche	Outstanding par value	Coupon rate
A	$150,000,000	9.00%
B	$50,000,000	9.00%

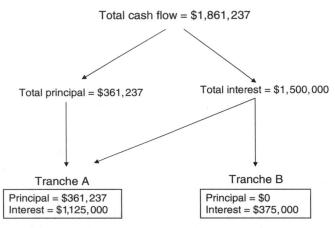

Figure 28.2   Example of cash flows to a two-sequential pay tranche CMO

For the purpose of illustrating how the cash flows are allocated to Tranches A and B, let us suppose that in month 1 a total of $361,237 is paid from the underlying collateral as principal repayments (notice that these include both scheduled repayments and any prepayments made by borrowers), and that $1,500,000 is paid as interest payments (i.e. 9%/12 × $200,000,000), for a total cash flow of $1,861,237. The cash flows to this sequential pay tranche are shown in Figure 28.2.

Figure 28.2 illustrates that, in month 1, both Tranche A and Tranche B receive their corresponding interest payments of $1,125,000 (i.e. $150,000,000 × 9%/12) and $375,000 (i.e. $50,000,000 × 9%/12), respectively, for a total of $1,500,000 in interest payments. The remaining cash flow of $361,237 (principal repayments) received from the underlying collateral is used only to pay principal to Tranche A, as this is a two-sequential pay tranche CMO where principal payments are made first to Tranche A and will only be made to Tranche B once the principal of Tranche A has been fully paid off. Therefore, at the end of month 1, the principal balance for Tranche A is equal to $149,638,763 (i.e. $150,000,000 − $361,237), while the principal balance of Tranche B remains at the initial $50,000,000.

The mechanics of the payments in the following months will be the same, with each tranche receiving its corresponding interest payments (in the case of Tranche A these interest payments will be declining as the time passes because the total principal is decreasing). Principal repayments received from the underlying collateral would be used only to pay the principal for Tranche A. The principal for Tranche B will start to be paid off only after the principal for Tranche A has been fully paid. If the prepayment rates of the mortgages underlying the CMO increase, Tranche A would be paid off faster and Tranche B would start to be amortized earlier (i.e. contraction risk). Contraction is desirable to the owner of a tranche when the tranche has a low coupon, but may be undesirable if the tranche's coupon is above current market rates on securities of similar risk and maturity.

Other CMOs

There are numerous variations that can be structured within a CMO issue. Here, we will briefly describe the following CMO types: Accrual tranches (Z-bonds), structured principal-only and interest-only tranches, floating rate tranches, and Planned Amortization Class (PAC) tranches.

Accrual tranches, or **Z-bonds**, receive no interest payments, effectively acting as a zero coupon bond. The interest payments scheduled for the accrual bond are instead redirected towards other tranches that are receiving principal payments to provide further principal reductions in those tranches.

Principal-only (PO) and **interest-only (IO) collateralized mortgage obligations** are bonds created by dividing the total cash flows from the mortgage collateral into the portion that is interest and the portion that is principal repayment. The principal repayment cash flows are distributed to one bond, which is the PO, and the interest cash flows are distributed to a second bond, which is the IO.

Investors in PO bonds are ultimately paid the face value of their bonds as homeowners make the principal payments on their mortgages. The logic behind a PO is that investors buy these bonds at a deep discount from face value and eventually receive the face value through the scheduled principal repayments and prepayments made by homeowners. An IO bond, in turn, has a notional principal, which is the remaining principal of the mortgages and is used to compute each interest payment. The cash flows received by investors in IOs decline as the principal is paid down.

Prepayment risk tends to be severe for POs and IOs, with one profiting when the other suffers. For example, in the case of POs on fixed rate mortgages, when interest rates decline, the speed of prepayments accelerates, thus reducing the life of the bond by paying the face value to investors faster, in effect generating an increased annualized return. On the other hand, when interest rates increase, the speed of prepayments declines, and the investor is paid the face value farther in the future, lowering its effective yield. Thus, prepayments are desirable from the perspective of the owner of a PO because the money is received earlier.

In the case of an IO on a fixed rate mortgage, its value generally increases when interest rates increase, because the speed of prepayments decreases and therefore the owner of the IO will receive interest payments for a longer period of time. However, when interest rates decline, the values of IOs decrease since the speed of prepayments accelerates and interest payments are reduced. As a result, prepayments are undesirable from the perspective of the owner of an IO because they lessen future interest income.

Interest-only loans, with both adjustable and fixed rates, became a very significant part of the mortgage market up to the beginning of the financial crisis in 2007. For instance, in 2005 and 2006, IOs accounted for close to 25% of the dollar volume of originations. The separation of mortgage cash flows into IO and PO securities does not change aggregate cash flows, but it partitions the cash flows into securities that, held individually, can be rather risky. The rapid growth in IOs leading up to 2007 explained part of the severe U.S. sub-prime and real estate crisis that started in 2007.

Planned Amortization Class (PAC) tranches receive principal payments in a more complex manner than sequential-pay CMOs. PAC CMOs have a main tranche (the PAC tranche) and a support or companion tranche. Until recent years, PAC tranches comprised more than 50% of newly-issued CMOs. The main rationale is to provide investors in the PAC tranche with more stable and predictable cash flows (in terms of the sensitivities to the prepayment rate). Investors in the PAC tranche have priority for receiving principal payments and interests and enjoy a relatively steady and predictable stream of cash flows. When prepayments diverge from what was originally projected, the support tranche first bears the variation. For example, when there are only modest prepayments most of the cash flows go first to the PAC tranche. With more prepayments, the PAC tranche collects the scheduled cash flows once again, but the support tranche receives distribution of the excess. The higher variability in the cash flows perceived by the support tranche is compensated by offering investors in this tranche a higher yield.

Some CMOs are structured so that they possess more than one PAC tranche having different levels of priorities. For example, a Type I PAC has the first priority and the most predictable and stable income. Type II and Type III PACs have fewer priorities, and income will be stable and predictable only over a narrower range.

Finally, **Floating-Rate tranches** earn interest rates that are linked to an interest-rate index, such as the London Interbank Offered Rate (LIBOR). Floating rates tranches can have rates that move even more than the underlying index and even in the opposite direction (inverse floaters). They also have a specified upper limit, and sometimes a lower limit too. Floating rates tranches are typically used to hedge interest-rate risks and can also be structured as sequential tranches or as a PAC.

Commercial mortgage-backed securities

Commercial mortgage-backed securities (CMBSs) are mortgage-backed securities secured by commercial property loans. CMBSs provide liquidity to commercial lenders and to real estate investors. As with other types of MBSs, the increased use of CMBSs can be attributable to the rapid rise in real estate prices over the years leading to 2006. Because they are not standardized, there are lots of details associated with CMBSs that make these instruments difficult to value. However, when compared to a residential mortgage-backed security (RMBS), a CMBS provides a lower degree of prepayment risk because commercial mortgages are most often set for a fixed term.

The CMBS market was initially slow to develop, although it has expanded rapidly over the last 10–15 years. As recently as 1992 in the U.S. only 3% of the $1 trillion of outstanding commercial mortgages were securitized. However, by the end of the decade, CMBS issues in that market exceeded $300 billion. The small scale of the CMBS market until the early 1990s was due to a number of reasons. First of all, there was a lack of both consistent underwriting standards and standard loan documentation for commercial real estate loans – two features that made the securitization of commercial loans more difficult when compared to the residential market. In addition, the historical performance of the loans tended to be poor. Finally, there was, until the early 1990s, an abundance of alternative sources of debt financing for commercial real estate, primarily flowing from insurance companies.

The emergence of the CMBS market in the U.S. in the early 1990s can be explained, at least partially, by similar factors that affected the REITs sector, namely that the large market corrections in many U.S. real estate markets at that time caused a severe lack of liquidity in the sector. Not only did the correction in many real estate markets make traditional providers of capital to real estate more cautious, but the U.S. Savings and Loans crisis of the 1980s effectively took out of circulation a major source of debt capital. While REITs allowed a more liquid and a lower unit cost entry to the equity market, CMBSs allowed a similarly liquid entry to the debt market. Furthermore, the establishment of the Resolution Trust Corporation (RTC) helped to liquidate the loan books of failed financial institutions from the late 1980s to the early 1990s and gave the CMBS market a boost, as the RTC securitized many of the loans that it had taken over. The nature of the market also shifted during the 1990s. While many of the early major security issues, such as those issued by the RTC, were primarily composed of troubled loans, increasing amounts of CMBSs were issued containing loans originated with the explicit aim of securitizing them. The 1990s also saw the increased use of conduit issues, which is examined later in this chapter. The issuance amounts of both CMBS and RMBS continued growing during 2000–2006. However, the financial and real estate crisis that started in 2007 caused a dramatic fall in the issuance of CMBS and RMBS.

As with the RMBS market, most CMBS issues are structured to include a variety of tranches. This process effectively breaks up the cash flows coming from the original mortgage loans into different components, each with slightly different characteristics designed to appeal to different clienteles of investors. Whereas investors in tranches in residential MBSs are frequently more concerned with the inherent prepayment risk, this is less of an issue in the case of the CMBS market. This is in part due to the fact that most commercial loans contain lockout provisions that limit the prepayment optionality of the loan. In addition, conduit loans usually contain clauses that give the borrower the right to *defease* future payments.[4] This process effectively allows the borrower to repay the loan by replacing the cash flows of the loan with payments from a portfolio of, for example, Treasury securities. This means that the primary issue for investors in CMBS tranches is default risk of loans that have not been defeased – not prepayment risk. Default risks are borne first by the most junior tranches and last by the most senior tranches.

As would be expected, credit ratings tend to differ quite considerably between the different tranches of a CMBS. This is because each tranche has different risk profiles, maturities and subordination. Due to subordination, credit ratings are lower for more junior tranches. Because they have a priority claim on the cash flows, the extra security imbedded means that it is quite common to see senior tranches with AAA credit ratings. It is also common to observe a large spread of ratings within a single issue. The most junior tranches, often referred to as first-loss tranches, are often rated at non-investment grades. This has the advantage of broadening the spread of possible interested investors. Furthermore, it changes the nature of the actual investment. The senior, investment-grade rated tranches, are generally viewed as fixed-income securities. In contrast, the junior tranches, and in particular the first-loss tranches are generally analyzed with more of an eye to the risk of the underlying real estate rather than to the risks of the broad bond market. Even a single large default can have a considerable impact on the performance of these securities. Therefore, in the case of CMBS, particular attention should be placed on the credit quality of the underlying pool of loans as well as on the value of the properties acting as collateral. Investors in CMBS also need to bear in mind that when tranches are narrow (e.g. 1% to 2% of loan exposure) pricing becomes even more complex and very difficult.

Figure 28.3 illustrates how a **conduit** creates a CMBS by purchasing commercial mortgages from loan originators and then issuing CMBSs with several tranches possessing different maturities and credit risks.[5] In Figure 28.3, the risk of default will go first to the residual class (which is the lowest seniority class and the one for which defaults first accrue), then to security four, then to security three, and so forth. Security one, which is the least risky security, will yield the lowest interest rate and will be rated highest by the credit rating agencies. The conduit will receive interest on the mortgages purchased from the originators, pay interest on the securities that it has issued, and make a profit on the weighted average difference between the two, as illustrated in Figure 28.4. As the seller of the securities, the conduit will try to get the buyers to pay the highest price (i.e. accept the lowest returns) possible. Furthermore, the conduit may decide to pay for pool insurance to help cover losses arising from loan defaults.

Figure 28.4 shows an example of how the interest rates may be structured under a hypothetical example of a CMBS. It can be seen that, for the last two classes, the conduit pays a rate that is higher than the rate received from the mortgage. This is because these last two classes bear most of the default risk. The conduit offsets these high rates by paying the other three classes a rate that is lower than that received from the pool of mortgages, which is possible because the classes have high seniority, high credit ratings and are attractive to investors seeking safety.

---

[4] A defeasance is a provision that annuls a loan when sufficient cash or bonds are saved by the borrower to service his debt.

[5] A conduit is a financial entity that buys financial assets from correspondents or issuers, repackages them and issues and sell interests in the new instruments to other parties.

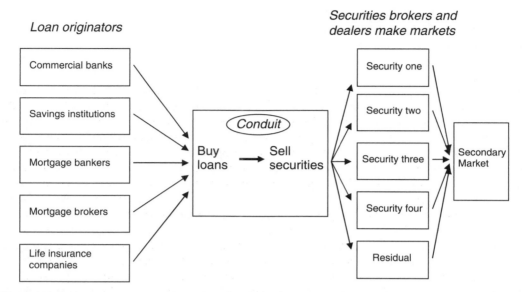

Figure 28.3   The securitization process of a CMBS

(Source: Adapted from Clauretie and Sirmans (2006))

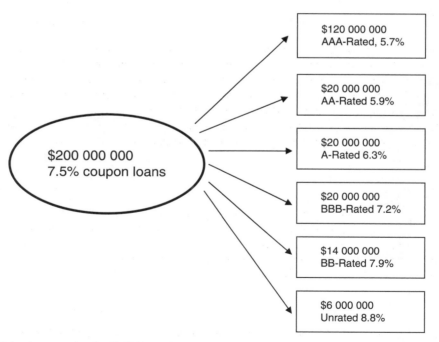

Figure 28.4   An example of a CMBS security creation

In this example, the conduit receives an average of 7.5% per year from a pool of $200,000,000 in commercial mortgages and pays a weighted average interest rate of 6.177% on the six classes of CMBS that were issued. This weighted average rate was calculated as follows:

$$5.7\%\frac{\$120\ M}{\$200\ M} + 5.9\%\frac{\$20\ M}{\$200\ M} + 6.3\%\frac{\$20\ M}{\$200\ M} + 7.2\%\frac{\$20\ M}{\$200\ M} + 7.9\%\frac{\$14\ M}{\$200\ M}$$

$$+ 8.8\%\frac{\$6\ M}{\$200\ M} = 6.177\%.$$

Therefore, the **conduit's average margin** or **"excess interest"** is 1.323% (i.e. 7.5% − 6.177%).

The tranching of a CMBS is set up so that the highly rated securities (i.e. AAA and AA rated bonds) comprise the largest tranches in terms of dollar amounts. CMBSs are created this way because of the high demand coming from most corporations, many mutual funds and money market mutual funds, some of which are restricted to invest only in highly rated securities. Conversely, there are only a few buyers of those tranches that are rated below investment grade (i.e. those rated below BBB).

While the RMBS and the CMBS markets have exposures to similar risk factors, there are important differences in their sources of risk. Many of these differences relate to the more heterogeneous nature of CMBS issues relative to RMBS issues, and also to their underlying real estate properties. In particular, default risks are more complex and heterogeneous for CMBSs than for the residential market due to the unique risks of commercial real estate assets and lending practices to the commercial sector. For instance, given the large size and indivisible nature of properties, CMBS issues will tend to contain fewer loans. This means that investors in the CMBS market are more exposed to a small number of potential defaults compared to the case of a standard RMBS. Factors that may affect CMBS default probabilities include:

- property type,
- location,
- borrower quality,
- tenant quality,
- lease terms,
- property management,
- property seasoning,
- property type,
- year of origination.

Given the importance of single properties in a CMBS issue, an investor should analyze the operational performance of each property (or at least the major properties in the pool), as this is a significant factor in the ability of the lender to repay the loan. Therefore, for underlying retail properties an investor should be concerned with operational issues such as tenant mix, quality of location, and economic viability. In the case of shopping centers, a crucial factor that must be examined is the quality of the anchor tenants. Office properties usually provide a level of reassurance to investors due to the longer leases generally used in the sector. However, this means that attention should be focused on issues such as technological obsolescence and the credit quality of the tenants. The mix of properties in the pool that forms the CMBS will be a factor in the analysis of the issue, not only by sector, but also by region. Investors should measure the diversification of the pool, as well as assess future cash flows. Analogous to the case of the RMBS market, different regional U.S. commercial real estate markets have different risk characteristics given that regional business cycles – one of the main factors affecting real estate prices through time – are not perfectly correlated. For these reasons rating agencies generally favor issues with less than 40% of the underlying pool in any one state or in any one-property sector in assigning higher credit ratings.

Loan-to-Value ratios play a big role in the analysis of CMBS issues as was the case with the residential sector. Most U.S. CMBS issues have had historical average LTV ratios in the region of 65–80%, although issues with average LTV ratios greater than 75% would be viewed as risky. However, what is probably more important to consider is the percentage of the individual loans in a CMBS with LTV ratios above 75%. In many cases, rating agencies allow for a maximum of 15% of loans having LTV ratios in excess of 75%. In the past, rating agencies looked for issues where no individual loan composed more than 5% of a specific issue. This has, however, changed in recent times primarily due to the growing use of notes that split a large loan into more than one note (e.g. *Pari Passu* Notes). These notes are designed to reduce large loan concentrations by splitting a large loan into cross defaulted segments of a more manageable size, where each segment is paid a pro rata share of cash flow payments. While used occasionally in the U.S. market since 1998, the years of 2003–2004 saw large increases in such issues. The issuance of such notes increased from 12 in 2002 to 81 in 2003, and to 112 in 2004.

Finally, CMBX indices have been introduced and have spawned a variety of derivatives-based products that facilitate risk transfers and risk management related to CMBSs. Each CMBX index is based on a basket of 25 tranches of the most recently issued CMBS deals rated by one of the three most important credit rating agencies. The CMBX indices were introduced in 2006 to facilitate CMBS market participants efforts to hedge their exposure to positions in commercial mortgages. The indices led to a considerable growth in the structured finance market. CMBX tranches trade over-the-counter, and liquidity is offered by a consortium of large investment banks.

Mezzanine loans

Mezzanine loans experienced exponential growth in the decade prior to the real estate and credit crisis of 2007–2008. These loans are usually second positions that lie in seniority between first mortgages and equity. The loans usually contain options to share in equity gains and are usually motivated when traditional commercial loans are being issued only up to conservative levels such as those creating LTVs of only 65% or 75%. Berman (2007) argues that mezzanine lenders face considerable risks both at the origination of their loans and later on if the borrower defaults due to intricate rules involving the liens on their collateral and difficulties in foreclosing on collateral.

THE U.S. REAL ESTATE AND MORTGAGE CRISIS OF 2007–2008

Real estate investments generated extraordinary performance during the decade prior to 2006–2007, not only in the U.S. but also in many other developed countries where two-digit yearly price increases became the norm. That performance has been followed by an unprecedented real estate market collapse in the U.S.[6] More specifically, according to the S&P Case-Shiller 20-City Composite Home Price Index, residential property prices declined a record 18.8% between June/July of 2006

[6] According to *The Economist* (2005), during the decade prior to 2006, real estate prices more than doubled in the U.S. and France, and tripled in the UK, to mention some of the countries where the "bubble" had been more prevalent. However, in the case of Japan, real estate prices had been declining year after year since 1990 as a result of that country's economic recession and its banking crisis experienced in the early nineties — and from which it had recovered only slowly at the beginning of this century.

and June of 2008. Real estate prices also declined from their peaks in other countries such as the United Kingdom and Spain. To many, this is the sign of a bubble bursting, not only in the U.S., but also in many other developed economies. To complicate matters, and related to this sharp decline in home prices, a mortgage crisis erupted in 2007. Once real estate prices in the U.S. started to deteriorate, the mortgage market began to experience declining prices, and several major financial institutions began experiencing financial distress. One of the largest U.S. banks, Washington Mutual, collapsed after making extraordinarily bad bets on the mortgage market and declared bankruptcy in September of 2008. The bank ran into trouble after having extended large amounts of **sub-prime mortgages**.[7] Troubles then spread to its option adjustable-rate mortgages. Countrywide Home Funding Corporation, the largest independent mortgage banker in the U.S. and responsible for the financing of 20% of all mortgages in the U.S. in 2006, suffered a similar fate earlier in 2008.

Mian and Sufi (2008) contend that a rapid expansion in the origination of mortgages prior to the crisis explains a large portion of the initial appreciation in U.S. house prices. Furthermore, this growth was driven especially by growth in sub-prime loans, a sector of the market that had been traditionally unable to borrow in the mortgage market. Sub-prime mortgage lending is said to have evolved from a small niche product to a mass market product. As a result, housing prices were pressed upwards and a significant decrease in the creditworthiness of borrowers took place. Subsequently, default rates increased in 2007 with the effect of depressing housing prices further.

Similarly, Dell'Ariccia, Igan and Laeven (2008) link the crisis to a reduction in lending standards associated with the fast growth experienced by the sub-prime market. They find that the lending standards were lower in those areas where there were stronger credit booms and where housing prices had increased faster. The authors also discovered that the entry of new and large lenders led to a lowering of lending standards and that this decline was more pronounced in those areas where mortgage securitization rates were higher. Increasing securitization and the entrance of new non-banking lender originators to the mortgage market made investors increasingly dependent on the ratings assigned by credit rating agencies. These agencies exacerbated the mortgage crisis by underestimating the actual risk of mortgage loans, particularly sub-prime loans.

Demyanyk and Van Hemert (2008) also find that the sub-prime mortgage market enjoyed a stellar growth between 2001 and 2006, and that this growth was fueled by the origination of privately-labeled MBSs. As noted above, even though these MBSs did not possess credit risk protection from the Government Sponsored Enterprises, demand for these private-label MBSs grew as investors were searching for higher yields in a relatively low interest rate environment. The increasing use of these new types of mortgages, which were different from traditional fixed-rate mortgage loans, also affected the intensity and later bursting of the real estate bubble. For example, in the case of variable-rate mortgages, it was common for the initial rate to be fixed and relatively low during an initial and short period of time (for example, two years). As a result of this, the sub-prime share of the mortgage market experienced a dramatic increase, from just 8% in 2001 to 20% in 2006, and the securitized portion of the sub-prime mortgage market grew from 54% in 2001 to 75% in 2006. Approximately two years after being issued, variable rate mortgages typically adjusted upward from the initial low "teaser" rates. In the case of the sub-prime mortgages, these variable rates mortgages experienced an average increase of 30–40% in the size of the monthly mortgage payment

---

[7] According to the U.S. Department of the Treasury (2001), "Subprime borrowers (are those that) typically have weakened credit histories that include payment delinquencies, and possibly more severe problems such as charge-offs, judgments, and bankruptcies. They may also display reduced repayment capacity as measured by credit scores, debt-to-income ratios, or other criteria that may encompass borrowers with incomplete credit histories."

when the rate adjustments took place. These loans were used extensively in 2006 and so the rate adjustments and payment increases in the face of declining home prices triggered the first wave of foreclosures.

Yet Demyanyk and Van Hemert (2008) determined that the high default rates of the mortgages that were originated in 2006 were not restricted to a particular section of the sub-prime mortgage market. They found that fixed-rate, adjustable-rate, low documentation, full documentation, and other types of mortgages originated in 2006 all recorded considerably higher delinquency and foreclosure rates than loans originated in the previous five years.

29

Real Estate and Asset Allocation

In this chapter, we focus our attention on the role of real estate as an asset class in an investor's portfolio. We start with an analysis of the empirical literature on the effects that macroeconomic variables have on real estate prices. We then analyze the potential benefits of real estate diversification, concentrating our attention on the case of REITs and the performance exhibited by investments in different real estate sectors (apartments, offices, retail and commercial) and U.S. regions (East, Midwest, South and West).

REAL ESTATE PRICES AND MACROECONOMIC VARIABLES

Commerical and residential real estate prices are determined by numerous factors. For example, according to Sabal (2005), real estate prices are affected by: 1) disposable income and availability of financing; 2) uniqueness of the property; 3) government planning and regulations on the use of land, which affect the real estate supply; 4) long-term population growth; 5) the cost of managing a property, maintenance costs, repairs and insurance costs; and 6) the tax treatment of real estate investments. Ling and Naranjo (1997) find that the following macroeconomic factors can explain real estate returns: growth in consumption, the term structure of interest rates, real interest rates, and unexpected inflation. However, the importance of unexpected inflation as a determinant of real estate prices is not supported by the mixed findings of others regarding the inflation-hedging potential of real estate investments (for a review on this topic see Goetzmann and Valaitis, 2006).

Empirical evidence suggests that real estate markets follow cycles. Furthermore, Eichholtz et al. (1998) and Eichholtz, Koedijk and Schweitzer (2001) identify strong continental factors in determining real estate returns in Europe and North America. The implication is that true international real estate diversification can only be achieved by investing inter-continentally. In the same vein, Case, Goetzmann and Rouwenhorst (2000) analyze returns in global real estate markets, including their integration and their relation to macroeconomic variables, especially local GNP and globally aggregated GNP. They find that, despite substantial correlation across world property markets due to fluctuations in the global economy, substantial diversification benefits can be attained through diversification across countries. However, a caveat suggested by Hoesli, Lekander, and Witkiewicz (2003) and Hoesli and Lekander (2005) is that those investing in real estate internationally should be aware that they suffer from an informational disadvantage over local investors.

THE ROLE OF REAL ESTATE IN AN INVESTOR'S PORTFOLIO

For most individual investors, their own homes, which typically represent a large portion of their net worth, are the starting point in terms of real estate investments. In such cases, the relevant question is to what extent adding commercial real estate investments to a homeowner's portfolio may be beneficial.

Modern Portfolio Theory predicts that, while individual assets tend to exhibit high volatility, a diversified portfolio of investments in those assets can have substantially lower risk levels, potentially without lowered expected returns, due to diversification. Academic research has shown that adding real estate to an investor's portfolio may reduce its risk and produce an improved combination of risk and return (mean vs. variance). This improvement is because real estate investments tend to have low correlations with traditional asset classes.

It has also been amply documented in the literature that property prices series tend to exhibit low volatility when compared to other assets. However, many authors caution that this apparently low volatility arises as a result of data smoothing, a phenomenon that was described in Chapter 24.

Given low correlations, low volatilities and reasonable historic average return levels, real estate would appear to be an attractive component of an institutional portfolio. Indeed, researchers estimating reasonable statistical parameters and using the mean-variance model of Markowitz find that optimized (efficient) portfolios tend to possess high real estate portfolio weights in the absence of other objectives or constraints. However, contrary to the predictions of such models, institutional investors normally have a real estate allocation of only between 5% and 10% of their total portfolios.

Although real estate represents a large proportion of the investable universe, there exists substantial disagreement on the role, if any, of real estate in strategic asset allocations. Goetzmann and Dhar (2005) conducted a questionnaire-based study through which they collected information about the real estate allocation choices and viewpoints of a group of leading U.S. investment managers. They found strong evidence suggesting that Modern Portfolio Theory forms the general basis for asset allocation decisions to real estate. Furthermore, even though investors placed real estate risk and return as lying between bonds and stocks, they also regarded the costs arising from real estate investing as relatively high when compared to traditional assets. Hudson-Wilson, Fabozzi and Gordon (2003) argue that real estate should be included in an investor's portfolios at their market weights (i.e. the percentage of investable wealth that real estate represents).

The most important constraint when allocating to real estate is often the inherent illiquidity of the asset. Accordingly, investors requiring liquidity should balance the disadvantages of real estate's illiquidity with the potential benefit of earning a liquidity return premium. A second constraint is that the time horizon for illiquid real estate investments such as direct property ownership should be long-term. This is because the costs of buying and selling properties are high and also because sellers usually have to wait at least a few months to be able to sell their properties (unless they are willing to offer a large discount, especially in bearish markets). A third constraint is that direct real estate investments usually require large amounts of capital. Therefore, to most individuals, investment in direct real estate implies that their aggregate portfolio (i.e. including real estate assets plus stocks and bonds) will not be well diversified.

The role of real estate in an investor's portfolio is a controversial issue that is far from being resolved. Opinions also differ with regard to allocations among types of real estate. Idzorek, Barad and Meier (2007) contend that the largest investors' recommended allocations should be more heavily concentrated in direct commercial real estate investments (such as acquiring and managing actual physical properties), and that smaller investors should obtain exposure to this asset class via investments in real estate investment trusts (REITs) and stocks of listed companies that belong to the real estate sector. These authors also suggest that relative weightings should be approximately equal to market capitalization-based weights.

REAL ESTATE AND DIVERSIFICATION

The heterogeneity of real estate assets means that real estate managers require a far greater number of assets to create a diversified portfolio defined in the conventional sense. There are, however, other considerations. First of all, given the high unit cost of real estate assets, a portfolio containing 30 properties (30 is often suggested as a reasonable number of stocks to hold in forming a diversified portfolio), particularly if concentrated in prime markets, will be very expensive. Another problem is that most of the research on diversification in equity and bond markets has assumed that the assets in the portfolios were equally weighted. However, the indivisible nature of direct real estate ownership means that real estate portfolios will have a value-weighting scheme. Brown and Matysiak (1998) and Byrne and Lee (2000) illustrate the implications of this issue in a portfolio construction context. Specifically, Brown and Matysiak (2000) show that if a value-weighting procedure is used then it will typically take far more properties to sufficiently eliminate unsystematic risk compared to the case where portfolios are created using an equal-weighting methodology.

The above discussion concerning real estate portfolio construction and diversification potential has largely concentrated on the elimination of most unsystematic risk. There is however another important element – that being the ability of a property portfolio to match the return of the market benchmark. As with the risk reduction issue, the heterogeneous nature of real estate means that the ability of a manager to track effectively a benchmark is problematic, to say the least. In the case of real estate, the range of performances around a benchmark is wider than in other asset classes (i.e. there are more extreme "winners" and more extreme "losers"). Furthermore, most real estate investors cannot merely buy an index to receive desired risk exposures to real estate assets.

Brown (1997) estimated that, on average, over 200 properties would be required in a portfolio for 95% of the variation in returns to be explained by the market (i.e. for 5% or less to be explained by unsystematic risk). Recent research by Oxford Property Consultants (OPC) estimates that to reduce the tracking error (i.e. the standard deviation of the difference between the portfolio's return and that of the benchmark) down below 5% requires an exponential increase in the number of properties. Based on UK data, OPC estimated that to construct a direct real estate portfolio with a 5% tracking error would require an investment of just over £500m. However, to reduce the tracking error down to 2% would require an increase in the size of the portfolio to over £3.7bn.

The implications of the often interlinked issues of heterogeneity and indivisibility therefore mean that it is not only extremely difficult to eliminate unsystematic risks but that it is even harder to match the benchmark's returns (the difference is from assuming that the benchmark contains unsystematic risks). Given that it will be nearly impossible for all but the largest institutions to do this, the vast majority of real estate funds are not well diversified in the conventional sense. This constraint begs the question of how real estate investors can best construct their portfolios. Historically, investors have tended to implement real estate portfolio strategies that have been analogous to bottom-up stock selection strategies: A major determinant of decisions is the real estate investor's examination of the "stand alone" attractiveness of individual potential investments. However, there are a number of additional issues that fund managers consider at a portfolio level. A number of commonly analyzed characteristics include income-based, yield-based and lease-based aspects. The portfolios are constructed in light of these characteristics to ensure that, insofar as possible, there are appropriate levels and variations in the types of properties held in the portfolio. The size of the fund will also influence the strategy adopted. Larger funds have advantages in terms of factors such as enhanced diversification abilities, the ability to invest in more expensive properties and the ability to undertake more development/refurbishment projects. However, larger funds are also limited in that it is harder for them to change significantly their portfolio allocations and structure easily and quickly due to the large sizes involved. Smaller funds, while being on average less diversified and limited in terms of the size of the properties that they can purchase, can alter their strategies far more quickly and also have the advantage that single transactions/deals can have a far larger impact upon the characteristics of the overall portfolio.

Diversification benefits of REITs investing

One of the main arguments for investing in REITs relates to their perceived diversification benefits, both from the real estate portfolio and from the capital market portfolio perspectives. A number of recent papers have shown that REITs provide adequate diversification opportunities even to mixed-asset portfolios that already contain an allocation to the private real estate market. For example,

Feldman (2003) finds that both public and private real estate have a place in a mixed-asset frame-work. Mueller and Mueller (2003) extend the analysis of Feldman (2003) to examine the impact of private and public real estate on the mixed-asset portfolio for various holding periods of five to 25 years ending in 2002. They find that for the full sample period the inclusion of private real estate, as measured by the NCREIF index, led to improvements in the performance of the efficient frontier at the lower risk levels, while REITs provided improvements to the entire frontier. Stevenson (2001) examines the improvement in portfolio performance from the inclusion of both REITs and international real estate securities into direct market portfolios and finds that not only do REITs receive substantial allocations in the optimal portfolios, but if a diversified private market portfolio is assumed, the improvement in portfolio performance from the addition of REITs is statistically significant.

Lee and Stevenson (2005) examine the consistency of the diversification benefits provided by REITs within a mixed-asset framework. Efficient frontiers were estimated for a range of four alternative rolling time periods (5, 10, 15 and 20 years). The analysis was concerned with both the potential risk reduction and the return enhancement benefits that REITs potentially provide to previously estimated equity and bond optimal portfolios. The results show that REITs consistently provide diversification benefits to the mixed-asset portfolio with substantial allocations to REITs in the efficient portfolios. Furthermore, these benefits tend to increase as the investment horizon is extended, thus suggesting that REITs may be more attractive to investors with longer holding periods. This higher attractiveness over longer holding periods may also arise as a result of the increasing linkages between REITs and the private real estate market with the use of longer horizons. Of further interest is that the diversification benefits of REITs appear to come from both their return enhancement and risk reduction benefits. While REITs have lower correlations with the general equity indices examined, this is not at the expense of increased correlations with bonds. REITs therefore effectively lie between the broad equity and fixed-income sectors both in terms of risk and return measures. It can be argued that perhaps many of the benefits of REITs in a portfolio context result from the mandatory high dividend payout that gives REITs fixed-income characteristics.

REITs diversification benefits in the period 1991–2007

Here we analyze the risk and total return performance of REITs (measured using the sum of capital appreciation and dividends from the FTSE NAIRET U.S. Real Estate Investment Trusts Index), compared to traditional U.S. equity and bond indices and to other alternative investments for the period 1991–2007. The NAREIT All-REIT index is calculated using actual trading prices on the stock exchanges. REITs are viewed as reflecting three effects. First, they are affected by the price evolution of the underlying real estate assets. Second, their returns also reflect a leverage effect because REITs usually borrow money to finance their real estate investment holdings. Finally, as was discussed in Chapter 25, REITs appear to "echo the behavior of the overall stock market rather than only reflecting the dynamics of the underlying private real estate market."

As can be seen in Table 29.1, the average annualized REIT Index returns were higher than all other asset classes except hedge funds and private equity. REITs exhibited a higher volatility than bonds, hedge funds and CTAs. However, REITs had comparable volatility to stocks and commodities and less volatility than private equity.

Results in Table 29.1 indicate little or no correlation between REITs and either traditional or alternative investments. These low correlations suggest that including real estate investments in an otherwise diversified portfolio can provide additional diversification benefits.

Figure 29.1 illustrates the mean returns and volatilities of Table 29.1. The illustration shows that, in general, there was a positive relationship between traditional and alternative investments' returns and risks, and that REITs offered one of the more attractive combinations.

Table 29.1   REITs and other investments' performances, 1991–2007

Stock, bond, and REIT performance	S&P 500	Lehman aggregate	3-Month LIBOR	Real estate
Annualized total return	11.4%	7.1%	4.5%	13.6%
Annualized standard deviation	13.4%	3.7%	0.5%	13.3%
Sharpe ratio	0.51	0.69		0.68
Maximum drawdown	−44.7%	−5.1%		−26.3%
Correlation with real estate	0.35	0.13	−0.06	1.00
Alternative asset performance	Hedge funds	CTA	Private equity	Commodities
Annualized total return	15.2%	7.9%	14.8%	8.9%
Annualized standard deviation	6.8%	9.1%	23.2%	13.9%
Sharpe ratio	1.57	0.38	0.45	0.31
Maximum drawdown	−11.6	−9.4%	−61.3%	−36.7%
Correlation with real estate	0.35	0.04	0.28	0.02

Source: Garay, 2008
Note:
"S&P 500" is a total return (capital appreciation and dividends) measure of U.S. stock returns calculated using the Standard and Poor's 500 Index;
"Lehman aggregate" is a measure of U.S. bond returns using the Lehman Aggregate Bond Index;
"3-month LIBOR" is a measure of short-term interest rates, estimated using the annualized 3-month London Interbank Offered Rate;
"REITs" is a measure of real estate investment trusts' total returns (capital appreciation and dividends) estimated using the FTSE NAIRET U.S. Real Estate Index;
"Hedge funds" represents the return of the CASAM/CISDM Hedge Fund Index (equally weighted);
"CTA" is the return of the CASAM/CISDM commodity trading advisors index;
"Private equity" is the return of the S&P Private Equity Index; and
"Commodities" is the return on a composite of commodities indices, taken as the average of the BCI, SPGSCI, and DJ-AIG commodity indices.

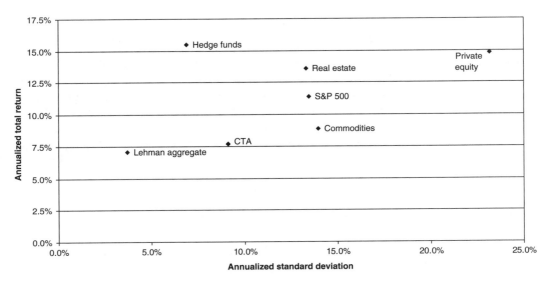

Figure 29.1 Return and risk characteristics for various assets, 1991–2007 (*Source:* Garay, 2008). For a definition of the variables included in this figure, see Table 29.1.

Table 29.2   Index performance 2001–2007

Stock, bond, and REIT performance	S&P 500	Lehman aggregate	3-Month LIBOR	Real estate
Annualized total return	3.3%	5.8%	3.3%	14.8%
Annualized standard deviation	13.3%	3.6%	0.5%	15.0%
Sharpe ratio	0.00	0.70		0.77
Maximum drawdown	−38.9%	−8.6%		−23.8%
Correlation with real estate	0.41	0.02	0.27	1.00
Alternative asset performance	Hedge funds	CTA	Private equity	Commodities
Annualized total return	9.7	7.5%	10.9%	10.5%
Annualized standard deviation	5.0%	8.4%	22.2%	15.7%
Sharpe ratio	1.30	0.50	0.35	0.46
Maximum drawdown	−5.3%	−8.7%	−45.8%	−24.5%
Correlation with real estate	0.40	0.09	0.46	−0.04

Source: Garay, 2008. For a definition of the variables included in this table, see Table 29.1.

REITs diversification benefits in the more recent past (2001–2007)

In this section, we present similar statistics as above except we include only the more recent years of 2001–2007. Table 29.2 shows that during this more recent time period, REITs exhibited a higher return than all other asset classes examined even after REIT prices had declined sharply in 2007 (and continued falling in 2008 after the study's time period). Compared to private equity, REITs had lower volatility, compared to stocks and commodities the volatility of REITs was roughly comparable, and compared to other asset classes REITs had higher volatility. Finally, Table 29.2 shows that the correlations between REITs and traditional and other alternative investments ranged from potentially negative to moderately positive during this more recent period of 2001–2007.

PERFORMANCE OF REAL ESTATE SECTORS

Here we examine the comparative performance of real estate sectors: apartments, industrial properties, offices and retail properties. The performance statistics shown in Table 29.3 (U.S.) suggest that returns and risks varied only slightly across the different real estate sectors throughout the 1995–2007 period. However, the figure also shows that offices yielded the highest Sharpe ratio with industrial yielding the lowest Sharpe ratio. It is also interesting to observe that the correlations between the four real estate sectors and inflation rates – either actual inflation or expected inflation – are near zero. This lack of correlation suggests that real estate investments may not have provided a hedge

Table 29.3   Performance of MIT/CRE real estate sector indices, 1995–2007

	All	Apartment	Industrial	Office	Retail
Annualized Return	15.2%	16.7%	15.8%	16.0%	15.8%
Annualized standard deviation	7.1%	8.1%	10.1%	6.9%	8.8%
Sharpe ratio	1.60	1.58	1.17	1.74	1.36
Correlation w/ unexpected inflation	−0.01	−0.01	−0.01	0.00	−0.01
Correlation w/ inflation	0.07	0.06	0.08	0.06	0.08

Source: Garay, 2008

Table 29.4   Geographical correlation of direct real estate returns, 1990–2007

	NCREIF Index	East	Midwest	South	West
NCREIF Index	1.00				
East	0.94	1.00			
Midwest	0.89	0.84	1.00		
South	0.91	0.83	0.82	1.00	
West	0.93	0.79	0.74	0.78	1.00

Source: Garay, 2008

against the risk of inflation during the considered period, but it should be noted that this was also a period of relatively low and steady inflation.

GEOGRAPHICAL DIVERSIFICATION

Another dimension affecting portfolio decisions is geography and the degree to which real estate returns of different regions are correlated. Table 29.4 shows the correlation matrix of total returns for four U.S. regions (East, Midwest, South, and West), using the NCREIF (National Council of Real Estate Investment Fiduciaries) geographical sub-indices and the combined NCREIF index for the period 1990–2007. The table shows that the correlations across all pairs of geographical sub-indices are relatively high, thus suggesting that the benefits of **geographical diversification** at the regional level were limited. However, analysis of finer divisions such as cities or metropolitan areas would be necessary to indicate whether there were substantial benefits of geographical diversification at finer geographic levels.

Some opportunities for geographical diversification in the U.S. may exist, but fewer can be found within other countries. This is because very few countries have the economic diversity of the U.S. Even major European economies such as the UK and France do not often have the necessary differences in regional economies to provide even as meaningful diversification results as the modest results indicated by this analysis.

The diversification benefits of geographic dispersion may vary based on the extent to which common factors drive returns of markets in diverse locations. For example, in the international office sector, many of the largest, most liquid global office markets are also key financial services centers, such as New York City, London, Toronto, Paris, Singapore and Sydney. These office real estate markets have many common forces driving demand. Furthermore, many of the largest financial companies rent substantial office space in several or all of these cities. This provides many common underlying demand drivers in these global markets, such as performance of the financial sector or even performance of a few large corporations. While naturally each of the markets will also be subject to the variation in local supply factors, the common underlying demand drivers in these international real estate markets feed into rental trends and tend to cause correlated return performance. Jones Lang LaSalle estimates that in every year since 2000 at least 40% of cross-border investment in Europe has been in the office sector. Furthermore, in 2005 alone, 45% of this investment went into the UK with by far the largest proportion entering the London market. It is estimated that in 2005 over 50% of purchasers in the City of London market were made by overseas investors, leading to 45% of all office space in the City of London being foreign-owned. This concentration is also seen to varying degrees in other global financial services centers. This indicates that although some real estate markets may not be in the same country, or even on the same continent, they may be highly correlated and may offer limited diversification benefits.

30

Alternative Real Estate Investment Vehicles

Several alternative real estate investment vehicles are available. Most of these products have been introduced recently. Other alternative real estate investment vehicles are anticipated to be launched in the coming years. These alternative investments include both private (i.e. non-exchange-traded) and exchange-traded products.

PRIVATE REAL ESTATE INVESTMENT VEHICLES

This section discusses the main characteristics of the following private real estate alternative investments: open-end real estate mutual funds, private equity real estate funds, commingled real estate funds, syndications, joint ventures, and limited partnerships.

Open-end real estate mutual funds

Open-end real estate mutual funds offer an alternative indirect non-exchange-traded means of obtaining access to the private real estate market. Open-end real estate funds are similar to REITs in that they allow investors to gain access to real estate investments with relatively small quantities of capital. Open-end real estate mutual funds are funds operated by an investment company that collects money from shareholders and invests in real estate assets following a set of objectives laid out in the fund's prospectus. Open-end funds initially raise money by selling shares of the funds to the public and generally continue to sell shares to the public when requested.

Even though open-end real estate funds usually allow investors to enter and exit the fund freely, there may be circumstances in which a fund may limit investors' ability to redeem units and exit the fund. This often occurs when, for example, a significant percentage of shareholders wishes to redeem their investments and if the fund is encountering liquidity problems. These liquidity problems can be exacerbated by the fact that they tend to occur as the real estate market is either booming or in a downturn. To make matters worse, these kinds of market conditions will often be characterized by an increased illiquidity in the underlying real estate asset market as well. Of course, these situations tend to be the exact circumstances under which fund investors most need the liquidity and thus limit the extent to which investors can view these open funds on a prospective basis as being liquid.

Open-end funds generally allow investors to redeem their shares (potentially subject to fees and limitations) at the fund's net asset value, which is computed on a daily basis. Given that downward phases in real estate market cycles tend to last for considerable periods of time, it is possible that real estate valuations used in some net asset value computations may be viewed by some analysts as trailing true market declines (and trailing true market increases in a bull market). Stale pricing of the assets of a fund provides an incentive for existing shareholders to sell during declining markets and new investors to enter during rising markets. During declining markets, therefore, an open-end fund may face redemption problems and may have to sell some of its real estate assets at deep discounts in order to obtain liquidity. To protect long-term investors and fund assets, many open-end real estate funds increasingly opt to reserve the right to defer redemption by investors to allow sufficient time to liquidate assets in case they need to do so.

In summary, investors in open-end mutual funds are typically offered daily opportunities to redeem their outstanding shares directly from the fund. This attempt to have high liquidity of open-end real estate funds shares contrasts to the illiquidity of the underlying real estate assets held in the fund's portfolio. As a result, a popular design for real estate mutual funds aimed for a broader public is the closed-end mutual fund (see Sebastian and Tyrell, 2006) –an alternative real estate investment that is explained later in this chapter.

Private equity real estate funds

Private equity real estate funds collect capital from investors with the objective of investing in the equity and/or the debt sides of the private real estate space. These funds follow active management real estate investment strategies such as property development or redevelopment. Private equity real estate funds usually have a life span of 10 years consisting of a two to three year investment period and a subsequent holding period during which the properties are expected to be sold.

The primary advantage to an investor is the access to private real estate, especially useful for smaller institutions that are limited in the size of the real estate portfolios that they are able to directly construct. However, even for larger institutions, there are advantages to investments in private equity real estate funds (and also in commingled real estate funds, explained in Section 30.1.3), as these investment vehicles can provide access to larger properties in which the institution may be reluctant to invest because of the unique asset risk they would need to bear and because of the fact that a single asset could account for a portfolio allocation that may be too high.[1] The use of private equity real estate funds can also provide access to local or specialized management, or to specific sectors and markets where the institution does not feel it has sufficient market knowledge or expertise.

Private equity real estate funds grew exponentially during the 1990s and up to the time of the real estate market crisis that started in 2007. However, investments through private equity funds do have some disadvantages. First of all, and similar to the case of REITs and open-end real estate funds, investors in private equity funds do not have direct control over the real estate portfolio and cannot make leasing decisions, strategic portfolio decisions, selling decisions or leverage decisions. The investors are primarily making the investment decisions based on their view of the fund manager's skills and the appropriateness of the investment objectives. In addition to the loss of control, private funds often lack a sufficiently liquid exit route, although it is fair to say that this problem varies across markets, fund types and time periods.

Another major issue with private equity funds is the difficulty of reporting the values of the underlying properties. As noted previously, incorrect asset valuation can create a number of problems. Most notably, the reported performance may not be accurate. Furthermore, the illiquidity in the underlying market implies that there could be considerable time or uncertainty in realizing reported performance. The finite life of this vehicle tends to make the funds a "hold to liquidation" instrument.

Commingled real estate funds

Commingled real estate funds (CREFs) consist of a pool of investment capital raised in the form of private placements that are "commingled" to purchase commercial properties. CREFs are the earliest established forms of real estate funds in the U.S. Investors in CREFs receive a negotiable, although non-exchange-traded, ownership certificate that represents a proportionate share of the

---

[1] It is not unusual, especially in the case of certain real estate sectors, to have real estate investments such as shopping malls or prime office markets in which an individual property has a value in the hundreds of millions of dollars.

real estate assets owned by the fund. CREFs are typically offered to pension funds by major banks, investment banks, life insurance companies, and real estate advisory firms. CREFs are generally closed-end in structure, with unit prices determined by annual or quarterly appraisals of the underlying properties. Ownership certificates in a CREF can be negotiated in a private sale as in the case of limited partnerships. Similar to the case of private equity real estate funds, for an investor utilizing commingled real estate funds, the primary advantage is the access that they provide to private real estate investments, especially in the case of smaller institutions. However, even for larger institutions, there are advantages to investments in commingled real estate funds, as these investment vehicles can provide access to larger properties that the institution may be unwilling to invest in because of the unacceptably large unique risk they would need to bear.

Similar to the CREF structure in the U.S., **property unit trusts** and **managed funds** have existed in other markets, such as the UK, for over four decades. Property unit trusts were established in the mid-1960s as a vehicle to allow tax-exempt institutions to invest indirectly in the real estate asset class. Resembling CREFs, these structures are particularly popular with smaller institutions that have insufficient internal resources to construct their own direct real estate portfolio. Unit trust prices are appraisal-based, usually on a monthly basis. Managed funds are similar but managed by insurance companies for their occupational pension fund clients. Both types of vehicles share an open-ended structure.

Syndications

Syndications are formed by a group of investors who retain a real estate expert with the intention of undertaking a real estate project. Usually developers who require extra equity capital to commence a project raise money through syndications. Legally, real estate syndications may operate as REITs, as a corporation, or as a limited or general partnership. A syndicate can be created to develop, acquire, operate, manage, or market real estate investments. According to Brueggeman and Fisher (2006) syndications can be thought of as a form of financing that offers smaller investors the opportunity to invest in real estate projects that would otherwise be outside their financial and management competencies. Syndicators profit from the fees they collect for their services and also from the interest they may preserve in the syndicated property.

Most real estate syndications are structured as limited partnerships with the syndicator performing as general partner and the investors as limited partners. This structure facilitates the pass through of depreciation deductions (which are normally high) directly to individual investors and therefore circumvents a potential double taxation.

Joint ventures

A real estate **joint venture** consists of the combination of two or more parties, typically represented by a small number of individual or institutional investors, embarking on a business enterprise such as the development of real estate properties. An example of a joint venture is the case of an institutional investor with no expertise in real estate but with an interest in investing in this area, who agrees to form a joint venture with a developer. A joint venture can be structured as a limited partnership, an important form of real estate investment that is explained in Section 30.1.6 below.

Limited partnerships

A partnership is defined as "an association of two or more persons who carry on a business for profit as co-owners." In real estate, partnerships can be used for many applications. **Limited partnerships** are business organizations that combine the limited liability characteristic of an investment in a corporation with the advantages of a partnership, such as tax advantages and the capability to make special distributions of income and cash to the partners. Whereas general partners in limited partnerships are supposed to have the competencies and knowledge of the real estate world and manage the business, including assuming its debts and obligations, limited partners strive to be liable only for the amount of their investments and typically are not further liable for the partnership's debts and obligations.

While fund structures such as CREFs have been in existence for a long period of time, the last decade has witnessed a major shift towards the use of other forms of private real estate investments. In particular, there has been an increased interest in limited partnership structures, similar in form to those commonly used in other areas such as private equity and hedge funds. Indeed, not only have real estate funds increasingly adopted limited partnership structures, but existing limited partnerships such as private equity and hedge funds have increasingly entered the real estate market. As with other limited partnership structures, a fund's sponsors act as the general partner and raise capital from institutional investors such as pension funds, endowments and from high net worth individuals (who serve as limited partners). Generally, the initial capital raised is in the form of commitments that are only drawn down when suitable investments have been identified. The three primary players, who act as fund sponsors, are large investment banks, investment houses that may run funds across a broad spectrum of asset classes and dedicated real estate fund managers.

Limited partnership funds in real estate have largely adopted a more aggressive investment style than their traditional counterparts. As the traditional forms of funds are primarily designed for institutional investment, they tend to adopt similar conservative investment strategies. This is particularly true with respect to **gearing**, which is defined as the ratio of the percentage of a fund's capital that is financed by debt and other long-term financing. Many such traditional real estate funds have limited, if any, gearing. In contrast, a large proportion of the new private equity real estate funds has gearing ratios in excess of 75%. This high level of gearing has been partially driven by the relatively low and stable interest rate environments that most industrialized markets have witnessed in the last 15 years.

Limited partnerships have also tended to adopt the fee structures commonly in place in private equity funds. In addition to an annual management fee, commonly in the region of 2% of assets under management, the newer funds have also introduced performance-related fees, in the common region of 20% of returns. Generally, the incentive-based performance fees are subject to some form of hurdle rate or preferred return. The incentive fee structure can be specified in a number of ways. General partners sometimes only take their incentive fee on returns in excess of the hurdle rate. Alternatively, the general partners might be eligible for the entire 20% of the total return, as long as the hurdle rate is exceeded. For example, assume that a fund has a stated preferred return of 10%, that the limited partners contribute $500m and that the profits of the fund are $125m, which equates to a 25% return. The general partners are clearly entitled to a performance-related fee because this 25% return exceeds the 10% preferred return. However, this performance fee could be calculated as either $15m, in the case that they are entitled to a 20% of the return in excess of the 10% hurdle rate, or $25m if the fund is structured such that, as long as the minimum 10% return is exceeded, then the fund sponsor would take 20% of the total profit. Net returns to the investor are therefore dependent on the fee structure.

The fund sponsors (or general partners) usually contribute some capital to the fund, thus benefiting not only from the explicit incentive and management fees, but also from their share of the limited partnership's return. Continuing with our example, assume that the sponsors contribute $200m in capital to the fund. If they are entitled to 20% of the return in excess of the 10% hurdle rate, they would take a $15m performance-related fee. This leaves the remaining $110m to be distributed among investors. Given that the sponsor contributed 40% of the capital, he would receive an additional $44m (40% of $110m). The remaining limited partners receive $66m, which would be distributed on a pro-rata basis.

Finally, the returns attained by private funds in real estate will vary considerably depending on the investment style adopted. More conservative funds, such as CREFs, that target core properties and do so with less gearing, will typically produce returns similar to those observed by benchmark indices such as the NCREIF. In contrast, more heavily geared funds and those targeting more high-risk property segments can deliver returns far different from those of the benchmark indices. Thus, an impact of gearing is to increase the volatility of returns.

For example, let us assume that an investor purchases a property for $100m. By the end of the first year, the property appreciates in value to $102m and the investor receives $8m in rental income. An ungeared investor receives a total return of 10%, comprised of a 2% capital gain ($2m/$100m) and an 8% income return ($8m/$100m). In contrast, if the property is purchased with a Loan-to-Value ratio of 60%, only $40m of equity is put into the property by the fund, and the return will be different. Assume that the debt of $60m carries an interest rate of 8%, thereby incurring annual interest payments of $4.8m. Given the original $8m of income, this leads to retained earnings of $3.2m ($8m – $4.8m). The total return for the geared investor is 13%, which is made up of a 5% capital gain ($2m/$40m) and an 8% income return ($3.2m/$40m). It can therefore be seen that, in this case, gearing enhances the return obtained. On the other hand, assume now that by the end of the year the property falls in value to $92m and that rental income is $7m rather than the anticipated $8m. The ungeared investor's total return is –1%. This is made up of a –8% capital return (–$8m/$100m) and a 7% income return ($7m/$100m). Continuing with the example of declining property values, the total return for the geared investor is −14.5%, which is made up of a −20% capital return (−$8m/$40m) and a 5.5% income return ($2.2m/$40m). This $2.2m net income is found by subtracting the interest ($4.8m) from the $7m income. Therefore, while geared funds can see returns enhanced while property returns are rising, losses are amplified during falling markets. Finally, private funds in real estate face the problem that they can generate tax liabilities without any cash distribution to cover the taxes.

PUBLIC REAL ESTATE INVESTMENT VEHICLES

Traditionally, REITs have been the most important public real estate investment vehicle. However, in recent years a number of new alternative public real estate investment vehicles have been launched. These other real estate investments include options and futures on real estate indices, exchange traded funds based on real estate indices, and closed-end real estate mutual funds.

Options and futures on real estate indices

Derivative products allow investors to transfer risk exposure related to either the equity or the debt sides of real estate investments without having to actually buy or sell properties. This is accomplished by linking the payoff of the derivative to the performance of a real estate return index, thus allowing investors to obtain exposures without engaging in real estate property transactions or real estate financing.

The CME Group began listing housing futures and options in May 2006. These contracts are based on the S&P/Case-Shiller Housing Index of 10 U.S. cities (Boston, Chicago, Denver, Las Vegas, Los Angeles, Miami, New York City, San Diego, San Francisco and Washington D.C.), as well as on the individual constituents (cities). It is expected that the recent introduction of these real estate derivatives products will help increase the transparency and liquidity in the real estate market in the coming years.

Exchange-traded funds based on real estate indices

Exchange-traded funds (or ETFs) represent a tradable investment vehicle that tracks a particular index by holding its constituent assets (or a sub-sample of them). ETFs trade on exchanges at approximately the same price as the net asset value of its underlying assets due to provisions that allow for the creation and redemption of shares at net asset value. ETFs have the advantage of being a relatively low cost investment vehicle (in the case of those ETFs that have reached a certain size or popularity among investors), they are tax efficient, and they offer stock-like features (such as liquidity, dividends, the possibility to go short or to use with margin, and in some cases the availability of calls and puts).

While the first ETFs were based on stock and bond indices, ETFs are now also based on other assets such as real estate, currencies and commodities. **Exchange-traded funds based on real estate indices** track a real estate index such as the *Dow Jones U.S. Real Estate*. Other ETFs, such as the *FTSE NAREIT Residential*, track a REITs index. Therefore, ETFs facilitate access to real estate assets for both small and large investors and, similar to options and futures on real estate indices, ETFs based on real estate indices can also be used either to hedge risks or to speculate.

Closed-end real estate mutual funds

A closed-end fund is an exchange-traded mutual fund that has a fixed number of shares outstanding. Closed-end funds issue a fixed number of shares to the general public in an initial public offering and, in contrast to the case of open-end mutual funds, shares in closed-end funds cannot be obtained from or redeemed by the investment company. Instead, shares in closed-end funds are traded on stock exchanges. Thus, unlike open-end funds, closed-end funds do not need to maintain liquidity to redeem shares and they do not need to establish a net asset value at which entering and exiting investors will transact. Since closed-end funds are not required to meet shareholder redemption requests they are generally more suitable for the use of leverage. Accordingly, the closed-end fund structure has advantages for investment in relatively illiquid assets such as foreign stocks and assets that investors often prefer to hold with leverage such as municipal bonds. **Closed-end real estate mutual funds** can exploit the advantages offered by the closed-end fund structure. Like other closed-end funds, they often trade at premiums or substantial discounts to their net assets values, especially when net asset values are not based on market values (such as REITs). Real estate closed-end funds usually liquidate their real estate portfolios and return capital to shareholders after an investment term (typically 15 years), the length of which is stated at the funds' inception. Closed-end real estate funds invest in properties (and/or REITs) and experienced significant growth up to the time of the real estate crisis of 2007–2008.

Finally, we conclude this section by presenting a summary of the main advantages and disadvantages (or potential shortcomings) of each of the alternative real estate investment vehicles discussed in this chapter (see Table 30.1).

CROSS-BORDER INVESTMENTS IN REAL ESTATE

The growth in real estate funds has had an impact on the increase in cross-border real estate investments. Historically, not only did institutions dominate real estate investment in most markets, but also in most countries, and the vast majority of holdings was held domestically. The primary

Table 30.1 Advantages and disadvantages of alternative real estate investments

Private real estate (RE) investment vehicles

	Open-end RE funds	Private equity (PE) RE funds	Commingled RE funds
Advantages	– Relatively liquid (compared to the rest of private RE) – Allow access to RE investments with little capital – Regulated by the Securities and Exchange Commission (SEC)	– Allow direct access to RE investments – Provide access to direct RE investments to small institutions – Can provide access to local management or specific sectors – Possibility to diversify into PE RE funds-of-funds	– Allow direct access to RE investments – Provide access to direct RE investments to small institutions – Can provide access to local management or specific sectors
Disadvantages/potential shortcomings	– Relatively illiquid (compared to closed-end funds) – Tend to be tax inefficient (compared to ETFs) – Difficult to obtain access to very specific markets or sectors – Potential transaction costs and commissions	– Illiquidity (PE RE funds often lack a sufficiently liquid exit route) – Capital constraints: This is not for small individual investors – Investors do not have direct control over RE portfolio – Reported performance will not necessarily be realizable	– Illiquidity – Capital constraints: This is not for small individual investors – Investors do not have direct control over RE portfolio – Reported performance may not necessarily be realizable

	RE syndications	RE joint ventures	RE limited partnerships
Advantages	– Allow direct access to RE investments – Provide access to small institutions to direct RE investments – Can provide access to local management or specific sectors	– Allow direct access to RE investments – Can provide access to local management or specific sectors	– Limited partners are liable only to the amount invested – Capability to make special distributions to the partners – Can provide access to local management or specific sectors
Disadvantages/potential shortcomings	– Illiquidity – Capital constraints: This is not for small individual investors – Investors do not have direct control over RE project	– Illiquidity – Capital constraints: This is not for small individual investors – Investors do not have direct control over RE project	– Illiquidity – Capital constraints: This is not for small individual investors

(Continued)

Table 30.1 (Continued)

Public real estate (RE) investment vehicles

	RE options and futures	ETFs on RE	Closed-end RE funds
Advantages	– Liquidity (since they are exchange-traded) – Investments in RE without having to buy actual properties – Possibility to go long or short – Regulated by the SEC and by the CFTC – Transparency brought by pricing in public capital markets – Relatively low transaction costs	– Liquidity (since they are exchange-traded) – Price and NAV are very close – They can be purchased with margin – Options exist in some ETFs on RE – Allow access to RE investments with little capital – Tax efficient (compared to open-and closed-end RE funds) – Possibility to take long or short positions – Regulated by the Securities and Exchange Commission – Transparency brought by pricing in public capital markets – Relatively low transaction costs	– Liquidity (since they are exchange-traded) – They can be purchased with margin – Allow access to RE investments with little capital – Regulated by the SEC – Less problems with redemptions – Transparency brought by pricing in public capital markets – Relatively low transaction costs
Disadvantages/potential shortcomings	– Still relatively new RE alternative investments – Complex instruments, not for unsophisticated investors	– Liquidity advantage is not that relevant for long-term investors – Difficult to obtain access to very specific markets or sectors	– Existence of a discount/premium between price and NAV – Discount/premium between price and NAV fluctuates – Liquidity advantage is not that relevant for long-term investors – Tend to be tax inefficient (compared to ETFs) – Difficult to obtain access to very specific markets or sectors

problems encountered with international investment include the lack of local knowledge, regulatory restrictions on foreign ownership, small scale markets, political risks and access to local services.

A number of studies have surveyed the involvement, motivation and problems encountered by institutional investors regarding international real estate investments. For example, Hines (1988) found that most investors preferred investing in nations that were geographically or culturally close to them. Worzala (1994) surveyed institutional investors (comprised of insurance companies, pension funds, publicly-traded companies, institutions and developers) in six countries (Germany, Japan, Netherlands, Sweden, the UK and the U.S.) and found that over half of them did not have any international real estate holdings at all.

This reluctance to invest in foreign real estate markets changed dramatically in the new millennium. For example, Jones, Lang, and LaSalle, a firm that specializes in real estate services and investment management, estimated that the overall volume of real estate investments in Europe increased from just over €60bn in 2000 to approximately €160bn by 2005. Furthermore, the growth was largely driven by an increase in cross-border investments. Indeed, in the first half of 2006, cross-border investments accounted for 68% of all investment volume. While an initial analysis may assume that this was perhaps due to the impact of using a single currency (i.e. the Euro zone), the market that has been the recipient of the largest share of this volume has been the UK, which remained outside the Euro zone. Furthermore, the figures for the first six months of 2006 showed that not only did 68% of volume include at least one non-domestic party, 38% included at least one non-European party. The importance of real estate funds can be illustrated by the fact that they accounted for 43% of purchases. However, in 2009, it is still too early to gauge the full impact of the real estate crisis that began in 2007 on the impetus of international real estate investments in the coming years.

The growth in international real estate investments, while widening the potential pool of properties available for purchase, does not come without challenges. In particular, real estate funds are exposed to foreign exchange risk. Currency exposure is particularly apparent in the case of international real estate investments given the relative low volatility of property returns when compared to other asset classes, particularly exchange-traded assets such as stocks.

The currency effect of international real estate investments can be illustrated by viewing international investment as effectively a two-asset portfolio, with the two assets being the asset itself and the foreign exchange rate. Analogous to the case of a two-stock portfolio, this international investment's variance can be decomposed as follows:

$$\sigma_d^2 = \sigma_{fx}^2 + \sigma_f^2 + 2\mathrm{cov}(fx, f).$$

Here, σ_d^2 is the variance of the international real estate investment return, expressed in domestic currency terms, σ_{fx}^2 is the variance of the foreign exchange rate, σ_f^2 is the variance of the foreign real estate asset return, and $2\mathrm{cov}(fx, f)$ is twice the covariance between the currency and the foreign real estate asset return. This equation illustrates the idea that investment in real estate domiciled in a location with a different currency can be viewed as adding foreign exchange rate risk – especially in instances where revenues are dominated by leases fixed in terms of the foreign currency and expenses such as interest expense that are specified in terms of the foreign currency.

PERFORMANCE OF ALTERNATIVE REAL ESTATE INVESTMENT VEHICLES

We conclude this chapter by analyzing the performance of U.S. mutual funds (open-end funds), hedge funds, closed-end funds and exchange-traded funds that invest in real estate. The summary statistics presented in Table 30.2 show that the performance of portfolios of each one of these asset classes

Table 30.2   Performance of real estate portfolios, 2001–2007

	Annualized return	Standard deviation	Sharpe ratio	Correlations	
				S&P 500	Lehman U.S. aggregate
Portfolio of mutual funds	23.3%	13.2%	1.58	0.41	0.15
Portfolio of hedge funds	16.9%	6.7%	2.17	0.59	−0.01
Portfolio of closed-end funds	11.1%	13.8%	0.63	0.31	0.27
Portfolio of exchange traded funds	11.0%	14.5%	0.59	0.42	0.13
S&P 500 Total Return Index	6.2%	12.4%	0.30	1.00	−0.28
Lehman U.S. aggregate	5.1%	3.8%	0.69	−0.28	1.00

Source: Garay, 2008.

was stellar compared to the performance of stocks and bonds indices over the period 2001–2007. The return volatilities of open-end funds, closed-end funds and exchange-traded funds that invest in real estate were similar to the volatility of stocks, while the volatility of real estate hedge funds was far lower than those of the other asset classes analyzed. These figures explain the considerable differences between the risk-adjusted performances of the portfolios of real estate funds versus stocks over this time interval. These results are also consistent with attributing the exceptional performance of REITs documented in Chapter 29 to the underlying private real estate of REITs rather than to their exchange-traded nature. The portfolios in Table 30.2 were, at best, moderately correlated with stocks while the correlations with bonds were low or negative. Once again, the sharp decline in real estate prices in the U.S., which started in 2007 and worsened dramatically in 2008, has negatively affected the performance of existing alternative real estate investment vehicles as well as the performance of most other traditional and alternative investment vehicles.

31

Real Estate Development

Real estate development is a complex business, encircling an array of operations that ranges from the acquisition of raw land or the sale of improved parcels to interested buyers, to the renovation and lease of existing properties. Normally, real estate development is an intricate process that entails:

- the acquisition of land or site,
- estimation of the marketing potential and profitability of the development project,
- development of a building program and design,
- procurement of the necessary public approvals and permitting,
- raising the necessary financing,
- building of the structure, and
- leasing, managing, and eventually selling the property.

In this chapter, we focus our attention on issues related to the appraisal and the financing of development projects. The development process can be depicted as shown in Figure 31.1.

Development is one of the most entrepreneurial and also one of the riskiest sectors in the real estate investments space. The primary risks involved in real estate development center around the exposure to factors such as vacancies and the inherent illiquidity of the underlying asset. Two key factors differentiate development projects from standing real estate investments. First, real estate development is a process in which a new asset is being created. Second, during the lifetime of the development, there is a high degree of uncertainty around the estimates of the revenues and costs of the investment. Even if a project is all equity financed, there is still the issue that, while many of the costs incurred are fixed, revenue relevant variables such as rental values and yields will most likely change during the lifetime of the development. Figure 31.2 depicts the evolution of the cumulative investment and risk/uncertainty during the following four states of a real estate development: 1) land assembly, planning process, design, zoning and permitting; 2) construction; 3) leasing and tenant finishing; and 4) stabilized operation.

As Figure 31.2 illustrates, as a project is being developed, the cumulative investment will tend to grow at a decreasing rate while much of the uncertainty associated with the development will have a tendency to decline as the "end picture" becomes clearer.

In the early stages of the development process, the uncertainty is very high, even though the developer has often still not incurred substantial costs. At this point, the developer is focused on issues such as assembling the site and obtaining the necessary zoning/planning permissions as well as financing. A key element affecting the degree of the project's risk and uncertainty is the accuracy of the timeline, which may need to be revised as the project progresses. It may take years for a real estate development to get under way, particularly for major projects. In the early preconstruction phases, the major risks center on the developer failing to get the project off the ground. Once the construction process has started, the developer has a firmer idea regarding the timeline of the project and can make more accurate estimates of both revenues and costs. As major costs are incurred, the project uncertainty is reduced.

Real estate developments affect the underlying dynamics of the real estate market because the supply of new developments may have a wide impact upon the local real estate market. A new development can change the urban fabric and can also have knock-on effects, either positive or

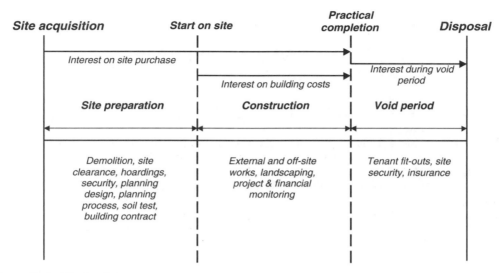

Figure 31.1 The development process

negative, on existing properties in the locality. They can be positive when they help regenerate an area, affecting not only the existing properties in terms of increased rental values, but also encouraging subsequent developments. The relationship between new supply and the rental cycle, particularly when examining a localized market, is well established. In general, periods of major new supply tend to have an adverse impact upon rental levels.

A crucial element in any successful development is that it must have a coherent underlying focus and aim. This first stage of a real estate development is vital – providing an initial assessment of the potential profitability of a development. Profitability will not only vary between projects but also

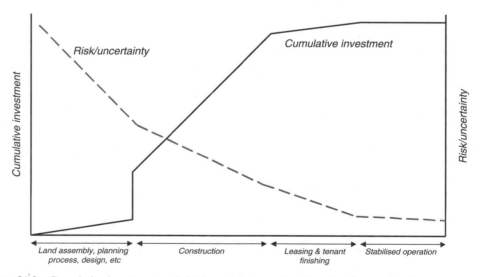

Figure 31.2 Cumulative investment and risk/uncertainty as a function of real estate development stages

between developers. The time and money spent assessing the viability of a potential development will naturally depend on the project in question. Projects such as an apartment block or a small neighborhood retail development will be relatively simple, quick and inexpensive to assess. In contrast, major projects such as a large speculative office development or a major shopping center will require extensive analysis. This is in part due to the fact that such large schemes are often those that are most controversial and may encounter delays in the zoning/planning process. We will now examine some of the key issues that need to be addressed in a variety of different property sectors.

RESIDENTIAL, RETAIL, OFFICE AND INDUSTRIAL DEVELOPMENTS

In the case of **residential developments**, one of the most important variables that ought to be considered is the target market. For single family units this will be reflected not only in the type and size of the property, but also in factors such as plot size, number of bedrooms and garage/parking facilities. An apartment developer will not only need to consider the size of the apartments but also the extent of services that are becoming standard in many high-end apartment complexes such as concierge services, closed-circuit TV entry systems and other security features. Indeed, the developers need to gauge the impact of additional features on prices and the target market.

In the case of residential developments where most of the units are expected to be sold to owner-occupiers, developers need to be concerned with the trends in residential prices in the respective locality. Since the income is expected to be generated from one-time sales of units rather than ongoing rents, timing is of utmost importance. This effectively reduces the time horizon of a developer when compared to either a commercial scheme or an investment-based residential scheme tied to ongoing rents. In these latter cases, even if the developer is planning to sell the completed development to an investor, it is more important that he or she ensures that the development is a viable ongoing standing investment.

Key factors that residential developers need to consider in their feasibility study include general housing trends in the local market, demographic and psychographic trends, mortgage financing trends, and political boundaries such as school districts and commuting trends. An analysis of these factors will help developers determine the best type of development.

Retail developments tend to be similar to residential developments in that they are affected by many of the same factors, particularly those that are of social and demographic nature. The primary issue with any retail development is the location of the proposed project. It is vital that any retail scheme be sufficiently accessible and attractive for the target market to which it is directed. The market targeted will depend on matters such as the site selected, which will be linked to issues such as transportation facilities and patterns, the estimated geographic extent of the catchments area (or area from which a region attracts customers or visitors), the scale and nature of competing centers and the demographic and economic trends in the catchments area.

In the case of **office** and **industrial sectors**, many of the factors to be considered in a feasibility analysis are similar, although there are some fundamental differences. Probably the most important element to consider is whether the development is a speculative build (i.e. projects that are not pre-leased or pre-sold). If so, the developer needs to undertake extensive work about who the potential target tenants are and their potential needs and requirements of the actual property space. Pure speculative builds introduce a large element of uncertainty into the development process. While the pre-leasing of properties to be developed does reduce this uncertainty, in particular with respect to vacancies, this practice may sometimes not be in the best interests of a developer. This is because if the developer estimates that the local market is going to continue to move in a positive direction in relation to occupancy demand, achievable rental levels and investor demand, a better financial outcome may result from waiting until the development is closer to completion before reaching an agreement with respect to either leasing or selling the property. In spite of this, it must be noted that the pre-leasing or the selling of a property being developed does reduce risk and uncertainty.

APPRAISAL OF A DEVELOPMENT PROJECT

A development project can be appraised using a number of alternative methodologies. Internationally, the most common approach consists in examining the projected cash flows in a **discounted cash flow (DCF) approach**. Even though all the methods have relative advantages and disadvantages, they all share the common problem of the difficulty in projecting accurate cash flow estimates (i.e. both revenues and costs). Not only the expected level of cash flow projections is important but also the timing of each is vital.

One of the most important factors in a development appraisal is the projected completed value of the development, and this projection differs slightly depending on the form of the development under consideration. For example, in the case of owner-occupied residential projects, developers will take a slightly shorter-term view of the project, as they do not have to be concerned about the viability of the development as a feasible ongoing standing investment. Key factors influencing the appraisal of a completed real estate development include local market conditions, the quality of building specification, anticipated occupancy demand, competing developments, broader supply measures, and general investment market conditions.

The length of the development process adds additional uncertainty concerning these projections, especially in the case of large-scale commercial schemes. Furthermore, the rental and development cycles are heavily interlinked. The supply of real estate is effectively fixed in the short-term, as new real estate developments will only add to the supply of new constructions in the medium term. Therefore, when the real estate market experiences a short-term positive demand shift, the impact will in all likelihood be felt in terms of upward pressure on rental values, as the supply of real estate cannot respond in the short-term. Developers need to ascertain whether these increased rental values may make a potential development more viable, as there is the risk that one of a number of events may occur prior to the project being completed. First, the developer is exposed to the demand shift being temporary, with rental values softening by the time the development comes into the market. Second, there is the risk that the increased rental values will also encourage other developers to go ahead and start their projects. The result could be a large increase in new construction and therefore the eventual presence of a more competitive supply. Even assuming that demand stays at these new higher levels, the supply increase will put a downward pressure on rents.

The worst case scenario is one similar to what occurred in many North American and European markets in the late 1980s and early 1990s, where the combined impact of reduced demand and increased supply for some types of real estate pushed down achievable rental values. Furthermore, the increased supply caused many developers to suffer from high vacancy rates that further exacerbated the decline in income. This type of scenario may also have the potential to reduce the attractiveness of real estate in that market to investors. Reduced investor demand may lead to upward pressure on required property yields (i.e. the rates of return demanded by investors to hold real estate). The combined result is a number of factors all reducing the value of the completed development.

A developer will often control many of the variables affecting the costs of the project, as they will typically have a relatively good idea about construction costs, professional fees and financing costs. However, even if provisions with contractors mean that any cost overruns are borne by the contractors there are still other potential risks, such as those represented by over-runs in relation to time (delays). Even if the contractor completes the development on budget, if delays mean that the project is completed six months late then the developer will be exposed to changing market conditions during that additional period of time and to additional financing costs.

Table 31.1 Example of a discounted cash flow appraisal of a real estate development (numbers in U.S.$)

Year		0	1	2	3	4	5
Anticipated sales value							37,596,036
EXPENDITURE							
Land							
Site value		−5000,000	0	0	0	0	0
Transaction costs		−200,000	0	0	0	0	0
Agent fees		−50,000	0	0	0	0	0
Legal fees		−25,000	0	0	0	0	0
Survey		−15,000	0	0	0	0	0
Finance arrangement fee		−200,000	0	0	0	0	0
Construction and other costs							
Construction costs		0	−1,033,110	−2,066,220	−3,099,330	−4,132,440	−4,132,440
Contingency		0	−51,655	−103,311	−154,966	−206,622	−206,622
Demolition costs		0	−80,000	0	0	0	0
Fees							
Architect		0	−41,324	−82,649	−123,973	−165,298	−165,298
Cost consultant		0	−25,828	−51,655	−77,483	−103,311	−103,311
Structural engineer		0	−20,662	−41,324	−61,987	−82,649	−82,649
Mechanical & electrical engineer		0	−20,662	−41,324	−61,987	−82,649	−82,649
Project management		0	−20,662	−41,324	−61,987	−82,649	−82,649
Misc. fees		0	0	0	0	0	0
Fund supervision		0	0	0	0	0	0
Other costs							
Road/site		0	0	0	0	0	0
Statutory costs		0	−23,214	−46,429	−69,643	−92,857	−92,857
Marketing		0	−5,714	−11,429	−17,143	−22,857	−22,857
LETTING & SALES COSTS							
Letting agents		0	0	0	0	0	−347,123
Letting – legal		0	0	0	0	0	−115,707
Sale costs – agent		0	0	0	0	0	−356,023
Sale costs – legal		0	0	0	0	0	−178,011
NET CASH FLOW		−5,490,000	−1,322,831	−2,485,665	−3,728,499	−4,971,332	31,627,839
PV @	7.00%	1.0000	0.9346	0.8734	0.8163	0.7629	0.7130
Present value		−5,490,000	−1,236,291	−2,171,076	−3,043,566	−3,792,605	22,550,212
NPV	6,816,674						
IRR	19.55%						

As mentioned above, the discounted cash flow approach is the most accepted method used for assessing the viability of a development. The rationale behind its application is that the use of present values ensures consistency with respect to the time value of money. The cash flows and discount rate in the DCF method can also be used to provide two investment decision-making rules: the net present value (NPV) rule and the internal rate of return (IRR) rule.

The example depicted in Table 31.1 illustrates the case of a relatively simply DCF appraisal of a real estate development expected to be completed in five years, at which time the project is expected to be sold. One of the most problematic issues with respect to DCF appraisal is the choice of the length of the time periods. If one uses quarterly, or even monthly, periods, there is a level of imprecision regarding the exact timing at which cash flows will occur. A further problem with the

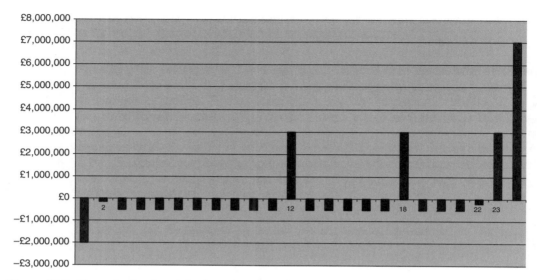

Figure 31.3 Example of a phased development where cash flows exhibit changing signs

DCF approach that is particularly apparent with the NPV decision-making rule is the determination of the discount rate to be used. Formally speaking, the discount rate used in a DCF calculation should be the risk-free rate plus a risk premium. It is important to bear in mind that while real estate investors in standing investments have the advantage of being able to observe market yields when determining appropriate discount rates, this is not the case with developments, where the respective project may well take years until it is completed.

According to the information provided in Table 31.1, the acquisition of land represents an expenditure (site value, transactions costs, fees and other expenses) of $5,490,000 to be paid today. The table also shows the estimates of a series of construction and other costs that will be incurred during the next five years and also that, at the end of this time period, the investment value of the development is estimated to be equal to $37,596,036. Assuming a discount rate of 7%, the table shows that the net present value (NPV) of this project is equal to $6,816,674. Given that this number is positive, the recommendation would be that this development should be undertaken. In fact, the estimated NPV indicates that the developer will experience an increase in current wealth equal to $6,816,674 by accepting the project. Finally, the internal rate of return (IRR) of this project, or rate of return that makes the net present value of the project equal to $0, is shown to be equal to 19.55%. According to the IRR rule the investment in this project should be accepted, as the IRR is greater than the discount rate of the project. The IRR of 19.55% may be interpreted as meaning that, risk aside, investing in the project is like investing in a bank that offers an 19.55% – which is well above the market rate of 7%.

Expanding our discussion on the use of the IRR, we must note that the development process is an area in finance where some of the difficulties in using this investment criterion become apparent.[1] A prime example of these problems is that multiple IRRs are obtained when the sign of cash flows change more than once. This is a common problem in the context of phased developments, as graphically depicted in Figure 31.3. It is also a potentially serious problem for projects that have final negative cash flows due to a need to clean up or restore a site.

---

[1] For a review of the potential problems that arise when using the internal rate of return see Bodie, Kane and Marcus (2008).

Table 31.2   Example of a decision between two mutually exclusive development projects (numbers in U.S.$)

Site purchase	−650,000				
Discount rate	13%				
Project A: Industrial					

Year	0	1	2	3	4
Net cash flow	−650,000	−1,900,000	−125,000	1,400,000	2,500,000
PV	−650,000	−1,681,416	−97,893	970,270	1,533,297
IRR	14.20%	← **Preferred scheme**			
NPV	74,258	← **Inferior scheme**			
Project B: Retail					

Year	0	1	2	3	4
Net cash flow	−650,000	−2,500,000	−2,500,000	−400,000	8,500,000
PV	−650,000	−2,212,389	−1,957,867	−277,220	5,213,209
IRR	13.97%	← **Inferior scheme**			
NPV	115,733	← **Preferred scheme**			

The IRR can also encounter difficulties in a development context when a developer is using this criterion in deciding between mutually exclusive projects. In this case, it is possible that the NPV and IRR rules will recommend the undertaking of different projects. We illustrate this problem by using the example shown in Table 31.2, which is based on two hypothetical development projects (project A is an industrial project and project B is a retail project). In this example, the site would cost the developer $650,000 and he or she has the choice of proceeding with either an industrial or a retail project. Each project will take an estimated four years to be completed. The estimated cash flows for each alternative are shown in the table. Based on a discount rate of 13% the NPV decision rule would point to the retail scheme being preferred. However, the IRR is indicating that the industrial project should be chosen. In this case the primary cause behind the discrepancy is the different magnitude of the two projects and the problem is that the IRR rule ignores the magnitude of the cash flows (i.e. the scale of the project). One way around this problem is to examine the differential cash flows (i.e. the cash flows from the retail project subtracted from those of the industrial scheme). If one estimates the IRR of these differential cash flows it provides a figure of 13.71%. Given that the developer's required rate of return is 13% (i.e. slightly less than the IRR of 13.71%) then the retail project will generate greater shareholder wealth than the industrial scheme.

However, the issue of mutually exclusive projects also raises issues with respect to the NPV rule. In particular, it may or may not be appropriate to use the same discount rate in the estimation of the financial viability of both projects. As noted earlier, as the discount rate is supposed to consist of the risk-free rate plus a risk premium it is not fair to assume that the risk premium related to both projects should be the same. Also, the NPV rule may not take into account differences in the lifetimes of projects and therefore may not properly value any advantage that a short-term project offers in providing a quicker ability to pursue new projects.

While the DCF approach is the methodology most commonly used in development appraisals, there are other alternatives. For instance, in many international markets a methodology referred to as the **residual method** is also commonly used. The residual method is calculated as simply the gross development value less the total development expenditure. If an estimate of the developer's profits is included in the expenditure estimates, then the end figure provides the value of the project ignoring the value of the site, and it can be viewed as the maximum acceptable cost of acquiring the site. Alternatively, if the site is either already purchased or the value of it is known with certainty, and this figure is included, then the residual value provides an estimate of the profit for the developer

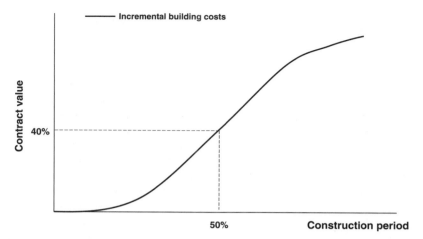

Figure 31.4 The S-curve and development financing

(in excess of any profits already included as expenditure estimates). The residual approach can be used for two alternative purposes. First, as with the conventional DCF approach, it can be used to assess the profitability of a development. Second, it can be used to estimate the maximum value that a developer can afford to pay for a site. While this method does have the advantage over a full DCF in that it is simpler to estimate, it also has a number of fundamental problems, as we will see shortly.

We can illustrate the use of the residual method with the following simple example. Let us assume that a developer has obtained permission to proceed with an industrial project. The developer estimates that the value of the completed development will be $4,572,000, while total costs will come to $3,135,089. These figures provide a residual value of $1,436,911. Note that the basic residual calculation does not take into account the timing of the cash flows. While the estimated market value of the completed scheme is based at the end of the development period, the costs incurred during the construction phase occur earlier and therefore the values are not adjusted for the time value of money. This represents the major disadvantage of the residual approach. Some practitioners may discount the final residual amount based on the total development period. However, this is highly inconsistent. For example, let us assume that the total development period is 18 months. Many of the costs incurred, including a large proportion of the construction costs, will have occurred prior to 18 months. Therefore, to discount these costs back 18 months actually results in an underestimation of the true costs of the development (because of the time value of money), in comparison to how the primary revenue figures are treated. Likewise, conventional residuals also deal with financing costs in a simplistic manner. As detailed periodic cash flows are not estimated, the conventional way of handling financing costs is to assume that the developer borrows the full amount for half of the period. However, for most developments, financing is drawn as and when required, and furthermore, for the most part costs follows an S-Curve, as illustrated in Figure 31.4. This shows that generally less than 50% of the costs would be incurred by the halfway point of the construction period. Therefore, the assumption made about the financing costs can also have an impact on the results.

BASICS OF DEVELOPMENT FINANCING

The majority of debt available for financing development projects is generally short term in focus. And even in the case when the development will continue to be held by the developer, refinancing typically occurs once the construction phase is completed. The amount that a lender will consider providing to a developer will depend on a number of factors, the primary one being the financial strength of the borrower. Lenders will consider the credit rating of the developer and also his or her past development history. The relative importance of these factors will vary slightly depending on the size of both the developer and the actual development project. For larger developers the corporate credit rating will be the primary factor. For smaller developers, more attention will be placed on their development history and track record.

Another major factor that will come into consideration is whether the development project is speculative or not. For speculative developments there is obviously greater uncertainty over the potential impacts of future market movements on the possible occupancy demand, vacancy rates and rental levels achieved, the ability to be able to lease the project and the value of the completed developments. Pre-leasing and pre-selling can reduce these uncertainties substantially. They not only provide a form of guarantees regarding vacancy and future cash flows but will also make the completed development more attractive for investors if the developer is planning to sell the development once it is completed. Even if the developer is planning on holding the project as a standing investment, he will generally need to refinance the project at completion.

The lender will also look at key terms, such as the amount to be borrowed, seniority, cross-collateralization, and recourse. Recourse is a key issue and involves the remedies available to the lender prior to completion. For mainstream development financing, lenders will generally look at loan-to-value ratios (LTV) below 75% for pre-let projects and below 65% for speculative developments. However, the exact figures will vary depending on the factors previously discussed and also on issues relating to the specific project and the overall real estate cycle. For projects that are developed in phases, where there is a greater opportunity for positive cash flows during the course of the project, it is more likely that these LTV ratio figures will be higher. In addition, residential schemes often obtain financing in excess of these figures. This is partly due to the fact that residential projects are often shorter in duration, and therefore there is less uncertainty regarding market movements. While it is possible that a residential project may receive 100% funding in relation to both the site purchase and the development costs, this will also be often accompanied by additional provisions that effectively allow the lender to participate as an equity partner. Common provisions include some form of profit share between the lender and the developer and the requirement of a specified minimum return for the lender.

In the case of large commercial developments, as lenders will rarely break the discussed LTV ratios, developers have increasingly turned to mezzanine financing as a means of increasing the level of funding that they receive. Mezzanine financing is a loan that usually provides the lender the rights to convert to an equity interest in the development project if the debt is not paid back fully and in a timely matter. Even though mezzanine financing can be structured in a number of different ways, the common element is that it is junior to the senior debt and effectively fills the gap between the senior debt and pure equity. As mezzanine financing will be junior to the main debt, it will generally be priced at higher interest rates to reflect the increased risk involved to the lender. This form of financing will also generally contain some form of equity potential for the lender. Therefore, the lender benefits not only from higher interest rates to reflect the increased risk; there is also an additional possible source of return. Given the equity position, even for well-established developers, lenders will place greater attention on the specific project and its projected profitability. The mix of debt and equity components means that the exact structure of the mezzanine financing will vary considerably among different projects.

In addition to the standard forms of financing, a developer can also obtain funding through alternative sources. Some of the most common sources are through some form of joint-venture with either a lender or with an institution that intends to purchase the complete development.

Two of the simplest forms are **forward sales** and **full forward funding**. In the case of forward sales the developer reaches an agreement wherein an investor will purchase the development on completion. Just as with pre-leasing and pre-selling, forward sales reduce the risks to the developer. Such agreements are effectively forward contracts on a development. The reduced uncertainty will generally reassure lenders and thus make project financing easier and possibly cheaper to obtain. These forward agreements will generally contain a variety of provisions. These will often include some formula that shares rental growth and guarantees on the part of the developer regarding the letting of the scheme. In addition, the agreed price is generally at a discount to the estimated full market value. This is to reflect the fact that the investors are effectively exposing themselves to the development risk through the agreement and that the developer is benefiting from the aforementioned reduced exposure. The alternative form, full forward funding, is a variation of the forward sale. In this case, rather than enter into an agreement to purchase the development on completion, short-term financing is also incorporated into the deal to cover development costs. Often the title of the site and project is also transferred prior to completion. This reduces the developer's risk to a large extent, as he no longer has to be concerned with obtaining development financing. However, as investors are taking on an even greater share of the risk, including letting and development costs, this will be reflected in the investors' demand for a larger share of the profits from the project. To some extent the developer is merely being hired for his entrepreneurial and managerial skills in completing the development.

References

Akers, K. "Timber Investment." *The Journal of Alternative Investments*. Summer, Vol. 5, No. 1, pp. 86–88. 2002.

Berman, A. "Risks and Realities of Mezzanine Loans." *Missouri Law Review*. Vol. 72, No. 4, Fall, p. 993. 2007.

Bianco Research LLC. "Financial Markets Outlook." Federal Reserve of Chicago, Economic Outlook Symposium. December 5, 2008.

Bodie, Z., A. Kane and A. Marcus. *Investments*. New York, McGraw-Hill, 7th edition, 2008.

Brown, G. R. "Reducing the Dispersion of Returns in U.K. Real Estate Portfolios." *Journal of Real Estate Portfolio Management*. Vol. 3, No. 2, pp. 129–140. 1997.

Brown G. R. and G. A. Matysiak. "Valuation Smoothing Without Temporal Aggregation." *Journal of Property Research*. Vol. 15, pp. 89–103. 1998.

Brown, G. R. and Matysiak, G. A. *Real Estate Investment: A Capital Markets Approach*, Financial Times-Prentice Hall, London. 2000.

Brueggeman, W. and J. Fisher. *Real Estate Finance & Investments*. New York, McGraw-Hill/Irwin, 13th edition, 2006.

Byrne, P. J. and S. L. Lee. "Risk Reduction in the United Kingdom Property Market" *Journal of Property Research*. Vol. 17, No. 1, pp. 23–46. 2000.

Campeau, F. "A Microstructure Analysis of the Information on Securitized and Unsecuritized Commercial Real Estate Markets." Cambridge University, Ph.D. 1994.

Case B., W. Goetzmann and K. Rouwenhorst. "Global Real Estate Markets-Cycles and Fundamentals." Working Paper 7566. National Bureau of Economic Research. February 2000.

Case, K. and R. Schiller. "Is There a Bubble in the Housing Market? An Analysis." Unpublished paper prepared for the Brookings Panel on Economic Activity. 2003.

Case, K., R. Shiller and A. Weiss. "Mortgage Default Risk and Real Estate Prices: The Use of Index-Based Futures and Options in Real Estate." Working Paper W5078. National Bureau of Economic Research. 1995.

Clauretie, T. and G. Sirmans. *Real Estate Finance Theory & Practice*. Thomson South-Western, 5th edition. 2006.

Damodaran, A. *Investment Valuation: Tools and Techniques for Determining the Value of Any Asset*. New York, John Wiley & Sons, Inc. 2nd edition. 2002.

Dell'Ariccia, G., D. Igan and L. A. Laeven. "Credit Booms and Lending Standards: Evidence From the Subprime Mortgage Market." http://ssrn.com/abstract=1100138. February 2008.

Demyanyk, Y. and O. Van Hemert. "Understanding the Subprime Mortgage Crisis." http://ssrn.com/abstract=1020396. August 2008.

The Department of the Treasury. *Expanded Guidance for Subprime Lending Programs*. 2001.

The Economist. "The Global Housing Boom." June 16, 2005.

Eichholtz, P., N. deGraaf, W. Kastrop and H. Veld. "Introducing the GRP 250 Property Share Index." *Real Estate Finance*. Vol. 15, No. 1, pp. 51–61. 1998.

Eichholtz, P. M. A., K. Koedijk and M. Schweitzer. "Global Property Investment and the Costs of International Diversification." *Journal of International Money and Finance*. Vol. 20, No. 3, pp. 349–366. June 2001.

Esaki, H. "Commercial Mortgage Defaults: 1972–2000." *Real Estate Finance*. Vol. 18, No. 4. Winter, 2002.

Fabozzi, F. *Bond Markets, Analysis, and Strategies*. Academic Internet Pub Inc., 6th edition, 2006.

Feldman, B. E. "Investment Policy for Securitized and Direct Real Estate." *Journal of Portfolio Management*, Special Real Estate Issue, Vol. 25, No. 5, pp. 112–21. 2003.

Garay, U. "The Benefits of Real Estate." Working Paper. Center for International Derivatives and Securities Markets. 2008.

Garay, U. and E. ter Horst. "Real Estate and Private Equity: A Review of the Diversification Benefits and Some Recent Developments." *The Journal of Alternative Investments*, Vol. 11, No. 4. 2009.

Genovese, D. and C. Mayer. "Loss Aversion and Seller Behavior: Evidence from the Housing Market." *Quarterly Journal of Economics*. Vol. 116. pp. 1233–1260. 2001.

Gentry, W., C. Jones and C. Mayer. "Do Stock Prices Really Reflect Fundamental Values? The Case of REITs." Working Paper 10850. National Bureau of Economic Research. October 2004.

Giliberto, M. and A. Mengden. "REITs and Real Estate: Two Markets Re-Examined." *Real Estate Finance*. Vol. 13, No. 1. pp. 56–60. 1996.

Girgis, J. "Mortgage Fraud, the Land Titles Act and Due Diligence: The Rabi v. Rosu Decision." *Banking and Finance Law Review*. Vol. 22, pp. 419–434. 2007.

Glascock, J. L., R. So and C. Lu. "REIT Returns and Inflation: Perverse or Reverse Causality Effects?" *Journal of Real Estate Finance and Economics*. Vol. 24, Issue 3. 2002.

Goetzmann, W. N. and R. Dhar. "Bubble Investors: What Were They Thinking?" Working Paper. Yale University. 2005.

Goetzmann, W. and E. Valaitis. "Simulating Real Estate in the Investment Portfolio: Model Uncertainty and Inflation Hedging." http://ssrn.com/abstract=889081. March 2006.

Harper, D. "Basic Valuation of a Real Estate Investment Trust (REIT)." Available at Investopedia.com. 2006.

Haurin, D. "U.S. Commercial Real Estate Indices: Transaction-Based and Constant-Liquidity Indices." Real Estate Indicators and Financial Stability from the Bank for International Settlements. Vol. 21. pp. 232–242. 2005.

Hines, M. "International Dimensions of Real Estate." *Appraisal Journal*. pp. 492–501. March, 1988.

Hoesli, M., J. Lekander and W. Witkiewicz. "Real Estate in the Institutional Portfolio: A Comparison of Suggested and Actual Weights." *The Journal of Alternative Investments*. Vol. 6, No. 3, pp. 53–59. 2003.

Hoesli, M. and J. Lekander, "Suggested Versus Actual Institutional Allocations to Real Estate in Europe: A Matter of Size?" *The Journal of Alternative Investments*. Vol. 8, No. 2, pp. 62–70. 2005.

Hudson-Wilson, S., F. J. Fabozzi and J. Gordon. "Why Real Estate?" *The Journal of Portfolio Management*. Vol. 29, Vol. 31, pp. 12–27. 2003.

Lee, S. and S. Stevenson. "The Case for REITs in the Mixed-Asset Portfolio in the Short and Long Run." *Journal of Real Estate Portfolio Management*. 11, pp. 55–80. 2005.

Ling D. and A. Naranjo. "Economic Risk Factors and Commercial Real Estate Returns." *Journal of Real Estate Finance and Economics*. Vol. 14, No. 3. pp. 283–301. 1997.

Idzorek, T. M., M. Barad and S. L. Meier. "Global Commercial Real Estate." *The Journal of Portfolio Management*. Special Issue, Vol. 5, No. 4, pp. 37–52. 2007.

Marcato, G. and T. Key. "Smoothing and Implications for Asset Allocation Choices." *The Journal of Portfolio Management*. Special Issue, Vol. 32, pp. 85–98. 2007.

Mian, A. and A. Sufi. "The Consequences of Mortgage Credit Expansion: Evidence from the 2007 Mortgage Default Crisis." http://ssrn.com/abstract=1072304. May 2008.

Mueller, A. G. and G. R. Mueller. "Public and Private Real Estate in the Mixed-Asset Portfolio." *Journal of Real Estate Portfolio Management*. Vol. 9, pp. 193–203. 2003.

Nussbaum, R. "Cash Flow Matters: DCF Analysis Suggests REITs are Fairly Valued...For Now." New York University REIT Center. 2006.

Roulac, S. "Due Diligence in Real Estate Transactions." *Handbook of Real Estate Portfolio Management*, J. Pagliari, ed. Boston, MA, Irwin. 1995.

Roulac, S. "Institutional Real Estate Investing Processes, Due Diligence Practices and Market Conditions." *Journal of Real Estate Portfolio Management*. Vol. 6, No. 4, pp. 387–416. 2000.

Sabal, J. "The Determinants of Housing Prices: The Case of Spain." Unpublished manuscript. 2005.

Sebastian, S. P. and M. Tyrell. "Open End Real Estate Funds – Diamond or Danger?" http://ssrn.com/abstract=893121. March 2006.

Shiller, R. "Derivatives Markets for Home Prices." Cowles Foundation Discussion Paper No. 1648. Working Paper 46. Yale Economics Department. March 2008.

Stevenson, S. "The Long-Term Advantages to Incorporating Indirect Securities in Direct Real Estate Portfolios." *Journal of Real Estate Portfolio Management.* Vol. 7, No. 1, pp. 5–16. 2001.

Wieder, M. "Due Diligence: A Not-So-Secret Weapon in Good Deal Making." *Real Estate Weekly.* April 30, 2008.

Worzala, E. "Overseas Property Investments: How Are They Perceived by the Institutional Investor?" *Journal of Property Valuation and Investment*, 1994, 12, pp. 31–47.

Part IV
Hedge Funds

François Lhabitant

Introduction

Hedge funds have been commonly regarded as investments that offer risk and return opportunities not easily attainable through traditional investments. Hedge funds enjoy such investment opportunities because they are able to participate in a broad selection of securities and markets and are capable of taking both long and short positions.

The hedge fund section in this Level II text consists of six chapters. Chapter 32 deals with convertible arbitrage, a strategy that attempts to exploit inefficiencies in the pricing of convertible bonds relative to their underlying stocks. In a classic example, convertible arbitrageurs buy cheap convertible bonds and hedge their market risk by selling short the underlying stock. More recently, the strategy has expanded to include volatility and credit trading elements. Chapter 33 covers global macro hedge funds. These funds have the broadest mandate of any of the major hedge fund strategies in terms of types of instruments, asset classes, markets and geographies. They can dynamically allocate their capital to the asset class, sector or region in which they think the best opportunities currently lie – hence the term "global". The term "macro" reflects the fact that these managers apply macroeconomic views to global markets, which are analyzed from a top-down perspective. The chapter supplies examples of trading strategies employed by global macro managers including currency bets, spread plays (carry trades), and contingent yield steepening trades. It also discusses the role of global macro funds in the Asian currency crisis of 1997, describes the strategy's evolution in terms of risk management and portfolio construction and concludes with analyses of the strategy's historical returns. Chapter 34 deals with the equity long/short strategy which is by far the largest in terms of assets and number of funds. The chapter illustrates a typical equity long/short position and presents evidence of the risk exposures of this strategy using the CISDM equity long/short index. Chapter 35 focuses on funds-of-hedge-funds – their characteristics, advantages and disadvantages. Most investors prefer to invest in hedge funds through this structure because individual fund selection, monitoring, portfolio construction, and risk management are all delegated to the fund-of- funds management team. This allows the investor to focus all their attention (due diligence) on choosing the appropriate fund-of-funds. The chapter concludes with a discussion of investible and non-investible hedge fund indices.

Chapter 36 focuses on strategy specific due diligence. Due diligence is considered by many to be the most critical stage in hedge fund investing because of the opaque nature of hedge funds and the difficulty in establishing reliable performance benchmarks. The chapter concentrates on due diligence as it pertains to the following strategies: long/short equity; convertible arbitrage; merger arbitrage; fixed income arbitrage; emerging markets; multi-strategy funds; and distressed securities. Finally, Chapter 37 deals with operational risk – an important area of concern highlighted in the

Basel II Accord, where it is defined as "the risk of loss resulting from inadequate or failed internal processes, people and systems". Using a case study approach, the chapter illuminates several early warning signals of operational failure brought to light by the infamous collapses of Bayou Amaranth and Madoff. The chapter concludes with an outline of the essential steps of a comprehensive operational due diligence review.

CAIA Association 2009

32

Convertible Arbitrage

EVOLUTION OF THE CONVERTIBLE ARBITRAGE STRATEGY

Convertible arbitrage is a classic arbitrage strategy that attempts to exploit inefficiencies in the pricing of convertible bonds relative to their underlying stock. Initially, convertible arbitrage started as a niche business for dedicated proprietary trading desks in large investment banks. Convertible arbitrageurs typically bought cheap convertible bonds and hedged their market risk by selling short the underlying stock. Subsequently, thanks to the development of sophisticated option pricing models and the availability of credit derivatives, the strategy expanded to include volatility and credit trading elements. Today, according to *Hedge Fund Research*, convertible arbitrage represents approximately 3% of the assets managed by hedge funds. Though quite small in comparison to, say, equity long/short, convertible arbitrage shares important features common to a variety of hedge fund strategies and serves as a valuable example.

In its simplest form, the convertible arbitrage strategy involves purchasing convertible bonds and hedging away various risks associated with the instrument, including the equity risk, credit risk, and interest rate risk. The ultimate objective is to isolate, underpriced options embedded in convertible bonds. Naturally, the question arises as to why corporations should issue underpriced securities. The answer is simple. In addition to raising capital through the issuance of debt, the corporation has the potential to raise capital through the issuance of equity. When a corporation issues convertible bonds, convertible arbitrage managers will short the underlying stock, effectively increasing the supply of shares. If the firm performs well and the convertibles expire in-the-money, the increase in the number of shares will become permanent as the convertibles are exchanged for shares. Therefore, the firm has effectively raised capital by issuing new equity without incurring the administrative costs associated with a straight equity issue. For firms that typically issue convertible bonds, raising capital through straight bonds or equity may prove to be too expensive. The straight bonds might have to carry a very high coupon that would negatively affect the cash flow of the firm. And while raising capital through equity alone may not have the negative cash flow impact, the size of the issue might have to be so large as to dilute the ownership of current shareholders. In short, convertible arbitrage managers provide a service to issuing corporations and get paid for this service. This provides a partial economic explanation for the potential source of alpha found within the convertible arbitrage strategy.

But this raises still another question: why wouldn't other investors step in to purchase these underpriced securities? The answer lies in the very nature of convertible bonds. They are neither stocks nor bonds but a hybrid of the two. As such, many traditional money managers do not have a natural place in their portfolio for them. Further, as we will see below, taking advantage of the mispricing of convertible securities requires managers to hedge a number of risks. This requires special skills traditional money managers may not possess. In addition, the investment strategy may not fall within the mandate of many traditional investment managers.

TERMINOLOGY

Convertible bonds give holders the right to exchange them for common shares of the issuer at some ratio during a particular period. They are complex securities that blend the characteristics found

Table 32.1   Summary of the terms offered by the XYZ convertible 2% 2012 bond

Fixed income features	
Issuer	XYZ Company Inc.
Rating	BBB
Coupon	$C = 2\%$ (annual)
Issue date	January 1, 2008 (today)
First coupon date	December 31, 2008 (in one year)
Accrued interest	0
Maturity	December 31, 2012 (in $T = 5$ years)
Nominal value	$1000
Risk-free rate	$R_F = 4\%$ per year
Issuer credit spread	$CS = 400$ bps above the risk free rate
Equity features	
Issuer	XYZ Company Inc
Stock price	$S_0 = \$100$ per share
Stock price change volatility	$\sigma = 30\%$ per year
Stock dividend	None
Conversion features	
Conversion ratio	$CR = 8$
Conversion price	112.50
Call protection	None
Market valuation	
Convertible market price	90 (i.e. 90% of face value)
Parity	80 (i.e. 80% of face value)
Conversion premium	12.5%

in equity, debt, and option securities. As a result, specialized terminology has been developed by traders and arbitrageurs to describe various aspects of the marketplace. For the sake of simplicity, assume it is now January 1, 2008 and that we have a hypothetical convertible bond denoted XYZ convertible 2% 2012. Table 32.1 describes the various parameters that characterize this convertible bond.

The fixed income features of our convertible bond are as follows:

- The *issuer* is the XYZ Company Inc., a company with a BBB *rating*.
- The convertible bond has a five-year *time to maturity*.
- The convertible bond pays a 2% *annual coupon*, with the first coupon paid in exactly one year.
- There is no *accrued interest:* the bond has just been issued.
- The *nominal* or *par value* of each bond is $1000. This is the amount for which each bond can be redeemed at maturity.[1]

The convertible bond can be converted into shares of the stock of the issuer. These shares have the following characteristics:

- The *issuer* is the XYZ Company Inc., i.e., the same issuer as the convertible bond.
- The stock price is currently $100 per share.
- The volatility of the stock price is 30% per year.
- The stock pays no dividend.

---

[1] The nominal value of convertible bonds is often 1000 units of the relevant currency in the Euro-convertible bond market and ¥1,000,000 in the Japanese domestic and Euro-yen markets.

The terms of the conversion are fixed in the convertible bond's indenture as follows:

- The **conversion ratio** denotes the number of shares obtained if one converts $1000 of face value of the bond. In our example, each bond with a $1000 face value can be converted into eight ordinary shares. The conversion ratio is therefore eight. This number usually remains fixed through the life of the instrument unless stock splits, special dividends, or other dilutive events occur.
- The **conversion price** denotes the price at which shares are indirectly purchased via the convertible security. It is equal to the market price of the convertible security divided by the conversion ratio, i.e. 900/8 = 112.50.
- **Call protections** grant the issuer the right to call back the convertible bond before its stated maturity. This can either be a *hard call*, where the issuer can call the bond at a pre-fixed price regardless of any other circumstances,[2] or a *soft call*, where the issuer can only call the bond if the equity price has risen significantly above the strike price or some other hurdle rate. In our example, for the sake of simplicity, we have assumed that there is no call protection.

The market valuation parameters of the convertible bond are observable in the market as follows:

- The **convertible price** denotes the quoted price of the convertible bond, which is usually expressed as a percentage of the nominal value (consistent with the traditional bond market). In our example, the convertible is quoted at 90% of its face value.
- **Parity** is the market value of the shares into which the bond can be converted. In our example, it is calculated as eight shares per bond × $100 per share = $800. Parity is normally quoted as a percentage of the par amount of the bond, i.e. $800/$1000 = 80 percent, or simply 80. Note that for a convertible bond to be in-the-money, its parity must be higher than 100.
- The **conversion premium** is the difference between the convertible bond price and parity, expressed as a percentage of parity. In our example, we would have (90−80)/80 = 12.5%. The premium expresses how much more an investor has to pay to control the same number of shares via a convertible. This premium also gives an indication of how a convertible should perform in relation to the underlying shares. All else being equal, convertibles with very low premiums will be much more sensitive to movements in the underlying share price (i.e. parity) than convertibles with higher premiums.

In addition to these standard features, convertible bonds may have more complex characteristics. Let us consider some of them:

- Zero-coupon convertible bonds are typically issued at a deep discount to par value and are redeemable at par. The most famous examples of such bonds are the Liquid Yield Option Notes (LYONs), which are both callable (redeemable prior to maturity by the issuer) and putable (redeemable prior to maturity by investors).
- Mandatory Conversion Securities (MCS) are convertibles whose conversion is mandatory at some stage. They tend to trade and behave like shares, although some may have additional features. For instance, a Preferred Equity Redemption Cumulative stock (PERC) is a mandatory preferred convertible with a pre-set cap level above which the conversion ratio is adjusted to keep the total return payoff constant (i.e. as the underlying stock price rises, the PERC becomes convertible into fewer and fewer underlying shares).
- Convertible preferred shares are preferred stocks that include an option for their holder to convert them into a fixed number of common shares, usually at any time after a predetermined date.

---

[2] Typically, the issuer must give public notice of its intention to redeem a convertible bond prior to maturity, and bondholders are given a limited period of time to decide whether to convert their convertible bond into shares.

In the following example, we largely ignore these features and focus on the arbitrage of plain vanilla convertible bonds.

VALUATION OF CONVERTIBLE SECURITIES

To identify convertible bond arbitrage opportunities, one must be able to calculate the fair value of a convertible bond.

The component approach

The component approach is the most intuitive valuation approach for simple convertible bonds. It essentially divides the convertible bond into a straight bond component and a call option:

Convertible bond = Straight bond + Call option on the underlying stock

The straight bond component refers to the pure fixed income portion of the convertible bond. It ignores the conversion possibility and its value is easily obtained by discounting all the future expected cash flows (coupons and final repayment) at an appropriate discount rate (the risk-free rate plus a credit spread). To illustrate, for our XYZ convertible bond we would obtain a discount rate of 8% (see Table 32.1) and a total present value of $760.44.

Time (years)	0	1	2	3	4	5
Cash flows		20	20	20	20	1,020.00
PV(CF) @ 8%		18.52	17.15	15.88	14.70	694.19
Total PV	760.44					

This pure bond price is, in a sense, the minimum value of a convertible bond. It is unaffected by the stock price level unless the latter falls so much that the issuer's ability to face its debt obligations is called into question.

The option component considers the conversion features of the convertible bond only. It is essentially an option to buy a certain quantity (the conversion ratio) of shares of stock by paying the value of the convertible bond. Such an option can be valued using the Black-Scholes (1973) Formula where S_t is replaced by the conversion ratio times the price of one share, and the strike price is set equal to the price of the bond to be delivered in exchange for the shares.[3] We have:

$$Call\ Option = S_t e^{-q(T-t)} N(d_1) - K e^{-r(T-t)} N(d_2)$$

where

$$d_1 = \frac{\ln\left(\frac{S}{K}\right) + (r - q + \frac{1}{2}\sigma^2)(T - t)}{\sigma\sqrt{T - t}}$$

$$d_2 = d_1 - \sigma\sqrt{T - t}$$

Note that $r = ln(1 + R_F)$ is the continuously compounded risk-free rate, q is the continuous annual dividend yield and $N(.)$ is the cumulative normal distribution function. For the option component of our XYZ bond, we would obtain a theoretical price of $202.23. The theoretical price of our

---

[3] Note that since the price of the bond is not constant, the Black-Scholes Model provides a very crude approximation for the price of the convertible bond. As seen below, the preferred approach is to use a binomial model.

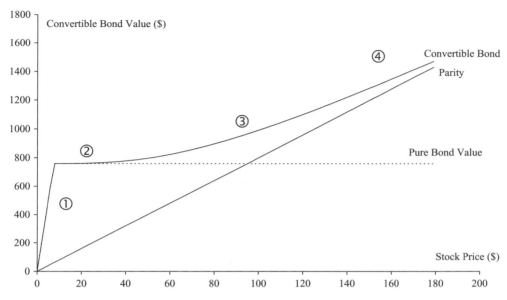

Figure 32.1   Behavior of a convertible bond at various stock price levels

convertible bond is obtained by summing the theoretical prices of its components, i.e. $760.44 + $202.23 = $962.67, or 96.27 percent of its face value.

The overall profile of a convertible bond can easily be obtained by calculating the theoretical prices of its components for various levels of the stock price. As can be seen from Figure 32.1, there are four possible states for a convertible bond:

- **Junk** or **distressed** *(area 1)*. When the stock price is so low as to indicate doubt about the issuer's ability to meet its debt obligations. The call option is worth zero and the convertible trades like a distressed bond. The parity is typically between 0% and 30% of the face value. The convertible is said to be "deep out-of-the-money."
- **Busted** *(area 2)*. When the stock price is low enough that conversion is unlikely. The value of the call option is negligible, and the convertible bond trades essentially similar to a straight bond with no equity sensitivity. The parity is typically between 30% and 80% of the face value. Such convertibles are said to be "out-of-the-money."
- **Hybrid** *(area 3)*. When the stock price is high enough that the option to convert gains value. The parity is typically between 80% and 120% of the face value, and the convertible is said to be "at-the-money."
- **Equity proxy** *(area 4)*. When the stock price is extremely high making conversion likely such that only the conversion value matters. Its equity sensitivity is high while its fixed income sensitivity is low. The parity is typically above 130% of the face value and the convertible is said to be "deep in-the-money."

Convertible arbitrageurs generally prefer hybrid convertibles because they exhibit both fixed-income and equity sensitivities. It may be recalled that the price of a call option can be broken into two parts, the intrinsic value and the time value (i.e. the optionality value). The optionality value tends to be highest for at-the-money options. For this reason, convertible arbitrage managers prefer hybrid convertibles because the optionality value is highest, increasing the profit potential.

The major drawbacks of the component approach are twofold: (i) it uses the Black-Scholes Model, which is only valid for European options and cannot deal with early termination (call and put) clauses; and (ii) it does not take the credit risk of the issuer into consideration.

Binomial model

To price convertible bonds, we need to model the possible evolution of the underlying stock price. The binomial tree approach introduced by Cox, Ross and Rubinstein (1979) is widely used in practice because it can deal with a wide range of contractual specifications while still remaining relatively simple.

Let us assume that the stock price process follows a binomial random walk. That is, over the next period, the stock price can either go up by a multiplicative factor u or go down by a multiplicative factor d, where $u > d$ (Figure 32.2).

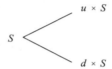

Figure 32.2   Possible stock price movements (one period)

This process can be repeated as many times as needed. For instance, over two periods we would obtain the following tree of discrete future possible underlying stock prices (Figure 32.3)

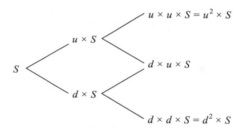

Figure 32.3   Possible stock price movements (two periods)

The parameters u and d are proportional to the volatility of the underlying asset and must be specified. As suggested by Cox, Ross and Rubinstein (1979), we set $u = \exp(\sigma\sqrt{\tau})$, where τ is the length of one period in the tree, and $d = 1/u$. This ensures that the resulting expected volatility of changes in stock price is σ.

Say we want to once again analyze our XYZ convertible bond. The life of the tree is set equal to the life of the convertible bond (five years). For the sake of simplicity, we will consider a tree made of $N = 5$ periods of $\tau = 1$ year, which implies that our convertible bond pays its coupon each period.[4] We have $u = \exp(0.30) = 1.3499$ and $d = 1/u = 0.7408$. The resulting stock price tree is given in Figure 32.4.

---

[4] In practice, a five-year time to maturity would need to be divided into several hundred periods to obtain an accurate bond price.

t = 0	t = 1Y	t = 2Y	t = 3Y	t = 4Y	t = 5Y
					448.17
				332.01	
			245.96		245.96
		182.21		182.21	
	134.99		134.99		134.99
100.00		100.00		100.00	
	74.08		74.08		74.08
		54.88		54.88	
			40.66		40.66
				30.12	
					22.31

Figure 32.4   Binomial tree for the stock price

As suggested by Cox, Ross and Rubinstein (1979), this binomial tree can be used to extract the **risk-neutral probability** of the stock price increasing (p) or decreasing $(1 - p)$. We have:[5]

$$p = [\exp(r\tau)\text{-}d]/[u - d] = 0.4926$$

and

$$1 - p = 0.5074.$$

The conversion value of the convertible bond is given by the stock price times the conversion ratio, thus we can easily construct the associated parity tree (Figure 32.5):

t = 0	t = 1Y	t = 2Y	t = 3Y	t = 4Y	t = 5Y
					358.54
				265.61	
			196.77		196.77
		145.77		145.77	
	107.99		107.99		107.99
80.00		80.00		80.00	
	59.27		59.27		59.27
		43.90		43.90	
			32.53		32.53
				24.10	
					17.85

Figure 32.5   Binomial tree for the parity

At time t = 5Y, the pure bond price of the convertible bond is its repayment value ($1000) plus the last coupon ($20). Conversion should only occur if the conversion value is higher than $1020. It is easy to verify that this is the case when the final stock price is $448.17, $245.96, or $134.99 (i.e. for the top three end-nodes). For the bottom three end-nodes, no conversion should occur. Therefore, we have a 100% probability of converting for the top three nodes at time t = 5Y and a 0% probability for the bottom three nodes.

---

[5] Note that R_F (4%) is used for r here, not $r = \ln(1 + R_F)$ as in the earlier Black-Scholes example.

For each node before time t = 5Y, the conversion probability can be calculated using backward induction (right to left) and the risk neutral probability p. We have:

$$\text{Prob.Conv.} = p \times \text{Prob.Conv.}_{up} + (1\text{-}p) \times \text{Prob.Conv.}_{down}$$

where Prob.Conv._{up} and Prob.Conv._{down} are the probabilities of converting in the next up-node and down-node, respectively. The resulting conversion probability tree is given in Figure 32.6.

t = 0	t = 1Y	t = 2Y	t = 3Y	t = 4Y	t = 5Y
					100%
				100%	
			100%		100%
		86.93%		100%	
	67.63%		74.25%		100%
48.61%		48.88%		49.26%	
	30.14%		24.26%		0%
		11.95%		0%	
			0%		0%
				0%	
					0%

Figure 32.6   Binomial tree for the conversion probability

Let us now find the theoretical value of our convertible bond. The only remaining complication is the choice of the discount rate used in conjunction with the tree. Fortunately, the conversion probability at each node can be used to determine the relevant discount rate. If conversion will occur with 100% probability, the discount rate should be the risk-free interest rate. But if the conversion is highly unlikely, the discount rate should reflect the credit spread of the issuer. In general, we have:

$$\text{Discount rate} = [\text{Prob.Conv.} \times (1 + R_F)] + [(1 - \text{Prob.Conv.}) \times (1 + R_F + CS)]$$

The resulting credit-adjusted discount rate tree is given in Figure 32.7.

t = 0	t = 1Y	t = 2Y	t = 3Y	t = 4Y	t = 5Y
					4.00%
				4.00%	
			4.00%		4.00%
		4.52%		4.00%	
	5.29%		5.03%		4.00%
6.06%		6.04%		6.03%	
	6.79%		7.03%		8.00%
		7.52%		8.00%	
			8.00%		8.00%
				8.00%	
					8.00%

Figure 32.7   Binomial tree for the credit-adjusted discount rate

As expected, the credit-adjusted discount rate increases as the stock price decreases.[6] We can now proceed with the calculation of the theoretical value for the convertible bond using backward

---

[6] Here again, for the sake of simplicity, we have assumed a constant credit spread even if the stock price decreases significantly. In practice, the credit spread is likely to vary throughout the tree.

induction. We already know the value of the convertible bond at expiration. At any given node prior to expiration, the convertible bond value is equal to the expected convertible bond value of the next two nodes discounted at the credit-adjusted discount rate of the current node, plus the coupon. That is:

$$\text{Convert.Value} = \frac{[p \times \text{Conv.Value}_{up} + (1\text{-}p) \times \text{Conv.Value}_{down}]}{1 + \text{Discount rate}} + \text{Coupon}$$

and we obtain the tree for the convertible bond value as shown in Figure 32.8.

t = 0	t = 1Y	t = 2Y	t = 3Y	t = 4Y	t = 5Y
					358.54
				267.82	
			201.00		196.77
		155.05		147.88	
	124.11		120.14		107.99
103.36		102.88		100.98	
	91.38		94.20		102.00
		88.24		96.44	
			91.30		102.00
				96.44	
					102.00

Figure 32.8 Binomial tree for the convertible bond value

According to our basic binomial tree approach, the theoretical value of our convertible bond is 103.36% of its face value. Of course, one could argue that our fictive XYZ bond was extremely simple. In reality, it is relatively easy to modify our tree to incorporate specific features and terms such as put and call clauses, reset features, varying interest rates and credit spreads, etc.

THE GREEKS

The "Greeks" are measures that represent the sensitivities of a convertible bond and, more generally, of any given portfolio to a variety of factors. The name "Greeks" is used because the parameters are often denoted by Greek letters.[7]

Delta and modified delta

Delta (Δ) measures the sensitivity of the value of a derivative security (e.g. convertible bond) to changes in its underlying asset (i.e. the stock price or parity level). Mathematically, it is the first order derivative of the convertible bond value with respect to the underlying stock price (Note that the following expression is strictly correct if the conversion ratio is one. More precisely, as shown below, delta measures the sensitivity of the bond to changes in its parity value):

$$\text{Delta} = \Delta = \frac{\partial \text{Derivative Price}}{\partial \text{Stock price}}$$

---

[7] The notation used in this section follows the conventions used for the Black-Scholes call option price in describing the component approach to valuing convertible securities.

t = 0	t = 1Y	t = 2Y	t = 3Y	t = 4Y	t = 5Y
				1.000	
			1.000		
		0.911		1.000	
	0.793		0.713		
0.672		0.532		0.123	
	0.406		0.126		
		0.108		0.000	
			0.000		
				0.000	

Figure 32.9 Binomial tree for the delta of the convertible bond

When using the Black-Scholes Formula, the delta is given by:

$$\text{Delta} = e^{-q(T-t)} N(d_1)$$

Since the underlying asset of a convertible bond is the stock price times the conversion ratio, the delta of a convertible is calculated using the sensitivity to parity. When using a binomial tree, the delta is also easily obtained by comparing the changes of the convertible value to changes in parity in the next two nodes. For instance, if we use the trees of Figures 32.8 and 32.5, at the initial node, we have:

$$\text{Delta} = (124.11 - 91.38)/(107.99 - 59.27) = 0.672$$

This means that a one point movement in the convertible's parity level will generate a 0.672 point movement in the convertible bond value.[8] By repeating the above procedure for each node prior to maturity, it is possible to build the delta tree as seen in Figure 32.9.

Note that as one moves along the convertible price curve, the value of delta varies between 0 and 1, which are the two bounds for the delta of a call option. At-the-money options generally have deltas of around 0.50. Deep-in-the-money call options have deltas that approach 1.00, while out-of-the-money call options have deltas approaching 0.0. As the underlying stock price moves, the embedded option becomes further in- or out-of-the-money changing the delta of the convertible bond.

Graphically, delta corresponds to the slope of the convertible bond price curve, as illustrated in Figure 32.10. A steeper slope indicates a higher sensitivity to the underlying stock price. When a convertible bond gets very deep-in-the-money, it begins to trade like the stock, moving almost dollar for dollar with the stock price (area 4, delta = 1). Meanwhile, out-of-the-money convertibles do not move much in absolute dollar terms (area 2, delta = 0), unless there are some serious bankruptcy concerns (area 1).

So far, we have implicitly assumed that nothing else changes; e.g. the volatility of the underlying stock, interest rates, or the passage of time. In reality, changes in any one of these quantities can affect the delta of the convertible bond, even if the price of the underlying stock remains the same. In fact, the more in-the-money or out-of-the-money the embedded option, the less sensitive the delta is to changes in volatility or time to expiration.

As we will see shortly, delta is a critical variable for convertible arbitrageurs for it indicates just how many shares of stock one should short to hedge a long position in the convertible bond.

---

[8] Although we calculate delta (and Gamma) in terms of changes in the parity level here, the numerical result would be similar if we used our earlier definition of delta (and Gamma) as a function of the change in the stock price.

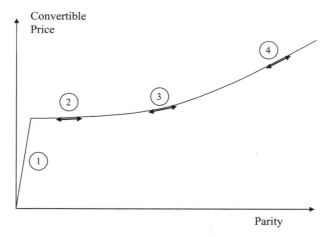

Figure 32.10   Delta as the slope of a tangent drawn on the convertible price line

Gamma

Delta only provides a linear approximation for the change in the convertible bond value. It is relatively accurate for small variations of the underlying stock price, but fails to capture the non-linearity of the convertible bond profile. To correct for this, it is necessary to introduce a convexity adjustment.

Gamma (Γ) measures the rate of change of the delta as the stock price changes. Mathematically, it is the second derivative of the convertible bond value with respect to the underlying stock price (assuming a conversion ratio of one):

$$Gamma = \Gamma = \frac{\partial^2 \text{Convertible value}}{\partial \text{Stock price}^2} = \frac{\partial \text{Delta}}{\partial \text{Stock price}}$$

When using the Black-Scholes Formula, the gamma is given by ($N'(d_1)$) denotes derivative of $N(d_1)$ with respect to stock price):

$$Gamma = \frac{e^{-q(T-t)} N'(d_1)}{S\sigma\sqrt{T-t}}$$

When using a binomial tree, the gamma is also easily obtained by looking at the change of delta in the next two nodes relative to changes in parity. For instance, if we use the trees of Figures 32.5 and 32.9 at the initial node, we have an initial delta of 0.672, an upside delta of 0.793, and a downside delta of 0.406. The gamma is therefore:

$$Gamma = (0.793 - 0.406)/(107.99 - 59.27) = 0.00796.$$

This indicates that the delta will change by 0.00796 for each point change in parity level.

Gamma is very important for convertible arbitrageurs as it indicates how much delta changes with regard to changes in the stock price. If gamma is large (i.e. delta is very sensitive to the underlying price), the portfolio will need to be adjusted frequently to maintain delta-neutrality. If gamma is small, delta changes slowly, and the portfolio will need to be adjusted less frequently to keep the portfolio delta-neutral.

Just as the delta changes, so does the gamma. Gamma is normally larger for at-the-money convertibles and gets progressively lower for both in- and out-of-the-money convertibles. This means that the delta of **at-the-money convertibles** changes the most when the underlying stock price moves up or down. In the case of distressed convertibles, gamma can even become negative.

In addition, gamma also changes as time passes and volatility changes, but in a more complex way than delta: time passing or a decrease in volatility normally increase the gamma of at-the-money convertibles, but decrease the gamma of in-the-money and out-of-the-money convertibles.

Vega

Vega (ν) measures the sensitivity of the convertible bond value to changes in the volatility of the underlying stock. Mathematically, it is the derivative of the option value with respect to the volatility of the underlying:

$$Vega = \nu = \frac{\partial \text{Convertible value}}{\partial \text{Volatility}}$$

When using the Black-Scholes Formula, vega is given by:

$$Vega = SN'(d_1)\sqrt{(T-t)}e^{-q(T-t)}.$$

Note that vega is always positive, as an increase in volatility will raise the value of all options on an asset while a decrease in volatility will lower their value. Convertibles that are trading near their conversion price are most sensitive to volatility and therefore display the highest vega.

Theta

The *theta* (θ), also known as time decay, is the change of the convertible price due to the passage of time. Mathematically, it is the derivative of the option value with respect to time:

$$Theta = \theta = \frac{\partial \text{Convertible value}}{\partial \text{Time}}$$

When using the Black-Scholes Formula, the theta is given by:

$$Theta = -\frac{\left[SN'(d_1)\sigma e^{-q(T-t)}\right]}{2\sqrt{T-t}} - rKe^{-r(T-t)}N(d_2) + qSN(d_1)e^{-q(T-t)}$$

Conventionally, theta is expressed as the percentage change in the convertible price for the passage of one day, other things being equal. Theta is used to estimate the degree to which a convertible bond option's time value is whittled away by the always-constant passage of time. For an at-the-money convertible, theta will be negative if the time decay of the option element outweighs any upward drift in the bond floor. Recall that the value of the straight bond component of the convertible serves as the floor for the price of the convertible bond because the value of the embedded option can never be negative.

Rho

Rho is an estimate of the sensitivity of a convertible value to movements in interest rates. Mathematically, it is the derivative of the option value with respect to interest rates:

$$Rho = \rho = \frac{\partial \text{Convertible value}}{\partial \text{Interest rate}}$$

When using the Black-Scholes Formula, the rho is given by:

$$Rho = K(T-t)e^{-r(T-t)}N(d_2)$$

Conventionally, it is expressed as the change in convertible price for a given 1 basis point move in interest rates (a parallel shift in the whole yield curve). Rho also evolves along the convertible curve – it increases when parity decreases, i.e. as the convertible starts trading more based on its fixed-interest characteristics.

Other Greeks

Convertible bond traders also use additional "Greeks" to measure the sensitivities of their positions to other market parameters:

- Chi is an estimate of the rate of change of a convertible's value to changes in the spot exchange rate.
- Omicron is an estimate of the rate of change of a convertible's value to changes in the credit spread.
- Upsilon is an estimate of the rate of change of a convertible's value to changes in the credit recovery rate.
- Phi is an estimate of the rate of change of a convertible's value to changes in the underlying stock's dividend rate.

It is worth noting that some arbitrageurs use a modified delta rather than the original delta. The modified delta is defined as follows:

$$Modified\ Delta = \frac{1}{2}\left[\frac{\text{Change in convertible value}}{\text{Positive change in stock price}} + \frac{\text{Change in convertible value}}{\text{Negative change in stock price}}\right]$$

For instance, an arbitrageur could set a 5% increase in the stock price, determine the convertible price change, and obtain the first term of the modified delta. Repeating the process with a 5% decrease in the stock price would provide the second term. The average would be the modified delta, which is no longer a pure delta since it implicitly incorporates the impact of other Greeks in the calculation, in particular the gamma.

The Greeks of mandatory convertibles behave very differently than those of ordinary convertibles. A mandatory convertible has a required conversion or redemption feature. Either on or before a contractual conversion date, the holder must convert the mandatory convertible into the underlying common stock. These securities offer higher yields to compensate investors for the additional risk incurred under the mandatory conversion structure. For mandatory convertibles, (i) the delta may actually increase as stock prices decline and decrease as stock prices rise; and (ii) gamma may turn negative for some stock price ranges. Hedging such convertibles therefore requires a precise analysis of the dynamics of their Greeks.

AN ARBITRAGE SITUATION

Our XYZ convertible bond had a theoretical value of 103.36% according to the binomial model. For the sake of illustration, let us assume that our XYZ convertible bond is quoted by the market at 90% of par. Given the current price and the estimated volatility of the underlying asset (stock), the convertible bond is clearly undervalued. The question is how can one exploit such a mispricing? Buying the cheap convertible is clearly part of the solution, but it is not sufficient. Simply waiting for market prices to adjust is not an arbitrage because the long convertible position comes with a variety of risks that could easily wipe out the expected gains. To arbitrage, it is necessary to buy the cheap convertible *and* hedge its risks – a dynamic process that is very similar to what option arbitrageurs do all day long.

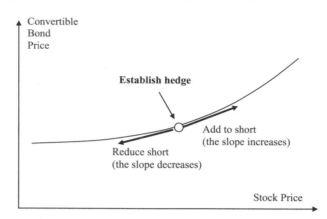

Figure 32.11   Delta hedging a convertible bond

The primary risk of holding a long convertible position comes from the potential variations in the underlying stock price. This equity risk can easily be eliminated by selling short an appropriate quantity of the underlying stock. This quantity corresponds to the convertible's delta times the number of shares into which the bond may be converted. If the stock price gains $1, the convertible bond will gain approximately *delta* dollars, and the short stock position will lose *delta* dollars, so that the overall variation will be nil. Conversely, if the stock price drops by $1, the convertible bond will lose approximately *delta* dollars, and the short stock position will gain *delta* dollars, so that the overall variation will again be nil. In both cases, the overall position's value no longer depends upon variations in the stock price.

We found that the delta of our CXZ convertible bond was 0.672. To hedge the equity risk, an arbitrageur would therefore need to sell short $0.672 \times 8 = 5.376$ shares of stock per $1000 face value of the convertible bond that he bought. For a small change in the price of the stock, the arbitrageur's position will be hedged. However, if the stock price changes by a large amount, the delta of the convertible bond will no longer be 0.672, and therefore the net delta of the position will no longer be equal to 0. In order to keep the position delta-hedged, a rebalancing of the hedge (re-hedging) is needed.

As the stock price increases and the option component moves further **in-the-money**, the convertible bond becomes more equity sensitive (see Figure 32.11). The delta of the convertible bond increases, so the arbitrageur must adjust his hedge by shorting more shares. Conversely, as the stock price declines and the option moves **out-of-the-money**, the delta of the convertible bond declines and the arbitrageur must reduce his hedge by buying back some shares. In any case, the hedge needs to be rebalanced repeatedly as the stock price moves. This investment approach, called dynamic "delta hedging" in options terminology, is the most common way of extracting value from convertibles without taking directional views on the underlying stock.

A key question for most arbitrageurs is how often they should rebalance their hedge. Theoretical **delta hedging** assumes that re-hedging is done continuously, i.e. infinitesimally small stock transactions are done for every infinitesimally small stock price movement. This is not feasible in the real world: stock prices change in finite increments, fractional shares are normally not traded, and even if they were, transaction costs would skyrocket along with the number of transactions. In practice, therefore, arbitrageurs re-hedge in discrete time, usually on a time-based or price-based basis. In the former case, re-hedging takes place at pre-specified time intervals, e.g. every day or every hour. In the latter case, re-hedging takes place whenever the stock price changes by a certain amount

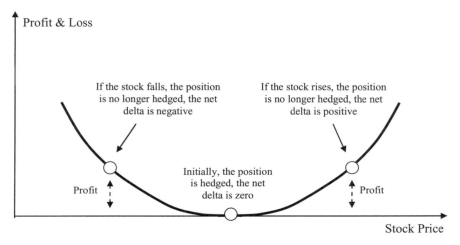

Figure 32.12 Profit on a delta hedged position (long convertible, short stock). The **net delta** is the slope of the curve

(e.g. every $1 move or every one percent move in the stock price) or when the size of the necessary adjustment reaches a certain threshold. If the selected re-hedging interval is small enough, the risk of running a poorly hedged position is limited. Of course, a combination of the two approaches can also be implemented, but in practice, the optimal choice of re-hedging strategy often varies, not only from stock to stock, but also over time depending on market conditions.

Of particular interest to convertible bond arbitrageurs is the asymmetric valuation profile generated by large movements in the underlying stock price. Due to the nonlinear nature of their payoff, most at-the-money convertible bonds exhibit a desirable property known as positive convexity or high gamma. That is, they appreciate in value more than they depreciate with respect to the same absolute change in the underlying stock price. Consequently, the delta hedged position will actually benefit from *any* large movement in the underlying stock. In other words, the position tends to become underhedged when the price of the stock (and consequently the convertible bond) increases – a good thing – and becomes overhedged when the stock price decreases, again a good thing! Convertible securities that demonstrate this property are attractive in volatile markets – all else being equal, the more volatile the stock price, the greater the expected profit of the position.

Figure 32.12, which shows the expected profit and loss of the hedged position as a function of the stock price, may give the impression that there is a pure arbitrage. The worst outcome seems to be a zero profit in the case of an unchanged stock price while a positive profit occurs in any other case. Unfortunately, this is not strictly true. We have considered stock price variations, but ignored other aspects of the convertible position, in particular the loss of time value of the option component.[9] This time decay offsets the convexity gains to such an extent that the expected return on the continuously delta-hedged position actually equals the risk-free rate. The curve in Figure 32.12 should therefore be shifted down to reflect the possibility of a loss around the current stock price.

Once the exposure to the underlying stock price is neutralized, the profitability of the transaction will be affected by a series of other factors, such as the volatility level of the embedded option, the

---

[9] This is understandable if one considers that a long-term American call option is always worth more than a short-term American option with the same exercise price. Other things being equal, as the maturity of the option draws closer, the option value decreases.

general level of interest rates, the cash flow stream generated by the position, and the credit spread inherent in the bond resulting from the issuer's credit quality.

Saying that a convertible bond is cheap is equivalent to saying that its implied volatility is too low. The exact shape of the profit and loss curve will therefore also depend on the *realized* volatility of the stock price versus its implied volatility. Since convertible bond arbitrageurs own the embedded call option, they are naturally long volatility. Any increase in the volatility of the stock's price should result in profits for the strategy. And if the realized volatility is higher than the implied volatility, the delta-hedged position will make a profit in excess of the risk-free rate. Conversely, if the realized volatility is below the implied volatility, the loss due to time decay will outweigh the profit made from the realized volatility and the position will underperform a risk-free investment, perhaps even incurring a loss.

Convertible arbitrageurs who are not willing to be exposed to volatility risk can hedge against volatility fluctuations. This is called **vega hedging**, or making the portfolio vega-neutral. Vega hedging in practice involves buying and selling other options or convertible bonds, since only these instruments exhibit convexity and hence have vega.[10] These option positions need to be adjusted on a regular basis, as their vega as well as the vega of the hedged convertible bond change continuously. Alternatively, arbitrageurs may opt to vega hedge by using volatility futures such as the VIX futures contracts, which provide a pure play on implied volatility independent of the direction and level of stock prices.

The interest rate factor is also important. A simple long convertible bond position is typically long duration and long convexity and will lose money if interest rates rise. Here again, if they want to, arbitrageurs can easily hedge this risk by selling interest rate futures contracts or by entering interest rate swaps.

The cash flow generated by the position is usually positive for arbitrageurs. Indeed, arbitrageurs receive not only the coupon payment from the bond, but also the interest on the proceeds from the stock sale less any cost associated with borrowing the stock, including the repayment of foregone dividends. This explains why non-dividend paying stock is more desirable for the strategy.

Credit considerations are also essential and they will be discussed in the next section.

CONVERTIBLE ARBITRAGE IN PRACTICE: STRIPPING AND SWAPPING

Once equity, volatility, and interest rate risks have been eliminated from the convertible position, our arbitrageur is left with credit risk, i.e. possible changes in credit spreads. This risk is important because the majority of convertible issuers are below investment grade, at least in the United States. Moreover, many convertible bonds are unsecured, subordinated, and issued by firms with high earnings volatility, high leverage, and/or intangible assets. They are particularly sensitive to the business cycle, so the arbitrageur cannot ignore credit risk.

Short selling the stock provides a partial hedge against credit risk – as spreads widen, stock prices generally decline. However, this hedge is imperfect and difficult to calibrate precisely. Moreover, to entirely eliminate the credit-spread risk with a short stock position, the arbitrageur would need to short considerably more stock than the delta hedge calls for, placing the position at considerable risk should spreads not widen and stock prices appreciate. One alternative is to sell short a straight bond of the same issuer. This is usually an effective hedge against credit risk, but it is only feasible if other bonds from the same issuer are still actively traded and can be borrowed easily. This is clearly

---

[10] Note that the delta and gamma of these other options would need to be hedged as well!

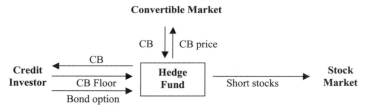

Figure 32.13 Typical flows in an asset swap

not the case for all issuers. Using credit default swaps might also be considered, but this practice exposes the arbitrageur to a serious call risk if the bond is callable – arbitrageurs who wish to unwind a default swap are reliant on finding a counterparty, but if the deliverable convertible bond has been called, there is unlikely to be a market. A workaround is to buy credit default swaps that mature before the call date, but there is no guarantee that the arbitrage profit will be realized by this date.

Until recently, it was almost impossible to properly hedge the credit risk of a specific convertible bond issuer. However, one has to remember that real arbitrageurs are not really interested in the fixed income/credit portion of convertible bonds. They are just keen to purchase the associated cheap equity call options that they can offset against either the equity or other equity-linked securities. On the other hand, many investment banks and prime brokers have clients who are interested in the fixed income portion of convertible securities but have no real desire to hold the associated call option. Once again, financial intermediation comes to the rescue: the **asset swap** is a key development that has boosted the demand for convertible bonds in recent years. This new instrument offers the ability to split a convertible bond into its two components: the fixed income part and the equity call option. Most of the time, the asset swap involves a "credit seller," who will keep the equity option, and a "credit buyer," who will acquire the fixed-income component. This unlocks the theoretical value of the convertible bond and greatly facilitates the implementation of arbitrage strategies.

Although asset swap arrangements can be technically complex, their basic construction is very simple. The process can be summarized by the following two steps (see Figure 32.13).

Step 1: A hedge fund manager identifies an undervalued convertible bond. He verifies with his prime broker that the underlying stock can be borrowed. If so, he purchases the convertible bond, which generally bears a fixed-rate coupon and an option for its holder to convert into equity. In terms of risk, the manager is now exposed to rising interest rates, falling equity prices, declining volatility, and widening credit spreads.

Step 2: The fund manager enters into an asset swap with a credit investor. This swap is usually made up of two transactions:

• The fund manager sells the convertible bond to the credit investor at a large discount to its market price. The selling price is typically set at the bond floor value, that is, the present value of the bond's future cash flow (coupons and repayment) discounted at LIBOR plus a fixed credit spread.
• In exchange for the discount on the sale price of the convertible bond, the credit investor gives the fund an over-the-counter call option. This option allows the fund to purchase the convertible bond back at a fixed exercise price. This is typically set at the present value of the bond's future cash flow (coupons and repayment) discounted at LIBOR plus a fixed recall spread. The recall spread is tighter than the one used for calculating the bond floor value to discourage rapid turnover of positions and to deliver a minimum return to the credit buyer. For instance, the swap terms could allow for a call at par value at the maturity of the bond.

Before proceeding further, let's verify that the asset swap has left each party with only their desired exposures. The hedge fund, for its part, still has the equity upside exposure inherent in the convertible bond by virtue of owning the call option, but is no longer exposed to the risk of widening credit spreads. This option is useless so long as the convertible bond is out-of-the-money, but allows for participation in the upside potential of the stock when the convertible bond is at- or in-the-money. Because the convertible bond is purchased below fair value and the straight bond component is sold at fair value, the hedge fund is left holding an option whose final purchase price is lower than its theoretical value. To capture the price difference, most hedge funds will simply delta hedge this option until it returns to fair value. Note that the hedge fund's loss is limited to the premium of the option, whose strike price depends on the credit spread initially agreed upon in the asset swap. On the other hand, the hedge fund can benefit if the credit trades to a tighter spread by calling the initial asset swap and simultaneously establishing a new one at a tighter spread.

After entering the asset swap, the credit investor holds a synthetic straight callable bond.[11] He has no equity exposure but now faces credit risk and interest rate risk. If he is solely interested in betting that the credit quality of the issuer will improve in the future, he can eliminate the interest rate risk by entering into another swap in which he pays a fixed rate equal to the convertible bond coupon and receives a floating rate, typically LIBOR plus a spread. This leaves him with only the credit exposure of the original convertible bond.

Now, let us consider what can happen at expiration. There are five basic cases to be considered:

- If the convertible bond matures out-of-the-money, the hedge fund manager lets his option expire. The credit investor redeems the convertible bond and is repaid at par by the issuer.
- If the convertible bond matures in-the-money, the hedge fund manager calls back the convertible bond and pays the par value to the credit investor. The hedge fund manager then exercises the conversion option and receives the parity value, which is higher than his payment to the credit investor.
- If the convertible bond is called out-of-the-money by the issuer, the hedge fund manager lets the option expire. The credit investor is then repaid at the call price by the issuer.
- If the convertible bond is called in-the-money by the issuer, the hedge fund manager calls back the convertible bond and pays the agreed call value to the credit investor. The hedge fund manager then exercises the convertible bond and receives the parity value, which is higher than his payment to the credit investor.
- If the issuer defaults, the hedge fund manager lets his option expire. The credit investor receives the recovery value of the convertible bond, if any, from the issuer.

In practice, asset swaps may take several alternative forms, but their basic function remains the same, i.e. to split the convertible bond into its two core components. Convertible bond arbitrageurs use these asset swaps to gain equity exposure to a company while avoiding credit and interest rate risk exposure.

HISTORICAL PERFORMANCE

The historical performance of the convertible arbitrage strategy is characterized by equity like returns with a low standard deviation. From January 1990 to December 2008, the CISDM Convertible Arbitrage Index exhibited an annualized return of 8.35% and an annualized return volatility of 5.11%. By comparison, the CISDM Equal Weighted Hedge Fund Index earned 12.59% per year

---

[11] The term "synthetic" is used because the position is not a straight callable bond, but it behaves exactly like a straight callable bond.

with a volatility of 8.23%, and the S&P 500 earned 7.33% per year with a volatility of 15.78%. The convertible arbitrage strategy exhibited moderate correlation to equity markets (0.43 versus the S&P 500) and a negatively skewed (−5.08) return distribution, indicating a high probability of earning significant negative returns. However, its worst drawdown (−22.46%) was still better than that experienced in equity markets (−44.73% for S&P 500 and −49.21% for MSCI EAFE).

Table 32.2 Historical performance of CISDM Convertible Arbitrage Strategy.

Year	BarCap Global Aggregate Bond (%Total Return)	S&P 500 (%Total Return)	MSCI Emerg (%Total Return)	MSCI EAFE (%Total Return)	CISDM Fund of Funds Diversified Index (%Total Return)	CISDM Fund of Funds Index (%Total Return)	CISDM Equal Weighted Hedge Fund Index (%Total Return)	CISDM Merger Arbitrage Index (%Total Return)	CISDM Global Macro Index (%Total Return)	CISDM Event Driven Multi-Strategy Index (%Total Return)	CISDM Equity Market Neutral Index (%Total Return)	CISDM Equity Long/Short Index (%Total Return)	CISDM Distressed Securities Index (%Total Return)	CISDM Convert Arbitrage Index (%Total Return)	CISDM CTA Asset Weighted Index (%Total Return)	CISDM CTA Asset Weighted Diversified Index (%Total Return)
1990	12.6	-3.1	-10.56	-23.2	7.51	7.47	6.54	-1.69	11.26	-3.31	10.18	-1.46	19.31	NA	27.29	19.8
1991	16.06	30.47	59.9	12.48	11.01	11.3	30.43	18.33	36.47	21.84	12.42	33.7	25.06	NA	16.82	11.34
1992	5.78	7.65	11.41	-11.85	12.04	11.93	16.83	17.37	22.35	19.36	7.92	17.38	18.25	16.68	9.9	-6.01
1993	11.08	10.08	74.86	32.94	23.33	24.21	30.29	26.38	40.88	26.47	9.73	21.56	31.25	16.56	19.86	22.12
1994	0.23	1.32	-7.31	8.06	-4.44	-4.42	3.53	5.23	-5.05	3.64	5.12	3.38	-4.3	2.2	-0.7	5.29
1995	19.67	37.57	-5.19	11.55	12.54	12.25	21.17	16.6	11.17	19.8	12.2	26.42	21.95	17.47	15.13	15.05
1996	4.92	22.96	6.04	6.34	16.83	16.68	23.24	15.97	9.86	22.31	13.69	22.34	21.05	14.75	14.64	12.73
1997	3.79	33.38	-11.59	2.05	17.09	17.2	21.79	18.17	15.97	23.56	14.87	23.74	18.67	14.25	10.06	7.09
1998	13.7	28.58	-25.33	20.34	1.71	1.65	3.97	5.5	8.11	3.9	11.16	9.57	-4.83	7.45	9.37	11.61
1999	-5.17	21.04	66.66	27.3	22.37	16.23	36.79	15.77	8.52	21.42	9.86	34.4	17.85	13.9	3.77	6.5
2000	3.18	-9.09	-30.71	-13.97	7.35	7.37	8.76	14.37	10.02	12.07	13.87	7.78	5.85	15.24	6.18	8.07
2001	1.57	-11.88	-2.37	-21.21	4.99	5.18	5.71	4.27	5.58	7.06	7.27	2.27	9.24	13.27	4.19	6.04
2002	16.52	-22.1	-6	-15.64	0.65	1.05	0.41	0.28	2.81	1.18	2.04	-4.72	6.85	8.89	11.95	12.38
2003	12.48	28.69	56.26	39.16	10.04	10.23	20.62	7.37	11.76	21.87	8.83	18.89	25.27	9.65	13.25	10.39
2004	9.27	10.87	25.94	20.69	7.23	7.12	9.97	7.01	4.48	12.12	4.97	9.86	16.64	2.47	4.24	3.95
2005	-4.48	4.89	34.53	14.01	6.36	6.47	9.84	5.77	6.65	6.63	7.11	8.86	7.44	-1.14	5	-1.08
2006	6.66	15.79	32.6	26.88	7.79	9.12	11.75	10.7	4.93	13.99	7.64	9.99	15.91	12.32	6.17	7.16
2007	9.48	5.5	39.78	11.62	9.52	8.69	10.5	3.74	12	6.57	6.5	8.48	5.26	3.97	9.14	12.01
2008	4.79	-36.99	-53.17	-43.06	-16.83	-17.05	-19.17	0.09	3.7	-19.05	0.61	-14.43	-19.55	-19.1	17.86	19.26

Source: CISDM

Table 32.3 Statistical properties of CISDM Convertible Arbitrage Index (1990–2008).

	N periods	Geometric mean (%)	Arithmetic mean (%)	Standard deviation (%)	Skewness	Information ratio	Maximum decline (%)	Correl against CISDM Convertible Arbitrage Index
BarCap Global Aggregate Bond Index	228	7.27	7.42	5.78	0.18	1.28	−10.07	0.23
S&P 500 Index	228	7.33	8.48	15.78	−0.69	0.54	−44.73	0.43
MSCI Emerging Mkts Index	228	7.81	11.03	26.64	−0.91	0.41	−59.5	0.47
MSCI EAFE Index	228	3.12	4.62	17.77	−0.57	0.26	−49.21	0.46
CISDM Fund of Funds Diversified Index	228	7.87	8.01	5.43	−0.89	1.48	−17.49	0.64
CISDM Fund of Funds Index	228	7.67	7.79	5.15	−1.34	1.51	−17.74	0.67
CISDM Equal Weighted Hedge Fund Index	228	12.59	12.89	8.23	−0.69	1.57	−21.13	0.61
CISDM Merger Arbitrage Index	228	9.81	9.91	4.55	−1.06	2.18	−5.74	0.57
CISDM Global Macro Index	228	11.18	11.37	6.66	1.15	1.71	−8.22	0.26
CISDM Event Driven Multi-Strategy Index	228	11.05	11.24	6.6	−1.55	1.70	−20.19	0.69
CISDM Equity Market Neutral Index	228	8.67	8.69	2.13	−0.52	4.08	−2.8	0.45
CISDM Equity Long/Short Index	228	11.82	12.2	9.27	−0.28	1.32	−17.04	0.48
CISDM Distressed Securities Index	228	11.77	12.04	7.7	−1.39	1.56	−21.24	0.67
CISDM Convertible Arbitrage Index	204	8.35	8.47	5.11	−5.08	1.66	−22.46	1.00
CISDM CTA Asset Weighted Index	228	10.55	11.04	10.55	0.63	1.05	−10.69	−0.04
CISDM CTA Asset Weighted Diversified Index	228	9.46	10.1	12.03	0.39	0.84	−16.55	−0.05
CISDM CTA Asset Weighted Discretionary Index	228	11.95	12.22	7.81	0.81	1.56	−5.6	0.25

Source: CISDM

33

Global Macro

Global macro managers have been around for more than 30 years, but their golden era culminated in the early 1990s when their strategy represented more than half of the hedge fund assets worldwide. This was the time when legendary managers such as George Soros (Quantum Fund) and Julian Robertson (Tiger Fund) were running multibillion dollar aggressive funds involved primarily in leveraged directional trades. Today, this strategy represents between 10% and 15% of the hedge fund industry's assets under management.

INTRODUCTION TO THE STRATEGY

Global macro hedge funds have the broadest mandate of any of the major fund strategies. Their mandate often has no limitations in terms of types of instruments, asset classes, markets, and geographies. They can dynamically allocate their capital to the asset class, sector, or region in which they think the best opportunities currently lie – hence the term "global." The second term, "macro," reflects the fact that these managers apply macro-economic views to global markets. Instead of analyzing "micro events" affecting companies or assets, they view the world from a top-down perspective. Their goal is to anticipate global macroeconomic changes and themes, detect trends and inflection points, and profit by investing in financial instruments whose prices are likely to be most directly impacted. They can go long or short, be concentrated or diversified, with or without leverage.

There are probably as many approaches to the strategy as there are global macro hedge fund managers, but they share a common desire to identify and exploit markets in severe disequilibrium. It is only when prices are more than one or two standard deviations away from fair value that macro traders deem that market presents a compelling opportunity.

Discretionary versus systematic

Discretionary global macro managers usually perform intensive fundamental research. They continuously analyze information from varied sources such as central bank publications, survey data, confidence indicators, asset flows statistics, liquidity measures, forecasting agencies, political commentators, and personal contacts. They look for markets that do not match the macroeconomic realities, identifying situations that are unsustainable, or asset classes that are likely to follow predictable trends. They spend hours forming their views on likely market scenarios while assessing the probabilities of alternative scenarios. Once interesting risk/reward opportunities have been identified, global macro managers determine appropriate entry points often by applying traditional technical analysis. The overall result is completely discretionary and highly dependent on the particular skills of the manager.

By contrast, systematic global macro managers apply a highly structured, disciplined, and repeatable investment process. They replace subjective macroeconomic analysis with a systematic way of looking at economic data and rely on mathematical models to evaluate markets, detect trading opportunities, generate signals, and establish entry and exit points. Many of them seek to identify specific fundamental data and key economic drivers that explain the long-term behavior of various markets and combine these elements with assessments of the current economic conditions and market forecasts. Others focus on identifying directional trends in markets that can be traded in large volumes and where capital is capable of moving quickly. Their systems can be based on moving averages, break-out systems, pattern recognition, or any combination of these. Some investors like to call them global trend followers as they are very close in spirit to trend-following commodity trading advisors (CTAs), particularly when they focus on longer-term trends.

The reality is that CTAs and some global macro funds share a fundamental source of returns, namely, long-term secular shifts in capital flows. Generally, both tend to participate in large trends in major equity, fixed income, foreign exchange markets, and to a lesser extent the energy, commodity, and precious metals markets. But they participate in these trends in different ways:

- Global macro funds are often anticipatory whereas CTAs are reactive. They therefore often overlap in the middle part of a well-established trend but their entry and exit points are fundamentally different.
- CTAs are purely price-based in their analysis and follow their systematic models regardless of fundamentals. Global macro managers prefer to look at the big picture and stand aside when market fundamentals do not appear to properly explain a trend.
- CTAs tend to exhibit the same views on markets at the same time as each other because their inputs and systems are similar. By contrast, global macro managers can be quite different from one another in how they evaluate data and make trading decisions.
- CTAs are generally momentum (technically driven) traders while their global macro counterparts focus on such fundamentals as value and relative value.
- Global macro funds often liquidate positions and suspend trading at a predetermined loss level or if market fundamentals are no longer attractive while CTAs will wait for a technical signal to confirm that a trend is over.

These disparities in approach help explain the disparity of returns and return volatility.

Schools of thought

Alternatively, one may also want to distinguish the sources of returns that global macro funds are trying to tap. In this case, according to Ahl (2001), there are essentially three possible schools of thought to be considered:

Feedback-based global macro managers assume that markets are rational most of the time, but that there can exist periods of severe irrationality. These can arise either because people have made money too easily and become complacent or because they have lost money too quickly and become stressed or distressed. As a result, feedback-based global macro managers attempt to read the financial market's psychology, sell in bursting bubbles, and buy into post-crash recoveries.

Information-based global macro managers rely primarily on collecting micro level information to better understand the global macro picture. Their hypothesis is that an information gap is created by the delay in release of official macro statistics. This gap then opens the door for pricing inefficiencies that will persist until the macro information has been disseminated into the public domain.

Model-based global macro managers rely primarily on financial models and economic theories to analyze market movements, detect policy mistakes of central banks and governments, or extract implied market expectations and compare them to sensible estimates. As discussed by Safvenblad (2003), examples of trades or models commonly used include:

- Carry trades, i.e. using interest rate differentials as indicators of positive carry positions – holding long maturity bonds against shorter instruments or long high-yielding currencies against low-yielding ones.

- **Yield curve relative value trades**, identifying the under/overvalued part of the yield curves, or trading the slope of one yield curve against the slope of another.
- **Purchasing power parity** (abbreviated as PPP) models – also called "law of one price" – are often used by global macro funds to assess the relative value of currencies.
- Valuations models, such as the dividend discount model used in trading equity markets. Such models are usually applied bottom-up, at each company level. Expected returns for each company are then aggregated and weighted to derive a market level expected return at a country level.
- Option pricing models, which can provide the market's implied views about the future volatility of some underlying asset.

For example, according to the 2008 edition of the Big Mac Index, the Euro was overvalued by 47% against the USD (i.e. a Big Mac sold in Europe at a price 47% greater than its price in the U.S. when both were converted into the same currency) while many Asian currencies were extremely cheap vis-à-vis the dollar. However, one could argue that these numbers are not necessarily reliable because they are calculated on the basis of a single perishable good. But if we use a basket of goods instead, the resulting PPP would be a much more reliable indicator of the exchange rate that would equalize the purchasing power of one currency (amount of goods and services that can be purchased with the currency) with that of another currency. One could then compare this PPP level with the current exchange rate level to identify possible future currency movements. For instance, the International Comparison Program of the United Nations collects data on the prices of goods and services for virtually all countries in the world and publishes PPP exchange rates for all currencies. Comparing these PPP levels with current spot levels allows one to calculate the deviation from PPP and rank currencies based on their level of expected overvaluation/undervaluation.

Another interesting relationship defined by the relative version of the PPP provides a one-to-one link between inflation differential and exchange rate changes. Essentially, relative PPP states that, over time, the change in the exchange rate between two countries should reflect the relative changes between local prices or, equivalently, the difference between the inflation rates of the two countries. Mathematically, we can write this as:

$$\frac{e_1}{e_0} = \frac{1 + \text{Inflation}_{\text{Domestic}}}{1 + \text{Inflation}_{\text{Foreign}}}$$

where e_t is the foreign exchange rate at time t (value of one unit of foreign currency in terms of the domestic currency). How can global macro managers use this relationship? Say for instance that the current spot exchange rate is 1.3600 USD = 1 EUR, and that the *anticipated* inflation rates for next year are 3% in the U.S. and 5% in Europe, therefore, $1.3600 \times 1.03/1.05 = 1.3341$ USD = 1 EUR. This means that, over time, one should expect the Euro to depreciate against the U.S. dollar. The next issue is to determine the timing and identify a potential catalyst for this to happen.

Multi-strategy global macro funds

Investing large sums of money is usually not an issue for global macro players given their flexibility and the depth and liquidity of the markets they trade in; however, the reality is that past a certain fund size, it becomes prudent to add more traders and strategies. Thus, it should come as no surprise that the larger global macro-oriented hedge funds have migrated to a multi-strategy model which in turn has increased their correlations with funds-of-hedge-funds. In such a case, identifying precisely which *school of thought* their manager belongs to may be difficult. For this reason, we have chosen to approach the global macro universe from a trading perspective rather than from a classification perspective.

A DIRECTIONAL CURRENCY BET: THE ERM CRISIS (1992)

One would be remiss in discussing the global macro strategy without mentioning George Soros and the Exchange Rate Mechanism (ERM) crisis of 1992–1993. This was likely the first time the general public became aware of the existence of global macro funds and their actions.

The European Monetary System (EMS) was formed in 1979 by several European countries to coordinate their monetary and exchange rate policies. Among other things, the EMS created a fictitious accounting unit called the European Currency Unit (ECU) using guidelines established by the Exchange Rate Mechanism (ERM) agreement. The ERM was essentially a managed floating exchange rate system where the currencies of participating countries were allowed to fluctuate within pre-specified bands around a reference point (±2.25% for most countries, ±6% for Italy, Spain, Portugal, and the UK). Central banks were charged with taking appropriate measures whenever needed to keep the exchange rate within these bands. Since the ECU was fictitious, in practice the unofficial reserve currency – the German mark – turned out to be the most stable currency of the group. That is, the bands were effectively maintained with respect to the German mark and central banks were usually intervening by selling or buying marks against their respective domestic currency. In a sense, the role of Germany within the ERM was similar to that of the U.S. within Bretton Woods. Since there were only ten "direct" exchange rates among the 11 member countries, Germany was free to set its monetary policy, often forcing other countries to follow their lead even when it ran counter to domestic interests. In practice, the countries had effectively lost all control over their own monetary policies. When an exchange rate approached one extreme of the pre-set bands, the respective central bank was forced to intervene, using the country's reserves to maintain the band.

Since its creation, the EMS achieved (to a large extent) its main objectives. In 1992 however, the policy interests of Germany and the rest of Europe began diverging dramatically. German reunification created strong domestic growth, which drove German interest rates higher and ultimately pushed other European currencies to the bottom of their respective bands. By contrast, the UK was in its worst recession since the end of World War II, with unemployment rates well in excess of 10%. In the absence of the ERM agreement, the UK would have resorted to an expansionary monetary policy or a devaluation to get out of the slump. Unfortunately, they were handcuffed by the fixed exchange rate system.

While most market participants thought that it was impossible to build up enough pressure to force the British authorities to abandon the bands, a few speculators, led by George Soros and his Quantum Fund, decided to launch a speculative attack. In the summer of 1992, they sold a huge amount of British pounds in exchange for other foreign currencies. The Bank of England rushed to defend the band through intervention, but rapidly depleted its foreign currency reserve holdings in the process. On September 3, to replenish these lost reserves, the Bank of England was forced to borrow ten billion ECUs (i.e. approximately $14.3 billion) on the international market. At the same time, speculators began attacking the Italian lira, forcing the Bank of Italy to raise its discount rate from 12% to 15%.

Speculation against the pound culminated on September 16, subsequently referred to as Black Wednesday.[1] Exacerbated by uncertainties over a French referendum on European construction, massive speculative flows continued to disrupt the functioning of the exchange rate mechanism. The Bank of England responded by raising its base lending rate from 10% to 12%, then to 15% the next day, but both announcements had little impact on the intense speculative pressure. Massive interventions in the foreign exchange markets proved futile as well. Ultimately, Germany agreed to

---

[1] Although Euro-skeptics like to call it "White Wednesday."

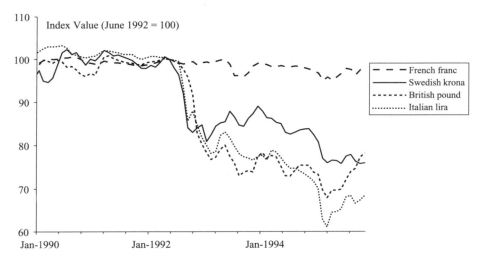

Figure 33.1 Evolution of exchange rates around the 1992 crisis

lower its discount rate by 50 bps and its Lombard rate by 25 bps, but by then it was too late. Although the Conservative government had repeatedly vowed otherwise, the Bank of England was forced to suspend participation of the pound in the ERM. Italy soon followed, causing a rapid and massive depreciation of both currencies. Spain too was pressured to devalue its currency by 5% and impose capital controls. The speculative attacks continued well into 1993 when the bands of several ERM currencies were widened temporarily to 15%, which meant they were effectively floating currencies. For George Soros and his $10 billion Quantum Fund, the result was a profit of more than a billion dollars in this directional bet against the British pound.

SPREAD PLAYS: CARRY TRADES

The basics

A **carry trade** is another very simple yet popular global macro strategy. In its simplest form, a carry trade consists of borrowing in a low-interest-rate currency and lending in a high-interest-rate currency without hedging the **exchange rate risk**. The goal of such a trade is to capture the interest rate differential, which can be quite substantial. As an illustration, if the funding currency carries an annual interest rate of 0.5% versus 5.25% in the target currency, a trader would borrow in the funding currency, convert the proceeds into the target currency, and buy bonds using the target currency. This would earn her a positive carry (or profit) of 4.75% *as long as the exchange rate does not change.* If the exchange rate does change, carry trading remains profitable as long as the target currency does not depreciate by more than the interest rate differential. This explains why global macro funds often establish carry trades between currencies that display *both* high interest rate differentials and low exchange rate volatility.

Currencies such as the Japanese yen and, more recently, the Swiss franc have been popular choices for the borrow side of carry trades due to their low interest rates. For instance, one can borrow yen at rates as low as 0.5%. By contrast, high-yielding currencies such as the South African rand, the New Zealand dollar, the Brazilian real or the Icelandic krona have been attractive currencies in which to invest.

Table 33.1   Example of the potential returns from carry trading against the yen (January 2005 to June 2007)

	Annual	Total
Brazilian real	41.8%	137.4%
New Zealand dollar	19.0%	53.9%
Australian dollar	18.1%	50.9%
Canadian dollar	17.2%	48.2%
British pound	15.3%	42.2%
U.S. dollar	12.6%	34.1%
Euro	10.7%	28.7%

Source: Bloomberg

When interest rate differentials are high, carry trades can be extremely profitable. As an illustration, Table 33.1, shows the potential returns of a yen-based carry trade (borrowing yen at the three-month rate and buying a three-month target currency) from January 2005 to June 2007.

To some extent, the profitability of a carry trade can be reinforced by the flows they generate. For instance, a yen-financed carried trade requires the trader to sell their borrowed yen to convert them into higher yielding assets in order to earn a profit. As large amounts of yen flow out of Japan into the global trading system, the yen weakens (all else being equal) while the target currency appreciates, thus reinforcing the cycle. However, we all know that at some point the carry trades will unwind. That is, traders will sell the assets in the target currency and convert the proceeds into the funding currency in order to pay back their initial loan. This typically occurs when one or more of the following happens:

- the funding currency interest rate rises, thereby increasing borrowing costs;
- the funding currency appreciates against the target currency; and
- the target currency investment does not yield as much as initially expected. This risk is particularly important in more aggressive carry trades where the investments made using the target currency consist of high-yielding assets, such as non-investment-grade corporate bonds or even equities.

When performed on a large scale, carry trade unwinding may be brutal and lead to significant amounts of financial market volatility, especially if many traders exit en masse from the same positions at the same time. For instance, in the summer of 1998, the Japanese yen, which had been depreciating versus the dollar for three years, started appreciating. Traders rushed to sell their high-yielding assets and their underlying currencies against yen to pay back their yen-denominated loans. Not only did the Japanese currency appreciate very sharply in early October as investors scrambled to buy yen, but prices of high-yielding assets tanked, forcing the Federal Reserve ("the Fed") to cut the Fed funds rate twice (for a total of 50 bps) in the subsequent month to bring liquidity back to the financial markets.

Carry trades: more advanced considerations

From an economic equilibrium perspective, it is interesting to note that carry trades should not be profitable. Indeed, investors at time t have the choice of holding risk-free assets denominated in their domestic currency or converting at the spot exchange rate into units of foreign currency, investing the proceeds in foreign risk-free assets and then reconverting into domestic currency at maturity. According to the **uncovered interest parity** (UIP), the interest differential between the two countries should equal the expected change in the exchange rate between their respective currencies. That is, the assumption of UIP postulates that markets will equilibrate the return on the domestic currency asset with the expected value at time t of the yield on an uncovered position in a foreign currency. Mathematically:

$$(1 + R_{\text{Domestic}}) = \frac{e_t}{E_t(e_{t+1})}(1 + R_{\text{Foreign}})$$

Thus, if the UIP holds, carry trades should essentially lose on the currency side what they expect to gain on the interest rate side.

For example, suppose the Euro is quoted at 1.2 USD, with one-year LIBOR rates quoted at 3% for USD and 3.5% for the Euro. The one-year rate is higher for the Euro implying that the market expects the Euro to depreciate versus the USD. Therefore if a U.S. investor attempts to borrow in USD and invest in the Euro, the extra 0.5% carry that is picked up will be lost when the transaction is reversed (i.e. when the proceeds from the investment in the Euro are converted back into USD). More precisely, using the above formula, the expected spot rate for the Euro is:

$$E(\text{Spot in 1 Year}) = \text{Spot Today} * (1 + \text{Euro}_{\text{1-Year Rate}})/(1 + \text{USD}_{\text{1-Year Rate}})$$
$$E(\text{Spot in 1 Year}) = 1.2 * (1 + .035)/(1 + .03) = 1.2058$$

Note that testing the UIP is relatively difficult as expectations of future exchange rates are not directly observable. It therefore usually requires additional assumptions on how market participants form their expectations. Nevertheless, in practice, data indicate a rejection of the UIP, particularly over medium-term time horizons. As evidence, a regression of exchange rate returns on the interest differential between two currencies often results in a statistically significant *negative* slope coefficient, which means that the currency with the higher interest rate tends to *appreciate*! As a result, carry trades (in which the investor borrows in the currency with the low interest rate and invests in the currency with a high interest rate) can be profitable on average over medium-term horizons.

An alternative version of the carry trade aims to exploit the **forward premium** of a given currency relative to another. Here again, the strategy is relatively simple and consists of comparing the forward exchange rate and the spot exchange rate between two currencies. If the forward exchange rate is higher than the spot exchange rate, there is a forward premium and it seems a priori profitable to sell the foreign currency forward. If the forward exchange rate is lower than the spot exchange rate, there is a forward discount and it seems a priori profitable to buy the foreign currency forward. Thus, currencies that are at a forward premium will be considered as funding currencies while those that are at a forward discount will be considered as target currencies.

Economists will argue that this new type of carry trade is in fact equivalent to the plain vanilla carry trade discussed previously. According to the **covered interest parity**, the forward premium of one currency relative to another is equal to the interest rate differential between them. This implies that currencies with a low interest rate are typically at a forward premium whereas currencies with a high interest rate are typically at a forward discount. Therefore, borrowing in currencies with low interest rates and lending in currencies with high interest rates is equivalent to selling currencies that are at a forward premium and buying currencies that are at a forward discount.

Another variation of the carry trade, the bond carry (yield curve) trade, typically consists of borrowing when short-term interest rates are low and reinvesting at higher longer-term interest rates *in the same currency*. As long as the overall funding cost does not exceed the yield on the long-term instrument, bond carry trades will generate a profit. These trades have been particularly attractive during periods when central banks have kept short-term interest rates low.

A MORE COMPLEX TRADE: CONTINGENT YIELD CURVE STEEPENING

Beyond the simple directional and relative value trades we have just presented, global macro funds often look for unusual price fluctuations that can be referred to as "far-from-equilibrium market conditions." These situations usually occur when a market's perceptions differ widely from the actual state of underlying economic fundamentals. They open the door to potentially profitable trades provided the fund manager can find the adequate instruments to express her view.

As an illustration, let us consider the following trade. In February 1999, following the 1998 Russian default and the collapse of Long Term Capital Management, financial markets were still experiencing tremendous volatility. The Fed had already lowered the Fed Funds rate twice to restore confidence and liquidity, but the European Central Bank (ECB) did not initially follow the second Fed cut. Although there was a high probability of further easing of interest rates in Europe should markets fail to stabilize, the implied volatility on the 2-year and 10-year German rates was priced at the same level. This essentially implied that markets had no opinion whether the yield curve would steepen or flatten on a sell-off. This was clearly a statistical anomaly, as illustrated in Figure 33.2.

To arbitrage this situation, several global macro funds started selling out-of-the-money puts on the 2-year swaps and buying out-of-the-money puts on the 10-year swaps. The result was essentially a zero cost bet on the yield curve steepening between 2 and 10 years. There were essentially four possible outcomes to this trade:

- German bond prices could continue to rally on the expectation of further cuts by the ECB. In this case, both option positions would remain out-of-the-money and the trade would expire worthless.
- German bonds prices could sell off in a parallel fashion. In this case, the gains on the 10-year swap puts would be offset by losses on the 2-year swap puts.
- The world stabilizes and German bond prices sell off led by the long end. This is the optimal case, as it leads to high profits for the strategy.
- The world stabilizes and markets sell off, led by the short end (i.e. rate hikes). The last scenario was highly unlikely given the market environment.

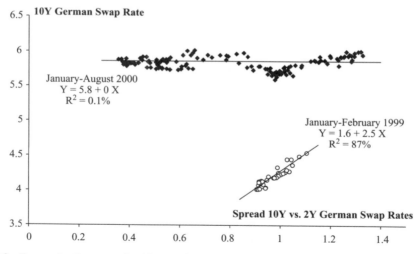

Figure 33.2 Regression between the 10-year German swap rate and the spread between the 10-year and 2-year German swap rate.

The overall result was therefore essentially a free contingent claim on the yield curve steepening. Global macro fund managers love these positions because they have very little downside and very large potential upside.

What was the final outcome of that position? As the international environment stabilized, yield curves began to steepen. Ultimately, the ECB did deliver a 50 bps "insurance" cut, which dramatically steepened the yield curve between very short-term instruments and two-year notes. Global macro funds were able to repurchase their short, two-year put position at almost no cost, leaving them long deep-in-the-money put position, which they ultimately monetized for a gain of up to 10%.

THE CASE OF EMERGING MARKETS

The 1997 Asian currency crisis brought to the foreground concerns about global macro funds and their possible role in exacerbating financial market volatility and disrupting emerging markets. Some Asian government officials explicitly accused hedge funds of attacking their currencies and causing their downfall. Specifically, Malaysia's Prime Minister, Mahathir Mohammad, argued that by accumulating very large and concentrated short speculative positions (referred to as "Big Elephants in Small Ponds"), hedge funds had destabilized the foreign exchange, money, and equity markets of Thailand, Malaysia, Indonesia and the Philippines. Several governments also raised concerns about aggressive and manipulative tactics used by some global macro hedge funds that might have compromised market integrity and interfered with a normal price-discovery process (see Brown, Goetzmann and Park (1998) for further discussion).

The International Monetary Fund (IMF) responded to these charges by examining the role of hedge funds in the Asian currency crisis. In the resulting study, Eichengreen et al. (1998) find no evidence that hedge funds played a major role in the events leading up to the Asian crisis, but many governments contested these conclusions as not fully coming to grips with the role played by hedge funds.

Political sensitivities aside, the reality is generally very difficult to fully assess the role and impact of hedge funds in emerging markets such as Asia. First, many hedge funds operate through over-the-counter (OTC) foreign exchange and money markets that are very opaque. Second, hedge funds themselves are opaque as they are not subject to mandatory reporting requirements. As a result, any assessment of the impact hedge funds may have had in Asia in the late 1990s needs access to some inside information (i.e. data), some market intelligence (such as off-the-record meetings with various prime brokers and traders), or requires making assumptions in order to build an econometric model.

Brown, Goetzmann and Park (1998) investigate the changing positions of the top ten global hedge funds vis-à-vis the Malaysian ringgit. They conclude that there were periods when hedge funds had large long and short currency exposures, but that changes in these positions had no relationship to exchange rate movements. In their opinion, there was no evidence to support a claim that hedge funds in general, or any particular hedge fund, led the charge against Asian currencies.

Using data on the returns of 27 large hedge funds during the Asian currency crisis, Fung, Hsieh and Tsatsaronis (2000) attempt to infer the currency positions held by the funds. They compare those inferred positions with the total capital flows for the Asian countries based on balance-of-payments accounts. They conclude that aggregate hedge fund positions were too small to have caused the collapse of the Asian currencies.

Lastly, the 2000 *Financial Stability Forum Report* on *Highly Leveraged Institutions* also attempts to assess the impact of hedge funds in Asia during the crisis. It expresses some concerns about the apparent large size and concentration of macro hedge fund positions and their implications for market dynamics especially during unsettled market conditions. It provides evidence on the aggressive activities of some hedge funds (talking their books, spreading rumors, aggressive trading at illiquid times, etc.) that could be seen as efforts to move markets. But it also points to the downside risk of using size to move a market. Large players such as global macro hedge funds face strong incentives to tailor position size-to-market size and liquidity to avoid moving prices too far when unwinding positions.

RISK MANAGEMENT AND PORTFOLIO CONSTRUCTION

In their youth, global macro funds were primarily one-man shops placing directional bets with a lot of leverage and very few risk controls. Their volatility was extremely high and large losses were frequent. For example, the Quantum Fund gained USD1 billion against the British pound in 1992, but lost USD2 billion during the Russian crisis of 1998. However, this old-style school of global macro fund gradually disappeared in the 1990s. Today's global macro managers still enjoy a high degree of flexibility, but risk management and a disciplined investment approach have become essential components of their activities.

The risk management culture has definitely changed the way global macro strategies are implemented. Most modern global macro managers aim to optimally diversify their portfolio holdings in order to reduce and control risk. In doing so, they often use a combination of Value-at-Risk measures and stop losses. The former quantifies the anticipated loss at different levels of probability and time horizons and has the advantage of being applicable across all asset classes and instruments, well as at the portfolio level. It is used to allocate risk capital across trade ideas and traders. The latter, stop-losses, are intended to impose rational and disciplined behavior, forcing a manager to exit from losing trades regardless of conviction. As summarized by Bruce Kovner, (the manager of Caxton Corporation), stop losses should be set "at a point that, if reached, will reasonably indicate that the trade is wrong, not at a point determined primarily by the maximum dollar amount you are willing to lose."

OVERALL STRATEGY RETURNS

Historical performance

From January 1990 to December 2008, global macro managers in the aggregate (as measured by the CISDM Global Macro Index) delivered an average return of 11.18% per year with a volatility of 6.66% per year. This gives the strategy an information ratio of 1.71, which compares favorably to the CISDM Equal Weighted Hedge Fund, the S&P 500 Index and Barclays Global Bond Index (Table 33.2).

Global macro exhibits a medium correlation to the average hedge fund (0.59 versus the CISDM Equal Weighted Hedge Fund Index) and equity markets (0.41 versus the S&P 500). Its return

Table 33.2   Performance statistics of the CISDM Global Macro Index

	CISDM global macro index	CISDM equal weighted hedge fund index	S&P 500	BarCap global aggregate bond index
Annualized return	11.18%	12.59%	7.33%	7.27%
Annualized volatility	6.66%	8.23%	15.78%	5.78%
Information ratio	1.71	1.57	0.54	1.28

Source: CISDM and Bloomberg

Table 33.3 Historical performance of CISDM Global Macro Index relative to traditional investments and to other hedge fund strategies

Year	BarCap Global Aggregate Bond (%Total Return)	S&P 500 (%Total Return)	MSCI Emerg (%Total Return)	MSCI EAFE (%Total Return)	CISDM Fund of Funds Diversified Index (%Total Return)	CISDM Fund of Funds Index (%Total Return)	CISDM Equal Weighted Hedge Fund Index (%Total Return)	CISDM Merger Arbitrage Index (%Total Return)	CISDM Global Macro Index (%Total Return)	CISDM Event Driven Multi-Strategy Index (%Total Return)	CISDM Equity Market Neutral Index (%Total Return)	CISDM Equity Long/Short Index (%Total Return)	CISDM Distressed Securities Index (%Total Return)	CISDM Convert Arbitrage Index (%Total Return)	CISDM CTA Asset Weighted Index (%Total Return)	CISDM CTA Asset Weighted Diversified Index (%Total Return)
1990	12.6	-3.1	-10.56	-23.2	7.51	7.47	6.54	-1.69	11.26	-3.31	10.18	-1.46	19.31	N A	27.29	19.8
1991	16.06	30.47	59.9	12.48	11.01	11.3	30.43	18.33	36.47	21.84	12.42	33.7	25.06	N A	16.82	11.34
1992	5.78	7.65	11.41	-11.85	12.04	11.93	16.83	17.37	22.35	19.36	7.92	17.38	18.25	16.68	9.9	-6.01
1993	11.08	10.08	74.86	32.94	23.33	24.21	30.29	26.38	40.88	26.47	9.73	21.56	31.25	16.56	19.86	22.12
1994	0.23	1.32	-7.31	8.06	-4.44	-4.42	3.53	5.23	-5.05	3.64	5.12	3.38	-4.3	2.2	-0.7	5.29
1995	19.67	37.57	-5.19	11.55	12.54	12.25	21.17	16.6	11.17	19.8	12.2	26.42	21.95	17.47	15.13	15.05
1996	4.92	22.96	6.04	6.34	16.83	16.68	23.24	15.97	9.86	22.31	13.69	22.34	21.05	14.75	14.64	12.73
1997	3.79	33.38	-11.59	2.05	17.09	17.2	21.79	18.17	15.97	23.56	14.87	23.74	18.67	14.25	10.06	7.09
1998	13.7	28.58	-25.33	20.34	1.71	1.65	3.97	5.5	8.11	3.9	11.16	9.57	-4.83	7.45	9.37	11.61
1999	-5.17	21.04	66.66	27.3	22.37	16.23	36.79	15.77	8.52	21.42	9.86	34.4	17.85	13.9	3.77	6.5
2000	3.18	-9.09	-30.71	-13.97	7.35	7.37	8.76	14.37	10.02	12.07	13.87	7.78	5.85	15.24	6.18	8.07
2001	1.57	-11.88	-2.37	-21.21	4.99	5.18	5.71	4.27	5.58	7.06	7.27	2.27	9.24	13.27	4.19	6.04
2002	16.52	-22.1	-6	-15.64	0.65	1.05	0.41	0.28	2.81	1.18	2.04	-4.72	6.85	8.89	11.95	12.38
2003	12.48	28.69	56.26	39.16	10.04	10.23	20.62	7.37	11.76	21.87	8.83	18.89	25.27	9.65	13.25	10.39
2004	9.27	10.87	25.94	20.69	7.23	7.12	9.97	7.01	4.48	12.12	4.97	9.86	16.64	2.47	4.24	3.95
2005	-4.48	4.89	34.53	14.01	6.36	6.47	9.84	5.77	6.65	6.63	7.11	8.86	7.44	-1.14	5	-1.08
2006	6.66	15.79	32.6	26.88	7.79	9.12	11.75	10.7	4.93	13.99	7.64	9.99	15.91	12.32	6.17	7.16
2007	9.48	5.5	39.78	11.62	9.52	8.69	10.5	3.74	12	6.57	6.5	8.48	5.26	3.97	9.14	12.01
2008	4.79	-36.99	-53.17	-43.06	-16.83	-17.05	-19.17	0.09	3.7	-19.05	0.61	-14.43	-19.55	-19.1	17.86	19.26

Source: CISDM

Table 33.4 Statistical properties of CISDM Global Macro Index relative to traditional investments and to other hedge fund strategies

1990–2008	N Periods	Geometric Mean (%)	Arithmetic Mean (%)	Standard Deviation (%)	Skewness	Information Ratio	Maximum Decline (%)	Correl Against CISDM Global Macro Index
BarCap Global Aggregate Bond Index	228	7.27	7.42	5.78	0.18	1.28	−10.07	0.15
S&P 500 Index	228	7.33	8.48	15.78	−0.69	0.54	−44.73	0.41
MSCI Emerging Mkts Index	228	7.81	11.03	26.64	−0.91	0.41	−59.5	0.47
MSCI EAFE Index	228	3.12	4.62	17.77	−0.57	0.26	−49.21	0.31
CISDM Fund of Funds Diversified Index	228	7.87	8.01	5.43	−0.89	1.48	−17.49	0.60
CISDM Fund of Funds Index	228	7.67	7.79	5.15	−1.34	1.51	−17.74	0.61
CISDM Equal Weighted Hedge Fund Index	228	12.59	12.89	8.23	−0.69	1.57	−21.13	0.59
CISDM Merger Arbitrage Index	228	9.81	9.91	4.55	−1.06	2.18	−5.74	0.45
CISDM Global Macro Index	228	11.18	11.37	6.66	1.15	1.71	−8.22	1.00
CISDM Event Driven Multi-Strategy Index	228	11.05	11.24	6.6	−1.55	1.70	−20.19	0.46
CISDM Equity Market Neutral Index	228	8.67	8.69	2.13	−0.52	4.08	−2.8	0.38
CISDM Equity Long/Short Index	228	11.82	12.2	9.27	−0.28	1.32	−17.04	0.57
CISDM Distressed Securities Index	228	11.77	12.04	7.7	−1.39	1.56	−21.24	0.49
CISDM Convertible Arbitrage Index	204	8.35	8.47	5.11	−5.08	1.66	−22.46	0.26
CISDM CTA Asset Weighted Index	228	10.55	11.04	10.55	0.63	1.05	−10.69	0.30
CISDM CTA Asset Weighted Diversified Index	228	9.46	10.1	12.03	0.39	0.84	−16.55	0.24
CISDM CTA Asset Weighted Discretionary Index	228	11.95	12.22	7.81	0.81	1.56	−5.6	0.35

Source: CISDM

distribution is positively skewed (+1.15), indicating relatively higher probability of large positive returns. Global macro has a relatively low maximum drawdown of −8.22%, or about one-fifth that of the S&P 500 Index and one-half that of the BarCap Global Aggregate Bond Index.

Good and bad years

Global macro funds generally had their best years in the 1990s, particularly during periods of currency or liquidity crises. In 1992−1993, as discussed previously, many successfully shorted the British pound and the Italian lira: average performance was +22% in 1992 and +41% in 1993. At that time, portfolios tended to be more concentrated and performance was highly dependent on the outcome of a very few trades that were often leveraged substantially. While high returns could be achieved, performance was extremely volatile. In time, managers significantly reduced their risk appetite. In 1997 for instance, they shorted several Asian currencies in the lead up to and aftermath of the Asian currency crisis, but only pocketed a 15.97% annual gain.

The only negative year so far for global macro was 1994 (−5.05%). In 1993, interest rates declined and bond markets rallied. As a result, most global macro funds built significant long positions in European bonds. But in early 1994, the Federal Reserve started aggressively raising rates, which caused global bond markets to crash, catching many funds wrong-footed.

While the late 1990s found most global macro funds in positive territory, several well-known funds closed their doors. Notably, Long Term Capital Management suffered significant losses as a result of the Russia crisis (1998) and Tiger Fund's value strategy struggled in the face of the growing NASDAQ bubble (1999).

Investors' appetite for global macro funds fell in mid-2000. High-profile operators such as George Soros and Julian Robertson shut down their macro funds and retired after posting disappointing performance numbers.[2] Other fund managers handed back capital to investors because they were losing their edge in large liquid markets and were too big to operate in illiquid markets. More importantly, by the mid-2000s, the lack of volatility across global markets had made it difficult for global macro funds to make money. Lastly, the number of liquid bond and currency markets (and hence opportunities) was drastically reduced with the introduction of the Euro.

After a long dry spell, the global macro strategy came back in favor in the second half of 2007 and in 2008 when global market volatility soared and the fear of a U.S.-led global recession became a real threat. Short dollar positions and long commodity trades became clear winners for global macro funds. But the global macro funds of today are very different from their parents' and grandparents'. Leverage is still employed, but the focus is more on consistency of returns and effective risk management.

---

[2] At their peaks, Soros and Robertson had assets of about $22 billion. Soros Fund Management announced a revamping of the Quantum Fund amid steep losses in technology stocks, billions in redemptions, and the departure of two top managers, Stanley Druckenmiller and Nicholas Roditi. Robertson announced in March that he was liquidating his funds and closing the doors on Tiger Management as his bets on value stocks backfired.

34

Equity Long/Short[1]

BRIEF DESCRIPTION OF STRATEGY

Equity long/short is an investment strategy associated with hedge funds whose managers buy equities that are expected to rise in value and sell equities that are expected to fall in value. Typically this strategy is implemented through successful fundamental stock selection and to a lesser extent by varying total net exposure.

Long/short managers generally find investments within the equity universe, though they may also employ derivative contracts. Their portfolios are typically much more concentrated in number of stocks (around 20−60), compared to equity market neutral or statistical arbitrage managers whose portfolios may have hundreds, or even thousands, of stocks. Additionally, long/short managers typically have much longer holding periods compared to the holding period of equity market neutral and statistical arbitrage managers.

Long/short managers may be broken into generalists and sector specialists. Generalists invest across a wide universe of stocks, whereas sector specialists tend to stay within a particular equity sector, such as financials, healthcare, technology, etc. Additionally, generalists may focus on a specific country or region.

Long/short managers have intimate knowledge of their stocks. For each stock within their portfolio, they are expected to know the company's business model, revenue generators, costs and expenses, product lines, comparative advantages, market opportunities, competition, and recent changes to the corporate structure. In establishing long positions, equity long/short managers look for solid companies with a defendable competitive advantage that are trading at a discount. It is common to hear long/short managers describe their strategy as "value with a catalyst" or "growth at a reasonable price."

Equity long/short managers are usually well trained in fundamental investing, often with previous experience at a large hedge fund (e.g. Tiger Fund) or as research analysts from top investment banks. Some long/short managers may come from the long-only mutual fund complexes or successful private equity shops. Regardless, these managers must be well equipped to analyze balance sheets and income statements, and make projections about a company's future earnings prospects in order to build discounted free cash flow models.

In addition to the general strategy described above, long/short managers may employ sector momentum, day-trading, corporate governance (activism), and market-timing strategies. Note that in practice, the classification of a long/short hedge fund is somewhat subjective, and therefore caution should be used when a hedge fund is categorized as such.

A SHORT HISTORY OF VALUE INVESTING

If Alford Winslow Jones is the grandfather of the hedge fund industry, then Tiger Fund's Julian Robertson should be the father of the long/short strategy. Only after his success with value investing did this sector truly grow to meaningful proportions, especially when a few of his top employees left

---

[1]This chapter was prepared by Jimmy Liew.

to start their own long/short hedge funds. Some of the former Tiger employees (referred to as Cubs) have enjoyed success employing this strategy, including Lee Ainslie of Maverick, Steve Mandel of Lone Pine, Andreas Halvorsen of Viking, and John Griffin of Blue Ridge.

Long/short managers are typically strong value investors who, like Warren Buffet, look to invest in a real business. Many times these managers are well-versed in analyzing 10-Ks and 10-Qs, income statements, balance sheets, and understanding their associated footnotes. They listen to company conference calls, perform independent research, and have a strong grasp of what it takes to run a successful company. Some have strong accounting backgrounds and others have law degrees, but the common skill amongst these long/short managers is that they can analyze a business in depth. Once they understand a business, they put together a forecasting model that predicts the future earnings and future cash flows. They value the company by determining an appropriate rate (commonly using the weighted average cost of capital (WACC)) to discount the projected future cash flows. They then compare this valuation with the market's assessment of the company. If the market's assessment is lower (higher) than the manager's, he would buy (short) the stock. A very important advantage for long/short managers is to have access to timely information through a strong network of contacts.

Value-investing techniques taught by Ben Graham and David Dodd at Columbia Business School have been around for many decades. But only a few of the top long/short managers have mastered the implementation of these techniques. Finding truly talented long/short managers is a challenging task. Disentangling alpha from beta in long/short returns is difficult due to the dynamic nature of their trading activities and positions.

Large-cap stocks are well covered by equity analysts making mispricings less likely. As a result, value-oriented equity long/short managers tend to focus their research on small and mid-cap companies. This is consistent with the empirical evidence indicating that these managers have a positive bias toward small-cap stocks.

It should be noted that knowledge of a manager's holdings is an important piece of information for an investor to use in evaluating the manager. Such knowledge is to some degree readily available for some of the hedge funds operating in the U.S. due to the Securities and Exchange Commission's mandatory reporting rule, otherwise known as form 13F. Filing of form 13F is required of institutional investment managers having discretion over $100 million or more in 13F securities. It requires them to disclose the names and positions of all 13F securities held long in their portfolio on a quarterly basis within 45 days after the quarter. A 13F security includes exchange-traded (e.g. NYSE, AMEX) or NASDAQ-quoted stocks, equity options and warrants, shares of closed-end investment companies, and certain convertible debt securities. It does not include, however, shares of open-end investment companies, i.e. mutual funds. To the extent that long/short managers do not change their positions frequently, the information obtained through the 13F reports will be current and relevant.

SIZE OF THE MARKET

As of December 31, 2008, the hedge fund industry had approximately $1.5 trillion of assets under management (AUM) according to Credit Suisse/Tremont. Credit Suisse/Tremont reports that the long/short sector represented 23.9% of the total, or roughly $358.5 billion of AUM.

Over time, the allocation to long/short has changed dramatically. According to Credit Suisse/Tremont estimates, long/short peaked in late 2000 when it represented over half of the AUM within the hedge fund industry (see Figure 34.1). Since then, however, it has fallen out of favor with investors, though it still represents a significant component of hedge fund assets.

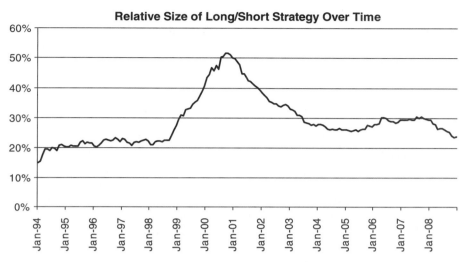

Figure 34.1   Long/short percent of total allocation to hedge funds over time. (*Source:* Credit Suisse/Tremont Hedge Fund Database)

MECHANICS OF THE STRATEGY

In this section, we discuss a traditional long/short investment process. Though the steps taken by any one manager will vary, essentially all long/short managers begin with an investment idea and end with portfolio risk management.

Idea generation

The first step, and by far the most critical, is to generate good ideas. Some managers screen the universe of stocks based on fundamental ratios or technical indicators so as to reduce the total number of stocks to a manageable size. Others read industry newsletters, research reports, market commentary, academic research, or other written sources of information to gain investment insights. Additionally, some managers attend investment conferences, trade conferences, and idea luncheons/dinners to develop new ideas. The value of a solid network of colleagues cannot be overestimated in uncovering and refining new ideas. Some may talk to friendly CEOs or CFOs while others may scrutinize form 13F reports for ideas. Any source that is publicly available can be employed for idea generation.

Optimal idea expression

This next step is instinctive to seasoned long/short managers. It consists of determining how best to express an idea. During this process, the manager may make the following inquires:

a. What trade should be executed to extract the highest return from their idea?
b. What price level will either confirm or negate the idea's validity?
c. Will the stock price move straight-up and become range-bound or will it slowly move upwards over many months?

For example, suppose a manager believes that the earnings of company XYZ will exceed the consensus forecast when released tomorrow. The manager must decide whether to buy the stock, buy call options, sell puts, or express the trade through sector Exchange Traded Funds (ETFs). In the interest of executing the optimal trade, the manager must further consider the downside risk and time frame.

Sizing the position

The next step works in conjunction with the prior step. Typically, a long/short manager has existing positions so she needs to understand how the new position fits within the context of her current portfolio. Sizing the position may require re-sizing the other opportunities within the portfolio. Positions are generally sized according to the level of the manager's conviction regarding the idea. If the long/short manager's conviction is high, she is likely to take a large position. On the other hand, if her conviction is low, she may build a toe-hold position to see whether the idea is a good one. She may then increase the size of the position, if the idea proves to be profitable.

Executing the trade

Many long/short managers will execute their own trades. That is, they will physically place the trade into the market via an electronic trading system or through their broker. The majority of long/short managers have extensive trading experience. They also tend to have a strong understanding of the intraday technical indicators and have experience determining when the technical environment is favorable for entering or exiting positions. When executing their trades, they must consider whether they should buy aggressively (lift offers), or sell aggressively (hit bids), or trade passively (join bids or offers). Other important considerations when executing trades include:

a. the liquidity of the underlying security at time of execution;
b. whether or not there is a major announcement due out that may move the market; and
c. the availability of the stock to be borrowed in the case of a short.

These managers possess a keen sense of the trade's potential market impact. Depending on the impact, there may be a trading cost associated with it. If a manager has a large order and tries to execute it all at once, she may move the market so violently that the ultimate average price paid would be very expensive. However, if she splits up the order into smaller pieces or executes at a time-weighted-average-price (TWAP) or volume-weighted-average-price (VWAP) throughout the day, she may achieve a better execution. The trade-off between alpha decay and order completion should be evaluated by asking what opportunity costs arise by waiting to execute. If the manager executes quickly, how much does she influence the market? For instance, the impact would be much greater for thinly traded stocks than for liquid stocks. Additionally, long/short managers should have a firm understanding of the fixed costs of commissions and exchange fees. Upon execution of the trade, long/short managers will usually examine their slippage reports (generated either internally or provided by the prime broker). Some trades may break (i.e. not be fully executed), requiring long/short managers to deal with their consequences.

Managing the risk

Once the order has been executed and the confirmations are checked, the portfolio positions are examined closely to see whether the investment idea is working. Corporate actions, such as merger announcements, spin-offs, and divestitures, require monitoring because they may change the risk profile of the company. Many long/short managers work with risk managers who go well beyond simply reporting the net and gross exposure of the fund. Many employ sophisticated risk models from various risk vendors such as Barra, Northfield, and/or Advanced Portfolio Technologies (APT), which assist them with the estimation and daily reporting of factor exposures. Additionally, standard risk reports are typically generated employing Value-At-Risk analysis (VaR). The VaR of the portfolio and all the various ways to slice the portfolio are examined, such as the VaR of the longs, shorts, sectors, regions, liquidity buckets, etc. Further, "what-if" scenarios are typically helpful in understanding the behavior of the portfolio in stressed markets (such as, "what-if this portfolio had been held during the tech-crash of 2000?"). Some of the smaller long/short managers may default to using their prime broker's risk reports since hiring a seasoned risk manager is expensive.

A brief commentary on the short position in a long/short portfolio is in order. Though short-selling is a defining characteristic of a successful long/short manager, long/short managers typically run net long. Empirical research has shown that on average long/short managers have positive net exposures to the overall market with a market beta around 0.5. Theoretically, a short position may lead to unlimited losses. Additionally, when a short position goes against the manager, it is far more painful than when a long position goes against the manager. This is best illustrated in the following example:

Suppose a long/short manager has two investments, A and B, and suppose he holds a long position of $100 in A and a short position of $100 in B. If both positions go against him by 10% in one day (A goes down from $100 to $90 and B goes up from $100 to $110), the manager loses $10 on the long A position and $10 on the short B position. Now if both positions go against him the next day by another 10%, he will lose $9 in A, as A goes down from $90 to $81 and $11 in B, as B goes up from $110 to $121.

Notice that the dollar losses in a long position become mitigated as the base decreases, whereas the dollar losses in the short position become magnified as the base increases. This subtle difference makes short-selling stocks more risky than buying stocks.

Long/short managers pay much more attention to their short-positions compared to the time spent managing their long positions. Other risks of short-selling include short-squeezes, forced covering, and regulatory measures aimed at limiting or preventing short-sales.

SOURCES OF RETURN/ALPHA

In this section, we examine the sources of returns from a long/short strategy. We begin with a macro perspective and finish with a simple illustrative example. The source of return that a long/short manager generates is a direct function of her investment universe, prowess, and process.

Since long/short managers typically invest in stocks, the investment opportunity set will be all possible combinations of stocks. For simplicity, we exclude derivatives and any private investments. Given that long/short managers can buy and sell short, we need to include all combinations of long stock positions and short stock positions. Additionally, long/short managers can be both under-invested and have a positive allocation to cash, as well as over-invested by borrowing cash to leverage. The possible number of combinations grows very large when we consider the continuum of allocation choices across long stocks, short stocks, and cash/leverage. Moreover, long/short managers can vary their exposures across time either by increasing and decreasing total leverage while holding the portfolio's composition constant, by changing the composition of the portfolio while holding the leverage constant, or a combination of both.

In summary, given the flexibility of long/short managers in making portfolio adjustments, their sources of returns are very dynamic. Below, we review basic investment approaches and investment opportunity sets.

Investment approach

Long/short managers have different styles of investing. Along one dimension long/short investment style classifications follow those of mutual funds such as value, growth, and blend. Their investment approach may also be classified as bottom-up versus top-down, or quantitative and technical versus fundamental valuation.

Value approach. Value long/short managers employ traditional valuation metrics, such as book-to-market, price-earnings ratios (P/E), dividend yield, and ratio of P/E to earnings growth rate (i.e. the PEG ratio) to look for undervalued companies. Managers following this approach tend to be contrarian and would invest in companies that are temporarily out of favor. Empirical evidence shows that value stocks tend to outperform growth stocks through many business cycles.[2]

Growth approach. Long/short growth managers look for companies with strong growth potential. They are attracted by top-line growth numbers and are willing to look past weak current earnings in the presence of aggressive sales growth. Often they invest in high-tech small companies because large companies in mature industries generally lack the same growth opportunities. Paying a reasonable price for growth companies is known as the "growth at a reasonable price" or GARP approach.

Blend approach. Finally, some long/short managers may employ both approaches, varying their investment process depending on the macro environment. Value stocks tend to have low betas relative to growth stocks. In down markets, managers may take a value investment approach while in rising markets, they increase their allocation to growth companies, thereby blending the two approaches. *Bottom-up approach.* Many long/short managers are **bottom-up** investors. They are essentially stock pickers who tend to have concentrated portfolios. They are less concerned with market timing and forecasting macro economic trends or relative industry performance. However, they are concerned with opportunities and threats faced by individual companies and focus on their strengths and weaknesses. This framework is referred to as a SWOT analysis (Strengths, Weaknesses, Opportunities, and Threats). It is common for these long/short managers to spend significant time away from their offices checking distribution channels, evaluating production lines, examining traffic at retail stores, etc. Bottom-up managers have researchers on the ground ferreting out any useful information that is not included in public documents. They perform detailed due diligence on the companies they hold in which they intend to invest. For example, managers may ask industry experts about their views on the company's products and processes, competitive advantages, patents, and political and regulatory risks. Typically, this strategy focuses on companies that have limited analyst coverage.

Top-down approach. Some long/short managers apply a **top-down** approach. A few broad investment themes drive this investment process. Managers seek to forecast macro-economic forces that would drive a sector's return and implement their views through diversified portfolios and ETFs. They tend to have strong views on the current stage of the business cycle, inflationary expectations, and monetary and fiscal policies. Real economy drivers are important to top-down managers. They spend less time on company specific analysis. Examples of the type of inquiries they may make are:

- When will the Baltic Exchange Dry Index (shipping rates) recover?
- What impact might Chinese government initiatives have on U.S. companies?
- Is India poised to lead the global recovery?
- As oil prices decline and global economic growth stalls, what are the implications for the U.S. stock markets and the oil sector performance?
- What is the impact of expansionary monetary policy on global financial institutions?

---

[2] For data on the performance of value versus growth stocks as well as return to momentum strategy, see http://mba.tuck.dartmouth.edu/pages/faculty/ken.french/

Top-down long/short managers have strong understanding of macro-economic forces and their impact of financial markets. They understand various interactions among different segments of capital markets: lead-lag relationships between fixed income, currency, commodities, real estate, and stock market sectors.

Quantitative approach. Some long/short managers start with a quant screen on the universe of stocks. These screens are generally based on self-constructed/proprietary rankings of various firm characteristics. Typically, these rankings employ historical balance sheet and income statement information variables, as well as forward estimates from analysts. For example, it is not uncommon to use future estimates of earnings, estimates of cash flow, estimates of sales, earnings surprises, and the strength of the analyst's prediction record in the construction of the final ranking. Analysts' rating of stocks may also be part of the initial inputs, such as Value Line and Investor's Business Daily ratings for U.S. stocks. Once the inputs have been determined, z-scoring and Winsorizing techniques are often performed in order to standardize firms' characteristics across the different measurement scales. Long/short managers will employ their own proprietary weighting scheme on the normalized variables and sort stocks belonging to their investment universe to obtain a short-list of stocks for further examination.

Z-scoring is a common technique that transforms the original data into standardized dimensionless quantities. Standardization occurs as original variables are transformed by subtracting the sample mean and then dividing this differential by the sample standard deviation. Practitioners often refer to z-scores as normalized variables because the variables have a mean of zero and a standard deviation of one. For instance, price-to-earnings ratios and price-to-sales ratios are significantly different in terms of scale. To rank stocks along these two dimensions, all price-to-earnings and price-to-sales ratios are normalized across all firms. Thus, a firm with a price earnings ratio of zero is considered to be in the middle quintile along its own dimension and so will be a firm with a price-to-sales ratio of zero.

A z-score of above three or below negative three may be **Winsorized** by setting outliers back to three or negative three, respectively. For example, suppose that upon z-scoring, we get values of -1.0, 2.4, 3.3, and -5.0 for price-to-earnings ratio of four different firms. After Winsorizing, we would get z-scores values of -1.0, 2.4, 3.0, and -3.0. Winsorizing the outliers is a common procedure employed to account for variables that are too extreme. The extreme outliers cause difficulties when z-scored variables are combined to produce a final score.

The quantitative screens are commonly the first step in the investment process of equity long/short managers. This step yields a shortlist of companies that are subject to further investigation by the portfolio manager and her research team. Some other approaches to portfolio construction discussed here may be considered to be part of the more general quantitative approach. For instance, value and momentum approaches to portfolio construction are considered to be a type of quantitative investment approach by Asness (2008) (see below).

Valuation based approach.[3] The goal of this approach is to determine the value of a company's stock based on forecasted sales, expenses, and earnings. These forecasts provide an estimated cash flow stream which is discounted to arrive at a value of the company. The equity value is found after subtracting the value of the company's debt. Given that forecasting the future is challenging at best, analysts may generate a set of valuations based on a good, medium, and bad scenarios, and then use the weighted average of these valuations, where weights correspond to the probability of the scenarios occurring. An example using of a good (bad) scenario is assuming a high (low) growth in company sales.

---

[3] Valuation techniques are readily available via a very useful website run by Professor Damodaran of NYU: http://pages.stern.nyu.edu/~adamodar/.

Momentum approach.[4] Academics have documented that one of the stronger existing anomalies is sector and company price **momentum**. That is, companies and sectors that have performed well in the past tend to continue to perform well in the future and sectors and companies that have performed poorly in the past tend to continue to underperform in the future. There is other literature that has extended this finding to include international sectors and companies as well. Some long/short momentum managers have capitalized on this persistence in good and bad performance across sectors by creating funds that aim to trade momentum across sectors.

As stated, individual stock momentum has been well documented in academic literature. Unfortunately, it appears that much of the momentum-based alpha at the stock level disappears once real-world constraints are added. Given that single-stock momentum tends to be a high-turnover trading strategy, much of the alpha vanishes once transaction costs and market impact costs are taken into account. The academic literature has also shown that trying to scale up such a strategy is very difficult since much of the alpha comes from thinly-traded stocks, which limits the capacity of such single-stock momentum strategy. Some managers who base their strategy purely on technical indicators such as trend, countertrend, momentum, and relative strength may be considered momentum investors. However, momentum signals will be one of many that these managers use to design their trading strategy.

Some managers may combine one or two of the above strategies. Perhaps the most well known of these combinations is momentum and value investing. The question that arises is, what are the sources of returns to these two strategies? Are there natural risk premiums attached to the stocks that are invested in based on these two strategies or are the sources of returns the result of market irrationality? Some would argue that value and momentum are associated with risk factors and thus returns to these two factors are consistent with efficient markets. Another argument is that returns to these factors represent market anomalies and therefore they are not consistent with efficient markets. Therefore, these returns may disappear once investors learn about them. Finally, some would argue that there are no systematic significant returns to these two investment strategies and observed returns are either too small to cover transaction and market impact costs or are just the result of data mining and will not be present going forward.

Asness (1997, 2008) argues that historical evidence is too strong and therefore the last argument can be ruled out. However, it is not possible to use available historical evidence to convincingly reject one of the other two arguments. Asness provides evidence that a momentum strategy based on buying stocks that have performed well during the last 12 months and shorting the stocks that have performed poorly during the same period has outperformed broad equity indices by about 150% between January 1990 and December 2008. Further these gains have been rather consistent during this time period. On the other hand, a value investment strategy based on buying stocks with high book-to-market ratios and shorting stocks with low book-to-market ratios has outperformed broad equity indices by 50% for the same time period. This strategy, however, performed poorly during the tech bubble of 1998−2000. Asness has argued that combining momentum and value strategies is much more effective than just employing momentum or value strategies separately. Given that these strategies are not perfectly correlated, diversification benefits are realized over time through the 50/50 combined portfolio of momentum and value strategies. A 50/50 combination of the two strategies ends up with a higher compounded rate of return because of the lower volatility of the combination (the combination's outperformance is 200% over the same time period). Furthermore, Asness (2008) states that momentum and value work across not only stocks, but also across bonds, currencies,

---

[4] For evidence supporting the presence of momentum, see Carhart (1997), Chan *et al.* (1996), Asness (1997, 2008). For evidence on momentum in international markets see Rouwenhorst (1998) and Ngo and Jory (2008). Finally, for references on the limits on momentum, see Conrad and Kaul (1993) and Lee and Swaminathan (2000).

and commodities. However, as pointed out by Asness, these results are likely to overestimate the performance of these two strategies because they do not account for transaction costs and market impact. Further, leverage has to be used to create these results. The interest cost of leverage is accounted for in generating these performance figures, the possibility that leverage may not be available at all times or that leverage may have to be reduced during periods of market stress has not been taken into account.

Sector investment approach. Sector funds are typically run by managers who used to be sector analysts for investment banks and brokerage firms. Most of these research analysts have been following a group of stocks within their industry specialization for many years. Portfolios are constructed by buying the stronger players within a given sector and selling the weaker ones. The popular sector funds focus on areas where highly specialized skills are necessary, such as in financials, health care, bio tech, technology, real estate, and energies, etc.

Corporate governance (activists) approach. Activists are long/short managers who take a very public stance on their investment. They are open about criticizing current management and the board. Research has shown that they are quite effective in changing the composition of a company's board of directors and they generally get existing management to adopt recommended changes to the corporate structure.[5] Such changes can favor one group of stakeholders over another. For example, an activist manager may recommend increasing dividends, benefiting shareholders to the detriment of bond holders. A recent study[6] uses data from 2001 to 2006 to report that activist hedge funds in the U.S. propose strategic, operational, and financial remedies and attain success or partial success in two-thirds of the cases. The excess (abnormal) stock return experienced by these target firms upon the announcement of the proposal made by an activist hedge fund that has taken a significant position in them is approximately 7%, with no reversal during the subsequent year. Further, it was reported that target firms experience increases in payout, operating performance, and higher CEO turnover after activism. The authors confirm that hedge funds who classify themselves as activist funds experienced significant positive return during the same time period. The excess returns earned by these funds significantly exceed the returns to all hedge funds and the returns earned by equity-oriented hedge funds.

Investment opportunity set

Examining a manager's investment opportunity set is another way to understand the sources of returns. Does the long/short manager tend to look for opportunities only in small cap stocks? Does the manager invest only in emerging markets? These questions reveal what underlying securities the manager may hold. Understanding the potential holdings of a long/short manager is a key component to understanding the sources of returns.[7]

Long/short managers typically have a comfort area of investing. Making the following types of inquiries can help in determining what that comfort area is.

- Do you invest in micro-caps, small-caps, medium-caps, or large-caps?
  - Which capitalization areas are you most comfortable with?
- What about the regional location of companies?
  - Do you invest in only domestic U.S. companies, or do you invest in pan-European or Asian companies?

---

[5] See Bray *et al.* (2008).

[6] See above.

[7] Standard and Poor's and MSCI are two companies that have very detailed classifications for equities. Their classification details can be found on their websites and a preview may be helpful to better understand the different classification schemes for equities as only a cursory review of the classification of equities will be discussed here.

Some long/short managers specialize in emerging markets and staff local offices within these markets to help research local companies. Others may trade emerging markets from abroad. For example, it is not uncommon to find long/short hedge funds based out of Singapore that trade across emerging Asia. As mentioned previously, some long/short managers are specialist investors remaining exclusively within certain sectors while others are generalists investing across sectors and countries. If one examines the long/short manager's prior experience and where she has been investing, one can obtain a good sense of where she will be investing going forward. Long/short managers typically stick to their comfort zones when it comes to their potential investment opportunity set. This is understandable considering that knowledge is accumulated over time with regard to specific equity markets.

Simplified example of return attribution

Total returns for long/short managers can be precisely decomposed and attributed to the following four components from the long positions and five components from the short positions.

- Returns/costs from long positions:
  - Price appreciation/depreciation
  - Dividends received
  - **Margin cost** of **longs** if leveraged
  - Interest earned on cash
- Returns/costs from short positions:
  - Price depreciation/appreciation
  - Short rebate
  - Cost to borrow shares, which is higher if securities are difficult to borrow
  - Dividend payments to buyers of borrowed shares
  - **Margin cost** of **shorts** if leveraged

Consider an overly simplified long/short manager with $100 of assets under management. The fund only has two positions:

- Long $100 of Company XYZ, where XYZ pays a $2 dividend.
- Short $50 of Company ABC, where ABC pays a $1 dividend.

Suppose we wanted to attribute the total performance of this long/short fund over a given specific period of one year. We also assume that no other trades were executed over that year.

Suppose XYZ goes up 10% over the year and ABC goes down by 5% over the same year. Also suppose that the **short rebate**[8] is 2% per year and the cost to borrow the ABC shares is 0.50% per year. To simplify the matter, suppose we were a good client so our prime broker charged us on only 30% of our total short amount at a rate of 3% per year.

Dollar returns from long position (XYZ):	
Price appreciation/depreciation	+$10 (= $110 − $100)
Dividends received	+$2
Margin cost of longs if leveraged	$0
Interest earned on cash	$0
Total dollar from long position:	+$12

---

[8] The rate of return paid on collateral when shares are borrowed.

Dollar returns from short position (ABC)

Price appreciation/depreciation	+$2.50 (= $50 − $47.50)
Short rebate	+$1 (= 0.02∗$50)
Cost to borrow shares	−$0.25 (= 0.005∗$50)
Dividend payments	−$1
Margin cost of shorts if leveraged	−$0.45 (= 0.3∗$50∗0.03)
Total dollar from short position:	+$1.8
Total dollars	+**$13.80**

In the above scenario, we would have earned 13.8% gross returns for our investors. Notice that we were fully invested on the long-side so we did not have any interest income earned on cash. It should be noted that margin requirements vary across long/short managers, with better capitalized funds typically receiving better rates.

The prime broker will normally examine the portfolio characteristics to determine margin specifications with more balanced long/short portfolios typically receiving lower rates. Many of these rates are negotiated and will vary with the perceived economic borrowing and lending conditions. We have seen periods where prime brokers cut back on the leverage they provide their hedge fund clients. As investment banks convert to commercial banks, we might see a further decline in leverage provided to hedge funds.

When returns from a long/short manager are decomposed by an attribution analysis, the largest contributors should typically be the price appreciation/depreciation corresponding to the underlying long and short positions, reflecting the manager's stock selection skills. If this is not the case, then the manager should be thoroughly reviewed, as long/short managers are typically hired for their stock-selection abilities, and not for their abilities to generate returns from non-stock-related activities.

COMPARISON TO OTHER EQUITY STRATEGIES

Equity market neutral strategy

In general, long/short managers generate returns that have a higher correlation to the market compared to those generated by equity market neutral managers. Equity market neutral managers are much more vigilant about keeping their long and short positions balanced. That is, equity market neutral managers are better at keeping the value of long positions ("dollar longs") equal to the value of short positions ("dollar shorts") and/or keeping the beta on the long-side equal to the beta on the short-side. Equity market neutral managers may be sector neutral as well, meaning that within a given sector they have long and short positions that are balanced. With all this neutrality, equity market neutral managers will run at a much higher leverage than long/short managers.

Equity market neutral managers are typically familiar with the latest academic and industry research on financial anomalies and behavioral finance. Some of these **anomalies** include:[9]

- Book-to-market: Stocks of companies possessing high book-to-market ratios tend to outperform stocks of companies with low book-to-market ratios.
- Market-capitalization: The finding that stocks of companies with low market capitalization (i.e. small stocks) on average outperform stocks of large capitalization companies.

---

[9] For a recent review of the literature on the most important anomalies, see Fama and French, "Dissecting Anomalies," *The Journal of Finance*, Volume 63, Issue 4, August 2008, pp. 1653–1678.

- Accruals: The finding that higher accruals predict lower stock returns. That is, those companies whose reported accounting profits are significantly higher (lower) than their reported cash flows tend to underperform (outperform) the market over the next 12 months.
- Post earning announcement drift: The continuation of abnormal returns in the direction of an earning's surprise for several months after earnings are announced.
- Momentum: The empirical finding that sectors and stocks that have performed well in the past tend to continue to perform well in the future and sectors and stocks that have performed poorly in the past tend to continue to underperform in the future.

Many of these anomalies were discovered by academics when they were testing the validity of the Capital Asset Pricing Model (CAPM). The CAPM states that an investment's expected return is directly related to its beta. The higher (lower) the beta, the higher (lower) the expected return. The CAPM is a cross-sectional relationship between risk as measured by beta and expected return. Beta, however, must be estimated using a time-series regression. Several anomalies have been found to contradict the CAPM's single factor assumption. The two of the most famous anomalies are firm market capitalization ("size") and book-to-market ("value"). In their work, Fama and French find evidence contradicting the CAPM by identifying the presence of the size factor and the value factor. Moreover, these factors were priced even in the presence of the market factor (the major source of risk in the CAPM).

Equity market neutral managers are well versed in employing multifactor models for both risk management purposes, as well as simplifying optimization procedures. Ross' Arbitrage Pricing Theory (APT) lays down the theoretical foundation for extending the single-factor CAPM to a multifactor model. The identity of the factors was left unanswered, however. Equity multifactor models are typically constructed from either fundamental factors, statistically-determined factors, macro factors, or return-based factors. In practice, factor models are typically purchased from well-known vendors or are constructed in-house.

In its simplest form, the APT assumes that stock returns are generated by a linear factor model of the following form:

$$r_i = a_i + \beta_{i1} \times F_1 + \ldots + \beta_{ik} \times F_k + e_i,$$

where, r_i is the monthly rate of return on stock i, a_i is the expected (average) rate of return on stock i, F_k for $k = 1, 2 \ldots$ is the unexpected rate of return on factor k, β_{ik} measures the exposure of stock i to unexpected changes in factor k, and e_i is that portion of the unexpected return on the stock that cannot be explained by the factors (idiosyncratic risk). It is important to note that the number of factors should be rather limited for the model to be of any use. The APT then argues that the risk premium on stock i is related to its exposures to various factors. In other words,

$$a_i - r_f = \lambda_1 \times \beta_{i1} + \ldots + \lambda_k \times \beta_{ik},$$

where r_f is the riskless rate and λ_k is the risk premium associated with factor k.

One potential application of APT is to tilt the portfolio in the direction of those factors that have relatively high risk premiums attached to them and then hedge the market risk of the portfolio by taking short positions in stocks that do not have large exposure to those high risk premium factors. Of course, if one agrees with the conclusion of the APT that sources of returns are related to factor exposures of funds, then funds will not be able to have alphas unless they are able to find stocks such that their current prices do not fully reflect their risk exposures. That is,

$$a_i - r_f > \lambda_1 \times \beta_{i1} + \ldots + \lambda_k \times \beta_{ik}$$

or

$$a_i - r_f < \lambda_1 \times \beta_{i1} + \ldots + \lambda_k \times \beta_{ik}$$

If such stocks can be identified, the portfolio manager may be able to create portfolios that have no or very little factor exposure while earning a rate of return that is above the riskless rate.

Equity market neutral managers have a good sense of mean-variance optimization benefits and shortfalls. One of these shortfalls arises from the large number of stocks that need to be incorporated in the optimization procedure. Factor models help reduce the dimensionality problem associated with optimizing over a large number of stocks. In practice, many of the top equity market neutral shops incorporate such models into their optimization procedures.

Equity market neutral "quants" typically spend their time forecasting expected returns and examining the stability of the correlations estimated by the variance-covariance matrix. When their models and preferred version of the mean-variance optimization generate targeted positions, the hope is that the positions are robust and not overly fit. A major problem in any optimization that is based on limited historical observations is to over-fit the data because this will result in poor out-of-sample performance of the model.

Equity market neutral managers constantly seek factors that are not well known because following the crowd can have disadvantages. Factors such as HML (high book-to-market minus low book-to-market), SMB (small stocks minus big stocks), and UMD (past winners minus past losers) are well understood and well utilized by this group of managers. When all the quants rushed for the exits in the great quant meltdown in August 2007, another factor emerged known as *quant-concentration*. Now some quants try to monitor other quants' positions so that they do not get into an overly popular position.

Applying less leverage and having a higher correlation to the market are two distinctions that differentiate long/short returns from equity market neutral returns. Additionally, long/short managers have a much deeper knowledge about the securities in their portfolios. For example, a long/short manager will likely have memorized all the important valuation ratios for the securities within her portfolios. Compare this to equity market neutral managers, many of which may not even know which securities they hold long and which they hold short. On the other hand, if an equity market neutral is asked about the nuances of optimization, he or she will give a thorough and comprehensive discussion of the matter.

To summarize, long/short and equity market neutral are two distinct strategies implemented by managers who have very different training and educational backgrounds. Long/short managers are typically skilled stock-pickers and have a very good sense of the realities of running and analyzing companies. Equity market neutral managers, on the other hand, are typically researchers who are more adept at computer programming, optimization procedures, and large empirical investigations. Both bring unique skills to the hedge fund industry and both have a large variation between their best and their average.

Long only and 130/30 mutual funds

Long/short funds typically generate returns that have lower correlation to the market, compared to that generated by long-only funds. This occurs because long/short funds can short and hedge away some of their net market exposure. Long-only funds do not have this ability to reduce their exposure to the market. Rather, a long-only fund can reduce its exposure to the market merely by increasing its cash allocation. This advantage to better control overall market exposure, as well as the ability to sell-short overvalued stocks, is such that the long/short strategy began threatening the traditional long-only world of mutual funds.

Given the popularity and effectiveness of the long/short strategy, the mutual fund industry has decided to offer similar long/short type investment strategies, known as **130/30 funds**. The main distinctions of the 130/30 fund structure compared to the traditional long-only mutual fund is that a 130/30 fund employs leverage and has the ability to short-sell. 130/30 funds have the ability to purchase stocks that are expected to appreciate in value as well as sell-short stocks that are expected to depreciate in value. This provides the 130/30 fund manager with the ability to express both positive and negative bets on stocks. This description is similar to how long/short funds operate. The 130/30 funds are the mutual fund industry response to the popularity of the long/short investment strategy.

Consider this oversimplified example: Suppose one invests $100 into a 130/30 fund. The $100 would be used to buy stocks similar to a $100 investment in a mutual fund. However, the 130/30 strategy implies that the fund will also short $30 of stocks and with the proceeds the fund will purchase another $30 of the long position.

One difference between long/short funds and 130/30 funds is the obvious constraint on the 130/30 regarding the size of the short position. Long/short funds are not restricted to a maximum leverage of 30% and a maximum shorting of 30%. Another important difference is government regulation in the U.S., where mutual funds are strictly regulated while hedge funds enjoy relatively lax oversight.

Advantages and disadvantages of four investment strategies

In this section, we discuss some of the advantages and disadvantages of four investment strategies. We compare equity long/short (LS), equity market neutral (EMN), 130/30, and long-only equity mutual funds (EMF). Our goal is to highlight the distinctions of each approach so that one gains a deeper understanding of these types of investment strategies. We offer general observations, and recognize that departures from our general descriptions may exist. The goal is to draw attention to distinctions between the typical LS, EMN, 130/30, and EMF strategies.

Correlation to market. EMF has highest correlation with the market, followed by the 130/30 strategy and then LS strategies, and finally EMN strategies. If an investor was looking for an investment with the lowest correlation with the market, of these four choices, she would look first to EMN managers. Alternatively, if an investor was only looking for the most market exposure, then she would look to EMF, and specifically index EMFs. EMN funds have a beta close to 0 while EMFs will have a beta equal to 1. The beta of LS strategies can vary. It is important to realize that 130/30 funds are designed to have a beta equal to 1.

Transparent daily NAVs. 130/30 and EMF are required to publish daily NAVs, while EMN and LS are not required to do so. If an investor needs daily NAVs for reporting purposes, then she would be inclined to examine the 130/30 and EMF. EMN and LS typically provide investors with monthly NAVs, perhaps weekly, but generally do not provide daily NAVs to investors. One alternative would be to use a managed account platform to invest in EMN and LS funds where daily NAVs are available.

Fees. Investors looking for low fees would be inclined to invest with 130/30 or EMF because their fee structures are typically fixed in the 0.5–2% per annum. LS and EMN typically charge the hedge fund standard, or a 2% per annum fixed fee and a 20% incentive fee. Incidentally, there has been heated debate over hedge fund fees. Many investors would like to drive them down below the 2%/20% standard, but there has been no meaningful change thus far.

Constrained max leverage and shorts. 130/30 fund managers, as previously discussed, have an explicit limit on how much shorting and leverage they can employ. If an investor needs to limit exposures, then she would favor 130/30 over LS. LS managers are not required to run their funds within strict guidelines. However, LS managers tend to stay within ranges of net positions and gross exposures that are consistent with the way they describe their particular strategy to investors.

Table 34.1 Summary statistics January 1990 to December 2008

	CISDM Equity Long/Short Index	CISDM Equity Market Neutral Index	CISDM Equal Weighted Hedge Fund Index	S&P 500
Annualized return	11.82%	8.67%	12.59%	7.33%
Annualized standard deviation	9.27%	2.13%	8.23%	15.78%
Information Ratio	1.32	4.08	1.57	0.54

Source: CISDM and Bloomberg

EMN will typically have the highest amount of leverage compared to LS, 130/30, and EMF. It is not uncommon for EMN to be 2- to 5-times leveraged. For example, if an investor invested $1, the manager may run $2 long and $2 short. Some may even run up to $5 long and $5 short. However, given recent market developments, the more highly leveraged EMN funds are becoming less prevalent.

Redemption/subscription liquidity. 130/30 and EMF have daily liquidity while LS and EMN generally have monthly, and sometimes quarterly, liquidity. LS and EMN often have notice periods for the return of capital, so the actual period of time it takes to receive those after submitting a redemption notice can be long. 130/30 and EMF, being mutual funds, are mandated to stand ready to honor redemptions on a daily basis.

Flexibility to vary net and gross exposures. LS managers have the most flexibility to vary their net and gross exposures. Typically, EMN funds run extremely neutral portfolios, and even if they vary their gross exposures, the net exposure should remain close to zero. EMFs cannot vary their gross exposures since they cannot leverage. 130/30 funds ostensibly overlay a long position of 100 with a neutralized position of 30 long and 30 short, so varying their nets and gross proves to be difficult.

It appears that 130/30 can be broken down into a long EMF and an EMN, i.e. for every $100, put $100 in EMF and $30 in an EMN that is levered 1 times. However, 130/30 managers are quick to point out that a portfolio created by combining a long-only portfolio with a 30 long/30 short portfolio is not the same as an integrated 130/30 portfolio. An integrated 130/30 portfolio accounts for correlations between individual long and short securities in its construction and will result in lower ex-ante tracking error with the market than the combined approach.

HISTORICAL PERFORMANCE

In this section, we present summary statistics of a long/short index and compare them to those of other indices. We employ the CISDM data and examine the CISDM Equity Long/Short Index, CISDM Equity Market Neutral Index, the CISDM Equal Weighted Hedge Fund Index, and the S&P 500. We examine the monthly returns over the period from January 1990 to December 2008, resulting in 228 observations for each index (see Tables 34.1, 34.5 and 34.6).

In Table 34.1, we find that over our sample period, the CISDM Equal Weighted Hedge Fund Index was the strongest performer with annualized returns of 12.59%. A close second was the CISDM Equity Long/Short Index, which had an annualized return of 11.82%. Following behind were the CISDM Equity Market Neutral Index and S&P 500, with annualized returns of 8.67% and 7.33%, respectively.

The S&P 500 was about 60% more volatile than the CISDM Equity Long/Short Index and CISDM Equal Weighted Hedge Fund Index while the CISDM Equity Market Neutral Index was much less volatile, with an annualized standard deviation of 2.13%. The low volatility in the CISDM Equity Market Neutral Index drove up its Information Ratio. It had the highest ratio of 4.08.

If we loosely interpret the S&P 500 as a proxy for long-only mutual fund performance, we can see the distinct benefits of the long/short strategy, represented by the CISDM Equity Long/Short Index. The Information Ratio of the long/short strategy was about three times better than the Information Ratio of the long-only mutual funds.

Next, we examine factor risk exposures for the above three CISDM hedge fund indices. We use the standard **Fama-French four factor model**.[10]

To review, the Fama-French four factor model is constructed by taking returns to four factor-mimicking portfolios of stocks. In general, factor-mimicking portfolios are used for two purposes. First, they can be utilized to measure the exposure of a portfolio or an asset to the factor that is represented by the factor-mimicking portfolio. For example, by running a regression of the excess return of a manager's return against the return to the factor-mimicking portfolio that represents the size factor, we measure the manager's exposure to this risk. Second, the factor-mimicking portfolio can be used to measure the return to the factor (i.e. its associated risk premium). For example, with the mean return to the factor-mimicking portfolio representing the size factor, we can measure the expected return to this factor. This can then be used to measure a manager's return from this source.

There are several methods for creating **factor-mimicking portfolios**.[11] The most common approach is to rank a large number of securities according to a characteristic that we wish to represent by a factor-mimicking portfolio. For example, suppose we wish to create a factor-mimicking portfolio that represents the price to earnings (P/E) factor. Also, suppose the universe of assets we wish to consider is the U.S. stock market. First, we calculate the P/E of all the stocks and then rank them according to their P/E. Next, we create two equally-weighted portfolios where the first will consist of 25% of the firms with the highest P/E and the second will consist of 25% of the firms with the lowest P/E. Finally, we short the high P/E portfolio and go long the low P/E portfolio. The return to this position, which requires no investment in theory, is the return to the factor-mimicking portfolio representing P/E. If the average return on this portfolio is positive, then we may conclude that the expected return to the P/E factor is positive. That is, low P/E stocks perform better than high P/E stocks. In the same manner, one can create factor-mimicking portfolios representing size, book-to-market value, beta, volatility, momentum, and so on.

In the case of Fama-French factors, the stocks are sorted on particular characteristics that have been shown to be priced in the cross-section of stock returns. The four factors are: excess return to the market; high book value minus low book value (HML); small minus big (SMB); and up minus down (UMD). That is, HML is the return to a long/short portfolio sorted on book-to-market, with high book-to-market stocks long and low book-to-market stocks short, SMB is return to a long/short portfolio, with small caps stocks long and large cap stocks short, and UMD is return to a long/short portfolio, with past winners long and past losers short.

For our hedge fund indices we estimate the following regression model:

$$r_{it} - r_{ft} = a_i + b_i \times (r_{mt} - r_{ft}) + h_i \times HML_t + s_i \times SMB_t + u_i \times UMD_t + e_{it}$$

That is, we regress the excess returns of our hedge fund indices, $r_{it} - r_{ft}$ (the dependent variable), on the excess returns of the market, $(r_{mt} - r_{ft})$, and Fama-French's three factor-mimicking portfolio

---

[10] Factor returns are readily available on Professor French's website: http://mba.tuck.dartmouth.edu/pages/faculty/ken.french/

[11] See Peter Zangari, "Equity Risk Factor Models," in *Modern Investment Management*, Bob Litterman (ed), John Wiley & Sons Inc., 2003, pages 334–398.

Table 34.2 Regression results for selected CISDM hedge fund indices January 1990 to December 2008

	b	h	s	u	R^2
CISDM Equity Long/ Short Index	0.438(23.69)	−0.021(−0.79)	0.213(9.01)	0.089(4.27)	80.9%
CISDM Equity Market Neutral Index	0.067(8.81)	0.046(4.23)	0.046(4.67)	0.057(6.59)	35.4%
CISDM Equal Weighted Hedge Fund Index	0.382(22.0)	0.038(1.54)	0.225(10.08)	0.106(5.40)	78.3%

returns: HML_t, SMB_t, and UMD_t. The residual e_{it} captures any other variation in excess returns that is orthogonal to the variations captured by our four factors.

We are interested in looking at the risk exposures given by the coefficients in the model. For this analysis, we are not interested in our intercept term a_i, which captures the risk-adjusted returns. Incidentally, the intercept would determine if a fund has statistically significant risk-adjusted returns sometimes known as alpha. The key to obtaining a meaningful estimate of a fund's alpha is to use excess returns on both sides of the regression equations. If the raw returns are used, then the impact of leverage and the cost associated with it is not accounted for.

Table 34.2 contains the regression coefficients of interest and associated t-statistics. We also include the coefficient of determination R^2 that captures how much variation in the hedge fund index excess returns is captured by variations from our four factor returns.

The results support our contention that the Fama-French model appears reasonable, as it explains 80.9% of total variation for CISDM Equity Long/Short Index. The positive loading on the excess return on the market of 0.438 says that CISDM Equity Long/Short Index is net long the market. The CISDM Equity Long/Short Index also has positive significant exposure to the SMB of 0.213, which implies that the long/short strategy on average has exposure to buying smaller stocks and selling larger stocks.

Table 34.3 Regression results for selected CISDM hedge fund indices (up S&P 500 months)

	b	h	s	u	R^2
CISDM Equity Long/ Short Index	0.453(10.41)	−0.007(−0.17)	0.219(6.92)	0.092(3.32)	60.0%
CISDM Equity Market Neutral Index	0.098(6.33)	0.074(5.48)	0.049(4.38)	0.068(6.97)	33.1%
CISDM Equal Weighted Hedge Fund Index	0.361(8.78)	0.087(2.41)	0.226(7.57)	0.117(4.50)	50.2%

Table 34.4 Regression results for selected CISDM hedge fund indices (down S&P 500 months)

	b	h	s	u	R^2
CISDM Equity Long/ Short Index	0.389(9.62)	−0.031(−0.78)	0.218(5.50)	0.090(2.57)	74.4%
CISDM Equity Market Neutral Index	0.048(2.50)	0.023(1.25)	0.050(2.66)	0.046(2.75)	25.9%
CISDM Equal Weighted Hedge Fund Index	0.450(12.74)	−0.020(−0.60)	0.200(5.79)	0.095(3.11)	81.2%

Table 34.5 Historical performance of CISDM equity long/short index relative to traditional investments and to other hedge fund strategies

Year	BarCap Global Aggregat Bond (%Total Return)	S&P 500 (%Total Return)	MSCI Emerg (%Total Return)	MSCI EAFE (%Total Return)	CISDM Fund of Funds Diversified Index (%Total Return)	CISDM Fund of Funds Index (%Total Return)	CISDM Equal Weighted Hedge Fund Index (%Total Return)	CISDM Merger Arbitrage Index (%Total Return)	CISDM Global Macro Index (%Total Return)	CISDM Event Driven Multi-Strategy Index (%Total Return)	CISDM Equity Market Neutral Index (%Total Return)	CISDM Equity Long/Short Index (%Total Return)	CISDM Distressed Securities Index (%Total Return)	CISDM Convert Arbitrage Index (%Total Return)	CISDM CTA Asset Weighted Index (%Total Return)	CISDM CTA Asset Weighted Diversified Index (%Total Return)
1990	12.6	-3.1	-10.56	-23.2	7.51	7.47	6.54	-1.69	11.26	-3.31	10.18	-1.46	19.31	NA	27.29	19.8
1991	16.06	30.47	59.9	12.48	11.01	11.3	30.43	18.33	36.47	21.84	12.42	33.7	25.06	NA	16.82	11.34
1992	5.78	7.65	11.41	-11.85	12.04	11.93	16.83	17.37	22.35	19.36	7.92	17.38	18.25	16.68	9.9	-6.01
1993	11.08	10.08	74.86	32.94	23.33	24.21	30.29	26.38	40.88	26.47	9.73	21.56	31.25	16.56	19.86	22.12
1994	0.23	1.32	-7.31	8.06	-4.44	-4.42	3.53	5.23	-5.05	3.64	5.12	3.38	-4.3	2.2	-0.7	5.29
1995	19.67	37.57	-5.19	11.55	12.54	12.25	21.17	16.6	11.17	19.8	12.2	26.42	21.95	17.47	15.13	15.05
1996	4.92	22.96	6.04	6.34	16.83	16.68	23.24	15.97	9.86	22.31	13.69	22.34	21.05	14.75	14.64	12.73
1997	3.79	33.38	-11.59	2.05	17.09	17.2	21.79	18.17	15.97	23.56	14.87	23.74	18.67	14.25	10.06	7.09
1998	13.7	28.58	-25.33	20.34	1.71	1.65	3.97	5.5	8.11	3.9	11.16	9.57	-4.83	7.45	9.37	11.61
1999	-5.17	21.04	66.66	27.3	22.37	16.23	36.79	15.77	8.52	21.42	9.86	34.4	17.85	13.9	3.77	6.5
2000	3.18	-9.09	-30.71	-13.97	7.35	7.37	8.76	14.37	10.02	12.07	13.87	7.78	5.85	15.24	6.18	8.07
2001	1.57	-11.88	-2.37	-21.21	4.99	5.18	5.71	4.27	5.58	7.06	7.27	2.27	9.24	13.27	4.19	6.04
2002	16.52	-22.1	-6	-15.64	0.65	1.05	0.41	0.28	2.81	1.18	2.04	-4.72	6.85	8.89	11.95	12.38
2003	12.48	28.69	56.26	39.16	10.04	10.23	20.62	7.37	11.76	21.87	8.83	18.89	25.27	9.65	13.25	10.39
2004	9.27	10.87	25.94	20.69	7.23	7.12	9.97	7.01	4.48	12.12	4.97	9.86	16.64	2.47	4.24	3.95
2005	-4.48	4.89	34.53	14.01	6.36	6.47	9.84	5.77	6.65	6.63	7.11	8.86	7.44	-1.14	5	-1.08
2006	6.66	15.79	32.6	26.88	7.79	9.12	11.75	10.7	4.93	13.99	7.64	9.99	15.91	12.32	6.17	7.16
2007	9.48	5.5	39.78	11.62	9.52	8.69	10.5	3.74	12	6.57	6.5	8.48	5.26	3.97	9.14	12.01
2008	4.79	-36.99	-53.17	-43.06	-16.83	-17.05	-19.17	0.09	3.7	-19.05	0.61	-4.43	-19.55	-19.1	17.86	19.26

Source: CISDM

Table 34.6 Statistical properties of CISDM equity long-short index relative to traditional investments and to other hedge fund strategies

1990–2008	N periods	Geometric mean (%)	Arithmetic mean (%)	Standard deviation (%)	Skewness	Information ratio	Maximum decline (%)	Correl against CISDM equity long/short index
BarCap Global Aggregate Bond Index	228	7.27	7.42	5.78	0.18	1.28	−10.07	0.06
S&P 500 Index	228	7.33	8.48	15.78	−0.69	0.54	−44.73	0.77
MSCI Emerging Mkts Index	228	7.81	11.03	26.64	−0.91	0.41	−59.5	0.67
MSCI EAFE Index	228	3.12	4.62	17.77	−0.57	0.26	−49.21	0.62
CISDM Fund of Funds Diversified Index	228	7.87	8.01	5.43	−0.89	1.48	−17.49	0.79
CISDM Fund of Funds Index	228	7.67	7.79	5.15	−1.34	1.51	−17.74	0.76
CISDM Equal Weighted Hedge Fund Index	228	12.59	12.89	8.23	−0.69	1.57	−21.13	0.92
CISDM Merger Arbitrage Index	228	9.81	9.91	4.55	−1.06	2.18	−5.74	0.67
CISDM Global Macro Index	228	11.18	11.37	6.66	1.15	1.71	−8.22	0.57
CISDM Event Driven Multi-Strategy Index	228	11.05	11.24	6.6	−1.55	1.70	−20.19	0.81
CISDM Equity Market Neutral Index	228	8.67	8.69	2.13	−0.52	4.08	−2.8	0.57
CISDM Equity Long/Short Index	228	11.82	12.2	9.27	−0.28	1.32	−17.04	1.00
CISDM Distressed Securities Index	228	11.77	12.04	7.7	−1.39	1.56	−21.24	0.68
CISDM Convertible Arbitrage Index	204	8.35	8.47	5.11	−5.08	1.66	−22.46	0.48
CISDM CTA Asset Weighted Index	228	10.55	11.04	10.55	0.63	1.05	−10.69	−0.05
CISDM CTA Asset Weighted Diversified Index	228	9.46	10.1	12.03	0.39	0.84	−16.55	−0.06
CISDM CTA Asset Weighted Discretionary Index	228	11.95	12.22	7.81	0.81	1.56	−5.6	0.14

Source: CISDM

Finally, some evidence exists that the CISDM Equity Long/Short Index has exposure to momentum, i.e. buying past winners and selling past losers, with a loading of 0.089 on UMD. Interestingly enough, the CISDM Equity Long/Short Index does not have statistically significant exposure to HML; the loading of −0.021 is not statistically significant with a t-statistic of −0.79. Long/short managers appear to be employing more sophisticated valuation techniques beyond just book value to market capitalization ratios.

The CISDM Equity Market Neutral Index, on the other hand, has a very different risk exposure to the Fama-French factors compared to the CISDM Equity Long/Short Index exposures. In particular, the CISDM Equity Market Neutral Index has a significant exposure to HML, indicating that these managers are net long value stocks and short growth stocks. As expected, the model does not explain as much of the variation of this strategy, the total variation explained being 35.4%.

Finally, the CISDM Equally Weighted Hedge Fund Index appears to yield results that are similar to the long/short strategy risk profile. That is, 0.382 exposure to the market, 0.225 exposure to long small cap and short large cap, and 0.106 exposure to buying winner and selling losers.

Up market and down market risks

In this section we examine how robust our risk exposures are over two different periods. We break our data into two periods, up S&P 500 months and down S&P 500 months. We then re-estimate our risk exposures (Tables 34.3 and 34.4). If the risk exposures are robust, then they should stay constant across our two sample periods. If the risk exposures are not constant, then we would expect to see large deviations across the two sample periods. Additionally, we examine whether long/short hedge funds are dynamically changing their exposure in anticipation of rising and falling S&P 500 monthly returns. By examining the results obtained from the up S&P 500 months and the down S&P 500 months, we find that our prior results for hedge fund indices are stable. For example, for the long/short strategy, the largest exposure was the excess return on the market. The estimated value of this exposure in up S&P 500 months is 0.453 and in down S&P 500 months is 0.389, compared to the full sample of 0.438. Also, the estimated exposure to SMB is 0.219 in up S&P 500 months and 0.218 in down S&P 500 months, compared to the full sample of 0.213. Finally, the estimated risk exposure to UMD in up S&P 500 months is 0.092 and in down S&P 500 months is 0.090, compared to the total sample estimate of 0.089. We can conclude that the full sample risk exposures are generally robust to segmenting the data by S&P 500 up and down months. Also, we may conclude that, on average, equity long/short managers do not appear to be timing the market by changing their factor exposures in down versus up markets.

35

Fund-of-Hedge-Funds and Investible Indices

APPROACHES FOR ACCESSING HEDGE FUNDS

There are essentially three approaches for qualified investors to obtain hedge fund exposure in their portfolios: self-managed, delegated, and indexed.

The self-managed approach consists of investing directly in a series of hedge funds. Unfortunately, this approach is not available for smaller investors who are constrained by the minimum wealth levels and sophistication standards required by regulators in many countries to invest in hedge funds. In addition, with more than 7000 funds in the hedge fund universe, many contend that this approach requires extensive resource capabilities to research the market, as well as sufficient experience and expertise to determine the appropriate blend of strategies and managers and to monitor them.

Many investors, therefore, prefer the delegated approach, which consists of buying shares in a fund-of-hedge-funds (FoHF). FoHF serve the following functions:

- **Manager selection**. The FoHF manager is responsible for selecting the strategies and the managers that will represent those strategies. FoHF managers may have access to "closed" managers and have insights with regard to strategies that are likely to perform better going forward.
- **Portfolio construction**. Once the strategies and managers have been selected, the FoHF manager has to decide on the allocation to each manager. The allocation will not only depend on risk return characteristics of the individual managers, but also on other features of each fund such as the lockup period, the liquidity of the positions, the size of the fund, and the length of its manager's track record.
- **Risk management and monitoring**. The FoHF manager will monitor each hedge fund to ensure that its performance profile is consistent with the fund's overall objectives.
- **Due diligence**. This is perhaps the most important function of the FoHF manager and it is the one that most investors tend to value most when choosing to invest in FoHF rather than directly in a portfolio of hedge funds.
- **Leverage and liquidity**. Some FoHF may offer their investors funding in order to leverage their investments. Also, some FoHF may offer liquidity terms that are more favorable to investors than those offered by the underlying hedge funds. In such a case, the FoHF may use their own lines of credit to allow investors to redeem their funds.

Investors who are uncomfortable with their FoHF selection skills can also select the third route: the indexed approach. In this case, they simply have to select a representative hedge fund index and buy a financial product (such as a FoHF, a certificate, a structured product, etc.) that aims to replicate the performance of that index. The advantages and disadvantages of each of these three approaches are discussed below.

CHARACTERISTICS OF FUNDS-OF-HEDGE-FUNDS

A FoHF is essentially an investment vehicle that pools the capital of several investors and allocates it to many different hedge funds with the goal of diversifying across a range of styles, strategies, and managers. When investing with a FoHF, investors delegate the management of their portfolio.

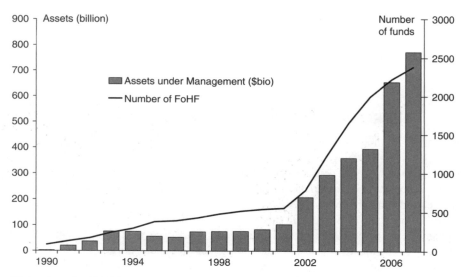

Figure 35.1 Growth of FoHF assets as a fraction of total assets in hedge funds. (*Source:* Data from Hedge Fund Research)

The FoHF manager is in charge of selecting individual hedge funds, performing a complete due diligence on them, obtaining capacity, monitoring risk and return, managing the overall portfolio, and reporting performance and other information to the investors.

According to *Hedge Fund Research Inc*, there were 2540 FoHF reporting to their database at the end of Q3 2008, versus 80 FoHF at the end of 1990 and 538 FoHF at the end of 2000. These FoHF controlled over USD772 billion, which is more than one-third of the hedge fund industry's assets (estimated at USD1.8 trillion). Their success was initially fueled by smaller investors who did not have the capital and resources to invest directly in hedge funds. More recently, the interest has been fueled by institutional investors such as pension funds, endowment funds, private banks, and family offices that are new to the alternative investment industry and prefer to utilize FoHF for their first allocation as a way for them to climb the learning curve.

Asset flow into the funds of funds industry (Figure 35.1) has been unevenly split between large and small managers. More than 80% of the assets run by FoHF are managed by less than 10% of the funds. Many of the smaller funds may have to close due to their inability to attract or retain adequate investment levels.

According to Xiong *et al.* (2007), FOHF performance, fund flows, and asset size are closely related. In particular, FoHF that have better performance experience greater capital inflows. The worst performing FoHF experienced net capital outflows while the top performing FoHF experienced net capital inflows. Moreover, 18-month Sharpe ratios have more explanatory power for capital inflows than Sharpe ratios measured over other durations or average raw returns, which seems to suggest that small funds that poorly perform literally have no future.

The approach to diversification is also a distinguishing characteristic in the universe of FoHF. Broadly speaking, FoHF can be grouped based on their number of underlying strategies and/or their number of underlying hedge fund managers:

- **Single-strategy FoHF** allocate their assets across several hedge funds following the same strategy, theme, or group of strategies. Their goal is to provide exposure to a particular subset of the hedge fund universe.

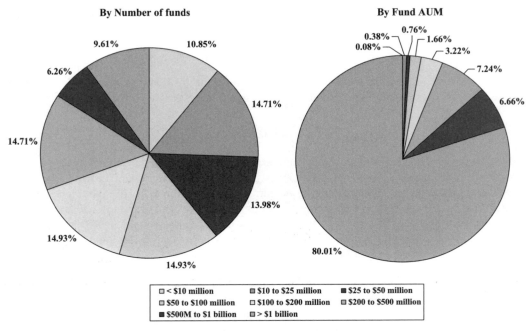

By Number of funds

10.85%

9.61%

6.26%

14.71%

14.71%

14.93%

14.93%

13.98%

By Fund AUM

0.76%
0.38% ─ ┌ 1.66%
0.08% ─ │ ┌ 3.22%

─ 7.24%

6.66%

80.01%

□ < $10 million	▣ $10 to $25 million	■ $25 to $50 million
□ $50 to $100 million	□ $100 to $200 million	▣ $200 to $500 million
■ $500M to $1 billion	□ > $1 billion	

Figure 35.2   Distribution of FoHF assets at the end of September 2008. (*Source:* Hedge Fund Research)

- **Multi-strategy FoHF** attempt to diversify their portfolio by allocating assets to several hedge funds that follow different strategies and are expected to be somewhat uncorrelated to each other.
- **Concentrated FoHF** typically allocate assets to a small number of hedge fund managers, i.e. five to 15.
- **Balanced FoHF** invest in a large number of hedge fund managers, i.e. more than 20 or 30.

Commercial FoHF databases are now widely available. This greatly facilitates information gathering and performance comparisons. Moreover, many experts feel that FoHF data are usually of a much better quality than data on individual hedge funds. In particular, some of the usual hedge fund "biases" are significantly reduced or even eliminated when applied to FoHF (see Fung and Hsieh (2002)):

- *No or little hedge fund* **survivorship bias**. FoHF provide audited track records that include allocations to both historical winners and losers, regardless of their individual reporting situation vis-à-vis a particular hedge fund database. For instance, the historical track record of a hedge fund that stops reporting to databases will remain included in the track record of all FoHF that have invested in that fund.
- *No* **selection bias**. An individual hedge fund may choose not to report to databases, but its track record is embedded in the performance of any FoHF invested in it. As a result, looking at FoHF databases increases the potential universe of funds captured.
- No **instant** history **bias**. When a FoHF adds a new hedge fund to its portfolio, the historical track record of that hedge fund will not be included in the historical track record of the FoHF.

Moreover, returns from FoHF are less susceptible to measurement biases:

- *Selection bias.* Most FoHF have an incentive to report their performance numbers to several databases in order to be on the radar screen of consultants and potentially attract new assets.

- *Survivorship bias.* The mortality rate of FoHF is much lower than the rate for individual hedge funds, and the performance differential between survivors and dead FoHF is also smaller when compared to single hedge funds. According to Liang (2003), the annual survivorship bias for hedge funds is 2.32% per year while the bias is 1.18% for FoHF.

As a result, FoHF returns are more likely to deliver a cleaner estimate of the actual investment experience of hedge fund investors than are single hedge fund returns or hedge fund indices.

BENEFITS OFFERED BY FOHF

Diversification. Prudent investing dictates that portfolios should be well diversified. Many investors lack the necessary asset size and expertise to invest directly in hedge funds and reach an appropriate level of diversification and risk reduction. By contrast, through a single FoHF investment investors can access a well-diversified portfolio, either in terms of managers and/or in terms of strategies.

However, the diversification level of a FoHF portfolio is not necessarily a straightforward function of the number of underlying funds and/or strategies. This is because hedge funds are not single securities. Instead, they are already-diversified portfolios of securities.

Numerous researchers have studied the impact of increasing the number of funds in a FoHF portfolio on various risk measures using a naïve diversification approach, i.e. random selection and equal weighting of the underlying managers. For single strategy FoHF, [1] the conclusion was that a portfolio consisting of approximately 3−5 equally-weighted hedge funds is usually highly correlated with its respective hedge fund strategy index. Moreover, such a portfolio reduces the overall strategy-specific portfolio risk to the level of the universe from which the funds are drawn. This clearly supports the idea, say researchers, of running relatively concentrated single strategy FoHF.

The same has been found to be true for multi-strategy FoHF. Lhabitant and Learned (2003, 2004) suggest that only 10−15 equally-weighted hedge funds are sufficient to diversify away most of the underlying manager-specific risk. Researchers conclude that this also supports the strategy of running relatively concentrated multi-strategy FoHF. *Accessibility and economies of scale.* The price of entry for investing in a single hedge fund is often a million U.S. dollars or even more, which makes them unaffordable for most individual investors. By comparison, minimum investment levels for FoHF are relatively low. This allows more individual investors and small institutions to gain access to hedge funds even though their capital base is comparatively small. Moreover, investors essentially share the costs associated with the manager selection process, reporting, and analysis with their FoHF co-investors. *Information advantage.* Because of their role as asset allocators, FoHF have the ability to access, collect, and interpret data gleaned from various channels such as data providers, prime brokers, and industry contacts. This gives them an informational advantage over non-professional investors. *Liquidity.* Investments in hedge funds are relatively illiquid, due to lockups, potential redemption gates, notice periods, and limited redemption dates. By comparison, the liquidity terms offered by FoHF are seen by some as more compelling. Most FoHF offer quarterly or monthly liquidity in normal market conditions.[2] Some FoHF even offer daily liquidity, either through a listing on an exchange or via an OTC secondary market that matches demand and supply. *Access to certain managers.* Access to the best talent and ideas in the hedge fund community is a scarce resource. The most desirable hedge funds are often closed to new investments. Most institutional investors do not have the necessary networks and protocol for obtaining investment capacity in

---

[1] See for instance Lhabitant and Learned (2003); Schneeweis, Kazemi, and Karavas (2003) or Schneeweis, Karavas and DuBose (2005).

[2] Note that many FoHF managers have provisions in their documents in order to limit redemptions if they need it.

these funds when it becomes available. Buying shares of an existing FoHF that is already allocated to these desirable hedge funds is the fastest way to participate immediately in their performance. **Negotiated fees**. Thanks to the power of their collective assets, some FoHF have successfully negotiated access to certain managers at reduced fees. This is normally beyond the capabilities of most individual investors. *Regulation.* In order to facilitate their distribution to a wider audience, some FoHF choose to register in locations that offer better investor protection than their underlying investments, even though the cost and administrative and operational burdens may be higher. This can often be reassuring for first-time investors and can ensure that they receive sufficient transparency, yearly oversight, and quarterly reports. *Currency hedging.* While the currency of choice in the hedge fund world is the U.S. dollar, several FoHF offer share classes denominated in various currencies with the currency risk hedged. Although institutional investors often wish to manage their own currency risks, many small or private investors prefer to be shielded from currency fluctuations and delegate the hedging aspects to professional managers. *Leverage.* Some FoHF provide leverage to their investors. They borrow money in addition to the capital provided by their investors and invest it into a portfolio of hedge funds. This allows them to produce higher returns in low-volatility periods than an unleveraged FoHF as long as the interest costs incurred are outweighed by the incremental out-performance generated by the leverage.

Educational role. Many first-time hedge fund investors look at FoHF not simply as an investment vehicle, but as a way of learning about hedge fund strategies and hedge fund managers. These investors typically switch to direct investments in hedge funds after a few years.

Professional management. Hedge funds are less transparent, less comprehensible, and less regulated than traditional mutual funds. It therefore requires dedicated resources to effectively seek out, analyze, select, carry out due diligence on hedge fund managers, construct portfolios, and monitor strategies and managers. These resources can be costly and many institutional investors do not have them, particularly when they just start investing in hedge funds.

DISADVANTAGES OF FOHF

Double layer of fees. An FoHF manager effectively passes on to his investors all fees charged by the underlying hedge funds in his portfolio, while also charging an extra set of fees for his own work. As an illustration, Ang, Rhodes-Kropf and Zhao (2008) estimate that in the TASS database, the average FoHF charges a 1.5% management fee and a 9.2% performance fee on top of the average hedge fund management fee of 1.4% and incentive fee of 18.4% for hedge funds.

Performance fees on portions of the portfolio. In a FoHF, the investor must pay performance fees for each of the underlying hedge funds regardless of the performance of the overall portfolio. So, if half the managers are down 10% and the other half are up 10% on a gross basis, the investor will still have to pay a performance fee to the positive performers despite no performance at all at the aggregate level.

Taxation. Because of their offshore registration, many hedge funds and FoHF may be tax-inefficient for certain investors in certain countries. As an illustration, in Germany, most FoHF invest in hedge funds that fail to meet the extensive notification and disclosure duties requested by German authorities. As a result, their gains are subjected to heavy penalty taxation which ultimately affects the investor.

Lack of transparency. Some FoHF managers do not disclose the content of their portfolio or their asset allocation. They contend that it represents what is colloquially called the "special sauce" they bring to the table and they are reluctant to reveal its ingredients. In such cases, it becomes relatively difficult for their investors to understand what is really happening in terms of risk and returns beyond the stream of net asset values.

Exposure to other investors' cash flows. FoHF commingle the assets of a number of investors. As a result, investors are affected jointly by inflows and outflows, since co-investors in the same fund may trigger cash increases or decreases or undesirable leveraging to finance redemptions. Custom portfolios for a single investor ("managed accounts") are not exposed to this type of problem. Further, to satisfy investors' requests for redemption, the FoHF manager will typically sell the most liquid funds first, leading to a potential change in the FoHF's style.

Lack of control. In an FoHF, investors give up control over how the assets are invested. Moreover, they lose the direct relationship with the hedge funds in which the FoHF invests.

Lack of customization. Direct investment in hedge funds allows investors to create allocations that fit their overall portfolio. For example, the pension fund of a bank may not wish to have exposure to distress or credit instruments because of the business risk of the pension fund's sponsor.

FOHF VERSUS INDIVIDUAL HEDGE FUNDS

One of the most important debates with respect to FoHF is whether or not they deserve their "fees on fees" and add value with respect to a randomly selected portfolio of, say, 20–40 hedge funds. In practice, there are essentially three ways for a FoHF manager to add value:

- *Strategically allocate to various hedge fund styles.* Running an FoHF is not just simply a matter of assembling a large collection of good managers. Even such a collection can still result in a concentration of risks, with somewhat illusory diversification if there is a high level of correlation in the trades or underlying exposures of these managers. The first and most important choice that an FoHF manager must make when organizing his portfolio is his long-term strategic asset allocation. This normally implies analyzing the long-term risk and return profiles of the different strategies, as well as examining the correlation of their observed and expected returns. The goal is then to determine an initial portfolio allocation consistent with the fund's long-term objectives and constraints. This task determines the long-run beta of the fund with respect to various sources of risks.

- *Tactically allocate across hedge fund.* Tactical Asset Allocation refers to active strategies that seek to enhance portfolio performance by opportunistically shifting the asset allocation in response to the changing environment. Many FoHF argue that they follow a top-down tactical style allocation process. In theory, this involves making three key decisions periodically: (i) what to do (e.g. overweight or underweight a particular investment style); (ii) when to do it (e.g. to implement the changes based on levels of certain indicators or factors); and (iii) how much to do (e.g. whether the overweight should be, for example, 1% or 3%). In practice, however, an FoHF is limited because of the underlying hedge funds' liquidity constraints, unless it invests only in the most liquid areas of alternative investments or uses managed accounts. This task therefore determines how the FoHF adjusts its long-term exposures in response to changes in market environment.

- *Select individual managers.* This involves the selection of individual managers within a strategy, as well as the decision of how much money to invest with each of them. While this seems very similar to a traditional stock selection activity, the reality is that FoHF managers often have to make a trade-off between their ability to add value through dynamic manager allocations in highly liquid funds and the potential contribution of less liquid funds (those with lockups, etc.). This task is the main source of added value for an FoHF manager.

Do these methods work in practice? As suggested by Ineichen (2002a), the potential to add value in a given market is often inversely proportional to the informational efficiency of the market and/or liquidity of the underlying instruments. It is fair to say that the hedge fund market is relatively

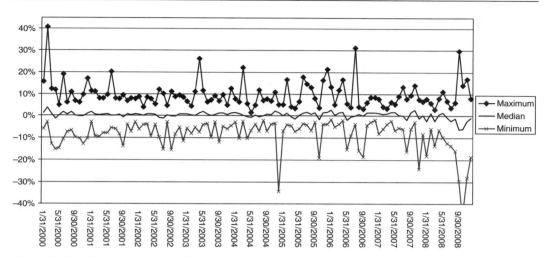

Figure 35.3 Dispersion of fund of funds returns (2000–2008): maximum, minimum and median. This chart includes FoHFs on CASM-CISDM that had data since 2000 (*Source:* CISDM)

inefficient – at least from an information perspective – and relatively illiquid. The result is a wide dispersion of returns between managers (see Figures 35.3 and 35.4) that seems to increase over time. As a result, it is no longer sufficient to have an average hedge fund allocation – one must select the managers in the first or second quartile. Investors with no "edge" face the risk of selecting lower quartile managers and are more likely to benefit from delegating the hedge fund selection to intermediaries with a competitive advantage.

To analyze whether actively-managed FoHF have, on average, generated substantial added value over noninvestible hedge fund indices, we can compare the performance of the CISDM Fund of

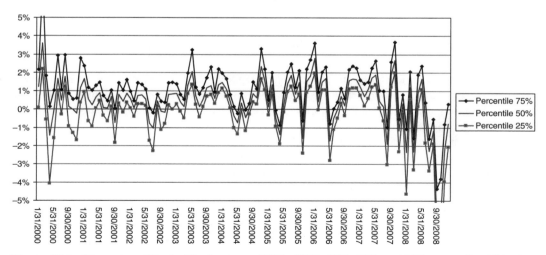

Figure 35.4 Dispersion of fund of funds returns (2000–2008): 75%, 50%, and 25% percentiles. This chart includes FoHFs on CASAM-CISDM that had data since 2000) (*Source:* CISDM)

Table 35.1   Analyzing FoHF versus single hedge funds.

1990–2008	Arithmetic mean (%)	Standard deviation (%)	Skewness	Information ratio	Maximum decline (%)	Correl against CISDM Fund of Funds Index
BarCap Global Aggregate Bond Index	7.42	5.78	0.18	1.28	−10.07	0.08
S&P 500 Index	8.48	15.78	−0.69	0.54	−44.73	0.57
MSCI Emerging Mkts Index	11.03	26.64	−0.91	0.41	−59.5	0.67
MSCI EAFE Index	4.62	17.77	−0.57	0.26	−49.21	0.54
CISDM Fund of Funds Diversified Index	8.01	5.43	−0.89	1.48	−17.49	0.98
CISDM Fund of Funds Index	7.79	5.15	−1.34	1.51	−17.74	1.00
CISDM Equal Weighted Hedge Fund Index	12.89	8.23	−0.69	1.57	−21.13	0.88
CISDM Merger Arbitrage Index	9.91	4.55	−1.06	2.18	−5.74	0.69
CISDM Global Macro Index	11.37	6.66	1.15	1.71	−8.22	0.61
CISDM Event Driven Multi-Strategy Index	11.24	6.6	−1.55	1.70	−20.19	0.83
CISDM Equity Market Neutral Index	8.69	2.13	−0.52	4.08	−2.8	0.61
CISDM Equity Long/Short Index	12.2	9.27	−0.28	1.32	−17.04	0.76
CISDM Distressed Securities Index	12.04	7.7	−1.39	1.56	−21.24	0.71
CISDM Convertible Arbitrage Index	8.47	5.11	−5.08	1.66	−22.46	0.67
CISDM CTA Asset Weighted Index	11.04	10.55	0.63	1.05	−10.69	0.13
CISDM CTA Asset Weighted Diversified Index	10.1	12.03	0.39	0.84	−16.55	0.10
CISDM CTA Asset Weighted Discretionary Index	12.22	7.81	0.81	1.56	−5.6	0.38

Source: CISDM

Funds Index[3] or CISDM Fund of Funds Diversified Index to the performance of the CISDM Equal Weighted Hedge Fund Index (Table 35.1).

Fund of funds provide significant diversification potential because they have fairly low drawdowns and standard deviations. This is particularly true of FoHF compared to individual hedge funds. This suggests that a fiduciary who is primarily concerned about the downside risk associated with hedge fund investment should consider a fund of funds vehicle. However, this risk reduction comes at the cost of lower annualized returns because average returns on FoHF are only a little more than half of those of single hedge funds over the same period of time. This is in line with the empirical literature and can be explained by the so-called "double layer of fees" and the survivorship impact that creates an upward bias in the reported performance of individual hedge funds.

---

[3] While the original FoHF were built around the concept of diversification, single strategy FoHF allocate up to 100% of their capital to a portfolio of funds following a specific hedge fund strategy. The CISDM Fund of Funds Index is used as a benchmark for such specialized hedge funds.

On a risk-adjusted basis, research also indicates that FoHF offer a slightly lower information ratio. This suggests either that FoHF managers have not done a particularly good job at selecting superior hedge funds or that the fees they charge wipe out the benefits they deliver. Several studies have confirmed these results and tend to confirm that on average, FoHF underperform hedge funds after fees (see Ackermann, McEnally and Ravenscraft (1999), Amin and Kat (2002), Brown, Goetzmann and Liang (2004), Capocci and Hubner (2004), Fung and Hsieh (2004)).

These results should be taken with caution, however. Comparing average risk-adjusted returns or alphas across two asset classes is valid only if they are directly comparable. Single hedge funds and FoHF are, however, not directly comparable. As stated by Ang, Rhodes-Knopf and Zhao (2008), the "average hedge fund" is not an investible quantity. This is because the best hedge funds are often closed to new investors. Even if an investor meets the high minimum requirements for investing in hedge funds, there is no guarantee that a successful hedge fund will take that investor as a client. Additionally, hedge funds are hard to find, evaluate, and monitor; they are relatively secretive, are legally prevented from marketing, and gathering information on them can be costly.

Ang, Rhodes-Knopf and Zhao (2008) built a model that assumes FoHF managers are skillful. Skilled investors with large amounts of capital and expertise directly invest in hedge funds, while unskilled investors with little capital or no expertise choose to use FoHF. Thus, the hedge funds that we can observe in databases are funded either directly by skilled investors or indirectly through skilled FoHF.

However, if there were no FoHF, all unskilled investors would be forced to directly invest in hedge funds, including the bad ones. These "bad" hedge funds would not receive any funding in a world where FoHF exist. As a result, we can say that most hedge funds receive funding either from skilled investors or indirectly from skilled FoHF. The hedge funds that we can observe in databases may be, therefore, biased upwards compared to the full hedge fund universe that would have existed if there were no FoHF. That is, by their mere presence, FoHF discourage "bad" hedge funds from being formed or, if formed, from staying in business for too long. This funding bias of hedge funds is very different from reporting biases. Many of the usual hedge fund database biases are based on whether funded hedge funds report or do not report to a database. By contrast, this funding bias involves the unobserved unfunded set of hedge funds.

According to Ang, Rhodes-Knopf and Zhao (2008), a true FoHF benchmark should include both funded and unfunded hedge funds available to unskilled investors. In addition, investors experience significant costs when accessing hedge funds such as search and due diligence costs, which are hard to measure, but should nevertheless be estimated and factored in. When these elements are taken into account, Ang, Rhodes-Knopf and Zhao concluded that FoHF, on average, deserve their "fees-on-fees", that the more skilled an investor is, the less likely he will find FoHF valuable, and that the less risk-averse an investor is, the less value an FoHF provides.

HEDGE FUND INDICES

In the universe of traditional assets, indexing has long been an ideal method of achieving broad-based, low-cost passive exposure to global equity and bond markets – often called "beta." As a result, there are countless investment vehicles based on the idea of tracking broad market indices, many of them with large assets under management. Until recently, indexing has not been applied to the world of hedge funds since hedge funds were historically marketed as following predominantly "alpha" oriented strategies (i.e. a rationale of absolute returns). It is only with increasing demand for hedge funds from institutional investors that the thinking has progressively shifted from "alpha generation" to "beta exposure" (i.e. a rationale of risk diversification). Not surprisingly, this shift has also generated a greater focus on how to capture the so-called hedge fund beta through indexation and passive strategies.

Desirable properties

Before discussing hedge fund indices in detail, let us recall the desirable properties of investment indices in general. Hedge fund indices that are used as yardsticks for investments should be:

- *Unambiguous*. The hedge funds included in the index must be specified with regard to their weight in the index, style, general partner, adviser, domicile, etc.
- *Verifiable*. Users should be able to verify all information and calculations used to construct the index. This is greatly facilitated when the construction methodology is publicly available.
- *Accountable*. The construction and the revisions of the index follow exact guidelines which should be approved by an independent committee.
- *Investible*. Investors should be able to replicate the index with reasonable costs and tracking errors. Note that investibility may be a subjective criterion as it might require large amounts of capital to access the index.
- *Reasonable*. The index should only contain funds which are reasonable investments for a typical client and are consistent with the investor's risk preference. The weighting and rebalancing rules should be compliant with the underlying investments or funds.

In addition, hedge fund indices should be *representative*. That is, they should accurately reflect the whole universe of hedge funds, or a universe focused on a particular style. In this regard, a potential conflict arises. While it is not difficult to create representative investible indices of traditional assets such as stocks and bonds, this goal is not attainable in the hedge fund world. Investments in hedge funds are lumpy, which means a truly diversified and representative investible index would require an enormous amount of capital to fund and monitor each manager. Even if the funding were available, some hedge fund managers may refuse to join an index platform. As a result, index providers have to strike a delicate balance between representativeness and economic efficiency.

Non-investible hedge fund indices

In theory, passive hedge fund investing could offer advantages over the FoHF approach. Indexing should offload much of the research and monitoring costs of FoHF, as well as remove the additional layer of fees and expenses charged by actively-managed FoHF. Additionally, an investment in a hedge fund index should protect investors from manager selection risk. Just like indices for stocks or bonds, hedge fund indices deliver the "normal" returns of the asset class or investment style — we could almost call it the "beta" of hedge funds. By contrast, selecting individual hedge funds exposes investors to the risk of significantly underperforming the aggregate return of the hedge fund industry. Indeed, both hedge funds and FoHF dispersions have been extremely high historically and both exhibit a clear widening trend. A wrong selection decision could, therefore, have a large impact on performance.

Unfortunately, identifying a representative hedge fund index is not a trivial task. The variety of index construction approaches and databases results in the extreme heterogeneity of performances among these indices. For instance, Amenc and Martellini (2003) analyzed 13 different style indices drawn from major index providers and observed a difference in performance of up to 22.04% in a single month for global long/short equity indices. In addition, some indices that were supposed to measure the same strategy were negatively correlated to each other during certain periods. This is clearly confusing for investors and casts serious doubt on the possibility of using such broad-based hedge fund indices as yardsticks in performance measurement. But the challenges for passive hedge fund investors do not end there.

Gaining exposure presents another significant hurdle, as tracking broad-based noninvestible hedge fund indices is complicated by the following issues:

- Most noninvestible hedge fund indices are not transparent. They do not disclose the list of their components, their weights, or even their construction methodology. This significantly complicates the work of a third-party indexer, unless it possesses privileged information from the index provider.
- Most noninvestible hedge fund indices are partially made up of funds that are already closed to new investment or will be closed at some point in the future once they reach their maximum capacity. A full replication (i.e. buying all the components in the index) is therefore often not feasible.
- Traditional indexing approaches (i.e. regularly rebalancing a portfolio of hedge funds to minimize the tracking error with respect to some index) are not applicable in practice because of the lack of liquidity of the underlying funds (lock-ups, redemption notice periods, lumpy investments).
- Attempts to replicate the returns of noninvestible hedge fund indices by dynamically trading traditional assets such as stocks and bonds, or even futures and options, usually result in significant tracking errors, essentially because the target is an index of *actively-managed portfolios*. Thus, although the funds in the index do not change, the funds' individual securities and their key characteristics change continuously.
- Most broad-based hedge fund indices often report their net asset value with a considerable delay, e.g. three weeks after the end of the month. This means that a third-party index always rebalances with considerable lag.

For all these reasons, several providers have recently decided to start from scratch with a new methodology and created *investible hedge fund indices*.

Investible hedge fund indices

The first *investible hedge fund indices* were launched in January 2001 by Zurich Financials and Schneeweis Partners[4] and was soon followed by several others (Standard and Poor's, MSCI, HFR, etc.). All investible hedge fund indices share the goal of offering investors the opportunity to hold the entire hedge fund market at a relatively low cost. But, as illustrated in Tables 35.2 and 35.3, their construction rules, weighting, and rebalancing policies differ widely, and this results in significant variations in their performances.

As mentioned before, index providers face a trade-off between including more funds, in order to be more representative, and using fewer funds to facilitate index tracking. Indeed, to be investible, hedge fund indices must select only a *limited number* of liquid and open hedge funds. The process of selecting hedge funds based on certain criteria leads to **access bias**. That is, it is likely that those hedge fund managers who are willing to belong to an investible index would have characteristics that are different from the universe of those managers. Access bias is likely to lead to lower return for the index, because it is often assumed that top-performing managers are less likely to

---

[4] These indices were later reintroduced under the name of Dow Jones Hedge Fund Indices.

Table 35.2 Key characteristics of investible indices

Index provider	Launch date	Start date	Number of indices	Strategy weighting	Fund weighting	Rebalancing
CS/Tremont	Aug. 03	Jan. 00	10+composite	Asset weighted	Asset weighted	Semi-annual
Dow Jones	Nov. 03	Jan. 02	5	n.a.	Equal weighting	Quarterly
EDHEC	Apr. 05	Apr. 02	5	n.a.	Optimized weights	Quarterly
FTSE	Apr. 04	Jan. 98	11+composite	Investability weighted	Investability weighted	Annual
HFRX	Mar. 03	Jan. 00	8+composite	Asset weighted	Optimized weights	Quarterly
MSCI	Jul. 03	Jan. 00	1	Adjusted median asset weighted	Equal weighting	Quarterly
RBC	Jul. 05	Jul. 05	9+composite	"representative of each strategy in the universe"	Equal weighting	Monthly
S&P	May 02	Jan. 98	5+composite	Equal weighted	Equal weighting	Annual

agree to belong to an index. Most index providers impose strict selection criteria (e.g. minimum track record, minimum assets under management, sufficient liquidity, absence of lock-up period, daily or weekly valuation, minimum transparency, willingness to accept additional investors and commitment to provide sufficient capacity) in order to select the funds that are eligible to enter their index. Several index providers go one step further and have signed partnerships with managed account[5] platforms or have developed their own platform in order to secure maximum capacity and liquidity on the components of their indices. Other providers have attempted to circumvent the problem by using quantitative methodologies – they typically partition the hedge fund universe into clusters and use various algorithms to select the funds that are the most representative of each cluster.

But regardless of the approach, the objective is to construct a representative sample of the hedge fund universe. As illustrated by Lhabitant (2007), the set of all investible indices included only four of the largest 25 hedge funds worldwide despite the fact that those funds managed more than $300 billion. Hedge funds with superior performance may find no need to be included in an investible index as they are already capable of attracting investors, while less successful hedge funds may be more willing to comply with strict selection criteria (e.g. more transparency, guaranteed capacity, and better liquidity) in order to increase their assets.

Beyond the question of representation, several criticisms of the selection process used by investible index providers have been raised. Since investible hedge fund indices are created with the implicit goal of launching a tracking vehicle, it is essential that their historical pro-forma performance looks attractive to potential investors. Therefore, index providers have a tendency to select index members among the funds with a good track record. However, this does not guarantee a good performance in the future. For most strategies and providers, a simple comparison between non-investible and

---

[5] A managed account is a discretionary account where a client has given specific written authorization to a hedge fund manager to select securities and execute trades on a continuing basis and for a fee. Most of the time, the managed account closely mirrors the main fund of the manager. Of course, the difficulty is that the number of fund managers willing to offer managed accounts is extremely limited and usually restricted to the most liquid strategies.

Table 35.3 Key characteristics of investible indices

Index provider	No. of funds in database (approx.)	No. of eligible funds (approx.)	No. of funds in index (approx.)	Pricing	Initial due diligence performed by	Uses managed accounts	Requirements
CS/Tremont	3300	420	60	Monthly	Tremont	No, uses actual hedge funds	member of the non-investible index accepts new investments and redemptions initial investment > $100,000 not U.S. domiciled no lock-up period monthly liquidity with at most one month notice, except for event-driven and convertible arbitrage (quarterly)/one of the six largest funds in the eligible funds in all 10 sectors
Dow Jones	300	100	35	Daily	CASAM	Apollo Capital Management	separate managed account AUM > $50m track record > 2 years
EDHEC	2300	130	60	Weekly	Lyxor	Lyxor	leverage constraint depending on the strategy high correlation with the first principal component calculated from extensive database of hedge funds
FTSE	6000	75	40	Daily	Harcourt	MSS Capital	AUM before leverage > $50m track record > 2 years monthly liquidity independently audited open and accepting investor subscriptions sufficient remaining capacity hedge fund does not belong to specialist interest strategies
HFRX	2300	unknown	varies	Daily	HFR	HFR	open for investment daily transparency pass extensive qualitative screening and due diligence
MSCI	105	unknown	97	Daily	Lyxor and MSCI	Lyxor	pass due diligence agree to offer frequent liquidity and sufficient capacity agree with MSCI on the classification funds should have other significant investors outside of those tracking the index

(continued)

Table 35.3 *(continued)*

Index provider	No. of funds in database (approx.)	No. of eligible funds (approx.)	No. of funds in index (approx.)	Pricing	Initial due diligence performed by	Uses managed accounts	Requirements
S&P	4700	300	40	Daily	Albourne Partners	PlusFunds	separated account AUM > $75m track record > 3 years additional investment capacity > $100m.
RBC	3500	300	254	Monthly	RBC	No, uses actual hedge funds	AUM > $10m can be categorized into one of the nine sub-strategies has a U.S.$ class redemptions no less frequently than annually max. 65-day notice to redeem domiciled outside of the U.S. lock-ups up to one year monthly subscriptions track record of at least 6 months dealing dates scheduled on the first or last business day of a month no redemption fee after 1 year no subscription fee minimum initial investment amount no greater than $250,000, minimum subsequent investment amount no greater than $50,000, and minimum redemption amount no greater than $50,000 no limit to the amount of redemptions over a particular period offers investments eligible to restricted persons for purposes of "new issues" as defined in NASD Rule 2790 passes a fund review process

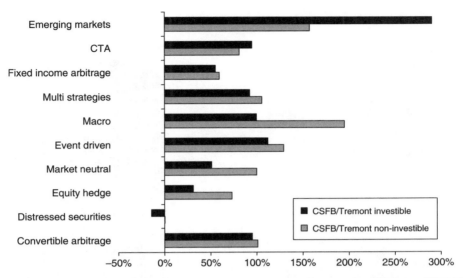

Figure 35.5 Total return achieved from December 31st, 1999 to January 31st, 2008 by CSFB/Tremont investible and non-investible indices. (*Source:* CSFB/Tremont)

investible indices *after* the creation date of the latter illustrates the underperformance of the investible index versus its non-investible cousin (see Figures 35.5 and 35.6).

Investible indices or FoHF?

Despite the fact that they are designed to *passively* measure the same universe, investible hedge fund indices tend to have considerably different strategic exposures. Consider, for instance, the long/short

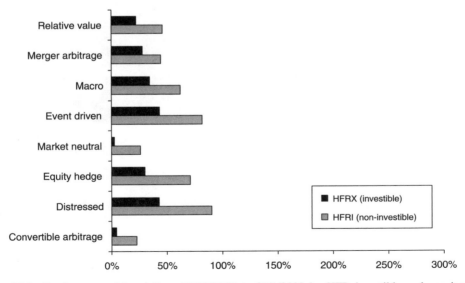

Figure 35.6 Total return achieved from 31/12/1999 to 31/1/2008 by HFR investible and non-investible indices. *Source: Hedge Fund Research*

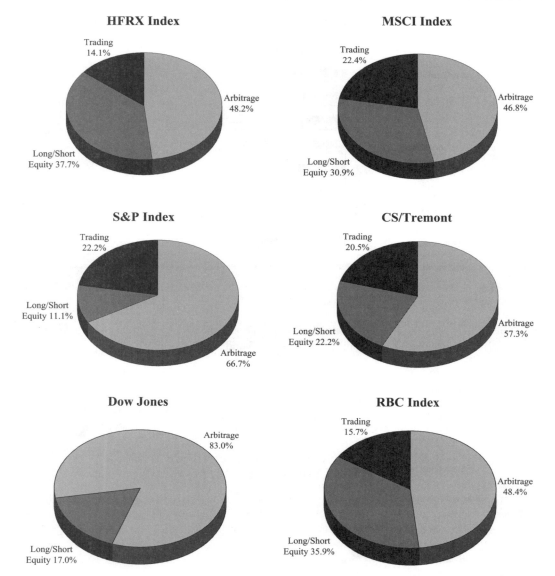

Figure 35.7 Strategic exposures of various investible hedge fund indices (Q1 2006). Note that FTSE and EDHEC do not disclose their asset allocation in terms of individual funds. (*Source:* Lhabitant (2007))

equity strategy. According to all databases, it is the largest hedge fund strategy, both in terms of number of funds and in terms of assets under management. However, its weight varies from only 11.1% of the S&P Investible Index to the 37.7% of the HFRX Index.

The disparity between investible indices is even more visible when one considers their individual components. At the end of March 2006, there were 297 distinct hedge funds/managed accounts in six major investible indices. The large majority of them (246 funds) were found in only one index, 32 funds were members of two indices, nine funds were in three indices, and 10 funds were in four indices. No fund was found in more than four indices (see Figures 35.7 and 35.8).

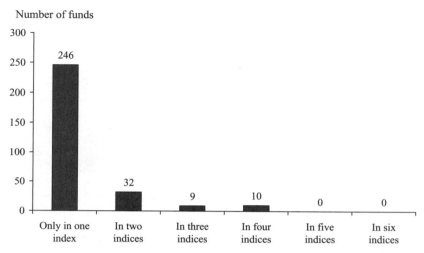

Figure 35.8 Number of funds in the intersection between various investible hedge fund indices as of March 2006. (*Source:* Lhabitant (2007))

The overlap between two different investible indices seems rather small – on average, only 7.8% of the funds covered by two of the major investible indices are common to both of them. These differences are comparable to those observed between *actively managed* funds-of-hedge-funds. Several researchers suggest that some investible hedge fund indices were in fact disguised FoHF that use the label "index" for their marketing efforts (Duc (2004a, 2004b) and Lhabitant (2007)). But despite these criticisms, hedge fund index products have generated some interest and continue to evolve as they address some of the most problematic elements of hedge fund investing.

DUE DILIGENCE ISSUES ARISING IN THE CONTEXT OF FUNDS-OF-FUNDS

The past few years have seen a significant proliferation of FoHF. With more than 3000 active FoHF in existence today, prospective investors now need to have a clear due diligence process to select one of them. A useful tool in this process is the Alternative Investment Management Association's (AIMA's) Illustrative Questionnaire for Due Diligence of Fund-of-Funds Managers. Most FoHF have adopted this questionnaire to provide investors with answers to standard questions.

The AIMA questionnaire is divided in the following 10 areas:

1. *Background.* Investors should review the history of the FoHF management firm and validate its business model. This requires reviewing items such as:
    a. The key milestones and significant events.
    b. The total assets under management and their evolution over time.
    c. The main clients and their type.
    d. The ownership and its evolution.
    e. The size of its staff and its recent changes, if any.
    f. The activities performed by this staff (via organizational chart).
    g. The qualification of the staff to perform its duties (such as education, professional background, etc.).

Table 35.4 Historical performance of CISDM Funds of Hedge Funds Index

Year	BarCap Global Aggregate Bond (%Total Return)	S&P 500 (%Total Return)	MSCI Emerg (%Total Return)	MSCI EAFE (%Total Return)	CISDM Fund of Funds Diversified Index (%Total Return)	CISDM Fund of Funds Index (%Total Return)	CISDM Equal Weighted Hedge Fund Index (%Total Return)	CISDM Merger Arbitrage Index (%Total Return)	CISDM Global Macro Index (%Total Return)	CISDM Event Driven Multi-Strategy Index (%Total Return)	CISDM Equity Market Neutral Index (%Total Return)	CISDM Equity Long/Short Index (%Total Return)	CISDM Distressed Securities Index (%Total Return)	CISDM Convert Arbitrage Index (%Total Return)	CISDM CTA Asset Weighted Index (%Total Return)	CISDM CTA Asset Weighted Diversified Index (%Total Return)
1990	12.6	-3.1	-10.56	-23.2	7.51	7.47	6.54	-1.69	11.26	-3.31	10.18	-1.46	19.31	NA	27.29	19.8
1991	16.06	30.47	59.9	12.48	11.01	11.3	30.43	18.33	36.47	21.84	12.42	33.7	25.06	NA	16.82	11.34
1992	5.78	7.65	11.41	-11.85	12.04	11.93	16.83	17.37	22.35	19.36	7.92	17.38	18.25	16.68	9.9	-6.01
1993	11.08	10.08	74.86	32.94	23.33	24.21	30.29	26.38	40.88	26.47	9.73	21.56	31.25	16.56	19.86	22.12
1994	0.23	1.32	-7.31	8.06	-4.44	-4.42	3.53	5.23	-5.05	3.64	5.12	3.38	-4.3	2.2	-0.7	5.29
1995	19.67	37.57	-5.19	11.55	12.54	12.25	21.17	16.6	11.17	19.8	12.2	26.42	21.95	17.47	15.13	15.05
1996	4.92	22.96	6.04	6.34	16.83	16.68	23.24	15.97	9.86	22.31	13.69	22.34	21.05	14.75	14.64	12.73
1997	3.79	33.38	-11.59	2.05	17.09	17.2	21.79	18.17	15.97	23.56	14.87	23.74	18.67	14.25	10.06	7.09
1998	13.7	28.58	-25.33	20.34	1.71	1.65	3.97	5.5	8.11	3.9	11.16	9.57	-4.83	7.45	9.37	11.61
1999	-5.17	21.04	66.66	27.3	22.37	16.23	36.79	15.77	8.52	21.42	9.86	34.4	17.85	13.9	3.77	6.5
2000	3.18	-9.09	-30.71	-13.97	7.35	7.37	8.76	14.37	10.02	12.07	13.87	7.78	5.85	15.24	6.18	8.07
2001	1.57	-11.88	-2.37	-21.21	4.99	5.18	5.71	4.27	5.58	7.06	7.27	2.27	9.24	13.27	4.19	6.04
2002	16.52	-22.1	-6	-15.64	0.65	1.05	0.41	0.28	2.81	1.18	2.04	-4.72	6.85	8.89	11.95	12.38
2003	12.48	28.69	56.26	39.16	10.04	10.23	20.62	7.37	11.76	21.87	8.83	18.89	25.27	9.65	13.25	10.39
2004	9.27	10.87	25.94	20.69	7.23	7.12	9.97	7.01	4.48	12.12	4.97	9.86	16.64	2.47	4.24	3.95
2005	-4.48	4.89	34.53	14.01	6.36	6.47	9.84	5.77	6.65	6.63	7.11	8.86	7.44	-1.14	5	-1.08
2006	6.66	15.79	32.6	26.88	7.79	9.12	11.75	10.7	4.93	13.99	7.64	9.99	15.91	12.32	6.17	7.16
2007	9.48	5.5	39.78	11.62	9.52	8.69	10.5	3.74	12	6.57	6.5	8.48	5.26	3.97	9.14	12.01
2008	4.79	-36.99	-53.17	-43.06	-16.83	-17.05	-19.17	0.09	3.7	-19.05	0.61	-14.43	-19.55	-19.1	17.86	19.26

Source: CISDM

Table 35.5 Statistical properties of CISDM Funds of Hedge Funds Index

1990–2008	N periods	Geometric mean(%)	Arithmetic mean(%)	Standard deviation (%)	Skewness	Infomtation ratio	Maximum decline (%)	Correl against CISDM Fund of Funds Index
BarCap Global Aggregate Bond Index	228	7.27	7.42	5.78	0.18	1.28	−10.07	0.08
S&P 500 Index	228	7.33	8.48	15.78	−0.69	0.54	−44.73	0.57
MSCI Emerging Mkts Index	228	7.81	11.03	26.64	−0.91	0.41	−59.5	0.67
MSCI EAFE Index	228	3.12	4.62	17.77	−0.57	0.26	−49.21	0.54
CISDM Fund of Funds Diversified Index	228	7.87	8.01	5.43	−0.89	1.48	−17.49	0.98
CISDM Fund of Funds Index	228	7.67	7.79	5.15	−1.34	1.51	−17.74	1.00
CISDM Equal Weighted Hedge Fund Index	228	12.59	12.89	8.23	−0.69	1.57	−21.13	0.88
CISDM Meiger Aibitrage Index	228	9.81	9.91	4.55	−1.06	2.18	−5.74	0.69
CISDM Global Macro Index	228	11.18	11.37	6.66	1.15	1.71	−8.22	0.61
CISDM Event Driven Multi-Strategy Index	228	11.05	11.24	6.6	−1.55	1.70	−20.19	0.83
CISDM Equity Market Neutral Index	228	8.67	8.69	2.13	−0.52	4.08	−2.8	0.61
CISDM Equity Long/Short Index	228	11.82	12.2	9.27	−0.28	1.32	−17.04	0.76
CISDM Distressed Securities Index	228	11.77	12.04	7.7	−1.39	1.56	−21.24	0.71
CISDM Convertible Arbitrage Index	204	8.35	8.47	5.11	−5.08	1.66	−22.46	0.67
CISDM CTA Asset Weighted Index	228	10.55	11.04	10.55	0.63	1.05	−10.69	0.13
CISDM CTA Asset Weighted Diversified Index	228	9.46	10.1	12.03	0.39	0.84	−16.55	0.10
CISDM CTA Asset Weighted Discretionary Index	228	11.95	12.22	7.81	0.81	1.56	−5.6	0.38

Source: CISDM

h. The sources of revenues and operating costs – some firms may have multiple business lines, or run multiple products.

i. The compensation scheme for key employees.

2. *Product information.* Investors should verify that the FoHF they are considering is compatible with their requirements and risk/return objectives. This requires reviewing items linked to the product such as:

a. Investment objective (including target return and target risk).

b. Target investors for the product.

c. Current size.

d. Date of inception.

e. Fee structure.

f. Liquidity.

3. *Performance.* Investors should obtain performance documentation for the FoHF they are considering, along with an explanation of what the performance represents. Typical matters of concern include:

a. Proforma versus real.

b. Net of fees versus gross of fees.

c. Rebalancing assumptions.

d. Use of leverage and its cost.

4. Asset allocation/style. Investors should understand how asset allocation decisions at the strategy level are made by the FoHF manager.

5. *Due diligence/manager selection.* Investors should review and validate the manager selection process of the FoHF. When possible, they should examine the reports and notes from the due diligence process in detail to better understand how a fund has been selected or rejected. Typical items to investigate are:

a. The minimum criteria a manager has to meet, if any, to pass the due diligence.

b. The time taken to perform due diligence on a manager.

c. The number of managers analyzed every year and the success ratio.

d. The process of verifying information provided by hedge funds.

e. The frequency of on-site visits with the managers.

f. The analysis of third party service providers (administrators, etc.).

g. The number of approved hedge funds.

6. *Portfolio construction.* Investors should understand how and why underlying hedge fund managers are hired and fired. Items to review include:

a. Annual turnover in the portfolio.

b. Reasons that warrant firing of a manager.

c. Use of quantitative tools.

d. Use of qualitative inputs.

7. *Risk management.* Investors should review and validate the risk management guidelines of the FoHF. This includes items such as:

a. Minimum number of underlying managers.

b. Maximum allocation per manager.

c. Maximum allocation per strategy (in terms of assets or the FoHF risk budget).

d. Maximum allocation into illiquid hedge funds, side pockets, etc.

e. Maximum leverage at the FoHF level, if any.

   Investors should also understand how risks are identified and what actions are taken to reduce unwanted risk.

8. *Administration/operations*. Investors should review and validate the activities performed in-house versus the activities delegated to external and independent service providers. Auditors and administrators are crucial with respect to valuation and their exact duties should be cautiously examined.

9. *Client information/reporting*. Prospects should always review the information they will obtain if they become investors and verify that it is sufficient for their needs. The easiest way to do it is by looking at sample reports.

10. *Compliance/legal*. This covers items such as the registration of the FoHF manager with its local regulatory and/or supervisory bodies, the result of the last inspection, if any, and the existence of a compliance officer. Investors should also validate the alignment of interests between the fund manager and his investors and the avoidance of conflicts of interests.

While this list appears comprehensive it is only a set of guidelines and FoHF due diligence should not stop once the investment has been made. Monitoring must continue to make sure the FoHF complies with the investment parameters and objectives specified in the initial due diligence.

36

Strategy Specific Due Diligence

Due diligence is the process by which a potential investor obtains a sufficient understanding of a hedge fund in order to make an informed decision on whether to invest in that fund. It typically covers the hedge fund's investment strategy, the character of the organization, the way the fund operates, the management of its associated risks, and the credibility of its business model. Not surprisingly, due diligence is considered by many as the most critical stage in hedge fund investing due to hedge funds' relative lack of oversight from regulators, the potentially limited information on what exactly is in a hedge fund portfolio, and the difficulty of establishing reliable performance benchmarks. Done well, due diligence can reduce risk, increase returns, and make investors more secure in their investment. Done poorly, it can put the investor's capital at risk.

Although there appears to be a wide variation in due diligence standards between different hedge fund investors, most generally agree that due diligence should include a review of the fund's marketing material, the investor correspondence, and legal/audit documents, the fund's regulatory and professional records, background checks, and investment performance. Generic due diligence questionnaires are also usually a good starting point to understand how a hedge fund operates. However, to be effective, due diligence must include more than just checking off items on a list. Interviews with the key professionals of the fund and discussions with its current investors are as important as the documents.

How long does a "typical" hedge fund due diligence take? Unfortunately, the answer is that the length of the due diligence process varies wildly, since it depends upon the complexity of the fund, its geographic location, the size of the organization, the availability and quality of the information supplied by the manager, and the sophistication and knowledge of the investor. According to Anson (2006), a thorough investor should expect to spend 75 to 100 hours in reviewing a hedge fund manager before investing. Andrew Golden, President of the Princeton University Investment Company, said that his organization spends at least 400 hours on initial due diligence before investing in a hedge fund, and then approximately 70 hours per year on ongoing due diligence (Testimony of Andrew Golden, 2007). A conservative estimate of the cost of due diligence is typically $50,000 to $100,000 per hedge fund – an amount that puts small funds-of-funds at a competitive disadvantage.

Overall, due diligence is a complex and iterative process that requires judgment, experience, and a variety of skills. In essence, one needs to be an accountant, a trader, an investment analyst, a psychotherapist, a business manager, a human resources manager, and a head hunter. Due diligence also requires a healthy dose of skepticism combined with strong common sense. Investors, therefore, have to conduct their own due diligence, either by themselves or by hiring others to do it for them. Consulting firms, law firms, accounting firms, and other third party providers offer a wide variety of due diligence services.

In this chapter, we focus on strategy-specific issues arising in such a due diligence process. Rather than being exhaustive, we concentrate on some of the major strategies and discuss only some specific questions that are related to each of them.

LONG/SHORT EQUITY

Long/short equity is the largest hedge fund category, both in number of funds and assets under management. It primarily involves buying equities that are expected to increase in value and selling short equities that are expected to decrease in value.

Essential due diligence questions for a long/short equity fund should include:

- *What is the exact strategy of the fund?* Whenever a strategy could have several substrategies, the investor should seek to understand the precise substrategy that the manager follows. Long/short equity funds now retain a large variety of strategies (e.g. bottom-up stock pickers, equity market timers, long biased concentrated activists, long/short sectors, and event-driven equities). It is essential to know how the hedge fund can be categorized as well as, how its strategy changes over time, if at all. The substrategy followed by the manager will indicate the investment universe that the manager follows. Some long/short equity managers will focus on one sector, country, or market capitalization range, while others will adopt a generalist perspective and invest on a global basis. Knowing the investment universe is useful for both manager assessment and portfolio construction.

- *How is the portfolio constructed?* Portfolio construction provides great insights into the thought process and risk management attitude of the fund manager. Some long/short equity managers take separately outright positions on the long and short side and hedge the residual risks at the portfolio level. Others are split into sectors, where each sector is run (and hedged) as a "mini hedge fund." Still others use a pairs trading strategy with a short position for each corresponding long position.

- *Do the manager and his team have sufficient shorting experience?* Many long only managers who shift to hedge funds underestimate the skills necessary to sell short. First, short selling requires the ability to identify flaws in a business before its share price drops – contrary to the aim of traditional managers. Second, short sellers need to borrow shares from willing lenders via their broker, manage collateral exposure, deal with dividends payments, and handle the risk that the lenders may recall their stock at any time. Third, short selling exposes the portfolio to additional risk of loss. Losses in a long-only portfolio are limited to what you paid for the stock; when you go short, losses are technically unlimited as the price at which you can buy back the stock rises ever higher above the price at which you sold the stock. All these risks tend to make short selling more difficult than holding a security long. While examining the manager's skill in managing the short positions of the portfolio, attention must be paid to the role of the prime broker or brokers in providing the manager with borrowed shares. It must be determined whether the manager uses one or more sources for borrowed shares and whether those sources are able to secure hard-to-borrow shares.

- *Is the manager doing naked short selling, covered short selling, or both?* **Naked short selling** refers to short sales by persons who, at the time of selling, are neither the owner of the relevant security nor have put appropriate arrangements in place to meet their delivery obligations. It is much riskier than **covered short selling**, particularly in terms of settlement risk.[1] By contrast, a covered short seller will first secure the borrowing of the stock before they sell it. In many countries, naked short selling is restricted or even prohibited.

- *What are the typical ranges for gross and net exposures?* **Gross exposure** represents the absolute level of investment bets and is measured as the total of the long and short positions. **Net exposure** represents the implicit amount of directional market risk that resides "unhedged" in the portfolio. It is defined as the total of the long minus the total of the short positions. For instance, a manager

---

[1] It is important to note that naked short selling may be illegal in some jurisdictions and therefore must be evaluated very carefully.

who is 120% long and 50% short would have a gross exposure of 170% and a net exposure of 70%. Knowing the gross and net exposure of a fund is essential to understanding its investment style as well as the possible downside risk that the fund is taking.

- *What are the expected sources of return?* This question could be asked from all hedge fund managers regardless of their style. In most cases, there are multiple sources of returns. In the case of long/short equity managers, the key concern is role of market risk (beta) as a source of return. Long/short equity managers have primarily three sources of return in their portfolios:
  - **Static returns** are the gains of the portfolio in the absence of change in the price of the underlying stocks. These are essentially received dividends and earnings on the proceeds of the short sales minus borrowing costs to leverage and the dividends paid to the lender of borrowed stocks.
  - **Market-linked returns** are coming from the residual net long or net short market exposure.
  - **Manager alpha** can arise because of stock picking and/or market timing activities.

  In examining the sources of return of the hedge fund, one must also determine if the manager uses short positions as a source of return or whether short positions are primarily used to hedge the risk of long positions. Understanding the sources of returns is essential because static returns and market-linked returns can easily be obtained with relatively simple replicating portfolios at a fraction of the cost charged by hedge funds.

- *How liquid are the stocks in the portfolio?* The liquidity of underlying assets of a hedge fund is always a source of concern for investors. Recent hedge fund failures have highlighted the danger of hedge funds running large positions in relatively illiquid stocks. When the fund buys an illiquid stock, its price can rise dramatically. This could have a great impact on the fund's overall performance. In these cases, selling these positions without affecting their price is almost impossible, which means that the paper gains may never be realized. In that respect, liquidity should always be considered as having three dimensions: how much of a stock the fund can trade in normal market conditions, how quickly it can sell its position, and how much the price will move as a result. Related to liquidity is the issue of the uniqueness of the manager's strategy. If a manager follows some of the better known strategies (e.g. momentum or book-to-market), then he may face the systemic risk that if a large number of hedge funds operating in the same space decide to liquidate their positions, he will face a market where it will be hard to find buyers or sellers. This is exactly what happened in August 2007 when stocks that were considered to be highly liquid were negatively impacted by the mass liquidation of a few large equity long/short and equity market-neutral funds.

- *What is the manager policy regarding non-listed stocks?* The case of non-listed stocks must be carefully analyzed with particular attention to issues such as liquidity, valuation, and deal flow access. The latter is particularly relevant for shares in companies that are privately owned or are being prepared for initial public offerings (IPOs). Do the key investment professionals possess the specialized knowledge and experience to invest successfully in such securities?

- *Is the fund restricted in some positions?* Investment restrictions are mandatory as soon as private information is made available to the fund manager. This is typically the case if the manager sits on the board of a company and means that the position cannot generally be traded as easily as others.

- *Which types of derivative instruments are being used?* Some long/short equity funds make heavy use of derivatives to implement their views or hedge their positions. While this may be perfectly rational from an investment perspective, derivatives may have three impacts on a hedge fund portfolio that need to be assessed:
  - They may create excessive leverage. When buying derivatives such as call options, the fund pays only a premium and benefits from the implicit leverage of the option.
  - They may create excessive liabilities. When selling call or put options, the fund pockets a premium, but needs to consider the resulting potential risk of future losses.

- ○ They create counterparty risk. Several funds use Over-the-Counter (OTC) derivatives such as swaps to enter in positions either for regulatory reasons (e.g. easier access, possibility to create synthetic short positions, etc.) or for tax reasons (e.g. avoid a stamp tax). But this exposes the fund to the risk of the default of its counterparty.
- *How is foreign exchange risk managed?* Funds investing abroad face the risk of having net foreign currency exposures. Some managers systematically hedge their foreign exchange exposure. Others consider it as a potential additional source of returns. In the latter case, one needs to ask what expertise the manager has to make these bets.
- *Is the fund manager engaged in shareholder activism?* In the recent past, several hedge funds have engaged in shareholder activism, arguing that they lack some of the conflicts of interests that have deterred traditional institutional shareholders from becoming active in corporate governance. Activism often implies owning significantly large positions for long time periods and ultimately being restricted in terms of trading.
- *Are there stop-loss rules in the portfolio?* How are they set and adjusted? Stop losses are predetermined rules that automatically reduce a portfolio's exposure after reaching a certain threshold of cumulative losses. Trailing stop losses are **stop-loss** orders that are adjusted upward as a stock moves higher. They are commonly used by some hedge fund managers to limit the downside risk of their investments, but other managers do not like them because they automatically lock in losses and prevent participation in a rebound.
- *Does the manager file form 13F reports with the SEC?* In the U.S., investment managers who exercise investment discretion over $100 million or more of assets must make quarterly disclosures of their holdings on form 13F with the SEC. Form 13F is publicly available and contains the names and class of the securities, the CUSIP number, the number of shares owned, and the total market value of each security. Form 13F filings can provide insight into the various securities owned by a hedge fund as well as changes in their positions.

CONVERTIBLE ARBITRAGE

As previously discussed, convertible arbitrage strategy seeks to generate returns from the potential mispricing of a convertible security's equity, bond, and embedded call option features. Typically, the potential source of alpha for convertible arbitrageurs is the mispriced embedded option. Since other components of a convertible are normally priced fairly, convertible arbitrageurs hedge the risks associated with those components; i.e. convertible arbitrage managers buy the convertible bond and then hedge its equity, credit, and interest rate risks using various cash and derivative instruments.

Due diligence on a convertible arbitrage fund should first address the specific approach used by the fund:

- *What types of convertible bonds is the manager using?* Convertible bonds can be in the distressed or out-of-the-money range, in the hybrid or at-the-money range, or in the "equity alternatives" or in-the-money range.
- *What is the specific strategy of the fund?* Convertible arbitrage includes various substrategies, such as exploiting the mispricing of the bond, trading volatility, trading credit, and trading gamma. Each of these substrategies has different return expectations and risk profiles and requires different skill sets. In some cases, a fund manager may decide to split her portfolio between several substrategies. The issue is whether the manager has the background, skill set, infrastructure, and supporting services to implement various convertible arbitrage substrategies.

The success of the convertible arbitrage strategy is highly dependent on the quality of the manager's pricing model. Competition makes it difficult to identify cheap convertible bonds; further, not only must the manager's pricing model be able to identify the most profitable opportunities, it must estimate the appropriate hedge ratios for various risk components.

- *How good is the pricing and hedging model?* Sophisticated pricing models can more easily address real world market features (e.g. time varying interest rates and stochastic volatility) and special convertible bond features (e.g. special termination clauses and forced conversions). Convertible bond models have improved over the past several years and are still improving. As a rule, convertible arbitrageurs need to upgrade their models on a regular basis.
- *Is the same model used for pricing and hedging?* A model should compute not only the price of the convertible, but all of the relevant risk and sensitivity parameters. If different models are used for hedging and pricing, it is likely to result in inconsistencies and may lead the manager to unknowingly expose her portfolio to risks that she is not prepared to manage.
- *What procedure is used to mark the portfolio?* Investors should probe the pricing policies of their hedge fund managers and determine the level of oversight exercised over portfolio pricing. A good hedge fund manager should normally use several marks from various independent brokers and have documented rules to deal with differences between these quotes. The use of discretionary marks may be unavoidable due to a lack of viable pricing source, but they should represent a very small portion of the portfolio's value. All funds should have a documented policy regarding when and why discretionary marks instead of market quotes are used. This policy should include a requirement for approval from someone other than the portfolio manager (preferably a controller or risk manager). Finally, the fund manager should maintain records supporting her valuation recommendations.
- *How much of the portfolio is marked-to-market versus marked-to-model?* A fund manager may decide to mark-to-model (for instance, in the case of illiquid instruments where it may be difficult to obtain a recent market quote). In such cases, there is a risk that the fund's valuation differs significantly from the potential selling price — especially if the position has to be liquidated rather quickly. A mark-to-model is, by construction, less reliable than a mark-to-market since it depends on the accuracy of the assumptions in the model. Further, the model may not be able to account for abnormal market conditions. Recent experience of many convertible arbitrage managers has shown that even the most accurate pricing models may fail to account for the impact of market distress on prices of hard to value assets.

As an illustration of the importance of pricing models for convertible arbitrage, let us recall the case of Lipper Convertibles LP, once one of the largest convertible arbitrage hedge funds. Edward J. Strafaci managed the fund until January 2002 when he and another principal left to launch their own firm. Lipper undertook a bottom-up review of the convertible bond portfolio following the departure of Mr. Strafaci. On February 20, 2002, the firm reported that it was reducing the value of its onshore fund by approximately 40%. In this specific case, it turned out that the valuation error had been intentional – the previous fund manager had knowingly and recklessly overstated the value of convertible bonds and preferred stocks held by the funds, resulting in the dissemination of materially false and misleading fund valuations and performance figures from at least 1998 until his departure. Lipper ultimately decided to liquidate the fund after being swamped with redemption requests. The Lipper Convertible Fund, which had reported approximately $722 million in partnership capital before Strafaci's resignation, reported approximately $365 million in partnership capital upon liquidation. The manager was convicted, sent to prison, and fined $89 million for fraud. The Securities and Exchange Commission (SEC) also initiated proceedings against the external auditor of the fund for unquestioningly relying on a valuation process that was significantly flawed. This was a classic example of what can happen when simple checks and balances are not present in the pricing process – Lipper's policy did not address exceptions nor did it require justifications and documentation for setting valuations that differed from market consensus.

- *What is the quality of the pricing inputs?* A model is only as good as its inputs. With securities as complex as convertible bonds, it is essential to integrate information on volatility and credit spread levels into pricing models. Further, some inputs may not be observable and have to be estimated (e.g. volatility of the equity). The quality and the source of these inputs have to be carefully examined.
- *Can the manager override the model or its inputs?* Some arbitrageurs use pricing models as a support tool, but take discretionary hedging positions. If so, under what conditions does this occur, how often does this happen, when was the last time and why? Further, have these discretionary positions positively impacted past performance of the fund?

Also, there are several risk management questions that are particularly relevant to convertible arbitrage strategy:

- *What are the risk parameters of the fund?* Risks of convertible arbitrage usually include equity risk (delta, gamma), interest rate risk (rho), volatility risk (vega), and credit risk (liquidity risk, though very important, is not generally modeled explicitly). Most convertible arbitrageurs hedge these risks, but not necessarily completely since they aim to take advantage of some particular market anomalies. For example, the manager may decide not to hedge the credit risk of the bond completely if she believes that the market misprices the credit risk of the sector that the issuing firm belongs to. Understanding these risk limits is essential in assessing the overall risk of the portfolio.
- *What instruments are used for hedging?* There are a variety of instruments that can be used to hedge the long position in convertible bonds, including some from the OTC market that involve counterparty risk or leave some residual risk in the portfolio (e.g., the credit risk of a position may be hedged using a credit derivative where the underlying is an index rather than the issuing firm).
- *How often is a portfolio hedged?* As the market moves, arbitrage positions need to be rebalanced. There are various rebalancing strategies ranging from discretionary to systematic such as making changes at fixed trading time intervals, at fixed price intervals, or a combined approach. It is also essential to determine if rebalancing the hedge ratio is done via program trading or manually by a trader.
- *Is the fund using leverage?* Leverage varies greatly according to the underlying trading style of the fund manager and directly influences the risk. Leverage should also be analyzed with respect to the liquidity of the underlying positions. In measuring the leverage of the fund, attention must be paid to both implicit and explicit leverage. Certain derivative products such as options and futures have leverage embedded in them. If leverage is measured to understand the potential volatility of the fund, then both implicit and explicit leverage should be accounted for. However, if leverage is measured to determine the risk of funding, only explicit leverage may be looked at. While explicit leverage requires the fund to secure a source of funding, implicit leverage is automatically available whenever those derivatives are used.
- *How liquid is the portfolio?* Liquidity is a frequent concern in the convertible bond market. Many smaller bond issues tend to become less liquid once the initial flurry of post-issue trading has receded. As a result, traders should have limits on the ownership of positions related to one issuer or even a given sector. Also, the fund should have limits on the size of its position relative to the total size of the issue.

- *What is the fund's ability to borrow the underlying stock?* Convertible issuers are often small- to mid-size companies with a small float and a very narrow ownership base. Therefore, the cost of borrowing the required shares could be quite high or the fund may be exposed to short squeezes.
- *What stress tests are run on the portfolio?* Observing the risks the manager perceives as crucial to his portfolio is usually very instructive. Typical stress tests should include variations on the shape of the yield curve, on credit risk premium, and on the volatility of bond and equity markets, etc.

MERGER ARBITRAGE

Merger arbitrage involves profiting from the spread created between the share prices of two companies that are reorganizing. Generally, once a merger or takeover is announced, the stock of the acquiring firm declines and the stock of the target firm increases. However, the stock price of the target firm will not increase to the level of the offered price because there is always a chance that the merger may not go through. Some traditional asset managers are not prepared to manage the risks associated with failed mergers and, therefore, may sell their positions in the target firm. Merger arbitrage managers, on the other hand, are specialized in managing such a risk. They would take long positions in the stock of those target firms where, in their judgment, the merger has a reasonable chance to be completed. At the same time, merger arbitrage managers do not want to remain exposed to the risks associate with fluctuations in equity markets. In a cash deal, a fund will typically buy shares of the target company on the expectation that its stock price will rise to the offered price (the equity risk may be hedged by shorting an appropriate amount of an equity index or the acquiring firm's stock). In a stock deal, the fund will purchase the stock of the target company and simultaneously short the buyer on the expectation that the two stocks should converge if the deal is successful.

Essential due diligence questions for a merger arbitrage fund should include:

- *Is the fund investing only in announced deals or also in potential ones?* Taking positions in announced deals is much safer but provides lower expected returns. Taking long and short positions based on potential merger activities is more risky, but provides the potential for higher returns if successful. In the former case, it is essential to understand the size of positions that the manager is willing to take and whether the manager considers certain types of mergers (e.g. cash offers, friendly takeovers, etc). If the manager considers taking positions in potential deals, then one must further examine his skills in this area. For example, does the manager concentrate in particular sectors of the economy? Does the manager consider cross-border deals?
- *How diversified is the portfolio?* Running a diversified portfolio limits the impact of one unsuccessful merger deal falling through. On the other hand, a diversified portfolio is likely to contain positions related to deals that are not completed, leading to losses.
- *Is the fund doing reverse mergers?* **Reverse mergers** consist of taking the inverse of the usual position, i.e. buying the acquirer and selling short the target. This is a play that spreads will actually diverge because the deal will fail.
- *How does the fund hedge cash deals?* Cash deal arbitrage typically involves long-only positions in the stock of the target firm. So it is important to see how the fund manager hedges the long positions at the portfolio level.
- *How will the fund manager react in a scenario of reduced merger activity?* A decrease in merger activity obviously reduces the opportunity set and therefore the return. Since mergers are cyclical, this phenomenon will occur on a regular basis. Some managers will shrink the size of their fund; others will migrate towards other strategies. In the latter case, one has to determine if the manager has the skill to operate in the new area.

FIXED INCOME ARBITRAGE

Fixed income arbitrage refers to a broad set of market-neutral investment strategies followed by hedge funds. The objective is to exploit differences in valuation between various fixed income securities or derivatives. There are five major fixed income arbitrage strategies in the market (see Duarte, Longstaff and Yu (2006)):

- **Swap spread arbitrage**. Historically, this has been an important strategy. For example, it was reportedly the most important source of losses for Long-Term Capital Management in 1998. To implement this strategy, first an arbitrageur enters into a swap to receive fixed coupon and to pay floating coupon. Next, the arbitrageur takes a short position in a Treasury bond and invests the proceeds in a margin account earning the repo rate. Thus, the arbitrageur receives a net fixed coupon that is equal to the difference between what is paid on the Treasury and what is received from the swap. On the other hand, the arbitrageur pays a net floating coupon that is equal to the difference between what is paid on the swap and what is received on the margin account. This strategy is, therefore, a bet that the fixed net cash flow will exceed the floating net cash flow.
- **Yield curve arbitrage**. This simple strategy takes the form of assuming both long and short positions in Treasuries of the different maturities. For example, the arbitrageur may take a long position in a 4-year duration bond and short positions in 2-year and 6-year duration bonds. In this case, it is perceived that the 4-year duration bond is relatively cheap.
- **Mortgage arbitrage**. This strategy involves taking a long position in mortgage pass-through securities and hedging the interest rate risk of the position using swaps or futures contracts. The major risk in pass-through securities is the prepayment risk. The manager will need to have a reliable prepayment model in order to identify profitable trades and to hedge the interest rate risk of these instruments.
- **Volatility arbitrage**. This strategy is based on the available empirical evidence that on average implied volatilities of both fixed-income and equity derivatives tend to overestimate realized volatilities. Thus, volatility arbitrage involves taking long positions in fixed-income derivatives and delta hedging the market risk of the position. The arbitrageur will benefit if the implied volatility is indeed higher than the realized volatility.
- **Capital structure arbitrage**. This strategy, which is also referred to as credit arbitrage, attempts to take advantage of mispricing between various instruments that appear on a firm's balance sheet. For example, an arbitrageur may believe that a firm's debt is relatively cheap compared to its equity. In this case, the manager would take a long position in the firm's debt and then would hedge some of the position's risk by taking a short position in the equity of the same firm. Other risks may be hedged using other instruments such as interest rate futures.

Essential due diligence questions for a fixed income arbitrage fund should include:

- *What is the investment universe of the fund?* While pure fixed income arbitrage typically covers government and swap curves, some funds will extend it to include areas such as mortgages, inflation-linked bonds, and event credit or emerging market bonds.
- *How is leverage measured?* Measuring leverage in fixed-income securities is not trivial and it is important to understand how the manager uses it. Since the profit margin associated with most fixed-income arbitrage trades tends to be very small, fixed-income arbitrage managers have to use significant leverage to generate reasonable returns. Some fund managers use notional positions to measure leverage, but it is not necessarily indicative of risk – the same notional amount of 6-month and 30-year bonds have different risks. Some fund managers bring all their notional exposure to

one standardized quantity, for instance, 5-year or 10-year equivalents. Others prefer to bucket their notional exposures along the yield curve.

- *What is the maximum, average, and minimum leverage?* Fixed-income arbitrageurs tend to use a lot of leverage, as the expected gains of their positions are usually expressed in terms of basis points. This is particularly true for swap spread, yield curve, and volatility arbitrage strategies.
- *How large is the fund size in each of its underlying markets/instruments?* Fixed-income markets are large, but some specific products such as OTC derivatives or corporate debts trade on a narrow basis. It is therefore essential for fund managers to ensure that they do not represent a significant portion of one contract, one maturity or one issue.
- *What is the loss tolerance for a position?* Due to the high leverage, it is essential that funds have strict exit rules on each position.

One particular aspect of fixed-income arbitrage funds is that they use instruments that only require the payment of a small fraction of their underlying value upfront (e.g. futures, options, and swaps). As a result, a significant portion of their holdings that needs to be managed is held in cash. This should be carefully analyzed.

- *How important are the fund's cash balances?* Cash balances of 60% or more are quite common in fixed-income arbitrage. Investors should also question any significant changes in the cash position.
- *What are the return objectives on cash balances?* What is the maturity/duration and credit quality of cash investments? As a rule, cash should not be seen as an alpha generating center. The fund should primarily focus on having immediate liquidity (in case of margin calls) and only invest in top quality short-term instruments.
- *How well is the cash segregated?* How is the cash isolated from bankruptcy, default, and fraud? The fund manager should be prepared to explain the safeguards and procedures. Who is authorized to move cash and what are the limits for each authorized signature? How often is reconciliation of cash conducted? If differences are detected in reconciliation, what procedures are in place to reconcile the variance? Who signs off on differences?

EMERGING MARKETS

Emerging market hedge funds invest in equity or debt of companies in less developed countries or in the government debt of emerging market countries.

Typical questions for emerging market hedge funds include:

- *What is the focus of the fund?* There are numerous trading styles within the strategy such as equity large caps versus small caps, top-down versus bottom-up, technical versus fundamental, sovereign versus corporate debt, hard (e.g. USD or the Euro) versus local currency denominated debt, etc.
- *What are the fund's sources of research and competitive advantages?* In particular, does the fund have proprietary research, local contacts, and privileged access to senior management?
- *What instruments does the manager use to implement its strategy?* Does the fund trade local shares or American depositary receipts (ADRs) receipts for shares of a foreign company held by a U.S. bank, representing equity ownership in the company)? Does the fund invest only in publicly-traded instruments or would it consider taking positions in privately-placed instruments?
- *How liquid is the portfolio?* Emerging markets are thin and tend to exhibit significant bid–ask spreads. Liquidating a portfolio can be costly and take a long time.
- *Does the fund invest in frontier markets?* "**Frontier markets**" are small and less accessible but investible markets that are generally considered to be at an earlier stage of economic development. They offer the potential for higher returns, but are often associated with lack of information,

inadequate regulation, non-transparency, substandard reporting, market illiquidity, and the inability to transfer profit abroad in some cases.

- *How is short selling implemented?* Short selling is often difficult in emerging markets due to the lack of securities lending agreements, specific domestic rules, or even a prohibition of shorting. As a result, many hedge funds have a long bias or run imperfect hedges.
- *What is the quality of the fund's counterparties such as brokers, banks, and custodians?* The manager may have to deal with local institutions to implement this strategy. Investors should carefully analyze the potential risks that are involved in dealing with institutions that are governed by different laws and in some cases could be partially or completely owned by foreign governments.
- *How is currency risk managed?* Emerging market currencies are volatile and often subject to devaluation risk or convertibility restrictions.
- *How sensitive is the fund to* **contagion risk**? Emerging market economies have diverse characteristics (e.g. size of country, financial markets, and foreign exchange reserves) and experienced investors differentiate between members of this heterogeneous group. However, when financial markets are in distress, contagion becomes a serious issue. We have seen in the past that currency or credit crises in one emerging economy could quickly spill over into other emerging countries. The manager must demonstrate her knowledge of contagion risk and have policies in place to manage this risk.
- *How does the fund deal with corporate governance?* Corporate governance issues are particularly important when companies are controlled by governments and families − often the case in emerging markets. Issues such as minority shareholder protection and board quality are crucial in such cases.

MULTI-STRATEGY FUNDS

Multi-strategy hedge funds typically employ several strategies under a common organizational umbrella. Typical due diligence questions for multi-strategy hedge funds include:

- *What are the fund's different strategies and how complementary are they?* Multi-strategy and multi-manager funds can effectively diversify idiosyncratic risk (i.e. individual manager, strategy, region, or sector risk). However, a key determinant of this diversification is the degree of similarity between its various trading strategies, particularly in response to a common shock.
- *How is capital allocated across strategies?* Multi-strategy funds are characterized by their ability to dynamically allocate capital among various strategies. Understanding the target capital allocation, changes in the target over time and performance attribution is essential since this is ostensibly what investors are paying for. A fluid allocation of resources to the best performing strategies and geographies is what allows the portfolio to maximize the return for investors.
- *What are the key risks of the aggregate portfolio and what are the risk limits per strategy?* Each portfolio manager in a multi-strategy fund normally has the freedom to operate within predefined risk limits (e.g. VaR, stress tests, liquidity, and gross and net exposures). These limits should be monitored in real time by the risk management function. Investors should understand the risk metrics employed by a multi-strategy fund, including the implications and limitations of those measurements, and ascertain whether they are appropriate for the strategies and objectives of the fund.
- *How important is leverage and how is it allocated?* Some managers leverage the overall portfolio while others apply a different level of leverage for each strategy or even for each transaction. Investors should clearly understand how accounting and economic leverage are utilized in the hedge fund portfolio, based on absolute capital exposures, VaR, or similar measures.

- *What happens if one strategy blows up?* If the assets of each strategy are used to back the other strategies (so-called "cross collateralization"), then the failure of one strategy can have a dramatic impact on the overall portfolio. This is exactly what happened at Amaranth (see Chapter 37, Operational Risk, for further discussion), where the leverage of the massive natural gas bets was backed by the assets of the firm's other strategies so when those gas trades went awry, the whole firm collapsed. To prevent this, some funds cautiously segregate each strategy so that if one experiences difficulties, it will not affect the others.
- *How are the various portfolio managers remunerated?* Remuneration is essential to attract and retain talented employees, but it is also used to drive the capital allocation across a multi-strategy fund. For instance, there should be a clear incentive for a portfolio manager to return capital if she sees no opportunities in her space.
- *How does the fund deal with redemptions?* One unique risk in a multi-strategy fund is that the most liquid positions may have to be redeemed first, resulting in a higher concentration in the least liquid strategies.
- *How independent is the risk manager?* In a multi-strategy fund, it is essential to have an independent risk manager whose compensation is not directly tied to portfolio performance and who reports directly to the senior management of the fund. This function should be adequately resourced and staffed by qualified personnel and be supported by appropriate risk measurement systems with real time feeds. Investors should also understand how various recommendations of the risk manager will be implemented by portfolio managers and who is expected to monitor compliance with those recommendations.
- *What amount of information is available on each of the sub-portfolios?* In a multi-strategy fund, it is important to go beyond the total net performance of the fund and analyze performance and risk information on each of the sub-strategies.
- *How are fees charged?* Some multi-strategy funds charge incentive fees at the individual book level and not at the fund level. That is, instead of applying incentive fees on the total net performance of the fund, some fund managers charge an incentive fee on each strategy that posts a gain. Such a policy on fees eliminates one of the perceived values of multi-strategy funds when compared to funds-of-funds, where each manager receives a performance fee based on her performance.

DISTRESSED SECURITIES

Distressed securities hedge funds typically take long positions in the debt of companies that are experiencing financial distress, in bankruptcy, or in a major reorganization. Typical questions for distressed securities hedge funds include:

- *Is the fund manager active or passive?* An active distressed manager will participate in the creditor committee to determine the restructuring and refinancing plans of the underlying companies. This is very labor intensive and requires extensive legal, financial, and business know-how, and a strong network of relationships. By contrast, a passive manager will simply buy debt and equity of distressed companies at a discount and hold them until they appreciate in value. An active manager must have a broad business background and must be able to demonstrate her ability to add value by being an active participant in bankruptcy and reorganization processes.
- *How senior are the fund's positions in the capital structure of the firm?* Distressed hedge funds can trade a wide range of securities such as debtor-in-possession loans, senior secured bank debt, public high-yielding bonds, subordinated and junior debt, trade claims, sub-performing real estate loans and mortgages, letters of credit, mezzanine debt, convertible bonds, preferred stock

and common stock. The risk of the fund dramatically increases as the seniority of the positions decreases.

- *How are the positions valued?* Distressed positions are extremely difficult to value as they are illiquid and can be marked-to-market only when trades occur. As a result, returns tend to exhibit low volatility and high autocorrelation. It is therefore essential that prices are validated by a third party administrator or pricing agent.
- *What is the liquidity offered by the fund to investors?* Distressed positions are typically illiquid and require long holding periods. It is essential that the capital of the fund stays locked-in during this period to avoid having to liquidate some positions at inopportune times. A distressed fund that offers generous liquidity provisions to its investors will not be able to offer attractive returns to those investors who want to be paid for bearing risks associated with illiquid assets.
- *What is the level of leverage?* Leverage on top of distressed positions can turn into a disaster if the underlying positions are not liquid or are hard to value.
- *What is the net credit exposure of the fund?* Some distressed managers may decide to hedge some of the risks associated with their long positions. The manager must communicate the fund's general policy to investors. Also, the manager must be prepared to discuss the fund's exposure to changes in the overall credit environment of the economy. For example, what is the impact of a widening of credit spreads on the fund's performance?
- *How diversified is the fund?* For active managers, it may be difficult to hold diversified positions. On the other hand, passive managers must hold diversified positions to reduce the risk of an unexpected development in the bankruptcy or reorganization process.
- *Does the manager use "side pockets" and what is the policy with regard to the management and valuation of the side pocket?* A side pocket is a process where a hedge fund separates illiquid or relatively hard to value assets from the rest of the fund's more liquid portfolio. The side pocket is normally formed by creating a new class of shares, which gives current investors a pro rata claim to the potential payoffs from the side pocket. Management must have a clear policy about when and what can be segregated into side pockets. Since assets assigned to side pockets are not valued on a regular basis, there have to be sufficient controls with regard to when assets can be moved between the regular fund and the side pockets.

Next, we present an example of due diligence applied to a hypothetical distressed securities hedge fund.[2]

John Redford, CAIA, is an alternative investment analyst at Johnson University endowment (JU). The endowment's board believes that the credit cycle is turning, that the default rate will pick up within the next year, and that there will be an opportunity to make investments in distressed debt. In preparation for potential allocations that JU's board will make, John is conducting due diligence on distressed securities hedge funds. John has received back the completed questionnaire for Barner Partners, L.P.

Below is a list of pros and cons with regard to investing in the fund, highlighting and classifying any "cons" as either yellow or red flags.

Pros:

- The investor and fund gates match up liquidity fairly well for a control distressed fund.

Cons:

- Yellow Flag: The fund takes a quarterly incentive fee while marking its own portfolio in some cases, which is a conflict of interest.

---

[2] This example was prepared by James Gil.

AIMA/CAIA Due Diligence Questionnaire – Distressed	
General Information	
Fund Name	Barner Partners, L.P.
HQ Address	200 Park Ave, NY, NY 10017
Tel, F, Email	212.555.1212; 212.555.1213; info@barner.
Fund Terms	
Subscriptions	Monthly
Redemptions	Quarterly with 30 days notice
Lock-up	Soft lock up of 4% penalty in first 6 months; 2% penalty in next 6 months, and none thereafter
Fund Gate	10% per quarter with a 1-year cleanup provision
Investor Gate	25% per quarter. 100% can be redeemed in full with a 5% penalty paid to the Fund if the Fund gate is not up.
Management Fee	2%
Incentive Fee	20% paid quarterly subject to high water mark
Side Pocket	The manager may designate up to 20% of the Fund's NAV as a "side-pocket" investment. The manager may move designated investments in and out of the side pocket at any time at its sole discretion
Fund Strategy	
Is the strategy passive or active distressed?	The Fund pursues an active (control) distressed strategy. The Fund seeks to purchase senior secured bank loans of companies in or about to enter bankruptcy, chair the creditor committee, and install the Fund's management personnel as the board members of the company.
Where in the capital structure does the fund focus?	See above answer.
How much leverage will be used?	Loan Market Value (LMV) will initially represent 300% of NAV. As the cycle improves, LMV exposure can reach 600%. Leverage will be in the form of overnight Repo from the Fund's prime broker.
How are positions valued	Positions are valued either by the Fund manager or the Fund's prime broker.
How many positions does the fund have?	At the peak, the fund is expected to have between 8 and 10 positions.

- Yellow Flag: The fund can move investments in and out of the side pocket at will, which is a conflict of interest.
- Yellow Flag: The redemption and lockup terms seem very light for a control distressed fund.
- Red Flag: Massive amounts of leverage are being used in a control distressed strategy.
- Red Flag: The prime broker has the ability to mark the portfolio. Since they are the leverage counterparty for the Repo and the positions are illiquid, the prime broker can effectively put the fund out of business by marking positions to the point where the fund would face a margin call, and the prime broker can liquidate the fund, leading to a total loss end BL.

These questions are illustrative of some of the key aspects that should be investigated during a due diligence process. In practice, it is essential to understand that proper due diligence needs to be tailored to the particular circumstances of each hedge fund investment.

37

Operational Risk

The first efforts to measure risk in the financial industry focused on two areas:

- **Market risk**. The potential economic loss caused by the decrease in the market value of a portfolio due to adverse changes in the market prices of financial assets, including interest rates, foreign exchange rates, equity prices and commodity prices.
- **Credit risk**. The potential economic losses due to a counterparty's credit rating being downgraded or outright default by the counterparty (e.g. the failure to perform according to a contractual arrangement).

However, since the publication of the International Convergence of Capital Measurement and Capital Standards, known as Basel II Capital Accord, a new type of risk has received considerable attention, namely, operational risk. Operational risk is technically defined by Basel II as "the risk of loss resulting from inadequate or failed internal processes, people, and systems." When applied to hedge funds, the term operational risk usually applies to the risks associated with the operating environment of the hedge fund (trade processing, accounting, administration, valuation, risk management, people, systems/technology, data/information, interfaces with external service providers, etc.). Unlike investments risks, operational risks are primarily driven by people/operations, technology, and data/information rather than by traders or portfolio managers.

The measurement and modeling of market, credit, and operational risks vary widely among firms and, more importantly, funds use widely differing approaches to measure each of these risks. Market risk is measured by two popular quantitative metrics:

- Value at Risk (VaR) measures the worst expected loss under "normal" market conditions over a specific time interval and at a given confidence level.
- Conditional Value at Risk (CVaR) is an extension of VaR. In simple terms, CVaR is the average loss in circumstances that would lead to a loss exceeding the VaR; in other words, the expected loss under "abnormal" market conditions.

Credit risk can also be measured using quantitative metrics. Typical measures are (see Figure 37.1):

- **Expected Loss** measures the anticipated average loss of a portfolio over the relevant time horizon. It is the average amount of credit losses that a fund should expect to experience over a given period. It is normally calculated as the product of three factors: the probability of default, the expected exposure at the time of default, and the expected loss given default.
- **Economic Capital** measures the amount of capital a fund must maintain to cover "worst case" credit losses. In a sense, it captures the variance or the uncertainty of the credit losses around the average.

In comparison to the probabilistic concepts used in calculating market risk and credit risk, the more recent measurements of operational risk are significantly less advanced and thus more subjective and qualitative. They concentrate more on business processes, overall operational workflow, and reducing the frequency and/or the severity of events that can lead to operational losses.

Assessing operational risk and its sources is one of the most complex, but essential issues with which investors must contend. According to a study by Feffer and Kundro (2003), 54% of failed

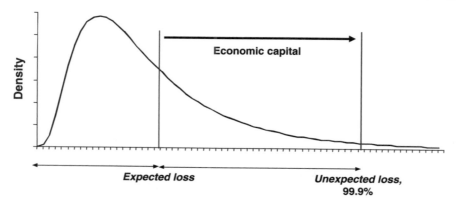

Figure 37.1   The metrics of credit risk.

hedge funds in the past 20 years had identifiable operational issues and half of all hedge fund failures could be attributed to operational risk alone. Of the funds in their study that were liquidated due to operational failures, 41% involved misrepresentation of investments and performance, 30% involved misappropriation of funds and general fraud, 14% involved unauthorized trading and style breaches, 6% involved inadequate resources and 9% involved other operational failures. Moreover, these statistics only describe the tip of the iceberg since they do not account for hedge funds that have incurred significant losses but have stayed in business. Prudent hedge fund investing shouldn't focus exclusively on the investment capabilities of fund managers, but should also avoid taking unnecessary operational risks.

The difficulty is that the type and quality of hedge fund management infrastructures vary widely, from small boutiques focused on niche strategies to large investment firms running multiple strategies in parallel. In the world of hedge funds, size is not necessarily a guarantee of operational quality; very successful hedge fund managers may have a tendency to grow rapidly beyond their own capacity to control risk.

Furthermore, the risk of failure is particularly acute in middle and back office functions because they are often a lower priority for expenditure, relative to other profit centers. Investors, therefore, need to scrutinize the organization managing the hedge fund (which includes their fund structure, their back office, the experience of operations personnel, as well as their valuation policy and independent oversight) before making the decision to invest.[1]

Well-publicized hedge fund "blow-ups" are usually the most extreme result of operational risk. Compared to blow-ups resulting from market or credit risks, there have been fewer blow-ups due to operation risk, but when they do happen, they can result in substantial losses to investors. Many such blow-ups could have been easily detected, or even avoided with more comprehensive operational due diligence and monitoring. In the following section we will discuss three recent high profile hedge fund failures, namely the Bayou Funds, Amaranth and Madoff. The Bayou Funds and Madoff cases

---

[1] As an illustration, a panel discussion on operational risk sponsored by the International Association of Financial Engineers was held on 20 September 2006. The panel identified four key operational risks that all investors should analyze: (i) valuation risk, which includes both intentional pricing misstatements to investors and errors or omissions associated with problematic inputs and calculations; (ii) fraud risk, which includes mismanagement, embezzlement and Ponzi schemes; (iii) challenges associated with securing robust and good quality data for the purpose of decision making, risk assessment and management; and (iv) the continuity of operations, both in terms of succession planning and key man risk, and traditional business continuity programs.

will illustrate frauds coupled with a massive "Ponzi scheme." Amaranth is provided as an example of a massive style drift in a multi-strategy fund with excessive risk taking.

CASE STUDY 1: THE BAYOU FUNDS

A review of the case

The first Bayou hedge fund was created in 1996 with $1.2 million of capital. Its founding partners, Samuel Israel III and Daniel E. Marino, were born within three months of each other in 1959 but had little else in common.

Samuel Israel grew up in New Orleans where his family ran a century-old commodities trading firm. Israel attended Tulane, but never graduated. He expected to join the family business, but his plans had to change when his father and grandfather sold their firm to Donaldson, Lufkin & Jenrette for $44 million in 1981. Israel joined the money management firm F.J. Graber & Co., as a simple trade executor. Over the years, his career never really progressed and he switched from one firm to the next, going from Graber to Midwood Securities Inc., then Gerard Klauer Mattison & Co. and finally Gruntal & Co. According to his employment record on file with the National Association of Securities Dealers, Israel left Gruntal in 1991 after a trade that resulted in a "substantial loss" after which he did not show up for work for several days. He then joined James Marquez, an ex-colleague from Graber, who had created a hedge fund called JGM Management. This new venture turned out very quickly to be a financial disaster and Israel abandoned it to join Leon Cooperman's Omega Advisors. He left Omega in 1995 and spent the next few months developing computer trading models.

His partner, Dan Marino, grew up on Staten Island. In 1981, Dan Marino graduated from Wagner College and joined Coopers & Lybrand as an auditor in New York. After a few years, he left Coopers & Lybrand to join Spicer & Oppenheim and later the hedge fund JGM Management as Chief Financial Officer. The poor performance at JGM Management forced James Marquez to shut down the firm in 1995.

In 1996, Israel created Bayou, recruiting both Marino and Marquez. His strategy of trading a stock portfolio with a turnover of about 200% per month was expected to generate an attractive performance of 1% to 3% a month with limited risk. But the first audit conducted by Chicago-based Grant Thornton LLP revealed a 12% loss for the first year. In order to keep their existing clients and attract new ones, Israel and Marino decided to lie about their results. First, they changed the date of inception of the fund, effectively erasing its debut losses. Second, to make the fund more attractive going forward, they waived their 2% management fee and only charged a performance fee (this should have been a red flag to investors). They then simultaneously established an affiliate broker dealer called Bayou Securities to execute all the fund's trades (a serious red flag to investors). As a result, the more they traded, the more they were pocketing in trading commissions – regardless of whether their trades were profitable or not.

In 1997, Bayou stumbled again. Once more Israel and Marino did not disclose trading losses to their clients. They even rebated a portion of the commissions that the fund had paid to Bayou Securities during that year. Bayou clients were therefore left with the false impression that they had made a trading profit.

In 1998, the Bayou Fund sustained a net trading loss of several million dollars. Rather than officially reporting these losses, Israel and Marino hid them again and continued to raise external capital. To avoid any external control, they terminated Bayou's independent auditor (a serious red flag that has to be investigated in every instance), Grant Thornton LLP, and created a fictitious accounting firm called Richmond-Fairfield Associates, CPA, PLLC ("Richmond-Fairfield") to pose as the fund's independent auditor. They then fabricated books and records that misrepresented their true financial performance and inflated the fund's net asset values. This was only possible because the Bayou Fund was self-administered and lacked a truly independent auditor. Finally, they generated false weekly performance summaries and sent them to investors and prospects. As Israel admitted later, the goal was "to induce people to invest in Bayou or continue to keep their money in Bayou."

With a few winning trades, the scheme could have remained undiscovered and losses recouped discreetly. Unfortunately, the Bayou Fund continued to accumulate trading losses and the two partners continued to conceal them and replace them with fictitious gains. In October 2000, they even decided to incorporate Richmond-Fairfield by filing with the New York Department of State, turning it into a real company. The reality was still that (i) the Bayou Fund was Richmond-Fairfield's only client and Marino was its only principal; (ii) from 1999 to 2003, the Bayou Fund continued to lose substantial amounts of money every year and never earned a profit; and (iii) Israel and Marino concealed the losses with false financial statements and a fictitious audit.

In February 2003, Israel and Marino attempted a big marketing coup. They liquidated the original Bayou Fund and created four separate hedge funds known as Bayou Accredited, Bayou Affiliates, Bayou No Leverage and Bayou Superfund. All existing investors were offered a transfer of their investment in the Bayou Fund to one of the new hedge funds. However, losses continued to accumulate in the new entities and were still concealed through the dissemination of false investment performance reports and false financial statements under cover of purported "audits" by Richmond-Fairfield.

In 2004, Israel and Marino stopped trading and attempted to recoup their losses by investing in private placement transactions in Europe. They drained virtually all of the funds' prime brokerage accounts and wired approximately $150 million into Bayou Management's account at Citibank, and later into Israel's name in European bank accounts for use in prime bank note trading programs. As usual, the transaction was not disclosed to the funds' investors. Instead, Israel and Marino falsely communicated to investors that the usual trading was still being conducted. Over the next 12 months, they undertook a number of transfers that eventually culminated with a $101 million transfer to a Wachovia bank account. Bank officials notified the Arizona Attorney General that there was reason to believe the transfer was made in connection with a fraud. After a brief inquiry, the Arizona Attorney General seized the funds and opened an investigation.

In a letter dated 27 July 2005, Israel and Marino abruptly advised their investors and creditors that the Bayou Funds were voluntarily liquidating. All were promised a full redemption of their investments, which purportedly had grown in value, upon completion of a final audit. In mid-August 2005, a second letter was sent to ensure that 90% of the total value of the fund shares would be distributed within one week. However, the Bayou Funds did not repay any money and the remaining funds vanished in a final act. Redemption checks tendered to clients in August 2005 were returned for insufficient funds – documents obtained from Bayou-related bank accounts later evidenced that the accounts had been overdrawn before the liquidation and redemption checks were drafted.

Israel and Marino were rapidly arrested. Both pleaded guilty to conspiracy, wire fraud and investment advisory fraud. Marquez, who had left the fund earlier, also pleaded guilty to persuading people to invest in the funds by telling them the funds were profitable when they were in fact losing large sums of money.

Early warning signs

Bayou is often cited as the perfect example of a hedge fund fraud case. The reality is that, lulled by financial statements showing annual returns of as much as 33%, many investors and financial advisors missed all the red flags at Bayou. Let us mention some of them:

Background checks

Before founding Bayou, Israel claimed to have worked for four years as a head trader for Leon Cooperman's Omega Advisors where, according to one of the Bayou Fund's marketing presentations, he "was responsible for all equity and financial futures executions (. . .) as well as sharing responsibility for hedging the portfolio through the use of futures and options." The reality was that Israel had misrepresented the length of his employment at Omega and overstated his position. A simple telephone call to verify Israel's credentials would have evidenced these two points. Additional calls would have revealed the losses at Gruntal. Moreover, when a very talented trader leaves a company to create his own hedge fund, it is common to see an initial investment from his former employer. This was not the case for Bayou – none of the two Omega funds of hedge funds invested in Bayou.

More interestingly, according to LexisNexis (a subscription data base), Israel had been arrested in New York State in 1999 and accused of "driving under the influence" and charged with criminal possession of a "controlled substance." Although the case was discontinued a year later, potential investors might also have been concerned if they had learned this.

Questionable operational setup

A serious operational due diligence on Bayou would have shown that the fund had no independent auditors, wired funds to unreported bank accounts, and had abnormal levels of expenses.

- Every financial statement from the Bayou Funds was accompanied by a report of the auditors, Richmond-Fairfield Associates. The latter was a completely unknown auditing firm – in fact, even a sham entity for many years. No investors seem to have verified the existence of Richmond-Fairfield Associates. Furthermore, in 2002, Bayou told some clients that Grant Thornton was overseeing its books. A phone call would have revealed that Grant Thornton had not audited Bayou since the late 1990s.
- Bayou Management maintained primary bank accounts at Citibank and then at Wachovia Bank on behalf of the Bayou Funds despite lacking a specified rationale. These accounts were later used to siphon money out of the Bayou Funds.
- Even though Bayou Securities' financial position was teetering, it was paying consulting fees to stock research firms ($60,000 a month), limousine services ($5000 a month), restaurant meals ($4000 a month), the lease of a private jet ($100,000 a month), and even the services of a counter-espionage consultant ($20,000 a month).

Conflicts of interest with own broker-dealer

The Bayou Funds' assets were traded through accounts maintained by Bayou Securities, the broker-dealer owned by Israel. According to Israel and Marino, this benefited the funds because of the quality of execution, reduced clearing costs and shared expenses. In practice, Bayou Securities did little, as it cleared all its trades through an arrangement with another registered broker-dealer that acted as the funds' prime broker. In fact, Israel was making dozens of very large trades every month that yielded enormous commissions for Bayou Securities, from which he and Marino paid themselves annual salaries and profit distributions. As an illustration, in 2003 alone, while the Bayou Funds lost approximately $49 million of investors' money, Bayou Securities earned approximately $29 million in commissions. No investors seemed to have verified or questioned the activity of Bayou Securities.

Some due diligence on Bayou Securities would have also shown the firm held insufficient capital; regulators require that a brokerage firm conducting business with clients maintain a certain amount

Table 37.1 Performance of the Bayou Fund (January 2000 to December 2004).

	Annualized return	Standard deviation
Bayou	13.1%	4.6%
CSFB Tremont HFI Long Short Equity	4.8%	9.0%
HFRI Equity Hedge Index	6.3%	8.7%
CISDM Equity Long Short Index	5.7%	6.6%

Source: Gupta and Kazemi (2007)

of capital on hand. In March 2004, Bayou Securities had a net capital position of $5.9 million and had borrowed 9% of that amount, according to its filings. By December 2004, however, the firm's net capital had declined to $259,731. By the end of March, it was negatively capitalized: it held $164,237 and its borrowings represented 161% of that.

Extravagant lifestyle

Most of the money siphoned off the Bayou Funds by Israel and Marino was used to finance their extravagant lifestyle. As an illustration, Israel rented a 1920's-era stone mansion in Mount Kisco, N.Y. for $32,000 a month and bought himself a Bentley. In October 2003, Marino bought a six-bedroom colonial-style home in Westport for $2.9 million, paying mostly in cash. Most common background checks performed during the due diligence process would have revealed these facts, which would have led to further investigations into the operations of the fund.

Exit recommendations from consultants

In 2002, some consultants, who had initially recommended the funds to their clients, advised them to withdraw their funds. For example, Tremont asked officials at Bayou about some discrepancy between the onshore and the offshore fund. The answer was that Bayou had shifted profitable trades made in its United States funds to the offshore portfolios in an attempt to increase the offshore funds' performance. Tremont decided to withdraw immediately.[2]

"Too good to be true" performance

Table 37.1 shows the summary statistics of Bayou's reported returns over the period January 2000 to December 2004, as well as those of comparable CASAM CISDM, CSFB and HFR long/short equity indices. With twice the return and half the risk, Bayou's performance was hardly in line with its peers. This should have tipped investors off that something unusual was happening at the fund.

Despite their official stunning performance, the Bayou Funds had very favorable terms for investors: (i) no management fee with just a 20% performance fee; (ii) low minimum investment of

---

[2] Note that investors who redeemed early were actually paid with the capital of new investors based on false valuation statements. After Bayou collapsed, Jeff J. Marwil of the law firm Winston & Strawn sued 122 redeemers for fraudulent conveyance and asked them to return all their money (principal as well as profits) so it could be split among *all* investors. His claim was backed by the U.S. bankruptcy law, which can force unwitting participants to forfeit their redemption proceeds if they had known about a scam because of red flags. In such a case, the burden of proof is on the accused, forcing redeemers to show they could not have suspected fraud from such clues.

$250,000; and (iii) monthly liquidity with no lockup period. These terms should have been perceived as unusually generous for a very successful hedge fund.

This long series of red flags should obviously have raised some concerns about Bayou before it started writing bad checks to its investors. Several investors who were led to invest in Bayou by outside investment consulting firms sued for not having exercised an appropriate level of due diligence. As a result, many FoHF beefed up their due diligence processes by performing background checks and probing valuation procedures on both their existing and potential investments.

CASE STUDY 2: AMARANTH

The case of Amaranth is fundamentally different from Bayou. There was no fraud, but rather there was a lack of appropriate risk management in a very large multi-strategy fund. The result was a loss of approximately $6 billion for the fund investors – one of the largest blow-ups so far in the hedge fund world.

A review of the case

The Amaranth Fund was created in September 2000 with 27 employees and $450 million in capital. Its founder, Nicholas Maounis, grew up in Stamford, Connecticut and graduated from the University of Connecticut. He started his finance career as a convertible bond arbitrageur at LF Rothschild, Unterberg, Towbin (1985–1989), then moved to Angelo, Gordon & Co. (1989–1990), and Paloma Partners (1990–2000). At Paloma, he ultimately became a portfolio manager, responsible for trading a large convertible arbitrage portfolio and managing up to 25 traders and assistants active in a variety of investment strategies.

In late 1998, Paloma Partners experienced liquidity problems as a result of the Russian crisis. Maounis' portfolio, although profitable, had to be liquidated to meet the fund's margin calls. Maounis and several members of his team decided to leave Paloma on amicable terms and create a new firm, which they called Amaranth International Advisors LLC. Amaranth contracted Paloma to provide infrastructure and back office servicing for the firm. Consequently, Donald Sussman, the founder of Paloma, took a 15% stake in the management company. He also gave Amaranth a substantial amount of seed capital in exchange for favourable redemption terms and no management fees.

During the first years of its existence, Amaranth relied strongly upon Paloma to provide compliance, infrastructure, and back-office services (settlement, reconciliation, accounting, valuation services and NAV production). Throughout 2003, the fund made significant investments in systems and staff, with the goal of becoming operationally independent of Paloma. It progressively expanded beyond Maounis' initial expertise (convertible arbitrage) and became a multi-strategy hedge fund, using a variety of trading strategies (statistical arbitrage, equity volatility arbitrage, energy/commodities trading, merger arbitrage, and long/short equity and credit products). Maounis remained in charge, opportunistically allocating capital among the various strategies used at Amaranth; but the non-trading aspects of the firm (i.e. accounting, treasury, administration, compliance, investor relations, legal, marketing, technology, back-office operations and human resources) were under the direction of Charles Winkler, the Chief Operating Officer. Winkler was formerly the Chief Operating Officer for Citadel Investment Group (at the time a $5 billion hedge fund), a member of its Management Committee and the Chairman of its Operations Committee.

Amaranth initially posted excellent returns: +21.4% in 2001, +10.6% in 2002, +15.1% in 2003. But in 2004, arbitrage strategies were lagging and the fund only delivered +8.3% to its investors. Maounis decided to increase exposure to potentially higher yielding markets such as energy. He hired Brian Hunter, a Canadian gas trader, to co-head the group of former Enron traders that had joined his firm in 2003.

JPMorgan Chase, which served as Amaranth's clearing firm for its commodity trades, described its energy trading initiative as follows: "The Fund has hired a couple of former Enron energy traders to build an Energy Arbitrage desk. Energy arbitrage opportunities can also take a number of forms due to the significant amount of available "Energy" products. A generic geographical energy arbitrage can be trading the difference of price in a given commodity either in the same location or in a different geographical location. Other arbitrage opportunities include grade arbitrage which encompasses trading the difference in price of two related crude oil based commodities such as the spread between WTI and Brent Crude. Generally these arbitrage opportunities are created by fundamental news affecting production and inventory. In addition, trades may also be on the perceived price volatility of crude oil and other crude products such as gasoline, jet fuel and heating oil and/or the correlation between one another. These views have been expressed through calendar spreads. In addition, deep out-of-the-money call options are purchased as a cheap way to take advantage of price shocks. Leverage ranges from 5–8×." JPMorgan Chase also indicated that "initially only 2% of Amaranth's capital will be allocated to energy related trading".

In 2005, Brian Hunter had positioned his trading book in the anticipation of soaring natural gas prices. This strategy proved successful when hurricane Katrina smashed into the Gulf Coast, wreaking havoc in New Orleans and disrupting dozens of natural gas refineries. As a result, Amaranth gained $1.3 billion from energy trading and posted a +18.6% gain in 2005, a great figure given that most of the "usual" arbitrage strategies did not perform very well in that year. JPMorgan Chase reported[3] that for the domestic Amaranth fund, "the majority of the positive performance for 2005 came from profits in the energy book; approximately 98% of the funds' [year-to-date] performance was related to energy trades. Energy trading profits/losses are derived primarily from natural gas calendar swaps". Brian Hunter pocketed a $75 million bonus and was named head of Amaranth's energy trading operations. Maounis let him move back to Calgary along with eight traders and run the energy trading desk from there.

By 2006, due to its energy trading successes, Amaranth had grown significantly in terms of number of employees (400), assets under management ($8 billion) and locations (Greenwich, Connecticut, London, Toronto, Singapore, Calgary and Houston). Its staff included a chief risk officer and 12 risk specialists to monitor the risks in the various trading books. The fund was now marketed as a low-risk multi-strategy hedge fund, but the reality was that most of the risk was allocated to Brian Hunter and his team.

At the beginning of the year, Hunter expected gas supply shortages, delivery bottlenecks and weather-related disruptions to develop during the winter, boosting gas prices. His forecast was based on an increase in domestic demand for natural gas, and the possibility of another tough hurricane season. Indeed, historically, winter natural gas prices had always been much higher than summer natural gas prices as natural gas prices typically increase as temperatures fall and the demand for natural gas for residential heating rises. Prices typically fall after March as consumer demand weakens (note that such a predictable pattern does not necessarily lead to profitable opportunities because natural gas is expensive to store and move). Moreover, his view was also clearly priced by the market in the "**forward curve**" (see Figure 37.2), i.e. the price of each natural gas NYMEX futures contract for successive future delivery months.

Hunter implemented his view on seasonal changes in gas prices through two major trading positions. To bet that January prices would be much higher than November prices, he bought gas futures contracts for January 2007 and sold such contracts for November 2006. In order to express

---

[3] Source: JPMorgan Chase, CP Leveraged Funds Due Diligence, Annual Review 2005.

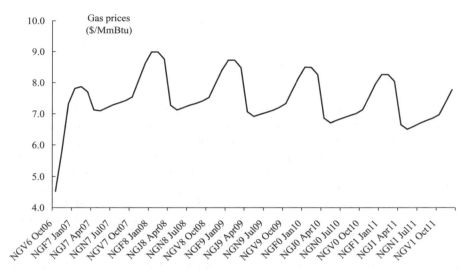

Figure 37.2   The natural gas forward curve as of 9/26/2006 peaks in the winter months and falls in the summer months. (*Source:* Bloomberg)

his view that March prices would be higher than April prices, he bought gas futures contracts for March 2007 and sold them for April 2007.

By the end of the summer of 2006, Brian Hunter's energy trades accounted for about half of Amaranth's capital and had generated more than $2.2 billion of profit. This time, however, success had been accompanied by massive volatility.

In April, Amaranth gained 14.42% and was up 30.73% YTD. In his monthly letter sent to investors, Maounis explained that: "Our energy and commodities portfolios generated outsized returns due to unusual volatility across the crude oil, natural gas, and metals businesses. Primary drivers of returns included (1) natural gas spread trades, which benefited from the significant increase in crude oil prices and the glut of summer 2006 natural gas relative to storage capacity and prospective summer demand, and (2) a profound increase in base metals prices (copper in particular) with an associated volatility spike. As volatility increased during the month, we took the opportunity to reduce exposure in our natural gas and metals portfolios and realized profits."

In May, Hunter suffered losses of approximately $1 billion as a result of a natural gas spread compression. When the fund tried to reduce some of its positions, it found it difficult to find enough buyers willing to pay the prevailing market prices. Maounis had to ask traders in other areas to cut their positions to raise cash, but allowed Hunter to keep his positions and attempt to recoup his losses. In his monthly letter to investors, Maounis said: "Historically, the market has provided sufficient liquidity and opportunity for us to tailor the portfolio as desired despite rapidly changing market dynamics. This "expansion/contraction" approach has enabled us to generate more profits than if we had required the team to unwind trades aggressively whenever markets moved in our favor. In this case, as we endeavored to monetize gains (and reduce risk) within the portfolio, liquidity in the market seized up due to high volumes of producer hedging that oversaturated market demand for forward natural gas. While this was a humbling experience that has led us to recalibrate how we assess risk in this business, we believe certain spread relationships remained disconnected from their fundamental value drivers."

In practice, Amaranth's inability to find buyers at the prevailing prices was not surprising. According to the U.S. Senate Permanent Subcommittee on Investigations (2007), during the spring and summer of 2006, Amaranth controlled between 25% and 48% of the outstanding contracts (open interest) in all NYMEX natural gas futures contracts for 2006; about 30% for 2007; between 25% and 40% for 2008; between 20% and 40% for 2009; and about 60% for 2010. Amaranth's large-scale trading was one of the major drivers behind the rise of the spreads it was betting on. More importantly, the size of Amaranth's losses also alerted the market to the potential size of its natural gas holdings.

In June and July 2006, Amaranth did not pare down its spread positions – it actually enlarged them as falling prices and spreads were seen as an opportunity to increase positions. As an illustration, Amaranth's position in January 2007 futures alone represented the entire amount of natural gas that was actually used by U.S. residential consumers nationwide during January 2007. In early August, on several occasions, the NYMEX directed Amaranth to reduce its positions. Amaranth ultimately responded by moving its positions to the unregulated ICE market and further increased them. But in late August, the hurricane season had been quiet, production had not been distorted, inventories were relatively high and gas prices started falling. As a result, Amaranth faced increasing margin requirements. Its non-energy traders had to again reduce the size of their books to generate cash, which further concentrated the fund's overall portfolio in gas spread play. When Hunter was forced to reduce the fund's September contract exposure, he represented such a significant share of the overall volume on the exchange that his trades pushed prices further down. Several hedge funds took large opposing positions to Amaranth's, knowing that prices were essentially driven by large-scale trading rather than market forces.[4] On August 29, Amaranth lost nearly $600 million – a sum that was far larger than its target daily VaR figure. But despite this enormous one-day loss, the fund still finished August with a net monthly gain of $631 million.

Markets continued to play against Amaranth in September. For example, the price of the NYMEX futures contract to deliver natural gas in October 2006 fell from a high of $8.45 per MMBtu[5] in late July to just under $4.80 per MMBtu in September, the lowest level for that contract in two and a half years. The March/April 2007 spread collapsed from a high of nearly $2.50 per MMBtu in July, to less than 60 cents in September, a drop of 75%. On August 31, Amaranth's margin requirements on ICE and NYMEX exceeded $2.5 billion; by September 8 they had surpassed $3 billion. In an ultimate attempt to reduce its market risk, in early September, Amaranth bought the opposing positions of MotherRock, a $300 million hedge fund in an attempt to reduce its exposure,[6] but it was too late. Amaranth was no longer able to face new margin calls. During the weekend of September 16, Amaranth was forced to sell its energy positions to its clearing firm (JPMorgan Chase) and another hedge fund (Citadel) and started liquidating the rest of its holdings.

Amaranth's end was rather chaotic. With a loss estimated at more than 35% for the year, most investors expected Amaranth to close. Yet on September 22, Maounis announced that he had "every intention of continuing in business". He suspended all redemptions for September and October "to enable the Amaranth funds to generate liquidity for investors in an orderly fashion, with the goal of maximizing the proceeds of asset dispositions". On the night of September 26, Maounis sent a four sentence e-mail to his 420 employees that started with "I want to thank all of you for your years of loyalty and support, especially during this especially difficult time for all of us" and continued with

---

[4] Amaranth sent a letter to the NYMEX on August 30, 2006, claiming that certain market participants were "not trading in a responsible manner."

[5] Natural gas is measured by volume (cubic feet) and by energy content (British Thermal Unit, or Btu). One Btu is the amount of heat required to raise the temperature of one pound of water by one degree Fahrenheit. Natural gas usually is measured in quantities of thousands of Btu (MBtu) or millions of Btu (MMBtu).

[6] MotherRock was a $300 million hedge fund headed by the former NYMEX chairman Bo Collins. MotherRock essentially took the opposite bet of Amaranth (i.e. that futures prices for winter contracts would fall in relation to the summer prices) and failed during the summer 2006. ABN Amro, its clearing firm, temporarily assumed its portfolio before selling it to Amaranth.

"I am quite sure that the Amaranth spirit will live on in all of us as nothing can ever take that away from us." Within an hour, Stanley Friedman, the head of human resources, sent out his own message explaining that the previous e-mail "was not intended to say goodbye." A few days later, under considerable pressure from his investors, Maounis finally agreed to liquidate the fund. Interestingly, most Amaranth employees have since joined other hedge funds. In particular, Brian Hunter and his former colleagues Shane Lee, Matthew Calhoun and Karl Koster launched their own fund in the beginning of 2007, Solengo Capital, to play in the commodity space.

Early warning signals

Here again, one could argue that numerous red flags could have been identified if Amaranth's investors had done their homework.

Background checks

Before joining Amaranth, Hunter was at Deutsche Bank's natural-gas trading desk where he personally generated $17 million in profit in 2001 and $52 million in 2002. Under his supervision, the gas desk cumulated $76 million in profits in 2003 until it lost $51.2 million in a single week in December. Hunter blamed "an unprecedented and unforeseeable run-up in gas prices" along with "well-documented and widely known problems with (Deutsche Bank's systems)," which limited his ability to extricate himself from bad trades. He argued that he personally created $40 million in profits that year and insisted on a commensurate bonus. Deutsche Bank denied its systems were to blame, demoted Hunter to an analyst role, and locked him out of the trading system. Hunter ultimately left Deutsche Bank in April 2004, subsequently sued over the withheld bonus, and claimed the bank defamed him. The suit was still pending when he joined Amaranth.

At Amaranth, there were also some conflicts and departures that should have been investigated. The former Enron trader Harry Arora joined Amaranth in 2002 as the head of the energy group. He was relatively conservative and sought to make diversified and relative value commodities investments. Under his leadership, the energy group posted steady returns. As Hunter, then his employee, wanted the ability to take on large directional bets, Arora had a falling out with Maounis over the risks the firm was taking. Arora separated his own book from Hunter's so that each could control his own trades. He ultimately left Amaranth to start his own energy trading outfit, Arcim Advisors. Hunter then became the head of the energy trading desk at Amaranth and moved the operations up to Calgary.

Suspect return pattern

Most investors saw no reason to worry about Amaranth's performance as long as it continued to provide strong returns – even when the returns were too good to be true for the strategy the investors believed the fund was pursuing. As an illustration, Gupta and Kazemi (2007) have compared Amaranth's performance with various hedge fund indices (Figure 37.3). Until May 2005, there is a relatively good tracking between Amaranth and the CASAM CISDM Equal Weighted Hedge Fund Index. However, the stellar returns generated in late 2005 and early 2006 indicate a clear change in strategy.

Gupta and Kazemi (2007) also observe that the magnitude of the kurtosis figure of Amaranth's return distribution signaled a fat tail compatible with an extremely volatile asset such as natural gas but certainly not with a multi-strategy hedge fund.

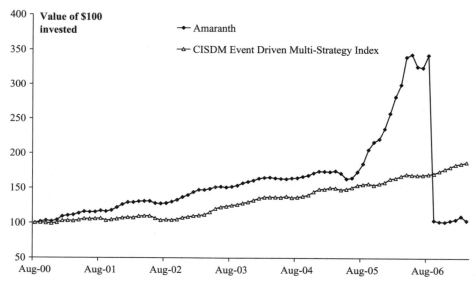

Figure 37.3 Comparison between the performance of Amaranth and the CISDM Event Driven Multi-Strategy Index. (*Source:* Gupta and Kazemi (2007))

Excessive position size

By 2005, Amaranth was no longer what it had marketed itself as – a diversified multi-strategy fund. Indeed, more than 55% of the fund's capital was effectively in one single concentrated, undiversified position. Most investors should have been aware of the large proportion of energy trades in the overall P&L since it was clearly revealed in the fund's monthly reports.

Amaranth accumulated such large positions and traded such large volumes of natural gas that it literally drove the market up as long as it was buying. Ultimately, the fund's positions became illiquid to the point that even the NYMEX had to step in and request some reduction.[7] To avoid the NYMEX speculative limits, Hunter moved its positions to the unregulated ICE market and used OTC contracts. By doing so, he lost anonymity as well as the ability to trade with many counterparties. More importantly, he concentrated large natural gas positions with counterparties who were in effect his direct competitors. After it collapsed, Amaranth could not exit its positions due to the lack of liquidity. It had to sell them to other hedge funds at a large discount to their mark-to-market value, compounding the losses to investors.

Non-independent administration

Amaranth's administrator was MQ Services Ltd. (MQS), an affiliate of the Fund's Bermuda legal counsel Wakefield Quin. In fact, MQS was a relatively small firm that only provided Amaranth with share registration servicing. All transaction level accounting records, intra-month reconciliations and

---

[7] As an illustration, the CFTC defines a "large trader" for reporting purposes in the natural gas market as a trader who holds at least 200 contracts, and the NYMEX examines a trader's position if it exceeds 12,000 natural gas contracts in any one month. Amaranth held as many as 100,000 natural gas contracts in a single month. Each variation of one cent in a position of 100,000 contracts changes a trader's profit or loss by $10 million.

Table 37.2 Summary statistics for Amaranth LLC. The top panel examines the period Jan 2003–Sept 2006, the middle panel examines the period Jan 2003–Aug 2006, and the bottom panel examines the period Jun 2005–Aug 2006.

	CISDM Equal Weighted Hedge Fund Index	CISDM Convertible Arbitrage Index	Amaranth
Jan 2003–Sept 2006			
Annualized return	11.82%	5.31%	3.54%
Annualized volatility	4.33%	3.18%	37.16%
Skewness	−0.30	−0.72	−5.56
Kurtosis	−0.29	1.09	34.91
Minimum return	−1.68%	−2.45%	−66.0%
Maximum return	3.54%	2.34%	14.42%
Jan 2003–Aug 2006			
Annualized return	12.09%	5.18%	21.62%
Annualized volatility	4.34%	3.21%	12.60%
Skewness	−0.35	−0.69	−0.02
Kurtosis	−0.24	1.01	6.29
Minimum return	−1.68%	−2.45%	−11.66%
Maximum return	3.54%	2.34%	14.42%
Jun 2005–Aug 2006			
Annualized return	12.23%	10.23%	42.98%
Annualized volatility	4.67%	2.24%	19.41%
Skewness	−0.68	0.38	−1.06
Kurtosis	0.16	0.73	3.93
Minimum return	−1.68%	−0.17%	−11.66%
Maximum return	3.28%	2.34%	14.42%

Source: Gupta and Kazemi (2007)

month-end NAV accounting computations were prepared internally by Amaranth.[8] From Amaranth's point of view, given the complexity of the securities traded, it was impossible to have an independent competent offshore administrator. Although this was not an issue in the collapse of the fund, it should have been a red flag for most investors as the NAV was not subject to independent control and oversight.

Early redemptions

Many independent FoHF and advisors either took a look at Amaranth and rejected or redeemed their investments. For instance, Donald Sussman, the founder of Paloma and former boss and seed investor for Nick Maounis, withdrew three years before the collapse. A due diligence report completed more than a year prior to its failure identified significant operational risk factors at Amaranth, including "the lack of an independent third-party administrator verifying returns, insufficient risk controls, and the passing through of company expenses to the fund." (Hosking, 2006). This report led at least one investor to pull its money out of the fund at a significant financial penalty.

---

[8] To give comfort to investors and mitigate their concerns, Amaranth engaged GlobeOp to perform an independent review of its net asset value calculation, including pricing at each month-end valuation date. Approximately one month after each valuation date, GlobeOp issued a one page letter stating their opinion of the accuracy of the pricing used in the Manager's valuation. These letters were made available to the fund's investors on request.

Inadequate risk management

In its investor conference calls, Maounis repeatedly mentioned that they had experienced professionals monitoring the risk of the firm's positions. Maounis' original expertise was convertible arbitrage so essentially Amaranth had a convertible arbitrage trader trying – and failing – to supervise an energy trader. The two strategies are fundamentally different. In particular, convertible arbitrage is essentially a long gamma strategy once the credit risk has been hedged whereas a long gas spread is effectively a short gamma strategy.

Moreover, Brian Hunter was in Calgary, Alberta, while the chief risk officer was in Greenwich, Connecticut, more than 2,000 miles away. Hunter was a profit maker whereas risk was seen as a cost center. As a result, Amaranth's management recklessly permitted large positions and ignored the early warning signals. Chincarini (2007a, 2007b) provides a detailed investigation of Amaranth's failure and finds that Amaranth may have been chasing a potential expected profit of about $1 billion in September 2006 for a market risk VaR of about $3.781 billion with a leverage of about 7.28 times capital. By every measure this was a highly risky trade which, in addition to high levels of market risk, involved significant exposure to liquidity risk.

Moreover, external risk systems such as Riskdata FOFiX delivered three clear quantitative signals long before the first May draw down which indicated that Amaranth's risk exposure had increased significantly:

- A rapidly increasing risk level began in 2006, culminating in a level that was 45% above that of the S&P 500 before the first draw down in May and 89% above the S&P 500 by the end of August.
- A persistent and significant exposure to energy related factors (Oil, Equity, Energy and Material Sectors) followed by a surprising factor profile drift in August.
- A very strong risk concentration in gas from the beginning of the year when the analysis was expanded to include gas factors. This was again followed by a surprising profile drift in August, with a significant downside risk.

These signals did not require anything other than an analysis of Amaranth's track record. Due to strict lockup terms (up to four years), many investors could not have exited anyway, but they should have nevertheless reacted to the style drift of the fund. One could argue that the price movements observed on gas spreads were highly unlikely based on historical analysis, but in reality the size of Amaranth's positions made such movements inevitable when it tried to reduce its exposure.

CASE STUDY 3: MADOFF

With Madoff, we are back to a fraud case but on a much larger scale – financial experts call it one of the most detrimental Ponzi schemes in history. Surprisingly, many large and otherwise sophisticated bankers, hedge funds, and funds-of-funds have been hit by his alleged fraud despite obvious red flags that any operational due diligence and quantitative analysis should have identified as a concern prior to investing. The following discussion is based on Gregoriou and Lhabitant (2009).

A review of the case

First, it is important to note that, technically, Bernard Madoff did not run a hedge fund or a series of hedge funds – this was an essential feature of the Madoff scheme. Madoff operated a brokerage firm called Bernard L. Madoff Investment Securities, LLC (hereafter: BMIS). With over 200 employees, it was one of the largest market makers on the New York Stock Exchange.

Through BMIS and in parallel to its market making activity, Madoff was managing discretionary accounts for a very small number of clients. All accounts were investing in the same strategy called split-strike conversion. This strategy can be summarized as follows:

- Buy a basket of stocks whose performance would be highly correlated to the performance of the S&P 100 Index.
- Sell out-of-the-money call options on the S&P 100 Index with a notional value similar to that of the long equity portfolio. This creates a ceiling value beyond which further gains in the basket of stocks are offset by the increasing liability of the short positions in the call options.
- Buy out-of-the money put options on the S&P 100 with a notional value similar to that of the long equity portfolio. This creates a floor value below which further declines in the value of the basket of stocks are offset by gains in the long put options.

The result was essentially a collar with limited upside and downside and some index participation in the middle. Officially, Madoff claimed to implement this strategy over short-term horizons –usually less than a month. The rest of the time, the portfolio was allegedly in cash.

Madoff's promise was to return 8–12% a year reliably, no matter what the markets did. And he did – at least officially. Over his 17-year track record, Madoff delivered an impressive total return of 557%; i.e. 11.2% per year with a volatility of 2.5%, no down year, and almost no negative months. This extremely attractive performance attracted numerous investors, in particular "feeder funds" that essentially allocated all their assets to BMIS and marketed the strategy all over the world.

On December 10, 2008, Madoff confessed to his two sons, his brother and his wife that his investment advisory business was "a giant Ponzi scheme." In the evening, his sons turned him in to the U.S. authorities. Madoff was arrested the next day and charged with securities fraud. The SEC filed a complaint in Federal court in Manhattan seeking an asset freeze and the appointment of a receiver for BMIS. Overall, the cost of the fraud has been estimated to be as high as $60 billion.

Early warning signals

Madoff is likely to remain a case study of poor due diligence as there were numerous obvious red flags that should have prevented an investment. Let us mention some of them.

Lack of segregation amongst service providers

Madoff only offered his strategy through managed accounts at his affiliated broker-dealer BMIS, which also executed and cleared the underlying trades. More importantly, all assets were held in custody and administered within the BMIS organization, which also produced all documents showing the performance of the underlying investments.

Obscure auditors

BMIS was audited by a small accountancy firm called Friehling and Horowitz, with only one active accountant.

Unusual fee structure

BMIS charged no fees for running the strategy, but only a "market rate" commission charged on each trade. This was very attractive to feeder funds, as they were able to charge significant management and performance fees without being criticized for a double layer of fees.

Extreme secrecy

While most brokers provide their customers with timely, electronic access to their accounts, Madoff never did so. Access to Madoff's offices for on-site due diligence was very limited or was even denied, and Madoff systematically refused to answer questions about his business or about his investment strategies. Nobody ever knew how many feeder funds there were or the total size of their assets. In addition, at the feeder fund level, most private placement memoranda and marketing materials never mentioned Madoff or BMIS.

Incoherent 13F filings

Interestingly, Madoff's 13F forms (a form that is filed with the U.S. SEC and describes long holdings of large investors) usually contained only a smattering of small positions in small (non-S&P 100) equities. Madoff's implausible explanation was that his strategy was mostly in cash at the end of each quarter to avoid publicizing information concerning the securities he was trading on a discretionary basis.

Clearly, some may have thought the returns were too good to pass up or Madoff was too respectable to question. Perhaps some gained confidence from personal relationships with the manager or word-of-mouth endorsements from friends. All chose faith over evidence. The reality is that the warning signals were there and the salient operational features common to best-of-breed hedge funds were missing.

ASSESSING THE OPERATIONAL RISK OF A HEDGE FUND

As highlighted with the cases of Bayou, Amaranth and Madoff, the consequences of operational risk in hedge funds can be dramatic for investors. Sadly, investors are structurally exposed to such risk. Hedge fund managers are typically people who used to rely on the infrastructure provided by a large organization, such as an investment bank or an asset management firm, and have little experience in running an independent asset management firm. They may have the talent to identify good trades or market trends, but usually have no experience running a company. They lack operational focus and expertise in the supportive tasks inherent in securities operations such as settlement, clearing, booking or internal control. More importantly, they tend to launch their funds with a very small staff base, which raises questions about independent oversight, the "four eyes" requirement, conflict of interest management, etc.

However, operational risk is not limited to start-ups. If a hedge fund is successful, the manager may be tempted to develop new strategies, hire new teams, grow the assets under management and investor base, launch new funds, extend the jurisdictional spread, etc. In such cases, the risk is that middle and back office functions may have a lower priority for expenditure versus profit centers of the business. This can result in trade confirmation backlogs, insufficient risk management or, more generally, over-stretched staff.

Thus, for investors, the only effective approach to reducing exposure to operational risk and avoiding fraud cases is to conduct an extensive and time-consuming operational due diligence process on *each* fund potentially considered for investment. This should be completed before any initial investment/exposure, and on an ongoing basis.

A typical operational due diligence process

Giraud (2004) suggests a three-phase approach to standardize the operational due diligence process on hedge funds (Figure 37.4):

- The **focus phase** aims at ensuring sufficient preparation of the diligence process itself and allowing for a targeted approach to questioning the fund representatives.

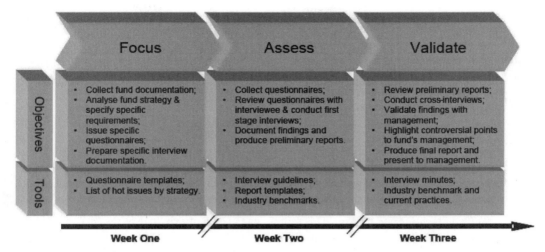

Figure 37.4   Baseline for industrializing operational due-diligence. (*Source:* Giraud (2004))

- The **assessment phase** combines interviews and questionnaires, which should be cross checked with collected documents.
- The **validation phase** reports the main findings and identifies the potential issues with the fund, if any.

Let us focus more specifically on some of the most important aspects of this process.

Review of the key fund documents

The desk review of the major fund documents typically includes:

- The memorandum and articles of association. The memorandum is akin to a certificate of incorporation; the articles of association are akin to a corporation's by-laws.
- The **private placement memorandum** and its supplements, if any. These documents explain the relevant trading strategies, the associated risks, and the biographies of key personnel. They disclose the names of the attorneys, accountants, administrators and other key service providers, as appropriate.
- The investment management agreement, which regulates the interaction between the fund and the portfolio manager.
- The **Form ADV**, if available.[9] This is a two part regulatory filing that is required of all types of fund advisers in the United States. Part 1 contains information about the adviser's education, business and disciplinary history within the last 10 years. Part 2 includes information on an adviser's services, fees and investment strategies.
- Other documents. These documents are particularly important during the interview process. A well-managed fund will have updated copies of these documents and the key employees of the

---

[9] In December 2004, the SEC adopted a new rule under the Investment Advisers Act of 1940 that required most hedge fund managers to register as investment advisers by February 2006. As a result, all registered hedge fund managers had to file a Form ADV with the SEC. In June 2006, the U.S. Court of Appeals for the District of Columbia Circuit vacated the rule changes and many hedge funds decided to deregister, but their 2006 Form ADV is still available. Still, today over half of U.S. hedge funds remain voluntarily registered with the SEC.

fund should thoroughly familiar with them. These documents may include:
o the administration agreement;
o the previous audit reports;
o the organizational chart;
o the disaster recovery plan;
o the compliance manual and internal control procedures;
o any marketing materials.

Onsite visits and interviews

Although each hedge fund may claim to have its own internal structure, there are generally eight main functional areas of responsibility that require investigation during an operational due diligence process:

- *Investment management and trading.* This represents the area of expertise of the fund manager. It covers research and development of trading ideas as well.
- *Portfolio financing.* This requires interaction with a prime broker and other sources of financing. The financing may be needed to increase leverage or to honor redemptions.
- *Risk management.* An independent risk manager is essential.
- *Reporting and performance measurement.* Return attribution and reporting should be performed regularly under a consistent set of guidelines.
- *Trade processing, settlement and asset servicing.* Proper management of operational risk requires that someone other than the person who initiates the trade monitors orders and reconciles them with the broker.
- *Accounting and portfolio valuation.* This deals with valuation of the fund and calculation of fees for various share classes. Investors should carefully examine the procedures employed to value the fund in order to ensure that the fund uses accepted principles while calculating the fees and that expenses charged to the fund are appropriate.
- *Business management.* This area comes under the control of the Chief Operating Officer and deals with areas such as human resources, information technology, security, compliance, etc.

Each of these areas should be described in terms of responsibilities of key employees and details of the relevant activities in each area along with the work flow process. These should be analyzed, verified and compared to best practices and available benchmarks.

This step of the due diligence process is usually performed using a mix of questionnaires and interviews. As discussed by Giraud (2004), both approaches have pros and cons. Questionnaires allow for detailed and systematic questioning, but suffer from the fact that an experienced respondent can think through the questions and establish the answers that will most likely satisfy the investor. This is particularly true if the questionnaire is a "standard" one, such as the one designed by AIMA. Interviews allow for direct contact with the key operational people at the hedge fund (Chief Operating Officer, Chief Financial Officer, Compliance Officer, Head of Risk Management, etc.) and hence for building a sense of how the fund's operations are *really* managed. The downsides are that very often they suffer from a lack of structure and an inexperienced interviewer may yield sterile findings.

Analysis of third party service providers

It is common practice to ask the manager to allow direct contact with third party service providers such as the administrator, the auditor, prime brokers, etc. The goal of these direct contacts is to understand and independently verify their roles in the fund's operations.

Key focus areas

There are several types of operational risks that should be considered in the due diligence process (some of these areas of focus provide valuable information with regard to other risks faced and managed by the fund).

External and internal administration

The due diligence process should examine all internal and external administration processes and procedures of a hedge fund. This includes, for instance, the trade confirmation, settlement, financial reporting and investor relations processes, the checks and safeguards to wire funds, etc.

Valuation

This is a cornerstone of hedge fund operations. From a legal perspective, the fund's general partners (U.S.) or board of directors (offshore) have a fiduciary responsibility to provide accurate and appropriate valuations to all investors. Although the general partners or the board may delegate valuation calculation to third-party agents, they remain ultimately responsible for ensuring that valuations are accurate.

The examination of the fund valuation process is a critical step in due diligence for two key reasons: (i) the net asset value of the fund must be determined precisely when subscriptions and redemptions take place, and (ii) the NAV of the fund is the main factor in calculating a managers' fees. The due diligence process should, therefore, ensure the following:

- Hedge fund managers have a clearly written valuation policy that formalizes the manner and calculation frequency of the fund's net asset value and makes appropriate disclosures in the offering documents.
- The valuation policy is consistently applied for similar securities at a point in time and thereafter, is reproducible, transparent and verifiable.
- The fund's back office has ownership and control of the pricing process. Neither portfolio managers nor traders should be responsible for marking their own books at month-end (nor directly compensate those who do so).
- The different types of outside sources used for pricing are fully documented. If judgment calls need to be made, these should be documented, disclosed and available for inspection.
- If possible, the fund administrator should ultimately price the securities for each net asset value calculation.

Note that the importance of independence, transparency and consistency is heightened when dealing with difficult to value or illiquid positions.

Auditors

The independence and qualification of the auditors and the audit firm employed should be reviewed. Opinions rendered on each audit should be reviewed and questioned if needed. Clear, credible explanations should be sought *and verified* whenever the auditor has been changed. It is worth remembering that the financial statements should come directly from the auditor.

Prime brokers

The due diligence process should examine the scope of the brokerage relationship, identify possible conflicts of interest and assess the general credit quality of the prime broker(s) used by the fund. Items such as soft dollar arrangements, record keeping, margin lending agreements, quality of systems and connections to the fund manager and other crucial service providers should be reviewed.

Compliance

A good hedge fund should provide evidence of a commitment to the highest standards of integrity and professionalism. The due diligence process should therefore assess the fund manager's overall compliance program, as well as the adherence to this program and the promotion of a compliance culture. Key elements to review include: the content of the fund's written compliance manual; a written code of ethics; the experience, qualifications and effectiveness of the Chief Compliance Officer and other compliance personnel; the existence of a robust training program to educate personnel on the fund's policies; and the use of third-party regulatory service providers. It is also useful to review all documents that substantiate the adherence to the compliance rules, e.g. compliance checklists, exception reports, internal audits and other pertinent documents.

Conflicts of interest

There are numerous situations in which a hedge fund manager could face conflicts of interest. Examples include cases where an employee or entity controlled by the manager is affiliated with another type of financial institution such as a broker-dealer, mutual fund, or limited partnership, or has proprietary interest in transactions, sales interest in transactions, brokerage discretion, custody of client assets, etc. Note that a conflict of interest in itself does not imply any wrongdoing, and in many cases is normal occurrence in the course of business. Many of these can easily be addressed with specific policies. They should, however, be fully disclosed to investors so that they may question and gauge the overall effect on the operational risk of the fund.

Personal trading

What is the policy for personal trading accounts? If trading is permitted, what is the process to review personal account activity? Who reviews it and how often? Is there potential for any individual to front-run the fund's trading or investment activity?

Human resources

As competition for talent across the industry escalates, recruiting and retaining skilled people is increasingly difficult for most hedge funds. The due diligence process should therefore:

- Verify that all employees are qualified to perform their assigned tasks. This normally involves the confirmation of: post high school education; licenses (CPA); designations (e.g. CAIA or CFA); and work experience, as well as **background checks** for key personnel. Carefully assess the quality of work experience of those individuals and be wary of unexplained gaps in resumes.
- Validate the compensation structure used to retain support staff and to align incentives between senior staff and investors. A large disparity in the distribution of performance fees between senior investment professionals often leads to future dissension and turnover. Analyze ownership positions in the management company, as this affects the commitment of the team.

- Examine the staff turnover experienced by the fund and understand the reasons behind this. Portfolio managers unable to preside over a stable organization should be evaluated with greater scrutiny.
- Assess the degree of "key man" risk. What happens if a portfolio manager becomes incapacitated or deceased? Is there a liquidation process for extraordinary events? How long would such liquidation take? What would be its impact on the portfolio and on the markets the manager invests in? Is there a key man clause, and is it adequate? What are the provisions for the absence of the key man? Who has the ability to fill in on a short-term or long-term basis?

Past behavior of the firm

Any past regulatory or legal problems of both the hedge fund management company and any of its related advisors should be carefully investigated. For U.S. registered funds, Form ADV, when available, provides detail on the nature, severity, and disposition of past criminal charges against the management personnel, and the disclosure of past regulatory actions taken against the firm or its personnel, including the regulatory body and the nature of the sanction. It also requires disclosure of past civil judicial action, past bond action, and past arbitration relating to the firm. In the absence of Form ADV, this information must be compiled by looking at various regulatory websites and doing background checks. This type of information does not necessarily capture personnel-related operational risk, but it provides evidence of past adverse behavior by the firm or by those the firm currently employs.

Risk reporting and control

Risk management systems are integral to most hedged strategies. The operational due diligence process should validate how well market risk is reported and controlled within the fund's self-prescribed risk limits. This typically includes verifying:

- The existence of a designated qualified risk manager role and its independence from the portfolio management team.
- The usefulness of the risk manager and the systems used in the identification, monitoring, and reporting of the portfolio's risk exposures.
- The level of commitment of the key individuals to the risk control process.

Fees

In the evaluation of the fee structure and terms, it is important to understand the value proposition of a particular hedge fund investment. Unreasonable and unfair terms may reveal something important about the motives of the fund's principals. Typical questions should include:

- What are the management and incentive fees of the fund that is being evaluated? If there are several share classes, what are the various fees and terms for each of them?
- How are these fees calculated and accrued? Is there a high watermark? Is it fixed or rolling? Is there a clawback account? Is there a hurdle rate?
- Who participates in the carry, and how much of it is reinvested in the fund?
- What expenses are charged to the fund, in addition to management and performance fees? Items such as administration, audit, and other professional expenses are normally taken out of the management fee. However, some managers will expense a portion of the firm's overhead to the fund, including travel, rent, salaries, and bonuses.

Investor base

Investors should attempt to understand the relative stability and sophistication of the fund's investor base, and consider the risk posed by the behavior of other investors in the same fund or even in the same fund family. Large redemptions by other investors could adversely affect the stability of the manager's business. Furthermore, large redemptions may affect the style of the manager since liquid assets are most likely to be sold first.

Liquidity risk

A very important risk that is closely related to operational risk for hedge funds and their investors is liquidity risk, i.e. the risk of not being able to sell investments within a reasonable timeframe and at a reasonable price. Historically, this risk was essentially theoretical because liquidity was abundant and was fueled by a greater use of debt to purchase assets, rising prices, and a growing number of financial institutions acting as brokers and market makers. However, since the middle of 2007, liquidity has dried up in several markets due to the subprime crisis and the pull back/collapse of several banks and prime brokers.

Liquidity risk is particularly high for hedge funds that invest in *very illiquid* or non-traded securities while simultaneously allowing investor redemptions on a periodic basis. Liquidity risk arises in this case because of the serious liquidity mismatch between their assets and liabilities. Further, securities that are liquid in a normal market could become highly illiquid during periods of market stress, and it is exactly during such periods that investors may elect to redeem their shares.

As an illustration, let us consider the example of a hedge fund with $100 in capital, offering monthly redemptions to its investors and having a portfolio split between illiquid distressed securities (75%) and cash (25%). For the sake of illustration, say the fund receives a redemption that corresponds to 25% of its capital, i.e. $25. Let us examine the various solutions for the fund manager.

- The fund manager may raise new capital ($25) and use the proceeds to pay for redemptions ($25). However, such a perfect match in terms of timing and amounts is highly unlikely.
- The fund manager may sell its liquid securities ($25) and use the proceeds to pay the redeemed capital ($25). As a result, the remaining portfolio becomes completely illiquid, and faithful investors will have to live with this going forward.
- The fund manager may decide to use leverage and borrow money to pay for redemptions. In such a case, faithful investors would have to bear the cost of leverage and live with a more volatile portfolio.

The fund manager may attempt to sell some of its illiquid securities to pay for redemptions. However, selling is fine only if the market price of these securities is insensitive to the increased supply. If this is not the case, then selling will affect the valuation of these securities and therefore the valuation of the overall portfolio. As a result, the fund's net asset value will decrease, which may then trigger additional redemptions from other investors, etc. Here again, faithful investors will have to face the consequences of the actions of early redeemers.

Alternatively, the fund manager may choose not to pay out redeeming investors by pursuing one of the following options:

- *Activation of a "redemption gate"*. Gates essentially allow a hedge fund manager to limit the proportion of assets investors can withdraw at one redemption date. This proportion can be at the investor level, the fund level, or both.
- *Suspension of redemptions*. Hedge funds may slow withdrawals or ignore them altogether, urging investors to be patient until market conditions improve.

- *Creation of a liquidation trust*. The assets of redeemers may be placed in a segregated vehicle managed for liquidity and realization while the rest of the assets are managed for long-term value and capital appreciation.
- *Payment in specie*. Rather than having to liquidate some illiquid underlying assets at fire sale prices, hedge funds can also decide to distribute them in specie to the redeeming investors.

To separate their liquid and illiquid assets, hedge funds may also opt for the creation of side pockets. As mentioned previously, the term "side pocket" refers to a portion of the hedge fund that is segregated from the remainder of the assets. It usually contains certain illiquid investments determined by the manager. In a sense, a side pocket is a single-asset private equity fund and operates as follows: Once the fund manager decides to make an illiquid investment, a special class of shares (the side pocket) is created and distributed to the present participants in the hedge fund. The side pocket will only hold that specific illiquid investment. So investors coming into the fund after the creation of the side pocket cannot obtain an ownership interest in the segregated investment and are therefore not able to participate in its performance. The side pocket exists as long as the illiquid investments are not realized. Thus, its holders have no opportunity to redeem the capital invested in it (investors may withdraw from the main fund, but they have to keep their side pocket investments until they are liquidated). Upon its realization, holders of the side pocket will receive either the corresponding cash or an allocation of the same amount back into the original fund.

All these options are often provided by a hedge fund's articles of association, either at the discretion of the manager or as a mechanism exercisable only under specific circumstances. These clauses should be carefully analyzed by potential investors so that their activation, if any, does not come as a complete surprise.

The case of managed accounts

As discussed by Giraud (2004, 2005), various managed account platforms may substantially increase transparency of the investment and reduce investors' exposures to operational risks. There are essentially four forms of managed accounts:

- *Standard custodial arrangements*. The investor's assets are held in the name of the fund in a dedicated and segregated account operated by the manager of the hedge fund.
- *Prime brokerage custody*. Assets are held in the name of the fund in a dedicated and segregated account operated by the manager. A bank acts as an independent provider of controls on behalf of the board of directors.
- *Basic managed accounts*. Assets are held in the name of the investor within the books of a custodian bank. The manager operates the account according to a specific mandate. The bank has no duty of control on the assets or the investment decisions, but can issue independent reporting directly to the investor.
- *Managed account platforms*. Assets are held in the name of investors in a segregated account. The manager gives the sub-adviser (hedge fund) instructions to be executed on the account according to a specific mandate. The bank operates back office and risk control functions on behalf of the board of directors of the hedge fund.

Managed accounts have several advantages over traditional hedge fund structures. In particular:

- They strongly reduce the level of risks related to misappropriation of assets. With a managed account, all assets are completely segregated and the manager only receives a mandate to trade on behalf of the account owner.

- They can offer an independent valuation on the assets, usually from the prime broker, without any possible interference by the manager.
- They can provide full transparency on the daily profit, loss, and risk exposures.
- They can offer daily liquidity, which allows an immediate liquidation of positions if the investor wished to redeem. Note, however, that if the underlying positions are illiquid, the investors may have to sell them at substantial discount.

However, managed accounts also come with a few disadvantages:

- The cost of monitoring a series of managed accounts can be extremely high and time consuming.
- Daily transparency on positions is only useful if the final investor has the team, knowledge, and system to analyze and verify each position in the portfolio.
- The investor must reconcile the gross trading performance of the managed account to the performance of the benchmark hedge fund.
- The fund manager may not be able to allocate a portion of all profitable trades to every single managed account. As a result, the performance of the managed account may turn out to be different from the manager's overall performance.
- Not all managers are willing to offer managed accounts. As a result, using only managed accounts reduces the potential universe of managers.
- The investor has to decide whether or not to incur the additional cost of an audit and whether the services of an administrator are needed.
- Assets are held by a custodian and therefore the investor is exposed to concentrated counterparty risk. If the custodian bank experiences difficulties, there is a risk that the investor may lose control of the assets (at least temporarily).

Whether the benefits of liquidity, transparency, fraud controls and controls over cash movements outweigh the associated costs and challenges of running separately managed accounts often needs to be determined on a case-by-case basis.

Operational ratings

Over recent years, operational due diligence by investors is reportedly increasing in quality, led by some endowments, pension funds and particularly well-run large funds-of-funds. Nevertheless, many investors state that adequate operational due diligence is still difficult to execute because they feel that they do not have the resources and competency to perform it. Therefore, they often prefer to seek expert advice from consultants. Moreover, the process is highly inefficient for hedge funds because, although each investor normally asks the same questions, the answers are confidential and not shared between investors. As a result, several intermediaries have stepped in to offer an objective independent third party initial and ongoing due diligence process dedicated to hedge funds.

The result of this due diligence usually takes the form of a rating that expresses the intermediary's opinion of a hedge fund's *operational* environment. Note that this rating says nothing about a hedge fund's debt, its return, market risk, or investment strategy. It does not guarantee that the hedge fund will not fail. It is simply assigning a rating to the "operational risk" of the hedge fund; essentially, how well it runs the nuts and bolts of its business, from its back-office systems to the controls it has in place to avoid sudden losses.

As an illustration, Moody's started issuing operational ratings for hedge funds in September 2006. Moody's five levels of operational rating are described in Table 37.3. They are scaled from OQ1 (excellent) to OQ5 (poor). Where appropriate, a "+" or "−" modifier may be appended to the OQ2,

Table 37.3 Description of Moody's operational ratings for hedge funds.

OQ1: Excellent	Funds at this level must have a very strong valuation process tailored to their investment strategy. Operations policies and procedures are extensively documented, precisely executed, and strongly enforced. All key service providers are judged to be independent of the fund, highly proficient, and well-qualified. Compliance risk is judged to be minimal. The investment manager's internal risk reporting and control is comprehensive, independent of portfolio management, and appropriate to the strategy. Background checks revealed no unresolved issues of concern.
OQ2: Very Good	Funds at this level have a strong valuation process appropriate for their investment strategy. Operations policies and procedures are well-documented, well-executed and enforced. All key service providers are judged to be independent of the fund, proficient in their contracted areas of responsibility, and well-qualified. Compliance risk is judged to be low. The investment manager's internal risk reporting and control is independent of portfolio management and appropriate to the strategy. Background checks revealed no unresolved issues of concern.
OQ3: Good	Funds at this level have sound operations throughout and a valuation process that is credible given their investment strategy. Key service providers are judged to be of generally good quality and not dependent on the fund in any discernable way. Compliance risk is not judged to be high. The investment manager has an internal process to systematically report and control risk. Background checks revealed no unresolved issues of concern.
OQ4: Fair	The valuation process of funds at this level is adequate but may have some deficiencies. Key service providers are judged to be of generally acceptable quality and are not dependent of the fund in any obvious way. Compliance risk may be moderately high. The investment manager's internal risk reporting may lack independence or may not be practiced systematically. Background checks revealed no unresolved issues of concern.
OQ5: Poor	Funds at this level may have an inadequate valuation process. Some key service providers could be of low quality and/or dependent of the fund. Compliance risk may be high. Risk reporting may be lacking or absent. Background checks could have revealed unresolved issues of concern.

Source: Moody's

OQ3, and OQ4 rating category and a "−" modifier may be appended to the OQ1 rating category. The "+" modifier indicates the fund ranks in the higher end of the designated rating category, while the "−" modifier indicates the fund ranks in the lower end of the designated rating category.

So far, most of the few hedge funds rated by Moody's have achieved the highest "OQ1" or "excellent" rating. This is not surprising as (i) there's obviously little appetite from the hedge fund community to pay to be rated as "poor" and (ii) a manager does not have to release the final rating if he does not like it. If widely adopted, then hedge funds that choose not to report a rating may be deemed to be too risky.

ASSESSING THE OPERATIONAL RISK OF A FoHF MULTI-STRATEGY FUND

Because investing directly into a single-strategy fund is beyond the reach of most investors, multi-strategy funds (MSHFs) and fund-of-hedge-funds are often the primary vehicles used to access hedge funds. From a functional perspective, both fulfill the same role, i.e. pooling investors' capital and allocating it to a series of investment strategies. From an implementation perspective, however, they are quite different. FoHFs outsource their investments by making multiple investments in (typically)

Table 37.4 Historical performance of CISDM Multi-Strategy Index relative to traditional investments and to other hedge fund strategies

Year	BarCap Global Aggregate Bond (%Total Return)	S&P 500 (%Total Return)	MSCI Emerg (%Total Return)	MSCI EAFE (%Total Return)	CISDM Fund of Funds Diversified Index (%Total Return)	CISDM Fund of Funds Index (%Total Return)	CISDM Equal Weighted Hedge Fund Index (%Total Return)	CISDM Merger Arbitrage Index (%Total Return)	CISDM Global Macro Index (%Total Return)	CISDM Event Driven Multi-Strategy Index (%Total Return)	CISDM Equity Market Neutral Index (%Total Return)	CISDM Equity Long/Short Index (%Total Return)	CISDM Distressed Securities Index (%Total Return)	CISDM Convert Arbitrage Index (%Total Return)	CISDM CTA Asset Weighted Index (%Total Return)	CISDM CTA Asset Weighted Diversified Index (%Total Return)
1990	12.6	-3.1	-10.56	-23.2	7.51	7.47	6.54	-1.69	11.26	-3.31	10.18	-1.46	19.31	NA	27.29	19.8
1991	16.06	30.47	59.9	12.48	11.01	11.3	30.43	18.33	36.47	21.84	12.42	33.7	25.06	NA	16.82	11.34
1992	5.78	7.65	11.41	-11.85	12.04	11.93	16.83	17.37	22.35	19.36	7.92	17.38	18.25	16.68	9.9	-6.01
1993	11.08	10.08	74.86	32.94	23.33	24.21	30.29	26.38	40.88	26.47	9.73	21.56	31.25	16.56	19.86	22.12
1994	0.23	1.32	-7.31	8.06	-4.44	-4.42	3.53	5.23	-5.05	3.64	5.12	3.38	-4.3	2.2	-0.7	5.29
1995	19.67	37.57	-5.19	11.55	12.54	12.25	21.17	16.6	11.17	19.8	12.2	26.42	21.95	17.47	15.13	15.05
1996	4.92	22.96	6.04	6.34	16.83	16.68	23.24	15.97	9.86	22.31	13.69	22.34	21.05	14.75	14.64	12.73
1997	3.79	33.38	-11.59	2.05	17.09	17.2	21.79	18.17	15.97	23.56	14.87	23.74	18.67	14.25	10.06	7.09
1998	13.7	28.58	-25.33	20.34	1.71	1.65	3.97	5.5	8.11	3.9	11.16	9.57	-4.83	7.45	9.37	11.61
1999	-5.17	21.04	66.66	27.3	22.37	16.23	36.79	15.77	8.52	21.42	9.86	34.4	17.85	13.9	3.77	6.5
2000	3.18	-9.09	-30.71	-13.97	7.35	7.37	8.76	14.37	10.02	12.07	13.87	7.78	5.85	15.24	6.18	8.07
2001	1.57	-11.88	-2.37	-21.21	4.99	5.18	5.71	4.27	5.58	7.06	7.27	2.27	9.24	13.27	4.19	6.04
2002	16.52	-22.1	-6	-15.64	0.65	1.05	0.41	0.28	2.81	1.18	2.04	-4.72	6.85	8.89	11.95	12.38
2003	12.48	28.69	56.26	39.16	10.04	10.23	20.62	7.37	11.76	21.87	8.83	18.89	25.27	9.65	13.25	10.39
2004	9.27	10.87	25.94	20.69	7.23	7.12	9.97	7.01	4.48	12.12	4.97	9.86	16.64	2.47	4.24	3.95
2005	-4.48	4.89	34.53	14.01	6.36	6.47	9.84	5.77	6.65	6.63	7.11	8.86	7.44	-1.14	5	-1.08
2006	6.66	15.79	32.6	26.88	7.79	9.12	11.75	10.7	4.93	13.99	7.64	9.99	15.91	12.32	6.17	7.16
2007	9.48	5.5	39.78	11.62	9.52	8.69	10.5	3.74	12	6.57	6.5	8.48	5.26	3.97	9.14	12.01
2008	4.79	-36.99	-53.17	-43.06	-16.83	-17.05	-19.17	0.09	3.7	-19.05	0.61	-14.43	-19.55	-19.1	17.86	19.26

Source: CISDM

Table 37.5 Statistical properties of CISDM Multi-Strategy Index (1990–2008) relative to traditional investments and to other hedge fund strategies

1990–2008	N Periods	Geometric Mean (%)	Arithmetic Mean (%)	Standard Deviation (%)	Skewness	Information Ratio	Maximum Decline (%)	Correl. Against CISDM Event Driven Multi-Strategy Index
BarCap Global Aggregate Bond Index	228	7.27	7.42	5.78	0.18	1.28	−10.07	0.02
S&P 500 Index	228	7.33	8.48	15.78	−0.69	0.54	44.73	0.69
MSCI Emerging Mkts Index	228	7.81	11.03	26.64	−0.91	0.41	−59.5	0.68
MSCI EAFE Index	228	3.12	4.62	17.77	−0.57	0.26	49.21	0.58
CISDM Fund of Funds Diversified Index	228	7.87	8.01	5.43	−0.89	1.48	−17.49	0.82
CISDM Fund of Funds Index	228	7.67	7.79	5.15	−1.34	1.51	−17.74	0.83
CISDM Equal Weighted Hedge Fund Index	228	12.59	12.89	8.23	−0.69	1.57	−21.13	0.87
CISDM Merger Arbitrage Index	228	9.81	9.91	4.55	−1.06	2.18	−5.74	0.84
CISDM Global Macro Index	228	11.18	11.37	6.66	1.15	1.71	−8.22	0.46
CISDM Event Driven Multi-Strategy Index	228	11.05	11.24	6.6	−1.55	1.70	−20.19	1.00
CISDM Equity Market Neutral Index	228	8.67	8.69	2.13	−0.52	4.08	−2.8	0.58
CISDM Equity Long/Short Index	228	11.82	12.2	9.27	−0.28	1.32	−17.04	0.81
CISDM Distressed Securities Index	228	11.77	12.04	7.7	−1.39	1.56	−21.24	0.76
CISDM Convertible Arbitrage Index	204	8.35	8.47	5.11	−5.08	1.66	−22.46	0.69
CISDM CTA Asset Weighted Index	228	10.55	11.04	10.55	0.63	1.05	−10.69	−0.09
CISDM CTA Asset Weighted Diversified Index	228	9.46	10.1	12.03	0.39	0.84	−16.55	−0.12
CISDM CTA Asset Weighted Discretionary Index	228	11.95	12.22	7.81	0.81	1.56	−5.6	0.15

Source: CISDM

nonaffiliated third-party single-strategy managers, while MSHFs employ *their own managers and traders* who execute a variety of different investment strategies under a common organizational umbrella. Not surprisingly, the collapse of Amaranth (self-described as an MSHF) sparked the debate as to which of these two solutions was better. The answer is "it depends," as both have strengths and weaknesses.

The advantages of multi-strategy hedge funds

Flexibility

MSHFs often argue that, since they own and control their underlying investments, they have the ability to quickly reallocate assets from one strategy to another. This gives them more control over the investment profile of the fund and allows them to react quickly to changing market trends by dynamically allocating capital in the short-term. This ability to time investments may enable them to earn higher returns. By contrast, FoHFs managers cannot engage in frequent reallocation because they are restricted by the liquidity and redemption terms of their underlying fund managers.

Single layer of fees

MSHFs charge a fee that incorporates the cost of the underlying strategies while FoHFs have a double layer of fees. Moreover, MSHFs normally net their incentive fees across strategies while FoHF still have to pay performance fees on appreciating funds regardless of the FOHFs return. As an illustration, suppose that there are two managers/strategies with no management fee and a 20% performance fee. In a given year, the first manager gains $10 gross of fees while the second manager loses $10. In an MSHF, the overall gross profit would be zero and the fund would not charge a performance fee. In an FoHF, the winning manager would still get her performance fee ($2) while the losing manager would not charge anything. The overall result for the FoHF would therefore be a net loss due to the performance fee of $2, despite an overall flat gross return for the investor. Not surprisingly, MSHFs have become increasingly popular with institutional investors who want diversification but do not like paying the extra layer of fees charged by FoHFs.

Many MSHFs claim that their risk management capacity is a source of added value compared to FoHFs. They claim that since all their trades and portfolios are centralized on a common system, they can control risk in real time. Some MSHFs also offer enhanced transparency into the underlying strategies. They can afford to do this because their value added is not only in the selection of underlying managers, but is also in the allocation among various strategies (which is a difficult process to replicate).

The weaknesses of multi-strategy hedge funds

However, MSHFs also come with some weaknesses compared to FoHFs. Let us mention some of them.

Agency risk

The strategies used by underlying managers in an MSHF are relatively opaque and are usually not observable. By contrast, an FoHF invests in other hedge funds and investors may be able to observe the performance of these hedge funds separately. As a result, FoHFs investors are able determine the success of the FoHF manager at deploying capital into profitable hedge fund strategies.

Excessive span of control

MSHFs managers are expected to be experts in several if not all hedge fund investment strategies. There is a risk that an MSHF manager will take on investment tasks at which he/she is less skilled. This is exactly what happened at Amaranth, whose portfolio manager drifted from convertible arbitrage (his area of expertise) to energy trading.

Potential for sub-par managers

An MSHF is a closed architecture investment and is therefore restricted to the managers that are available on the platform. An FOHF, on the other hand, is able to use a "best of breed" approach. In practice, it may also prove difficult to reduce the capital managed by a co-founder or partner. Moreover, an MSHF has a natural disincentive (and in some situations the inability) to fire an underperforming manager.

Talent retention

An institutionally-owned MSHF might have difficulties retaining its best managers, particularly if they do not like corporate environments or if their capital allocation is reduced. Further, these managers may receive reduced incentive fees because of the poor performance of other managers who are on the same platform.

Operational risk

The most important risk faced by an MSHF is probably *operational risk* and more specifically *blow-up risk*. Investors may achieve diversification in terms of underlying strategies, but they are still exposed to the operations of a single hedge fund company as all the underlying managers are owned or controlled by that shop. In particular, sub-portfolios and positions are usually cross-collateralized by the fund as a whole. MSHFs therefore carry a single-business risk and are more likely to suffer blow-ups (which is exactly what happened at Amaranth). In contrast, when a blow-up happens in one of the funds of an FoHF, performance suffers but the overall business does not usually collapse.

Did Amaranth's blow-up impact other multi-strategy hedge funds? It is difficult to say. First, it is a misnomer to call Amaranth a multi-strategy fund – as discussed above, it was actually a highly leveraged single-strategy fund. Second, several large MSHFs actually benefited from being on the other side of Amaranth's underlying energy trades. Third, many FoHFs actually held Amaranth as one of their core positions.[10] In any case, investors must realize and accept that investing with an MSHF means accepting some degree of manager blow-up risk. The lesson from Amaranth's implosion, if any, is to understand the importance of both diversification and stringent risk control in MSHF.

Historical performance

The historical performance of MSHFs as a group has been relatively good (see Tables 37.4 and 37.5). From January 1990 to December 2008, MSHF (as measured by the CISDM Event Driven Multi-Strategy Index) delivered an average return of 11.05% per year with a volatility of 6.6%

---

[10] Martin (2007) provides an interesting analysis of 80 FoHFs that were significantly invested in Amaranth in September 2006. He observes that these FoHF lost 5.7 years worth of their alpha production in the month of September 2006.

per year. This gives an Information Ratio of 1.70, which compares favorably to the CISDM Equal Weighted Hedge Fund Index, the CISDM Fund of Funds Diversified Index, the S&P 500 and the Barclays Global Bond Index.

The event-driven multi-strategy index has high correlations to most other strategies, a rather high correlation to equity markets (0.69 versus the S&P 500) and a low correlation to bond markets (0.02). Its return distribution is negatively skewed (−1.55) and its maximum draw down is about half as much as the S&P 500 Index.

References

Ackerman, C., R. McEnally and D. Ravenscraft. "The Performance of Hedge Funds: Risk, Return, and Incentives." *Journal of Finance*. 54, pp. 833–874. 1999.

Ahl, Peter. "Global Macro Funds: What Lies Ahead?" *AIMA Newsletter*. April 2001,

Amenc, N. and L. Martellini. "The Brave New World of Hedge Fund Indices." Working Paper. EDHEC. 2003.

Amin, G. and H. Kat. "Portfolios of Hedge Funds: What Investors Really Invest In." Working Paper. City University London. 2002.

Ang, A., M. Rhodes-Kropf and R. Zhao. "Do Funds-of-Funds Deserve Their Fees-on-Fees?" Working Paper. National Bureau of Economic Research. 2008.

Anson, M. *Handbook of Alternative Assets*. New York, John Wiley & Sons, Inc. 2006.

Asness, C. S. "The Interaction of Value and Momentum Strategies." *Financial Analysts Journal*. pp. 29–36. March/April 1997.

Asness, C. S. "The Past and Future of Quantitative Asset Management," CFA Institute Conference Proceedings Quarterly. pp. 47–55. December 2008.

Black, F. and M. Scholes. "The Pricing of Options and Corporate Liabilities," *Journal of Political Economy*, Vol. 81 Issue 3, pp. 637–654. 1973.

Black, F. and M. Scholes. "The Effects of Dividend Yield and Dividend Policy on Common Stock Prices and Returns." *Journal of Finance*. Vol. 1 Issue. 1, pp. 1–22. 1974.

Brav, A., W. Jiang, F. Partnoy and R. Thomas. "The Returns to Hedge Fund Activism." ECGI Working Paper Series in Law, Working Paper No. 098/2008. March 2008.

Brown, S., W. Goetzmann and B. Liang. "Fees on Fees in Funds of Funds." *Journal of Investment Management*. Vol. 2, No. 4. 2004.

Brown, S., W. Goetzmann and J. Park. "Hedge Funds and the Asian Currency Crisis of 1997." New York University, Leonard N. Stern School Finance Department Working Paper Series 98−014. 1998.

Capocci, D. and G. Hubner. "An Analysis of Hedge Funds Performance." *Journal of Empirical Finance*. 11, pp. 55–89. 2004.

Carhart, M. M. "On Persistence in Mutual Fund Performance." *The Journal of Finance*. Vol. 52, No. 1. pp. 57–82. March 1997.

Chan, L. K. C., J. Narasimhan and L. Josef. "Momentum Strategies." *The Journal of Finance*. Vol. 51, No. 5, pp. 1681–1713. December 1996.

Chincarini, L. "The Amaranth Debacle: Failure of Risk Measures or Failure of Risk Management." Working Paper. Georgetown University. 2007a.

Chincarini, L. "The Amaranth Debacle: What Really Happened?" Working Paper. Georgetown University. 2007b.

Conrad, J. and G. Kaul. "Long-Term Market Overreaction or Biases in Computed Returns?" *The Journal of Finance*. Vol. 48, No. 1, pp. 39–63. March 1993.

Cox, J. C., S. A. Ross and M. Rubenstein. "Options Pricing; A Simplified Approach." *Journal of Financial Economics*. 7, pp. 229–263. 1979.

Duarte, J., F.A. Longstaff and F. Yu, "Risk and Return in Fixed Income Arbitrage: Nickels in Front of a Steamroller?," Available at SSRN: http://ssrn.com/abstract=872004. 2006.

Duc, F. "Hedge Fund Indices: Status Review and User Guide." Working Paper. 3A Alternative Investments, Geneva, Switzerland. 2004a.

Duc, F. "Investable Indices: A Viable Alternative to Funds of Funds?" Working Paper. 3A Alternative Investments, Geneva, Switzerland. 2004b.

Eichengreen, B.J., A. Jansen, B. Chadha, L. Kodres, D. Mathieson and S. Sharma. "Hedge Funds and Financial Market Dynamics," IMF Occasional Papers 166, International Monetary Fund. 1998.

Fama and French. "Dissecting Anomalies." *The Journal of Finance*, Volume 63, Issue 4, pp. 1653–1678. 2008

Feffer, S. and C. Kundro. "Understanding and Mitigating Operational Risk in Hedge Fund Investments: A Capco White Paper." Working Paper. Capco. 2003.

Financial Stability Forum, "Report of the Working Group on Highly Leveraged Institutions." Available on http://www.fsforum.org/publications/ r_0004a.pdf. 2000.

Fung, W. and D. Hsieh. "Hedge-Fund Benchmarks: Information Content and Biases." *Journal of Alternative Investments*. Vol. 58 (1), pp. 22–34. 2002.

Fung, W. and D. Hsieh. "Hedge Fund Benchmarks: A Risk-Based Approach." *Financial Analyst's Journal*. 60 (5), p. 65–80. 2004.

Fung, W., D. Hsieh and K. Tsatsaronis. "Do Hedge Funds Disrupt Emerging Markets?" Brookings-Wharton Papers on Financial Services. 2000.

Giraud J. R. "The Management of Hedge Funds' Operational Risks." Working Paper. EDHEC. 2004.

Giraud J. R. "Mitigating Hedge Funds' Operational Risks: Benefits and Limitations of Managed Account Platforms." Working Paper. EDHEC. 2005.

Gregoriou G. and F.S. Lhabitant. "Madoff: A Riot of Red Flags." Working Paper. Available at SSRN: http://ssrn.com/abstract=1335639. 2009

Gupta R. and H. Kazemi. "Factor Exposures and Hedge Fund Operational Risk: The Case of Amaranth." Working Paper. Center for International Securities and Derivatives Markets. 2007.

Hosking, P. "Investor Paid Out Extra Penalties to Quit Amaranth." *The Times*. p. 50. October 13, 2006.

Ineichen, A. "Fund of Hedge Funds: Industry Overview." Working Paper. UBS Warburg. 2002a.

JP Morgan Chase. "CP Leveraged Funds Due Diligence, Annual Review." 2005.

Lee, C. M. C. and B. Swaminathan. "Price Momentum and Trading Volume." *The Journal of Finance*. Vol. 55, No. 5, pp. 2017–2069. October 2000.

Lhabitant, F. and M. Learned. "Hedge Fund Diversification: How Much is Enough?" *Journal of Alternative Investments*. Vol. 5 (3), p. 23–49. 2003.

Lhabitant, F. and M. Learned. "Hedge Fund Diversification: Not a Free Lunch." In: *Hedge Funds: Strategies, Risk Assessment, and Returns*. G. Gregoriou, V. Karavas, and F. Rouah (eds). Frederick, MD, Beard Books. 2004.

Lhabitant, F. S. "Hedge Fund Indices for Retail Investors: UCITs Eligible or Not Eligible?" *Derivatives Uses, Trading and Regulation*, 12. pp. 275–289. 2007.

Liang, B. "On the Performance of Alternative Investments: CTAs, Hedge Funds, and Funds-of-Funds." Working Paper. University of Massachusetts at Amherst. 2003.

Martin, G. "Who Invested in Amaranth? A Flash Analysis of Fund of Funds." *Journal of Alternative Investments*. Spring 2007.

Ngo, T. and S. Jory. "International Evidence on the Relationship Between Trading Volume and Serial Correlation in Stock Returns." *Global Journal of Finance and Banking Issues*. Vol. 2, No. 2, pp. 1–13. July 2008.

Rouwenhorst, K. G. "International Momentum Strategies." *The Journal of Finance*. Vol. 53, No. 1, pp. 267–284. February 1998.

Safvenblad, Peter. "Global Macro and Managed Futures Strategies." Working Paper. Stockholm School of Economics. 2003.

Schneeweis, T., H. Kazemi and V. Karavas. "Fund Diversification in Fund of Funds Investment: How Many Hedge Funds Are Enough?" Working Paper. Center for International Securities and Derivatives Markets. 2003.

Schneeweis, T., V. Karavas and R. DuBose. "Diversification in Fund of Funds Investment: How Many Hedge Fund Managers are Enough to Represent a Strategy?" Working Paper. Center for International Securities and Derivatives Markets. 2005.

Schneeweis, T., H. Kazemi and G. Martin. "Understanding Hedge Fund Performance: Research Issues Revisited – Part I." Journal of alternative Investments, Vol. 5 (3), pp. 6–72. 2002.

Schneeweis, T., H. Kazemi and G. Martin. "Understanding Hedge Fund Performance: Research Issues Revisited – Part II." Journal of alternative Investments, Vol. 5 (4), pp. 8–30, 2003.

"Testimony of Andrew K. Golden, President of the Princeton University Investment Company. Presented to the Financial Services Committee, United States House of Representatives." http://www.house.gov/apps/list/hearing/financialsvcs_dem/ht031307.shtml. 2007.

Xiong, J., Th. Idzorek, P. Chen and R. Ibbotson. "Dynamics of Fund of Hedge Funds: Flow, Size, and Performance," Ibbotson Associates Research Paper, October 2007.

Zangari, Peter. "Equity Risk Factor Models." In: *Modern Investment Management*, Bob Litterman (ed.). John Wiley & Sons Inc., pp. 334–398. 2003.

Index

Notes